Microcontroller System Design Using PIC18F Processors

University of Balamand, Lebanon

A volume in the Advances in Systems Analysis,
Software Engineering, and High Performance
Computing (ASASEHPC) Book Series

www.igi-global.com

Published in the United States of America by
   IGI Global
   Information Science Reference (an imprint of IGI Global)
   701 E. Chocolate Avenue
   Hershey PA, USA 17033
   Tel: 717-533-8845
   Fax: 717-533-8661
   E-mail: cust@igi-global.com
   Web site: http://www.igi-global.com

                      Library of Congress Cataloging-in-Publication Data

Names: Haddad, Nicolas K., 1962- author.
Title: Microcontroller system design using PIC18F processors / by Nicolas K.
   Haddad.
Description: Hershey, PA : Information Science Reference, 2017. | Includes
   bibliographical references and index.
Identifiers: LCCN 2016047024| ISBN 9781683180005 (hardcover) | ISBN
   9781683180012 (ebook)
Subjects: LCSH: Programmable controllers--Design and construction. |
   Programmable controllers--Equipment and supplies. | PIC
   microcontrollers--Programming.
Classification: LCC TJ223.P76 H336 2017 | DDC 629.8/5--dc23 LC record available at https://lccn.loc.gov/2016047024

This book is published in the IGI Global book series Advances in Systems Analysis, Software Engineering, and High Performance Computing (ASASEHPC) (ISSN: 2327-3453; eISSN: 2327-3461)

British Cataloguing in Publication Data
A Cataloguing in Publication record for this book is available from the British Library.

For electronic access to this publication, please contact: eresources@igi-global.com.

Advances in Systems Analysis, Software Engineering, and High Performance Computing (ASASEHPC) Book Series

Vijayan Sugumaran
Oakland University, USA

ISSN:2327-3453
EISSN:2327-3461

MISSION

The theory and practice of computing applications and distributed systems has emerged as one of the key areas of research driving innovations in business, engineering, and science. The fields of software engineering, systems analysis, and high performance computing offer a wide range of applications and solutions in solving computational problems for any modern organization.

The **Advances in Systems Analysis, Software Engineering, and High Performance Computing (ASASEHPC) Book Series** brings together research in the areas of distributed computing, systems and software engineering, high performance computing, and service science. This collection of publications is useful for academics, researchers, and practitioners seeking the latest practices and knowledge in this field.

COVERAGE

- Engineering Environments
- Computer System Analysis
- Virtual Data Systems
- Distributed Cloud Computing
- Enterprise Information Systems
- Software Engineering
- Human-Computer Interaction
- Computer Networking
- Performance Modelling
- Computer graphics

IGI Global is currently accepting manuscripts for publication within this series. To submit a proposal for a volume in this series, please contact our Acquisition Editors at Acquisitions@igi-global.com or visit: http://www.igi-global.com/publish/.

Titles in this Series

For a list of additional titles in this series, please visit: www.igi-global.com

Comparative Approaches to Using R and Python for Statistical Data Analysis
Rui Sarmento (University of Porto, Portugal) and Vera Costa (University of Porto, Portugal)
Information Science Reference • copyright 2017 • 197pp • H/C (ISBN: 9781683180166) • US $180.00 (our price)

Developing Service-Oriented Applications Using the Windows Communication Foundation (WCF) Framework
Chirag Patel (Charotar University of Science and Technology, India)
Information Science Reference • copyright 2017 • 487pp • H/C (ISBN: 9781522519973) • US $200.00 (our price)

Resource Management and Efficiency in Cloud Computing Environments
Ashok Kumar Turuk (National Institute of Technology Rourkela, India) Bibhudatta Sahoo (National Institute of Technology Rourkela, India) and Sourav Kanti Addya (National Institute of Technology Rourkela, India)
Information Science Reference • copyright 2017 • 352pp • H/C (ISBN: 9781522517214) • US $205.00 (our price)

Handbook of Research on End-to-End Cloud Computing Architecture Design
Jianwen "Wendy" Chen (IBM, Australia) Yan Zhang (Western Sydney University, Australia) and Ron Gottschalk (IBM, Australia)
Information Science Reference • copyright 2017 • 507pp • H/C (ISBN: 9781522507598) • US $325.00 (our price)

Innovative Research and Applications in Next-Generation High Performance Computing
Qusay F. Hassan (Mansoura University, Egypt)
Information Science Reference • copyright 2016 • 488pp • H/C (ISBN: 9781522502876) • US $205.00 (our price)

Developing Interoperable and Federated Cloud Architecture
Gabor Kecskemeti (University of Miskolc, Hungary) Attila Kertesz (University of Szeged, Hungary) and Zsolt Nemeth (MTA SZTAKI, Hungary)
Information Science Reference • copyright 2016 • 398pp • H/C (ISBN: 9781522501534) • US $210.00 (our price)

Managing Big Data in Cloud Computing Environments
Zongmin Ma (Nanjing University of Aeronautics and Astronautics, China)
Information Science Reference • copyright 2016 • 314pp • H/C (ISBN: 9781466698345) • US $195.00 (our price)

Emerging Innovations in Agile Software Development
Imran Ghani (Universiti Teknologi Malaysia, Malaysia) Dayang Norhayati Abang Jawawi (Universiti Teknologi Malaysia, Malaysia) Siva Dorairaj (Software Education, New Zealand) and Ahmed Sidky (ICAgile, USA)
Information Science Reference • copyright 2016 • 323pp • H/C (ISBN: 9781466698581) • US $205.00 (our price)

IGI GLOBAL
DISSEMINATOR OF KNOWLEDGE

www.igi-global.com

701 E. Chocolate Ave., Hershey, PA 17033
Order online at www.igi-global.com or call 717-533-8845 x100
To place a standing order for titles released in this series, contact: cust@igi-global.com
Mon-Fri 8:00 am - 5:00 pm (est) or fax 24 hours a day 717-533-8661

Table of Contents

Foreword vii

Preface viii

Acknowledgment x

Chapter 1
Introduction 1

Chapter 2
CPU Architecture 7

Chapter 3
Instruction Set 25

Chapter 4
Macros and Subroutines 49

Chapter 5
Migrating from Assembly to C 72

Chapter 6
Input/Output Ports 94

Chapter 7
Interrupts and Applications 120

Chapter 8
Alphanumeric Liquid Crystal Displays 144

Chapter 9
Analog-to-Digital Conversion 166

Chapter 10
Timers and Associated Hardware 181

Chapter 11
State Machines 200

Chapter 12
Asynchronous Serial Communications 222

Chapter 13
The Serial Peripheral Interface 240

Chapter 14
I2C Interface 263

Appendix 1 283

Appendix 2 288

Appendix 3 353

Appendix 4 359

Appendix 5 375

Appendix 6 395

Appendix 7 400

Appendix 8 412

Appendix 9 421

Compilation of References 425

About the Author 426

Index 427

Foreword

No doubt if you are interested in microcontrollers you have heard the saying "they will be in everything" and that is why Dr. Haddad's new book is so timely. They are showing up in everything: from drones to running shoes. The current estimate is that most cars being produced this year will have up to 50 microcontrollers. They work in consort to manage everything in the car from the safety systems, to the engine management, to the entertainment system and to the average person, "it's all just magic". It's not enough to say "I know about microcontrollers" these days. You need to know how they function, how to program them and how to interface them in real world applications.

This book utilizes a unique combination of theory, practical examples, software, and real world exercises, to cover complex topics such as programming in assembly and C as well as interfacing to real world devices such as switches, LEDs, LCDs, keypads, relays and more. It also covers complex subjects such as serial communications, I²C and SPI. Of course all of this would be of very little benefit if you don't understand the core of how the microcontroller and its peripherals functions work. The book will take you from the lower most instruction set all the way to how to use the complex timers, analog to digital converter and the ports.

Throughout the book the Microchip PIC18F45K22 and its companion parts are used. Microchip is a market leader and the K22 is a leading edge part to work with. The many complex peripherals in the K22 are covered in-depth with logic diagrams and detailed schematics of their operation.

The examples in the book are presented using Proteus VSM. Proteus is a PC based tool that lets you design and debug your code for the micro in your PC. This eliminates the need for a lot of hardware and test equipment as Proteus includes meters, a 4-channel oscilloscope, a logic analyzer and specialized debugging tools for understanding I²C and SPI communications.

If your goal is to work with microcontrollers, and learn programming for real world applications, then this is the book for you.

Don Jackson
Labcenter Electronics North America, USA

Preface

Microcontroller System Design with PIC18 Processors is totally geared towards microprocessor-based electronic system design. In this sense, the PIC18 microcontroller family by Microchip is taught as a tool in the development of state of the art electronic systems spanning a variety of areas: on/off control, data acquisition, instrumentation, telemetry, communications, motor control, sensing and measurement, etc.

Throughout this textbook, readers will acquire strong software and hardware skills. Software modularity, efficiency and compactness will be emphasized through the aid of the following additions and innovations:

- Employment of elaborate data structures to simplify the logic of programs and hence enhance their readability.
- Development of dedicated libraries for handling peripheral devices such as Liquid Crystal Displays, serial I/O devices, I²C components, etc. As a result, programs will have a compact appearance and will hide the intricacies of peripheral devices. For instance, if a user were to design a digital thermostat, the program should mainly highlight the control related algorithm rather than delve into LCD or keypad routines used as I/O devices.
- Mimicking state machines in the implementation of complex systems. This is consistent with the hardware alternative engineers are familiar with.
- Evaluation of code size and efficiency will be a dominant aspect of the textbook, set aside clarity, human readability, simple logic, comments, etc.
- Retrospection is also a major facet of software skills this textbook is trying to promote. A programmer who designs a function will have to ask the following questions: could I have done it better? Is this routine efficient? If I were to use this function with other programs, would it be general enough? Is my logic redundant? Etc.

As to the software platform, PROTEUS electronic circuit simulator along with MPLAB X and the C18 C compiler will be utilized. PROTEUS is an advanced software package that can emulate any electronics circuit board. Here is a list of some of the I/O devices that are supported by PROTEUS:

- Toggle switches, push buttons and LEDs.
- Multiplexed displays.
- Alphanumeric dot-matrix displays plus serial drivers.
- Serial real-time clock chips.
- High-precision temperature sensors.

- Serial 7-segment multiplexed display/driver/decoder interface.
- Graphics LCD display.
- DC motor, stepper motor and servomotor plus support chips.
- High voltage input/output interfaces with optoisolation.
- I^{2}C support chips.

The textbook intends to provide the reader with an in-depth knowledge of peripheral interface devices and components: alphanumeric LCD, piezoelectric buzzer, RS232 interface, I^{2}C temperature sensors, etc. It exposes designers to a wide variety of electronic components that can be used in different applications. A thorough coverage of the on-chip I/O subsections such as timers, A/D, SPI, USART, CCP, etc. will be presented along with pertinent applications.

With this combination of software/hardware support, engineers will be able to put together state-of-the-art electronic systems in a very short time span. In addition to this, they are provided with simulation tools that will prove very effective in troubleshooting a malfunctioning or faulty system.

Programmers are also expected to extend the software libraries according to their needs. Add-on modules can also be prototyped to support evolving technology such as CAN, USB, 1-wire interface components, codecs, touch screens, etc.

The book assumes a basic knowledge in combinational and sequential circuits. A basic course in C language programming will help but is not a must. An introductory course in computer architecture will be of tremendous help but is not a requirement as well. The author intends to start with the basics and build up a strong pedagogical infrastructure aiming at allowing practicing engineers to develop advanced applications swiftly.

Nicolas K. Haddad
University of Balamand, Lebanon

Acknowledgment

I would like to express my gratitude to the many people who went through this long process with me; to all those who provided support and advice, read, wrote, and offered constructive comments.

I would like to thank IGI Global Publishing for enabling me to publish this book. Above all I want to thank my family members: my wife Nelly and my children Roula, Ryan and Rhea who supported me and encouraged me in spite of all the time it took me away from them. It was a long and time-consuming journey for all of us.

I would like to thank Engineers Majdi Richa and Don Jackson for their endless support and encouragement. Thanks to Ms Kelsey Weitzel-Leishman from IGI Global Publishing for providing on-going encouragement and support.

Last but not least, I thank the University of Balamand for providing me with all the needed support throughout this process.

Chapter 1
Introduction

WHERE ARE MICROCONTROLLERS USED?

Microcontrollers reside in almost any gadget you carry or use nowadays. Whether it is a cell phone, a digital camera, a wireless telephone, a camcorder, a digital watch, a remote control, a multimeter, etc., it is certain that it has some sort of embedded microcontroller. Contemporary automobiles can have at least ten of them: The engine is controlled by one, as are the anti-lock brakes, the cruise control, the electric car seats, the air conditioner, the dashboard, etc. Home appliances such as microwave ovens, washing and drying machines, modern refrigerators, satellite receivers, climate controllers, dishwashers, and the list goes on and on; all of these have some kind of microcontroller buried inside. All office equipment: printers, scanners, coffee makers, copy machines, etc. have microcontroller-based electronics. Home automation products (KNX, Modbus, etc.) along with Programmable Logic Controllers (PLC) are designed with microcontrollers too. You get the point. Basically, any product or device that interacts with its user has a microcontroller inside.

WHAT IS A MICROCONTROLLER?

A microcontroller is a small computer integrated on a single chip. It can be programmed to implement just about anything a consumer wants. It is also known as a single-chip microcomputer or simply a microcontroller unit (MCU).

Regardless of the MCU manufacturer, complexity or throughput, microcontrollers have several things in common:

- All microcontrollers have a central processing unit (CPU) in charge of executing programs. Computer programs consist of instructions designed to execute arithmetic and logic operations. A CPU can also execute data move and control instructions.

DOI: 10.4018/978-1-68318-000-5.ch001

- Microcontrollers have two different memory types: Random Access Memory (RAM) and Read Only Memory (ROM). RAMs hold variables and alterable data. ROMs hold non-volatile information such as a computer program or setpoints. Different ROM technologies (PROM, EPROM, EEPROM) are available on the market.
- Microcontrollers are interfaced to I/O devices like push buttons, keypads, Liquid Crystal Displays (LCD), touch screens, relays, etc.

In essence, a microcontroller is very much similar in functionality to a general purpose processor like a Pentium chip. The difference is in scale. A general purpose computer employing a "heavy-duty" microprocessor is capable of executing a large number of programs concurrently through time sharing techniques or via the multi-core technology. A microcontroller generally runs a single program on a single core and is mostly dedicated to handheld devices and dedicated applications. Besides this,

- Microcontrollers are equipped with several I/O subfunctions: serial and parallel ports, A/D and D/A converters, internal memory, timers, etc. Electronic designers use internal blocks to implement sophisticated gadgets with minimal external components. A microcontroller is often called an "embedded controller" since it can be embedded inside a consumer product.
- Microcontrollers are dedicated to a single task and hence run one program perfectly well. The program is stored in non-volatile memory (ROM type) and remains there throughout the lifetime of the processor.
- Since microcontrollers are mostly used in battery-based handheld devices, they are designed to consume only a few milliwatts of power. Nowadays microcontrollers can be supplied from a tiny 3V battery and are armed with many features that optimize power consumption such as the *sleep* mode and the *Watchdog Timer* among others.
- A microcontroller is best suited to read data from sensors (analog/digital), process the data, and then control outputs (relays, switching transistors etc.). For instance, the MCU inside a TV receives a command from a remote control via its infrared sensor. It processes the command and sends the appropriate control signals to switch to a new channel, increase/decrease the volume, etc. The engine controller in a car receives data from sensors and accordingly it controls the car speed (cruise control), the spark plug timing, the fuel mix, etc. The controller inside a microwave oven decodes a keypad command and consequently it activates the relay that turns on the oven for the specified time duration.
- Microcontrollers are often small and inexpensive. In our time, it is common to purchase a low pin count MCU, suitable for small applications, for a cost as low as a few dimes.
- Microcontrollers are generally designed to work in harsh environments. For instance, an MCU controlling a car's engine should be able to operate at a wide temperature range. Hence, it should function properly in Siberia at temperatures below 32 °F as well as in the midst of the Mojave Desert where summer average temperatures surpass 120 °F. On the contrary, a microcontroller embedded in a modern TV ought not to be ruggedized at all since it operates at moderate temperatures.

This textbook covers a line of popular controllers called "PIC microcontrollers" manufactured by Microchip Technology Inc. By today's standards, these CPUs are incredibly minimal in size; plus they are extremely inexpensive when purchased in large quantities and can often meet the needs of a device's designer with just one chip.

The smallest Microchip microcontroller (PIC10F200) has 256 words of ROM (program memory) and 16 bytes of RAM (data memory) on the chip, along with four I/O pins. In large quantities, the cost of this chip is less than fifty cents. You certainly are never going to run a Web Server on such a chip and a processor that can run millions of instructions per second would not be appropriate for a microwave oven controller. With a microcontroller, you have one specific task you are trying to accomplish, and low-cost, low-power performance is what is important.

PIC18F45K22 MICROCONTROLLER

PIC is a family of Harvard architecture microcontrollers made by Microchip Technology. The name PIC initially referred to *Programmable Interface Controller*, but shortly thereafter was renamed *Programmable Intelligent Computer*. PICs are popular with developers and hobbyists alike due to their low cost, wide availability, large user base, extensive collection of application notes, availability of low cost or free development tools, and serial programming (and re-programming with flash memory) capability.

This textbook emphasizes the PIC18 family of processors. Special attention will be given to the PIC18F45K22 microcontroller (see figure 1.1) which is an 8-bit processor with a powerful instruction set. Its popularity stems from a number of features listed subsequently:

- Optimized instruction set: 75 standard instructions and 8 extended instructions.
- Linear program memory addressing: up to 16,384 single-word instructions.
- Linear data memory addressing: 1,536 bytes of on-chip RAM.
- 256 bytes of EEPROM with a typical retention time of 100 years.
- Operating frequency: up to 16 million instructions per second.
- 16-bit wide instructions: the majority of these instructions are single-word.
- 8-bit wide data path. Statistically, most applications do not require a wider data path.
- 8x8 single cycle hardware multiplier.
- 35 I/O pins plus one input-only pin with high current sink/source capability of about 25 mA. Nine of these pins have internal pull-ups.
- Wide operating voltage range: 2.0 V to 5.5 V.
- External interrupt pins: three external interrupts INT0/1/2 plus four interrupt-on-change pins.
- A number of timing capabilities: seven timers, two Capture/Compare/PWM (CCP) modules and three Enhanced CCP (ECCP) modules.
- An extended Watchdog Timer (WDT) with a programmable period of 4 ms to 131 seconds.
- Serial communication ports: two Master Synchronous Serial Port (MSSP) modules with SPI (Synchronous Peripheral Interface) and I²C (Inter-Integrated Circuit) modes, two Enhanced Universal Synchronous Asynchronous Receiver Transmitter (EUSART) modules.
- Analog features: one 10-bit Analog-to-Digital Converter (ADC) with up to 30 external channels, one Digital-to-Analog converter (DAC), one Fixed Voltage Reference (FVR), two analog comparator modules in addition to a Charge Time Measurement Unit (CTMU) for touch screen sensing and capacitive switches.
- A Set-Reset (SR) latch with multiple set/reset input options.

Figure 1. Pin diagram of PIC18F45K22/ PIC18F46K22 Microcontroller

Pin	Signal	Signal	Pin
2	RA0/C12IN0-/AN0	RC0/P2B/T3CKI/T3G/T1CKI/SOSCO	15
3	RA1/C12IN1-/AN1	RC1/P2A/CCP2/SOSCI	16
4	RA2/C2IN+/AN2/DACOUT/VREF-	RC2/CTPLS/P1A/CCP1/T5CKI/AN14	17
5	RA3/C1IN+/AN3/VREF+	RC3/SCK1/SCL1/AN15	18
6	RA4/C1OUT/SRQ/T0CKI	RC4/SDI1/SDA1/AN16	23
7	RA5/C2OUT/SRNQ/SS1/HLVDIN/AN4	RC5/SDO1/AN17	24
14	RA6/CLKO/OSC2	RC6/TX1/CK1/AN18	25
13	RA7/CLKI/OSC1	RC7/RX1/DT1/AN19	26
		RD0/SCK2/SCL2/AN20	19
33	RB0/INT0/FLT0/SRI/AN12	RD1/CCP4/SDI2/SDA2/AN21	20
34	RB1/INT1/C12IN3-/AN10	RD2/P2B/AN22	21
35	RB2/INT2/CTED1/AN8	RD3/P2C/SS2/AN23	22
36	RB3/CTED2/P2A/CCP2/C12IN2-/AN9	RD4/P2D/SDO2/AN24	27
37	RB4/IOC0/T5G/AN11	RD5/P1B/AN25	28
38	RB5/IOC1/P3A/CCP3/T3CKI/T1G/AN13	RD6/P1C/TX2/CK2/AN26	29
39	RB6/IOC2/PGC	RD7/P1D/RX2/DT2/AN27	30
40	RB7/IOC3/PGD		
		RE0/P3A/CCP3/AN5	8
		RE1/P3B/AN6	9
		RE2/CCP5/AN7	10
		MCLR/VPP/RE3	1

PIC18F45K22/PIC18F46K22

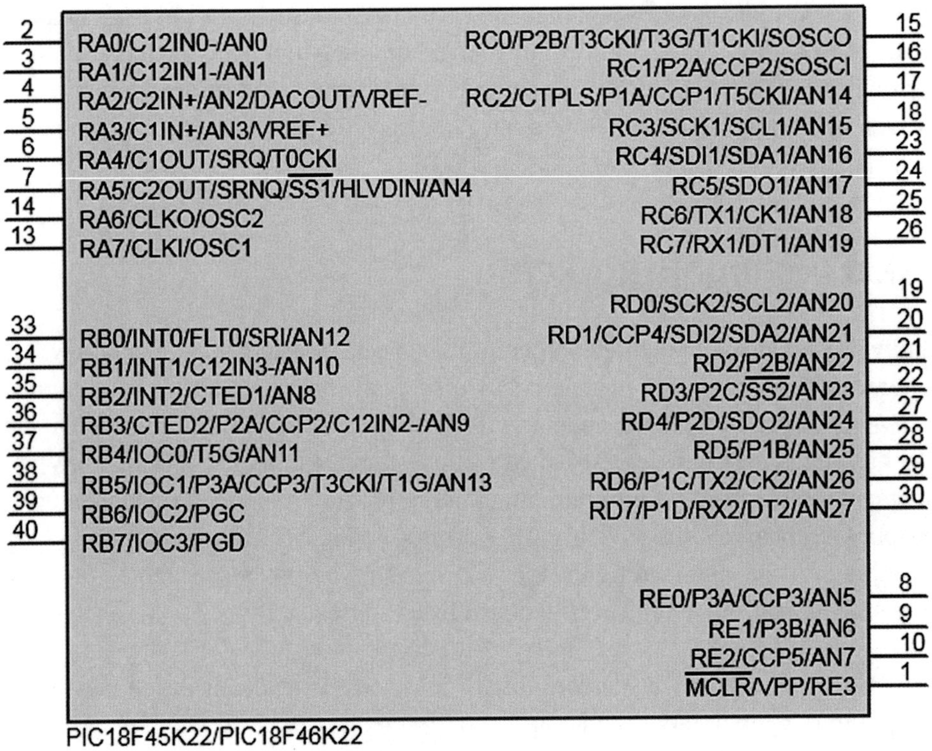

MICROCONTROLLER APPLICATIONS

Microcontrollers have invaded most engineering applications. Here is a non-exhaustive list of the numerous fields where microcontrollers have been applied:

- Data acquisition.
- Instrumentation.
- Telemetry.
- Automation products.
- Robotics.
- Handheld devices: cell phones, GPS, pagers, etc.
- Digital communications.
- Control systems.
- I/O devices: printers, scanners, fingerprint detector, etc.

DEVELOPMENT TOOLS

The cover page of the textbook shows the EasyPIC v7 demonstration board by MikroElekronika. This setup allows users to program the PIC18F45K22 chip (among many others) on the board. It also allows software debugging. The user is strongly recommended to use the MPLAB as a debugging tool. Besides this, the textbook highlights PROTEUS as the software platform employed to simulate hardware design. It covers a wide variety of applications simulated via this software. Here is a list of some of them:

- LCD interface.
- Multiplexed displays.
- Keypad encoding.
- Programmable timer.
- Digital thermostat.
- Real-time clock applications.
- Remote control.
- Pager.

NOMENCLATURE AND TECHNICAL TERMS

Appendix 1 explains the technical terms pertaining to the microcontroller field. The reader is strongly recommended to skim through this appendix in order to learn the basic literature and nomenclature used in this area. Here is a list of the essential terms the reader should be familiar with before exploring the upcoming chapters:

- Hardware, software.
- Bit, Byte, Kilobyte and Megabyte.
- Pin-out.
- Microprocessor (MPU), Microcontroller (MCU).
- Control unit and control bus.
- Arithmetic Logic Unit (ALU)
- Register and working register.
- Fetch and execute.
- Volatile and non-volatile memory.
- RAM, ROM, EPROM, EEPROM.
- Address/Data bus.
- Addressing mode: absolute versus relative.
- Assembler, assembly language and assembler directive.
- Instructions, program and machine code/language.
- Source code and object code.
- Operation code (OPCODE) and operand.
- Subroutine.

- Interrupt.
- Input/Output port.
- Serial I/O.
- Interface circuitry, peripheral.
- Signed and unsigned binary numbers.
- Binary-Coded-Decimal (BCD)
- ASCII code.

Chapter 2
CPU Architecture

INTRODUCTION

This chapter focuses on the block diagram of PIC18(L)F2X/4XK22 microcontrollers. The difference between the *Von Neumann* and *Harvard* architectures will be outlined. In the context of efficient execution of instructions, a comparison between a *Reduced Instruction Set Computer* (RISC) and a *Complex Instruction Set Computer* (CISC) will be presented. Pipelining which greatly enhances the processor's throughput will be covered as well. The chapter also discusses the special features of the CPU: oscillator options, Brown-out reset, reset circuitry, watchdog timer, etc.

VON NEUMANN ARCHITECTURE

The philosophy of this architecture is based upon the fact that instructions and data share the same memory as shown in Figure 1. Since the data bus is 8-bit wide, an instruction consisting of an opcode[1] (operation code) and one or more operands[2] obviously occupies more than one byte in memory. Consequently, an instruction occupying 3 bytes of storage elapses 3 cycles to be read plus additional cycles to be executed.

Figure 1. Von Neumann basic architecture

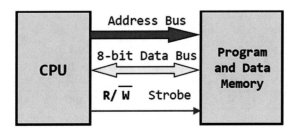

DOI: 10.4018/978-1-68318-000-5.ch002

This slows down the CPU tremendously and limits its operating bandwidth. Traditionally, microcontroller manufacturers used the *Von Neumann* architecture. In order to further understand this architecture, let us consider the Freescale 68HC11 microcontroller instruction stored at memory address 0x0100:

```
LDAA    0x1234    ; load accumulator A with contents of 0x1234
```

This instruction occupies 3 bytes of memory: the opcode (0xB6) followed by the high-order and low-order bytes of the address (0x12 and 0x34). This implies that the CPU requires 3 cycles to read the instruction plus one additional cycle to execute it; a total of 4 cycles. This is quite a waste of time and resources from a *Harvard machine* point of view whose basic philosophy is to read the instruction in one cycle.

Table 1 illustrates the cycle-by-cycle execution of the instruction. In the first cycle, the CPU puts the instruction's address 0x0100 on the address bus to read its opcode 0xB6. Then the processor reads the instruction's operand (memory address 0x1234) in 2 additional cycles. Subsequently, the CPU puts address 0x1234 on the address bus in order to read its contents. In a microprocessor system, instructions occupy non-volatile memories of the ROM (*Read Only Memory*) type whereas variables reside in alterable memories of the RWM (*Read Write Memory*) type. Therefore, in a Von Neumann machine, memory is a mixture of ROM for instructions and lookup tables, and RAM[3] (modified acronym of RWM) for variables.

HARVARD ARCHITECTURE

In reference to Figure 2, the Harvard architecture uses physically separate memories: program memory (PM) to store instructions and data memory (DM) to allocate variables. This requires dedicated address

Table 1.

Address	Data	Meaning
0x0100	0xB6	Opcode of the instruction
0x0101	0x12	High-order byte of 16-bit address
0x0102	0x34	Low-order byte of 16-bit address

(a)

Cycle	Address	Data	$R/\overline{W}$	Meaning
1	0x0100	0xB6	1	Opcode of the instruction
2	0x0101	0x12	1	Read high-order byte of 16-bit address
3	0x0102	0x34	1	Read low-order byte of 16-bit address
4	0x1234	(0x1234)	1	Read contents of 0x1234 into accumulator A

(b)

(a) LDAA 0x1234 storage in memory.
(b) Cycle-by-cycle execution.

Figure 2. Harvard architecture block diagram

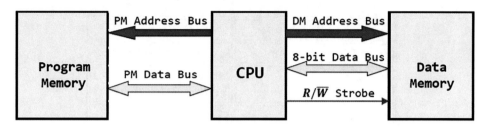

and data buses for each of them. As a result, the CPU is able to fetch instructions from program memory and operate on variables from data memory simultaneously.

Since data and instructions are now in separate memories, the instruction width in program memory is made wide enough to fit an opcode along with its operands. Therefore, the CPU can read the majority of instructions in one cycle. This increases the throughput of the machine tremendously as compared to the Von Neumann alternative.

RISC VS. CISC

RISC (*Reduced Instruction Set Computer*) is a microprocessor that has a limited number of instructions. Until the mid-80s, the trend among computer manufacturers was to design complex CPUs with large instruction sets. Other manufacturers decided to reverse this tendency by building CPUs capable of executing only a limited and essential set of instructions. RISC computers can execute their instructions very fast, typically in one cycle, because of the instructions simplicity. Another important appeal of RISC processors is the fact that they require fewer transistors, which makes them inexpensive to design and manufacture. Ever since RISC computers emerged on the market, conventional computers have been referred to as CISCs *(Complex Instruction Set Computers)*.

Advocates of RISC processors claim that these machines are cheaper and faster, and hence should be the ones adopted in the future. The counter argument made by opponents is that by making the hardware simpler, RISC architectures waste the extra cycles in software. They contend that conventional processors are becoming increasingly fast and cheap anyhow.

To a certain degree, this argument is becoming disputable because CISC and RISC implementations are converging at some point. Nowadays, several RISC processors are equipped with as many instructions as traditional CISC chips. By the same token, CISC chips use many new hardware techniques formerly linked with RISC chips.

CISC *(Complex Instruction Set Computer)* is a processor that recognizes a large set of complex instructions. This traditional architecture can complete a task in as few lines of assembly language instructions as possible. This is achieved by building a processor with a complex ALU. The primary advantage of this machine is that the compiler can translate a high-level statement into a relatively smaller number of instructions. Because the length of the code is relatively short, very little memory is required to store instructions. Table 2 illustrates the main differences between CISC and RISC architectures.

Table 2. CISC vs. RISC summary

CISC	RISC
Emphasis on hardware	Emphasis on software
Includes multi-cycle complex instructions	Single-cycle, reduced instruction only
Small code sizes, high cycles per second	Low cycles per second, large code sizes
Transistors used for storing complex instructions	Spends more transistors on memory registers

PIPELINING

In a CISC machine an instruction requires several cycles to be executed. There are a number of *fetch* and *execute cycles*. Execution cycles fall into one of the following categories:

- Read data.
- Process data.
- Write data.

The instruction overhead (1 or more bytes of storage) in a Von Neumann machine along with the non-uniform number of execution cycles, required by a CISC machine, makes this combination the worst candidate from an efficiency point of view. The fact that a Harvard machine fetches instructions in one cycle and that RISC allows instruction execution in one cycle, makes this union the ultimate choice for a high efficiency processor. To increase the throughput of the processor even further, designers have added the *pipelining* feature to the machine. It consists of fetching the next instruction to be executed while the current instruction is being executed (see Figure 3). This is feasible on a Harvard machine having two separate memories: program memory (PM) and data memory (DM). Consequently, the combination: Harvard, RISC and pipelining is the ultimate solution for high speed processing. Microchip Technology Inc. is the leader in the design of high-speed microcontrollers based upon this 3-feature fusion.

Figure 3. Instruction pipeline flow

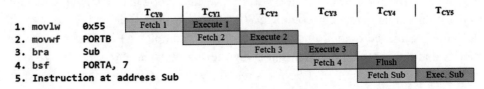

All instructions are single cycle, except for program branches. Branch instructions take two cycles. This is because during execution of a `bra` instruction, another instruction is fetched. Since the branch instruction loads the **PC** with a new address, the latest fetched instruction is "flushed" from the pipeline. This extra cycle is counted as a part of the `bra` instruction.

OVERALL PICTURE

Figure 4 shows the block diagram of PIC18(L)F2X/4XK22 microcontrollers. This section elaborates on the following topics: program and data memories, hardware stack, ALU, control unit, oscillator and reset circuitry, and power requirements.

Program Memory

The 21-bit address bus of program memory implies that the CPU can access up to 2^{21} (2 Meg) memory locations in PS. Since one-word instructions (16-bit) require 2 bytes of memory, program space can store up to 1 Meg of single-word instructions. The implemented memory storage on the PIC18F45K22 consists however of 32 Kbytes only. This translates into a maximum capacity of 16,384 single-word instructions. The reader may refer to the device's datasheet to get the memory size of other PIC18 devices.

When executing a program, the upper left multiplexer in Figure 4 selects the *program counter* (PC) to drive the address bus of program memory. The PC is a 21-bit register that points to the instruction to be fetched from PM into the instruction register (IR). The IR holds the instruction to be executed by the processor. In fact, the control unit observes the instruction in the IR and accordingly it gives appropriate commands to the ALU or other hardware to execute it. The IR is obviously 16-bit wide to match the instruction width[4]. When an instruction is read from PM, the PC is automatically incremented to point to the next instruction to be executed. By the time the current instruction is executed, a new instruction awaiting execution would have been read. This is the advantage of *pipelining*: no time is lost.

When reading data from PS, the upper left multiplexer routes the *Table Pointer* register (TBLPTR) to the address bus. The *table read* instruction (tblrd) reads the 8-bit data addressed by TBLPTR into the *Table Latch* register (TABLAT). Note that a new read operation overwrites the previous byte, therefore TABLAT must be saved before another tblrd instruction destroys its contents.

Hardware Stack

The program counter PC has a direct connection to the so-called *hardware stack* which is a group of 32 21-bit registers. This stack is used to save *return addresses* in subroutine calls. It is associated with a 5-bit *stack pointer* SP (initially cleared) used to index one of 32 registers (Figure 5). A subroutine is a set of instructions used to perform a certain task. It is usually placed after the main program and is invoked via the call or rcall (relative call) instructions (see Table 3). The *return address* is the address of the instruction to be executed upon exit from a subroutine. In other words, it is the address of the instruction succeeding the call or rcall instruction in the main program. Retrieving the *return address* from the stack is accomplished via the return instruction. Consider the code snippet:

```
        org     0x0000
        rcall   Subr        ; Stack[++SP] ← 0x0002, PC ← 0x0124
here    bra     here        ; instruction at address 0x0002

        org     0x0124
Subr    movlw   2           ; occupies addresses 0x0124:0x125
        ...
        return              ; PC ← Stack[SP--] = 0x0002
```

Figure 4. PIC18(L)F2X/4XK22 family block diagram

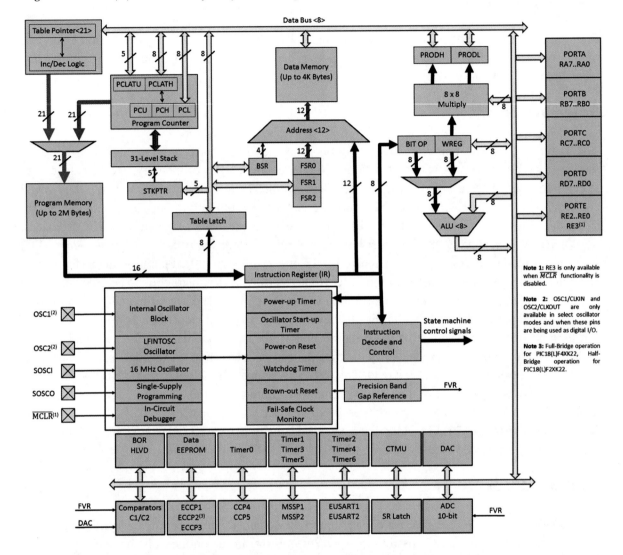

Upon execution of the rcall (relative call) instruction, the SP is incremented by 1 and the address of the subsequent instruction 0x0002 is saved on the stack at the SP position (Figure 5). Then the destination address 0x0124 is loaded into the PC. This guides the CPU to execute the first instruction in the subroutine (movlw instruction). When the return[5] instruction is encountered, the *return address* 0x0002 is popped from the stack and loaded into the PC. The SP is then decremented by 1 and the stack is said to be *purged*. Loading the PC with the return address directs the CPU to resume program execution at address 0x0002.

The hardware stack can handle up to 31 nested subroutines. A nested subroutine is one that is invoked by another subroutine. The stack is said to be 31-level deep because the first memory location on the stack (address 00000_2) is never used.

Figure 5. Illustration of a LIFO type (Last In First Out) hardware stack

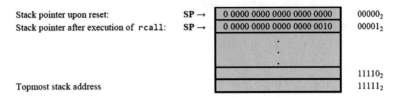

Table 3. Summary of major instructions affecting the stack

Instruction	CPU Operation	Size	Cycles
`rcall n`	Stack[++SP] ← PC+2, PC ← PC + 2 + 2n	1 word	2
`call n`	Stack[++SP] ← PC+4, PC<20:1> ← n	2 words	2
`return`	PC ← Stack[SP--]	1 word	2

Data Memory

Data memory (DM) is a RAM based memory in charge of storing variables. It is also called data space DS, data RAM or *register file*. It is 8-bit wide with an address bus of 12 bits. This means that the CPU can access up to $2^{12} = 4096$ bytes or 4 Kbytes of data RAM. This address could be direct (specified by the instruction itself) or indirect as indicated by one of the *file-select registers* FSR0, FSR1 and FSR2. Chapter 3 discusses the addressing modes available on PIC18 processors along with the role of the *Bank Select Register* BSR in the segmentation of data memory. Note that data memory of the PIC18F45K22 microcontroller consists of only 1536 bytes.

Arithmetic Logic Unit

As implied by its name, the Arithmetic Logic Unit (ALU) is responsible for arithmetic and logic operations. Arithmetic instructions perform operations such as: addition, subtraction, multiplication, negation, etc. while logic operations are responsible for OR, XOR, AND, 1's complement operations, etc. Chapter 3 elaborates on the ALU and explains all the instructions it can perform. The STATUS register, not shown on the block diagram, provides information about the result of an arithmetic or logic operation.

Instruction Decode and Control Unit

The control unit regulates the operation of the CPU. Its function is to cause the proper sequence of events to occur during the execution of instructions. This is done by providing appropriate timing and control signals to the hardware: ALU and other circuits. Case in point, when the instruction addwf (add WREG to f) is executed, the control unit:

- Applies the address f to the address bus of DM, which in turn puts the contents of this address on the data bus. Therefore, the ejected data byte goes straight to the right input of the ALU.
- Routes WREG to the left input of the ALU. Then it instructs the ALU to perform an add operation. The result goes to WREG or back to f as specified by the destination option of the instruction.
- Instructs the hardware to read a new instruction from program memory. Then it increments the PC to point to the next instruction in program space.

Oscillator Circuit

The CPU, which is essentially a complex state machine, requires a clock to trigger it to advance from one state to another. Figure 6 illustrates the crystal-based oscillator circuit required to generate this clock. Note that the instruction frequency F_{cy} equals the operating frequency divided by four ($F_{cy} = F_{osc} / 4$). In other words, if the oscillator (or crystal) frequency F_{osc} is say 4 MHz, the instruction frequency F_{cy} is 1 MHz. In this case the CPU executes 1 million single-cycle instructions per second and the instruction cycle has a duration of $T_{cy} = 1$ μsec.

Each instruction cycle is subdivided into 4 internal clock cycles Q1, Q2, Q3 and Q4 with time duration $T_{osc} = 1/F_{osc} = 0.25$ μs for $F_{osc} = 4$ MHz. For instance, the instruction:

```
subwf      0x040, F   ; subtract WREG from register f (address 0x040)
```

is executed as follows:

Q1- Instruction Decode: This cycle is in charge of interpreting the instruction to decide that it is indeed a subtract operation.

Q2 - Read Register: During this cycle, address 0x040 is applied to data memory. The contents of this memory location are fed to one of the ALU inputs via the data bus.

Figure 6. Crystal oscillator for the following modes: LP (Low Power Crystal), XT (Crystal/Resonator), and HS (High Speed Crystal). Typical values of C1 and C2 are 22 pF.

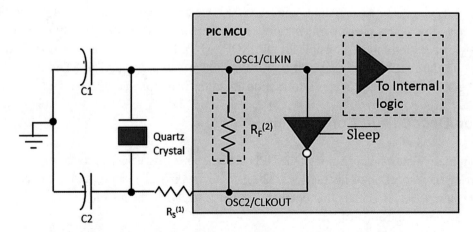

Note 1: A series resistor R_S may be required for quartz crystals with low drive level.

Note 2: The value of R_F varies with the oscillator mode selected (typically between 2 MΩ to 10 MΩ).

Q3 - Process Data: This is the cycle during which the ALU is given appropriate control signals to subtract WREG from data memory register 0x040.

Q4 - Write to Destination: During this cycle, the ALU output is written to the destination register (0x040).

The External clock (EC) mode depicted in Figure 7 requires an external clock source to be connected to the OSC1/RA7 pin. In this case, OSC2/RA6 is available for general purpose I/O pin.

The External Clock (EC) features different power modes, Low Power (ECLP), Medium Power (ECMP) and High Power (ECHP), selectable by the FOSC<3:0> bits in the configuration register CONFIG1H (Table 4). Each mode is suitable for a frequency range as shown subsequently:

- **ECLP:** Below 500 KHz.
- **ECMP:** Below 500 KHz and 16 MHz.
- **ECHP:** Above 16 MHz.

In applications where timing accuracy is not crucial, the RC/RCIO options of Figure 8 provide additional cost savings. In RC mode, pin OSC2/RA6 outputs the clock signal $F_{osc}/4$ whereas in RCIO mode OSC2/RA6 pin becomes a general purpose I/O pin. The RC oscillator frequency is a function of the supply voltage, R_{EXT} and C_{EXT} as well as the operating temperature. In order to determine the oscillation frequency of the RC oscillator, the reader is referred to the device's datasheet.

Figure 7. External Clock (EC) mode

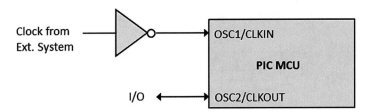

Figure 8. RC/RCIO modes (RA6: external clock or I/O pin)

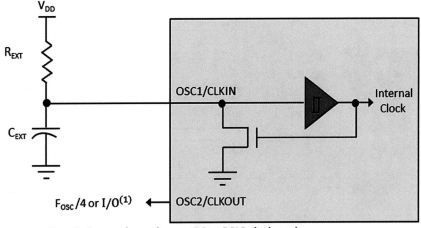

Note1: Output depends upon RC or RCIO clock mode.

Figure 9 illustrates the overall block diagram of the oscillator. The clock emanating from the primary clock module may optionally be passed through a Phase Locked Loop (PLL). The PLL multiplies the oscillator frequency by 4 and is controlled via software (see CONFIG1H register in Table 4). For instance, if F_{osc} = 10 MHz the internal clock frequency will be 40 MHz when the PLL is enabled.

Figure 9. Simplified oscillator system block diagram

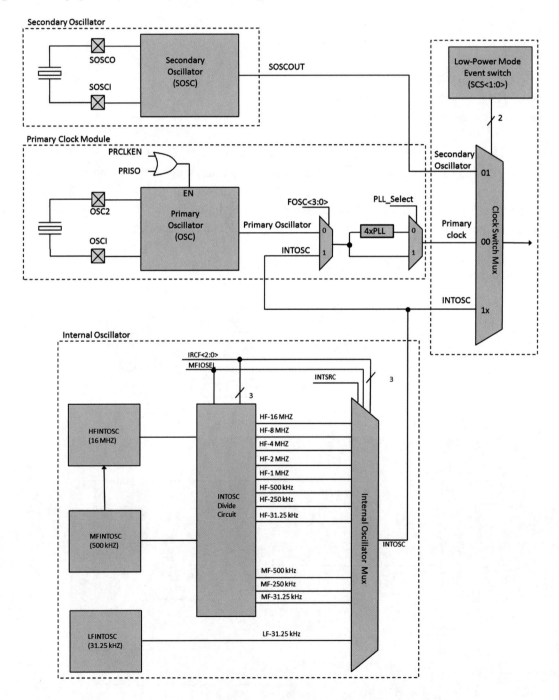

Table 4. Configuration register used to configure the oscillator clock

CONFIG1H: CONFIGURATION REGISTER 1 HIGH

R/P-0	R/P-0	R/P-1	R/P-0	R/P-0	R/P-1	R/P-0	R/P-1
IESO	FCMEN	PRICLKEN	PLLCFG	FOSC<3:0>			
bit 7							bit 0

R = Readable bit   P = Programmable bit   U = Unimplemented bit, read as '0'
-n = Value when device is not programmed   x = Bit is unknown

bit 7   **IESO** [1]: Internal/External Oscillator Switchover bit
             1 = Oscillator Switchover mode enabled
             0 = Oscillator Switchover mode disabled

bit 6   **FCMEN** [1]: Fail-Safe Clock Monitor Enable bit
             1 = Fail-Safe Clock Monitor enabled
             0 = Fail-Safe Clock Monitor disabled

bit 5   **PRICLKEN**: Primary Clock Enable bit
             1 = Primary Clock is always enabled
             0 = Primary Clock can be disabled by software

bit 4   **PLLCFG**: 4 x PLL Enable bit
             1 = 4 x PLL always enabled, Oscillator multiplied by 4
             0 = 4 x PLL is under software control, PLLEN (OSCTUNE<6>)

bit 3-0   **FOSC<3:0>** : Oscillator Selection bits
             1111 = External RC oscillator, CLKOUT function on RA6
             1110 = External RC oscillator, CLKOUT function on RA6
             1101 = EC oscillator **(low power, ≤ 500 kHz)**
             1100 = EC oscillator, CLKOUT function on OSC2 **(low power, ≤ 500 kHz)**
             1011 = EC oscillator **(medium power, 500 kHz-16 MHz)**
             1010 = EC oscillator, CLKOUT function on OSC2 **(medium power, 500 kHz - 16 MHz)**
             1001 = Internal oscillator block, CLKOUT function on OSC2
             1000 = Internal oscillator block
             0111 = External RC oscillator
             0110 = External RC oscillator, CLKOUT function on OSC2
             0101 = EC oscillator **(high power, > 16 MHz)**
             0100 = EC oscillator, CLKOUT function on OSC2 **(high power, > 16 MHz)**
             0011= HS oscillator **(medium power, 4 MHz - 16 MHz)**
             0010= HS oscillator **(high power, >16 MHz)**
             0001= XT oscillator
             0000= LP oscillator

Note 1:   When FOSC<3:0> is configured for HS, XT, or LP oscillator and FCMEN bit is set, then the IESO bit should also be set to prevent a false failed clock indication and to enable automatic clock switch over from the internal oscillator block to the external oscillator when the OST times out.

It is worthwhile noting at this point that the maximum oscillator frequency for PIC18F2X/4XK22 microcontrollers is $F_{osc} = 64$ MHz or $F_{cy} = 16$ MHz. As a result, this processor can execute a maximum of 16 Million Instructions Per Second (MIPS).

PIC18F2X/4XK22 microcontrollers can also be clocked from an internal clock source as illustrated in the internal oscillator block. The different frequencies employed herein are factory calibrated. They are selected via flags ICRF<2:0>, MFIOSEL, and INTSRC in register OSCCON (Table 5).

Another feature associated with the clock is the so-called *Oscillator Start-up Timer* (OST) intended to keep the chip in RESET mode until the crystal oscillator is stable. When the oscillator block is con-

Table 5. Register OSCCON used to select an internal frequency option

OSCCON: OSCILLATOR CONTROL REGISTER

R/W-0	R/W-0	R/W-1	R/W-1	R-q	R-0	R/W-0	R/W-0
IDLEN		IRCF<2:0>		OSTS [1]	HFIOFS	SCS<1:0>	
bit 7							**bit 0**

R = Readable bit   W = Writable bit   U = Unimplemented bit, read as '0'
-n = Value at POR   '1' = Bit is set   '0' = Bit is cleared   x = Bit is unknown

bit 7   **IDLEN:** Idle Enable bit
               1 = Device enters Idle mode on SLEEP instruction
               0 = Device enters Sleep mode on SLEEP instruction

bit 6-4   **IRCF<2:0>:** Internal RC Oscillator Frequency Select bits[2]
               111 = HFINTOSC – (16 MHz)
               110 = HFINTOSC/2 – (8 MHz)
               101 = HFINTOSC/4 – (4 MHz)
               100 = HFINTOSC/8 – (2 MHz)
               011 = HFINTOSC/16 – (1 MHz)[3]

               If INTSRC = 0 and MFIOSEL = 0:
               010 = HFINTOSC/32 – (500 kHz)
               001 = HFINTOSC/64 – (250 kHz)
               000 = LFINTOSC – (31.25 kHz)

               If INTSRC = 1 and MFIOSEL = 0:
               010 = HFINTOSC/32 – (500 kHz)
               001 = HFINTOSC/64 – (250 kHz)
               000 = HFINTOSC/512 – (31.25 kHz)

               If INTSRC = 0 and MFIOSEL = 1:
               010 = MFINTOSC – (500 kHz)
               001 = MFINTOSC/2 – (250 kHz)
               000 = LFINTOSC – (31.25 kHz)

               If INTSRC = 1 and MFIOSEL = 1:
               010 = MFINTOSC – (500 kHz)
               001 = MFINTOSC/2 – (250 kHz)
               000 = MFINTOSC/16 – (31.25 kHz)

bit 3   **OSTS:** Oscillator Start-up Time-out Status bit
               1 = Device is running from the clock defined by FOSC<3:0> of the CONFIG1H register
               0 = Device is running from the internal oscillator (HFINTOSC, MFINTOSC or LFINTOSC)

bit 2   **HFIOFS:** HFINTOSC Frequency Stable bit
               1 = HFINTOSC frequency is stable
               0 = HFINTOSC frequency is not stable

bit 1-0   **SCS<1:0>:** System Clock Select bit
               1x = Internal oscillator block
               01 = Secondary (SOSC) oscillator
               00 = Primary clock (determined by FOSC<3:0> in CONFIG1H).

Note 1:   Reset state depends on state of the IESO Configuration bit.
Note 2:   INTOSC source may be determined by the INTSRC bit in OSCTUNE and the MFIOSEL bit
               in OSCCON2.
Note 3:   Default output frequency of HFINTOSC on Reset.

figured for LP, XT or HS modes, the OST counts 1024 oscillations from OSC1. This happens after a Power-on Reset (POR) and when the Power-up Timer PWRT has expired (if option is selected), or a wake-up from sleep. During this time, the CPU will not execute instructions. The OST insures that the oscillator provides a stable clock before it applies it to the CPU.

Finally, PIC18 microcontrollers are provided with an interesting feature known as *oscillator switching* which allows the system clock to be switched from the main oscillator to an alternate low frequency clock source on SOSCI-SOSCO pins at run-time. The rightmost multiplexer of Figure 9 is responsible for this switching (see SCS<1:0> in OSCCON register).

Power Considerations

PIC18F2X/4XK22 microcontrollers operate under a wide voltage range (2.3 V to 5.5 V) and can tolerate high temperatures (industrial and extended range). They are implemented with CMOS technology and hence they consume low power as listed subsequently:

- Less than 3 mA typically at V_{DD} = 5V and F_{osc} = 20 MHz for -40 °C $\leq$ T $\leq$ 125 °C.
- 8.4 µA typically for V_{DD} = 3V and F_{osc} = 31 KHz at room temperature.
- Less than 13 µA typical standby current at V_{DD} = 5V in the SLEEP mode.

PIC18 MCUs have a current sinking/sourcing capability of 25 mA. This means that an I/O pin can drive up to 25 mA into a load with no interface device such as a transistor or a light emitting diode.

The supply stability is monitored by the *Power-up Timer* PWRT. When enabled the PWRT insures that the chip is kept in RESET for at least 65.5 ms after *Power-on Reset* POR. This allows V_{DD} to rise to an acceptable level.

Reset

Resetting the CPU means clearing the program counter in order to run the program stored in program memory starting at address 0x0000. This also means loading control registers with reset values. For instance, some registers (TRISA, TRISB, TRISC, etc.) are set upon reset to insure that all parallel ports are initially configured as inputs. Some other flags such as those pertaining to interrupts are disabled at reset so that no interrupt occurs inadvertently. There are different kinds of RESET:

1. **Power-on Reset (POR):** This occurs when the CPU detects a rise in V_{DD}. In this case, the $R/\overline{W}$ pin may be directly tied to V_{DD}. This has the advantage of eliminating external RC components usually needed to create a delay upon reset as in Figure 10.
2. $\overline{MCLR}$ **Reset during Normal Operation:** This occurs when the user decides to apply a hardware reset while the CPU is running a program. This is done by connecting a normally open push button across capacitor C in Figure 10. Pressing this push button will force a reset condition.
3. $\overline{MCLR}$ **Reset during Sleep (Figure 11):** When the CPU is placed in the *sleep* mode, the clock is halted. The $\overline{MCLR}$ reset re-enables the clock to trigger the processor and restarts program execution right from the beginning.

Figure 10. RC circuit to reset the CPU at power-up only

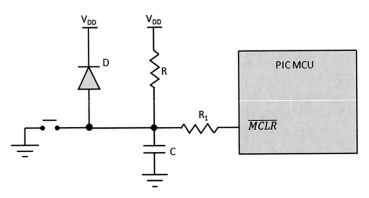

Figure 11. Simplified block diagram of on-chip reset circuit

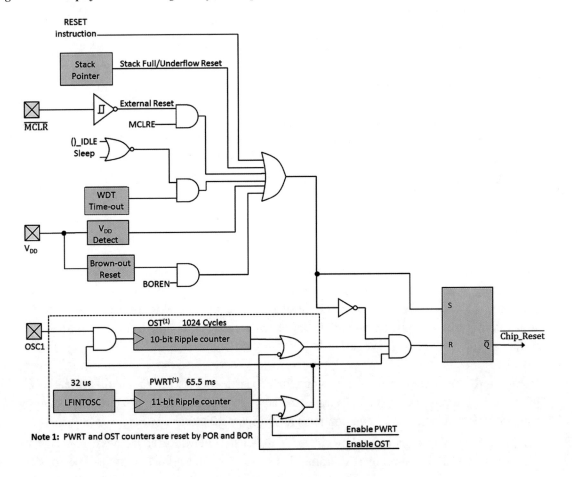

4. **Watchdog Timer (WDT) Reset (Figure 11):** When enabled, the WDT acts like a chronometer that resets the CPU when it times out. In order not to reset the CPU, the instruction clrwdt must be executed before the preset period elapses. This feature is used to keep the processor running properly. The watchdog timer is also called COP (Computer Operating Properly).

5. **Programmable Brown-Out Reset (BOR) (Figure 11):** The BOR uses the threshold voltage V_{BOR} to control the operation of the CPU. This threshold voltage is configured in BORV<1:0> of CONFIG2L register (Table 6). If BOR is enabled (BOREN<1:0> of CONFIG2L different from 00), any drop of V_{DD} below V_{BOR} for greater than T_{BOR} will reset the device. The microcontroller will remain in Brown-out reset until V_{DD} exceeds V_{BOR}.

    If the Power-up Timer is enabled, it will incur an extra delay TPWRT after V_{DD} rises above V_{BOR}. If V_{DD} drops below V_{BOR} while the Power-up timer is still running, the MCU will re-enter the BOR state and the Power-up Timer will reset. As soon as V_{DD} rises above V_{BOR}, the Power-up Timer will go through the additional time delay. In brief, the processor is fully protected against fluctuations in the power supply.

6. **RESET Instruction:** When executed, this instruction restarts program execution at address 0x0000 and hence it provides a handy way of resetting the CPU.

Table 6. CONFIG2L register used to configure the Brown-out reset feature

CONFIG2L: CONFIGURATION REGISTER 2 LOW

U-0	U-0	U-0	R/P-1	R/P-1	R/P-1	R/P-1	R/P-1
-	-	-	BORV<1:0>[1]		BOREN<1:0>[2]		$\overline{PWRTEN}$ [2]
bit 7							bit 0

R = Readable bit   P = Programmable bit   U = Unimplemented bit, read as '0'
-n = Value when device is not programmed   x = Bit is unknown

bit 7-5   **Unimplemented**: Read as '0'

bit 4-3   **BORV<1:0>:** Brown-out Reset Voltage bits[1]
                 11 = V_{BOR} set to 1.90 V nominal
                 10 = V_{BOR} set to 2.20 V nominal
                 01 = V_{BOR} set to 2.50 V nominal
                 00 = V_{BOR} set to 2.85 V nominal

bit 2-1   **BOREN<1:0>:** Brown-out Reset Enable bits[2]
                 11 = Brown-out Reset enabled in hardware only (SBOREN is disabled)
                 10 = Brown-out Reset enabled in hardware only and disabled in Sleep mode
                     (SBOREN is disabled)
                 01 = Brown-out Reset enabled and controlled by software (SBOREN is enabled)
                 00 = Brown-out Reset disabled in hardware and software

bit 0   **$\overline{PWRTEN}$:** Power-up Timer Enable bit[2]
                 1 = PWRT disabled
                 0 = PWRT enabled

Note 1:   See datasheet's section 27.1 "DC Characteristics: Supply Voltage, PIC18(L)F2X/4XK22" for specifications.
Note 2:   The Power-up Timer is decoupled from Brown-out Reset, allowing these features to be independently controlled.

7. **Stack Full and Stack Underflow Reset:** The underflow occurs when the stack is empty (SP = 00000_2) and the return is executed. The overflow happens when the stack is full (SP = 11111_2) and a subroutine is invoked. In both cases, the CPU resets itself. More on the hardware stack will be explained in chapter 3.

High/Low Voltage Detect (HLVD)

This feature is of special importance. It gives the CPU the capability of detecting when V_{DD} exceeds (or drops below) any of 15 threshold values (see Figure 12). In fact, when the voltage exceeds (or drops below) the specified threshold, it can generate a high/low-voltage detect (HLVD) interrupt that can be used to carry out any housekeeping tasks. In other words, the interrupt is used to save crucial data to EEPROM and then the CPU is shut down via the sleep instruction. This feature allows the processor to recuperate important system parameters when it recovers from the *sleep* mode. Register HLVDCON (Table 7) is used to configure the High/Low Voltage Detect feature.

Ports and Peripherals

Figure 4 displays a number of parallel I/O ports: PORTA through PORTC for PIC18(L)F2XK22 series and PORTA through PORTE for PIC18(L)F4XK22 series. The figure also highlights peripheral devices such as the A/D converter, the serial ports, the Capture/Compare/PWM units, etc. Ports are used to communicate with the outside world. They can be configured both as input or output. Peripheral devices are

Figure 12. HLVD module block diagram (with external input)

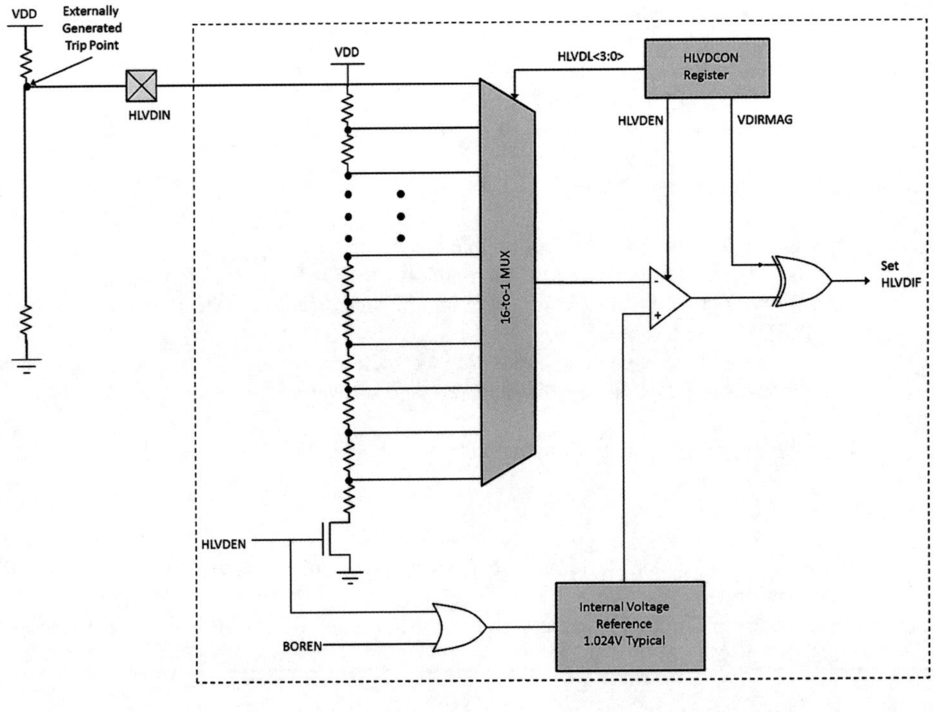

Table 7. HLVDCON register used to configure the High/Low Voltage Detect feature

HLVDCON: HIGH/LOW-VOLTAGE DETECT CONTROL REGISTER

R/W-0	R-0	R-0	R/W-0	R/W-0	R/W-1	R/W-0	R/W-1
VDIRMAG	BGVST	IRVST	HLVDEN	HLVDL<3:0>			
bit 7							bit 0

bit 7   **VDIRMAG:** Voltage Direction Magnitude Select bit
1 = Event occurs when voltage equals or exceeds trip point (HLVDL<3:0>)
0 = Event occurs when voltage equals or falls below trip point (HLVDL<3:0>)

bit 6   **BGVST:** Band Gap Reference Voltages Stable Status Flag bit
1 = Internal band gap voltage references are stable
0 = Internal band gap voltage reference is not stable

bit 5   **IRVST:** Internal Reference Voltage Stable Flag bit
1 = Indicates that the voltage detect logic will generate the interrupt flag at the specified voltage range
0 = Indicates that the voltage detect logic will not generate the interrupt flag at the specified voltage range and the HLVD interrupt should not be enabled

bit 4   **HLVDEN:** High/Low-Voltage Detect Power Enable bit
1 = HLVD enabled
0 = HLVD disabled

bit 3-0   **HLVDL<3:0>:** Voltage Detection Level bits[1]
0000 = 1.84 V (minimum setting)
0001 = 2.07 V
0010 = 2.28 V
0011 = 2.44 V
0100 = 2.54 V
0101 = 2.74 V
0110 = 2.87 V
0111 = 3.01 V
1000 = 3.30 V
1001 = 3.48 V
1010 = 3.69 V
1011 = 3.91 V
1100 = 4.15 V
1101 = 4.41 V
1110 = 4.74 V (maximum setting)
1111 = External analog input is used (input comes from the HLVDIN pin)

Note 1:   The tabulation shows typical values. See datasheet for complete specifications.

used for data acquisition, control applications, serial communications, timing, etc. In the past, peripheral devices used to be external chips. Nowadays, these devices are integrated on the microcontroller chip. Here is a list of the different peripheral devices and features available on PIC18(L)F4XK22 microcontrollers:

- **Two Enhanced Universal Synchronous Asynchronous Receiver Transmitter:** EUSART1 and EUSART2.
- **Two Master Synchronous Serial Ports:** MSSP1 and MSSP2. The MSSP operates in one of two modes: Synchronous Peripheral Interface (SPI) and Inter-Integrated Circuit (I^2C).

- Five Capture/Compare/PWM (CCP) units three of which are enhanced (ECCP). These are: ECCP1, ECCP2, ECCP3, CCP4 and CCP5.
- Two programmable analog comparators C1 and C2.
- One Set Reset (SR) latch.
- A 10-bit Analog-to-Digital Converter (ADC) with an internal Sample-and-Hold (SAH) circuit. It can convert one of 32 analog channels through an analog multiplexer.
- One charge time measurement unit (CTMU) ideal for interfacing with capacitive-based sensors.
- A 5-bit Digital-to-Analog (DAC) converter.
- **Seven Timers:** Timer0 through Timer6. Timer0 may be used in 8-bit or 16-bit modes. Timers 2/4/6 are 8-bit timers employed by the PWM units. Timers 1/3/5 are 16-bit timers used in collaboration with the Capture and Compare modules.
- A non-volatile data EEPROM used to retain crucial data. It is 8-bit wide and contains 256 memory locations for PIC18F(L)25K22/PIC18F(L)45K22 microcontrollers and 1024 memory locations for PIC18F(L)26K22/PIC18F(L)46K22.
- Brown-out Reset (BOR) and High/Low Voltage Detect (HLVD) features discussed earlier in the chapter.

SUMMARY

This chapter went through an overview of the architecture of PIC18 processors. In particular, PIC18F(L)2XK22/PIC18F(L)4XK22 microcontrollers were described. Chapter 3 elaborates further on this architecture in the context of instructions.

ENDNOTES

1   The opcode (operation code) is a set of bits interpreted by the control unit of the processor. Its purpose is to specify the type of instruction to be executed (multiply, add, subtract, etc.).

2   The operands of an instruction specify the registers or data to be operated on. For instance, the instruction LDAA 0x1234 which loads accumulator A with the contents of memory location 0x1234 has 0x1234 as its operand. This is a 3-byte instruction: opcode (1 byte) plus operand (2 bytes).

3   RAM is the acronym of Random Access Memory. It is used instead of RWM for simplicity. This acronym may imply that ROMs are not accessed randomly as is the case in RAMs. However, this is not true since the address lines can be modified electronically to hop from one address to another for both ROMs and RAMs.

4   In a set of 75 standard instructions, there are only six 2-word instructions that occupy 2 consecutive 16-bit words in PM. These instructions obviously require 2 cycles to be executed.

5   In addition to what return does, retlw k (covered in chapter 3) stores the constant k in WREG. The retfie instruction does exactly what return does, but also it re-enables interrupts (see chapter 7).

Chapter 3
Instruction Set

INTRODUCTION

This chapter covers the instruction set by tracing each processor block apart. The different addressing modes available on PIC18 processors will be discussed. The role and importance of the STATUS register in the context of arithmetic and logic instructions will be covered as well. In order to introduce the reader to computer architecture, an overview of *instruction encoding* is covered. Last but not least, the relationship between high level statements, namely C language constructs, and assembly language is explained.

ADDRESSING MODES

Figure 1 shows the processor's blocks: control unit, ALU, multiplier, I/O ports, and data and program memories along with pertinent hardware. You may refer to it in subsequent sections.

Direct Addressing Mode

Consider the instruction movwf of Table 1. This instruction transfers the contents of the working register WREG to the data memory location specified by operand f. The most significant byte of the instruction (0110111a) is the opcode. Since the 12-bit address does not fit within an instruction word, only the eight least significant bits of the data address (AD7 ... AD0) are stored within the instruction. This is shown as ffffffff in the instruction encoding. The 4 most significant bits of the address (AD11 ... AD8) must be stored in the so-called Bank Select Register BSR. This direct addressing mode is known as *Banked Addressing*. Another alternative to this addressing mode is known as *Access Bank Addressing*. It consists of sign-extending the 8-bit address at run-time in order to form the 12-bit address. Further elaboration on these modes is given subsequently.

DOI: 10.4018/978-1-68318-000-5.ch003

Figure 1. PIC18(L)F2X/4XK22 family block diagram

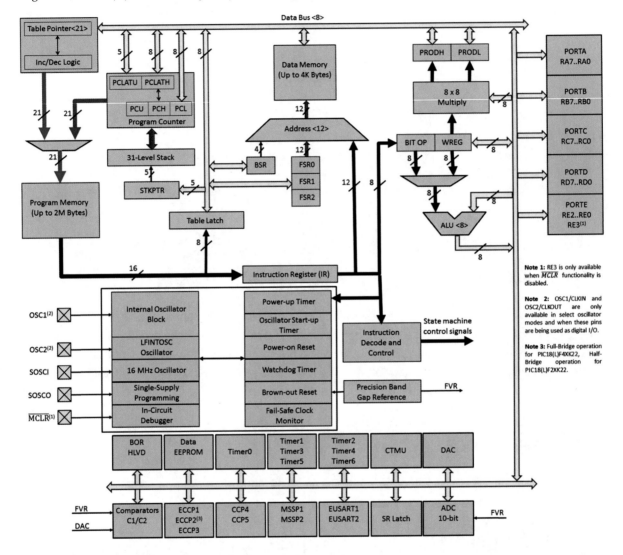

Banked Addressing

Since the address bus of data memory is 12-bit wide, the CPU may access up to 2^{12} bytes or 4 Kbytes of data memory (address range: 0x000 and 0xFFF). This memory is subdivided into 16 banks (256 bytes each) as shown in Table 2.

When using banked addressing, the bank number (0 … 15) is stored in BSR. This is done via the instruction *move literal to BSR* as in:

```
movlb      2        ; select bank 2
```

Table 1. Move WREG to the specified register f in data memory

MOVWF	Move W to f
Syntax:	movwf f{,a}
Operands:	0 ≤ f ≤ 255
	a ∈ [0, 1]
Operation:	f ← (W)
Status affected:	None
Encoding:	`0110` `111a` `ffff` `ffff`
Description:	Move data from W to register 'f'. Location 'f' can be anywhere in the 256-byte bank. If 'a' is '0', the Access Bank is selected. If 'a' is '1', the BSR is used to select the GPR bank (default).

Thereafter, the user refers to the address (say 0x234) as follows:

```
movwf      0x234          ; WREG is moved to address 0x234
```

In the above instruction only 0x34 is stored in the address field of the instruction. The assembler figures out that address 0x234 is in bank 2 and therefore it sets the a-bit (a = 1) in the instruction. This indicates to the processor that banked addressing is being used. It is the sole responsibility of the programmer (not the assembler) to select the appropriate bank. Note that there is no need to specify to the assembler that banked addressing is employed. It will figure this out from the specified 12-bit address. As a matter of fact, the 2 subsequent instructions are equivalent. Their encoding in accordance with Table 1 is 0x6F34.

```
movwf      0x234          ; no need to specify banked
movwf      0x234, BANKED  ; BANKED may be omitted
```

Table 2. Banks 0 to 15 of data memory and their address ranges

Bank0	0x000 - 0x0FF
Bank1	0x100 - 0x1FF
Bank2	0x200 - 0x2FF
...	...
Bank14	0xE00 - 0xEFF
Bank15	0xF00 - 0xFFF

Access Bank Addressing

As shown in Table 3, the *access bank* consists of the first 96 bytes of memory (0x000 – 0x05F) in Bank0 and the last 160 bytes of memory (0xF60 – 0xFFF) in Bank15. The lower portion of the *access bank* (address range: 0x000 – 0x05F) is known as the General Purpose Registers (GPRs). The upper portion (address range: 0xF60 – 0xFFF) is where the device's *Special Function Registers* (SFRs) reside. Given the 8 least significant bits (AD7:AD0) of the address, the most significant nibble (AD11:AD8) of the 12-bit address is generated at run-time in accordance with the following criterion:

```
if (AD7:AD0 < 0x60)
        AD11:AD8 = 0000₂              // address 0x000 - 0x05F
else
        AD11:AD8 = 1111₂              // address 0xF60 - 0xFFF
```

The a bit is cleared (a = 0) by the assembler if the specified 12-bit address is in the *access bank*. Some SFRs (addresses 0xF38 – 0xF5F) belong to bank 15 but are not part of the *access bank*. These must be addressed via the BANKED mode (BSR = 15).

The SFRs (PORTA, PORTB, PORTC, etc.) occupy addresses: 0xF38 – 0xFFF. Only addresses 0xF60 – 0xFFF as well as addresses (0x000 – 0x05F) form the *access bank* (refer to Appendix 2). The latter range is employed for user-defined variables. There is no need to specify to the assembler that the access bank is employed. It will figure this out from the specified 12-bit address. Hence, the two subsequent instructions are equivalent:

```
movf        0xF62, W              ; no need to specify access
movf        0xF62, W, ACCESS      ; ACCESS may be omitted
```

Their encoding in accordance with Table 4 is 0x5062.

Memory-To-Memory Move (MOVFF Instruction)

The movff instruction specifies the complete 12-bit source and destination addresses within the 2-word instruction as depicted in Table 5. These addresses are referenced directly since they both fit within the

Table 3. Access Bank area shadowed in pink; address bits are labeled AD11:AD0

Bank0 (lower partition)	0x000 - 0x05F	Access RAM
Bank0 (upper partition)	0x060 - 0x0FF	
...	...	
Bank14	0xE00 - 0xEFF	
Bank15 (lower partition)	0xF00 - 0xF5F	0xF38 – 0xF5F are also SFRs
Bank15 (upper partition)	0xF60 - 0xFFF	Special Function Registers

Table 4. Move f to WREG or back to f

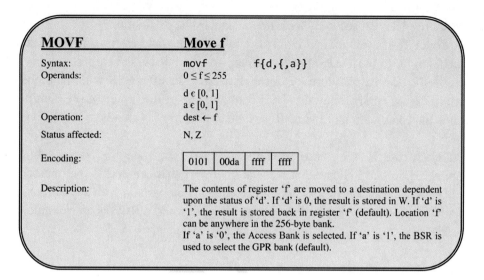

MOVF   **Move f**

Syntax:	movf f{d,{,a}}
Operands:	$0 \le f \le 255$
	$d \in [0, 1]$
	$a \in [0, 1]$
Operation:	dest ← f
Status affected:	N, Z

Encoding:

0101	00da	ffff	ffff

Description: The contents of register 'f' are moved to a destination dependent upon the status of 'd'. If 'd' is 0, the result is stored in W. If 'd' is '1', the result is stored back in register 'f' (default). Location 'f' can be anywhere in the 256-byte bank.
If 'a' is '0', the Access Bank is selected. If 'a' is '1', the BSR is used to select the GPR bank (default).

Table 5. Move source register f_s to destination register f_d

MOVFF   **Move f to f**

Syntax:	movff fs, fd
Operands:	$0 \le f_s \le 4095$, $0 \le f_d \le 4095$
Operation:	$f_d \leftarrow (f_s)$
Status affected:	None

Encoding:

1100	ffff	ffff	ffff$_s$
1111	ffff	ffff	ffff$_d$

Description: The contents of source register 'f_s' are moved to destination register 'f_d'. Location of source 'f_s' can be anywhere in the 4096-byte data space (0x000 to 0xFFF) and location of destination 'f_d' can also be anywhere from 0x000 to 0xFFF.
movff is particularly useful for transferring a data memory location to a peripheral register (such as the transmit buffer or an I/O port).
The movff instruction cannot use the PCL, TOSU, TOSH or

instruction. This operation transfers the contents of the source address to the destination without using WREG as a mediator.

Summary

Here is a summary of the three different ways the 12-bit address is formed when *direct addressing* is used:

- **Dual Address:** The 12-bit source and destination addresses are stored within the 2-word movff instruction. During execution, the address is changed twice within the instruction cycle: first to read the source data and secondly to write the data to the destination.
- **Access Mode:** The 12-bit address in formed by appending address bits ffffffff within the instruction with 0000_2 or 1111_2 in accordance with the criterion discussed earlier.
- **Banked Mode:** The 12-bit address is formed by concatenating BSR with the 8 bits ffffffff in the instruction. Figure 1 may imply that BSR could be one of the inputs of the multiplexer while in reality it is the combination of the BSR with the 8-bit address **f** that is fed to the bus.

We should finally note that ports and peripherals are part of data memory. They are shown as separate blocks in Figure 1 simply to indicate that these are registers that can access the microcontroller pins. There is no distinction as to how an I/O port is accessed in comparison with any other register. This is commonly known as *memory-mapped I/O*. The working register WREG is an example of a *memory-mapped* register.

Indirect Addressing Mode

When using indirect addressing, the programmer makes a roundabout reference to the address via the *File Select Register* (FSR). In the instruction:

```
movf        INDF0, W              ; WREG = *FSR0
```

The acronym INDF0 means INDirect addressing via FSR0. Upon execution, the above operation transfers the contents of the address stored in FSR0 to WREG. FSR0, which is a 16-bit register (FSR0 = FSR0H:FSR0L), is hence employed to store the 12-bit address of a register. Commonly, it is said that FSR0 *points* to a memory location. PIC18 designers were generous enough to provide users with 3 of these pointers: FSR0, FSR1 and FSR2.

Note that registers INDFx (x = 0, 1, 2) are not physically implemented. A reference to INDFx simply implies indirect addressing via FSRx. For instance, if FSR0 holds address 0x100, the movf instruction above transfers the contents of address 0x100 to WREG.

Indirect addressing in PIC18 processors allows pointer arithmetic within the same instruction and without incurring additional instruction cycles. Table 6 elaborates further on these addressing modes. In brief, the pointer may be:

- Postincremented (**POSTINCx**, x = 0, 1, 2).
- Postdecremented (**POSTDECx**, x = 0, 1, 2).
- Preincremented (**PREINCx**, x = 0, 1, 2).
- Indexed with respect to **WREG** (**PLUSWx**, x = 0, 1, 2).
- Left intact (**INDFx**, x = 0, 1, 2).

Table 6. Indirect addressing modes using FSR0 as a pointer

movf POSTINC0, W	Move contents of memory location pointed to by **FSR0** to **WREG**, then increment **FSR0**. **WREG = *FSR0++.**
movf POSTDEC0, W	Move contents of memory location pointed to by **FSR0** to **WREG**, then decrement **FSR0**. **WREG = *FSR0--.**
movf PREINC0, W	Increment **FSR0** then move contents of memory location pointed to by **FSR0** to **WREG**. **WREG = *(++FSR0).**
movf PLUSW0, W	Move contents of memory location pointed to by (**FSR0 + WREG**) to **WREG**, and leave **FSR0** intact. **WREG = *(FSR0 + WREG).** The addition of **FSR0** and **WREG** is signed.
movf INDF0, W	Move contents of memory location pointed to by **FSR0** to **WREG**. **FSR0** is left intact. **WREG = *FSR0.**

Note that a reference to two pointers within the same instruction is possible as in:

```
movff       POSTINC0, POSTINC1              ; *FSR1 = *FSR0
```

This powerful instruction moves the contents of the register pointed to by FSR0 to the register addressed by FSR1. This is a 2-word/2-cycle instruction. In order to load a pointer with a certain address, the *load fsr* (lfsr) instruction is used as follows:

```
lfsr        0, 0x100              ; FSR0 = 0x100
```

STATUS REGISTER

This register reflects the status of the ALU after an arithmetic or a logical operation is executed. It is not shown in Figure 1 for the sake of simplicity but it is associated with the ALU block. It contains a number of flags (or indicators) whose purpose is to inform the user of the outcome of an operation. These flags are affected by the result of specific instructions (see Appendix 3). Here is a description of how these flags work:

Zero Bit (Z)

This bit (or flag) is set if the 8-bit result of an arithmetic or logic operation is zero; otherwise, it is cleared. Testing of the Z bit is done via the bz (branch if zero, Z = 1) and bnz (branch if not zero, Z = 0) instructions. Here is an indirect way to branch to a label if the Z bit is set:

```
btfsc       STATUS, Z              ; skip if Z = 0
bra         Label                  ; branch if Z = 1
```

31

Carry Bit (C)

The C bit is set by the ALU when the result of an addition operation (i.e. addwf or addlw) is greater than 255_{10}; if not, the C bit is cleared. The carry bit is set to indicate that the 9-bit result does not fit in an 8-bit register and hence this should be accounted for in software.

In the context of subtract operations (subwf and sublw), this flag is also called $\overline{BORROW}$ (active low). It is cleared to indicate that the *subtrahend* is greater than the *minuend*; or else it is set. In short, the operation of the carry bit C when it comes to a subtract operation is best described with the following C language statement:

```
WREG = RegA - RegB              // compare RegA against RegB
if (RegA >= RegB)
        STATUSbits.C = 1;       // RegA >= RegB (unsigned compare)
else
        STATUSbits.C = 0;       // RegA < RegB (unsigned compare)
```

The carry bit is also affected by rotate-through-carry instructions (rrcf and rlcf). When an 8-bit register is rotated the carry bit is fed into one end of the register and the bit that is shifted out at the opposite end goes into the carry. Other instructions such as incf, decf, etc. affect the carry bit as well (see Appendix 3). The instructions that test the C bit are bc (branch if carry) and bnc (branch if not carry).

Negative Bit (N)

The N bit mirrors the sign bit resulting from an arithmetic operation on signed numbers in two's complement notation. It is set to point out that the result of the instruction is negative (most significant bit of the result is set); otherwise, it is cleared. The conditional branch/skip instructions that test the N bit are bn (branch if negative, N = 1) and bnn (branch if not negative, N = 0).

Digit Carry Bit (DC)

The DC bit is set by the CPU when an add operation generates a carry-out from bit 3 to bit 4 in the addition. This flag finds its applications in arithmetic operations on *packed* BCD (binary-coded-decimal) numbers. BCD numbers represent the decimal digits 0 through 9 with a 4-bit binary equivalent ($0_{10} = 0000_2$, $3_{10} = 0011_2$ etc.). Packed BCD numbers concatenate 2 BCD digits in one 8-bit register ($68_{10} = 0110\ 1000_2$, $95_{10} = 1001\ 0101_2$, etc.). When two packed BCD numbers are added together, the CPU will treat them as binary numbers. Any carry from bit 3 to bit 4 will be stored in the DC flag. In order to transform the result to a BCD notation, the daw instruction (decimal adjust WREG) makes use of DC, C and the 8-bit result in WREG in order to correct the result.

In order to check the status of the DC flag, one can clearly use the bit test instructions for there are no branch-type instructions for the digit carry.

Overflow Bit (OV)

The OV bit is affected by additions, subtractions, and increment/decrement instructions. This flag responds to operations on 8-bit signed numbers ranging from -128_{10} to $+127_{10}$. OV is set when the addition of two 8-bit binary numbers of the same sign generates a result of the opposite sign; otherwise, OV is cleared. For example, the addition of 126_{10} (0x7E) to 6_{10} (0x06) sets OV since the result 132_{10}, coded as 0x84 in hexadecimal, represents a negative number in signed 8-bit arithmetic.

The conditional branch/skip instructions that test the OV bit are bov (branch if overflow, OV = 1) and bnov (branch if no overflow, OV = 0).

DATA MOVE INSTRUCTIONS

These instructions transfer data from one place to another inside the microcontroller. They are summarized in Table 7 and allow the following:

- The transfer of constant k from program memory (movlw k) to WREG.
- The transfer of a variable from data memory (movf instruction) to WREG or back to data memory.
- The transfer of a constant k to BSR (movlb instruction).
- The transfer of data from WREG to data memory (movwf instruction).
- The transfer of data from a source register to a destination register in data memory (movff instruction).

ALU-ORIENTED INSTRUCTIONS

The Arithmetic Logic Unit (ALU) is responsible for arithmetic and logic operations. Arithmetic instructions perform addition, subtraction, multiplication, negation, increment, etc. whereas logic operations are responsible for OR, XOR, AND, 1's complement, etc. PIC18 instructions are subdivided into different categories as shown subsequently.

Table 7. Summary of the move instructions

Instruction	Meaning	Cycles
movlw k	Move literal k stored within the instruction to WREG	1
movf f, d	Move f to WREG or back to f	1
movlb k	Move literal k to BSR<3:0>	1
movwf f	Move WREG to f	1
movff f_s, f_d	Move source register f_s to destination register f_d.	2

Operations on WREG and Register F

All instructions having wf or fw in their mnemonic fall under this category, as illustrated Table 8. These instructions essentially perform logic or arithmetic operations on WREG and a register f. The result of these operations is stored in either WREG or f as specified by the instruction. For instance, assuming that RegA is declared at address 0x040, the instructions underneath add the contents of address 0x040 to WREG. The sum is stored in either 0x040 (,F option) or WREG (,W option).

```
addwf        RegA, F      ; RegA = RegA + WREG
addwf        RegA, W      ; WREG = RegA + WREG
```

Only the multiply instruction mulwf, which multiplies WREG by f, uses PRODH:PRODL as the destination register in order to fit the 16-bit result. Although the last three logic instructions in Table 8 do not have wf or fw in their mnemonic, they perform an unsigned comparison of f against WREG. If the comparison is true (f = WREG, f > WREG, f < WREG) the subsequent instruction is skipped, otherwise the instruction is executed.

Operations on WREG and Literal K

As depicted in Table 9, the instructions having lw in their mnemonic fall under this category. Essentially, they perform a logic or arithmetic operation on WREG and an 8-bit constant k specified by the instruction. With the exception of the mullw instruction, the result is stored in WREG as in Table 9.

A special case of this category of instructions is the multiply instruction mullw which multiplies WREG by a constant k and stores the 16-bit result in PRODH:PRODL.

Table 8. 2-operand byte-oriented file register operations

Instruction	Meaning	Cycles	Type
addwf f, d	Add WREG and f	1	Arithmetic
addwfc f, d	Add WREG and Carry bit to f	1	Arithmetic
subwf f, d	Subtract WREG from f	1	Arithmetic
subwfb f, d	Subtract WREG from f with borrow	1	Arithmetic
subfwb f, d	Subtract f from WREG with borrow	1	Arithmetic
mulwf f, d	Multiply WREG with f	1	Arithmetic
andwf f, d	AND WREG with f	1	Logical
iorwf f, d	Inclusive OR WREG with f	1	Logical
xorwf f, d	Exclusive OR WREG with f	1	Logical
cpfseq f	Compare f with WREG skip if f = WREG	1 (2 or 3)	Logical
cpfsgt f	Compare f with WREG skip if f > WREG	1 (2 or 3)	Logical
cpfslt f	Compare f with WREG skip if f < WREG	1 (2 or 3)	Logical

Table 9. Literal operations

Instruction	Meaning	Cycles	Type
addlw k	Add literal k to **WREG**	1	Arithmetic
sublw k	Subtract **WREG** from literal k	1	Arithmetic
mullw k	Multiply **WREG** with literal k	1	Arithmetic
andlw k	AND **WREG** with literal k	1	Logical
iorlw k	Inclusive OR **WREG** with literal k	1	Logical
xorlw k	Exclusive OR **WREG** with literal k	1	Logical

Byte-Oriented Operations on F

This is a set of arithmetic or logical operations that have strictly f in their acronym. A summary of these instructions is shown in Table 10. Note that the instructions clrf, setf, and negf do not provide a destination choice whereas the remaining instructions provide a selection between F and W.

The last five instructions in Table 10 perform arithmetic operations and program counter modification. Case in point, the instruction incfsz (increment f skip if zero) increments register f by 1. If the incremented register is zero, the next instruction is skipped, otherwise it is executed.

Similarly, the instruction tstfsz (test f skip if zero) tests whether a register is zero. If the condition is true, the next instruction is skipped, otherwise it is executed. The hardware essentially controls the offset added to the PC. If the condition is false, the offset is 2 (no skip). For a true condition, the offset is 4 if the skipped instruction is 1 word and 6 if the skipped instruction is 2 words. Note that the majority of these instructions affect the flags (see Appendix 3).

> **Example 1:** Verify the effect of the last instruction in each sequence of Table 11 on the flags. Refer to Appendix 3 to figure out the functionality of instructions and their effect on status bits.

Table 10. Single-operand byte-oriented file register operations

Instruction	Meaning	Cycles	Type
clrf f	Clear f	1	Arithmetic
comf f, d	Complement f	1	Logical
incf f, d	Increment f by 1	1	Arithmetic
decf f, d	Decrement f by 1	1	Arithmetic
negf f	Negate f	1	Arithmetic
rlcf f, d	Rotate left f through Carry	1	Logical
rrcf f, d	Rotate right f through Carry	1	Logical
rlncf f, d	Rotate left f (no Carry)	1	Logical
rrncf f, d	Rotate right f (no Carry)	1	Logical
setf f	Set f	1	Logical
swapf f, d	Swap nibbles in f	1	Logical
tstfsz f	Test f, skip if 0	1 (2 or 3)	Logical
incfsz f, d	Increment f, skip if 0	1 (2 or 3)	Arithmetic
infsnz f, d	Increment f, skip if not 0	1 (2 or 3)	Arithmetic
decfsz f, d	Decrement f, skip if 0	1 (2 or 3)	Arithmetic
dcfsnz f, d	Decrement f, skip if not 0	1 (2 or 3)	Arithmetic

Table 11. Effect of arithmetic/logic instructions on the STATUS register. x means not affected

```
;initial value of RegA: 0x02        ;initial value of RegA: 0xA0

        movlw       0xFE                    movlw       0x0F
        addwf       RegA, W                 andwf       RegA, F

  WREG = 0x00, RegA = 0x02            WREG = 0x0F, RegA = 0x00
  (N,OV,Z,DC,C) = (0,0,1,1,1)         (N,OV,Z,DC,C) = (0,x,1,x,x)
;initial value of RegA: 0xFF
                                            movlw       6
        comf    RegA, F                     sublw       5

  RegA = 0x00                          WREG = 0xFF
  (N,OV,Z,DC,C) = (0,x,1,x,x)         (N,OV,Z,DC,C) = (1,0,0,0,0)
;initial value of RegA: 0x01        ;initial value of RegA: 255

        decf    RegA, F                     incf    RegA, W

  RegA = 0x00                          WREG = 0x00, RegA = 0xFF
  (N,OV,Z,DC,C) = (0,0,1,1,1)         (N,OV,Z,DC,C) = (0,0,1,1,1)
;initial value of RegA: 0xD1        ;initial value of RegA: 0xC4

        bcf     STATUS, C                   bcf     STATUS, C
        rlcf        RegA, W                 rlncf       RegA, F

  WREG = 0xA2, RegA = 0xD1            WREG = 0xC4, RegA = 0x89
  (N,OV,Z,DC,C) = (1,x,0,x,1)         (N,OV,Z,DC,C) = (1,x,0,x,x)
;initial value of RegA: 0xCA        ;initial value of RegA: 0xAB

        movlw       0x0F                    movlw       0x55
        xorwf       RegA, W                 iorwf       RegA, W

  WREG = 0xC5, RegA = 0xCA            WREG = 0xFF, RegA = 0xAB
  (N,OV,Z,DC,C) = (1,x,0,x,x)         (N,OV,Z,DC,C) = (1,x,0,x,x)
        setf    RegA                        movlw       B'11000011'
        movff       RegA, RegB              setf    RegA
        negf    RegA                        comf    RegA, F

  RegA = 0x01, RegB = 0xFF            WREG = 0xC3, RegA = 0x00
  (N,OV,Z,DC,C) = (0,0,0,0,0)         (N,OV,Z,DC,C) = (0,x,1,x,x)
```

Bit-Oriented File Register Operations

These instructions allow bitwise operations such as setting, clearing, toggling or testing a bit inside a register (Table 12). They specify the bit to be affected or tested by reserving three bits bbb in the machine code (see bsf instruction in Table 13). The hardware uses these three bits to generate an 8-bit *mask* then performs one of the bitwise operations: OR, XOR and AND.

Table 12. Bit-oriented operations. AND $\equiv$ ·, OR $\equiv$ $^+$, XOR $\equiv$ $\oplus$

Instruction		Meaning	ALU operation	Cycles
bcf	f, b	Clear bit b in f	$f = f \cdot \overline{mask}$	1
bsf	f, b	Set bit b in f	$f = f + mask$	1
btg	f, b	Toggle bit b in f	$f = f \oplus mask$	1
btfsc	f, b	Bit test f, skip if clear	*Skip if* $(f.mask) = 0$ *else* $PC \leftarrow PC + 2$	1/2/3
btfss	f, b	Bit test f, skip if set	*Skip if* $(f.mask) = 1$ *else* $PC \leftarrow PC + 2$	1/2/3

Table 13. Bit set instruction

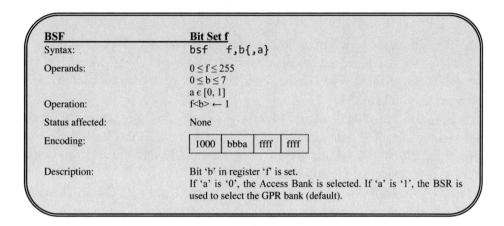

BSF	Bit Set f
Syntax:	bsf f,b{,a}
Operands:	$0 \leq f \leq 255$ $0 \leq b \leq 7$ a ϵ [0, 1]
Operation:	f<b> ← 1
Status affected:	None
Encoding:	1000 | bbba | ffff | ffff
Description:	Bit 'b' in register 'f' is set. If 'a' is '0', the Access Bank is selected. If 'a' is '1', the BSR is used to select the GPR bank (default).

The 8-bit mask is related to the bit number bbb in the following fashion: 000 → 00000001, 001 → 00000010, 010 → 00000100, 011 → 00001000, 100 → 00010000, 101 → 00100000, 110 → 01000000, 111 → 10000000.

The daw Instruction

This instruction (*decimal adjust* WREG) falls under the category of *inherent* for it operates on register WREG implied by the instruction. It adjusts the 8-bit value in WREG resulting from the earlier addition of 2 numbers (each in packed BCD format). This is a needed instruction because the ALU can only add in binary. For instance, the addition of 0x08 to 0x04 results in 0x0C which is the correct value in binary form. The decimal adjust instruction converts this result to 0x12. The used criterion is explained in the subsequent if statements:

```
if (WREG[3:0] > 9) or (DC = 1)
      WREG[3:0] ← WREG[3:0] + 6;
if (WREG[7:4] > 9) or (C = 1)
      WREG[7:4] ← WREG[7:4] + 6;
```

The carry bit is affected by the daw instruction and is used as a carry in for 16-bit packed BCD additions. Note that the above if statements are performed in sequence within one cycle.

Example 2:	How can the additions below be adjusted to provide packed BCD results?								
	1.	**2.**	**3.**	**4.**	**5.**	**6.**	**7.**	**8.**	**9.**
Operands	0x19	0x18	0x92	0x83	0x86	0x89	0x89	0x29	0x23
	0x04	0x09	0x45	0x95	0x64	0x97	0x92	0x99	0x34
Result	0x1D	0x21	0xD7	0x18	0xEA	0x20	0x1B	0xC2	0x57

Solution:

1. W[3:0] > 9, adding 0x06 to WREG adjusts it to 0x23 and no carry is generated.
2. DC = 1, adding 0x06 to the result adjusts it to 0x27 and no carry is generated.
3. W[7:4] > 9, adding 0x60 to WREG adjusts it to 0x37 and a carry is generated (C = 1) to indicate that the overall result is 0x137.
4. C = 1, adding 0x60 to WREG adjusts it to 0x78 and no carry is generated (C = 0). The carry generated before the adjustment indicates that the overall result is 0x178.
5. W[3:0] > 9 and W[7:4] > 9, adding 0x66 to the result would adjust it to 0x50 and a carry is generated (C = 1) to indicate that the overall result is 0x150.
6. DC = 1 and C = 1, adding 0x66 to the result adjusts it to 0x86 with C = 0. The carry generated before the adjustment indicates that the overall result is 0x186.
7. W[3:0] > 9 and C = 1, adding 0x66 to WREG adjusts it to 0x81 with C = 0. The carry generated before the adjustment implies that the overall result is 0x181.
8. W[7:4] > 9 and DC = 1, adding 0x66 to the result would adjust it to 0x28 and a carry is generated (C = 1) to indicate that the overall result is 0x128.
9. None of the conditions checked in the daw instruction are true and hence the decimal adjust instruction does not modify the result in this case.

CONTROL AND PC-RELATED INSTRUCTIONS

The instructions tabulated in Table 14 fall under the category of control and PC-related operations. The latter have the capability of loading or modifying the program counter conditionally or unconditionally. The last three instructions (reset, sleep and clrwdt) are categorized as control type for they can directly affect the microcontroller's hardware.

The goto Instruction

The goto instruction is a 2-word instruction that loads the program counter with the address of the instruction to be executed next (refer to Table 15). The upper 20 bits of the "jump" address (bits 20..1) are stored within the instruction. When goto Label is executed, the CPU loads bits 20 through 1 of the PC with the 20-bit field in the instruction. The least significant bit of the PC is always 0 since instructions are word aligned.

The address specified by the goto instruction is in a way "written in stone" in the sense that if a piece of code is moved to another location in memory the goto instruction does not track the new *jump* address. This is because the destination address is determined by the assembler during compilation. So, if one were to design an operating system in which *relocatable* code is a big issue, goto will definitely not do the job. The relative branch instruction bra is used instead.

It is important to note that with a 20-bit address field, the goto instruction allows an unconditional branch anywhere within the entire memory range of program space. As a result, there is no restriction as to how far the jump address is from the goto instruction.

Table 14. Control instructions that modify the program counter

Instruction	CPU Operation	Cycles	Type
goto k	$PC<20:1> \leftarrow k$, $PC<0> = 0$	2	Unconditional jump
bra n	$PC \leftarrow PC + 2 + 2n$	2	Unconditional branch
bc n	If $C = 1$, $PC \leftarrow PC + 2 + 2n$ else $PC \leftarrow PC + 2$	1 (2)	Conditional branch
bn n	If $N = 1$, $PC \leftarrow PC + 2 + 2n$ else $PC \leftarrow PC + 2$	1 (2)	Conditional branch
bnc n	If $C = 0$, $PC \leftarrow PC + 2 + 2n$ else $PC \leftarrow PC + 2$	1 (2)	Conditional branch
bnn n	If $N = 0$, $PC \leftarrow PC + 2 + 2n$ else $PC \leftarrow PC + 2$	1 (2)	Conditional branch
bnov n	If $OV = 0$, $PC \leftarrow PC + 2 + 2n$ else $PC \leftarrow PC + 2$	1 (2)	Conditional branch
bnz n	If $Z = 0$, $PC \leftarrow PC + 2 + 2n$ else $PC \leftarrow PC + 2$	1 (2)	Conditional branch
bov n	If $OV = 1$, $PC \leftarrow PC + 2 + 2n$ else $PC \leftarrow PC + 2$	1 (2)	Conditional branch
bz n	If $Z = 1$, $PC \leftarrow PC + 2 + 2n$ else $PC \leftarrow PC + 2$	1 (2)	Conditional branch
rcall n	$TOS \leftarrow PC + 2$, $PC \leftarrow PC + 2 + 2n$	2	Subroutine call
call n,s s $\in$ [0,1]	$TOS \leftarrow PC + 4$, $PC<20:1> \leftarrow n$, $PC<0> = 0$ If $s = 1$, $WS \leftarrow W$, $STATUSS \leftarrow STATUS$, $BSRS \leftarrow BSR$	2	Subroutine call
return s s $\in$ [0,1]	$PC \leftarrow (TOS)$, $PC<20:1> \leftarrow n$, $PC<0> = 0$ If $s = 1$, $W \leftarrow WS$, $STATUS \leftarrow STATUSS$, $BSR \leftarrow BSRS$ Note: PCLATU, PCLATH are unchanged	2	Subroutine return
retlw k	$W \leftarrow k$, $PC \leftarrow (TOS)$ Note: PCLATU, PCLATH are unchanged	2	Subroutine return
retfie s	$PC \leftarrow (TOS)$, set GIE or PEIE If $s = 1$, $W \leftarrow WS$, $STATUS \leftarrow STATUSS$, $BSR \leftarrow BSRS$ Note: PCLATU, PCLATH are unchanged	2	Return from interrupt
reset	Reset registers flags that are affected by a $\overline{MCLR}$ reset.	1	Hardware control
sleep	Processor is put into SLEEP mode with the oscillator stopped. Watchdog timer and its postscaler are cleared.	1	Hardware control
clrwdt	Resets Watchdog timer and its postscaler.	1	Hardware control

Table 15. Description of the goto instruction

GOTO	Unconditional Branch		
Syntax:	goto k		
Operands:	$0 \leq k \leq 1048575$		
Operation:	$PC<20:1> \leftarrow k;$		
Status affected:	None		

Encoding:

1110	1111	k_7kkk	$kkkk_0$
1111	$k_{19}kkk$	kkkk	$kkkk_8$

Description: goto allows an unconditional branch anywhere within entire 2-Mbyte memory range. The 20-bit value k is loaded into $PC<20:1>$. GOTO is a two-cycle instruction.

Words: 2

Table 16. Description of the bra instruction

BRA	**Unconditional Branch**
Syntax:	**bra** n
Operands:	$-1024 \leq n \leq 1023$
Operation:	PC ←(PC) + 2 + 2n
Status affected:	None
Encoding:		1101	0nnn	nnnn	nnnn	
Description:	The 2's complement '2n' is added to the PC. Since the PC will have incremented to fetch the next instruction, the new address will be PC + 2 + 2n. This instruction is then a two-cycle instruction.
Words:	1
Cycles:	2

The bra Instruction

The bra instruction computes the effective address at *run-time* and loads it into the PC as shown in Table 16. This is done by adding a signed offset 2n to PC+2. n, which is an 11-bit signed number stored within the instruction, is determined by the assembler. The signed offset 2n is sign-extended then added to PC+2.

When the CPU fetches the bra instruction, it assumes the next instruction in sequence will be executed next. Therefore the PC is automatically incremented by 2. Upon deciding it has to branch out of sequence, the processor adds 2n (sign-extended offset) to PC+2. The 2n even offset insures that the effective address is always word-aligned.

The offset is signed in order to give the CPU the option of branching forward or backward. The main advantage of the bra instruction is the fact that it is perfectly suitable for *relocatable code*. In other words, if the user decides to relocate a piece of code in memory, the bra instruction would still be able to compute the new destination address with respect to its new position in the program. It is generally recommended to use the bra instruction instead of the goto because the former occupies one instruction word instead of two. Since n is coded with 11 bits, the bra instruction allows a forward leap of 1023 instructions and a backward leap of 1024 instructions.

It is important to note that both bra and goto instructions require two execution cycles. The CPU wastes an extra cycle to fetch the *out-of-sequence* instruction. In computer architecture jargon, this is known as *pipeline stalling*.

Example 3: Using Tables 15 and 16, verify the encoding of the **bra/goto** instructions below.

a. Assume the **movlw** instruction is at address **0x7254** in program space

```
                goto        Label       ; Encoding: 0xEF2A
                ...                      ;           0xF039
    Label       movlw       5
```

b. Assume the **movwf** instruction is at address **0x2A8** in program space

```
                org         0x0000
                bra         Label       ; Encoding: 0xD153
                ...
    Label       movwf       RegA
```

c. Assume the **movff** instruction is at address **0x152** and the **bra** instruction is at address **0x3B4** in program space.

```
    Label       movff       RegA, RegB
                ...
                bra         Label       ; Encoding: 0xD6CE
```

Conditional Branch Instructions

The operand of conditional branch instructions:

- bz (*branch if zero*), bnz (*branch if not zero*)
- bc (*branch if carry*), bnc (*branch if not carry*)
- bn (*branch if negative*), bnn (*branch if not negative*)
- bov (*branch if overflow*) and bnov (*branch if not overflow*)

is a signed 8-bit offset n. These instructions test the relevant flag (Z, C, N, or OV) in the STATUS register. If the test condition is true, the branch address PC+2+2n is loaded into the PC. If the condition is false, the PC is loaded with PC+2 (address of subsequent instruction). Equation 1 shows how the CPU computes the branch address at run-time: the offset n is multiplied by 2 (logical shift left once), 2n is sign-extended then added to PC+2 (instruction address). This sum, which is the destination or branch address, is loaded into the PC at run-time.

$$Branch\ Address = Instruction\ Address + 2 + 2n \qquad (1)$$
$$n = [Branch\ Address - (Instruction\ Address + 2) \gg 1 \qquad (2)$$

Equation 2 is used by the assembler to compute the offset **n** given the instruction address and the branch address. Conditional branch instructions require 1 word of storage in memory. They execute in 2 cycles if the "branch" takes place; otherwise, only one cycle is elapsed. The 8-bit offset **n** implies conditional branch operations can leap forward and backward no more than 127 and 128 instruction words respectively.

Example 4: Find the offset n for the `bnz` instruction in the loop construct below:

```
            org       0x0000
            movlw     10          ; address 0x0000
            movwf     RegA        ; address 0x0002
Loop        nop                   ; address 0x0004
            nop                   ; address 0x0006
            nop                   ; address 0x0008
            decf      RegA, F     ; address 0x000A
            bnz       Loop        ; address 0x000C
```

Solution:

- Branch Address = 0x0004, Instruction Address = 0x000C.
- Branch Address - (Instruction Address + 2) = 0xFFF6 = 2n (sign extended).
- 2n shifted right once and truncated to eight bits = $1111\ 1011_2$ = 0xFB (negative offset).
- Instruction encoding: 0xE1FB
- Branch Address = 0x000C + 2 + 0xFFFB << 1 = 0x000E + 0xFFF6 = 0x0004

Example 5: Find the offset n for the `bn` instruction in the code sequence below:

```
            org       0x0200
            lfsr      0, 0x100    ; 4 bytes
            movf      INDF0, F    ; address 0x0204
            bn        Label       ; address 0x0206
            movlw     2           ; address 0x0208
            addwf     RegA, F     ; address 0x020A
            nop                   ; address 0x020C
Label       nop                   ; address 0x020E
```

Solution:

- Branch Address = 0x020E, Instruction Address = 0x0206.
- Branch Address - (Instruction Address + 2) = 0x0006 = 2n (sign-extended).
- 2n shifted right once and truncated to 8 bits = $0000\ 0011_2$ = 0x03 (positive offset).
- Instruction encoding: 0xE603
- Branch Address = 0x0206 + 2 + 0x0003 << 1 = 0x0208 + 0x0006 = 0x020E

The call, rcall, and return Instructions

These instructions are used to invoke subroutines. In computer programming, a *subroutine* is a sequence of instructions that perform a specific task. It can be used in programs wherever that particular task should be performed. The instructions call and rcall, described in Tables 17 and 18, are similar to goto

Table 17. Description of the call instructions

CALL	Subroutine Call		
Syntax:	`call  k{,s}`		
Operands:	$0 \le k \le 1048575$, $s \in [0, 1]$		
Operation:	$TOS \leftarrow (PC) + 4$, $PC<20{:}1> \leftarrow k$;		
	If $(s = 1)$, $WS \leftarrow (W)$, $STATUSS \leftarrow (STATUS)$, $BSRS \leftarrow (BSR)$		
Status affected:	None		
Encoding:			

1110	110s	k_7kkk	$kkkk_0$
1111	$k_{19}kkk$	kkkk	$kkkk_7$

Description:	Subroutine call of entire 2-Mbyte memory range. First, return address (PC+ 4) is pushed onto the return stack. If 's' = 1, the W, STATUS and BSR registers are also pushed into their respective shadow registers, WS, STATUSS and BSRS. If 's' = 0, no update occurs (default). Then, the 20-bit value k is loaded into PC<20:1>. `call` is a two-cycle instruction.		

Table 18. Description of the rcall instructions

RCALL	Relative Call		
Syntax:	`call  n`		
Operands:	$-1024 \le n \le 1023$		
Operation:	$TOS \leftarrow (PC) + 2$		
	$PC \leftarrow (PC) + 2 + 2n$		
Status affected:	None		
Encoding:			

1101	1nnn	nnnn	nnnn

Description:	Subroutine call with a jump up to 1K from the current location. First, return address (PC + 2) is pushed onto the stack. Then, the 2's complement number '2n' is added to the PC. Since the PC will have incremented to fetch the next instruction, the new address will be PC + 2 + 2n. This is a two-cycle instruction.
Words:	1
Cycles:	2

and bra. They are used to load the PC with the subroutine's address. In addition to this, they save the *return address* on the *hardware stack*.

The *return address* is the address of the instruction to be executed upon exiting a subroutine. The hardware stack consists of 32 21-bit wide registers. It keeps track of the *return address* to be retrieved by the CPU when it encounters the return instruction. Note that return loads the PC with the most recent *return address* pushed on the stack and thereby directs the CPU to resume program execution right after the call or rcall instruction. The depth of the stack (31-level deep) is designed to handle up to 31 nested subroutines.

There is a slight distinction between call and rcall. The former uses a 20-bit absolute address stored within the instruction and appends to it 0 (least significant bit) to form the 21-bit effective address at run-time. The latter (*relative call*) computes the address with respect to the current position of the PC. It adds a 12-bit signed offset 2n to PC+2. Consequently, the call instruction can jump to any address in PS whereas rcall can hop no more than 1 kiloword forward or backwards in PS.

Furthermore, the call instruction allows a *fast call* (call Label, FAST) as specified by a single bit s in the instruction. If s = 1 (FAST), W, STATUS and BSR are saved in their equivalent shadow registers WS, STATUSS and BSRS. The user may recover the original values of these registers upon exit from subroutine via the return FAST instruction. The purpose of the "FAST" call and return is the protection of registers WREG, STATUS and BSR from being modified inside the subroutine. This happens with no overhead. Finally, both call and rcall execute in 2 cycles, but differ in storage: the first is a 2-word instruction whereas the second occupies a single word.

The easiest way to abuse the logical flow of programs happens when goto and bra are employed as substitutes for call and rcall, and vice versa. This is because the former instructions do not save the return address on the stack. As a result, when the return instruction is encountered, the wrong address is pulled from the stack and the program runs out of control. Also, care must be taken to insure that every subroutine call is matched with a return instruction. Otherwise, the program is guaranteed an erroneous behavior.

The retlw Instruction

The retlw instruction operates like the return instruction. Besides this, it sends back a constant value via the working register. It is similar to the C return statement in the following function. Note that the assembly language subroutine func, sends back the value of 4 in WREG if RegA > RegB; otherwise, WREG returns 8 to the calling routine.

```
int func(int RegA, int RegB)     func        movf      RegB, W
{                                             cpfsgt    RegA
        if (RegA > RegB)                      retlw     8
                return 4;                     retlw     4
        else
                return 8;
}
```

There are a couple of ways one can access array elements in program space: (a) using a *computed goto* and (b) via the tblrd instruction. A *computed goto* is accomplished by adding an index in WREG to the PC thereby redirecting program flow to the new position of the PC. The subsequent program elucidates the concept:

```
        org     0x0000
        movlw   2               ; WREG = 2 (array index)
        rcall   Table           ; read Table[2]
        movwf   RegA            ; store 0x56 in RegA
        bra     $

Table   addwf   WREG, W         ; multiply W by 2
        addwf   PCL, F          ; PCL ← PCL + 2 + 2*W
        retlw   0x12            ; Table[0] = 0x12
        retlw   0x34            ; Table[0] = 0x34
        retlw   0x56            : Table[0] = 0x56
```

Subroutine Table is invoked via the rcall instruction with the index ($i = 2$) sent in WREG. This index is then multiplied by 2. This way, the PC hops by an even offset to account for word aligned instructions. Adding 2*i to the PC guides the CPU to jump to the last retlw instruction. Upon executing it, the table entry 0x56 is stored in WREG and the return address is retrieved from the hardware stack. This means that the CPU will resume program execution at the movwf instruction with Table[2] stored in WREG.

Note that the alteration of PCL (say via the addwf PCL, F instruction) has the side effect of loading the reset values of PCLATU and PCLATH (all 0s) into bits 20 through 8 of the PC. If the lookup table happens to originate at an address greater than 8 bits (0x0100 and above), the computed goto technique will no longer work. This is because, latching 0's in the upper part of the PC will redirect the CPU to execute instructions in the first page of program memory (0x0000 - 0x00FF). As a result, no retlw instruction will be executed. To remedy this problem, one must update the contents of PCLATH and PCLATU via a dummy read of PCL (movf PCL, F). This way the PC is loaded with the appropriate 21-bit address when an offset is added to it. Here is the proposed solution:

```
        org     0x0100          ; or 0x0200, etc.
Table   movf    PCL, F          ; update PCLATU:PCLATH
        addwf   WREG, W         ; multiply W by 2
        addwf   PCL, F          ; PC<20:8> ← PCLATH/U
                                ; PCL ← PCL + 2 + 2*W
        dt      0x12, 0x34, 0x56
```

Note that dt (*define table*) is an assembler directive used to enumerate a large number of retlw instructions. For instance, if one were to store a null-terminated string of ASCII characters in program space, the following directive is employed:

```
dt          "Hello World\0"
```

The retfie Instruction

This instruction is very much similar to the return instruction with the addition that it sets the global interrupt enable bit GIE or PEIE. It is used to return from an *interrupt service routine*. Interrupts will be discussed in chapter 6 in detail.

The reset, sleep, and clrwdt Instructions

These instructions fall under the category of control instructions. They have the ability of directly affecting the hardware. Here is a description of their operation:

- **reset:** Provides a way to do a $f = f \cdot \overline{mask}$ reset of the CPU in software. This has the effect of clearing the **PC** thereby restarting the program at address 0. Besides this, all control registers will be loaded with their initial values (see Appendix 2).
- **sleep:** The processor is put in SLEEP mode with the oscillator stopped. In this mode, the microcontroller saves power for it consumes a current less than 100 nA typically.
- **clrwdt:** Resets the watchdog timer and its prescaler as well. When enabled, it elapses a preset period of time (from 4 ms to 131.072 secs) before it times out. When this occurs, the CPU is reset and the program starts all over again. Normally, the user resets the WDT before it times out via the clrwdt instruction. If for some reason this instruction is not reached, the CPU resets itself, provided of course that the watchdog timer is enabled.

PROGRAM MEMORY READ/WRITE INSTRUCTIONS

There are essentially two instructions dealing with program memory: tblrd and tblwt along with their variants. The registers involved in reading from or writing to PM are TBLPTR and Table Latch (or TABLAT) shown in Figure 1.

The tblrd Instruction

This instruction is one of the novelties of PIC18 microcontrollers for it allows reading of data bytes stored side by side in program space. This is done by:

1. Loading the 21-bit register TBLPTRU:TBLPTRH:TBLPTRL with the address of the memory location to be read.
2. Executing instruction tblrd which moves the contents of the location pointed to by TBLPTR into TABLAT. This instruction allows pointer update (see Table 19).

Table 19. The tblrd instruction and its variants

Instruction	CPU Operation
tblrd*	TABLAT ← (Prog Mem(TBLPTR)), TBLPTR - no change
tblrd*+	TABLAT ← (Prog Mem(TBLPTR)), TBLPTR = TBLPTR + 1
tblrd*-	TABLAT ← (Prog Mem(TBLPTR)), TBLPTR = TBLPTR - 1
tblrd+*	TBLPTR = TBLPTR + 1, TABLAT ← (Prog Mem(TBLPTR))

The db (define byte) directive is used to store a set of consecutive table entries in PS as in:

```
            org         0x1234
Table       db          0x12, 0x34, 0x56, 0x78   ; hex values
Message     db          "Hello World\0"          ; string
```

In order to let TBLPTR point to address Table declared at address 0x1234 in PS, the following sequence of instructions will do the job.

```
        movlw       upper(Table)        ; upper(0x1234) = 0x00
        movwf       TBLPTRU             ; TBLPTRU = 0x00
        movlw       high(Table)         ; high(0x1234) = 0x12
        movwf       TBLPTRH             ; TBLPTRH = 0x12
        movlw       low(Table)          ; low(0x1234) = 0x34
        movwf       TBLPTRL             ; TBLPTRL = 0x34
```

Six instructions may seem cumbersome to point to a memory location in PS. In chapter 4, these instructions are encapsulated in macroinstruction Point. Finally, note that the tblrd instruction does not affect the STATUS bits. Therefore, in order to check whether a table entry is zero, use the following code:

```
        tblrd*                          ; read entry into TABLAT
        movf        TABLAT, F           ; affect flags
        bz          Label               ; bra if TABLAT = 0
```

Example 6:   Assuming **TBLPTR** holds the address **Table+2** initially, verify the values stored in **TABLAT** and **TBLPTR** upon execution of the subsequent code.

```
                org         0x0000
                tblrd*+
                movf        TABLAT, W
                tblrd+*
                bnz         $

                org         0x0050
    Table       db          "012345"
```

TABLAT = 0x34 (ASCII of 4), **TBLPTR** = 0x000054, **WREG** = 0x32

The tblwt Instruction

This instruction allows writing data bytes in program space. This is not as straight forward as reading data. Since writing to EEPROM cells will be discussed when covering the data EEPROM in chapter 4, the tblwt instruction will not be explained in this textbook. Interested readers may refer to the manufacturer's datasheet for a detailed explanation of this instruction.

CONCLUSION

This chapter outlined the majority of PIC18 instructions. The extended instruction set, not covered in this chapter, is hardly ever used by system developers.

Finally, it is important to remember that assembly language programming is both a science and an art. It is a science because one can learn systematic ways to implement high level statements. It is an art in the sense that the user may write attractive and readable code by properly subdividing code sequences, writing clarifying comments and even choosing adequate variable names.

Chapter 4
Macros and Subroutines

This chapter highlights sound programming habits particularly those pertaining to *modularity* and *code readability*. Modularity is the art of designing independent software modules or subprograms better known as subroutines.

SUBROUTINES

A subroutine is a set of instructions designed to perform a specific and usually repetitive task. The user's program may execute the subroutine simply by "calling" its name. Upon termination of the subroutine's chore, the CPU resumes execution of remaining jobs. The main advantages of subroutines in programming languages are:

- Staying away from re-inventing the wheel. In fact many useful and elaborate routines have been written by other programmers and are available to "cut-and-paste" free of charge. This speeds up software development and frees the programmer from the burden of re-designing a piece of code from scratch.
- The utilization of subroutines makes programs more compact since an instruction sequence does not have to be reproduced over and over if one intends to perform the same task repetitively. The logical thing to do is to design a subroutine and invoke it as needed in a program.
- Subroutines make programs more readable for they divide big tasks into smaller ones that the user can easily trace. For instance, someone interested in designing a digital thermostat would have to perform the following steps:
  - Read the temperature from a sensor.
  - Display it on a Liquid Crystal Display (LCD).
  - Compare it against a set point for HVAC control.

DOI: 10.4018/978-1-68318-000-5.ch004

The programmer may then design three autonomous subroutines namely: ReadTemp, DispTemp and Control. This way if a fault is detected in one of these software modules, it can be corrected independently of the other modules. Thus programmers can concentrate on debugging one subroutine at a time, reminiscent of how humans normally tackle life difficulties: "I will cross that bridge when I get to it".

A *macro* is a set of instructions framed between the two assembler directives: *macro* and *endm*. It allows programmers to extend the instruction set to handle more complex operations such as 16-bit manipulations, BCD arithmetic, etc. When the assembler encounters a macro call, it inserts the instructions constituting the macro into the program. This is not the case for subroutines; instructions forming a subroutine have only one occurrence in the program and are executed upon demand.

Macros allow programmers to hide certain intricacies inside software blocks and hence they give programs a compact appearance and improved *readability*. In fact, tracing and debugging a long program is rather overwhelming whereas a concise and structured program attracts its reader and is easier to trace. In upcoming sections, macros and subroutines will be developed with the following goals in mind: instruction set extension, program compactness and improved readability.

PRE-DECLARED VARIABLES

Using the same variable name in several subprograms has the benefit of reducing memory storage and also improving program readability. In order to eliminate side effects, variables must be properly protected in nested subroutines. The *software stack*, introduced in a later section, allows saving and retrieving these variables. In this textbook, a set of variables starting at address 0x040 (access bank) are pre-declared as shown:

```
cblock      0x040                   ; variables in access RAM
    RegA, RegB, RegC, RegD          ; 8-bit GP registers
    RegE:2, RegF:2                  ; 16-bit GP registers
    RegG:2, RegH:2                  ; 16-bit GP registers
    wE:2                            ; 16-bit working register
endc
```

This *constant block*[1] (cblock) declaration will be part of the file <MyMacros.asm>. This file essentially contains all the *macros* to be developed throughout this chapter. You need to include it in each assembly language program of this book via the directive:

```
#include     <MyMacros.asm>
```

BASIC MACROS

MPASM[2] assembler macros have the following generic syntax:

```
<macroname>        macro                 [<arg1>, <arg1>, … ,<argn>]
                   instruction sequence
                   endm
```

where <macroname> is a valid assembler label used to invoke the macro, and <arg$_i$> is any number of optional arguments supplied to the macro. Hence a macro allows the user to pass parameters as in high level languages. The endm directive terminates the macro. Note that macros must be defined before the org directive in order for the program to invoke them when needed.

As mentioned before, a macro replaces a frequently repeated sequence of instructions to provide programs with a higher level of readability. For instance, it is very common to move constant data or *literal* from program memory to data memory as in:

```
        movlw       val                 ; move val to WREG
        movwf       reg                 ; move WREG to reg
```

The repetition of these instructions makes it worthwhile designing the Load macro:

```
Load        macro       reg, val        ; load reg with val
            movlw       val             ; move val to WREG
            movwf       reg             ; move WREG to reg
            endm
```

The *formal arguments* reg and val will be substituted with *actual arguments* whenever the Load macro is invoked. For instance, the assembler will replace

```
        Load        PORTB, 0x55
```

with

```
        movlw       0x55                ; move 0x55 to WREG
        movwf       PORTB               ; move WREG to PORTB
```

Note that the Load macro has the side effect of modifying WREG. In order to distinguish between instructions and macroinstructions, the convention of capitalizing the first letter of a macro has been adopted throughout this textbook.

> **Example 1** The PIC18F instruction set does not allow incrementing or decrementing a packed BCD variable directly. For example, if variable `Temp` storing `0x59` is incremented by 1, the result would be `0x5A`. This result is corrected to `0x60` via the **daw** instruction.
>
> a. Design the macro **IncBcd** that increments a packed BCD variable by 1. Make sure the incremented variable rolls over from `0x99` to `0x00`.
>
> b. Design a macro **DecBcd** that decrements a packed BCD variable by 1. Ensure the decremented variable rolls back from `0x00` to `0x99`. *Hint*: In order to decrement a variable by 1, one can add the 10's complement of 1 to the variable and then do the decimal adjust.
>
> c. Show how you can invoke the macros of parts (a) and (b) to emulate the `if` statement:
>
> ```
>         if (PORTBbits.RB0 == 0)        // test bit 0 of PORTB
>             increment BCD counter by 1
>         else
>             decrement BCD counter by 1
> ```
>
> d. Use the macros **Brset** or **Brclr**, defined subsequently, to simplify part c.
>
> ```
> ; Branch to label if flag (or bit number) in reg is set.
> Brset           macro       reg, flag, label
>                 btfsc       reg, flag
>                 bra         label
>                 endm
>
> ; Branch to label if flag (or bit number) in reg is clear.
> Brclr           macro       reg, flag, label
>                 btfss       reg, flag
>                 bra         label
>                 endm
> ```

Solution:

a. As is the case with the Load macro, IncBcd assumes the register being used is in *access bank*. This is a fair assumption to make since the special function registers commonly employed belong to the *access bank*. The user is then constrained to declare variables in this bank. This is not such a great sacrifice to make.

```
IncBcd          macro       f
                incf        f, W        ; store incremented f in W
                daw                     ; decimal adjust W
                movwf       f           ; store adjusted value in f
                endm
```

b. The 10's complement of 1 is obtained by evaluating the 9's complement of 1 then adding 1 to the result: $(0x99 - 0x01) + 0x01 = 0x99$. Therefore, to subtract 1 from a packed BCD variable, one can simply add 0x99 to it. This trick is used simply because the daw instruction does not adjust a decremented register. The macro is shown below:

```
DecBcd          macro       f
                movlw       0x99            ; 10s complement of -1: 0x99
                addwf       f, W            ; store decremented f in W
                daw                         ; decimal adjust W
                movwf       f               ; store adjusted value in f
                endm
```

c. Since btfsc/btfss skip only one instruction, care must be taken when skipping a macro consisting of more than one instruction. Note that in order to use PORTB and RB0, you must include the file <P18F45K22.inc> at the beginning of the program.

```
                btfsc       PORTB, RB0
                bra         Dec
Inc             IncBcd      RegA            ; RB0 = 0
                bra         GoOn            ; to endif
Dec             DecBcd      RegA            ; RB0 = 1
GoOn            ...
```

d. Here is a better approach that simplifies the code and makes it more compact.

```
                Brset       PORTB, RB0, Dec
Inc             IncBcd      RegA            ; RB0 = 0
                bra         GoOn            ; to endif
Dec             DecBcd      RegA            ; RB0 = 1
GoOn            ...
```

> **Example 2** Code the macros, part of <MyMacros.asm>, whose prototypes are given in Table 1 These allow you to implement structured if statements in assembly language.

Solution: These macroinstructions are more versatile than the instructions cpfslt, cpfseq, cpfsgt for they can branch to any address within the limits of the bra instruction. This is a good recipe for avoiding "spaghetti code". This set of macroinstructions perform *unsigned comparisons*. The coding of these macros is listed in Table 2.

> **Example 3** Using the macros coded in Table 2, write a macro-based program to sort the three registers a, b and c in ascending order.

Table 1. Compare and branch macros

Macro Prototype	Performed Task
Cpfblt reg, label	PC ← label if reg < WREG, else execute next instruction
Cpfbeq reg, label	PC ← label if reg = WREG, else execute next instruction
Cpfbgt reg, label	PC ← label if reg > WREG, else execute next instruction
Cpfbneq reg, label	PC ← label if reg != WREG, else execute next instruction

Table 2. Coding of compare and branch macros

Compare reg against WREG, branch to label if reg < WREG (unsigned comparison)			
Cpfblt	macro	reg, label	
	cpfslt	reg	
	bra	$+4	; skip next instruction
	bra	label	
	endm		
Compare reg against WREG, branch to label if reg = WREG			
Cpfbeq	macro	reg, label	
	cpfseq	reg	
	bra	$+4	; skip next instruction
	bra	label	
	endm		
Compare reg against WREG, branch to label if reg > WREG (unsigned comparison)			
Cpfbgt	macro	reg, label	
	cpfsgt	reg	
	bra	$+4	; skip next instruction
	bra	label	
	endm		
Compare reg against WREG, branch to label if reg != WREG			
Cpfbneq	macro	reg, label	
	cpfseq	reg	; skip next instruction if equal
	bra	label	; else branch
	endm		

Solution: The algorithm leads to the design of the macros Swap, Sort2 and Sort3 coded in Table 3. The directive local (in Sort2) implies that ExitAddr will be computed with respect to the position of the macro call inside the program. Therefore, this label will not cause conflict if the macro is employed more than once in the program.

In brief, macros allow you to extend the capability of a programming language and give programs a compact look reminiscent of high-level languages.

16-BIT MACROS

The 18F family of microcontrollers is a native 8-bit family. Although 8-bit arithmetic and logic operations constitute the vast majority of operations in a microcontroller program, 16-bit manipulations find their application in double precision arithmetic.

In this section, we propose to develop some useful "16-bit macros". In order to distinguish between 8-bit and 16-bit macros, the capital letter "E" (**Extended**) will be associated with the macro name. Furthermore, the so-called *little endian* notation will be adopted. This means that if a 16-bit variable Temp:2 is declared at address 0x000, then Temp (address 0x000) will store the least significant byte of the variable and Temp+1 (address 0x001) will store the most significant byte.

As a start, the macro LoadE (*load extended*) is used to load a 16-bit constant (e.g. 0x1234) into a 16-bit register (e.g. RegE). It is coded as follows:

Table 3. Program to sort three variables in ascending order

```
Sorting 3 variables in ascending order using macros
 1  #include     <MyMacros.asm>
 2
 3  Swap         macro       arg1, arg2         ; swap arg1 & arg2
 4               movf        arg1, W
 5               movff       arg2, arg1
 6               movwf       arg2
 7               endm
 8
 9  Sort2        macro       arg1, arg2
10               local       ExitAddr
11               incf        arg2, W            ; W = arg2 + 1
12               Cpfblt      arg1, ExitAddr     ; arg1 <= arg2
13               Swap        arg1, arg2         ; arg1 > arg2
14  ExitAddr
15               endm
16
17  Sort3        macro       arg1, arg2, arg3
18               Sort2       arg1, arg2         ; sort arg1 & arg2
19               Sort2       arg1, arg3         ; sort arg1 & arg3
20               Sort2       arg2, arg3         ; sort arg2 & arg3
21               endm
22
23               org         0x0000
24               Sort3       RegA, RegB, RegC   ; single statement
25               bra         $
26               end
```

```
LoadE        macro       reg, val
             Load        reg+1, high(val)    ; high(val) = MS byte
             Load        reg+0, low(val)     ; low(val) = LS byte
             endm
```

Another useful macro is MovffE (*movff extended*). It transfers the contents of a 16-bit register to another.

```
MovffE       macro       SrcReg, DstReg
             movff       SrcReg+0, DstReg+0
             movff       SrcReg+1, DstReg+1
             endm
```

Example 4   Using the macros developed in Example 1, design two macros IncBcdE and DecBcdE to perform a similar task on 16-bit registers.

Solution: When incrementing a 16-bit register, the least significant byte (reg+0) is incremented first. If a carry is generated, the most significant byte (reg+1) is then incremented. As to decrementing a 16-bit register, if the decrementation of the least significant byte leads a result of 0x99, then the most significant byte must be decremented as well. These macros are listed subsequently:

```
Increment 16-bit packed BCD register (little-endian format)
IncBcdE      macro        reg
             local        ExitAddr
             IncBcd       reg
             bnc          ExitAddr
             IncBcd       reg+1
ExitAddr
             endm
Decrement 16-bit packed BCD register (little-endian format)
DecBcdE      macro        reg
             local        ExitAddr
             DecBcd       reg
             movlw        0x99
             subwf        reg, W
             bnz          ExitAddr
             DecBcd       reg+1
ExitAddr
             endm
```

Table 4 summarizes 16-bit macros pertaining to double precision arithmetic and data move operations. These adopt the little-endian notation and are coded in Table 4 in Appendix 4.

Another useful set of macros comprise the capability of comparing a 16-bit register against zero and branching to an address accordingly. By analogy with the instructions: bnz and tstfsz, the macros BnzE (branch if 16-bit register is nonzero) and TstEsz (test extended skip if zero) are coded as follows:

```
Branch to label if 16-bit register reg is different than zero
BnzE     macro     reg, label
         movf      reg+0, F    ; Set Z if lower byte = 0
         bnz       label       ; if LS byte != 0, bra to label
         movf      reg+1, F    ; Set Z if upper byte = 0
         bnz       label       ; if MS byte is != 0, bra to label
         endm                  ; else next
Test 16-bit register reg, skip next instruction if zero
TstEsz   macro     reg
         movf      reg+0, F    ; Set Z if lower byte = 0
         bnz       $+4         ; if LS byte is != 0, don't skip
         tstfsz    reg+1       ; if MS byte is != 0, don't skip
         endm
```

Example 5 Code the macro BltE (*branch if less extended*) with the following header:

```
    BltE        macro        reg, val, label
```

which makes a 16-bit unsigned comparison of reg against val. If reg is strictly less than val, the branch to label takes place, otherwise the **PC** points to the first instruction after the macro.

Solution: The subsequent code sequence consists of making two unsigned 8-bit comparisons starting with (reg+1) against high(val) then (reg+0) against low(val).

Table 4. 16-bit arithmetic and data move macros (see code in Table 4 (Appendix 4))

Macro Prototype		Performed Task	Cycles
LoadE	reg, val	Load extended register with 16-bit literal	4
MovffE	Src, Dst	Extended move of Src to Dst	4
ClrE	reg	Clear 16-bit register	2
ComE	reg	1's complement 16-bit register	2
IncE	reg	Increment 16-bit register by 1	2
NegE	reg	Negate 16-bit register (2's complement)	4
AddE	reg, val	Add 16-bit value to 16-bit register	4
AddwfE	reg	Add WREG to 16-bit variable register	3
AddwEf	reg	Add 16-bit wE to 16-bit variable register	4
DecE	reg	Decrement 16-bit register by 1	3
SubE	reg, val	Subtract 16-bit literal from 16-bit register	4
SubwfE	reg	Subtract WREG from 16-bit register	3
SubwEf	reg	Subtract 16-bit wE from 16-bit register	4
IncBcdE	reg	Increment 4-digit packed BCD register by 1	6/8
DecBcdE	reg	Decrement 4-digit packed BCD register by 1	8/11

```
Compare 16-bit register against 16-bit value, branch if reg < val (unsigned comparison)
BltE        macro       reg, val, label
            local       ExitAddr
            movlw       high(val)    ; put high order data in W
            subwf       reg+1, W     ; compare (reg)hi with (val)hi
            bnc         label        ; reg < val, goto label
            bnz         ExitAddr     ; result != 0, bra to ExitAddr
            movlw       low(val)     ; compare (reg)lo with (val)lo
            subwf       reg+0, W     ; if reg >= val, bra to ExitAddr
            bnc         label        ; else branch to label
ExitAddr
            endm
```

Table 5 summarizes all 16-bit unsigned *compare and branch* type of macros. These macros are coded in Table 6 (Appendix 4).

Table 5. 16-bit unsigned compare/test instructions (see code in Table 6 (Appendix 4))

Macro Prototype		Performed Task	Cycles
BnzE	reg, label	PC ← label if reg ≠ 0, else execute next instruction	3/4/5
BzE	reg, label	PC ← label if reg = 0, else execute next instruction	3/4/5
BltE	reg, val, label	PC ← label if reg < value, else execute next instruction	4/5/7/8
BgeE	reg, val, label	PC ← label if reg ≥ value, else execute next instruction	4/5/7/8
BeqE	reg, val, label	PC ← label if reg = value, else execute next instruction	4/6/7
CpEblt	reg, label	PC ← label if reg < wE, else execute next instruction	4/5/7/8
CpEbeq	reg, label	PC ← label if reg = wE, else execute next instruction	4/6/7
CpEbgt	reg, label	PC ← label if reg > wE, else execute next instruction	4/5/8/9
TstEsz	reg	Skip next instruction if reg = 0, else execute it	3/4
TstEsnz	reg	Skip next instruction if reg ≠ 0, else execute it	4/5

SOFTWARE STACK AND RELATED MACROS

Since the hardware stack of PIC18 processors is used to store return addresses in subroutine calls, the user cannot save variables on it. In many applications, there is a need to save subroutine parameters in data memory for later retrieval. A user defined *software stack* is designed specifically for that purpose.

PIC18 MCUs do not directly provide users with a *software stack* and an associated *stack pointer*. They do on the other hand supply them with three pointers FSR0, FSR1 and FSR2 along with abundant data memory. If FSR2 is sacrificed for utilization as a software stack pointer SP, then a stack data structure can be easily implemented. The two remaining pointers FSR0 and FSR1 are usually sufficient in most programs. The advantage of adding the stack data structure for protecting variables generally outweighs the inconvenience of losing only one pointer out of the three.

When an 8-bit variable is saved or pushed on the stack, it is written at the location pointed to by the SP (FSR2 in this case). Then the SP is decremented to point to the next available address on the stack. The type of stack being described here grows from upper data memory towards lower data memory as shown in Figure 1. It is assumed that the initial position of the stack pointer is 0x0FF which happens to be the uppermost address in bank 0.

In order to retrieve an 8-bit value from the stack, the SP is incremented to point to the data item to be read. The value addressed by the SP is then read into a specified variable. To distinguish between 8-bit and 16-bit variables, PushB and PullB (B stands for Byte) versus PushD and PullD (D stands for Double byte) are employed. Table 6 lists all the stack related operations including the code.

> **Example 6**   Rewrite the Swap macro of Example 4 without modifying **WREG**.

Solution: The approach shown underneath uses the stack as a temporary variable and hence WREG will not be altered. Never forget to initialize the SP using InitSP when the stack is used. Otherwise, you will be overwriting undesired memory locations.

```
Swap        macro       arg1, arg2
            PushB       arg1
            movff       arg2, arg1
            PullB       arg2
            endm
```

Figure 1. The initial position of the SP and its position after three variables are pushed onto the stack; this stack is a LIFO type (Last In First Out).

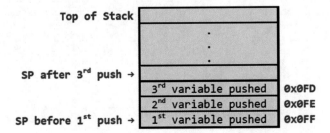

Table 6. Stack related macros

Macro Implementation			Performed Task	Cycles
InitSP	macro lfsr endm	2, 0x0FF	SP ← 0x0FF, initialize SP to 0x0FF	2
PushB	macro movff endm	reg reg, POSTDEC2	*SP ← reg, SP--	2
PullB	macro movff endm	reg PREINC2, reg	SP++, reg ← *SP	2
PushD	macro movff movff endm	reg reg+1, POSTDEC2 reg+0, POSTDEC2	*SP ← reg+1, SP--, *SP ← reg, SP--	4
PullD	macro movff movff endm	reg PREINC2, reg+0 PREINC2, reg+1	SP++, reg ← *SP, SP++, reg+1 ← *SP	4

SUBROUTINES

A subroutine is a set of instructions designed to perform a specific task. These instructions are framed between the subroutine name and the return instruction. When a subroutine is invoked with the call/rcall instruction, the following occurs:

1. The *return address* is saved on the hardware stack.
2. The PC is loaded with the subroutine's address. As a result, the CPU will execute the first instruction in the subroutine and proceed with subsequent instructions.

When the return instruction is encountered, the return address is pulled from the hardware stack into the PC. This means that the CPU will resume execution at the instruction located right after the call/rcall instruction.

Subroutines help subdivide large tasks into smaller ones that are more tractable and hence easier to trace. In a way, the calling routine passes the buck to specialized subprograms in order to solve these smaller tasks. In essence, a large program consists of a number of subroutines invoked in sequence by the main program. A set of subroutines relevant to a particular task or peripheral constitute a *library*. Throughout this chapter, a number of subroutines dealing with *Binary-to-BCD* conversion are packaged in an *include* file namely <BCDlib.asm>. This way, all conversion related peculiarities are hidden in the library. The textbook promotes the utilization of libraries in accordance with the approach used in high level languages.

> **Example 7**   Subroutine Sub1 uses RegA as a loop counter to invoke subroutine Sub2 10 times. Sub2 uses RegA as a temporary register. Show how this can be done without incurring side effects.

Solution: This example shows how RegA can be used as a local variable in two subroutines where one (Sub1) invokes the other (Sub2). Obviously, the stack is an ideal place to save local variables and retrieve them later.

```
Sub1        Load        RegA, 10
Loop        rcall       Sub2
            decf        RegA, F
            bnz         Loop
            return

Sub2        PushB       RegA
            ...
            PullB       RegA
            return
```

> **Example 8**   The subroutine CopyBuff transfers a buffer of size Len (Len < 65536) starting at address SrcB to a destination buffer at address DstB. Different versions are shown for comparative purposes.

Solution: Version 1 keeps track of the number of iterations via a loop counter. If Len <= 255, the 8-bit loop counter RegA may be used. If the iterations exceed 255, the 16-bit loop counter RegE must be used instead (version 2). In this case, the DecE macroinstruction must be coupled with the BnzE macro in order to iterate Len number of times. Note that DecE does not affect the Z-bit when RegE is decremented. Hence BnzE tests if RegE is not zero. If this is the case, the branch address Next is loaded into the PC.

Version 3 is a more compact version. It compares the pointer FSR0 against the last address in the buffer. If it exceeds it (FSR0 = SrcB+Len), the loop is exited. Otherwise, looping occurs until the last data item is transferred. The BltE uses FSR0L in the comparison simply because the macro compares FSR0 = FSR0H:FSR0L against SrcB+Len (see implementation of BltE).

```
┌──────────────────────────────────────────────────────────────────────────────┐
│ Version 1: Len <= 255, loop counter is used                                    │
├──────────────────────────────────────────────────────────────────────────────┤
│ CopyBuff   lfsr      0, SrcB            ; point FSR0 to SrcB                    │
│            lfsr      1, DstB            ; point FSR1 to DstB                    │
│            Load      RegA, Len          ; 8-bit counter                        │
│ Next       movff     POSTINC0, POSTINC1 ; DstB[i] = SrcB[i]                     │
│            decf      RegA, F            ; RegA--, affect Z-bit                  │
│            bnz       Next               ; branch if RegA != 0                   │
│            return                                                              │
├──────────────────────────────────────────────────────────────────────────────┤
│ Version 2: Len <= 65,535, loop counter is used                                 │
├──────────────────────────────────────────────────────────────────────────────┤
│ CopyBuff   lfsr      0, SrcB            ; point FSR0 to SrcB                    │
│            lfsr      1, DstB            ; point FSR1 to DstB                    │
│            LoadE     RegE, Len          ; 16-bit counter                       │
│ Next       movff     POSTINC0, POSTINC1 ; DstB[i] = SrcB[i]                     │
│            DecE      RegE               ; RegE--                               │
│            BnzE      RegE, Next         ; branch if RegE != 0                   │
│            return                                                              │
├──────────────────────────────────────────────────────────────────────────────┤
│ Version 3: Len <= 65,535, no loop counter is used                              │
├──────────────────────────────────────────────────────────────────────────────┤
│ CopyBuff   lfsr      0, SrcB            ; point FSR0 to SrcB                    │
│            lfsr      1, DstB            ; point FSR1 to DstB                    │
│ Next       movff     POSTINC0, POSTINC1 ; DstB[i] = SrcB[i]                     │
│            BltE      FSR0L, SrcB+Len, Next ; pointer arithmetic                 │
│            return                                                              │
└──────────────────────────────────────────────────────────────────────────────┘
```

The upcoming macro does essentially the same thing in a high level syntax. The buffer length Len along with the source and destination addresses (SrcB and DstB) are passed as arguments.

```
CopyBuff    macro     SrcB, DstB, Len
            local     Loop
            PushD     FSR0L
            PushD     FSR1L
            PushD     RegE
            lfsr      0, SrcB            ; point FSR0 to SrcB
            lfsr      1, DstB            ; point FSR1 to DstB
            LoadE     RegE, Len          ; 16-bit counter
Loop        movff     POSTINC0, POSTINC1 ; DstB[i] = SrcB[i]
            DecE      RegE               ; RegE--
            BnzE      RegE, Loop         ; branch if RegE != 0
            PullD     RegE
            PullD     FSR1L
            PullD     FSR0L
            endm
```

Notice that FSR0, FSR1 and RegE are protected via appropriate *Push* and *Pull* macroinstructions. Although saving local variables on the stack and retrieving them later may seem to be a hassle, this is the only guarantee for removing side effects.

Example 9 Design a subroutine `FindAve` to compute the rounded average value of a buffer `Buff` of size Len = 256 bytes. The average value is stored in variable **Ave**.

Solution: The code is listed in Table 7. FindAve computes the sum of the buffer elements first. Since the maximum sum is 16-bit wide (256 x 255 = 65280 < 65536), RegE is used as an accumulator. AddwfE adds the 8-bit array element Buff[i] to the sum.

Table 7. Program to compute the rounded average value of a 256-byte buffer in DM

Finding the rounded average value of a buffer using a subroutine call.				
1	#include	<P18F45K22.inc>		
2	#include	<MyMacros.asm>		
3				
4	#define	Buff	0x100	
5	#define	Len	256	
6				
7		cblock	0x000	
8			Ave	
9		endc		
10				
11		org	0x0000	
12		rcall	FindAve	
13		bra	$	
14	FindAve	PushD	FSR0L	
15		PushD	RegE	
16		lfsr	0, Buff	
17		ClrE	RegE	; sum = 0
18	Next	movf	POSTINC0, W	
19		AddwfE	RegE	; sum += Buff[i]
20		BltE	FSR0L, Buff+Len, Next	
21		movff	RegE+1, Ave	; divide by 256
22		btfsc	RegE+0, 7	
23		incf	Ave	; rounding result
24		PullD	RegE	
25		PushD	FSR0L	
26		return		

To divide by 256 (or 2^8), the decimal point is placed in the middle of RegE. This implies that the average value is in RegE+1. The lower byte RegE+0 holds the bits after the decimal point and hence the 7th bit, with weight 2^{-1}, is tested for rounding purposes.

Example 10   The C snippet below converts an 8-bit number N to BCD. It computes the number of 100s, 10s and units. These are stored in a[0], a[1] and a[2] respectively.

```
a[0] = 0; a[1] = 0;         // a[] and N are global
CompDig(100, 0);            // a[0] = Most significant digit
CompDig(10, 1);             // a[1] = Middle digit
a[2] = N;                   // a[2] = Least significant digit

void CompDig(unsigned char temp, unsigned char i) {
        while (N >= temp) {
                N = N - temp;
                a[i] = a[i] + 1;
        }
}
```

a. Write a subroutine _Bin2Bcd to convert the 8-bit number stored in RegA to unpacked BCD. The result is stored in 3 consecutive registers pointed to by **FSR0**. Also design a macro Bin2Bcd with two parameters SrcReg and DstAddr where SrcReg holds the number to be converted and DstAddr is the starting address in the destination array.

b. Repeat part (a) for a 16-bit binary number passed as an argument in RegE. Make use of the 16-bit macros dicsussed earlier in the chapter.

c. Write a small program to test the macros of part (a) and (b).

Solution:

a. The C code above is converted to the macro and subroutine listed in Table 8. The subroutine will be part of a library named <BCDlib.asm>[3] whereas the macro is added to <MyMacros.asm>. RegA, used as an input parameter, is saved and retrieved in order for the subroutine not to create undesirable side effects in the calling routine.

b. This algorithm is similar to that of part a, except that 16-bit RegE is used to pass the value of N instead of RegA. Besides this, macros dealing with 16-bit manipulations and comparisons are used instead of their 8-bit equivalent (see Table 9).

c. The program of Table 10 illustrates an 8/16-bit down counter as an example. As you can see, there are minor modifications between both programs. Load is substituted by LoadE, Bin2Bcd by Bin2BcdE and so forth (see comments on the right). Also note that RegA and RegE were used as counters in the main program as well as local variables in Bin2Bcd and Bin2BcdE. Thanks to the stack there will not be any conflict whatsoever.

Table 8. Macro and subroutine used to convert 8-bit binary register to unpacked BCD

Convert SrcReg to 3 BCD digits at DstAddr, DstAddr+1 and DstAddr+2 (MSB first).			
Bin2Bcd	macro	SrcReg, DstAddr	
	PushB	RegA	
	PushD	FSR0L	
	movff	SrcReg, RegA	; RegA = binary value
	lfsr	0, DstAddr	; FSR0 = destination address
	call	_Bin2Bcd	; subroutine in "BCDlib.asm"
	PullD	FSR0L	
	PullB	RegA	
	endm		
Convert RegA to 3 BCD digits stored at the address pointed to by **FSR0**.			
_Bin2Bcd	clrf	POSTINC0	
	clrf	POSTDEC0	
	movlw	100	; compute 100s
	rcall	CmpDig	
	movlw	10	
	rcall	CmpDig	; compute 10s
	movff	RegA, POSTDEC0	; get single digit
	movf	POSTDEC0, F	; adjust pointer
	return		
CmpDig	Cpfblt	RegA, ExitCmp	
	incf	INDF0, F	
	subwf	RegA, F	; subtract 100 or 10
	bra	CmpDig	
ExitCmp	movf	POSTINC0, F	; increment pointer
	return		

Table 9. Macro and subroutine used to convert 16-bit binary register to unpacked BCD

Convert SrcReg to BCD digits DstAddr, DstAddr+1 ... DstAddr+4 (MSB first).			
Bin2BcdE	macro	SrcReg, DstAddr	
	PushD	RegE	
	PushD	FSR0L	
	MovffE	SrcReg, RegE	; RegE = binary value
	lfsr	0, DstAddr	; FSR0 = destination address
	call	_Bin2BcdE	; subroutine in "BCDlib.asm"
	PullD	FSR0L	
	PullD	RegE	
	endm		
Convert RegE to 5 BCD digits stored at the address pointed to by FSR0.			
_Bin2BcdE	PushD	FSR0L	
	fill	(clrf POSTINC0), 4*2	; 4 instructions
	PullD	FSR0L	; recover initial ptr value
	LoadE	wE, 10000	; compute 10 Ks
	rcall	CmpDigE	
	LoadE	wE, 1000	
	rcall	CmpDigE	; compute Ks
	LoadE	wE, 100	
	rcall	CmpDigE	; compute 100s
	LoadE	wE, 10	
	rcall	CmpDigE	; compute 10s
	movff	RegE, INDF0	; get single digit
	return		
CmpDigE	CpEblt	RegE, ExitCmpE	
	incf	INDF0, F	
	SubwEf	RegE	; subtract 10K, 1K, 100, 10
	bra	CmpDigE	
ExitCmpE	movf	POSTINC0, F	; increment pointer
	return		

Table 10. Program to test the binary-to-BCD conversion routines

	Test Bin2Bcd/Bin2BcdE using a down counter. Place a breakpoint at the bnz instruction.				
1	#include	<P18F45K22.inc>			
2	#include	<MyMacros.asm>			
3					
4		cblock	0x000		
5		digits:3		; digits:5	
6		endc			
7					
8		org	0x0000		
9		InitSP			
10		Load	RegA, 255	; LoadE	RegE, 65535
11	Loop	Bin2Bcd	RegA, digits	; Bin2BcdE	RegE, digits
12		decf	RegA, F	; DecE	RegE
13		bnz	Loop	; BnzE	RegE, Loop
14		bra	$		
15					
16	#include	<BCDlib.asm>			
17		end			

DELAY ROUTINES

If we were to blink a LED interfaced to a pin by toggling the pin continuously, we will not see it blink due to the slow response of the eye. The only way we can detect the blinking is in slowing down the CPU by introducing a delay between toggles. In this section, a couple of macros, one to handle short delays and another one for long delays, will be developed.

In designing delay routines, one has to select a time base first. This is done by answering the question: What is the minimum delay required for an application? Milliseconds, seconds, minutes, etc. Once a time base is chosen, say msecs, a sequence of instructions that elapses one millisecond is coded. If a time delay of 60 msecs is required, the 1 ms time base is invoked 60 times. The subsequent code snippet executes in 1 ms for $F_{cy} = 1$ MHz:

```
            movlw     250            ; 1 µs
InnerLoop   nop                      ; 1 µs
            addlw     -1             ; 1 µs
            bnz       InnerLoop      ; 1(2) µs
```

The loop is executed 250 times. Note that only in the 250th iteration the bnz instruction elapses 1 cycle (2 cycles otherwise). The 1 ms delay is computed as follows:

$$1\mu s + 250* (1\mu s + 1\mu s + 2\mu s) - 1\mu s = 1000 \ \mu s = 1ms$$

In order to wait a number of milliseconds, the code sequence above is repeated msecs times as depicted in the macro DelayS (short delay) of Table 11. In order not to create any side effect, RegA is saved on the software stack at the beginning of the macro and retrieved upon exit.

DelayL, listed in Table 11 as well, is essentially the same thing with the difference that RegE is used instead. This necessitates a 16-bit compare via the macros DecE and BnzE.

It can be easily shown that the delay error does not exceed 1% for DelayS and DelayL. This is pretty accurate from a practical point of view. Using delay loops is not the ideal way of timing events since they tend to take time away from more important CPU tasks. Chapter 7 shows how *timers* and the *interrupt* feature can provide accurate time delays with minimal CPU time.

> **Example 11** Write a code sequence to flash a LED connected to pin **RB0** of **PORTB** every ¼ second. You may assume that this pin is configured as an output pin.

Solution: Although I/O ports will be discussed formally in chapter 6, the following code snippet shows how to flash a LED connected to RB0.

```
Loop        btg       PORTB, RB0     ; toggle LED
            DelayS    250            ; wait 250 ms
            bra       Loop           ; loop infinitely
```

Table 11. DelayS and DelayL macroinstructions

Macro DelayS: provides short delays (1ms to 255 ms)			
DelayS	macro	msecs	
	local	InnerLoop, OuterLoop	
	PushB	RegA	
	Load	RegA, msecs	; RegA = msecs
OuterLoop	movlw	250	; to elapse 1 ms
InnerLoop	nop		
	addlw	-1	
	bnz	InnerLoop	
	decf	RegA, F	; msecs down counter
	bnz	OuterLoop	
	PullB	RegA	
	endm		
Macro DelayL: provides long delays (1 ms to 65,535 msecs = 65.535 sec)			
DelayL	macro	msecs	
	local	InnerLoop, OuterLoop	
	PushD	RegE	
	LoadE	RegE, msecs	; RegE = msecs
OuterLoop	movlw	250	; to elapse 1 ms
InnerLoop	nop		
	addlw	-1	
	bnz	InnerLoop	
	DecE	RegE	; msecs down counter
	BnzE	RegE, OuterLoop	
	PullD	RegE	
	endm		

It is important to use the following directive (in <MyMacros.asm>) so that 250 specifies a decimal number:

```
        radix     dec                    ; choose base 10
```

STRINGS IN PROGRAM SPACE

As mentioned in chapter 3, program memory can store data bytes in addition to instructions. This way, tables and strings stored in PM will not be lost when the microcontroller is no longer supplied with power. Non-volatile data is useful particularly for constant strings and look-up tables. This section develops some useful macros illustrating how to handle data in program memory.

Example 12 Given the macro `Point` (point to specified address in program space):

```
Point       macro      AddrPS              ; load TBLPTR with AddrPS
            Load       TBLPTRU, upper(AddrPS)
            Load       TBLPTRH, high(AddrPS)
            Load       TBLPTRL, low(AddrPS)
            endm
```

a. Design a macro to transfer a null-terminated string from **PS** to data memory. Assume `AddrPS` and `AddrDS` are the starting addresses of the string in **PS** and data space respectively. The null-terminated string is padded with `'\0'` whose ASCII character is `0x00`. This character is used as a sentinel to exit the loop.

b. Write a program to test the designed macro and test it on the MPLAB simulator.

Solution:

a. MoveString coded in Table 12 uses TBLPTR and FSR0 to point to PM and DM respectively. These pointers are auto incremented within the loop. The iterative process terminates when '\0' is encountered. Since movff does not affect the STATUS flags, the instruction:

```
movf        TABLAT, F
```

is used simply to affect the Z-bit based upon the value read in TABLAT. This instruction might seem useless (TABLAT ← TABLAT) unless one takes into consideration the affected flags.

b. The test program is listed in Table 13. The simulation snapshot is shown in Figure 2.

Table 12. MoveString macroinstruction

```
Macro MoveString: moves a string from program space to data space
MoveString  macro      StringPS, StringDS
            local      Loop
            PushD      FSR0L                ; save FSR0 on stack
            Point      StringPS             ; point to string in PS
            lfsr       0, StringDS          ; point to string in DS
Loop        tblrd*+                         ; TABLAT = StringPS[i++]
            movff      TABLAT, POSTINC0     ; StringDS[j++] = TABLAT
            movf       TABLAT, F            ; is TABLAT == '\0'?
            bnz        Loop                 ; loop back
            PullD      FSR0L                ; recover FSR0 from stack
            endm
```

Table 13. Program to test the MoveString macroinstruction

Test the `MoveString` macro by transferring a number of strings from **PS** to **DS**.		
1	`#include`	`<P18F45K22.inc>`
2	`#include`	`<MyMacros.asm>`
3		
4		`org` `0x0000`
5		`InitSP`
6		`MoveString    HelloMsg, 0x100`
7		`MoveString    HowRuMsg, 0x110`
8		`bra           $`
9		
10	`HelloMsg`	`db        "Hello Everybody\0"`
11	`HowRuMsg`	`db        "How're you pal?\0"`
12		`end`

Figure 2. Snapshot of the simulation result of Example 12

Address	00	01	02	03	04	05	06	07	08	09	0A	0B	0C	0D	0E	0F	ASCII
0E0	00	00	00	00	00	00	00	00	00	00	00	00	00	00	00	00	....
0F0	00	00	00	00	00	00	00	00	00	00	00	00	00	00	00	00	....
100	48	65	6C	6C	6F	20	45	76	65	72	79	62	6F	64	79	00	Hello Ev erybody.
110	48	6F	77	27	72	65	20	79	6F	75	20	70	61	6C	3F	00	How're y ou pal?.

Example 13 Given the macro `StringLen` (string length) whose header is:

`StringLen   macro      StrAddr, reg`

a. Code the macro so that it counts the length (number of characters excluding the null-terminator) of a string stored in **PS**. The count is returned into the specified register `reg`.

b. Write a program to test the designed macro.

Solution:

a. The StringLen macro coded in Table 14 uses reg as an output parameter; therefore, there is no point in saving it on the stack. This is similar to a C function with a non-void return type. The input to this function is the address of the string StrAddr.

b. The test program is listed in Table 15. The user may use the simulator to add a watch and observe the results in RegA and RegB. The macro should return 15 and 11 in RegA and RegB respectively.

PIC18F45K22 DATA MEMORY MAP

Table 16 illustrates the organization of data memory. The manufacturer subdivided memory into banks that use either the access mode (256 blue addresses) or banked addressing (black addresses). We partitioned Bank0 into three portions: (a) User-defined variables, (b) Pre-declared variables, and (c) Software stack.

Table 14. StringLen macroinstruction returns the length of a string

Macro StringLen: returns the string length (excluding '\0') in the argument reg.			
StringLen	macro	StrAddr, reg	
	local	Loop	
	Point	StrAddr	; Point to string in PS
	Load	reg, -1	; reg: # of chars
Loop	incf	reg, F	
	tblrd*+		; TABLAT = StringPS[i++]
	movf	TABLAT, F	; is TABLAT == \0?
	bnz	Loop	
	endm		

Table 15. Program to test the StringLen macroinstruction

Test the StringLen macro with two strings stored in program space.			
1	#include	<P18F45K22.inc>	
2	#include	<MyMacros.asm>	
3			
4		org	0x0000
5		InitSP	
6		StringLen	HelloMsg, RegA
7		StringLen	HowRuMsg, RegB
8		bra	$
9			
10	HelloMsg	db	"Hello Everybody\0"
11	HowRuMsg	db	"How're you?\0"
12		end	

CONCLUSION

This chapter covered macros with one goal in mind: structured assembly language. As you might have deduced, low-level programming does not have to be mal-structured if you use these modular blocks we called macros. As a matter of fact, macros help you organize and structure assembly language programs and parameterize your subroutines.

Subroutines are also modular blocks that are invoked as needed from a calling routine. They do not incur code insertion like macros. Instead, there is one occurrence of the subroutine code in the program. This code is used over and over whenever it is called. It is strongly recommended to use a combination of both: a macro that calls a subroutine. The macro provides the capability of passing arguments as in high level languages whereas the subroutine reduces the program size for it does not cause code repetition.

To make the modular blocks (e.g. MoveString, Bin2Bcd, etc.) independent and reliable, the software stack was introduced to make local variables truly "local". This way, the invoked macro and the calling routine may use the same variable without causing any side effects.

The language was also extended to handle 16-bit instructions. Thus, it can be dealt with the 8-bit processor as if it were a 16-bit one. Of course, this comes at the cost of lower processing speed. Nonetheless, these macros will do the job.

Table 16. PIC18F45K22 memory organization and partitions

Address	Name	Address	Name	Address	Name
0x000	speed	0x300		0x600	
0x001	torque	0x301		0x601	
0x002	current	0x302		0x602	
	. . .				
0x040	RegA				
0x041	RegB				
0x042	RegC				
0x043	RegD		BANK3		
0x044	RegE				
0x045					
	. . .				
0x05F					BANKS 6 THROUGH 14 NOT IMPLEMENTED
0x060	Top of Stack				
	. . .	0x3FD			
		0x3FE			
0x0FF	Stack bottom	0x3FF			
0x100		0x400			
0x101		0x401			
0x102		0x402			
	BANK1		BANK4		
0x1FD		0x4FD		0xEFD	
0x1FE		0x4FE		0xEFE	
0x1FF		0x4FF		0xEFF	
0x200		0x500		0xF00	
0x201		0x501		0xF01	
0x202		0x502			. . .
				0xF38	ANSELA
				0xF39	ANSELB
	BANK2		BANK5		. . .
				0xF5F	CCPR3H
				0xF60	SLRCON
				0xF61	WPUB
					. . .
0x2FD		0x5FD			
0x2FE		0x5FE		0xFFE	TOSH
0x2FF		0x5FF		0xFFF	TOSU

Note 1: Bank 0: user-defined variables (yellow), pre-declared variables (orange), software stack (red).
Note 2: Banks 1 to 5: physically implemented (light blue). Banks 6 to 14: not implemented (blue).
Note 3: Bank 15: GPRs (light blue), SFRs not in access bank (light green), SFRs in access bank (green).
Note 4: Access bank (blue addresses); all other addresses (black) employ banked mode or indirect addressing.

Perhaps the most important reason assembly language is popular among hard-core programmers, is the fact that efficiency cannot be beaten by C compilers. The software developer knows exactly how many cycles his/her program will require for execution. No matter how efficient a C compiler might be, it can never outdo an optimized assembly language program written by an experienced programmer.

One disadvantage of assembly language is machine dependency. On the contrary, a C language program can run on any processor with minor modifications (if any); provided of course it gets compiled to the machine code of the processor it will run on.

Another drawback of assembly language is its lack of universality. That is to say, it might be difficult for someone to read your assembly language program even if you have meaningful names for your macros. In this respect, C is more like a universal language that has been adopted by most microcontroller manufacturers. So your C program can be read and used by other programmers throughout the world.

It is worthwhile adding that C language is easier for handling complicated data structures and mathematical computations (e.g. trigonometric functions). Plus, it is unbeatable when it comes to modularity and readability. For this reason, we will migrate smoothly from assembly to C in Chapter 5. Nevertheless, we will resort to assembly language when efficiency is required through the well-known feature named *inline assembly*.

ENDNOTES

1   A constant block is an assembler directive that allows the enumeration of a set of variables starting at a certain address in data memory. These variables occupy consecutive memory locations.

2   MPASM is the acronym of Microchip assembler.

3   Subroutines and macros dealing with Binary-to-BCD (Bin2Bcd) and BCD-to-Binary (Bcd2Bin) conversions are summarized in Appendix 4.

Chapter 5
Migrating from Assembly to C

INTRODUCTION

This chapter introduces the C18 compiler used to convert C language programs into PIC18 machine code. It is assumed that the reader has a basic background in C language or any other programming language. A number of elucidating examples are given in order to quick start you in this area. You may refer to the C18 Reference Guide in Appendix 5 for an elaborate overview of this programming language. This chapter highlights the following topics:

- Conversion routines: Binary-to-BCD and vice versa.
- Inline assembly language.
- Delay functions.
- I/O ports read/write access.
- EEPROM read/write operations.
- Built-in and user-defined macros.
- 16-bit arithmetic.

INTEGER AND FLOATING-POINT TYPES

The MPLAB C18 compiler supports the standard ANSI-defined integer types. It also supports a 24-bit integer type short long int in both a signed and unsigned variety. The ranges of integer data types are documented in Table 1.

Note that int data types require two bytes of storage in data memory on PIC18 processors. Consequently, this slows down processing speed. For instance, if two int variables are added together, then two 8-bit additions are required at the machine level. As a result, given the choice between int and unsigned char data types for a loop counter that does not exceed 255 iterations, the user should opt for the unsigned char type to speed up execution. Be aware that a plain char data type is signed by default.

DOI: 10.4018/978-1-68318-000-5.ch005

Table 1. Integer data types sizes and limits

Type	Size	Minimum	Maximum
char	8 bits	-128	127
signed char	8 bits	-128	127
unsigned char	8 bits	0	255
int	16 bits	-32,768	32,767
unsigned int	16 bits	0	65,535
short	16 bits	-32,768	32,767
unsigned short	16 bits	0	65,535
short long	24 bits	-8,388,608	8,388,607
unsigned short long	24 bits	0	16,777,215
long	32 bits	-2,147,483,648	2,147,483,647
unsigned long	32 bits	0	4,294,967,295

Also note that short long (24-bit) and long data types (32-bit) require 3 and 4 bytes of storage respectively. Utilization of these data types must be avoided, unless there is no other alternative, due to their slow processing speed and large storage requirement.

As to 32-bit floating-point types, the user may employ either double or float data types. The ranges of the floating point types are documented in Table 2.

C LANGUAGE OPERATORS

The standard C operators are essentially categorized as follows:

- **Arithmetic Operators:** Addition (+), subtraction (-), multiplication (*), division (/) and modulus (%).

Table 2. Floating-point data types sizes and limits

Data Type	Data Size	Minimum Exponent	Maximum exponent	Minimum Normalized	Maximum Normalized
float	32 bits	-126	128	$2^{-126} \approx$ 1.17549435e-38	$2^{128}*(2-2^{-15}) \approx$ 6.80554349e+38
double	32 bits	-126	128	$2^{-126} \approx$	$2^{128}*(2-2^{-15}) \approx$

- **Relational Operators:** Greater than (>), greater than or equal to (>=), less than (<), less than or equal to (<=), equal to (==) and not equal to (!=).
- **Logical Operators:** AND (&&), OR (||) and NOT operator (!).
- Increment (++) and decrement (--) operators.
- **Bitwise Operators:** AND (&), OR (|), XOR (^), shift left (<<) and shift right (>>).
- Assignment operator (=).

Table 3 outlines operator priority from highest to lowest. Associativity resolves the issue of operators having the same priority.

Table 4 lists all the operators with a brief explanation of each. The reader is referred to a C language textbook to learn more about operators and their priority levels.

ELEMENTARY EXAMPLES

Table 5 attempts to leap the reader into C language through a comparative approach. C is one of the few languages that allow stress-free hopping between high level constructs and low level manipulations (i.e. bitwise operations).

Note that IncBcd(f) and DecBcd(f) are macros that use inline assembly language. They are part of the "homemade" library <BCDlib.h> (Table 1 in Appendix 6). Since the address f of the C variable is assigned by the compiler, banked mode (a = 1) must be used. The instruction (movlb f) stores the bank address specified by f by into the BSR. C18 has its own assembler directives syntax which differs slightly from mpasm.

Table 3. Operator precedence chart

Operator Type	Operator	Associativity
Unary Operator	*, &, +, -, !, ~, sizeof	right-to-left
Binary Operators	*, /, %	left-to-right
	+, -	
	>>, <<	
	<, >, <=, >=	
	==, !=	
	&	
	^	
	|	
	&&	
	||	
Assignment Operators	=, +=, -=, *=, /=, %=, >>=, <<=, &=, ^=, |=	right-to-left

Table 4. C language operators

Operator	Operator Meaning
+	Addition operator
+=	Addition assignment operator, x += y, is the same as x = x + y
&=	Bitwise AND assignment operator, x &= y, is the same as x = x & y
&	Bitwise AND operator
^=	Bitwise XOR assignment operator, x ^= y, is the same as x = x ^ y
^	Bitwise XOR operator
|=	Bitwise inclusive OR assignment operator, x |= y, is like x = x | y
|	Bitwise inclusive OR operator
?:	Conditional expression operator
--	Decrement
/=	Division assignment operator, x /= y, is the same as x = x / y
/	Division operator
==	Equality
>	Greater than operator
>=	Greater than or equal to operator
++	Increment
*	Indirection operator
!=	Inequality
<<=	Left shift assignment operator, x <<= y, is the same as x = x << y
<	Less than operator
<<	Left shift operator
<=	Less than or equal to operator
&&	Logical AND operator
!	Logical negation operator
||	Logical OR operator
%=	Modulus assignment operator, x %= y, is the same as x = x % y
%	Modulus operator
*=	Multiplication assignment operator, x *= y, is the same as x = x * y
*	Multiplication operator
~	One's complement operator

Table 5. Assembly to C language conversion table

Declaring a 1-byte *unsigned* variable count and a 2-byte *unsigned* variable speed	

`cblock    0x000`
 	
`        count, speed:2`
 	
`endc`
	`unsigned char count;`
	
	`unsigned int speed;`

Declaring a 1-byte *signed* variable count and a 2-byte *signed* variable speed	

`cblock      0x000`
`    count, speed:2`
`endc`
	`char count;`
	
	`int speed;`

Main program	

`org    0x0000`
`...`
`end`
	`void main(void) {`
	`    …`
	`}`

Variable assignment, count is 8-bit wide (char) whereas speed is 16-bit wide (int)	

`movlw      135`
 	
`movwf      count`
 	
`movlw      0x34`
 	
`movwf      speed+0`
 	
`movlw      0x12`
 	
`movwf      speed+1`
	`count = 135;`
	
	`speed = 0x1234;`

Logical operation (logical shift left 4 times)	

`rlncf      Temp, F`
 	
`rlncf      Temp, F`
 	
`rlncf      Temp, F`
 	
`rlncf      Temp, W`
 	
`andlw      0xF0`
 	
`movwf      Temp`
	`Temp <<= 4;`

Logical operation (1's and 2's complement)	

`comf       PORTB, F`
 	
`negf       Temp`
	`PORTB = ~PORTB;`
	
	`Temp = -Temp;`

Bitwise operations (inclusive OR, XOR and AND)	

`movlw      B'10110011'`
 	
`iorwf      PORTA, F   ; IOR`
 	
`movlw      0xF0`
 	
`xorwf      PORTB, F   ; XOR`
 	
`movlw      B'10101111'`
 	
`andwf      PORTC, F   ; AND`
	`PORTA = PORTA | 0b10110011;`
	
	`PORTB = PORTB ^ 0xF0;`
	
	`PORTC = PORTC & 0b10101111;`

continued on following page

Table 5. Continued

Logical expression		
movlw	0xF0	PORTC = (PORTC & 0xF0) | (PORTB >> 4);
andwf	PORTC, W	
movvf	Temp	
swapf	PORTB, W	
andlw	0x0F	
iorwf	Temp, W	
movwf	PORTC	

Bitwise operations (bit set, bit clear, bit toggle)		
bsf	PORTB, RB0	PORTBbits.RB0 = 1;
bcf	TRISB, TRISB5	TRISBbits.TRISB5 = 0;
btg	PORTC, RC2	PORTCbits.RC2 = !PORTCbits.RC2;
bsf	Temp, 7	Temp = Temp | 0b10000000;
btg	Temp, 3	Temp = Temp ^ 0b00001000;
bcf	Temp, 6	Temp = Temp & 0b10111111;

if statement plus arithmetic expressions (all registers used are 8-bit wide)			
movf	RegB, W		if (RegA == RegB)
	subwf	RegA, W	RegC = 5 - RegD;
	bnz	NotEq	else
Equal	movf	RegD, W	RegA = RegA + RegB;
	sublw	5	
	movwf	RegC	
	bra	GoOn	
NotEq	movf	RegB, W	
	addwf	RegA, F	
GoOn	...		

Conditional expression operator (all registers are declared as unsigned char)			
	movlw	145	RegA = RegB > 145? ~RegB: -RegA;
	cpfsgt	RegB	
	bra	FalseC	
TrueC	comf	RegB, W	
	movwf	RegA	
	bra	GoOn	
FalseC	negf	RegA	
GoOn	...		

continued on following page

Table 5. Continued

for loop: storing the first 100 odd numbers in a buffer of size 100 (`unsigned char Buffer[100]`)			
	movlw	100	`for (i = 0; i < 100; i++)`
	movwf	RegA	`    Buffer[i] = 2 * i + 1;`
	lfsr	0, Buffer	
	movlw	1	
Loop	movwf	POSTINC0	
	addlw	2	
	decf	RegA, F	
	bnz	Loop	

do ... while loop: moving a null-terminated string `SrcStr` (in RAM) to `DstStr` (in RAM)			
	lfsr	0, SrcStr	`i = 0;`
	lfsr	1, DstStr	`do`
Loop	movff	INDF0, POSTINC1	`    DstStr[i] = SrcStr[i];`
	movf	POSTINC0, F	`while (SrcStr[i++] != '\0');`
	bnz	Loop	

while loop: waiting for **PORTB**<0> to become '0' and then back to '1'			
Wait0	btfsc	PORTB, RB0	`while (PORTBbits.RB0);`
	bra	Wait0	`while (!PORTBbits.RB0);`
Wait1	btfss	PORTB, RB0	
	bra	Wait1	

Inline assembly to increment a packed BCD variable using the daw instruction - 4 cycles
`#define IncBcd(f) {_asm movlb f  incf f,0,1  daw  movwf f,1  _endasm}`

Inline assembly to decrement a packed BCD variable by adding the 10s complement of 1 - 5 cycles
`#define DecBcd(f) {_asm movlb f movlw 0x99 addwf f,0,1 daw movwf f,1 _endasm}`

Example 1 The PIC18 instruction set does not allow incrementing or decrementing a packed BCD variable directly. For example, if variable `Temp` storing 0x59 is incremented by 1, the CPU result would be 0x5A. This result is to be adjusted to 0x60.

a. Design the function

    void BcdInc(unsigned char *reg)

that increments the packed BCD register `reg` by 1. The function should not use any inline assembly instructions and should roll over to 0x00 when 0x99 is incremented.

b. Design the function

    void BcdDec(unsigned char *reg)

that decrements the packed BCD register `reg` by 1. The function should not use any inline assembly instructions and should roll back to 0x99 when 0x00 is decremented.

c. Given the hardware setup of Figure 1, write a program to perform the following:

  • Wait for the push button CLK to be pressed.
  • If DIR = 1, increment PORTC in packed BCD, else decrement it.
  • Wait for push button CLK to be released.
  • Repeat the three previous steps infinitely.

d. Compare the execution cycles of the `IncBcd()` macro which uses inline assembly versus the C implemented function `BcdInc()`. Repeat the same comparison for the decrement BCD function and macro.

Figure 1. Hardware setup to increment/decrement a 2-digit counter in packed BCD format

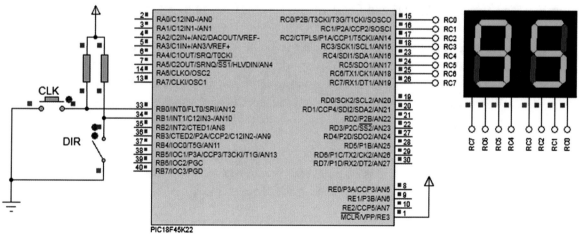

PIC18F45K22

Solution:

a. Assume reg is a pointer to an 8-bit variable holding a packed BCD number. In order to convert this variable to binary, it is sufficient to multiply its most significant nibble (*reg / 16) by 10 then add the result to the variable's least significant nibble (*reg % 16). Then the CPU increments the variable in binary via the + operator. The result is converted back to BCD: the number of 10s (*reg / 10) is shifted left 4 times (or multiplied by 16) and packed with the units (*reg % 10). Here is the implementation:

```
void BcdInc(unsigned char *reg) {
        *reg = (*reg / 16) * 10 + (*reg % 16);      // BCD to binary
        *reg = *reg != 99? *reg + 1: 0;             // add 1 to reg
        *reg = (*reg / 10) * 16 + (*reg % 10);      // binary to BCD
}
```

b.   This is similar to part (a) with the only difference in the decrementation logic.

```
void BcdDec(unsigned char *reg) {
    *reg = (*reg / 16) * 10 + (*reg % 16);      // BCD to binary
    *reg = *reg != 0? *reg - 1: 99;             // sub 1 from reg
    *reg = (*reg / 10) * 16 + (*reg % 10);      // binary to BCD
}
```

c.   This part provides two alternatives listed in Table 6: the first uses the C functions designed in this example. The second uses the macros IncBcd(f) and DecBcd(f) of Table 5.

d.   IncBcd(PORTC) and DecBcd(PORTC) elapse 4 and 5 cycles respectively whereas the functions designed in this example (BcdInc() and BcdDec()) require 285 cycles. This measurement was done through the MPLAB simulator.

> **Example 2** Redo Example 1 to match the hardware of Figure 2. Make sure you use the macros `IncBcd()` and `DecBcd()`to design `IncBcdE()` and `DecBcdE()` (E stands for *extended* and implies 4 digits in this case). Compute the execution cycles of these macros.

Solution: The macros IncBcdE() and DecBcdE() (part of <BCDlib.h>) are listed in Table 7.

We will note here that when a 16-bit variable f (type int) is declared in C18, the compiler allocates 2 consecutive bytes at addresses f and f+1. These addresses hold data in *little endian* format. That is to say, f stores the least significant byte and f+1 stores the most significant byte. A cycle count shows that IncBcdE() and DecBcdE() require 10 and 13 cycles respectively (for the worst case scenario). The test program is listed in Table 8.

> **Example 3** In order to refresh your knowledge of pointers and arguments by reference, write a program to sort the three signed variables a, b and c (of type char) in ascending order. To test the code, you may enter the values of a, b and c via the MPLAB simulator.

Solution: The algorithm leads to the design of the functions Sort2() and Sort3() coded in Table 9. Note that variables a, b and c are passed by reference in the main program because their contents are to be modified. Since they are declared as ordinary variables, their addresses &a, &b and &c must be sent as actual arguments. The same thing is true when passing arguments between Sort3() and Sort2(). However, in this case, the arguments arg1, arg2 and arg3 are already declared as pointers (or addresses). Therefore, if the contents of these memory locations are to be modified, a reference to *a, *b and *c must be employed.

Table 6. Two different implementations of Example 1 part (c)

```
First alternative: uses BcdInc() and BcdDec() functions in <BCDlib.h>
1    #include    <p18cxxx.h>
2    #include    <BCDlib.h>
3
4    void main(void)
5    {
6        unsigned char PORTCdata = 0x00;
7
8        TRISC = 0x00; ANSELC = 0x00;    // PORTC: output port
9        PORTC = PORTCdata;              // start count with 00
10       while (1) {
11           while (PORTBbits.RB0);      // wait PB press
12           if (PORTBbits.RB1)          // choose direction
13               BcdInc(&PORTCdata);
14           else
15               BcdDec(&PORTCdata);
16           PORTC = PORTCdata;
17           while (!PORTBbits.RB0);     // wait PB release
18       }
19   }
```

```
Second alternative: uses IncBcd() and DecBcd() functions in <BCDlib.h>
1    #include    <p18cxxx.h>
2    #include    <BCDlib.h>
3
4    void main(void)
5    {
6        TRISC = 0x00; ANSELC = 0x00;    // PORTC: output port
7        PORTC = 0x00;                   // start count with 00
8
9        while (1) {
10           while (PORTBbits.RB0);      // wait PB press
11           if (PORTBbits.RB1)          // choose direction
12               IncBcd(PORTC)
13           else
14               DecBcd(PORTC)
15           while (!PORTBbits.RB0);     // wait PB release
16       }
17   }
```

Figure 2. Hardware setup to increment/decrement a 4-digit counter in packed BCD format

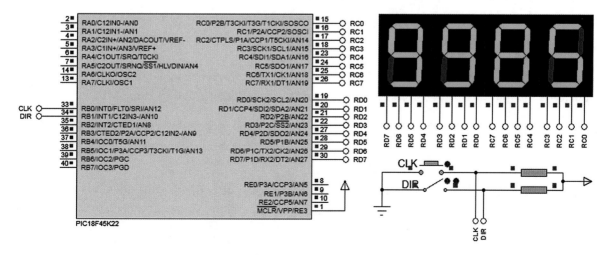

Table 7. Listing of the macros IncBcdE( ) and DecBcdE( )

Inline assembly to increment a 16-bit packed BCD variable (10 cycles maximum)
| ```
#define    IncBcdE(f)      {IncBcd(f)                      \
                           _asm                            \
                                    tstfsz  f, 1           \
                                    bra     4              \
                           _endasm                         \
                           IncBcd(f+1)}
``` |
| Inline assembly to increment a 16-bit packed BCD variable (10 cycles maximum) |
| ```
#define    DecBcdE(f)      {DecBcd(f)                      \
                           _asm                            \
                                    movlw   0x99           \
                                    subwf   f, 0, 1        \
                                    bnz     5              \
                           _endasm                         \
                           DecBcd(f+1)}
``` |

Table 8. Program listing of Example 2

Testing the macros IncBcdE( ) and DecBcdE( ) in <BCDlib.h>
| ```
1   #include   <p18cxxx.h>
2   #include   <BCDlib.h>
3
4   void main(void)
5   {
6       TRISC = 0x00; ANSELC = 0x00;      // PORTC: output port
7       TRISD = 0x00; ANSELD = 0x00;      // PORTD: output port
8       PORTC = 0x00; PORTD = 0x00;       // start count with 00
9
10      while (1) {
11          while (PORTBbits.RB0);        // wait PB press
12          if (PORTBbits.RB1)            // choose direction
13              IncBcdE(PORTC)            // increment PORTD:PORTC
14          else
15              DecBcdE(PORTC)            // decrement PORTD:PORTC
16          while (!PORTBbits.RB0);       // wait PB release
17      }
18  }
``` |

The while loop in the main program helps in the testing phase. A breakpoint is placed at the Sort3(&a, &b, &c) function call (line 9). Arguments a, b and c are entered interactively via the MPLAB simulator.

> **Example 4** Write a program to compute the rounded average value of the 256-byte buffer that starts at address 0x100 in DM. The average value is stored in variable **Ave**.

Solution: There is no need to allocate (or declare) a 256-byte buffer in this case since it is already part of data memory and may be filled up via MPLAB. Therefore, we need to declare a pointer p to the buffer and initialize it with 0x100. Since the buffer size is 256, the loop counter has to be of
```

Table 9. Program to sort 3 variables in ascending order

```
Program to sort three 8-bit signed variables a, b and c.
1      void Sort3(char *, char *, char *);
2      void Sort2(char *, char *);
3
4      void main(void)
5      {
6          char a, b, c;              // load arguments from simulator
7
8          while (1)
9              Sort3(&a, &b, &c);
10     }
11
12     void Sort3(char *arg1, char *arg2, char *arg3)
13     {
14         Sort2(arg1, arg2);     // arg1 is lowest of arg1 & arg2
15         Sort2(arg1, arg3);     // arg1 is lowest of all
16         Sort2(arg2, arg3);     // arg2 is lowest of arg2 & arg3
17     }
18
19     void Sort2(char *arg1, char *arg2)
20     {
21         char temp;
22
23         if (*arg1 > *arg2) {
24             temp = *arg1;                // swap arg1 with arg2
25             *arg1 = *arg2;
26             *arg2 = temp;
27         }
28     }
```

type int. Also the accumulated sum would have to be of type int cause the sum of 256 bytes will not fit into an 8-bit register. Note that the maximum value that can be stored in the sum is 256 * 255 = 65,280 which is less than 65,536. As a result, there is no point in declaring a 24-bit register to store the sum.

The program is listed in Table 10. Note the use of indirect addressing via the pointer. This notation *(p++) implies that the content of the memory location pointed to by p is added to sum. The pointer is then incremented to point to the next memory location. The reader should not confuse this syntax with (*p)++ which increments the content of the memory location pointed to by p. Rounding is done by adding 0.5 = 128/256 to the average value sum/256.

Another alternative to compute the rounded average value is via the statements:

```
sum = sum + 128;
ave = *(&sum + 1);
```

instead of the statement on line 13. This takes advantage of the fact that an int variable is stored in little endian format and hence dividing by 256 is done by ignoring the least significant byte. The Sleep() macro invokes the sleep instruction which freezes the clock and reduces power consumption.

Table 10. Program to compute the average value of the 256-byte buffer

```
Program to compute the rounded average of 256 bytes starting at address 0x100
1   #include    <p18cxxx.h>
2
3   void main(void)
4   {
5       unsigned int i, sum;        // loop counter, sum
6       unsigned char ave;          // rounded average
7       unsigned char *p;           // buffer pointer
8
9       sum = 0;
10      p = (unsigned char *) 0x100; // point to address 0x100
11      for (i = 0; i < 256; i++)
12          sum = sum + *(p++);
13      ave = (sum + 128) / 256;    // rounding (128 / 256 = 0.5)
14      Sleep();                    // halt the program
15  }
```

DELAY ROUTINES

Table 11 lists the delay functions provided by the C18 compiler. These functions, coded in assembly language, do nothing but elapse CPU cycles when they are invoked. They all belong to the library <delays.h>. Refer to the detailed description in Appendix 6.

If we were to blink a LED interfaced to a pin by toggling the pin continuously, we will not see it blink due to the slow response of the eye. We can detect the blinking by slowing down the CPU through introducing a delay between toggles as shown in the succeeding example.

Example 5 Write a program to flash a LED connected to pin **RB0** of **PORTB** every ¼ second. You may assume that F_{osc} = 4 MHz.

Solution: $F_{CY} = F_{osc} / 4 = 1$ MHz implies $T_{cy} = 1 / F_{CY} = 1$ μsec. Therefore, the unit delay in Delay10KT-CYx() is 10,000 μsecs = 10 ms. To elapse 250 ms, the function's argument is set to 25 (25 x 10 ms = 250 ms). The code is listed in Table 12.

Table 11. Delay functions

Function	Description
Delay1TCY()	Delay one instruction cycle
Delay10TCYx()	Delay in multiples of 10 instruction cycles
Delay100TCYx()	Delay in multiples of 100 instruction cycles
Delay1KTCYx()	Delay in multiples of 1,000 instruction cycles
Delay10KTCYx()	Delay in multiples of 10,000 instruction cycles.

Table 12. Delay functions

```
1    #include    <p18cxxx.h>
2    #include    <delays.h>
3
4    void main(void)
5    {
6        TRISBbits.TRISB0 = 0;                // RB0: output
7        ANSELBbits.ANSB0 = 0;                // RB0: digital
8
9        while (1) {                          // infinite loop
10           PORTBbits.RB0 = !PORTBbits.RB0;  // toggle RB0
11           Delay10KTCYx(25);                // 250 ms delay
12       }
13   }
```

CONVERSION ROUTINES

This section covers the algorithms employed to convert from binary to BCD and vice versa through the following set of examples.

Example 6 *Binary-to-BCD* conversion

a. Code the function

   void Bin2Bcd(unsigned char N, char *a)

   to convert the 8-bit number N to unpacked BCD. The result is stored in a 3-byte char array whose starting address is passed as a parameter (formal argument char *a).

b. Code the function

   void Bin2BcdE(unsigned int N, char *a)

   to convert the 16-bit number N to unpacked BCD. The result is stored in a 5-byte char array whose starting address is passed as a parameter (formal argument char *a).

c. Write a program to test the designed functions. Use the hardware setup of Figure 3.

Solution:

a.   Converting an 8-bit number from binary to BCD requires counting the 100s, the 10s and the units. For instance, the 8-bit number 0xFE (254_{10}) consists of 2 hundreds, 5 tens, and 4 units. The function Bin2Bcd() receives the 8-bit number N by value and returns the BCD digits in an array a of 3 bytes. The most significant BCD digit is stored in a[0], the middle in a[1] and the least significant in a[2]. Refer to the solution in Table 13.

b.   Converting a 16-bit number from binary to BCD requires counting the number of 10s of thousands, 1000s, 100s, 10s and units. For instance, the 16-bit number 0xFFFE ($65,534_{10}$) consists of 6 tens of thousands, 5 thousands, 5 hundreds, 3 tens and 4 units. The function Bin2BcdE() receives the 16-bit number N by value and returns the BCD digits in an array a of 5 bytes. The most significant BCD digit is stored in a[0] whereas the least significant digit is stored in a[4]. The solution is listed in Table 13.

Table 13. Binary-to-BCD conversion routines, 8-bit and 16-bit input argument

Convert 8-bit N to 3 BCD digits. Result at a[0] (MSB), a[1] & a[2]

```
void Bin2Bcd(unsigned char N, char *a)
{
        a[2] = N % 10;                          // least significant digit
        N = N / 10;
        a[1] = N % 10;                          // middle significant digit
        a[0] = N / 10;                          // most significant digit
}
```

Convert 16-bit N to 5 BCD digits. Result at a[0] (MSB), a[1], ..., a[4]

```
void Bin2BcdE(unsigned int N, char *a)
{
        unsigned char i;

        for (i = 0; i < 4; i++) {
                a[4-i] = N % 10;                // rem of division by 10
                N = N / 10;
        }
        a[0] = N;
}
```

c.   The programs listed in Table 14 are suitable for testing both the 8/16 bit conversion routines. For this purpose, a 3-digit and a 4-digit up counters are employed. A time delay of 250 ms between counts is used to slow down the counter's frequency.

The 8-bit counter (3 digits) program rolls over to 000 naturally when 255 is incremented by 1. The 16-bit counter (4 digits) rolls over to 0000 when 9999 is incremented by 1. This is handled by an if statement in software. Also note the use of bitwise operations to pack BCD numbers in one register (PORTC and PORTD). The conversion routines Bin2Bcd() and Bin2BcdE() are added to the library <BCDlib.h>.

Figure 3. Hardware setup to test the binary-to-BCD conversion routines

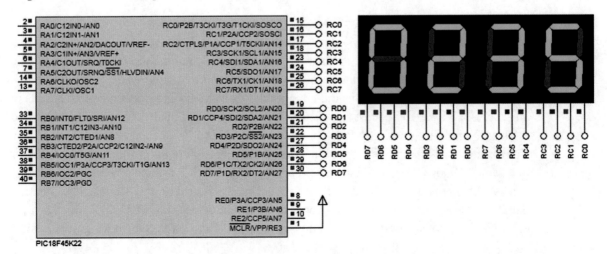

Table 14. Programs to test the binary-to-BCD conversion routines

Program to test `Bin2Bcd()` using an up counter with a 250 ms delay between counts

```
1    #include    <p18cxxx.h>
2    #include    <delays.h>
3    #include    <BCDlib.h>
4
5    void main(void) {
6        unsigned char N = 0;                        // init. count
7        char digits[3];                             // 3-byte array
8
9        TRISC = 0x00; ANSELC = 0x00;                // PORTC: output
10       TRISD &= 0xF0; ANSELD &= 0xF0;              // <RD3:0> outputs
11
12       while (1) {
13         Bin2Bcd(N++, digits);                     // convert to BCD
14         PORTD = (PORTD & 0xF0) | digits[0];       // output D2 (MSB)
15         PORTC = (digits[1] << 4) | digits[2];     // output D1:D0
16         Delay10KTCYx(25);                         // wait 250 ms
17       }
18   }
```

Program to test `Bin2BcdE()` using an up counter with a 250 ms delay between counts

```
1    #include    <p18cxxx.h>
2    #include    <delays.h>
3    #include    <BCDlib.h>
4
5    void main(void) {
6        unsigned int N = 0;                         // init. count
7        char digits[5];                             // 5-byte array
8
9        TRISC = 0x00; ANSELC = 0x00;                // PORTC: output
10       TRISD = 0x00; ANSELD = 0x00;                // PORTD: output
11
12       while (1) {
13         Bin2BcdE(N++, digits);                    // convert to BCD
14         if (N == 10000) N = 0;                    // roll over to 0
15         PORTD = (digits[1] << 4) | digits[2];     // output D3:D2
16         PORTC = (digits[3] << 4) | digits[4];     // output D1:D0
17         Delay10KTCYx(25);                         // wait 250 ms
18       }
19   }
```

Example 7 *BCD-to-Binary* conversion

a.   Code the function:

$$\text{unsigned int Bcd2Bin(char *a)}$$

to convert the 3-byte unpacked BCD array **a** to a binary number. Since the array may hold {9, 9, 9}, the returned value is of type `unsigned int`.

b.   Code the function:

$$\text{unsigned int Bcd2BinE(char *a)}$$

to convert the 4-byte unpacked BCD array **a** to a binary number. Since the array may hold {9, 9, 9, 9}, the returned value is of type `unsigned int`.

Solution: The solution is straight forward and is listed in Table 15. Note the importance of casting to convert a char data type to int when the product is greater than 255.

EEPROM READ/WRITE ROUTINES

Although the data EEPROM constitute an I/O subsection of the microcontroller, functions allowing EEPROM read/write operations blend in nicely with the spirit of this chapter.

The data EEPROM consists of 256 bytes of EEPROM cells with address range: 0x00 – 0xFF as shown in Figure 4. The control registers used to access the data EEPROM are:

- EEADR (*EEPROM address register*) which specifies the EEPROM address to read from or to write to.
- EEDAT (*EEPROM data register*) which holds the value to be written to EEPROM in a write operation or the value read from EEPROM in a read operation.
- EECON1 and EECON2: EEPROM configuration registers 1 and 2.

In order to read a byte from EEPROM at the address specified by EEADR, the control register EECON1 is used in the following manner:

- Clear flags EEPGD and CFGS in EECON1.
- Set the RD bit to initiate a read command.

Immediately thereafter, the result is stored in EEDAT. Refer to the implementation ReadEE (library EEPROM.h) of Table 16.

To write a byte in EEDAT to data EEPROM at address EEADR, the PIC18 datasheet specifies the following steps to be done:

- Clear flags EEPGD and CFGS in EECON1.
- Set WREN bit in EECON1 to enable EEPROM write.
- Clear the GIE bit in the INTCON register to disable interrupts.

Table 15. BCD-to-Binary conversion routines

Convert a 3-byte unpacked BCD array to binary. Maximum value returned is 999.
| ```
unsigned int Bcd2Bin(char *a)
{      return (int) a[0] * 100 + a[1] * 10 + a[2];}
``` |
| Convert a 4-byte unpacked BCD array to binary. Maximum value returned is 9999. |
| ```
unsigned int Bcd2BinE(unsigned char *a)
{
       return (int) a[0] * 1000 + (int) a[1] * 100 + a[2] * 10 + a[3];
}
``` |

Figure 4. Data EEPROM block diagram with all cells erased (0xFF)

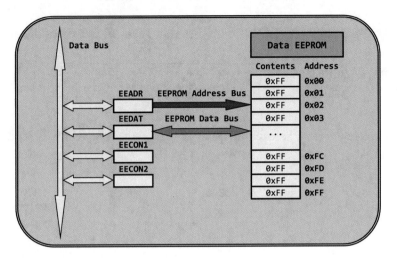

Table 16. EEPROM read and write routines

Function that returns value read from EEPROM address SrcReg.

```c
unsigned char ReadEE(unsigned char SrcReg)
{
    EEADR = SrcReg;                 // select EE address to read from
    EECON1bits.EEPGD = 0;           // access Data EEPROM memory
    EECON1bits.CFGS = 0;            // do not access config. regs
    EECON1bits.RD = 1;              // initiates an EEPROM read
    return EEDATA;                  // return read value
}
```

Function to transfer the contents of SrcReg (in RAM) to DstReg (in EEPROM).

```c
void Wrt2EE(unsigned char SrcReg, unsigned char DstReg) {
    char interruptSet = 0;          // indicates GIE state

    EEADR = DstReg;                 // specify destination register
    EEDATA = SrcReg;                // store SrcReg in EEDATA
    EECON1bits.EEPGD = 0;           // access Data EEPROM memory
    EECON1bits.CFGS = 0;
    EECON1bits.WREN = 1;            // enable EEPROM write
    if (INTCONbits.GIE) interruptSet = 1;  // used to recover GIE state
    INTCONbits.GIE = 0;             // disable interrupts
    EECON2 = 0x55;                  // required sequence
    EECON2 = 0xAA;                  // required sequence
    EECON1bits.WR = 1;              // initiates a write cycle
    while (EECON1bits.WR);          // wait for write to terminate
    if (interruptSet) INTCONbits.GIE = 1;  // recover GIE state
    EECON1bits.WREN = 0;            // disable write
}
```

- Load EECON2 with 0x55 then 0xAA.
- Set bit WR in EECON1 to initiate the write cycle.
- Once the write cycle is initiated, interrupts may be re-enabled by setting the GIE bit.
- Wait until WR is cleared, an indication that the write operation has been completed.

- Clear WREN bit so that accidental EEPROM writes are inhibited.

The function Wrt2EE (in library EEPROM.h) listed in Table 16 translates the above steps.

> **Example 8** Write a program to transfer a null-terminated string from **DS** to **EEPROM**. The string is padded with `'\0'`. This character is used as a sentinel to exit the loop.

Solution: The complete program is listed in Table 17. The following syntax is used to declare a string in data EEPROM.

```
#pragma romdata eeAddress = 0xF00000    // address 0x00 in EEPROM
rom char eeString[];                    // string array in EEPROM
```

In order to modify a variable declared in EEPROM, one must transfer the variable to a RAM location, alter it and then write it back. For instance, given the following declaration:

```
#pragma romdata eeAddress = 0xF00000    // address 0x00 in EEPROM
rom unsigned char eeVar;                // variable in EEPROM
unsigned char dmVar;                    // variable in data memory
```

The subsequent code snippet is used to add 5 to eeVar.

```
dmVar = ReadEE((char) &eeVar);          // read EE variable into RAM
dmVar += 5;                             // add 5 to DM variable
Wrt2EE(dmVar, (char) &eeVar);           // save DM variable in EEPROM
```

Or simply,

```
Wrt2EE(5 + ReadEE((char) &eeVar), (char) &eeVar);
```

The syntax: (char) &eeVar, means address of eeVar (0xF00000) casted to an 8-bit value (0x00). The compiler uses the address range (0xF00000 - 0xF000FF) to denote the EEPROM address range (0x00 - 0xFF). This has the effect of removing any contention with address ranges of data memory (0x000 - 0xFFF) and program memory (0x000000 - 0x1FFFFF).

> **Example 9** Write a program to demonstrate that **EEPROM** variables are indeed non-volatile. For this purpose, you will be displaying a 2-digit binary counter on **PORTC** (Figure 5). The count is read from an **EEPROM** variable eeVar. Any time you reset the system or you restart its power supply, the counter should resume where it left off.

Table 17. Program to test the routine Wrt2EE() in <EEPROM.h>

```
Program to transfer a null-terminated string from data memory to EEPROM.
1    #include    <p18cxxx.h>
2    #include    <EEPROM.h>
3
4    #pragma romdata eeAddress = 0xF00000    // EEPROM address 0x00
5    rom char eeString[];                    // EEPROM string array
6
7    void main(void) {
8        char dmString[] = "Hello World";    // DM string array
9        unsigned char i = 0;                // string index
10
11       do {
12           Wrt2EE(dmString[i], (char) &eeString[i]); // address cast
13       } while (dmString[i++] != '\0');
14       Sleep();
15   }
```

Figure 5. Hardware setup to demonstrate EEPROM data retention

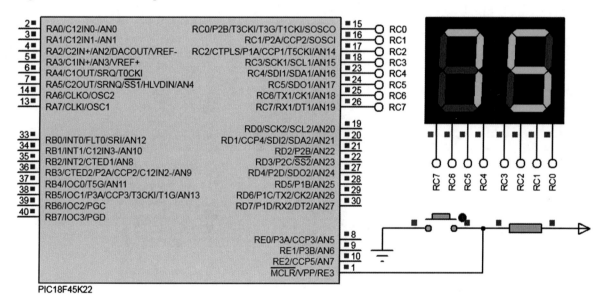

Solution: The code is listed in Table 18. When the MCU is reset while it is running, the counter resumes as soon as the reset button is released. The same thing occurs when the power supply is switched off and back on.

BUILT-IN C18 MACROS

Table 19 lists the predefined macros of the C18 compiler. These are defined in the library P18F45K22.h and cover the instructions: nop, clrwdt, sleep, reset, swapf and rotate; all of which do not have a direct equivalent in C language. Therefore, they use inline assembly to gain the best of both worlds: high level for structured programming and low level for efficient programming.

Table 18. Program to demonstrate EEPROM data preservation

```
Program to implement an EEPROM-based up counter.
1   #include    <p18cxxx.h>
2   #include    <EEPROM.h>
3   #include    <delays.h>
4
5   #pragma romdata eeAddress = 0xF00000    // address 0x00 in EEP
6   rom unsigned char eeVar;                // variable in EEP
7
8   void main(void) {
9       TRISC = 0x00; ANSELC = 0x00;        // TRISC: output port
10      PORTC = ReadEE((char) &eeVar);      // PORTC = EEP value
11      while (1) {
12          Delay10KTCYx(25);               // 250 ms delay
13          Wrt2EE(++PORTC, (char) &eeVar); // ++PORTC then save
14      }
15  }
```

Table 19. C macros of some PIC18 MCU instructions

Instruction Macro[1]	Action
Nop()	Executes a no operation (nop)
	{_asm nop _endasm}
ClrWdt()	Clears the WatchDog Timer (clrwdt)
	{_asm clrwdt _endasm}
Sleep()	Executes a sleep instruction
	{_asm sleep _endasm}
Reset()	Executes a device reset (reset)
	{_asm reset _endasm}
Rlcf(f,d,a) [2,3]	Rotates f to the left through the carry bit
	{_asm movlb f rlcf f,d,a _endasm}
Rlncf(f,d,a)[2,3]	Rotates f to the left without going through the carry bit
	{_asm movlb f rlncf f,d,a _endasm}
Rrcf(f,d,a) [2,3]	Rotates f to the right through the carry bit
	{_asm movlb f rrcf f,d,a _endasm}
Rrncf(f,d,a)[2,3]	Rotates f to the right without going through the carry bit
	{_asm movlb f rrncf f,d,a _endasm}
swapf(f,d,a)[2,3]	Swaps the upper and lower nibble of f
	{_asm movlb f swapf f,d,a _endasm}

GUIDELINES FOR SOUND PROGRAMMING HABITS

Programming microcontrollers is undoubtedly a delicate issue that requires patience and care. The first requirement is to devise a plan by dividing the program into self-contained manageable subprograms. The guidelines proposed herein provide a starting point towards sound programming habits with two goals in mind: modularity and style.

1. When designing separate software modules or functions, meticulous testing is required. The programmer must ensure the designed routine never fails. The code must be efficient and readable by humans.

2. A set of functions pertaining to a certain I/O device such as an LCD display or others must be placed in a library and included in a program as needed.

3. Functions requiring arguments must be carefully designed. The user must make appropriate decisions as to whether arguments are passed by *reference* or by *value*.

4. Avoid unreadable code. Make sure your program is easy to read and is self-explanatory. This helps tremendously in making changes and updates.

5. As far as style is concerned, make sure you indent and align statements and comments. Meaningful comments improve program readability and eases debugging.

6. Use symbolic pin names. For example if a motor is driven by RB0 via an appropriate interface, use the following definition for improved program readability:

```
#define        Motor       PORTBbits.RB0
```

This way the statement: Motor = 1, turns on the motor and Motor = 0 turns it off.

7. Write programs as if you are implementing hardware state machines. This approach applies to rather substantial programs and will be elaborated upon in Chapter 11.

ENDNOTES

[1] Using any of these macros in a function affects the ability of the MPLAB C18 compiler to perform optimizations on that function.

[2] f must be an 8-bit quantity (i.e., char) and not located on the stack.

[3] If d is 0, the result is stored in WREG, and if d is 1, the result is stored in f. If a is 0, the access bank will be selected, overriding the BSR value. If a is 1, then the bank will be selected as per the BSR value.

Chapter 6
Input/Output Ports

INTRODUCTION

This chapter discusses the different I/O ports available on PIC18 microcontrollers. A detailed description of the underpinning hardware behind these ports as well as their features, limitations and applications will be covered. Figure 1 shows the pin diagram of PIC18F25K22/26K22 processors having 3 ports (PORTA, PORTB and PORTC) as well as PIC18F45K22/46K22 processors having as many as 5 ports (PORTA, PORTB, PORTC, PORTD and PORTE). Throughout the chapter, you need to refer to Appendix 2 for bit-by-bit description of special function registers as well as Appendix 7 (configuration registers).

PORTA

A parallel port such as PORTA allows the processor to interface with the outside world. It may be used both as input or output. When used as output, a port consists of a set of 8 flip-flops with the D-inputs connected to the data bus and the Q-outputs connected to the port pins. It is accessible via a write operation (e.g. movwf PORTA).

Similarly, data appearing on the input pins of a port may be acquired via a read operation (e.g. movf PORTA, W). Using a port pin both as input and output is illustrated in Figure 2. When the TRIS latch is cleared $(Q_{TRIS} = 0)$, the output buffer acts like a closed switch. This allows the data latch output Q_{DATA} be routed to the output pin.

A port pin is treated as a digital I/O pin if the corresponding bit in ANSEL register is 0. For instance, if RA2 (PORTA, bit 2) is to be used as a digital I/O pin, then ANSELA<2> (ANSELA register, bit 2) must be cleared. If not, this pin is treated as analog (default value) and is read as logic '0'. Table 1 lists the status of I/O pins for all different possibilities.

When the pin is configured as input $(Q_{TRIS} = 1)$, the output buffer behaves like an open circuit. This isolates, electrically speaking, the data latch from the input pin and hence no data contention occurs.

DOI: 10.4018/978-1-68318-000-5.ch006

Figure 1. Pin diagram of PIC18F25K22/26K22 and PIC18F45K22/46K22

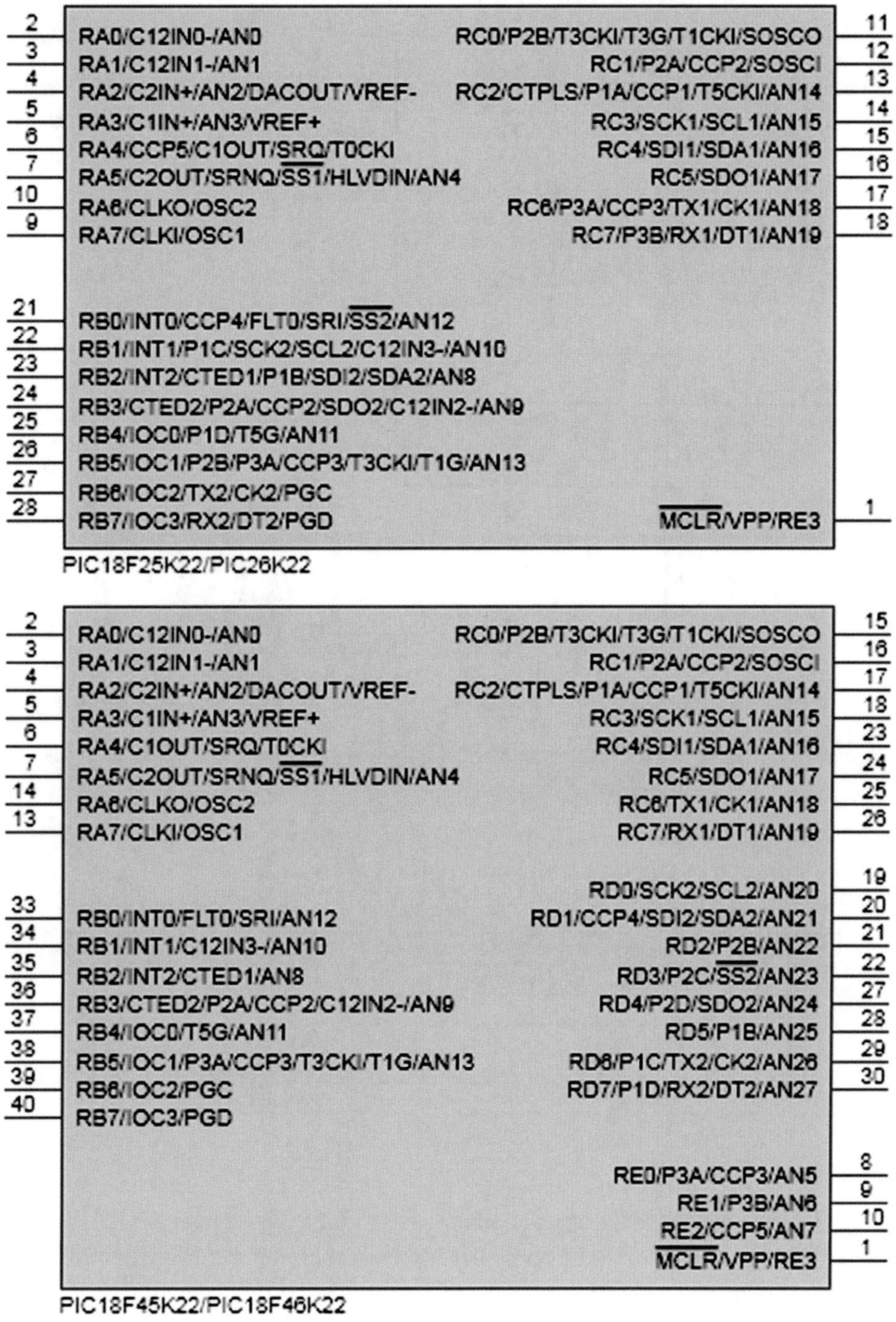

```
 2  — RA0/C12IN0-/AN0              RC0/P2B/T3CKI/T3G/T1CKI/SOSCO  — 11
 3  — RA1/C12IN1-/AN1                        RC1/P2A/CCP2/SOSCI  — 12
 4  — RA2/C2IN+/AN2/DACOUT/VREF-   RC2/CTPLS/P1A/CCP1/T5CKI/AN14  — 13
 5  — RA3/C1IN+/AN3/VREF+                   RC3/SCK1/SCL1/AN15   — 14
 6  — RA4/CCP5/C1OUT/SRQ/T0CKI               RC4/SDI1/SDA1/AN16  — 15
 7  — RA5/C2OUT/SRNQ/SS1/HLVDIN/AN4               RC5/SDO1/AN17  — 16
10  — RA6/CLKO/OSC2               RC6/P3A/CCP3/TX1/CK1/AN18      — 17
 9  — RA7/CLKI/OSC1               RC7/P3B/RX1/DT1/AN19           — 18

21  — RB0/INT0/CCP4/FLT0/SRI/SS2/AN12
22  — RB1/INT1/P1C/SCK2/SCL2/C12IN3-/AN10
23  — RB2/INT2/CTED1/P1B/SDI2/SDA2/AN8
24  — RB3/CTED2/P2A/CCP2/SDO2/C12IN2-/AN9
25  — RB4/IOC0/P1D/T5G/AN11
26  — RB5/IOC1/P2B/P3A/CCP3/T3CKI/T1G/AN13
27  — RB6/IOC2/TX2/CK2/PGC
28  — RB7/IOC3/RX2/DT2/PGD                   MCLR/VPP/RE3        —  1
```

PIC18F25K22/PIC26K22

```
 2  — RA0/C12IN0-/AN0              RC0/P2B/T3CKI/T3G/T1CKI/SOSCO  — 15
 3  — RA1/C12IN1-/AN1                        RC1/P2A/CCP2/SOSCI  — 16
 4  — RA2/C2IN+/AN2/DACOUT/VREF-   RC2/CTPLS/P1A/CCP1/T5CKI/AN14  — 17
 5  — RA3/C1IN+/AN3/VREF+                   RC3/SCK1/SCL1/AN15   — 18
 6  — RA4/C1OUT/SRQ/T0CKI                    RC4/SDI1/SDA1/AN16  — 23
 7  — RA5/C2OUT/SRNQ/SS1/HLVDIN/AN4               RC5/SDO1/AN17  — 24
14  — RA6/CLKO/OSC2                        RC6/TX1/CK1/AN18      — 25
13  — RA7/CLKI/OSC1                        RC7/RX1/DT1/AN19      — 26

                                          RD0/SCK2/SCL2/AN20    — 19
33  — RB0/INT0/FLT0/SRI/AN12               RD1/CCP4/SDI2/SDA2/AN21 — 20
34  — RB1/INT1/C12IN3-/AN10                       RD2/P2B/AN22   — 21
35  — RB2/INT2/CTED1/AN8                          RD3/P2C/SS2/AN23 — 22
36  — RB3/CTED2/P2A/CCP2/C12IN2-/AN9              RD4/P2D/SDO2/AN24 — 27
37  — RB4/IOC0/T5G/AN11                           RD5/P1B/AN25   — 28
38  — RB5/IOC1/P3A/CCP3/T3CKI/T1G/AN13     RD6/P1C/TX2/CK2/AN26  — 29
39  — RB6/IOC2/PGC                         RD7/P1D/RX2/DT2/AN27  — 30
40  — RB7/IOC3/PGD

                                          RE0/P3A/CCP3/AN5      —  8
                                          RE1/P3B/AN6           —  9
                                          RE2/CCP5/AN7          — 10
                                          MCLR/VPP/RE3          —  1
```

PIC18F45K22/PIC18F46K22

Electrical isolation is extended to the data bus as well. In fact, the control signals RD TRISA, RD LATA and RD PORTA allow only one input at a time to be fed to the data bus: Q_{TRIS}, Q_{DATA} or Q_{in} (logic level of RAx) respectively.

Figure 2. Bit slice of PORTA; only RA<3:0> and RA5 may be used as analog.

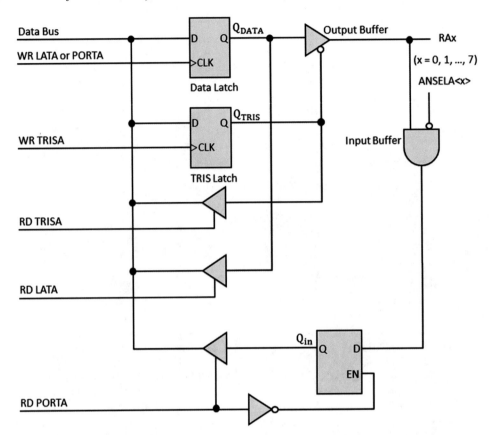

Table 1. Pin configuration of ports; applicable to ports A through E

ANSEL	Data Latch	TRIS Latch	Pin Level	Pin Status
0	0	0	0	Output
0	1	0	1	Output
0	X	1	Digital input	Input
1	X	1	Analog input	Input
1	X	0	Analog output	Output

Five of PORTA pins have a dual purpose: analog and digital. These pins are RA0/AN0, RA1/AN1, RA2/AN2, RA3/AN3 and RA5/AN4. Upon power-up reset, these pins are configured as analog inputs. The bits in charge of configuring PORTA pins as analog versus digital reside in ANSELA (see Table 2).

The TRISA register controls the drivers of the PORTA pins, even when they are being used as analog inputs. The user should ensure the bits in the TRISA register are maintained set when using them as analog inputs.

RA0 through RA5 may also be used as comparator inputs or outputs by setting the appropriate bits in the CM1CON0 and CM2CON0 registers.

Table 2. PORTA Analog Select Register (ANSELA)

ANSELA:	PORTA ANALOG SELECT REGISTER						
U-0	U-0	R/W-1	U-0	R/W-1	R/W-1	R/W-1	R/W-1
-	-	ANSA5	-	ANSA3	ANSA2	ANSA1	ANSA0
bit 7							bit 0

R = Readable bit   W = Writable bit   U = Unimplemented bit, read as '0'
-n = Value at POR   '1' = Bit is set   '0' = Bit is cleared   x = Bit is unknown

bit 7-6   **Unimplemented**: Read as '0'

bit 5   **ANSA5**: RA5 Analog Select bit
1 = Digital input buffer disabled (analog pin)
0 = Digital input buffer enabled (digital pin)

bit 4   **Unimplemented**: Read as '0'

bit 3-0   **ANSA<3:0>**: RA<3:0> Analog Select bit
1 = Digital input buffer disabled (analog pin)
0 = Digital input buffer enabled (digital pin)

As to I/O pins RA7 and RA6, they are normally used as the oscillator pins $OSC1$ and $OSC2$. These pins are configured as I/O pins by programming CONFIG1H<3:0> to 1000_2 (see CONFIG1H in Appendix 7 for further details). When they are not used as port pins, RA6 and RA7 and their associated TRIS and LAT bits are read as '0'.

The RA4 pin is multiplexed with the Timer0 module clock and one of the comparator outputs to become RA4/T0CKI/C1OUT. When used as a clock input for Timer0, RA4 is fed through a Schmitt Trigger. All other PORTA pins have TTL input levels and full CMOS output drivers.

Finally all I/O pins are protected against high input voltages and negative voltages. For that purpose, 2 diodes D1 and D2 are connected between the supply voltage V_{DD} and ground as illustrated in Figure 3. When an input voltage greater than 5.6 V is applied to the input pin, only diode D1 conducts with

Figure 3. (a) Applied input voltage ≥ 5.6 V: pin voltage is limited to 5.6 V; (b) applied input voltage ≤ -0.6V: pin voltage is limited to -0.6 V; (c) applied input within range: pin voltage equals applied voltage

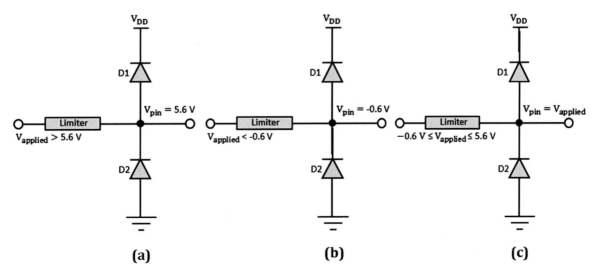

a forward drop of 0.6 V. This limits the pin voltage to 5.6 V for V_{DD} = 5V (Figure 3 (a)). Figure 3 (b) depicts the effect of a negative applied voltage. In this case, only D2 conducts and the pin voltage is limited to -0.6 V. Figure 3 (c) shows the output whenever an "in-range" voltage is applied. Both D1 and D2 are off and the pin voltage equals the applied voltage.

Example 1: Figure 4 shows the hardware/software implementation of a 4-bit binary up/down counter displayed on 4 LEDs and controlled by **RA4**. If **RA4** = 1, **PORTA** is incremented, else it is decremented. The counter frequency is 2 Hz or a period of 500 ms. *Note:* the forward voltage across green LEDs is around 1.8 V and hence the current limiting resistors (typically 330 Ω) limit the current to 9.7 mA.

Figure 4. Hardware setup for up/down binary counter

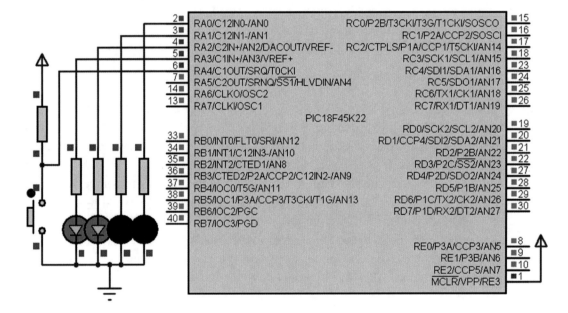

Table 3. Software implementation of up/down binary counter

Program to implement a binary counter on PORTA. Direction is controlled by RA4.

```
1   #include      <p18cxxx.h>
2   #include      <delays.h>
3
4   void main(void)
5   {
6       ANSELA &= 0xE0;          //  PORTA<4:0>: digital pins
7       LATA &= 0xF0;            //  PORTA<3:0> = 0000
8       TRISA &= 0xF0;           //  RA3:RA0 outs, RA4 input
9
10      while (1) {
11          Delay10KTCYx(50);    // 500 ms delay, Fosc = 4 MHz
12          if (PORTAbits.RA4)
13              LATA++;          // RA4 = 1, increment
14          else
15              LATA--;          // RA4 = 0, decrement
16      }
17  }
```

Solution: The program listing of Table 3 is self-explanatory.

Table 4 summarizes the pin functions of PORTA whereas Table 5 lists the registers associated with PORTA.

Table 4. Summary of PORTA pins

PORTA I/O SUMMARY

Pin	Function	TRIS Setting	ANSEL Setting	I/O	I/O Type	Description
RA0/C12IN0/AN0	RA0	0	0	O	DIG	LATA<0> data output; not affected by analog input.
		1	0	I	TTL	PORTA<0> data input; disabled when analog input enabled.
	C12IN0-	1	1	I	AN	Comparators C1 and C2 inverting input.
	AN0	1	1	I	AN	Analog input 0.
RA1/C12IN1/AN1	RA1	0	0	O	DIG	LATA<1> data output; not affected by analog input.
		1	0	I	TTL	PORTA<1> data input; disabled when analog input enabled.
	C12IN1-	1	1	I	AN	Comparators C1 and C2 inverting input.
	AN1	1	1	I	AN	Analog input 1.
RA2/C2IN+/AN2/ DACOUT/VREF-	RA2	0	0	O	DIG	LATA<2> data output; not affected by analog input. Disabled when DACOUT enabled.
		1	0	I	TTL	PORTA<2> data input; disabled when analog input enabled; Disabled when DACOUT enabled.
	C2IN+	1	1	I	AN	Comparators C2 non-inverting input.
	AN2	1	1	I	AN	Analog input 2.
	DACOUT	x	1	O	AN	DAC reference output.
	VREF-	1	1	I	AN	A/D reference voltage (low) input.
RA3/C1IN+/AN3/ VREF+	RA3	0	0	O	DIG	LATA<3> data output; not affected by analog input.
		1	0	I	TTL	PORTA<3> data input; disabled when analog input enabled.
	C1IN+	1	1	I	AN	Comparator C1 non-inverting input.
	AN3	1	1	I	AN	Analog input 3.
	VREF+	1	1	I	AN	A/D reference voltage (high) input.

Legend: DIG = Digital level output; AN = Analog input or output; TTL = TTL compatible input; HV = High Voltage; OD = Open Drain; XTAL = Crystal; CMOS = CMOS compatible input or output; DIG = Digital level output; ST = Schmitt Trigger input with CMOS levels; I²C = Schmitt Trigger input input with I²C; x = Don't care.

Pin	Function	TRIS Setting	ANSEL Setting	I/O	I/O Type	Description
RA4/CCP5/C1OUT/SRQ/T0CKI	RA4	0	-	O	DIG	LATA<4> data output.
		1	-	I	ST	PORTA<4> data input; default configuration.
	CCP5	0	-	O	DIG	CCP5 Compare output /PWM output, takes priority over RA4 output.
		1	-	I	ST	Capture 5 input/Compare 5 output/PWM5 output.
	C1OUT	0	-	O	DIG	Comparator C1 output.
	SRQ	0	-	O	DIG	SR Latch Q output; takes priority over CCP5 output.
	T0CKI	1	-	I	ST	Timer0 external clock input
RA5/C2OUT SRNQ/$\overline{SS1}$ HLVDIN/AN4	RA5	0	0	O	DIG	LATA<5> data output; not affected by analog input.
		1	0	I	TTL	PORTA<5> data input; disabled when analog input enabled.
	C2OUT	0	0	O	DIG	Comparator C2 output.
	SRNQ	0	0	O	DIG	SR Latch $\overline{Q}$ output.
	$\overline{SS1}$	1	0	I	TTL	SPI slave select input (MSSP1).
	HLVDIN	1	1	I	AN	High/Low-Voltage Detect input.
	AN4	1	1	I	AN	A/D input 4.
RA6/CLKO/OSC2	RA6	0	-	O	DIG	LATA<6> data output; enabled in INTOSC mode when CLKO is not enabled.
		1	-	I	TTL	PORTA<6> data input; enabled in INTOSC mode when CLKO is not enabled.
	CLKO	x	-	O	DIG	In RC mode, OSC2 pin outputs CLKOUT which has ¼ the frequency of OSC1 and denotes the instruction cycle rate.
	OSC2	x	-	O	XTAL	Oscillator crystal output; connects to crystal or resonator in crystal oscillator mode
RA7/CLKI/OSC1	RA7	0	-	O	DIG	LATA<7> data output. Disabled in external oscillator modes.
		1	-	I	TTL	PORTA<7> data input. Disabled in external oscillator modes.
	CLKI	x	-	I	AN	External clock source input; always associated with pin function OSC1.
	OSC1	x	-	I	XTAL	Oscillator crystal input or external clock source input ST buffer when configured in RC mode; CMOS otherwise.

Legend: TTL = TTL compatible input; HV = High Voltage; OD = Open Drain; XTAL = Crystal; CMOS = CMOS compatible input or output; DIG = Digital level output; ST = Schmitt Trigger input with CMOS levels; I²C = Schmitt Trigger input with I²C; x = Don't care.

Table 5. Registers associated with PORTA

SUMMARY OF REGISTERS ASSOCIATED WITH PORTA

Name	Bit 7	Bit 6	Bit 5	Bit 4	Bit 3	Bit 2	Bit 1	Bit 0
ANSELA	–	–	ANSA5	–	ANSA3	ANSA2	ANSA1	ANSA0
CM1CON0	C1ON	C1OUT	C1OE	C1POL	C1SP	C1R	C1CH1	C1CH0
CM2CON0	C2ON	C2OUT	C2OE	C2POL	C2SP	C2R	C2CH1	C2CH0
VREFCON1	DACEN	DACLPS	DACOE	–	DACPSS1	DACPSS0	–	DACNSS
VREFCON2	–	–	–	DACR4	DACR3	DACR2	DACR1	DACR0
HLVDCON	VDIRMAG	BGVST	IRVST	HLVDEN	HLVDL3	HLVDL2	HLVDL1	HLVDL0
LATA	LATA7	LATA6	LATA5	LATA4	LATA3	LATA2	LATA1	LATA0
PORTA	RA7	RA6	RA5	RA4	RA3	RA2	RA1	RA0
SLRCON	–	–	–	SLRE	SLRD	SLRC	SLRB	SLRA
SRCON0	SRLEN	SRCLK2	SRCLK1	SRCLK0	SRQEN	SRNQEN	SRPS	SRPR
SSP1CON1	WCOL	SSPOV	SSPEN	CKP	SSPM3	SSPM2	SSPM1	SSPM0
T0CON	TMR0ON	T08BIT	T0CS	T0SE	PSA	T0PS2	T0PS1	T0PS0
TRISA	TRISA7	TRISA6	TRISA5	TRISA4	TRISA3	TRISA2	TRISA1	TRISA0

CONFIGURATION REGISTER ASSOCIATED WITH PORTA

Name	Bit 7	Bit 6	Bit 5	Bit 4	Bit 3	Bit 2	Bit 1	Bit 0
CONFIG1H	IESO	FCMEN	PRICLKEN	PLLCFG	FOSC<3:0>			

Legend: – = unimplemented cells, read as '0'. Yellow shaded cells are not used by **PORTA**.

PORTB

PORTB, whose bit slice is shown in Figure 5, is an 8-bit digital/analog port. When used as a digital port, TRISB specifies the port direction. When a TRIS latch is cleared the pertinent pin is configured as output. When the TRIS latch is set, the pin is configured as input.

Only pins RB<5:0> may be used as analog and digital channels. Therefore, the user must clear the corresponding bit in ANSELB in order to use them as digital I/O.

The PMOS transistor plays the role of a weak pull-up resistor. To turn it on, the following conditions must be met:

- The I/O pin must be configured as input (TRISB<x> = 1). This is the default status.
- Bit WPUB<x> in WPUB (Weak Pull-up PORTB Register) must be set. See Table 6 for further details on WPUB.
- The PORTB pull-up enable bit $\overline{RBPU}$ is to be cleared.

Under these conditions, the PMOS channel is enhanced and V_{DD} is connected to the input pin via the channel resistance (2 KΩ ≤ $R_{channel}$ ≤ 5 KΩ). This feature allows direct connection of a switch or push button to any of PORTB pins without the need of an external pull-up resistor.

The tri-state buffers controlled by RD TRISB, RD LATB and RD PORTB play the role of inhibiting bus contention. The data latch, the TRIS latch and the pin level may be selectively read on a single wire.

Figure 6 shows the added hardware of RB<7:4> or the *Interrupt-On-Change* pins IOC<3:0>. The bottom circuitry of the figure is designed to detect a level change on RB7/IOC3, RB6/IOC2, RB5/IOC1 and RB4/IOC0. Here is how this feature works:

Figure 5. Bit slice of PORTB; only RB<5:0> may be used as analog.

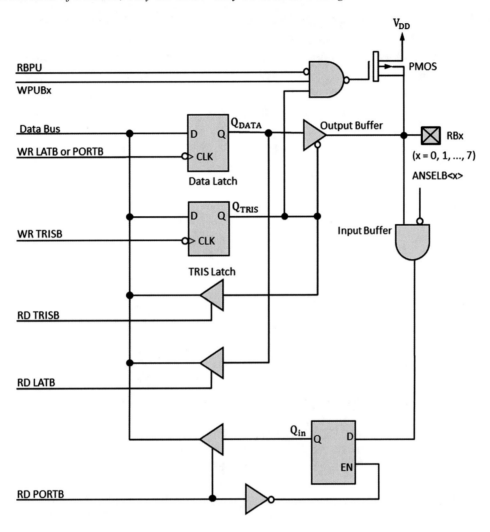

Table 6. Register used to enable/disable the weak pull-ups on PORTB

WPUB: **WEAK PULL-UP PORTB REGISTER**

R/W-1	R/W-1	R/W-1	R/W-1	R/W-1	R/W-1	R/W-1	R/W-1
WPUB7	WPUB6	WPUB5	WPUB4	WPUB3	WPUB2	WPUB1	WPUB0
bit 7							**bit 0**

R = Readable bit   W = Writable bit   U = Unimplemented bit, read as '0'
-n = Value at POR   '1' = Bit is set   '0' = Bit is cleared   x = Bit is unknown

bit 7-0   **WPUB<7:0>**: Weak Pull-up Register bits
                 1 = Pull-up enabled on PORT pin
                 0 = Pull-up disabled on PORT pin

- The bottom latch in the figure feeds the pin's logic level to its output only when PORTB is read. The AND gate insures the input pin is latched during the Q3 cycle of a read instruction (e.g. movf PORTB, W).
- The top latch, enabled at all times, reads the pin status continuously. The XOR gate fires a logic '1' when the pin's current logic level differs from the previously read pin level.
- If the pin changes voltage level, the 4-input OR gate outputs a '1' which in turn is memorized in flip-flop RBIF (PORTB change interrupt flag).

In order to check whether any of the pins RB<7:4> (or IOC<3:0>) has changed its logic level, the user may poll RBIF in the INTCON register as follows:

```
btfss       INTCON, RBIF      ; exit when RBIF = 1
bra         $-2               ; else loop back
```

or via the C statement:

```
while (!INTCONbits.RBIF);      // exit when RBIF = 1
```

To clear RBIF, the user must first access PORTB. Any read or write of PORTB, except with the movff instruction, will end the mismatch condition between the "Top Latch" and the "Bottom Latch". Secondly, the CPU must execute at least one instruction, typically a nop. Finally, RBIF must be cleared via the instruction (bcf INTCON, RBIF) or the equivalent C statement (INTCONbits.RBIF = 0).

> **Example 2:** Figure 7 illustrates the hardware/software needed to display the logic levels of input pins **RB7:RB4** on **RB3:RB0**. Note that the code does not update the display until the switch positions change. To minimize the hardware, internal pull-ups are enabled.

> **Example 3:** The hardware/software setup of Figure 8 is used to display the position of the pressed push button on the LEDs. The figure shows the push button tied to **RB6** pressed. Internal pull-ups are enabled in order to minimize the external hardware. The code is listed in Table 8.

Three of PORTB pins (RBx/INTx; x = 0, 1, 2) are designed to capture an event of the type: falling or rising edge. The associated hardware, illustrated in Figure 9, employs a Schmitt trigger to sharpen any slow rising or falling edge applied to the pin.

Figure 10 demonstrates how a falling edge (INTEDGx = 0) or a rising edge (INTEDGx = 1) is detected and captured into the INTxIF D flip-flop. This flip-flop is cleared at reset. Upon detection of an edge, the logic high D input is fed to the output and consequently INTxIF is set. The user can poll this flag to detect the occurrence of an edge. When INTxIF is set, the code should service the event. In order to wait for the re-occurrence of a similar event, INTxIF must be cleared before proceeding.

Furthermore, PORTB pins have protective diodes similar to those of PORTA. Tables 9 and 10 summarize the pin functions and the registers associated with PORTB.

It is worthwhile re-iterating that PORTB has 6 dual purpose channels: analog and digital. These channels are RB0/AN12, RB1/AN10, RB2/AN8, RB3/AN9, RB4/AN11 and RB5/AN13. These channels

Figure 6. Bit slice of RB<7:4> or IOC<3:0>; only RB<5:4> may be used as analog.

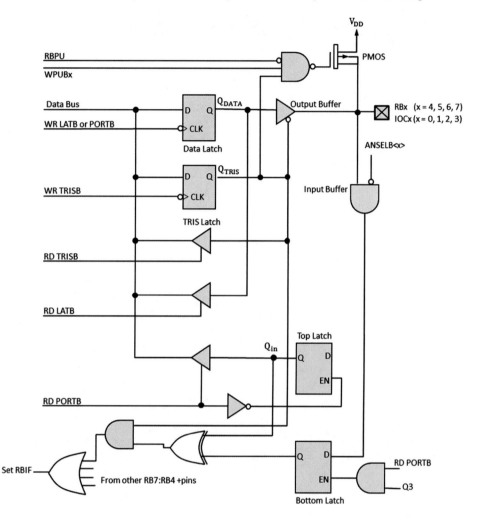

Figure 7. Hardware setup to display the status of RB7:RB4 on RB3:RB0

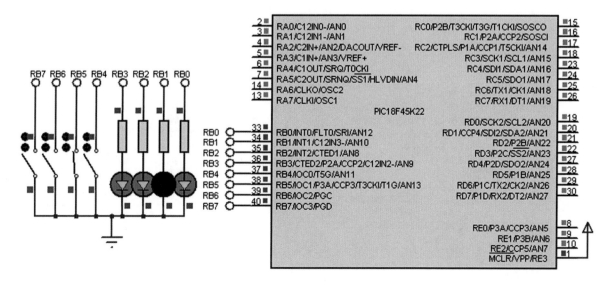

Table 7. Program to display the status of RB7:RB4 on RB3:RB0 (example 2)

```
     Program to display the status of the switches tied to RB7:RB4 on RB3:RB0.
 1   #include    <p18cxxx.h>
 2
 3   void main(void)
 4   {
 5       INTCON2bits.RBPU = 0;          // enable PORTB pull-ups
 6       TRISB = 0xF0;                  // PORTB<3:0> outputs
 7       ANSELB = 0x00;                 // all digital pins
 8
 9       while (1) {
10           PORTB >>= 4;               // removes mismatch too
11           INTCONbits.RBIF = 0;       // clear RBIF
12           while (!INTCONbits.RBIF);  // wait for change
13       }
14   }
```

Figure 8. Hardware setup to display the position of the pressed button

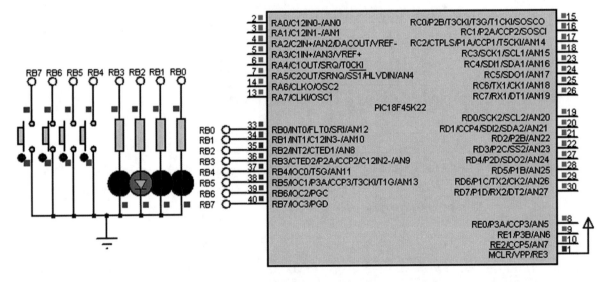

Table 8. Program that displays the position of the pressed button (example 3)

```
     Program to display position of the pressed PB on the LEDS of PORTB. Pull-ups are used.
 1   #include    <p18cxxx.h>
 2
 3   void main(void)
 4   {
 5       INTCON2bits.RBPU = 0;          // enable PORTB pull-ups
 6       PORTB &= 0xF0;                 // all LEDs are off
 7       TRISB &= 0xF0;                 // PORTB<3:0> outputs
 8       ANSELB = 0x00;                 // all digital pins
 9
10       while (1) {
11           while (!INTCONbits.RBIF);  // wait for change
12           PORTB = ~PORTB >> 4;       // complement then swap
13           INTCONbits.RBIF = 0;       // clear RBIF
14       }
15   }
```

Figure 9. Bit slice of RBx/INTx (x = 0, 1, 2)

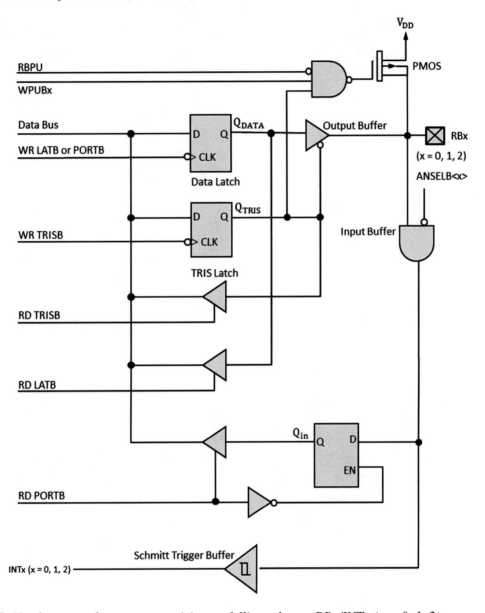

Figure 10. Hardware used to capture a rising or falling edge on RBx/INTx (x = 0, 1, 2)

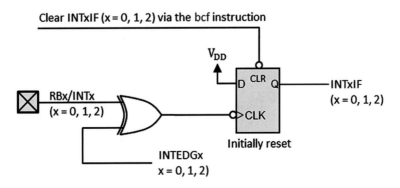

Table 9. PORTB I/O summary

PORTB I/O SUMMARY

Pin	Function	TRIS Setting	ANSEL Setting	I/O	I/O Type	Description
RB0/INT0/CCP4/ FLT0/SRI/$\overline{SS2}$/ AN12	RB0	0	0	O	DIG	LATB<0> data output; not affected by analog input.
		1	0	I	TTL	PORTB<0> data input; disabled when analog input enabled.
	INT0	1	0	I	ST	External interrupt 0 input.
	CCP4[3]	0	0	O	DIG	Compare 4 output / PWM 4 output.
		1	0	I	ST	Capture 4 input.
	FLT0	1	0	I	ST	PWM Fault input for ECCP auto-shutdown.
	SRI	1	0	I	ST	SR Latch input.
	$\overline{SS2}$[3]	1	0	I	TTL	SPI slave select input (MSSP2)
	AN12	1	1	I	AN	A/D input channel 12.
RB1/INT1/P1C/ SCK2/SCL2/ C12IN3-/AN10	RB1	0	0	O	DIG	LATB<1> data output; not affected by analog input.
		1	0	I	TTL	PORTB<1> data input; disabled when analog input enabled.
	INT1	1	0	I	ST	External interrupt 1 input.
	P1C[3]	0	0	O	DIG	Enhanced CCP1 PWM output 3.
	SCK2[3]	0	0	O	DIG	MSSP2 SPI Clock output.
		1	0	I	ST	MSSP2 SPI Clock input.
	SCL2[3]	0	0	O	DIG	MSSP2 I²C™ Clock output.
		1	0	I	I²C	MSSP2 I²C™ Clock input.
	C12IN3-	1	1	I	AN	Comparators C1 and C2 inverting input.
	AN10	1	1	I	AN	A/D input channel 10.
RB2/INT2/CTED1/ P1B/SDI2/SDA2/ AN8	RB2	0	0	O	DIG	LATB<2> data output; not affected by analog input.
		1	0	I	TTL	PORTB<2> data input; disabled when analog input enabled.
	INT2	1	0	I	ST	External interrupt 2 input.
	CTED1	1	0	I	ST	CTMU Edge 1 input.
	P1B[3]	0	0	O	DIG	Enhanced CCP1 PWM output 2.
	SDI2[3]	1	0	I	ST	MSSP2 SPI data input.
	SDA2[3]	0	0	O	DIG	MSSP2 I²C™ data output.
		1	0	I	I²C	MSSP2 I²C™ data input.
	AN8	1	1	I	AN	A/D input channel 8.
RB3/CTED2/P2A/ CCP2/SDO2/ C12IN2-/AN9	RB3	0	0	O	DIG	LATB<3> data output; not affected by analog input.
		1	0	I	TTL	PORTB<3> data input; disabled when analog input enabled.
	CTED2	1	0	I	ST	CTMU Edge 2 input.
	P2A	0	0	O	DIG	Enhanced CCP1 PWM output 1.
	CCP2[2]	0	0	O	DIG	Compare 2 output / PWM 2 output.
		1	0	I	ST	Capture 2 input.
	SDO2[2]	0	0	O	DIG	MSSP2 SPI data output.
	C12IN2-	1	1	I	AN	Comparators C1 and C2 inverting input.
	AN9	1	1	I	AN	A/D input channel 9.
RB4/IOC0/P1D/ T5G/AN11	RB4	0	0	O	DIG	LATB<4> data output; not affected by analog input.
		1	0	I	TTL	PORTB<4> data input; disabled when analog input enabled.
	IOC0	1	0	I	TTL	Interrupt-on-pin change.
	P1D	0	0	O	DIG	Enabled CCP1 PWM output 4.
	T5G	1	0	I	ST	Timer5 external clock gate input.
	AN11	1	1	O	DIG	Analog input channel 11.
RB5/IOC1/P2B/ P3A/CCP3/T3CKI/ T1G/AN13	RB5	0	0	O	DIG	LATB<5> data output; not affected by analog input.
		1	0	I	TTL	PORTB<5> data input; disabled when analog input enabled.
	IOC1	1	0	I	TTL	Interrupt-on-pin change pin 1.
	P2B[1][3]	0	0	O	DIG	Enabled CCP2 PWM output 2.
	P3A[1]	0	0	O	DIG	Enhanced CCP3 PWM output 1.
	CCP3[1]	0	0	O	DIG	Compare 3 output / PWM 3 output.
		1	0	I	ST	Capture 3 input.
	T3CKI[2]	1	0	I	ST	Timer3 external clock input
	T1G	1	0	I	ST	Timer1 external clock gate input.
	AN13	1	1	O	DIG	Analog input channel 13.
RB6/IOC2/PGC	RB6	0	-	O	DIG	LATB<6> data output; not affected by analog input.
		1	-	I	TTL	PORTB<6> data input; disabled when analog input enabled.
	IOC2	1	-	I	TTL	Interrupt-on-pin change pin.
	TX2[3]	1	-	O	DIG	EUSART asynchronous transmit data output.
	CK2[3]	1	-	O	DIG	EUSART asynchronous serial clock output.
		1	-	I	ST	EUSART asynchronous serial clock input.
	PGC	x	-	I	ST	In-Circuit Debugger and ICSP™ programming clock input.
RB7/IOC3/PGD	RB7	0	0	O	DIG	LATB<7> data output; not affected by analog input.
		1	0	I	TTL	PORTB<7> data input; disabled when analog input enabled.
	IOC3	1	-	I	TTL	Interrupt-on-pin change pin.
	RX2[2][3]	1	-	I	ST	EUSART asynchronous receive data input.
	DT2[2][3]	1	-	O	DIG	EUSART synchronous receive data output.
		1	-	I	ST	EUSART synchronous receive data input.
	PGD	x	-	O	DIG	In-Circuit Debugger and ICSP™ programming data output.
		x	-	I	ST	In-Circuit Debugger and ICSP™ programming data input.

Legend: DIG = Digital level output; AN = Analog input or output; TTL = TTL compatible input; HV = High Voltage; OD = Open Drain; XTAL = Crystal; CMOS = CMOS compatible input or output; DIG = Digital level output; ST = Schmitt Trigger input with CMOS levels; I²C = Schmitt Trigger input with I²C; x = Don't care.

Note 1: Default pin assignment for PB2, T3CKI, CCP3 and CCP2 when Configuration bits PB2MX, T3CMX, CCP3MX and CCP2MX are set.

Note 2: Alternate pin assignment for P2B, T3CKI, CCP3 and CCP2 when Default pin assignment for PB2, T3CKI, CCP3 and CCP2 when Configuration bits PB2MX, T3CMX, CCP3MX and CCP2MX are clear.

Note 3: Function on PORTD and PORTE for PIC18(L)F4XK22.

Table 10. Summary of the registers associated with PORTB

SUMMARY OF REGISTERS ASSOCIATED WITH PORTB

Name	Bit 7	Bit 6	Bit 5	Bit 4	Bit 3	Bit 2	Bit 1	Bit 0
ANSELB	–	–	ANSB5	ANSB4	ANSB3	ANSB2	ANSB1	ANSB0
ECCP2AS	CCP2ASE	CCP2AS2	CCP2AS1	CCP2AS0	PSS2AC1	PSS2AC0	PSS2BD1	PSS2BD0
CCP2CON	P2M1	P2M0	DC2B1	DC2B0	CCP2M3	CCP2M2	CCP2M1	CCP2M0
ECCP3AS	CCP3ASE	CCP3AS2	CCP3AS1	CCP3AS0	PSS3AC1	PSS3AC0	PSS3BD1	PSS3BD0
CCP3CON	P3M1	P3M0	DC3B1	DC3B0	CCP3M3	CCP3M2	CCP3M1	CCP3M0
INTCON	GIE	PEIE	TMR0IE	INT0IE	RBIE	TMR0IF	INT0IF	RBIF
INTCON2	RBPU	INTEDG0	INTEDG1	INTEDG2	–	TMR0IP	–	RBIP
INTCON3	INT2IP	INT1IP	–	INT2IE	INT1IE	–	INT2IF	INT1IF
IOCB	IOCB7	IOCB6	IOCB5	IOCB4	–	–	–	–
LATB	LATB7	LATB6	LATB5	LATB4	LATB3	LATB2	LATB1	LATB0
PORTB	RB7	RB6	RB5	RB4	RB3	RB2	RB1	RB0
SLRCON	–	–	–	SLRE[1]	SLRD[1]	SLRC	SLRB	SLRA
T1GCON	TMR1GE	T1GPOL	T1GTM	T1GSPM	T1GGO/DONE	T1GVAL	T1GSS1	T1GSS0
T3CON	TMR3CS1	TMR3CS0	T3CKPS1	T3CKPS0	T3SOSCEN	T3SYNC	T3RD16	TMR3ON
T5GCON	TMR5GE	T5GPOL	T5GTM	T5GSPM	T5GGO/DONE	T5GVAL	T5GSS1	T5GSS0
TRISB	TRISB7	TRISB6	TRISB5	TRISB4	TRISB3	TRISB2	TRISB1	TRISB0
WPUB	WPUB7	WPUB6	WPUB5	WPUB4	WPUB3	WPUB2	WPUB1	WPUB0
CONFIG3H	MCLRE	–	P2BMX	T3CMX	HFOFST	CCP3MX	PBADEN	CCP2MX
CONFIG4L	DEBUG	XINST	–	–	–	LVP[1]	–	STRVEN

Legend: – = unimplemented cells, read as '0'. Yellow shaded cells are not used by **PORTB**.
Note 1: Can only be changed when in high voltage programming mode.

are controlled by PBADEN (PORTB A/D Enable). When PBADEN is on (reset value), RB5:RB0 are configured as analog channels; otherwise, these pins work as digital channels. The directive

```
#pragma     config     PBADEN = OFF
```

has been added to the file <p18F45K22.h> to insure RB5:RB0 start up as digital channels. This way, there will be no need to clear flag ANSBx in ANSELB to configure these pins as digital.

Finally, note that the *Interrupt-On-Change* feature (RB7:RB4 or IOC3:IOC0) as well as the edge-triggered pins INT0/1/2 have the capability of provoking interrupts and thereby make programs more efficient. The topic of interrupts is rather substantial and will be covered thoroughly in chapter 7.

> **Example 4:** Given the hardware setup of Figure 11, write a program to display an up/down counter running at a frequency of 2 Hz on the hexadecimal display. Program the counter to count up initially. When push button **RB0/INT0** is pressed, the counter changes direction. Use a flag named **UpDown** to keep track of the counter direction. Enable the internal pull-ups on input pins to minimize the hardware.

Solution: The program listed in Table 11 is self-explanatory. A counter frequency of 2 Hz implies a rate of ½ sec or 500 ms per counter cycle. The following FLAGS bit structure:

```
struct {
    unsigned B0:1, B1:1, B2:1, B3:1;        // Bits 0..3
    unsigned B4:1, B5:1, B6:1, B7:1;        // Bits 4..7
} FLAGS;
```

Figure 11. Hardware circuitry for Examples 4 and 5

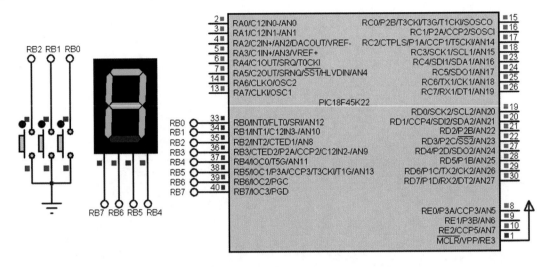

has been added to the file <p18cxxx.h> for your convenience. This structure allows programmers to use variables of the Boolean type which is not part of the standard C data types. Hence the statement:

```
#define    UpDown      FLAGS.B0
```

allocates a 1-bit variable UpDown in FLAGS<0>. This flag can be easily set, cleared or toggled in C language.

Table 11. Implementation of Up/Down counter with direction control via toggle PB

```
Up/Down counter. PB tied to RB0 changes direction and acts like a toggle switch.
1   #include    <p18cxxx.h>
2   #include    <delays.h>
3
4   #define     UpDown      FLAGS.B0        // UpDown = 1, count up
5                                           // UpDown = 0, count down
6   void main(void)
7   {
8       INTCON2bits.RBPU = 0;               // enable PORTB pull-ups
9       INTCON2bits.INTEDG0 = 0;            // react to -ve edge
10      PORTB &= 0x0F;                      // start count at 0
11      TRISB &= 0x0F;                      // PORTB<7:4> outputs
12      ANSELB = 0x00;                      // all digital pins
13      UpDown = 1;                         // count up initially
14
15      while (1)
16      {
17          Delay10KTCYx(50);              // 500 ms (Fosc = 4 MHz)
18          if (INTCONbits.INT0IF)          // wait for change
19          {
20              UpDown = !UpDown;           // change direction
21              INTCONbits.INT0IF = 0;      // acknowledge PB
22          }
23          PORTB += UpDown ? 0x10 : 0xF0;  // add 1 or -1 to MSBs
24      }
25  }
```

Example 5: Given the hardware setup of Figure 11, the program (Table 12) implements an up/down counter controlled by **RB1/INT1** (count up) and **RB2/INT2** (count down). The counter initially displays a count of 0. The program is event driven in the sense that when **RB1** is pressed, the counter is incremented. Similarly, when **RB2** is pressed, the counter is decremented.

Table 12. Implementation of Up/Down counter with 2 push buttons

```
Up/Down counter with 2 push buttons
 1  #include     <p18cxxx.h>
 2
 3  void main(void)
 4  {
 5      INTCON2bits.RBPU = 0;             // enable Pull-ups
 6      INTCON2bits.INTEDG1 = 0;          // INT1: -ve edge
 7      INTCON2bits.INTEDG2 = 0;          // INT2: -ve edge
 8      PORTB &= 0x0F;                    // start count at 0
 9      TRISB &= 0x0F;                    // PORTB<7:4> outputs
10      ANSELB = 0x00;                    // all digital pins
11
12      while (1)
13      {
14          if (INTCON3bits.INT1IF)       // increment
15          {
16              INTCON3bits.INT1IF = 0;
17              PORTB += 0x10;
18          }
19          else if (INTCON3bits.INT2IF)  // decrement
20          {
21              INTCON3bits.INT2IF = 0;
22              PORTB += 0xF0;
23          }
24      }
25  }
```

PORTC

PORTC is an 8-bit bidirectional port with no internal pull-ups. In this respect, its hardware configuration looks like a bit-slice of PORTA. It has 6 analog channels RC7:RC2 or AN19:AN14. Its pins are multiplexed with peripheral devices such as: USART1, SPI1, I2C port1, CCP modules, the clock inputs of Timer1, 3, 5 etc. Table 13 describes the pins functionality and Table 14 lists the registers associated with PORTC.

Some of these pin functions can be relocated to alternate pins using the control fuse bits in CONFIG3H. RC0 is the default pin for T3CKI. Clearing the T3CMX bit moves the pin function to RB5. RC1 is the default pin for the CCP2 peripheral pin. Clearing the CCP2MX bit moves the pin function to the RB3 pin.

Two other pin functions, P2B and CCP3, can be relocated from their default pins to PORTC pins by clearing the control fuses in CONFIG3H. Clearing P2BMX and CCP3MX moves the pin functions to RC0 and RC6/RE0, respectively.

This chapter will stick to the functionality of PORTC as a digital I/O port. The upcoming example illustrates a practical application.

Table 13. PORTC I/O summary

PORTC I/O SUMMARY

Pin	Function	TRIS Setting	ANSEL Setting	I/O	I/O Type	Description
RC0/P2B/T3CKI/T3G/ T1CKI/SOSC0	RC0	0	-	O	DIG	LATC<0> data output.
		1	-	I	ST	PORTC<0> data input.
	PB2[2]	0	-	O	DIG	Enhanced CCP2 PWM output 2.
	T3CKI[1]	1	-	I	ST	Timer3 clock input.
	T3G	1	-	I	ST	Timer3 external clock gate input.
	T1CKI	1	-	I	ST	Timer1 clock input.
	SOSC0	X	-	O	XTAL	Secondary oscillator output.
RC1/P2A/CCP2/ SOSCI	RC1	0	-	O	DIG	LATC<1> data output.
		1	-	I	ST	PORTC<1> data input.
	P2A	0	-	O	DIG	Enhanced CCP2 PWM output 1.
	CCP2[1]	0	-	O	DIG	Compare 2 output / PWM 2 output.
		1	-	I	ST	Capture 2 input.
	SOSCI	x	-	I	XTAL	Secondary oscillator input.
RC2/CTPLS/P1A/ CCP1/T5CKI/AN14	RC2	0	0	O	DIG	LATC<2> data output; not affected by analog input.
		1	0	I	ST	PORTC<2> data input; disabled when analog input enabled.
	CTPLS	0	0	O	DIG	CTMU pulse generator output.
	P1A	0	0	O	DIG	Enhanced CCP1 PWM output 1.
	CCP1	0	0	O	DIG	Compare 1 output / PWM output 1.
		1	0	I	ST	Capture 1 input.
	T5CKI	1	0	I	ST	Timer 5 clock input.
	AN14	1	1	I	AN	Analog input 14.
RC3/SCK1/SCL1/AN15	RC3	0	0	O	DIG	LATC<3> data output; not affected by analog input.
		1	0	I	ST	PORTC<3> data input; disabled when analog input enabled.
	SCK1	0	0	O	DIG	MSSP1 SPI Clock output.
		1	0	I	ST	MSSP1 SPI Clock input.
	SCL1	0	0	O	DIG	MSSP1 I²C™ Clock output.
		1	0	I	I²C	MSSP1 I²C™ Clock input.
	AN15	1	1	I	AN	Analog input 15.
RC4/SDI1/SDA1/AN16	RC4	0	0	O	DIG	LATC<4> data output; not affected by analog input.
		1	0	I	ST	PORTC<4> data input; disabled when analog input enabled.
	SDI1	1	0	I	ST	MSSP1 SPI data input.
	SDA1	0	0	O	DIG	MSSP1 I²C™ data output.
		1	0	I	I²C	MSSP1 I²C™ data input.
	AN16	1	1	I	AN	Analog input 16.
RC5/SDO1/AN17	RC6	0	0	O	DIG	LATC<5> data output; not affected by analog input.
		1	0	I	ST	PORTC<5> data input; disabled when analog input enabled.
	SDO1	0	0	O	DIG	MSSP1 SPI data output.
	AN17	1	1	I	AN	Analog input 17.
RC6/P3A/CCP3/TX1/ CK1/AN18	RC6	0	0	O	DIG	LATC<6> data output; not affected by analog input.
		1	0	I	ST	PORTC<6> data input; disabled when analog input enabled.
	P3A[2],[3]	0	0	O	CMOS	Enhanced CCP3 PWM output 1.
	CCP3[2],[3]	0	0	O	DIG	Compare 3 output / PWM 3 output.
		1	0	I	ST	Capture 3 input.
	TX1	1	0	O	DIG	EUSART asynchronous transmit data output.
	CK1	1	0	O	DIG	EUSART synchronous serial clock output.
		1	0	I	ST	EUSART synchronous serial clock output.
	AN18	1	1	I	AN	Analog input 18.
RC7/P3B/RX1/DT1/ AN19	RC7	0	0	O	DIG	LATC<7> data output; not affected by analog input.
		1	0	I	ST	PORTC<7> data input; disabled when analog input enabled.
	P3B	0	0	0	CMOS	Enhanced CCP3 PWM output 2.
	RX1	1	0	I	ST	EUSART asynchronous receive data input.
	DT1	1	0	O	DIG	EUSART synchronous receive data output.
		1	0	I	ST	EUSART synchronous receive data input.
	AN19	1	1	I	AN	Analog input 19.

Legend: DIG = Digital level output; AN = Analog input or output; TTL = TTL compatible input; HV = High Voltage; OD = Open Drain; XTAL = Crystal; CMOS = CMOS compatible input or output; ST = Schmitt Trigger input with CMOS levels; I²C™ = Schmitt Trigger input with I²C.

Note 1: Default pin assignment for PB2, T3CKI, CCP3 and CCP2 when Configuration bits PB2MX, T3CMX, CCP3MX and CCP2MX are set.

Note 2: Alternate pin assignment for P2B, T3CKI, CCP3 and CCP2 when Default pin assignment for PB2, T3CKI, CCP3 and CCP2 when Configuration bits PB2MX, T3CMX, CCP3MX and CCP2MX are clear.

Note 3: Function on PORTD and PORTE for PIC18(L)F4XK22.

Table 14. Summary of the registers associated with PORTC

SUMMARY OF REGISTERS ASSOCIATED WITH PORTC

Name	Bit 7	Bit 6	Bit 6	Bit 4	Bit 3	Bit 2	Bit 1	Bit 0
ANSELC	ANSC7	ANSC6	ANSC5	ANSC4	ANSC3	ANSC2	–	–
ECCP1AS	CCP1ASE	CCP1AS2	CCP1AS1	CCP1AS0	PSS1AC1	PSS1AC0	PSS1BD1	PSS1BD0
CCP1CON	P1M1	P1M0	DC1B1	DC1B0	CCP1M3	CCP1M2	CCP1M1	CCP1M0
ECCP2AS	CCP2ASE	CCP2AS2	CCP2AS1	CCP2AS0	PSS2AC1	PSS2AC0	PSS2BD1	PSS2BD0
CCP2CON	P2M1	P2M0	DC2B1	DC2B0	CCP2M3	CCP2M2	CCP2M1	CCP2M0
CTMUCONH	CTMUEN	–	CTMUSIDL	TGEN	EDGEN	EDGSEQEN	IDISSEN	CTTRIG
LATC	LATC7	LATC6	LATC5	LATC4	LATC3	LATC2	LATC1	LATC0
PORTC	RC7	RC6	RC5	RC4	RC3	RC2	RC1	RC0
RCSTA1	SPEN	RX9	SREN	CREN	ADDEN	FERR	OERR	RX9D
SLRCON	–	–	–	SLRE[(1)]	SLRD[(1)]	SLRC	SLRB	SLRA
SSP1CON1	WCOL	SSPOV	SSPEN	CKP	SSPM3	SSPM2	SSPM1	SSPM0
T1CON	TMR1CS1	TMR1CS0	T1CKPS1	T1CKPS0	T1SOSCEN	T1SYNC	T1RD16	TMR1ON
T3CON	TMR3CS1	TMR3CS0	T3CKPS1	T3CKPS0	T3SOSCEN	T3SYNC	T3RD16	TMR3ON
T3GCON	TMR3GE	T3GPOL	T3GTM	T3GSPM	T3GGO/DONE	T3GVAL	T3GSS1	T3GSS0
T5CON	TMR5CS1	TMR5CS0	T5CKPS1	T5CKPS0	T5SOSCEN	T5SYNC	T5RD16	TMR5ON
TRISC	TRISC7	TRISC6	TRISC5	TRISC4	TRISC3	TRISC2	TRISC1	TRISC0
TXSTA1	CSRC	TX9	TXEN	SYNC	SENDB	BRGH	TRMT	TX9D

Legend: – = unimplemented, read as '0'. Yellow shaded cells are not used by **PORTC**.
Note 1: Available on PIC(L)18F4XK22 devices.

CONFIGURATION REGISTER ASSOCIATED WITH PORTC

Name	Bit 7	Bit 6	Bit 5	Bit 4	Bit 3	Bit 2	Bit 1	Bit 0
CONFIG3H	MCLRE	–	P2BMX	T3CMX	HFOFST	CCP3MX	PBADEN	CCP2MX

Legend: – = unimplemented cells, read as '0'. Yellow shaded cells are not used by **PORTC**.

Example 6: Implement a 2-digit programmable timer as illustrated in Figure 12. The user specifies the timer duration (00 to 99) via the up and down push buttons. The start push button turns on the device and initiates the countdown process of the timer. When the time elapses, the device is turned off, the buzzer is triggered intermittently for 3 seconds and the display is flashed.

Figure 12. 2-digit programmable timer; the display is interfaced to PORTC

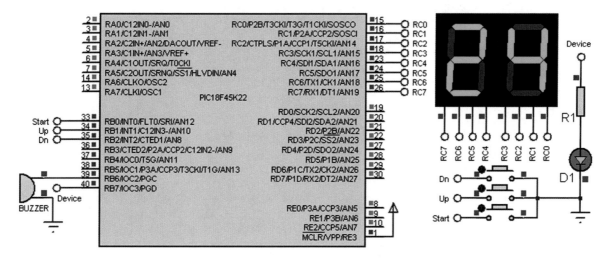

Solution: The program, listed in Table 15, is subdivided into three functions and a main program.

Table 15. 2-digit programmable timer

```
2-digit programmable timer with Up/Dn push buttons and data retention in RAM
1   #include      <p18cxxx.h>
2   #include      <BCDlib.h>
3   #include      <delays.h>
4
5   #define       Device   PORTBbits.RB7        // device pin
6   #define       Buzzer   PORTBbits.RB6        // buzzer pin
7   #define       Up       INTCON3bits.INT1IF   // Up push button
8   #define       Dn       INTCON3bits.INT2IF   // Dn push button
9   #define       Start    INTCONbits.INT0IF    // Start push button
10
11  void Setup(void);
12  void IncDec(void);
13  void TurnOn(void);
14
15  unsigned char i;                            // loop counter
16  unsigned char seconds = 0x25;               // seconds variable
17
18  void main(void) {
19      Setup();                                // system setup
20      while (1) {
21          IncDec();                           // set time
22          TurnOn();                           // elapse selected time
23      }
24  }
25
26  void Setup(void)
27  {
28      Device = 0;                             // turn device off
29      Buzzer = 0;                             // turn buzzer off
30      TRISBbits.TRISB7 = 0;                   // RB7 output pin
31      TRISBbits.TRISB6 = 0;                   // RB6 output pin
32      TRISC = 0x00;                           // PORTC is output
33      ANSELB = ANSELC = 0x00;                 // ports B & C digital
34      INTCON2 = 0b00000101;                   // RBPU = 0, INTx: -ve edge
35  }
36
37  void IncDec(void)
38  {
39      PORTC = seconds;                        // start with initial value
40      while (1) {
41          if (Up)
42          {
43              Up = 0;                         // acknowledge flag
44              IncBcd(PORTC);                  // increment
45          }
46          else if (Dn)
47          {
48              Dn = 0;                         // acknowledge flag
49              DecBcd(PORTC);                  // decrement
50          } else if (Start) {
51              Start = 0;                      // acknowledge flag
52              if (PORTC != 0) {
53                  seconds = PORTC;            // save set value
54                  return;
55              }
56          }
57      }
58  }
59
60  void TurnOn(void)
61  {
62      Device = 1;                             // turn device on
63      do {
64          Delay10KTCYx(100);                  // 1 second delay, Fosc = 4 MHz
65          DecBcd(PORTC);                      // count down
66      } while (PORTC != 0);
67
68      Device = 0;                             // turn device off
69      for (i = 0; i < 6; i++) {
70          Delay10KTCYx(50);                   // 1/2 second delay
71          TRISC = ~TRISC;                     // flash display
72          Buzzer = ~Buzzer;                   // beep intermittently
73      }
74  }
```

- **Setup():** It initializes the I/O ports of the system and configures the interrupt pins INT0/1/2 to react to falling edges. The internal pull-ups are enabled as well.
- **IncDec():** This function is used to set the time via the Up/Dn push buttons. Upon termination, the user initiates the counting process via the Start button. The set time is memorized in variable seconds.
- **TurnOn():** To turn on the device and display a down counter until the count of 00 is reached. At this point the device is turned off and the user can start all over again. Also, the buzzer is triggered intermittently for 3 seconds and the display is flashed.
- **main():** To invoke the above functions.

Table 16. PORTD pin functions

PORTD I/O SUMMARY

Pin	Function	TRIS Setting	ANSEL Setting	I/O	I/O Type	Description
RD0/SCK2/SCL2/ AN20	RD0	0	0	O	DIG	LATD<0> data output; not affected by analog input.
		1	0	I	ST	PORTD<0> data output; disabled when analog input enabled.
	SCK2	0	0	O	DIG	MSSP2 SPI Clock output.
		1	0	I	ST	MSSP2 SPI Clock input.
	SCL2	0	0	O	DIG	MSSP2 I²C™ Clock output.
		1	0	I	I²C	MSSP2 I²C™ Clock input.
	AN20	1	1	I	AN	Analog input 20.
RD1/CCP4/SDI2/ SDA2/AN21	RD1	0	0	O	DIG	LATD<1> data output; not affected by analog input.
		1	0	I	ST	PORTD<1> data output; disabled when analog input enabled.
	CCP4	0	0	O	DIG	Compare 4 output/PWM 4 output.
		1	0	I	ST	Capture 4 input.
	SDI2	1	0	I	ST	MSSP2 SPI data input.
	SDA2	0	0	O	DIG	MSSP2 I²C™ data output.
		1	0	I	I²C	MSSP2 I²C™ data input.
	AN21	1	1	I	AN	Analog input 21.
RD2/P2B/AN22	RD2	0	0	O	DIG	LATD<2> data output; not affected by analog input.
		1	0	I	ST	PORTD<2> data output; disabled when analog input enabled.
	P2B[1]	0	0	O	DIG	Enhanced CCP2 PWM output 2.
	AN22	1	1	I	AN	Analog input 22.
RD3/P2C/$\overline{SS2}$/AN23	RD3	0	0	O	DIG	LATD<3> data output; not affected by analog input.
		1	0	I	ST	PORTD<3> data output; disabled when analog input enabled.
	P2C	0	0	O	DIG	Enhanced CCP2 PWM output 4.
	$\overline{SS2}$	1	0	I	TTL	MSSP2 SPI slave select input.
	AN23	1	1	I	AN	Analog input 23.
RD4/P2D/SDO2/ AN24	RD4	0	0	O	DIG	LATD<4> data output; not affected by analog input.
		1	0	I	ST	PORTD<4> data output; disabled when analog input enabled.
	P2D	0	0	O	DIG	Enhanced C`CP2 PWM output 3.
	SDO2	0	0	O	DIG	MSSP2 SPI data output.
	AN24	1	1	I	AN	Analog input 24.
RD5/P1B/AN25	RD6	0	0	O	DIG	LATD<5> data output; not affected by analog input.
		1	0	I	ST	PORTD<5> data output; disabled when analog input enabled.
	P1B	0	0	O	DIG	Enhanced CCP1 PWM output 2.
	AN25	1	1	I	AN	Analog input 25.
RD6/P1C/TX2/ CK2/AN26	RD6	0	0	O	DIG	LATD<6> data output; not affected by analog input.
		1	0	I	ST	PORTD<6> data output; disabled when analog input enabled.
	P1C	0	0	O	DIG	Enhanced CCP1 PWM output 3.
	TX2	1	0	O	DIG	EUSART asynchronous transmit data output.
	CK2	1	0	O	DIG	EUSART synchronous serial clock output.
		1	0	I	ST	EUSART synchronous serial clock input.
	AN26	1	1	I	AN	Analog input 26.
RD7/P1D/RX2/ DT2/AN27	RD7	0	0	O	DIG	LATD<7> data output; not affected by analog input.
		1	0	I	ST	PORTD<7> data output; disabled when analog input enabled.
	P1D	0	0	O	DIG	Enhanced CCP1 PWM output 4.
	RX2	1	0	I	ST	EUSART asynchronous receive data input.
	DT2	1	0	O	DIG	EUSART synchronous receive data output.
		1	0	I	ST	EUSART synchronous receive data input.
	AN27	1	1	I	AN	Analog input 27.

Legend: DIG = Digital level output; AN = Analog input or output; TTL = TTL compatible input; HV = High Voltage; OD = Open Drain; XTAL = Crystal; CMOS = CMOS compatible input or output; ST = Schmitt Trigger input with CMOS levels; I²C™ = Schmitt Trigger input with I²C.

Note 1: Default pin assignment for PB2, T3CKI, CCP3 and CCP2 when Configuration bits PB2MX, T3CMX, CCP3MX and CCP2MX are set.

PORTD

PORTD is an 8-bit wide bidirectional port. Its direction is controlled by the data direction register TRISD. A bit slice of PORTD resembles that of PORTA. All pins of PORTD are implemented with Schmitt Trigger input buffers and can have either digital or analog functionality. Register ANSELD controls this option as is the case with the other ports discussed so far. Table 16 describes the pins functionality and Table 17 lists the registers associated with PORTD.

> **Example 7:** Redo Example 6 using a 3-digit display (Figure 13). The time duration is set by the up and down push buttons is to be memorized in EEPROM. This way when the system is turned on, it reads the previously stored value from EEPROM variable eeSeconds.

Table 17. Summary of the registers associated with PORTD

SUMMARY OF REGISTERS ASSOCIATED WITH PORTD

Name	Bit 7	Bit 6	Bit 6	Bit 4	Bit 3	Bit 2	Bit 1	Bit 0
ANSELD[1]	ANSD7	ANSD6	ANSD5	ANSD4	ANSD3	ANSD2	ANSD1	ANSD0
BAUDCON2	ABDOVF	RCIDL	DTRXP	CKTXP	BRG16	–	WUE	ABDEN
CCP1CON	P1M1	P1M0	DC1B1	DC1B0	CCP1M3	CCP1M2	CCP1M1	CCP1M0
CCP2CON	P2M1	P2M0	DC2B1	DC2B0	CCP2M3	CCP2M2	CCP2M1	CCP2M0
CCP4CON	–	–	DC4B1	DC4B0	CCP4M3	CCP4M2	CCP4M1	CCP4M0
LATD[1]	LATD7	LATD6	LATD5	LATD4	LATD3	LATD2	LATD1	LATD0
PORTD[1]	RD7	RD6	RD5	RD4	RD3	RD2	RD1	RD0
RCSTA2	SPEN	RX9	SREN	CREN	ADDEN	FERR	OERR	RX9D
SLRCON[1]	–	–	–	SLRE	SLRD	SLRC	SLRB	SLRA
SSP2CON1	WCOL	SSPOV	SSPEN	CKP	SSPM3	SSPM2	SSPM1	SSPM0
TRISD[1]	TRISD7	TRISD6	TRISD5	TRISD4	TRISD3	TRISD2	TRISD1	TRISD0

Legend: – = unimplemented, read as '0'. Yellow shaded cells are not used by **PORTD**.
Note 1: Available on PIC18(L)F4XK22 devices.

CONFIGURATION REGISTER ASSOCIATED WITH PORTD

Name	Bit 7	Bit 6	Bit 5	Bit 4	Bit 3	Bit 2	Bit 1	Bit 0
CONFIG3H	MCLRE	–	P2BMX	T3CMX	HFOFST	CCP3MX	PBADEN	CCP2MX

Legend: – = unimplemented cells, read as '0'. Yellow shaded cells are not used by **PORTD**.

Figure 13. 3-digit programmable timer; the set time is memorized in EEPROM.

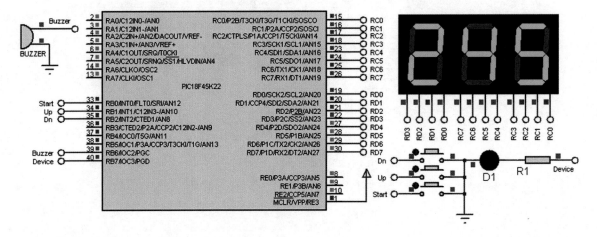

Solution: The program, listed in Table 18, starts by reading variable eeSeconds from EEPROM to variable seconds in RAM. Whenever the user presses the start push button, the set time in variable seconds is saved in EEPROM variable eeSeconds and then the device is turn on.

Table 18. 3-digit programmable timer program listing

```
3-Digit programmable timer with Up/Dn push buttons and data retention in EEPROM
 1  #include       <p18cxxx.h>
 2  #include       <BCDlib.h>
 3  #include       <EEPROM.h>
 4  #include       <delays.h>
 5
 6  #pragma        romdata eeAddress = 0xF00000    // EEPROM address 0x00
 7  rom char       eeSeconds;                      // EEPROM seconds
 8
 9  #define        Device  PORTBbits.RB7           // device pin
10  #define        Buzzer  PORTBbits.RB6           // buzzer pin
11  #define        Up       INTCON3bits.INT1IF     // Up push button
12  #define        Dn       INTCON3bits.INT2IF     // Dn push button
13  #define        Start    INTCONbits.INT0IF      // Start push button
14
15  void Setup(void);
16  void IncDec(void);
17  void TurnOn(void);
18  void DisplaySeconds(void);
19
20  unsigned char i;                               // loop counter
21  char digits[3];                                // array of BCD digits
22  unsigned char seconds;                         // seconds counter
23
24  void main(void)
25  {
26      Setup();                                   // system setup
27      while (1) {
28          IncDec();                              // set time
29          TurnOn();                              // turn on device
30      }
31  }
32
33  void Setup(void) {
34      Device = 0; TRISBbits.TRISB7 = 0;          // turn device off
35      Buzzer = 0; TRISBbits.TRISB6 = 0;          // turn buzzer off
36      INTCON2 =  0b00000101;                     // RBPU = 0, INTx: -ve edge
37      TRISC = 0x00; TRISD &= 0xF0;               // configure output pins
38  }
39
40  void IncDec(void) {
41      seconds = ReadEE((char) &eeSeconds);       // from EEPROM to RAM
42      DisplaySeconds();                          // display initial value
43      while (1) {
44          if (Up) {                              // increment
45              Up = 0;                            // acknowledge flag
46              seconds++;
47              DisplaySeconds();
48          } else if (Dn) {                       // decrement
49              Dn = 0;                            // acknowledge flag
50              seconds--;
51              DisplaySeconds();
52          } else if (Start) {
53              Start = 0;                         // acknowledge flag
54              if (seconds != 0) {                // save seconds in EEPROM
55                  Wrt2EE(seconds, (char) &eeSeconds);
56                  return;
57              }
58          }
59      }
60  }
61
62  void TurnOn(void) {
63      Device = 1;                                // turn device on
64      do {
65          Delay10KTCYx(100);                     // 1 sec for Fosc = 4 MHz
66          seconds--;                             // count down
67          DisplaySeconds();
68      } while (seconds != 0);
69
70      Device = 0;                                // turn device off
71      for (i = 0; i < 6; i++) {
72          Delay10KTCYx(50);                      // 500 msecs, Fosc = 4 MHz
73          TRISC = ~TRISC; TRISD ^= 0x0F;         // blink display
74          Buzzer = ~Buzzer;                      // beep intermittently
75      }
76  }
77
78  void DisplaySeconds() {
79      Bin2Bcd(seconds, digits);
80      PORTD = (PORTD & 0xF0) | digits[0];        // MS digit
81      PORTC = (digits[1] << 4) | digits[2];      // LS digits
82  }
```

If you try this program on PROTEUS, you will notice that each time you turn on the system, it starts with a display of 000. This is because a variable declared in EEPROM is cleared by the compiler. You will not experience this effect if you try the code on a real hardware.

PORTE

PORTE is a 4-bit wide port. Only three of its pins (RE0/P3A/CCP3/AN5, RE1/P3B/AN6 and RE2/CCP5/AN7) can be configured as inputs or outputs. These pins can be used as analog inputs. When selected as an analog input, these pins will read as '0's. All three of them have Schmitt Trigger input buffers for edge-triggered hardware options.

RE3 is an input only pin. Its operation is controlled by the MCLRE Configuration bit. When selected as a port pin (MCLRE = 0), it functions as a digital input pin. Otherwise (MCLRE = 1), it functions as the $\overline{MCLR}$ reset. For this reason, it does not have TRIS or LAT bits associated with it. RE3 also functions as the programming voltage during programming. Table 19 describes the pins of PORTE and Table 20 lists all the registers associated with PORTE.

For PIC18F2XK22 devices, PORTE is only available when Master Clear functionality is disabled (MCLRE = 0). In these cases, PORTE is a single bit, input only port comprised of RE3 only. The pin operates as described previously.

The RE3 pin has an individually controlled weak internal pull-up. When set, the WPUE3 (TRISE<7>) bit enables the RE3 pin pull-up. The $\overline{RBPU}$ bit of the INTCON2 register controls pull-ups on both PORTB and PORTE. When $\overline{RBPU} = 0$, the weak pull-ups become active on all pins which have WPUE3 or WPUBx bit set. When set, the $\overline{RBPU}$ bit disables all weak pull-ups. The pull-ups are dis-

Table 19. PORTE pin functions

PORTE I/O SUMMARY

Pin	Function	TRIS Setting	ANSEL Setting	I/O	I/O Type	Description
RE0/P3A/CCP3/AN5	RE0	0	0	O	DIG	LATE<0> data output; not affected by analog input.
		1	0	I	ST	PORTE<0> data input; disabled when analog input enabled.
	P3A[1]	0	0	O	DIG	Enhanced CCP3 PWM output.
	CCP3[1]	0	0	O	DIG	Compare 3 output/PWM 3 output.
		1	0	I	ST	Capture 3 input.
	AN5	1	1	I	AN	Analog input 5.
RE1/P3B/AN6	RE1	0	0	O	DIG	LATE<1> data output; not affected by analog input.
		1	0	I	ST	PORTE<1> data input; disabled when analog input enabled.
	P3B	0	0	O	DIG	Enhanced CCP3 PWM output.
	AN6	1	1	I	AN	Analog input 6.
RE2/CCP5/AN7	RE2	0	0	O	DIG	LATE<2> data output; not affected by analog input.
		1	0	I	ST	PORTE<2> data input; disabled when analog input enabled.
	CCP5	0	0	O	DIG	Compare 5 output/PWM 5 output.
		1	0	I	ST	Capture 5 input.
	AN7	1	1	I	AN	Analog input 7.
RE3/V$_{PP}$/$\overline{MCLR}$	RE3	–	–	I	ST	PORTE<3> data input; enabled when MCLRE configuration bit is clear.
	VPP	–	–	P	AN	Programming voltage input. Always available regardless of pin mode.
	$\overline{MCLR}$	–	–	I	ST	Active-low Master Clear (device Reset) input, enabled when MCLRE configuration bit is set.

Legend: DIG = Digital level output; AN = Analog input or output; TTL = TTL compatible input; HV = High Voltage; OD = Open Drain; XTAL = Crystal; CMOS = CMOS compatible input or output; ST = Schmitt Trigger input with CMOS levels; I²C™ = Schmitt Trigger input with I²C.

Note 1: Alternate pin assignment for P3A/CCP3 when Configuration bit CCP3MX is clear.

Table 20. Summary of registers associated with PORTE

SUMMARY OF REGISTERS ASSOCIATED WITH PORTE

Name	Bit 7	Bit 6	Bit 6	Bit 4	Bit 3	Bit 2	Bit 1	Bit 0
ANSELE[1]	–	–	–	–	–	ANSE2	ANSE1	ANSE0
INTCON2	$\overline{RBPU}$	INTEDG0	INTEDG1	INTEDG2	–	TMR0IP	–	RBIP
LATE[1]	–	–	–	–	–	LATE2	LATE1	LATE0
PORTE	–	–	–	–	RE3	RE2[1]	RE1[1]	RE0[1]
SLRCON	–	–	–	SLRE[1]	SLRD[1]	SLRC	SLRB	SLRA
TRISE	WPUE3	–	–	–	–	TRISE2[1]	TRISE1[1]	TRISE0[1]

Legend: – = unimplemented, read as '0'. Yellow shaded cells are not used by **PORTE**.
Note 1: Available on PIC18(L)F4XK22 devices.

CONFIGURATION REGISTERS ASSOCIATED WITH PORTE

Name	Bit 7	Bit 6	Bit 5	Bit 4	Bit 3	Bit 2	Bit 1	Bit 0
CONFIG3H	MCLRE	–	P2BMX	T3CMX	HFOFST	CCP3MX	PBADEN	CCP2MX
CONFIG4L	*DEBUG*	XINST	–	–	–	LVP[1]	–	STRVEN

Legend: – = unimplemented cells, read as '0'. Yellow shaded bits are not used by **PORTE**.
Note 1: Can only be changed when in high voltage programming mode.

abled on a Power-on Reset. When the RE3 port pin is configured as $\overline{MCLR}$, (CONFIG3H<7>, MCLRE = 1 and CONFIG4L<2>, LVP = 0), or configured for Low Voltage Programming, (MCLRE = x, and LVP = 1), the pull-up is always enabled and the WPUE3 bit has no effect.

> **Example 8:** Based upon Figure 14, write a program to do the following:
> - If the SPDT switch is connected to logic 0, the LED must be turned off.
> - If the SPDT switch is connected to logic 1, the LED must be blinked at a rate of 250 ms per cycle.
>
> Use an internal clock of 4 MHz to run your program.

Figure 14. State machine to employ RE3 as an input pin; it uses an internal oscillator.

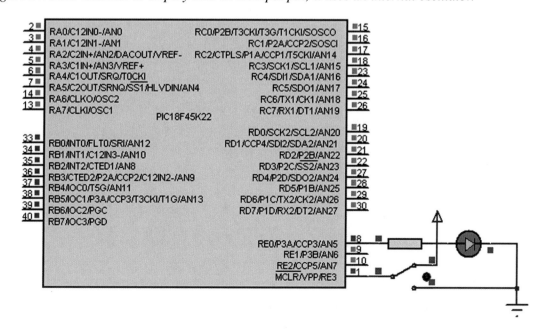

Solution: In order to use RE3 as an input pin with internal pull-up, the following directive:

```
#pragma    config    MCLRE = INTMCLR      // MCLR disabled
```

is needed in addition to the C statements:

```
ANSELEbits.ANSE0 = 0;             // digital pin
TRISEbits.TRISE0 = 0;             // output pin
INTCON2bits.RBPU = 0;             // enable PUs
```

Table 21. Implementation of Up/Down counter with 2 push buttons

	2-state state machine to employ **RE3** as an input pin. It uses a 4 MHz internal oscillator.

```
1    #include    <p18cxxx.h>
2    #include    <delays.h>
3
4    void Setup(void);
5
6    #pragma    config      FOSC = INTIO67    // internal oscillator
7    #pragma    config      MCLRE = INTMCLR   // MCLR disabled
8
9    #define    SPDT        PORTEbits.RE3     // SPDT pin
10   #define    LED         PORTEbits.RE0     // LED pin
11
12   enum {FlashLED, ClearLED} State = FlashLED; // first state: FlashLED
13
14   void main(void)
15   {
16       Setup();
17
18       while (1) {
19           switch (State) {
20               case FlashLED:
21                   LED = !LED;
22                   Delay10KTCYx(25);
23                   if (!SPDT) State = ClearLED;   // SPDT = 0
24                   break;
25               case ClearLED:
26                   LED = 0;
27                   if (SPDT) State = FlashLED;     // SPDT = 1
28                   break;
29           }
30       }
31   }
32
33   void Setup(void)
34   {
35       OSCCON = 0b01010000;                  // 4 MHz internal ck
36       ANSELEbits.ANSE0 = 0;                 // digital pin
37       TRISEbits.TRISE0 = 0;                 // output pin
38   }
```

To use the 4 MHz internal oscillator, the directive:

```
#pragma    config    FOSC = INTIO67        // internal oscillator
```

along with the C statement:

```
        OSCCON = 0b01010000;                // 4 MHz internal clock
```

will do the job. Again, the SFRs and configuration registers are listed in Appendix 2 and Appendix 7 respectively with all needed details. All these directives are generated by a utility under MPLAB. All you need to do is select the configuration setting from a menu and then "Generate Source Code to Output". You can then copy these directives (or pragmas) and paste them in your program. The complete program is listed in Table 21.

CONCLUSION

This chapter showed how the microcontroller can be interfaced to external I/O devices (pushbuttons, switches, displays, etc.) for full-blown system design. Chapter 7 will proceed to cover these I/O concepts on an interrupt basis. Case in point: keyboard encoding and multiplexed 7-segment displays. Chapter 8 covers the Liquid Crystal Display (LCD) which is a famous output device.

Chapter 7
Interrupts and Applications

INTRODUCTION

An interrupt is an event that causes the CPU to temporarily suspend the job it is performing in order to service a more urgent task. When an interrupt occurs, the program counter is loaded with the address of the routine to be executed. This address is commonly known as *interrupt vector* and the routine carried out by the processor is called *interrupt service routine* (ISR). In a way, an ISR is like a function with the exception that it is not invoked by the program itself but rather by the hardware upon occurrence of a specific event. The event may be caused by the arrival of a new byte to the serial port, the detection of an edge on an interrupt pin, the rollover of a timer, etc.

INTERRUPT MECHANISM

To facilitate the understanding of interrupts, we propose some real-life analogies. Suppose you are expecting someone to pay you a short visit. Imagine how inefficient it would be if you were to wait for your guest to show up on your front door while doing nothing. In order not to waste valuable time, you decide in the process to read an interesting book. When your guest appears at the front door of your house, he/she would ring the bell to indicate arrival. This bell ringing act signals an *event*: the arrival of your guest. Normally, you would respond right after you finish reading the current sentence. When you open the door and host your guest, your reading is interrupted. After servicing your guest by responding to his/her requests, you resume your reading at the point you left off. Normally, you would use a book marker to tell you where to continue.

At the microcontroller level, a similar process occurs. The CPU is normally busy running a certain task. The event that can interrupt it may occur periodically or intermittently. For example, if the MCU were to output a 1 KHz square wave, it would have to toggle a microcontroller pin, say RB0, every 500 μs. Timer0 which is an 8/16-bit counter may be programmed to generate a periodic interrupt every 500 μs. This interrupt event is indicated by setting a flag, namely TMR0IF. When the CPU responds to it

DOI: 10.4018/978-1-68318-000-5.ch007

and toggles RB0, an interrupt takes place. The CPU has the option to respond to an event by executing the corresponding ISR (interrupt-driven approach) or simply ignore it.

The first condition that must be satisfied in order for an interrupt to take place is the emergence of an event (external or internal). The hardware indicates the event to the CPU by setting a flip-flop or flag. For example, when Timer0 rolls over to a count of zero, flag TMR0IF (*Timer0 interrupt flag*) is set. All event indicating flags are "sticky" bits and hence they must be cleared within the interrupt service routine.

The occurrence of an event does not necessarily trigger an interrupt. There are two barriers that must be surmounted. These barriers are called interrupt masks and may be either global or local. A global mask acts very much like a university main gate. If it is open, everybody can get into the university. A local mask behaves much like the front gate of a faculty building. So in essence, a device requesting interrupt must have its local mask enabled in addition to the global mask. A programmer may wish to disable all interrupts by simply clearing the global mask.

Table 1. Interrupt sources, indicator flags, local and global masks

Interrupt source	Event Indicator	Local Mask	Global mask(s)[1]
INT0 pin edge	INTCON, INT0IF	INTCON, INT0IE	GIE
INT1 pin edge	INTCON3, INT1IF	INTCON3, INT1IE	GIE
INT2 pin edge	INTCON3, INT2IF	INTCON3, INT2IE	GIE
PORTB pin change	INTCON, RBIF	INTCON, RBIE	GIE
Timer0 overflow	INTCON, T0IF	INTCON, T0IE	GIE
Timer1 overflow	PIR1, TMR1IF	PIE1, TMR1IE	GIE and PEIE
Timer1 gate interrupt	PIR3, TMR1GIF	PIE3, TMR1GIE	GIE and PEIE
Timer2 count = PR2	PIR1, TMR2IF	PIE1, TMR2IE	GIE and PEIE
Timer3 overflow	PIR2, TMR3IF	PIE2, TMR3IE	GIE and PEIE
Timer3 gate interrupt	PIR3, TMR3GIF	PIE3, TMR3GIE	GIE and PEIE
Timer4 count = PR4	PIR5, TMR4IF	PIE5, TMR4IE	GIE and PEIE
Timer5 overflow	PIR5, TMR5IF	PIE5, TMR5IE	GIE and PEIE
Timer6 gate interrupt	PIR3, TMR5GIF	PIE3, TMR5GIE	GIE and PEIE
Timer6 count = PR6	PIR5, TMR6IF	PIE5, TMR6IE	GIE and PEIE
CCP1 interrupt	PIR1, CCP1IF	PIE1, CCP1IE	GIE and PEIE
CCP2 interrupt	PIR2, CCP2IF	PIE2, CCP2IE	GIE and PEIE
CCP3 interrupt	PIR4, CCP3IF	PIE4, CCP3IE	GIE and PEIE
CCP4 interrupt	PIR4, CCP4IF	PIE4, CCP4IE	GIE and PEIE
CCP5 interrupt	PIR4, CCP5IF	PIE4, CCP5IE	GIE and PEIE
A/D conversion done	PIR1, ADIF	PIE1, ADIE	GIE and PEIE
EUSART1 receive	PIR1, RC1IF	PIE1, RC1IE	GIE and PEIE
EUSART1 transmit	PIR1, TX1IF	PIE1, TX1IE	GIE and PEIE
EUSART2 receive	PIR3, RC2IF	PIE3, RC2IE	GIE and PEIE
EUSART2 transmit	PIR3, TX2IF	PIE3, TX2IE	GIE and PEIE
MSSP1 data transfer	PIR1, SSP1IF	PIE1, SSP1IE	GIE and PEIE
MSSP1 Bus Collision	PIR2, BCL1IF	PIE2, BCL1IE	GIE and PEIE
MSSP2 data transfer	PIR3, SSP2IF	PIE3, SSP2IE	GIE and PEIE
MSSP2 Bus Collision	PIR3, BCL2IF	PIE3, BCL2IE	GIE and PEIE
Low voltage detect	PIR2, HLVDIF	PIE2, HLVDIE	GIE and PEIE
Oscillator Fail Interrupt	PIR2, OSCFIF	PIE2, OSCFIE	GIE and PEIE
Compare C1 Interrupt	PIR2, C1IF	PIE2, C1IE	GIE and PEIE
Compare C2 Interrupt	PIR2, C2IF	PIE2, C2IE	GIE and PEIE
EEPROM Write Interrupt	PIR2, EEIF	PIE2, EEIE	GIE and PEIE

As far as the global mask is concerned, there are actually two of them: the *global interrupt enable* bit (GIE) and the *peripheral interrupt enable* bit (PEIE). GIE enables the traditional interrupt sources similar to those of the older PIC16F84 microcontroller. The added interrupt sources pertaining to peripheral devices are enabled by asserting both GIE and PEIE. Table 1 lists the 33 interrupt sources along with their *event indicator* flags and *local/global masks* bits. Figure 2 shows the control register INTCON (*Interrupt configuration register*) pertaining to the following interrupt sources:

- Detection of a rising or falling edge on INT0.
- Detection of a level change on RB7... RB4.
- Roll over of Timer0 from 0xFF (8-bit mode) or 0xFFFF (16-bit mode) to zero.

Table 2. INTCON: interrupt control register

INTCON: INTERRUPT CONTROL REGISTER

R/W-0	R/W-0	R/W-0	R/W-0	R/W-0	R/W-0	R/W-0	R/W-x
GIE	PEIE	TMR0IE	INT0IE	RBIE	TMR0IF	INT0IF	RBIF
bit 7							**bit 0**

R = Readable bit   W = Writable bit   U = Unimplemented bit, read as '0'
-n = Value at POR   '1' = Bit is set   '0' = Bit is cleared   x = Bit is unknown

bit 7   **GIE:** Global Interrupt Enable bit
             1 = Enables all unmasked interrupts
             0 = Disables all interrupts including peripherals

bit 6   **PEIE:** Peripheral Interrupt Enable bit
             1 = Enables all unmasked peripheral interrupts
             0 = Disables all peripheral interrupts

it 6   **TMR0IE:** Timer0 Overflow Interrupt Enable bit
             1 = Enables the TMR0 overflow interrupt
             0 = Disables the TMR0 overflow interrupt

bit 4   **INT0IE:** INT0 External Interrupt Enable bit
             1 = Enables the INT0 external interrupt
             0 = Disables the INT0 external interrupt

bit 3   **RBIE:** Port B Interrupt-On-Change (IOCx) Interrupt Enable bit[2]
             1 = Enables the IOCx port change interrupt
             0 = Disables the IOCx port change interrupt

bit 2   **TMR0IF:** Timer0 Overflow Interrupt Flag bit
             1 = TMR0 has overflowed (must be cleared in software)
             0 = TMR0 register did not overflow

bit 1   **INT0IF:** INT0 External Interrupt Flag bit
             1 = The INT0 external interrupt occurred (must be cleared in software)
             0 = The INT0 external interrupt did not occur

bit 0   **RBIF:** RB Port Change Interrupt Flag bit[1]
             1 = At least one of the IOC<3:0> (RB<7:4>) pins changed state (must be cleared in software)
             0 = None of the IOC<3:0> (RB<7:4>) pins have changed state

Note 1:   A mismatch condition will continue to set the RBIF bit. Reading PORTB will end the
               mismatch condition and allow the bit to be cleared.
Note 2:   RB port change interrupts also require the individual pin IOCB enables.

In summary, when an interrupt flag (such as TMR0IF, INT0IF, etc.) is set and the pertinent masks (local and global) are enabled, the MCU performs the following interrupt sequence:

1. It completes execution of the current instruction then it saves the return address on the hardware stack. In a way, the stack is the CPU's book marker that will tell it where to resume execution after the interrupt is completed.
2. It saves WREG, STATUS and BSR in their so-called shadow registers WREGS, STATUSS and BSRS respectively. Therefore, WREG, STATUS and BSR may be modified without worry within the interrupt service routine.
3. The GIE bit is cleared to disable further interrupts while one is being serviced.
4. The PC is loaded with address 0x0008 thereby directing the CPU to execute the interrupt service routine at that address.

Inside the interrupt service routine:

1. The flags corresponding to the interrupt sources (in the case of multiple interrupt sources) must be polled to determine what caused the interrupt. The flag that is set indicates the interrupt source. It must be cleared in software to acknowledge the event. Otherwise, the ISR will be invoked over and over and the processor will enter an infinite loop.
2. The user may decide to disable the interrupt by clearing the local mask if no further interrupts from that particular source must be handled.
3. Next the user writes the code in charge of servicing the event that triggered the interrupt.
4. Finally, the assembly instruction retfie s (s = 0 or 1) terminates the ISR. It is equivalent to } or return in C. It simply recovers the return address from the stack and sets the GIE bit to enable pending interrupts (if any). If s = 1 (FAST option), the initial values of WREG, STATUS and BSR are recovered from their shadow registers.

It is important to note that in the case of multiple interrupt sources, the user may poll the flags according to a user-selected priority level as illustrated in the first alternative of Table 3.

This approach services one request at a time. If there is a pending event requesting service, it will be serviced right after the current ISR is exited. This is an efficient tactic since statistically it is rare to have more than one device requesting service simultaneously. The second alternative consists of servicing all events (if any) before exiting the ISR as illustrated in Table 3.

As to the overall code employing interrupts, Table 4 shows a program skeleton. When power saving mode is desired, the infinite loop should be substituted by the statement:

```
while (1)          // wait for interrupt
    Sleep();       // to leave sleep mode
```

Upon execution of the Sleep() macro (or sleep instruction), the next instruction (at address PC+2) is fetched. Then the clock is halted and the processor is put into low power mode. All internal registers retain their data in the *sleep* mode. When the processor wakes up from sleep[2], due to a set event indicator flag, it executes the interrupt service routine then it resumes with the while statement. This puts the

Table 3. Two alternatives of polling interrupt flags in multi-interrupt scenario

First alternative: polling interrupt flags when multi-interrupt sources are in use.

```
#pragma code ISR = 0x0008           // ISR at 0x0008
#pragma interrupt ISR               // ISR is an interrupt

void ISR(void)
{
    if (INTCONbits.T0IF)            // first priority
    {
        INTCONbits.T0IF = 0;
        ...                         // service Timer0 interrupt
    }
    else if (INTCONbits.INT0IF)     // second priority
    {
        INTCONbits.INT0IF = 0;
        ...                         // service INT0 interrupt
    }
    else if (INTCON3bits.INT1IF)    // third priority
    {
        INTCON3bits.INT1IF = 0;
        ...                         // service INT1 interrupt
    }
}                                   // retfie FAST
```

Second alternative: polling interrupt flags when multi-interrupt sources are in use.

```
#pragma code ISR = 0x0008           // ISR starts at 0x0008
#pragma interrupt ISR               // ISR is an interrupt

void ISR(void)
{
    if (INTCONbits.T0IF)            // first priority
        Timer0ISR();
    if (INTCONbits.INT0IF)          // second priority
        Int0ISR();
    if (INTCON3bits.INT1IF)         // third priority
        Int1ISR();
}                                   // retfie FAST

void Timer0ISR(void)
{
    INTCONbits.T0IF = 0;
    ...                             // service Timer0 interrupt
}                                   // return

void Int0ISR(void)
{
    INTCONbits.INT0IF = 0;
    ...                             // service INT0 interrupt
}                                   // return

void Int1ISR(void)
{
    INTCON3bits.INT1IF = 0;
    ...                             // service INT1 interrupt
}                                   // return
```

Table 4. Skeleton of a program utilizing interrupts

```
Overall program showing the main program and the interrupt syntax.
void main(void) {
    Setup();
    while (1);            // wait for interrupt
}

void Setup(void) {        // system setup & interrupt(s) enable
    ...
}

#pragma code ISR = 0x0008
#pragma interrupt ISR

void ISR(void)                        // service interrupt(s)
{
    ...
}
```

processor back in the sleep mode. The power saving advantage is tremendous when the Sleep() macro is used. This is because the CPU consumes only a few number of μA in this mode.

CASE STUDY 1: TIMER0

As implied by its name, Timer0 is a hardware unit designed to generate periodic interrupts and time delays without the need to count instruction cycles. Figure 1 shows the hardware configuration of Timer0 in 8-bit mode. The unit consists of a counter TMR0L that may be clocked internally or externally as specified by T0CS (*Timer0 Clock Select* bit). The *prescaler assignment* bit PSA selects between the clock signal and a prescaled version of it in accordance with the *prescaler select* bits: T0PS2, T0PS1, and T0PS0. *Timer0 Source Edge Select* bit T0SE specifies whether the counter advances on a rising

Figure 1. Timer0 block diagram in 8-bit mode

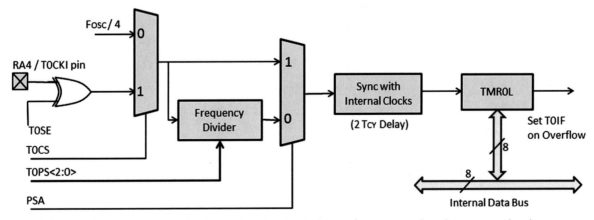

Note: Upon Reset, **Timer0** is enabled in 8-bit mode with clock input from **TOCKI** and maximum pre-scale value.

Figure 2. Timer0 block diagram in 16-bit mode

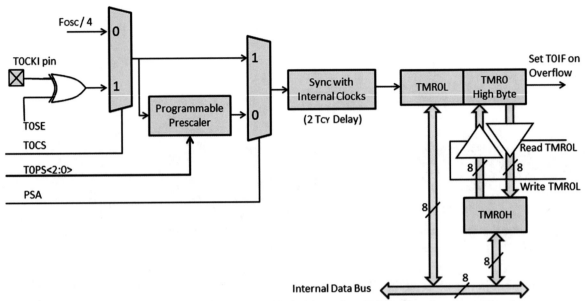

Note: Upon Reset, **Timer0** is enabled in 8-bit mode with clock input from **T0CKI** and maximum prescale value.

or falling edge of RA4/T0CKI. TMR0L is accessible for read/write operations via the data bus. It can be started off with any 8-bit value written to it. Note that when the user writes a value to TMR0L, a 2-cycle delay is incurred (see "Sync with Internal Clocks" block in Figure 1). Therefore, if 256 – N is written to TMR0L, the overflow will take N+2 cycles to occur. When the counter rolls over from 0xFF to 0x00, TMR0IF (also called T0IF) is set and an interrupt will take place if the local and global masks TMR0IE and GIE are both set.

Figure 2 illustrates Timer0 operation in 16-bit mode. The only variant now is the utilization of a 16-bit counter. In practice, this translates into longer time delays.

In order to write a 16-bit value to the counter, the user should first write the most significant byte to TMR0H. This value is not latched into TMR0 high byte until the user writes to TMR0L. This latching scheme ensures writing a 16-bit value in one shot. Similarly, when TMR0L is read, the upper byte of the counter is transferred to TMR0H and hence a 16-bit count is read in one shot.

Figure 3 illustrates how an interrupt is generated with Timer0. When the timer is used in 8-bit mode (T08BIT = 1), the most significant bit Q7 of TMR0L produces a falling edge only when it rolls over

Figure 3. Q7 /Q15 is the MSB of Timer0 in 8-bit/16-bit mode respectively

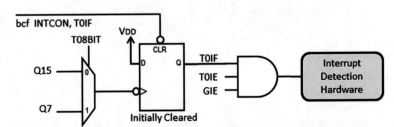

Table 5. T0CON: Timer0 control register

T0CON: TIMER0 CONTROL REGISTER

R/W-1	R/W-1	R/W-1	R/W-1	R/W-1	R/W-1	R/W-1	R/W-1
TMR0ON	T08BIT	T0CS	T0SE	PSA	TOPS<2:0>		
bit 7							bit 0

bit 7   **TMR0ON**: Timer0 On/Off Control bit
             1 = Enables Timer0
             0 = Stops Timer0

bit 6   **T08BIT**: Timer0 8-Bit/16-Bit Control bit
             1 = Timer0 is configured as an 8-bit timer/counter
             0 = Timer0 is configured as a 16-bit timer/counter

bit 5   **T0CS**: Timer0 Clock Source Select bit
             1 = Transition on T0CKI pin
             0 = Internal instruction cycle clock (CLKOUT)

bit 4   **T0SE**: Timer0 Source Edge Select bit
             1 = Increment on high-to-low transition on T0CKI pin
             0 = Increment on low-to-high transition on T0CKI pin

bit 3   **PSA**: Timer0 Prescaler Assignment bit
             1 = Timer0 prescaler is not assigned. Timer0 clock input bypasses prescaler.
             0 = Timer0 prescaler is assigned. Timer0 clock input comes from prescaler output.

bit 2-0   **T0PS<2:0>**: Timer0 Prescaler Select bits
             111 = 1:256 Prescale value
             110 = 1:128 Prescale value
             101 = 1:64   Prescale value
             100 = 1:32   Prescale value
             011 = 1:16   Prescale value
             010 = 1:8   Prescale value
             001 = 1:4   Prescale value
             000 = 1:2   Prescale value

from 0xFF to 0x00. This edge is captured by the D flip-flop once every 256 cycles. As a result, the event indicator flag T0IF (or TMR0IF) is set and an interrupt occurs if T0IE (or TMR0IE) and GIE are both set. Table 5 lists the control bits of T0CON needed in programming Timer0.

Example 1: Write a program to flash the LEDs of Figure 4 every ¼ second using Timer0 in interrupt mode. LEDs are toggled from 10101010_2 to 01010101_2 and vice versa.

Figure 4. Hardware setup used in Examples 1, 2 and 3

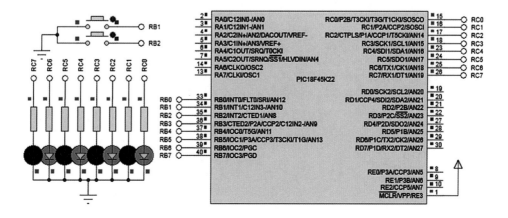

Solution: The complete program is listed in Table 6. For a prescale value of 1/16, Timer0 should count:

$$250,000 \ \mu s \ / \ (16 \ \mu secs/cycle) = 15,625 \ cycles$$

so that ¼ second is elapsed. It should count up from $(2^{16} - 15,625)$ until it rolls over to 0. When this happens, an interrupt occurs and the programmed time delay is attained. In the ISR, the LEDs are toggled and Timer0 is reloaded with the same initial value $(2^{16} - 15,625)$ in order for the 250 ms interrupt to repeat periodically.

Since the number of cycles exceeds 256, Timer0 must be employed in 16-bit mode. Here is how the 16-bit value $(2^{16} - 15,625)$ is written to it in one shot:

Table 6. Program to flash LEDs on an interrupt basis using periodic cycles of Timer0

```
Flashing LEDs on an interrupt  basis using periodic cycles of Timer0
1    #include      <p18cxxx.h>
2
3    void Setup(void);
4
5    void main(void)
6    {
7          Setup();                      // system initialization
8          while (1);                    // wait for interrupt
9    }
10
11   #pragma code ISR = 0x0008
12   #pragma interrupt ISR
13
14   void ISR(void)
15   {
16       TMR0H = (65536 - 15625) / 256;  // 15625 * 16 us = 250ms
17       TMR0L = (65536 - 15625) % 256;
18       INTCONbits.T0IF = 0;            // acknowledge interrupt
19       PORTC = ~PORTC;                 // toggle bits
20   }
21
22   void Setup(void)
23   {
24       PORTC = 0b10101010;             // on-off-on-off
25       TRISC = ANSELC = 0x00;          // ports C: digital output port
26       T0CON =  0b10010011;            // 1/16, 16-bit mode
27       TMR0H = TMR0L = 0xFF;           // speed up first interrupt
28       INTCONbits.TMR0IE = 1;          // enable local mask
29       INTCONbits.GIE = 1;             // enable global mask
30   }
```

```
TMR0H = (65536 - 15625) / 256;        // TMR0H = MS byte (first)
TMR0L = (65536 - 15625) % 256;        // TMR0L = LS byte (second)
```

> **Example 2:** Write a program to turn on a device interfaced to **RC0** for 15 minutes upon reset. Use a time base of 1 second to elapse 60 seconds or 1 minute.

Solution: The complete program is listed in Table 7. For a prescale value of 1/16, Timer0 should count:

$$1,000,000 \ \mu s \ / \ (16 \ \mu secs/cycle) = 62,500 \text{ cycles}$$

so that one second is elapsed. Variable seconds, is used to count 60 seconds or 1 minute. Each time a minute is elapsed, the minutes counter, whose initial value is 15, is decremented. This process goes on until 15 minutes are scheduled. At that time the device is turned off.

Table 7. Program to turn a device on for 15 minutes

Program to turn on a device on for 15 minutes using periodic interrupts of Timer0

```
 1  #include      <p18cxxx.h>
 2  #define       Device        PORTCbits.RC0       // device pin
 3
 4  void Setup(void);
 5
 6  unsigned char seconds = 60, minutes = 15;       // 15 minutes timer
 7
 8  void main(void) {
 9      Setup();                                    // system initialization
10      while (1);                                  // wait for interrupt
11  }
12
13  #pragma code ISR = 0x0008
14  #pragma interrupt ISR
15
16  void ISR(void) {
17      TMR0H = (65536 - 62500) / 256;              // 62,500 * 16 us = 1 sec
18      TMR0L = (65536 - 62500) % 256;
19      INTCONbits.TMR0IF = 0;                      // acknowledge interrupt
20      if (--seconds != 0)                         // decrement seconds
21          return;
22      if (--minutes != 0)                         // decrement minutes
23          seconds = 60;                           // count 60 more seconds
24      else {
25          Device = 0;                             // turn off device
26          INTCONbits.TMR0IE = 0;                  // disable TMR0 interrupt
27      }
28  }
29
30  void Setup(void) {
31      Device = 1;                                 // turn on device
32      TRISCbits.TRISC0 = 0;                       // RC0: output pin
33      TMR0H = (65536 - 62500) / 256;              // 62,500 * 16 us = 1 sec
34      TMR0L = (65536 - 62500) % 256;
35      T0CON = 0b10010011;                         // 1/16, 16-bit mode
36      INTCONbits.TMR0IE = 1;                      // enable local mask
37      INTCONbits.GIE = 1;                         // enable global mask
38  }
```

CASE STUDY 2: INT0, INT1, AND INT2

RB0/INT0, RB1/INT1 and RB2/INT2 can be configured to generate interrupts when a rising/falling edge is detected. Figure 5 shows the hardware associated with RB0/INT0 (RB1 and RB2 are similar). The D flip-flop is initially reset. Upon detection of a falling edge on its clock input, the flip-flop is set (INT0IF = 1). If INT0IE and GIE are both set, an interrupt occurs. INT0IF will remain set until the flip-flop is cleared. This is done via the instruction:

```
bcf          INTCON, INT0IF
```

or the C statement:

```
INTCONbits.INT0IF = 0;
```

The exclusive OR gate configures the D flip-flop to react to either a rising edge (INTEDGE0 = 1) or a falling edge (INTEDGE0 = 0). The control registers pertaining to these pins are INTCON (Table 2), INTCON2 (Table 8) and INTCON3 (Table 9).

> **Example 3:** Using the hardware of Figure 3, write an interrupt-based program to implement a binary up/down counter displayed on the LEDs of **PORTC**. The counter is controlled by **RB1/INT1** (Up) and **RB2/INT2** (Down).

Solution: The program, listed in Table 10, employs the interrupt pins of PORTB in addition to the internal pull-ups of this port. Since the push-buttons are normally open, both INT1 and INT2 were configured to react to a falling edge. There is also a need to decide on the interrupt source by testing flags INT1IF and INT2IF.

As opposed to programs dealing with Timer0, the MCU may be put in the sleep mode. Upon detection of an edge on INT1 or INT2, it wakes up to execute the ISR. Afterwards, it resumes program execution at the while statement which takes the processor back to the sleep mode.

Figure 5. Block diagram of RB0 pin; RB1 and RB2 are similar.

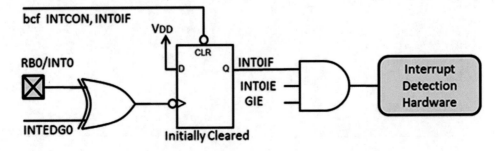

Table 8. INTCON2 register

INTCON2:   INTERRUPT CONTROL REGISTER 2

R/W-1	R/W-1	R/W-1	R/W-1	U-0	R/W-1	U-0	R/W-1
$\overline{RBPU}$	INTEDG0	INTEDG1	INTEDG2	–	TMR0IP	–	RBIP
bit 7							bit 0

bit 7   **$\overline{RBPU}$**: PORTB Pull-up Enable bit
1 = All PORTB pull-ups are disabled
0 = PORTB pull-ups are enabled provided that the pin is an input and the corresponding WPUB
bit is set.

bit 6   **INTEDG0**: External Interrupt 0 Edge Select bit
1 = Interrupt on rising edge
0 = Interrupt on falling edge

bit 5   **INTEDG1**: External Interrupt 1 Edge Select bit
1 = Interrupt on rising edge
0 = Interrupt on falling edge

bit 4   **INTEDG2**: External Interrupt 2 Edge Select bit
1 = Interrupt on rising edge
0 = Interrupt on falling edge

bit 3   **Unimplemented**: Read as '0'

bit 2   **TMR0IP**: Timer0 Overflow Interrupt Priority bit
1 = High priority
0 = Low priority

bit 1   **Unimplemented**: Read as '0'

bit 0   **RBIP**: RB Port Change Interrupt Priority bit
1 = High priority
0 = Low priority

Table 9. INTCON3 register

INTCON3:   INTERRUPT CONTROL REGISTER 3

R/W-1	R/W-1	U-0	R/W-0	R/W-0	U-0	R/W-0	R/W-0
INT2IP	INT1IP	–	INT2IE	INT1IE	–	INT2IF	INT1IF
bit 7							bit 0

bit 7   **INT2IP**: INT2 External Interrupt Priority bit
1 = High priority
0 = Low priority

bit 6   **INT1IP**: INT1 External Interrupt Priority bit
1 = High priority
0 = Low priority

bit 5   **Unimplemented**: Read as '0'

bit 4   **INT2IE**: INT2 External Interrupt Enable bit
1 = Enables the INT2 external interrupt
0 = Disables the INT2 external interrupt

bit 3   **INT1IE**: INT1 External Interrupt Enable bit
1 = Enables the INT1 external interrupt
0 = Disables the INT1 external interrupt

bit 2   **Unimplemented**: Read as '0'

bit 1   **INT2IF**: INT2 External Interrupt Flag bit
1 = The INT2 external interrupt occurred (must be cleared in software)
0 = The INT2 external interrupt did not occur

bit 0   **INT1IF**: INT1 External Interrupt Flag bit
1 = The INT1 external interrupt occurred (must be cleared in software)
0 = The INT1 external interrupt did not occur

Note: Interrupt flag bits are set when an interrupt condition occurs, regardless of the state of its
corresponding enable bit or the global enable bit. User software should insure the appropriate
interrupt flag bits are clear prior to enabling an interrupt.

Table 10. Interrupt-driven program to increment/decrement a binary counter

```
┌─────────────────────────────────────────────────────────────────────────┐
│ Binary Up/Down counter on an interrupt basis. The count is displayed on the LEDs of PORTC. │
├───┬───────────────────────────────────────────────────────────────────────┤
│ 1 │ #include      <p18cxxx.h>                                             │
│ 2 │                                                                        │
│ 3 │ void Setup(void);                                                      │
│ 4 │                                                                        │
│ 5 │ void main(void)                                                        │
│ 6 │ {                                                                      │
│ 7 │     Setup();                          // system initialization        │
│ 8 │     while (1)                                                          │
│ 9 │         Sleep();                      // wait for -ve edge on RB1/RB2  │
│ 10│ }                                                                      │
│ 11│                                                                        │
│ 12│ #pragma code ISR = 0x0008                                             │
│ 13│ #pragma interrupt ISR                                                 │
│ 14│                                                                        │
│ 15│ void ISR(void) {                                                       │
│ 16│     if (INTCON3bits.INT1IF) {                                         │
│ 17│         INTCON3bits.INT1IF = 0;                                       │
│ 18│         PORTC++;                                                       │
│ 19│     } else {                                                           │
│ 20│         INTCON3bits.INT2IF = 0;                                       │
│ 21│         PORTC--;                                                       │
│ 22│     }                                                                  │
│ 23│ }                                                                      │
│ 24│                                                                        │
│ 25│ void Setup(void) {                                                     │
│ 26│     ANSELB = ANSELC = 0x00;           // ports B and C are digital     │
│ 27│     PORTC = 0x00;                      // start with a count of 0       │
│ 28│     TRISC = 0x00;                      // configure PORTC as output     │
│ 29│     INTCON2bits.RBPU = 0;              // enable pull-ups               │
│ 30│     INTCON2bits.INTEDG1 = 0;           // RB1 reacts to -ve edge        │
│ 31│     INTCON2bits.INTEDG2 = 0;           // RB2 reacts to -ve edge        │
│ 32│     INTCON3bits.INT1IE = 1;            // enable INT1 interrupt         │
│ 33│     INTCON3bits.INT2IE = 1;            // enable INT2 interrupt         │
│ 34│     INTCONbits.GIE = 1;                // enable global mask            │
│ 35│ }                                                                      │
└───┴───────────────────────────────────────────────────────────────────────┘
```

CASE STUDY 3: INTERRUPT-ON-CHANGE AND KEYBOARD ENCODING

A level change on any pin of PORTB<7:4> sets RBIF in INTCON. Figure 6 shows the hardware responsible for this feature. For an interrupt-on-change to occur, RBIE and GIE must be set (see 3-input AND gate). To clear RBIF, the user must first remove the mismatch by reading the current value of PORTB (see Bottom Latch and the AND gate that controls it). Having done this, RBIF is cleared via the instruction: INTCONbits.RBIF = 0. The manufacturer recommends that at least one cycle (typically a nop instruction) must be wasted between removing the mismatch and clearing RBIF.

The leftmost AND gate insures that the interrupt occurs only if the pin is configured as input. The latches along with the XOR gate allow detection of a level change. RB4 is continuously sampled by the top latch and is sampled by the bottom latch only when PORTB is read. The XOR gate fires a '1' when the current value of RB4 differs from the previously read value.

The interrupt-on-change feature has many applications. One of which is the ability to connect a hexadecimal keypad to PORTB with no other external components as shown in Figure 7.

Figure 6. Interrupt-on-change hardware for RB4/IOC0; RB6:RB7 are similar.

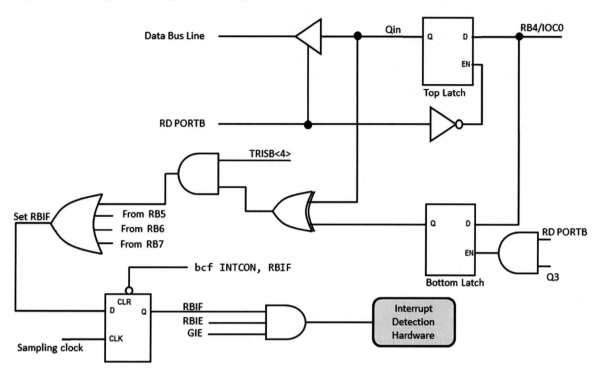

The keypad's internal structure is displayed in Figure 8. It consists of an array of normally open push buttons organized in a grid of 4 rows (Row0 to Row3) and 4 columns (Col0 to Col3).

When a key is pressed, the row and column where the key resides will be connected together. Keyboard encoding consists of converting a key press to a hexadecimal number. Here is a summary of the algorithm:

1. Clear PORTB's output latches and enable all its internal pull-ups.
2. Configure RB<7:4> (keypad columns) as inputs and RB<3:0> (keypad rows) as outputs. In accordance with step 1, this implies that RB7… RB4 will initially be pulled up to a logic high whereas RB3…RB0 will be tied to a soft ground (see Figure 9).

Figure 7. Hex keypad connection to PORTB

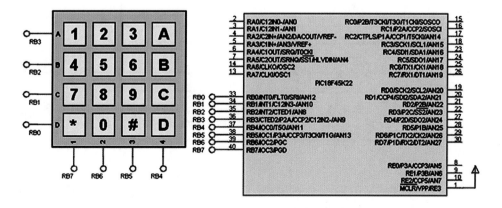

Figure 8. Internal structure of a hex keypad and its connection to PORTB

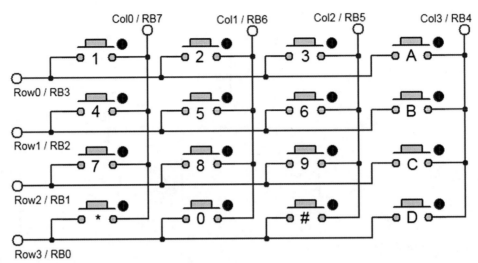

3. Put the processor in the sleep mode waiting to be awakened by a key stroke. It is assumed that the local mask RBIE and the global one GIE are enabled.
4. When a key is pressed, the row-column intersection at the key position is short circuited (Figure 10). This implies that the column in which the key resides will be tied to ground. This level change

Figure 9. RB<7:4> are inputs with internal pull-ups and RB<3:0> are logic low outputs.

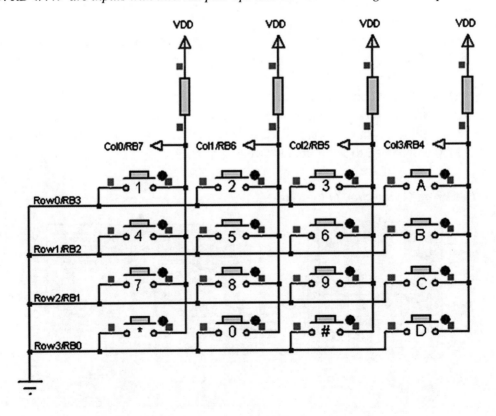

Figure 10. Determining the key's column number; red line indicates current flow.

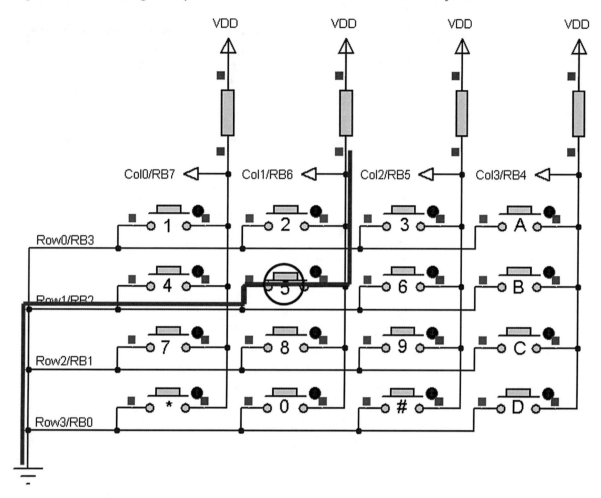

from high to low generates an interrupt-on-change and the processor is awakened to execute the associated interrupt service routine.

5. Inside the interrupt service routine, the following steps are performed:

    a. The switch is debounced in software. This necessitates waiting about 20 ms till the push button stops bouncing before proceeding.

    b. Then the mismatch is removed via a dummy read of PORTB followed by clearing RBIF.

    c. PORTB is read to determine the column position (0, 1, 2 or 3). For instance, if key 5 is pressed, PORTB will read 10110000_2 (col 1) whereas if key 7 is pressed, reading PORTB gives 01110000_2 (col 0).

    d. To determine the row where the key resides, RB<3:0> are configured as inputs and RB<7:4> as outputs (see Figure 11). This connects the columns to a "soft" ground and pulls-up the rows to logic high except the one in which the key is pressed. Reading PORTB for keys 5 and 7 gives 00001011_2 (row1) and 00001101_2 (row2) respectively.

    e. The reading of PORTB in part c is added to that of part d. The sum is called the "raw" code which provides information about both the row and column positions. Keys 5 and 7 have "raw" codes of 10111011_2 and 01111101_2 respectively.

Figure 11. Determining the key's row number; red wire indicates current flow.

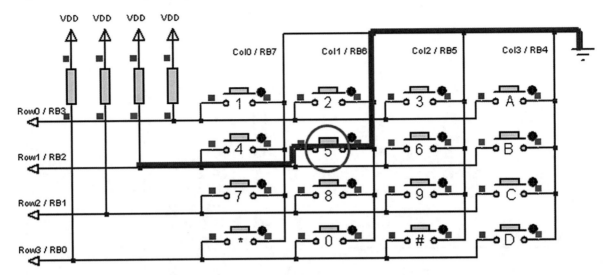

 f. Proceed to encode the key via a lookup table.

 g. Display the digit pressed on a 7-segment display, LEDs or LCD.

6. Go back to step (2) and wait for a new key to be pressed.

This algorithm is translated to C in Table 11. The 7-segment codes and the "raw" keycodes are stored in RAM. The key pressed is displayed on a common-cathode 7-segment display connected to PORTC (Figure 12). Note that # and * are displayed as E and F respectively.

The char array KeyCodes[] stores all possible "raw" keycodes. The function HexCode() converts a pressed keycode to hexadecimal (0, 1, …, F). Normally in a lookup table, the user supplies the index and gets the table entry. HexCode(), however, receives the table entry RawKey as an argument, determines the index of the matching entry in the lookup table, then returns it to displayed on a 7-segment display (see Figure 12). Current-limiting resistors of 330 Ω limit the current-per-segment to 10 mA which is well below the current sourcing capability of 25 mA per pin.

Figure 12. Common-cathode 7-segment display and its connection to PORTC

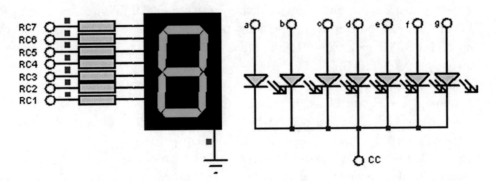

Table 11. Hex keypad encoder program

```
Keypad encoding, wake-up on keystroke, unordered  keys
1    #include <p18cxxx.h>
2    #include <delays.h>
3
4    // Dummy read of PORTB, 1 nop instruction, then clear RBIF
5    #define      ClearRBIF()  {WREG = PORTB; Nop(); INTCONbits.RBIF = 0;}
6
7    char KeyCodes[] = {0b10111110,0b01110111,0b10110111,0b11010111,   // 0,1,2,3
8                       0b01111011,0b10111011,0b11011011,0b01111101,   // 4,5,6,7
9                       0b10111101,0b01011101,0b11100111,0b11101011,   // 8,9,A,B
10                      0b11101101,0b11101110,0b11011110,0b01111110}; // C,D,E,F
11
12   // Table of seven segment codes
13   char SSCodes[] = {0xFC, 0x60, 0xDA, 0xF2, 0x66, 0xB6, 0xBE, 0xE0,
14                     0xFE, 0xF6, 0xEE, 0x3E, 0x9C, 0x7A, 0x9E, 0x8E};
15   char HexKey;
16
17   void Setup(void);
18   char HexCode(char);
19
20   void main(void)
21   {
22       Setup();
23       while (1) Sleep();
24   }
25
26   void Setup(void)
27   {
28       ANSELB = ANSELC = 0x00;     // ports B and C are digital
29       PORTC = 0x00;               // initialize display to 0
30       TRISC = 0x00;               // PORTC<7:1> to 7-seg a..g
31       PORTB = 0x00;               // connect rows to ground
32       TRISB = 0xF0;               // cols are inputs, rows are outs
33       INTCON2bits.RBPU = 0;       // enable internal pull-ups
34       ClearRBIF();                // just in case it was set
35       INTCONbits.RBIE = 1;        // local mask
36       INTCONbits.GIE = 1;         // global mask
37   }
38
39   #pragma code GetKey = 0x0008
40   #pragma interrupt GetKey
41
42   void GetKey(void) {
43       char RawKey;
44
45       Delay10KTCYx(2);            // wait 20 ms for switch to settle
46       if ((~PORTB & 0xF0) != 0) {
47           RawKey = PORTB;         // RawKey has column position
48           TRISB = 0xFF;           // only on PROTEUS
49           TRISB = 0x0F;           // rows are inputs, cols are outs
50           RawKey |= PORTB;        // RawKey has row & column positions
51           HexKey = HexCode(RawKey); // find equivalent hex code
52           PORTC = SSCodes[HexKey]; // SScode to 7-segment display
53           TRISB = 0xF0;           // back to status quo
54       }
55       ClearRBIF();
56   }
57
58   char HexCode(char RawKey)                 // unordered keys (uses KeyCodes)
59   {
60       i = 0;                                // index in KeyCodes table
61       while (RawKey != KeyCodes[i++]);      // search code in table
62       return --i;                           // return index of matching entry
63   }
```

Example 4: The keypad keys are re-ordered and re-labled as illustrated in Figure 13. This is done through a minor surgical procedure on the keypad. Verify that the hex code is related to the row and column via the expression: $Hexcode = col + 4 * row$. Update HexCode() to match the reordered keypad.

Solution: The expression, $Hexcode = col + 4 * row$, is computed in the listing of Table 12. The column is determined from the position of the zero in the most significant nibble of RawKey whereas the row is obtained from the least significant nibble of RawKey.

Figure 13. Keypad with re-ordered and re-labeled keys

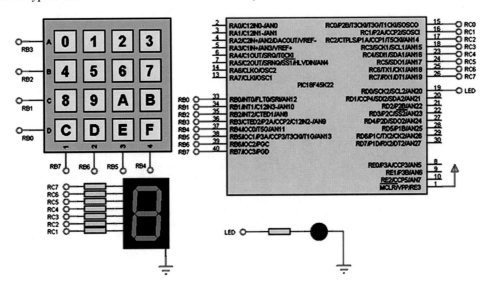

Table 12. New HexCode() function to match the keypad of Figure 13

Keyboard encoding, ordered keys, HexKey = col + 4 * row

```
1    char HexCode(char RawKey)          // ordered keys
2    {
3        char i, row, col;              // row and column indicators
4
5        for (i = 0; i < 4; i++, RawKey <<= 1)
6            if ((RawKey & 0x80) == 0)  // search column
7                col = i;
8
9        for (i = 0; i < 4; i++, RawKey <<= 1)
10           if ((RawKey & 0x80) == 0)  // search row
11               row = i;
12
13       return col + 4 * row;          // row + 4 * col if keys are
14   }                                  // transposed diagonally
```

Table 13. Additions made to Table 11 to implement combination lock program

Definitions to be added before the program: LED, Done flag and number of digits in hidden code.

```
#define          LED            PORTDbits.RD0
#define          Done           FLAGS.B0
#define          NumOfDigs      5     // number of digits to be keyed in
```

Lookup table for the hidden code 1AB4C plus the index (new variable declaration) of this table.

```
char HiddenCode[] = {0x01, 0x0A, 0x0B, 0x04, 0x0C}; // Hidden code
char HexKey, index = 0;                             // index of HiddenCode
```

Forward declaration of the new function CompDigits().

```
void CompDigits(void);
```

New statements in the Setup() routine, preferably at the beginning of the routine.

```
LED = 0;                        // LED initially off
ANSELDbits.ANSD0 = 0;           // RD0 is a digital pin
TRISDbits.TRISD0 = 0;           // LED pin is output
Done = 0;                       // Done flag is initially false
```

CompDigits() is added to the ISR right after the newly designed HexCode() is invoked.

```
HexKey = HexCode(RawKey); // find equivalent hex code
PORTC = SSCodes[HexKey];  // SScode to 7-segment display
CompDigits();             // compare digits one by one
```

New function CompDigits() invoked from the interrupt service routine.

```
void CompDigits(void)
{
        if (!Done) {                               // exit if Done = 1
              if  (HiddenCode[index++] == HexKey)
                    {if (index == NumOfDigs) {LED = 1; Done = 1;}}
              else
                    Done = 1;
        }
}
```

Example 5: Show the required additions to the program of Table 11 in order to implement a combination lock. Upon entering the code 1AB4C, the lock is released. The LED in Figure 13 emulates an electronic lock. The code gives the user one chance only to enter the correct code.

Solution: The whole program is not shown here. Only the required additions are listed in Table 13. This is to emphasize the idea that if a program is written in a modular fashion, then any additions do not require restructuring of the whole code.

CASE STUDY 4: MULTIPLEXED DISPLAYS

Figure 14 shows a 4-digit multiplexed display used essentially to reduce power consumption and minimize "pin-appropriation" by the display.

The non-multiplexed scheme usurps 28 MCU pins (7 segments times 4 digits) whereas the multiplexed display requires only 11 pins (7 for the segments and 4 for the digit selectors). It illuminates one digit at a time at a fast rate. Due to the eye persistence, it looks as if all the digits are turned on concurrently. In order not to see the display flicker, the refresh time must not exceed 25 ms. For the 4-digit display, the "on-time" per digit must be around 6 ms. If only 3 digits were used, the on-time per digit would be 8 ms. As to the power saving gain, the 4-digit multiplexed display consumes only one-fourth the power absorbed by the non-multiplexed display.

Figure 14. Multiplexed display; current limiting resistors (330 Ω) for segments a..g are not shown.

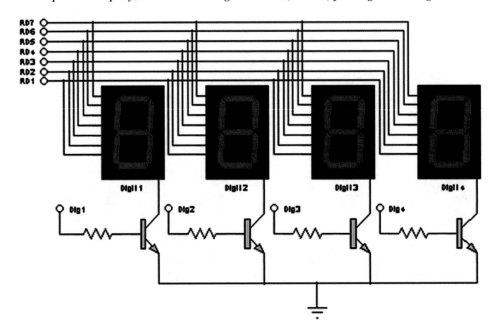

Limiting resistors in the order of 330 Ω should be placed in series with the segments (a, b, c, d, e, f, g) in order to protect the LEDs from burning out. This will drive a current of about 10 mA per LED segment which is well below the 25 mA maximum current that can be provided by a microcontroller pin. Note also that the total current drawn by a 7-segment display is about 70 mA under the current circumstances. Since this is well beyond the 25 mA current sinking capability of the MCU pin, a switching transistor is placed between the pin and the cathode of the 7-segment display. These transistors act like an open circuit when driven by a logic low level and like a short circuit when driven by a logic high level. The base resistor must be appropriately selected to insure the transistor operates in the saturation mode when switched on.

Example 6: Using the multiplexed display of Figure 15, write a program to display a 3-digit up counter running at a frequency of 1Hz. Use a periodic interrupt of 8 ms to refresh the display. Hint: one second = 125 * 8 ms. *Variations of this program*: digital voltmeter, digital thermometer, programmable timer, etc.

Solution: The 8 ms on-time provides a refresh time of 24 ms. If Timer0 is triggered at a rate of 64 μs/cycle (1:64 prescaler), it would have to count 8000 μs / (64 μs/cycle) = 125 cycles in order to elapse 8 ms. Since the periodic interrupt occurs every 8 ms, a 1 sec period of time is obtained by counting 1000 ms / (8 ms per interrupt) = 125 interrupts. The 8 ms period is used to refresh the display and also to time the 1 second interval for incrementing the counter. Table 14 lists the complete self-explanatory program.

Figure 15. Hardware for Examples 6 and 7; inverters are used instead of transistors.

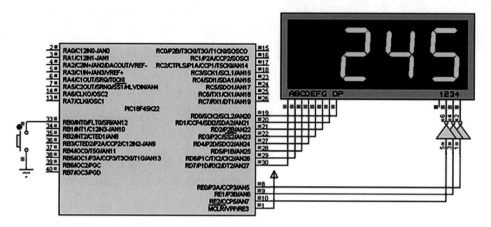

Table 14. Up counter program for 3-digit multiplexed display

```
Program to implement a 3-digit multiplexed display via periodic interrupts of Timer0,  Fcy = 1 MHz
1   #include    <p18cxxx.h>
2   #include    <BCDlib.h>
3
4   char digits[3];
5   unsigned char counter, Qstates, IntCounter, i;
6   char SSCodes[] = {0xFC, 0x60, 0xDA, 0xF2, 0x66, 0xB6, 0xBE, 0xE0, 0xFE, 0xF6};
7
8   void Setup(void);
9
10  void main(void) {
11      Setup();                        // system initialization
12      while (1);                      // wait for interrupt
13  }
14
15  #pragma code ISR = 0x0008
16  #pragma interrupt ISR
17
18  void ISR(void) {
19      INTCONbits.TMR0IF = 0;          // acknowledge interrupt
20      TMR0L = 256 - 125;              // 64us * 125 = 8ms
21      PORTD = 0x00;                   // remove shadowing
22      PORTE = Qstates;                // select 1 digit
23      PORTD = SSCodes[digits[i++]];   // send data to SS display
24      Qstates >>= 1;                  // get ready for next digit
25      if (i == 3) {
26          i = 0;                      // point to digits[0]
27          Qstates = 0b00000100;       // start with MSD
28      }
29      if (--IntCounter == 0) {
30          IntCounter = 125;           // 1 sec has elapsed, start anew
31          Bin2Bcd(++counter, digits); // increment counter & convert to BCD
32      }
33  }
34
35  void Setup(void) {
36      ANSELD = 0; TRISD = 0x00;       // PORTD is an output port
37      ANSELE = 0; TRISE = 0x00;       // RE2, RE1, RE0 output pins
38      counter = 0;                    // start with a count of 0
39      Bin2Bcd(counter, digits);       // convert to BCD
40      i = 0;                          // point to digits[0]
41      Qstates = 0b00000100;           // start with MSD
42      T0CON = 0b11010101;             // divide clock by 64, 8-bit mode
43      TMR0L = 256 - 125;              // 64us * 125 = 8ms
44      IntCounter = 125;               // 8ms * 125 = 1 sec
45      INTCONbits.TMR0IE = 1;          // enable real-time interrupt
46      INTCONbits.GIE = 1;
47  }
```

> **Example 7:** Modify the program of Example 6 to implement an up/down counter. **RB0** is driven by a normally open push button used as a toggle switch. When **RB0** is pressed, the counter changes status from up to down and vice versa. Use the internal pull-up transistor for **RB0**. Show the required modifications to Example 6.

Solution: To remember the switch status, a flag Up defined as follows:

```
#define     Up      FLAGS.B0
```

controls the counter's direction (Up $= 1$, count up else count down). The following statements should be added to the Setup() function:

```
Up = 1;                     // count up initially
ANSELBbits.ANSB0 = 0;       // RB0: digital input
INTCON2bits.INTEDG0 = 0;    // RB0 reacts to a falling edge
INTCON2bits.RBPU = 0;       // enable internal pull-up
```

The *if* statement below is added at the beginning of the interrupt service routine. This ISR is invoked due to an overflow of Timer0. This is the reason why the local mask INT0IE of INT0 has not been enabled in the Setup() routine.

```
if (INTCONbits.INT0IF)      // check if button is pressed
{
    INTCONbits.INT0IF = 0;  // acknowledge button
    Up = !Up;               // toggle counter direction
}
```

When it is time to increment or decrement the counter, one may check the status of the Up flag. Therefore, the statement Bin2Bcd(++counter, digits) in Table 14 should be substituted by the statements:

```
Up? counter++: counter--;   // Up = 1, count up else count down
Bin2Bcd(counter, digits);   // convert counter to BCD
```

CONCLUSION

Interrupt-driven programs are very efficient in nature. They allow the CPU to service an I/O device without the need to continuously check a flag. When the event indicator flag is set, an interrupt occurs immediately. The CPU services the request then resumes with normal operation. Interrupts allow power saving since the CPU may be put in the *sleep* mode and awakened upon the occurrence of an event. This is definitely a great advantage especially when designing battery operated gadgets.

When there is a need to wake up the processor periodically in order to perform a certain task, the watchdog timer (WDT) may be used in conjunction with the *sleep* mode.

Interrupt driven programs may be complicated sometimes. This complexity is mitigated by emulating hardware state machines in software. A systematic approach for working with many interrupt sources will be presented in Chapter 11.

ENDNOTES

[1]   These mask bits are in the interrupt configuration register INTCON shown in Table 2

[2]   When GIE and the local mask (i.e. INT0IE) are both set, the CPU leaves the sleep mode when the event indicator (i.e. INT0IF) is asserted. In this case, the CPU executes the ISR then resumes with the statement after the Sleep() statement. If only the local mask (i.e. INT0IE) is set, the CPU does not execute any ISR. It resumes with the statement after the Sleep() macro upon detection of an event.

Chapter 8
Alphanumeric Liquid Crystal Displays

INTRODUCTION

Alphanumeric liquid-crystal displays (LCDs) play a crucial role in microcontroller-based systems for the following reasons:

- They allow system designers to display text messages to monitor the status of the system.
- LCDs help transform electronic gadgets into interactive and user friendly ones. The displayed messages guide the user to properly operate the device or gadget.
- Since they allow users to display variables, LCDs are excellent debugging tools. Designers can trace the system and make decisions as to whether a hardware unit is functioning properly or not.
- As opposed to 7-segment displays, LCDs display numbers as well as letters at a lower cost per bit of information. The Character Generator RAM (CGRAM) of the LCD can be programmed to display special characters such as Greek, Japanese, etc.

Fortunately, all LCDs follow the protocol of the Hitachi HD44780 LCD controller chip. What differs from one LCD to another is the number of lines and the number of characters per line. Alphanumeric LCDs have three control signals E, RS and $R/\bar{W}$ and 8 data lines. They can be operated in 4-bit or 8-bit mode.

This chapter emphasizes 4-bit mode for its pin-saving advantage. A specialized set of functions, intended to isolate the user from LCD peculiarities, will be developed.

DOI: 10.4018/978-1-68318-000-5.ch008

Figure 1. 4-bit vs. 8-bit mode; V_{EE} is used for brightness control. It is usually connected to the output of a voltage divider to provide a voltage level between 0 and 5V. For maximum brightness, V_{EE} is tied to ground.

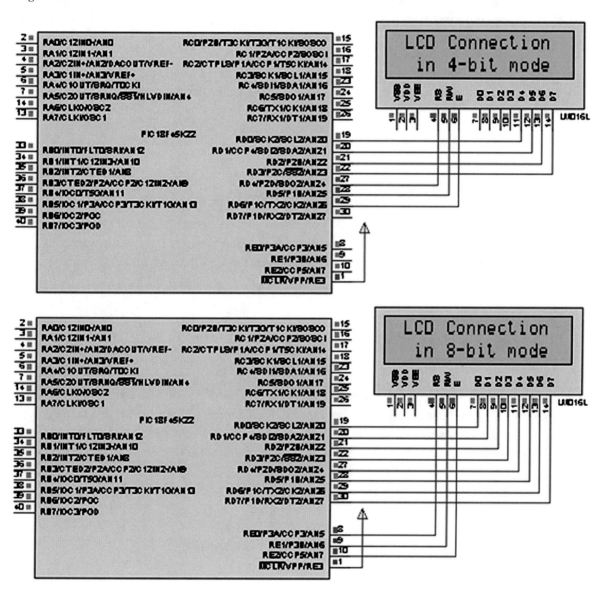

LCD INTERFACE AND FUNCTIONALITY

LCD modules can operate in 4-bit mode or 8-bit mode as shown in Figure 1. In the former, data is transferred one nibble at a time starting with the most significant nibble. In 8-bit mode, data transfer is done in one shot. The advantage of 4-bit versus 8-bit mode is pin-saving. On this basis, 4-bit data transfer will be emphasized in this chapter and will be the mode of choice throughout this textbook. Note that the 4-bit mode appropriates only 7 microcontroller pins (4 data lines plus 3 control lines) whereas the 8-bit mode usurps 11 microcontroller pins.

All alphanumeric LCD modules have three control signals:

- RS (Register Select Control):
  0 = LCD in command mode.
  1 = LCD in data mode.

Data mode allows the user to transfer ASCII characters to the LCD whereas command mode is in charge of transferring commands such as: clear the LCD, specify the position of the character to be displayed, etc.

- $R/\overline{W}$ (Read/Write Control):
  0 = MCU writes data to LCD.
  1 = MCU reads data from LCD.

When the MCU reads data from the LCD ($R/\overline{W} = 1$), it is generally to read the *busy* flag (BF) which signals whether the LCD is busy or not. If an appropriate delay is inserted between characters being sent to the LCD, the $R/\overline{W}$ pin may be tied to ground since there will no longer be any need to test the *busy* flag.

- E (Enable Signal):
  Rising Edge = Latches the control state (status of RS and $R/\overline{W}$).
  Falling Edge = Latches Data.

This signal works like a clock. It latches the status of RS and $R/\overline{W}$ into the LCD controller on the rising edge. On the falling edge, it latches the ASCII character (for $RS = 1$) or the command (for $RS = 0$). The latched data may be a byte or a nibble depending on whether 8-bit or 4-bit mode is used.

Figure 2 displays the LCD timing diagram in the write mode. Ambitious readers may refer to the device's datasheet for further details on timing parameters.

LCD commands, listed in Tables 1 and 2, are described subsequently:

- **Clear Display:** Clears entire display.
- **Return Home:** Returns display to original position if it was shifted.

Figure 2. Timing diagram in the write mode, timing parameters are not shown.

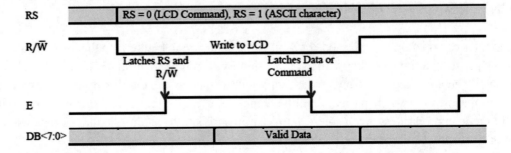

- **Entry Mode Set:** Sets cursor move direction and specifies display shift.
- **Display On/Off Control:** Sets entire display (D) on/off, cursor on/off (C), and blinking character at cursor position (B).
- **Cursor or Display Shift:** Moves cursor and shifts display without changing the display driver RAM (DDRAM) contents.
- **Function Set:** Sets interface data length (DL), number of display lines (N) and character font (F).
- **Set CGRAM Address:** Sets character generator RAM (CGRAM) address. CGRAM data is sent and received after this setting. This setting is used to add new patterns to be displayed as described extensively in the HD44780U datasheet.
- **Set DDRAM Address:** Sets display driver RAM address to specify character position on the LCD. Figure 4 elaborates on the command that specifies the character position on a 16-character x 2-line LCD.
- **CG/DD RAM Data Write:** Writes data into CGRAM or DDRAM. Normally an ASCII character is written to the DDRAM for display. The character may be sent as one entity or split into two nibbles starting with the most significant one.

Table 1. Major LCD commands and meaning of control bits

Instruction	RS	R/$\overline{W}$	D7	D6	D5	D4	D3	D2	D1	D0
Clear display	0	0	0	0	0	0	0	0	0	1
Return Home	0	0	0	0	0	0	0	0	1	-
Entry mode set	0	0	0	0	0	0	0	1	I/D	S
Display on/off control	0	0	0	0	0	0	1	D	C	B
Cursor or display shift	0	0	0	0	0	1	S/C	R/L	-	-
Function set	0	0	0	0	1	DL	N	F	-	-
Set CGRAM address	0	0	0	1	ACG					
Set DDRAM address	0	0	1	ADD						
CG/DD RAM data write	1	0	Write data							
Read Busy Flag & AC	0	1	BF	Address Counter						

Bits	I/D	S	D	C	B	S/C	R/L	DL	N	F
0	Decrement	Display Freeze	Display off	Cursor off	Character at cursor position does not blink	Cursor move	Left shift	4 bits	1 line	5x8 character font
1	Increment	Display Shift	Display on	Cursor on	Character at cursor position blinks	Display shift	Right shift	8 bits	Multiple lines	5x10 character font

Table 2. Specifying character position (DDRAM address) for a 16 x 2 LCD

1	LINE	Display Driver RAM Address
↑ Set DDRAM Address	↑ 0 = Line1 1 = Line2	↑ Specify address in DDRAM 000000_2 = char 0 on LCD 000001_2 = char 1 on LCD etc.

Display position	0	1	2	3	4	...	13	14	15
Line 1	0x80	0x81	0x82	0x83	0x84	...	0x8D	0x8E	0x8F
Line 2	0xC0	0xC1	0xC2	0xC3	0xC4	...	0xCD	0xCE	0xCF

Table 3. Basic commands required to configure the LCD

Command (RS = 0, R/W = 0)									Performed Task
0	0	1	DL	N	F	-	-		Function set: 4-bit interface data (DL = 0), 2 display lines (N = 1), 6x8 dot
0	0	1	0	1	0	0	0		character font (F = 0).
0	0	0	0	1	D	C	B		Display on/off control: display on (D = 1), cursor off (C = 0), blinking off
0	0	0	0	1	1	0	0		(B = 0)
0	0	0	0	0	0	0	1		Clear display and set DDRAM address 0 in address counter
0	0	0	0	0	1	I/D	S		Increment the DDRAM address by 1 when a character code is written into
0	0	0	0	0	1	1	0		DDRAM (I/D = 1), no shift (S = 0)

BASIC LCD ROUTINES

Using a LCD in 4-bit mode requires an initialization step before one can start sending ASCII characters to it for display. Table 3 lists the basic commands required to initialize the LCD.

For reasons having to do with the LCD start-up mode, the control codes 0x28, 0x0C, 0x01 and 0x06 of Table 3 are preceded by 0x33 and 0x32. You may refer to the datasheet for further details. As a result, the initialization string is defined as:

```
char LCDstr[] = {0x33, 0x32, 0x28, 0x0C, 0x01, 0x06, '\0'};
```

These bytes will be latched into the LCD one nibble at a time using the SendCmd() function. The null-terminator '\0' is appended to the stream of commands to be sent to the LCD. This way the commands in LCDstr[] will be sent one-by-one until the null-terminator is encountered.

In 4-bit mode, the LCD controller requires the reception of the upper nibble of the data/control code followed by its lower nibble. Table 4 lays out the fundamental functions used to display data on the LCD. Since data is output on PORTD<3:0>, care must be taken to keep the upper pins RD7:RD4 of PORTD intact. The following is a description of these subprograms:

- **InitLCD():** This function configures PORTD<6:4> (control pins E, $R/\overline{W}$ and RS) as outputs. The control commands stored in LCDstr[] are sent to the LCD one by one via SendCmd(). This goes on until the null-terminator is encountered.
- **SendCmd():** Routine in charge of latching a control command cmd into the LCD controller one nibble at a time. It waits until the busy flag BF is no longer asserted (BF = 0) before allowing a new command to be sent.
- **SendChar():** This function latches an ASCII character ch into the LCD controller one nibble at a time. It also waits until the busy flag BF is no longer asserted (BF = 0) before allowing a new character to be sent.
- **SendNibble():** Routine that latches one nibble of data (ASCII character or command) into the LCD. This is done without modifying PORTD<7:4>. It is invoked from SendCmd() and SendChar().
- **Wait4LCD():** It waits for the busy flag BF (active high) to become inactive. In order to do that, the LCD is put in read mode and the busy flag is polled. When BF is cleared, a new character/command may be sent to the LCD.

Table 4. Basic functions used to display data on the LCD in 4-bit mode

```
Basic LCD routines (4-bit mode). Uses the 4 LSBs of PORTD for data, RD<6:4>: control signals.
1    #include      <delays.h>
2    #include      <LCDdefs.h>
3
4    #define    E      PORTDbits.RD6
5    #define    RW     PORTDbits.RD5
6    #define    RS     PORTDbits.RD4
7
8    void SendCmd(char);
9    void SendNibble(char);
10   void Wait4LCD(void);
11
12   void InitLCD(void)               // initialize LCD in 4-bit mode
13   {
14       char LCDstr[] = {0x33, 0x32, 0x28, 0x0C, 0x01, 0x06, '\0'};
15       unsigned char i = 0;
16
17       ANSELD &= 0x80;              // RD<6:0> are digital pins
18       Delay10KTCYx(10);           // small initial delay
19       while (LCDstr[i] != '\0')
20           SendCmd(LCDstr[i++]);
21   }
22
23   void SendCmd(char cmd)           // send a command to the LCD
24   {
25       RS = 0; RW = 0; E = 0;       // set LCD in command mode
26       SendNibble((cmd >> 4) & 0x0F); // send upper nibble of command
27       SendNibble(cmd & 0x0F);     // send lower nibble of command
28       Wait4LCD();
29   }
30
31   void SendChar(char ch)           // send a character to the LCD
32   {
33       RS = 1; RW = 0; E = 0;       // set LCD in data mode
34       SendNibble((ch >> 4) & 0x0F); // send upper nibble of data
35       SendNibble(ch & 0x0F);      // send lower nibble of data
36       Wait4LCD();
37   }
38
39   void SendNibble(char ch)
40   {
41       TRISD &= 0b10000000;        // RD6..RD0 are output pins
42       PORTD = (PORTD & 0xF0) | ch; // upper nibble of not altered
43       E = 1;                      // latch control state (RS/R_W)
44       Delay10TCYx(2);             // 20 cycles delay
45       E = 0;                      // latch data/command
46   }
47
48   void Wait4LCD(void)              // Wait for busy flag to clear.
49   {
50       unsigned char LoNibble, HiNibble, status;
51
52       TRISD |= 0x0F;              // switch data port to input
53       RW = 1; RS = 0; E = 0;      // read busy flag
54       do {
55         E = 1;                           // provide logic high on E
56         Nop();                           // 1 cycle delay
57         HiNibble = PORTD << 4;           // read the high nibble
58         E = 0;                           // provide falling edge
59         E = 1;                           // provide logic high on E
60         Nop();                           // 1 cycle delay
61         LoNibble = PORTD & 0x0F;         // read the low nibble
62         E = 0;                           // provide falling edge
63         status = HiNibble | LoNibble;    // status<7> = busy flag
64       } while (status & 0x80);           // test busy flag
65   }
```

Example 1 Using the basic functions developed in Table 4,

a. Code the function

```
void DispRomStr(char StartPos, ROM *Str)
```

to display a null-terminated string `Str` stored in **PS** (ROM). The LCD starting position `StartPos` is passed as an argument. The string is of type ROM *. ROM is defined as:

```
typedef     const far rom char        ROM;     // strings in PS
```

b. Code the function

```
void DispRamStr(char StartPos, char *Str)
```

to display a null-terminated string `Str` stored in data space (RAM). The starting position `StartPos` on the LCD is passed as an argument to the function.

c. Implement the function

```
void DispVarStr(char *Str, char StartPos, unsigned char NumOfChars)
```

to display an n-byte string whose length is passed as a parameter in `NumOfChars`. The starting position `StartPos` on the LCD is passed as an argument as well.

d. Code the function

```
void DispBlanks(char StartPos, unsigned char NumOfChars)
```

to display blanks (spaces) on the LCD. The starting position is passed in `StartPos` and the number of blanks is passed in `NumOfChars`.

Solution: The ROM type is char in program space (rom char). This declaration tells the compiler that any pointer to this data type (ROM *) will access data via TBLPTR. Besides this, this new type may be stored at a far location in PS. This forces the compiler to employ TBLPTRU, TBLPTRH and TBLPTRL as a pointer to ROM. Finally, strings of type (ROM *) are not modifiable since the const specifier is utilized.

The *include* file <LCD4lib.h> has all the LCD functions (see Appendix 8) in 4-bit mode. Constant definitions stored in <LCDdefs.h>[1] allow the user to employ symbolic names for the LCD's starting position as in:

```
DispRomStr(Ln1Ch3, (ROM *) "Hello World");
```

where Ln1Ch3 is specified via the #define directive (in <LCDdefs.h>) as:

```
#define     Ln1Ch3     0x83          // line1, character 3
```

and (ROM *) is used to cast the constant string "Hello World" to a pointer to ROM.

Table 5 lists the designed functions. These functions permit the user to step back from the nitty-gritty details of the LCD and concentrate on the overall system being conceived. They belong to the LCD libraries <LCDxlib.h> (x = 4, 8) listed completely in Appendix 8. Also note that the ROM typedef has been added to the file <p18cxxx.h> so that this new data type may be used by all designed libraries.

Table 5. Routines to display strings, variables and blanks on the LCD (4/8-bit mode)

Display null-terminated string (in ROM) at position `StartPos` on the LCD.

```
void DispRomStr(char StartPos, ROM *Str)
{
    SendCmd(StartPos);
    while (*Str != '\0')
      SendChar(*Str++);
}
```

Display null-terminated string (in RAM) at position `StartPos` on the LCD.

```
void DispRamStr(char StartPos, char *Str)
{
    SendCmd(StartPos);
    while (*Str != '\0')
        SendChar(*Str++);
}
```

Display ASCII array of specified length at position `StartPos` on the LCD.

```
void DispVarStr(char *Str, char StartPos, unsigned char NumOfChars)
{
    unsigned char i;

    SendCmd(StartPos);
    for (i = 0; i < NumOfChars; i++)
      SendChar(*Str++);
}
```

Display a number of blank characters (`NumOfChars`) at position `StartPos` on the LCD.

```
void DispBlanks(char StartPos, unsigned char NumOfChars)
{
    unsigned char i;

    SendCmd(StartPos);
    for (i = 0; i < NumOfChars; i++)
      SendChar(' ');                        // send a blank character
}
```

Example 2 Write a program to test the LCD functions developed so far. You may display the same message of Figure 1 (4-bit or 8-bit mode) on the LM016L.

Solution: Table 6 lists two different versions of the program. The first stores the string in program space (ROM) whereas the seconds stores it in data space (RAM).

Table 6. Simple programs to test the LCD functions DispRomStr and DispRamStr

World's smallest LCD program. Displays 2 null-terminated strings stored in PS.

```
1   #include    <p18cxxx.h>
2   #include    <LCD4lib.h>          // Use LCD8lib.h in 8-bit mode
3
4   void main (void)
5   {
6       InitLCD();
7       DispRomStr(Ln1Ch0, (ROM *) " LCD Connection ");
8       DispRomStr(Ln2Ch0, (ROM *) "  in 4-bit mode ");
9       Sleep();
10  }
```

World's smallest LCD program. Displays 2 null-terminated strings stored in DS.

```
1   #include    <p18cxxx.h>
2   #include    <LCD4lib.h>          // Use LCD8lib.h in 8-bit mode
3
4   char Line1[] = " LCD Connection ";
5   char Line2[] = "  in 4-bit mode ";
6
7   void main (void)
8   {
9       InitLCD();
10      DispRamStr(Ln1Ch0, Line1);
11      DispRamStr(Ln2Ch0, Line2);
12      Sleep();
13  }
```

Example 3 For the sake of designing a complete set of functions helpful when working with LCD displays,

a. Code the function

$$\text{void Bcd2Asc(char *a, unsigned char Len)}$$

to convert the BCD array a of length Len to an ASCII array.

b. Code the function

$$\text{void Asc2Bcd(char *a, unsigned char Len)}$$

to convert the ASCII array a of length Len to a BCD array.

c. Code the function

$$\text{void PBCD2Asc(unsigned char SrcReg, char *DstArr)}$$

to convert a packed BCD byte in SrcReg to two ASCII characters in consecutive memory locations DstArr[0] (MSD) and DstArr[1] (LSD).

d. Code the function

$$\text{unsigned int Asc2Bin(char *a)}$$

to convert a 3-byte ASCII array a to binary. The array holds a 3-digit decimal number in unpacked ASCII format. For instance, the number 786_{10} is passed as an argument in array a as a[0] = 0x37 (hundreds), a[1] = 0x38 (tens) and a[2] = 0x36 (units). Since the conversion may return a number greater than 255_{10}, the return argument is of type int (16 bits).

e. Repeat part (d) for a 4-byte ASCII array. The function has the following prototype:

$$\text{unsigned int Asc2BinE(char *a)}$$

Table 7. Accessory functions to the LCD libraries (<LCD4lib.h> and <LCD8lib.h>)

```
Convert BCD array of length Len to ASCII
void Bcd2Asc(char *a, unsigned char Len)
{
    unsigned char i;
    for (i = 0; i < Len; i++)
        a[i] += '0';                        // convert to ASCII
}
```
```
Convert ASCII array of length Len to BCD.
void Asc2Bcd(char *a, unsigned char Len)
{
    unsigned char i;
    for (i = 0; i < Len; i++)
        a[i] &= 0x0F;                       // convert to BCD
}
```
```
Convert a packed BCD register SrcReg to unpacked ASCII (most significant in DstArr[0].
void PBCD2Asc(unsigned char SrcReg, char *DstArr)
{
    *DstArr++ = (SrcReg >> 4) | '0';        // upper nibble to ASCII
    *DstArr-- = (SrcReg & 0x0F) | '0';      // lower nibble to ASCII
}
```
```
Convert 3-digit ASCII array to binary.
unsigned int Asc2Bin(char *a)
{
    return (int) (a[0] & 0x0F) * 100 + (a[1] & 0x0F) * 10 +
                 (a[2] & 0x0F);
}
```
```
Convert 4-digit ASCII array to binary.
unsigned int Asc2BinE(char *a)
{
    return (int) (a[0] & 0x0F) * 1000 + (a[1] & 0x0F) * 100 +
                 (a[2] & 0x0F) * 10 + (a[3] & 0x0F);
}
```

Solution: These functions, listed in Table 7, are easy to understand.

Example 4 Modify the functions Bin2Bcd() and Bin2BcdE() of Example 6 in Chapter 5 to Bin2Asc() and Bin2AscE() in order to convert from binary to ASCII.

Solution: These functions are coded in Table 8 and are straightforward to comprehend.

Table 8. Bin2Asc() and Bin2AscE() routines in <LCD4lib.h> and <LCD8lib.h>

```
Convert 8-bit N to ASCII chars and store in array a (MSD first)
void Bin2Asc(unsigned char N, char *a) {
    a[2] = (N % 10) + '0';                  // least significant digit
    N = N / 10;
    a[1] = (N % 10) + '0';                  // middle significant digit
    a[0] = (N / 10) + '0';                  // most significant digit
}
```
```
Convert 16-bit N to ASCII chars and store in array a (MSD first)
void Bin2AscE(unsigned int N, char *a) {
    unsigned char i;
    for (i = 0; i < 4; i++) {
        a[4-i] = (N % 10) + '0';            // rem of N / 10 in ASCII
        N = N / 10;
    }
    a[0] = N + '0';
}
```

LCD APPLICATIONS

This section covers a number of examples pertaining to the LCD such as programmable timers, the Hi-Lo game and a frequency counter.

Example 5 Given the programmable timer setup of Figure 3,

a. Write a program to implement the programmable timer with only three push buttons: **Up** and **Down** to set the time, and **Start** to initiate the countdown process. The initial time is read from EEPROM address eeSeconds (0x00) into RAM address Seconds. After setting the time and pressing the **Start** command, the system will perform the following steps:

- First it memorizes the set time in EEPROM.
- Then it turns the device on and displays a down counter running at a rate of 1 Hz.
- When the time elapses, the device is turned off and the program starts all over again. A flashing display and intermittent beeps of a buzzer indicate timeout.

b. Use the voltage divider tied to analog channel **AN0** to specify the duration (0 s ≤ T ≤ 255 s). The **Start** push button turns on the device and initiates the countdown.

Solution:

a.   The program of Table 9 is subdivided into three routines:

○   **Setup():** Initializes the system ports and LCD.
○   **SetTime():** Sets the time with the Up/Down push buttons and waits for the Start command.
○   **TurnOn():** Turns on the device and displays a down counter until the time elapses. Upon termination, the device is turned off and the system is reset.

Figure 3. Programmable timer using push buttons or A/D converter to set the time

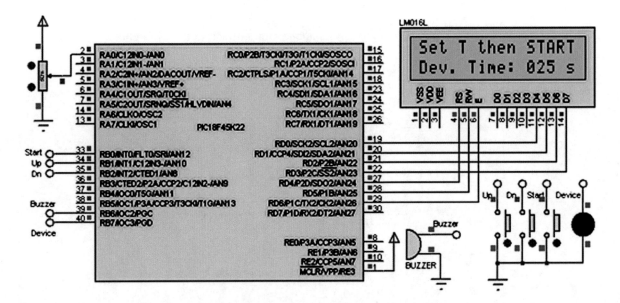

It is important to note that all local masks INT0IE, INT1IE and INT2IE are enabled in the Setup() function. However, the global mask GIE is not. This way the processor will not attempt to execute an interrupt service routine when awakened from sleep due to an INT0, INT1 or INT2 falling edge. In brief, the Sleep() macro in SetTime() halts the clock and the pressing of one of the buttons lets the program resume execution right after the Sleep() statement.

Table 9a. Programmable timer program using push buttons

```
3-digit programmable timer with push buttons. Set time is memorized in EEPROM.
1    #include      <p18cxxx.h>
2    #include      <LCD4lib.h>
3    #include      <EEPROM.h>
4
5    #define       eeSeconds    0x00                 // variable address in EEP
6    #define       Device       PORTBbits.RB7        // device pin
7    #define       Buzzer       PORTBbits.RB6        // buzzer pin
8    #define       Start        INTCONbits.INT0IF    // Start indicator
9    #define       Up           INTCON3bits.INT1IF   // Up indicator
10   #define       Dn           INTCON3bits.INT2IF   // Dn indicator
11
12
13   void Setup(void);
14   void SetTime(void);
15   void TurnOn(void);
16
17   char Digits[3]; unsigned char Seconds, i;       // i: loop counter
18
19   void main(void) {
20       Setup();
21       SetTime();
22       TurnOn();
23   }
24
25   void Setup(void)
26   {
27       ANSELB &= 0b11111000;                   // RB<2:0>: digital inputs
28       Device = 0; TRISBbits.TRISB7 = 0;       // turn device off
29       Buzzer = 0; TRISBbits.TRISB6 = 0;       // turn buzzer off
30       INTCON2 = 0x0F;                         // Pullups enabled, INTx: -ve edge
31       INTCON3bits.INT1IE = 1;
32       INTCON3bits.INT2IE = 1;
33       INTCONbits.INT0IE = 1;
34       Seconds = ReadEE(eeSeconds);            // read from EEPROM to RAM
35       InitLCD();                              // initialize LCD
36       DispRomStr(Ln1Ch0, (ROM *) "Set T then START");
37       DispRomStr(Ln2Ch0, (ROM *) "Dev. Time:    s");
38       Bin2Asc(Seconds, Digits);               // convert to 3 ASCII chars
39       DispVarStr(Digits, Ln2Ch11, 3);         // send Digits to LCD
40   }
```

Table 9b. Programmable timer program using push buttons continued

```
3-digit programmable timer with push buttons. Set time is memorized in EEPROM.
41
42  void SetTime(void)
43  {
44      while (1) {
45          Sleep();                            // wait for PB
46          if (Start) {
47              Start = 0;                      // acknowledge START PB
48              if (Seconds != 0)
49                  break;                      // exit loop
50          } else if (Up)                      // increment
51          {
52              Up = 0;                         // acknowledge Up PB
53              Bin2Asc(++Seconds, Digits);     // convert to ASCII
54              DispVarStr(Digits, Ln2Ch11, 3); // send Digits to LCD
55          } else                              // increment
56          {
57              Dn = 0;                         // acknowledge Dn PB
58              Bin2Asc(--Seconds, Digits);     // convert to ASCII
59              DispVarStr(Digits, Ln2Ch11, 3); // send Digits to LCD
60          }
61      }
62  }
63
64  void TurnOn(void)
65  {
66      Device = 1;                             // turn device on
67      Wrt2EE(Seconds, eeSeconds);             // save in EEPROM
68      DispRomStr(Ln1Ch0, (ROM *) "Left Time:   s");
69      do {
70          Bin2Asc(Seconds, Digits);           // convert to ASCII
71          DispVarStr(Digits, Ln1Ch11, 3);     // send Digits to LCD
72          if (Seconds == 0) break;
73          Delay10KTCYx(100);                  // 1000 ms delay
74          Seconds--;
75      } while (1);
76
77      Device = 0;                             // turn device off
78      for (i = 0; i < 6; i++) {
79          Delay10KTCYx(50);                   // 1/2 second delay
80          Buzzer = ~Buzzer;                   // intermittent beep
81      }
82      Reset();
83  }
```

b. Although the A/D converter is covered in chapter 9, it is introduced here. When 8-bit resolution is used, the A/D converts the voltage applied to RA0/AN0 to an 8-bit code. For a voltage between 0V and 5V, the digital code provided by the A/D ranges between 0x00 and 0xFF proportionally. The upcoming instructions are added to the Setup() routine to configure the A/D converter.

```
ADCON0bits.ADON = 1;     // A/D on, AN0: default channel
ADCON2 = 0b00001001;     // left justify, Tconv = 22 us, Tacq = 4 us
```

Table 10. Programmable timer with voltage divider applied to RA0/AN0

```
3-digit programmable timer. Set time is memorized via a voltage divider applied to ADC (AN0)
1    #include       <p18cxxx.h>
2    #include       <LCD4lib.h>
3
4    #define      Device       PORTBbits.RB7      // device pin
5    #define      Buzzer       PORTBbits.RB6      // buzzer pin
6    #define      Start        INTCONbits.INT0IF  // Start indicator
7
8    void Setup(void);
9    void SetTime(void);
10   void TurnOn(void);
11
12   char Digits[3]; unsigned char Seconds, I;     // i: loop counter
13
14   void main(void) {
15       Setup();
16       SetTime();
17       TurnOn();
18   }
19
20   void Setup(void)
21   {
22       ANSELBbits.ANSB0 = 0;                      // RB0: digital input
23       Device = 0; TRISBbits.TRISB7 = 0;          // turn device off
24       Buzzer = 0; TRISBbits.TRISB6 = 0;          // turn buzzer off
25       INTCON2bits.RBPU = 0;                      // enable pull-up
26       INTCON2bits.INTEDG0 = 0;                   // -ve edge of INT0
27
28       ADCON0bits.ADON = 1;                       // A/D on, chan AN0
29       ADCON2 = 0b00001001;                       // 8-bit, Tad = 2us
30
31       InitLCD();                                 // initialize LCD
32       DispRomStr(Ln1Ch0, (ROM *) "Set T then START");
33       DispRomStr(Ln2Ch0, (ROM *) "Dev. Time:    s");
34       DispVarStr(Digits, Ln2Ch11, 3);            // send Digits to LCD
35   }
36
37   void SetTime(void)
38   {
39       while (1) {
40           ADCON0bits.GO = 1;                     // start conversion
41           while (ADCON0bits.NOT_DONE);           // wait until EOC
42           Seconds = ADRESH;
43           Bin2Asc(Seconds, Digits);              // convert to ASCII
44           DispVarStr(Digits, Ln2Ch11, 3);        // send Digits to LCD
45           if (Start) {
46               Start = 0;                         // ack. START PB
47               if (Seconds != 0) break;
48           }
49       }
50   }
51
52   void TurnOn(void)
53   {
54       Device = 1;                                // turn device on
55       DispRomStr(Ln1Ch0, (ROM *) "Left Time:    s");
56       do {
57           Bin2Asc(Seconds, Digits);              // convert to ASCII
58           DispVarStr(Digits, Ln1Ch11, 3);        // send Digits to LC
59           if (Seconds == 0) break;
60           Delay10KTCYx(100);                     // 1000 ms delay
61           Seconds--;
62       } while (1);
63
64       Device = 0;                                // turn device off
65       for (I = 0; I < 6; i++) {
66           Delay10KTCYx(50);                      // ½ second delay
67           Buzzer = ~Buzzer;                      // intermittent beep
68       }
69       Reset();
70   }
```

In order to convert an analog voltage to digital code, the GO bit in ADCON0 must be set. Upon end-of-conversion (EOC), the $\overline{DONE}$ (NOT_DONE) bit in ADCON0 is cleared by the hardware. The user must poll this flag to test the *end-of-conversion* condition as follows:

```
ADCON0bits.GO = 1;                    // start conversion
while (ADCON0bits.NOT_DONE);          // wait until EOC
```

Upon conversion, the result is stored in ADRESH (A/D result high) for 8-bit resolution. The complete program is listed in Table 10.

Example 6 Implement the programmable timer of Figure 4. The hex keypad is interfaced to the MCU via the 74C922 keypad encoder chip. The chip's data available pin **DA**, tied to **RB0/INT0**, provides a rising edge when a key is pressed.

Solution: The program is listed in Table 11. In brief, the CPU is awakened when a key is pressed (INT0IF = 1). Consequently, the processor clears INT0IF and processes the key as follows:

- Keys C through F are ignored. Only BCD digits 0 through 9 are displayed.
- If the *BackSpace* (B) key is pressed, the previously entered key is erased.
- If the *Enter* (A) key is pressed, the device is turned on and the countdown is initiated.

Figure 4. Programmable timer using a hex keypad

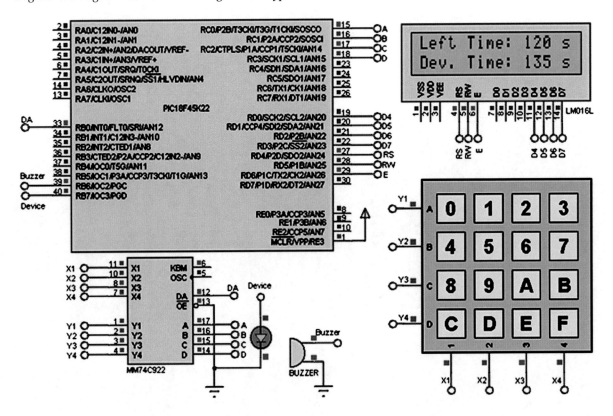

Table 11a. Programmable timer using hex keypad

```
3-digit programmable timer with hex keypad interface (hardware encoding).
1    #include      <p18cxxx.h>
2    #include      <LCD4lib.h>
3    #include      <string.h>
4
5    void Setup(void);
6    void GetTime(void);
7    void DispDashes(void);
8    void ProcessKey(void);
9    void TurnOn(void);
10
11   #define      Device      PORTBbits.RB7      // device pin
12   #define      Buzzer      PORTBbits.RB6      // buzzer pin
13   #define      TimeEnt     FLAGS.B0          // time entered indicator
14   #define      Enter       0x0A              // code of Enter key
15   #define      BkSpace     0x0B              // code of backspace key
16
17   char Digits[3], Key;
18   unsigned char i;                          // pointer to digits
19   unsigned int Seconds;                     // # of secs device is on
20
21   void main(void)
22   {
23       Setup();
24       GetTime();
25       TurnOn();
26   }
27
28   void Setup(void)
29   {
30       ANSELBbits.ANSB0 = 0;                 // RB0: digital input
31       Device = 0; TRISBbits.TRISB7 = 0;     // turn device off
32       Buzzer = 0; TRISBbits.TRISB6 = 0;     // turn buzzer off
33       ANSELC &= 0b11110011;                 // RC<3:2>: digital inputs
34
35       INTCONbits.INT0IE = 1;                // operate in sleep mode
36       TimeEnt = 0;                          // TimeEnt not asserted
37       InitLCD();                            // initialize LCD
38       DispRomStr(Ln1Ch0, (ROM *) "Set T then START");
39       DispRomStr(Ln2Ch0, (ROM *) "Dev. Time:     s");
40       DispDashes();
41   }
42
43   void GetTime(void)
44   {
45       do {
46           Sleep();                          // wait for data available
47           INTCONbits.INT0IF = 0;            // acknowledge DA
48           Key = PORTC & 0x0F;               // grab pressed Key
49           ProcessKey();
50       } while (!TimeEnt);                   // exit when TimeEnt = 1
51   }
52
53   void DispDashes(void)
54   {
55       memset(Digits, '_', 3);               // store _ _ _
56       DispVarStr(Digits, Ln2Ch11, 3);
57       i = 0;                                // point to Digits[0]
58   }
```

Table 11b. Programmable timer using hex keypad continued

```
3-digit programmable timer with hex keypad interface (hardware encoding).
59
60   void ProcessKey(void)
61   {
62       if (Key <= BkSpace)                      // BkSpace = 11
63           switch (Key) {
64               case BkSpace:                    // process BackSpace Key
65                   if (i != 0)
66                   {
67                       Digits[--i] = '_';       // store '_' at last digit
68                       DispVarStr(Digits, Ln2Ch11, 3);
69                   }
70                   break;
71               case Enter:                      // process Enter Key
72                   if (i == 3)
73                   {
74                       Seconds = Asc2Bin(Digits);// convert to binary
75                       if (Seconds > 255)
76                           DispDashes();         // invalid, start anew
77                       else if (Seconds == 0)
78                           DispDashes();         // invalid, start anew
79                       else
80                           TimeEnt = 1;
81                   }
82                   break;
83               default:                         // it is a BCD digit
84                   if (i != 3)
85                   {
86                       Digits[i++] = Key + '0';  // convert to ASCII
87                       DispVarStr(Digits, Ln2Ch11, 3); // display Digits
88                   }
89                   break;
90           }
91   }
92
93   void TurnOn(void)
94   {
95       Device = 1;                              // turn device on
96       DispRomStr(Ln1Ch0, (ROM *) "Left Time:   s");
97       do {
98           Bin2Asc(Seconds, Digits);            // convert to ASCII
99           DispVarStr(Digits, Ln1Ch11, 3);      // send Digits to LCD
100          if (Seconds == 0) break;
101          Delay10KTCYx(100);                    // 1000 ms delay
102          Seconds--;
103      } while (1);
104
104      Device = 0;                              // turn device off
106      for (i = 0; i < 6; i++) {
107          Delay10KTCYx(50);                     // 1/2 second delay
108          Buzzer = ~Buzzer;                     // intermittent beep
109      }
110      Reset();
111  }
```

Example 7 Use the hardware of Figure 4 to implement the Hi-Lo game as described in the steps below. Refer to the execution demonstration of Table 12.

- The processor chooses a random number between 0 and 255 inclusive. This is done by reading **TMR0L** when the user presses the first key.
- The user starts guessing the hidden number by entering a 3-digit guess at the position of the underscores (see upcoming illustrations).
- If the entered guess is greater than 255, the user is prompted for a new guess and the LCD displays: "**Out of Range ...**"
- If the entered guess is greater than the hidden number, the user is asked to enter a new guess and the LCD displays: "**Sorry! Too Large**".
- If the entered guess is smaller than the hidden number, the processor waits for a new guess and the LCD displays: "**Sorry! Too Small**".
- The user continues to play until guessing the hidden number. At this time, the LCD displays the number of guesses along with a congratulation message.

Solution: The complete program is listed in Table 13.

Table 12. Execution demonstration of the Hi-Lo game

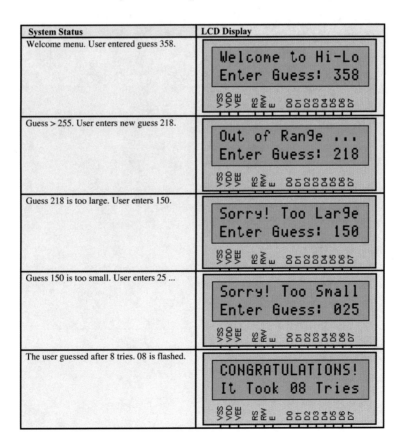

System Status	LCD Display
Welcome menu. User entered guess 358.	Welcome to Hi-Lo Enter Guess: 358
Guess > 255. User enters new guess 218.	Out of Range ... Enter Guess: 218
Guess 218 is too large. User enters 150.	Sorry! Too Large Enter Guess: 150
Guess 150 is too small. User enters 25 ...	Sorry! Too Small Enter Guess: 025
The user guessed after 8 tries. 08 is flashed.	CONGRATULATIONS! It Took 08 Tries

Table 13a. Software implementation of the Hi-Lo game

```
Hi-Lo Game with keypad and LCD display
1    #include      <p18cxxx.h>
2    #include      <LCD4lib.h>
3    #include      <string.h>
4
5    void Setup(void);
6    void PlayHiLo(void);
7    void GetGuess(void);
8    void DispDashes(void);
9    void ProcessKey(void);
10   void HiLo(void);
11
12   #define    Buzzer       PORTBbits.RB6    // buzzer pin
13   #define    GuessEnt     FLAGS.B0         // Guess entered indicator
14   #define    GameOver     FLAGS.B1         // Game over indicator
15   #define    Enter        0x0A             // code of Enter key
16   #define    BkSpace      0x0B             // code of backspace key
17
18   unsigned char Number, Tries, Key, i;
19   unsigned int Guess;
20   char Digits[3];                          // store ASCII array
21
22   void main(void) {
23       Setup();
24       PlayHiLo();                          // infinite loop
25   }
26
27   void Setup(void) {
28       ANSELBbits.ANSB0 = 0;                // RB0: digital input
29       Buzzer = 0; TRISBbits.TRISB6 = 0;    // turn buzzer off
30       ANSELC &= 0b11110011;                // RC<3:2>: digital inputs
31
32       T0CONbits.T0CS = 0;                  // internal clock
33       InitLCD();                           // initialize LCD
34   }
35
36   void PlayHiLo(void) {
37       while (1) {
38           GameOver = 0;                    // "GameOver" initially false
39           DispRomStr(Ln1Ch0, (ROM *) "Welcome to Hi-Lo");
40           DispRomStr(Ln2Ch0, (ROM *) "Enter Guess:     ");
41           Tries = 0;
42           do {
43               GetGuess();
44               if (Tries++ == 0)            // select RN if Tries = 0
45                   Number = TMR0L;          // get RN from TMR0
46               HiLo();                      // make a decision
47           } while (!GameOver);             // exit when GameOver = 1
48       }
49   }
```

Table 13b. Software implementation of the Hi-Lo game continued

```
Hi-Lo Game with keypad and LCD display
50
51   void GetGuess(void)
52   {
53       GuessEnt = 0;                           // Guess entered = false
54       DispDashes();                           // display _ _ _
55       do {
56           while (!INTCONbits.INT0IF);         // wait for data available
57           INTCONbits.INT0IF = 0;              // acknowledge DA
58           Key = PORTC & 0x0F;                 // read pressed key
59           ProcessKey();
60       } while (!GuessEnt);                    // exit if GuessEnt = true
61   }
62
63   void DispDashes(void) {
64       memset(Digits, '_', 3);                 // store _ _ _
65       DispVarStr(Digits, Ln2Ch13, 3);
66       i = 0;                                  // point to Digits[0]
67   }
68
69   void ProcessKey(void) {
70       if (Key <= BkSpace)                     // if valid key
71           switch (Key) {
72               case BkSpace:                   // process BackSpace Key
73                   if (i != 0) {
74                       Digits[--i] = '_';      // store underscore
75                       DispVarStr(Digits, Ln2Ch13, 3); // display Digits
76                   }
77                   break;
78               case Enter:                     // process Enter Key
79                   if (i == 3) GuessEnt = 1;
80                   break;
81               default:                        // it is a BCD digit
82                   if (i != 3) {
83                       Digits[i++] = Key + '0';    // convert to ASCII
84                       DispVarStr(Digits, Ln2Ch13, 3); // display Digits
85                   }
86                   break;
87           }
88   }
89
90   void HiLo(void) {
91       DispBlanks(Ln1Ch0, 16);                 // blank 1st line to give the
92       Delay10KTCYx(50);                       // impression MCU is thinking
93       Guess = Asc2Bin(Digits);
94       if (Guess > 255) {
95           DispRomStr(Ln1Ch0, (ROM *) "Out of Range ...");
96           DispDashes();
97       } else if (Guess > Number)
98           DispRomStr(Ln1Ch0, (ROM *) "Sorry! Too Large");
99       else if (Guess < Number)
100          DispRomStr(Ln1Ch0, (ROM *) "Sorry! Too Small");
101      else {
102          DispRomStr(Ln1Ch0, (ROM *) "CONGRATULATIONS!");
103          DispRomStr(Ln2Ch0, (ROM *) "It Took    Tries");
104          for (i = 1; i <= 5; i++) {          // flash display
104              Bin2Asc(Tries, Digits);
106              DispVarStr(&Digits[1], Ln2Ch8, 2);  // MSD not important
107              Delay10KTCYx(30);               // 300 ms delay
108              DispBlanks(Ln2Ch8, 2);
109              Delay10KTCYx(30);               // 300 ms delay
110          }
111          GameOver = 1;                       // assert "game over"
112      }
113  }
```

Figure 5. Frequency counter hardware setup

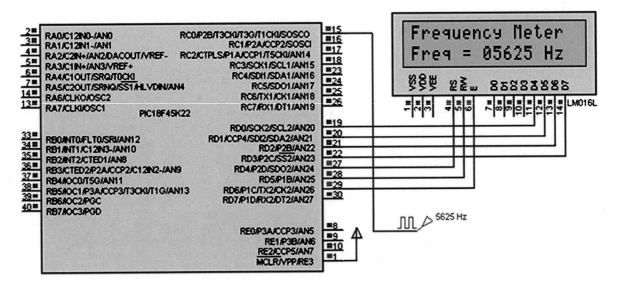

Example 8 The signal applied to **RC0/T1CKI** (Figure 5) drives a frequency counter that can measure frequencies up to 65,535 Hz. Write the code to implement this gadget. Use **Timer0** to time 1 second and **Timer1** to accumulate pulses for 1 second. Test your code by applying a range of frequencies within the constraints of the frequency counter.

Solution: The program of Table 14 accumulates cycles for a period of 1 second. Timer0 is used to provide an exact delay of 1 second via the polling mode. Timer1 is employed to count edges appearing on the clock input. Although Timer1 has not been covered yet, it operates very much like Timer0. You may refer to Appendix 2 (TxCON, x = 1) in order to configure Timer1 appropriately. In this example, Timer1 is triggered by an external clock: the signal whose frequency is to be measured. It works as a 16-bit counter and has no 8-bit option.

Note the use of the inline assembly code to read Timer1:

```
_asm
        movff       TMR1L, Cycles       // read low byte first
        movff       TMR1H, Cycles+1
_endasm
```

Table 14. Frequency counter program

```
Frequency counter: uses Timer0 to time 1 sec and Timer1 to accumulate pulses in 1 sec
1    #include    <p18cxxx.h>
2    #include    <LCD4lib.h>
3
4    unsigned int Cycles;                    // cycles counter
5    char Digits[5];                         // digits array
6
7    void main(void)
8    {
9        InitLCD();                          // initialize LCD
10       DispRomStr(Ln1Ch0, (ROM *) "Frequency Meter ");
11       DispRomStr(Ln2Ch0, (ROM *) "Freq = 00000 Hz ");
12
13       T0CON = 0b10010101;                 // CLK / 64, 16-bit mode
14       T1CON = 0b10000011;                 // external ck, no prescale
15
16       while (1)
17       {
18           TMR0H = (65535 - 15625) / 256;  // 64 us * 15,625 = 1 sec
19           TMR0L = (65535 - 15625) % 256;
20           INTCONbits.TMR0IF = 0;
21
22           TMR1H = 0x00; TMR1L = 0x00;     // write in one shot
23
24           while (!INTCONbits.TMR0IF);     // wait for 1 sec
25
26           _asm
27               movff TMR1L, Cycles         // read low byte first
28               movff TMR1H, Cycles + 1
29           _endasm
30
31           Bin2AscE(Cycles, Digits);
32           DispVarStr(Digits, Ln2Ch7, 5);
33       }
34   }
```

CONCLUSION

The use of an LCD in a gadget certainly adds value to it and makes it user friendly. A combination of this output device along with a small hex keypad is the ideal solution to menu-driven applications. It is strongly recommended to combine these 2 I/O devices whenever possible. With all the variety of LCDs available in the market, the user will always find the one that best suits his/her application. Appendix 8 summarizes the LCD libraries (<LCD4lib.h> and <LCD8lib.h>) as well as the LCD definitions <LCD-defs.h> used to specify the LCD positions in symbolic format.

ENDNOTE

[1]   <LCDdefs.h> is included in <LCD4lib.h> for convenience. This file is listed in Appendix 8 as well.

166

Chapter 9
Analog–to–Digital Conversion

INTRODUCTION

The purpose of the Analog-to-Digital converter (ADC) is to transform a voltage sample to a proportional digital code thereby allowing the measurement of physical quantities such as voltage, current, temperature, atmospheric pressure, etc. Most sensors transform physical quantities into voltage. For instance, the LM35 temperature sensor converts the temperature range (0 – 100 °C) into a linear voltage range between 0 and 1 Volt as described by the characteristic curve of Figure 1. Due to the digital nature of a microcontroller, the ADC serves as a mediator between the analog world in which we live and the digital world created by Man.

This chapter discusses the functionality of the ADC and its use in a variety of applications. The Sample-and-Hold (SAH) circuit and the Successive-Approximation (SAR) ADC will be explained and pertinent timing constraints will be covered as well.

Figure 1. Characteristic curve of LM35 temperature sensor

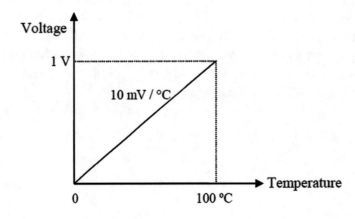

DOI: 10.4018/978-1-68318-000-5.ch009

SAMPLE-AND-HOLD CIRCUITRY

In order to convert a voltage sample to digital code, the sample is not allowed to change value during conversion. This is because analog-to-digital conversion is not an instantaneous process. The successive-approximation A/D converter, employed by the PIC18 family, is essentially a state machine requiring a number of clock cycles to complete the conversion procedure.

Since signals in general (e.g. audio signals) vary rapidly as a function of time, the need to track the input signal is performed via a Sample-and-Hold (SAH) circuit as depicted in Figure 2. The 5 pF capacitor (C_{in}) in the figure models the input capacitance of the SAH whereas C_{hold} is used to store or hold the input sample for conversion. In order to track an input signal, the sampling switch S is closed and the RC circuit formed by ($R_{ic} + R_{ss}$) and C_{hold} allows the holding capacitor to track the input signal within five time constants. This "tracking time" T_c has been computed to be 1.2 µs under the worst considerations. If other factors such as the amplifier settling time (T_{AMP} = 5 µs) and the temperature coefficient (T_{COFF} = 1.25 µs for an operating temperature of 50 °C) are taken into account, then the acquisition time (T_{ACQ} = $T_{AMP} + T_C + T_{COFF}$) adds up to 7.45 µs. Therefore, the sampling switch S must be closed for at least 7.45 µs for reliable data acquisition.

When the ADC is commanded to start conversion (GO = 1), S is opened and the input signal is disconnected from the hold capacitor. Simultaneously switch $\bar{S}$ is closed and the conversion process of the voltage sample stored across C_{hold} is initiated. Due to the high input impedance of the ADC, the voltage sample remains constant during conversion. Upon termination, an end-of-conversion flag ($\overline{DONE}$) is asserted to 0 and consequently $\bar{S}$ is opened and S is closed. This means that the SAH will go back to sampling mode. The charge holding capacitor C_{hold} is instantaneously discharged after each sample via a discharge switch (not shown in Figure 2). This feature helps to optimize the sampling process, as the circuit always needs to charge the capacitor, rather than charge/discharge based upon previously measured values.

Figure 2. Analog input model

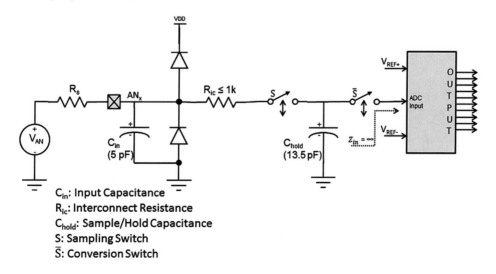

C$_{in}$: Input Capacitance
R$_{ic}$: Interconnect Resistance
C$_{hold}$: Sample/Hold Capacitance
S: Sampling Switch
$\bar{S}$: Conversion Switch

SUCCESSIVE APPROXIMATION ADC

In reference to Figure 3, the successive approximation analog-to-digital (SAR ADC) converter circuit typically consists of five chief sub-circuits:

1. A sample and hold circuit to acquire the input voltage (V_{in}).
2. A voltage comparator that compares V_{in} to the DAC's output. It outputs the comparison result to the successive approximation register (SAR).
3. A successive approximation register designed to supply an approximate digital code of V_{in} to the internal DAC.
4. An internal reference DAC that supplies the comparator with an analog voltage equivalent of the digital code supplied by of the SAR.
5. A register ADRES to store the ADC result upon end-of-conversion (*EOC*).

The successive approximation register is initialized so that the MSB b_9 is '1' and all other bits are '0'. This code is fed into the DAC which supplies its analog equivalent (V_{REF+} - V_{REF-}) / 2 into the comparator circuit for comparison. If this analog voltage V_- exceeds V_{in}, the comparator causes the SAR to reset this bit and set the next bit (b_8) to a digital 1. If V_- falls below V_{in}, then b_9 is left a 1 and the b_8 is set to 1. This binary search, illustrated in Table 1, continues until every bit is generated. The ADC result is the digital approximation of the input sample and is outputted by the ADC at the end of the conversion ($\overline{DONE}$ = 0). As shown in this algorithm, a successive-approximation ADC requires:

1. An input voltage sample V_{in}.
2. Two reference voltage sources V_{REF-} and V_{REF+} to specify the input range (V_{REF-} - V_{REF+}). The low reference voltage is usually ground.
3. A DAC to convert the ith approximation x_i to a voltage.
4. A comparator to compare the DAC's output with the input sample.
5. A register to store the output of the comparator and apply a new value to the DAC.

Figure 3. 10-bit successive approximation ADC block diagram

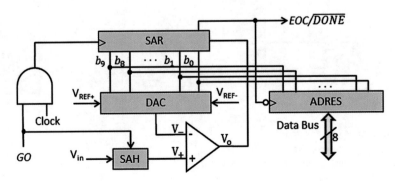

Table 1. Iterations of 10-bit SAR ADC for $V_+ = 4$ V, $V_{REF+} = 5$ V and $V_{REF-} = 0$ V

\multicolumn{6}{SAR ADC Operation for V_{in} = 4 V. ADRES = 0x333}		Thresholds Used in Search	
Cycle	Bit	$b_9b_8...b_1b_0$	V_+	V_-	V_o	DAC Input	DAC Output
1	b_9	10 0000 0000	4 V	2.5000000000 V	1	10 0000 0000	2.5000000000 V
2	b_8	11 0000 0000	4 V	3.7500000000 V	1	01 0000 0000	1.2500000000 V
3	b_7	11 1000 0000	4 V	4.3750000000 V	0	00 1000 0000	0.6250000000 V
4	b_6	11 0100 0000	4 V	4.0625000000 V	0	00 0100 0000	0.3125000000 V
5	b_5	11 0010 0000	4 V	3.9062500000 V	1	00 0010 0000	0.1562500000 V
6	b_4	11 0011 0000	4 V	3.9843750000 V	1	00 0001 0000	0.0781250000 V
7	b_3	11 0011 1000	4 V	4.0234375000 V	0	00 0000 1000	0.0390625000 V
8	b_2	11 0011 0100	4 V	4.0039062500 V	0	00 0000 0100	0.0195312500 V
9	b_1	11 0011 0010	4 V	3.9941406250 V	1	00 0000 0010	0.0097656250 V
10	b_0	11 0011 0011	4 V	3.9990234375 V	1	00 0000 0001	0.0048828125 V

The ADC of PIC18 microcontrollers generates a 10-bit approximation upon end-of-conversion. Figure 4 shows the timing diagram of the A/D converter after the GO bit has been asserted. The A/D conversion requires 11 T_{AD} per 10-bit conversion where T_{AD} is the A/D conversion time per bit. Upon termination, the 10-bit A/D result is saved in ADRESH:ADRESL (A/D result high and low). Simultaneously, the $\overline{DONE}$ bit is cleared by the hardware (end-of-conversion indicator) and the sampling switch is closed again to allow the capacitor to track the input signal in anticipation for conversion. When the next sample is to be converted, the GO bit is set once again. This disconnects the sampling switch from the input signal and initiates the conversion process. The charges held across the capacitor's plates will not discharge during conversion due to the high input impedance of the converter.

A/D FUNCTIONALITY AND ASSOCIATED REGISTERS

In reference to Figure 5, the A/D converter module of PIC18F45K22 devices has 28 external analog channels AN0 through AN27 (channel AN28 is reserved at this point) and 3 internal channels (FVR BUF, DAC and CTMU). The external channels occupy all the ports either partially or completely. The analog multiplexer allows selection of one channel at a time in accordance with the Channel Select bits

Figure 4. A/D conversion T_{AD} cycles; acquisition time $T_{ACQ} = 0$ (ACQT<2:0> = 000)

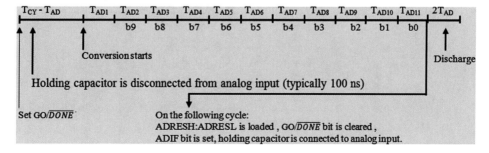

Figure 5. A/D block diagram

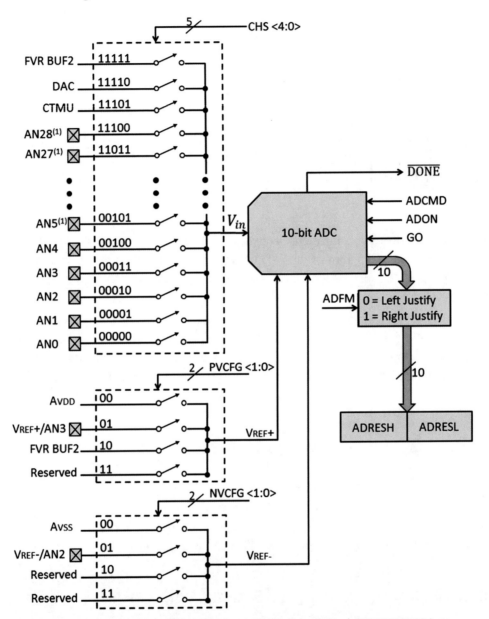

(1) Additional ADC channels AN5 – AN7 and AN20 – AN27 are only available on PIC18(L)F4XK22 devices.

CHS<3:0> in control register ADCON0 (Table 2). The user should first set ADON in ADCON0 to turn on the A/D. The chosen channel is fed to the A/D converter via the sample and hold circuit. The GO bit in ADCON0 initiates the conversion process. Upon end-of-conversion, the same bit (also named $\overline{DONE}$) is cleared and the 10-bit digital result is stored in ADRESH:ADRESL.

Table 2. ADCON0: A/D configuration register 0

ADCON0:   A/D CONTROL REGISTER 0

U-0	R/W-0	R/W-0	R/W-0	R/W-0	R/W-0	R/W-0	R/W-0
-	CHS<4:0>					GO/$\overline{\text{DONE}}$	ADON
bit 7							**bit 0**

R = Readable bit	W = Writable bit	U = Unimplemented bit, read as '0'
-n = Value at POR	'1' = Bit is set	'0' = Bit is cleared x = Bit is unknown

bit 7   **Unimplemented**: Read as '0'

Bit 6-2   **CHS<4:0>: Analog Channel Select bits**
        00000 = AN0
        00001 = AN1
        00010 = AN2
        00011 = AN3
        00100 = AN4
        00101 = AN5[1]
        00110 = AN6[1]
        00111 = AN7[1]
        01000 = AN8

        . . .

        10011 = AN19
        10100 = AN20[1]
        10101 = AN21[1]
        10110 = AN22[1]
        10111 = AN23[1]
        11000 = AN24[1]
        11001 = AN25[1]
        11010 = AN26[1]
        11011 = AN27[1]
        11100 = Reserved
        11101 = CTMU
        11110 = DAC
        11111 = FVR BUF2 (1.024V/2.048V/2.096V Volt Fixed Voltage Reference)[2]

bit 1   **GO/$\overline{\text{DONE}}$**: A/D Conversion Status bit
        1 = A/D conversion cycle in progress. Setting this bit starts an A/D conversion cycle.
           This bit is automatically cleared by hardware when the A/D conversion has completed.
        0 = A/D conversion completed / not in progress)

bit 0   **ADON:** ADC Enable bit
        1 = ADC is enabled
        0 = ADC is disabled and consumes no operating current

Note 1:   Available on PIC18(L)F4XK22 devices only.
Note 2:   Allow greater than 15 μs acquisition time when measuring the Fixed Voltage Reference.

The voltage configuration bits PVCFG<1:0> and NVCFG<1:0> in ADCON1 (see Table 3) select the reference voltages V_{REF+} and V_{REF-} of the A/D converter. These references essentially specify the minimum and maximum voltages that can be applied to the analog inputs. In most cases, the references used are $V_{REF+} = V_{DD} = 5V$ and $V_{REF-} = V_{SS} = 0V$ (internal references). This way a voltage range of 0 to 5V provides a digital code between 0x000 and 0x3FF for the 10-bit A/D.

Table 3. ADCON1: A/D configuration register 1

ADCON1:   A/D CONTROL REGISTER 1

R/W-0	U-0	U-0	U-0	R/W-0	R/W-0	R/W-0	R/W-0
TRIGSEL	–	–	–	PVCFG<1:0>		NVCFG<1:0>	
bit 7							**bit 0**

R = Readable bit   W = Writable bit   U = Unimplemented bit, read as '0'
-n = Value at POR   '1' = Bit is set   '0' = Bit is cleared   x = Bit is unknown

bit 7   **TRIGSEL**: Special Trigger Select bit
                   1 = Selects the special trigger from CTMU
                   0 = Selects the special trigger from CCP5

bit 6-4   **Unimplemented:** Read as '0'

bit 3-2   **PVCFG<1:0>:** Positive Voltage Reference Configuration bits
                   00 = A/D VREF+ connected to internal signal, AVDD
                   01 = A/D VREF+ connected to external pin, VREF+
                   10 = A/D VREF+ connected to internal signal, FVR BUF2
                   11 = Reserved (by default, A/D VREF+ connected to internal signal, AVDD)

bit 1-0   **NVCFG<1:0>:** Negative Voltage Reference Configuration bits
                   00 = A/D VREF- connected to internal signal, AVSS
                   01 = A/D VREF- connected to external pin, VREF-
                   10 = Reserved (by default, A/D VREF- connected to internal signal, AVSS)
                   11 = Reserved (by default, A/D VREF- connected to internal signal, AVSS)

Figure 6 illustrates the role of ADFM (A/D Format Select) in selecting whether the ADC result is right justified (ADFM = 1) or left justified (ADFM = 0). This control bit belongs to ADCON2 (Table 4). For 8-bit resolution, the 2 LSBs are dropped and hence left justification is recommended. This way the result to be processed is read from ADRESH. When 10-bit resolution is required, right justification of the result turns out to be easier in processing the information unless fractional arithmetic or fixed-point notation is used.

Bits ADCS2:ADCS0 specify the conversion time per bit T_{AD}. The conversion time T_{conv} is 11 T_{AD}. When the internal RC oscillator is used to trigger the A/D converter (ADCS<2:0> = x11), T_{AD} is guaranteed a typical value of 1.7 μs. The MCU manufacturer notes that for correct A/D conversion, T_{AD} must be at least 1 μs. Table 5 lists the conversion time per bit T_{AD} for all values of ADCS<2:0> and for different operating frequencies F_{osc}.

Figure 6. A/D result justification

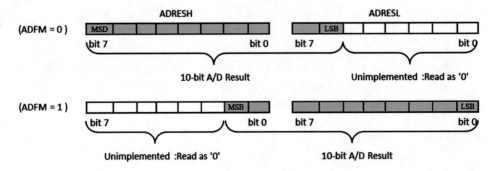

Table 4. ADCON2: A/D configuration register 2

ADCON2:   A/D CONTROL REGISTER 2

R/W-0	U-0	R/W-0	R/W-0	R/W-0	R/W-0	R/W-0	R/W-0
ADFM	–	ACQT<2:0>			ADCS<2:0>		
bit 7							bit 0

bit 7   **ADFM**: A/D Result Format Select bit
               1 = Right justified
               0 = Left justified

bit 6   Unimplemented: Read as '0'

bit 5-3   **ACQT<2:0>**: A/D Acquisition time select bits. Acquisition time is the duration that the A/D charge holding capacitor remains connected to A/D channel from the instant the $\overline{GO/DONE}$ bit is set until conversions begins.
               $000 = 0^{(1)}$
               $001 = 2\ T_{AD}$
               $010 = 4\ T_{AD}$
               $011 = 6\ T_{AD}$
               $100 = 8\ T_{AD}$
               $101 = 12\ T_{AD}$
               $110 = 16\ T_{AD}$
               $111 = 20\ T_{AD}$

bit 2-0   **ADCS<2:0>**: A/D Conversion Clock Select bits
               $000 = F_{OSC}/2$
               $001 = F_{OSC}/8$
               $010 = F_{OSC}/32$
               $011 = F_{RC}^{(1)}$ (clock derived from a dedicated internal oscillator = 600 kHz nominal)
               $100 = F_{OSC}/4$
               $101 = F_{OSC}/16$
               $110 = F_{OSC}/64$
               $111 = F_{RC}^{(1)}$ (clock derived from a dedicated internal oscillator = 600 kHz nominal)

Note 1:   When the A/D clock source is selected as F_{RC} then the start of conversion is delayed by one instruction cycle after the $\overline{GO/DONE}$ bit is set to allow the sleep instruction to be executed.

Table 5. ADC clock period vs. device operating frequencies

ADC Clock Period (T_{AD})		Device Frequency (F_{OSC})			
ADC Clock	**ADCS<2:0>**	**64 MHz**	**16 MHz**	**4 MHz**	**1 MHz**
$F_{osc}/2$	000	$31.25\ ns^{(2)}$	$125\ ns^{(2)}$	$500\ ns^{(2)}$	$2\ \mu s$
$F_{osc}/4$	100	$62.5\ ns^{(2)}$	$250\ ns^{(2)}$	$1\ \mu s$	$4\ \mu s^{(3)}$
$F_{osc}/8$	001	$400\ ns^{(2)}$	$500\ ns^{(2)}$	$2\ \mu s^{(3)}$	$8\ \mu s^{(3)}$
$F_{osc}/16$	101	$250\ ns^{(2)}$	$1\ \mu s$	$4\ \mu s^{(3)}$	$16\ \mu s^{(3)}$
$F_{osc}/32$	010	$500\ ns^{(2)}$	$2\ \mu s$	$8\ \mu s^{(3)}$	$32\ \mu s^{(3)}$
$F_{osc}/64$	110	$1\ \mu s$	$4\ \mu s^{(3)}$	$16\ \mu s^{(3)}$	$64\ \mu s^{(3)}$
F_{RC}	x11	$1 - 4\ \mu s^{(1,\,4)}$	$1 - 4\ \mu s^{(1,\,4)}$	$1 - 4\ \mu s^{(1,\,4)}$	$1 - 4\ \mu s^{(1,\,4)}$

Legend: Yellow shaded cells are outside of recommended range.
Note 1:   The F_{RC} source has a typical time of T_{AD} 1.7 μs.
Note 2:   These violate the minimum required T_{AD} time.
Note 3:   For faster conversion times, the selection of another clock source is recommended.
Note 4:   When the device frequency is greater than 1 MHz, the F_{RC} clock source is only recommended if the conversion will be performed during the *sleep* mode.

Figure 7. A/D conversion cycles; acquisition time $T_{ACQ} = 4\ T_{AD}$ (ACQT<2:0> = 010)

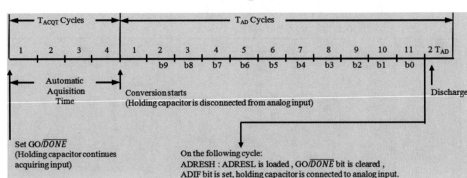

The acquisition time is programmable via ACQT<2:0> in ADCON2. It is the time the sampling switch tracks the input signal before conversion. The minimum required acquisition time has been computed to be 7.45 μs. Figure 7 shows the timing diagram of the conversion.

A/D OPERATION SUMMARY

The procedure to follow in using the A/D converter is outlined subsequently:

1. Configure the A/D module:
   a. Configure analog pins (ANSEL) and voltage references (ADCON1). The analog input channels must have their corresponding TRIS bits selected as inputs.
   b. Select A/D input channel (ADCON0).
   c. Select A/D conversion clock, acquisition time and data format (ADCON2).
   d. Turn on A/D module (ADON in ADCON0).
2. Configure A/D interrupt if desired. Set ADIE (PIE1), GIE and PEIE (INTCON).
3. Wait the required acquisition time.
4. Start conversion: set $GO\ /\ \overline{DONE}$ bit (ADCON0).
5. Wait for A/D conversion to complete, by either:
   a. Waiting for the $GO\ /\ \overline{DONE}$ bit to be cleared (interrupts disabled); or
   b. Waiting for the A/D interrupt.
6. Read A/D result registers (ADRESH/ADRESL). Clear bit ADIF if in interrupt mode.
7. Process A/D result then go back to step 3 if more samples are to be converted.

A/D TRANSFER FUNCTION

The A/D converter maps an analog voltage into an N-bit digital value. This mapping is described by a transfer function. An ideal transfer function is one in which there are no errors or non-linearity. Figure 8 describes the ideal behaviour of PIC18 A/D converters.

The transfer function shows the voltage axis subdivided into 2^n subdivisions or steps. The width of a step is 1 LSB defined as

$$1LSB = \frac{V_{REF+} - V_{REF-}}{2^n} \qquad (1)$$

where n is the A/D resolution in bits (n = 8 or 10). Throughout this chapter, we will assume that $V_{REF-} = 0V$ and $V_{REF+} = 5V = V_{REF}$. Hence Equation 1 becomes

$$1LSB = \frac{V_{REF}}{2^n} = \begin{cases} 19.5mV \; for \; n = 8 \\ 4.88mV \; for \; n = 10 \end{cases} \qquad (2)$$

The curve of Figure 8 shows the A/D transfer function for 10-bit resolution. One can easily see that if a voltage falls between -1/2 LSB and +1/2 LSB, the assigned digital code is 0x000. For a voltage between 1/2 LSB and 3/2 LSB, the assigned digital code is 0x001. In general,

$$If \left(2i-1\right)\left(\frac{LSB}{2}\right) \leq V_{in} < \left(2i+1\right)\left(\frac{LSB}{2}\right), then \; ADRES = i \; for \; (0 \leq i < 2^n) \qquad (3)$$

where V_{in} is the input voltage applied and ADRES is the A/D result stored in ADRESH:ADRESL. The red straight line crossing the staircase of Figure 8 is the line that best fits the points on the curve. It can be used to relate ADRES to V_{in}. This characteristic equation is given by:

$$ADRES = 2^n \, / \, V_{REF} \times V_{in} \qquad (4)$$

Figure 8. Ideal A/D transfer function for PIC18 microcontrollers (10-bit resolution)

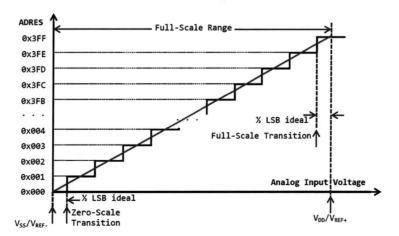

Solving for V_{in} as a function of ADRES, we get

$$V_{in} = V_{REF} / 2^n \times ADRES \qquad (5)$$

The upcoming examples illustrate how these equations can be used to design a digital voltmeter as well as a thermometer.

INSTRUMENTATION EXAMPLES

This section introduces the reader to the concept of instrumentation through a couple of examples. With the ADC, any physical quantity may be measured provided of course that there is an appropriate sensor for it.

> **Example 1** - *Digital Voltmeter:* Write a program to implement the 2-digit voltmeter of Figure 9 to measure an applied voltage between 0.0 V and 5.0 V.

Solution: In order to measure the voltage with one digit after the decimal point, we can multiply V_{in} of Equation (5) by 10 then place the decimal point on the LCD at the appropriate position. This removes the hassle of having to work with fractions. Therefore, the voltage to be displayed, for n = 8 and V_{REF} = 5 V, is given by:

$$V = 10V_{in} = 10V_{REF} / 2^n \times ADRES = 50ADRES / 256 \qquad (6)$$

which happens to be a nice equation from a coding point of view. The program is listed in Table 6. The precision can be easily updated for 2 digits after the decimal point.

Figure 9. Digital voltmeter with one digit after the decimal point

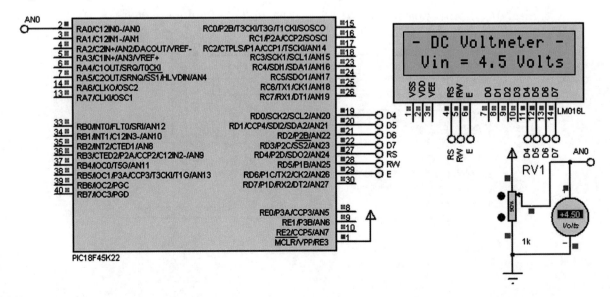

Table 6. Digital voltmeter program (precision: 1-digit after the decimal point)

```
Program that implements a digital voltmeter with 1 digit of precision after the decimal point.
1   #include    <p18cxxx.h>
2   #include    <LCD4lib.h>
3
4   void Setup(void);
5   void MeasureV(void);
6
7   void main(void) {
8       Setup();
9       while (1)
10          MeasureV();
11  }
12
13  void Setup(void) {
14      InitLCD();                                      // init LCD display
15      DispRomStr(Ln1Ch0, (ROM *) "- DC Voltmeter -"); // display line 1
16      DispRomStr(Ln2Ch0, (ROM *) " Vin = _._ Volts"); // display line 2
17
18      ADCON0bits.ADON = 1;        // turn on A/D, AN0: default channel
19      ADCON2 = 0b00001001;        // left justify, Tconv = 22 us, Tacq = 4 us
20  }
21
22  void MeasureV(void) {
23      unsigned char Result;
24      char Digits[3];
25
26      ADCON0bits.GO = 1;                              // start A/D conversion
27      while (ADCON0bits.NOT_DONE);                    // wait until EOC
28      Result = ((unsigned) 50 * ADRESH + 128) / 256;  // 128/256 (rounding)
29      Bin2Asc(Result, Digits);                        // convert to ASCII
30      DispVarStr(&Digits[1], Ln2Ch7, 1);              // digit before DP
31      DispVarStr(&Digits[2], Ln2Ch9, 1);              // digit after DP
32  }
```

The concept of measuring DC voltage can be easily employed to measure AC voltages. In fact, the high voltage can be dropped down to a low level (say around 12 Vrms) via a step down transformer (isolated case) or a voltage divider (non-isolated case). From this point on, the voltage can be converted to DC via a bridge rectifier followed by a capacitor filter. The overall interface circuit can be designed to provide a DC voltage level between 0 and 5V for an AC input between 0 and 255 Vrms. Since the A/D reading provides a digital code proportional to the applied voltage, a value of ADRESH = 255 (8-bit mode) is equivalent to an applied AC voltage of 255 Vrms, and so forth. For further precision of the voltage measurement, one would resort to the 10-bit A/D resolution.

Example 2 – *Digital Thermostat:* In reference to Figures 10 and 11, it is desired to implement a digital thermostat using the LM35 temperature sensor which provides an output voltage of 10 mV per degree Celsius. In this example, the sensor is intended to measure a temperature range between 0 and 100 °C. This means that its output voltage will vary between 0V to 1 V. Since the ADC converter generally uses the internal references V_{DD} and V_{SS}, an amplifier with a gain of 5 is placed between the sensor and the ADC input in order to take advantage of the full-scale range of the ADC.

a. Write a program to implement the digital thermometer on the LCD. *Hint:* The relationship between the temperature and the ADC input V_{in} is given by:

$$T_C = 100 \, V_{in} \, / \, 5 = 20 \, V_{in} \qquad (7)$$

This relationship, along with the A/D equation (9.5), leads to the following equation:

$$T_C = 100 \, ADRES \, / \, 256 \qquad (8)$$

b. Add the option of displaying the temperature in Celsius or Fahrenheit. Initially, the system displays degree Celsius. When the user presses the PB, the temperature unit is toggled (Celsius to Fahrenheit and vice versa). Recall that F = 1.8C + 32. To avoid floating point computations, you need to compute 10F = 18C + 320.

c. Add a the function `Control()` that turns on the LEDs: Hi, Lo and Med in accordance with the following algorithm:

0°C ≤ T_C < 20°C,	Turn on Lo LED
20°C ≤ T_C ≤ 30°C,	Turn on Med LED
30°C < T_C ≤ 100°C,	Turn on Hi LED

Figure 10. Digital thermostat displaying T = 25 °C or 77.0 °F (20 °C ≤ T ≤ 30 °C)

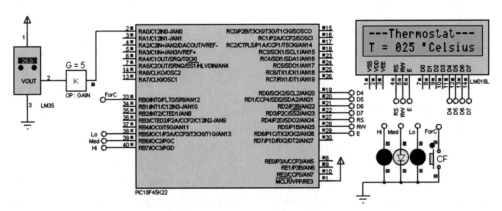

Figure 11. Digital thermostat displaying T = 96.8 °F or 36 °C (T > 30 °C)

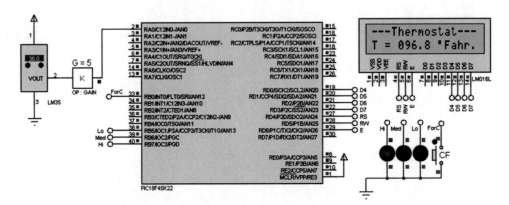

Solution: The complete program is listed in Table 7. It is self-explanatory and modular. The temperature thresholds used (20 °C and 30 °C) are converted to their equivalent A/D reading (LoTemp = 51 and HiTemp = 76) by solving for ADRES in Equation 8. This gives

$$ADRES = 256 T_C / 100 \qquad (9)$$

Table 7. Program listing of the digital thermostat

```
Program that implements a digital thermometer (Celsius/Fahrenheit) on a Liquid Crystal Display.
1    #include      <p18cxxx.h>
2    #include      <LCD4lib.h>
3
4    #define    Hi        PORTBbits.RB7       // High temperature indicator
5    #define    Med       PORTBbits.RB6       // Medium temp. indicator
6    #define    Lo        PORTBbits.RB5       // Low temperature indicator
7
8    #define    DegC      FLAGS.B0            // DegC = 1, C else F
9    #define    HiTemp    76                  // A/D reading for T = 30 C
10   #define    LoTemp    51                  // A/D reading for T = 20 C
11
12   void Setup(void);
13   void Control(void);
14   void C_or_F(void);
15   void TestPB(void);
16
17   char Digits[5];
18
19   void main(void) {
20       Setup();
21       while (1) {
22           Control();                      // indicate hi, lo or medium temperature
23           C_or_F();                       // use current A/D result
24           TestPB();                       // start A/D & test PB
25   //      Sleep();                        // awakened by WDT reset (if enabled)
26       }
27   }
28
29   void Setup(void) {
30       InitLCD();                          // init LCD display
31       DispRomStr(Ln1Ch0, (ROM *) "---Thermostat---"); // display top line
32       DispRomStr(Ln2Ch0, (ROM *) "T =        Celsius"); // initially in C
33       DegC = 1;                           // display Celsius initially
34
35       ADCON0bits.ADON = 1;                // turn on A/D, AN0: default channel
36       ADCON2 = 0b00001001;                // left justify, Tconv = 22 us, Tacq = 4 us
37
38       ANSELB = 0x00; TRISB &= 0x1F;// RB7..RB5 are output pins
39       INTCON2bits.INTEDG0 = 0;            // RB0 reacts to a falling edge
40       INTCON2bits.RBPU = 0;               // use internal pull-up resistor
41   }
42
43   void Control(void) {
44       PORTB &= 0b00011111;                // turn off Hi, Med & Lo
45       if (ADRESH > HiTemp)
46           Hi = 1;                         // T > HiTemp, turn on high LED
47       else if (ADRESH >= LoTemp)
48           Med = 1;                        // LoTemp <= T <= HiTemp, turn on med. LED
49       else
50           Lo = 1;                         // else T < LoTemp, turn on low LED
51   }
52
53   void C_or_F(void) {
54       unsigned char Celsius;
55       unsigned int Fahrenheit;
56       char Degree = 0xDF;         // ASCII character of degree symbol
57
58       Celsius = ((unsigned) 100 * ADRESH + 128) / 256; // ( plus rounding)
59       if (DegC) {
60           Bin2Asc(Celsius, Digits);                // convert voltage to BCD
61           if (Digits[0] == '0')                    // compare against ASCII of 0
62               Digits[0] = '+';                     // display '+' instead of '0'
63           DispVarStr(Digits, Ln2Ch4, 3);
64           DispVarStr(&Degree, Ln2Ch8, 1);          // display degree symbol
65       } else {
66           Fahrenheit = ((unsigned) 18 * Celsius + 320); // F = (1.8C+32)*10
67           Bin2AscE(Fahrenheit, Digits);            // Digits+0 is ignored
68           if (Digits[1] == '0')                    // compare against ASCII of 0
69               Digits[1] = '+';                     // display '+' instead of '0'
70           DispVarStr(&Digits[1], Ln2Ch4, 3);       // digits before DP
71           DispVarStr(&Digits[4], Ln2Ch8, 1);       // digits after DP
72           DispVarStr(&Degree, Ln2Ch10, 1);         // display degree symbol
73       }
74   }
75
76   void TestPB(void) {
77       ADCON0bits.GO = 1;                       // conversion for next iteration
78       if (INTCONbits.INT0IF) {
79           INTCONbits.INT0IF = 0;
80           DegC = ~DegC;                        // toggle indicator
81           if (DegC)
82               DispRomStr(Ln2Ch0, (ROM *) "T =        Celsius");
83           else
84               DispRomStr(Ln2Ch0, (ROM *) "T =    .   Fahr.");
85       }
86   }
```

Figure 12. LM35 (10 mV/°C) used to measure a temperature range between 0 and 100 °C

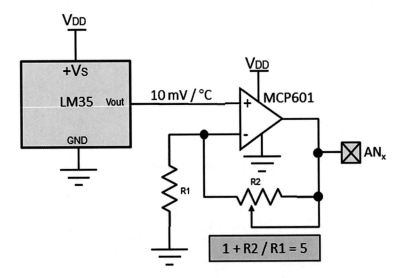

This program may be operated in the *sleep* mode and can be periodically interrupted via the watchdog timer every 64 ms or so. This insures the device consumes minimum power.

Figure 12 shows the actual amplifier circuit with a gain of 5. The MCP601 by Microchip is an operational amplifier that can be powered up with a single supply of +5V. The potentiometer is used to calibrate the temperature. It can be shown that the error on the measurement is ± 0.2 °C for n = 8 and ± 0.05 °C for n = 10.

CONCLUSION

The A/D converter is such a crucial device in microcontroller systems. Its applications span the areas of digital signal processing, digital communication, instrumentation and digital control. Hence a good understanding of its functionality and constraints is indispensable.

Chapter 10
Timers and Associated Hardware

INTRODUCTION

This chapter discusses timers 1 through 6. Timers 1, 3 and 5 are 16-bit timers and are very much alike. They are used in conjunction with the CCP (Capture/Compare/PWM) modules. The capture unit is employed to measure pulse durations or clock periods. The compare unit is used to generate periodic signals or pulses. Timers 2, 4 and 6, are 8-bit timers used essentially to generate PWM (Pulse Width Modulation) signals. These signals are important in speed control of motors, dimmers, wireless communications and frequency synthesizers.

TIMER1/3/5

Like Timer0, TimerX[1] is designed to generate periodic interrupts and time delays without burdening the CPU. Figure 1 shows that TimerX is a 16-bit counter that may be clocked internally or externally as specified by TMRxCS<1:0> (*TimerX Clock Select* bits). When triggered by an external clock, the processor can be operated in the *sleep* mode. There are two options for the external clock:

- The clock is generated externally via a crystal oscillator or an RC oscillator (e.g., 555 timer chip in astable mode). In this case, the clock signal is fed to the TxCKI pin. Note that T1CKI = RC0, T3CKI = RB5 and T5CKI = RC2.
- The internal oscillator circuit is completed by placing a low frequency crystal (32.768 KHz) between RC0/SOSCO (*Secondary Oscillator Output*) and RC1/SOSCI (*Secondary Oscillator Input*). In order to turn on this low power oscillator circuit, TxSOSCEN (*Secondary Oscillator Control* bit) in TxCON (*TimerX Control* register) must be set. Besides this, TMRxCS<1:0> (also in TxCON) must be loaded with 10_2 as illustrated in Table 1.

DOI: 10.4018/978-1-68318-000-5.ch010

Figure 1. Timer1/3/5 block diagram

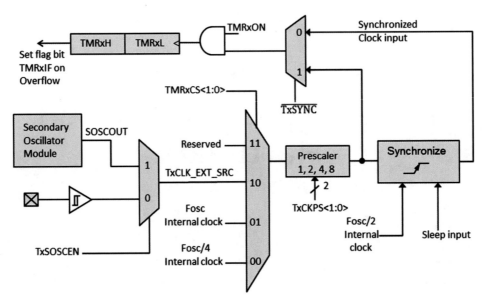

Table 1. Clock source selection

TMRxCS1	TMRxCS0	TxSOSEN	Clock Source
0	1	x	System Clock (F_{OSC})
0	0	x	Instruction Clock ($F_{OSC}/4$)
1	0	0	External Clocking on TxCKI Pin
1	0	1	Osc. Circuit On SOSCI/SOSCO Pins

Figure 1 also shows the prescaler (frequency divider) with 4 options: divide by 1, 2, 4 and 8. It is controlled by TxCKPS<1:0> in TxCON. The external clock may be fed through a synchronizer $\left(\overline{TxSYNC} = 0\right)$ circuit or may simply bypass this block $\left(\overline{TxSYNC} = 1\right)$. When operating in the sleep mode, the synchronizer must be bypassed. TimerX can be cleared by a special event trigger from the CCP modules.

The figure also shows that TMRxON is used as a clock enable pin. The default value of this flag is logic '0'. This means that TimerX is disabled upon reset. When the counter rolls over from 0xFFFF to 0x0000, TMRxIF is set and an interrupt will take place if TMRxIE, GIE and PEIE are all set.

Figure 2 illustrates how TimerX can be read from or written to in one shot. In order to write a 16-bit value to the counter, the user should first write the most significant byte to TMRxH. This value is not latched into TimerX high byte until the user writes to TMRxL. This latching scheme is important in providing the capability of writing a 16-bit value in one shot. By the same token, when TMRxL is read, the upper byte of the counter is transferred to TMRxH and hence a 16-bit count is read in one shot. Table 2 shows the main control register TxCON used to program TimerX. Note that TxRD16 gives the user the option of writing to TimerX in one 16-bit operation or in two 8-bit operations.

Figure 2. Schematic showing how Timer1/3/5 can be read from or written to in one shot

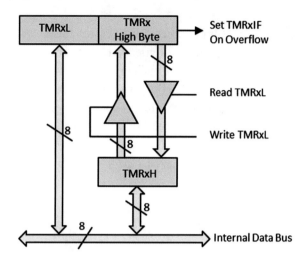

Table 2. TxCON: Timer1/2/3 control register

TxCON:	TIMER1/3/5 CONTROL REGISTER (x = 1, 3, 5)						
R/W-0/u	R/W-0/u	R/W-0/u	R/W-0/u	R/W-0/u	R/W-0/u	R/W-0/0	R/W-0/u
TMRxCS<1:0>		TxCKPS<1:0>		TxSOSCEN	$\overline{\text{TxSYNC}}$	TxRD16	TMRxON
bit 7							bit 0

R = Readable bit   W = Writable bit   U = Unimplemented bit, read as '0'
u = Bit is unchanged   x = Bit is unknown

bit 7-6   **TMRxCS<1:0>:** Timer1/3/5 Clock Source Select bits
            11 =Reserved. Do not use.
            10 =Timer1/3/5 clock source is pin or oscillator:
            <u>If TxSOSCEN = 0:</u>
            External clock from TxCKI pin (on the rising edge)
            <u>If TxSOSCEN = 1:</u>
            Crystal oscillator on SOSCI/SOSCO pins
            01 =Timer1/3/5 clock source is system clock (FOSC)
            00 =Timer1/3/5 clock source is instruction clock (FOSC/4)

bit 5-4   **TxCKPS<1:0>:** Timer1/3/5 Input Clock Prescale Select bits
            11 = 1:8 Prescale value
            10 = 1:4 Prescale value
            01 = 1:2 Prescale value
            00 = 1:1 Prescale value

bit 3   **TxSOSCEN:** Secondary Oscillator Enable Control bit
            1 = Dedicated Secondary oscillator circuit enabled
            0 = Dedicated Secondary oscillator circuit disabled

bit 2 $\overline{\text{TxSYNC}}$**:** Timer1/3/5 External Clock Input Synchronization Control bit
            <u>TMRxCS<1:0> = 1X</u>
            1 = Do not synchronize external clock input
            0 = Synchronize external clock input with system clock (FOSC)
            <u>TMRxCS<1:0> = 0X</u>
            This bit is ignored. Timer1/3/5 uses the internal clock when TMRxCS<1:0> = 1X.

bit 1   **TxRD16:** 16-Bit Read/Write Mode Enable bit
            1 = Enables register read/write of Timer1/3/5 in one 16-bit operation
            0 = Enables register read/write of Timer1/3/5 in two 8-bit operation

bit 0   **TMRxON:** Timer1/3/5 On bit
            1 = Enables Timer1/3/5
            0 = Stops Timer1/3/5. Clears Timer1/3/5 Gate flip-flop

TIMER2/4/6

TimerX[2], illustrated in Figure 3, is an 8-bit counter driven by the internal clock $F_{osc}/4$. The clock signal is passed through a prescaler with 3 selections: divide by 1, 4, or 16. The counter is compared against the 8-bit period register PRx on each clock cycle. When TimerX reaches the value stored in PRx, the comparator detects this equality and resets the counter on the next clock cycle. The postscaler determines how often TMRxIF is set. That is to say, if the postscaler's selection is 1:n (n = 1, 2, 3, ..., 16), TMRxIF is set every n true compares. When TMRxIF is set, an interrupt occurs if TMRxIE, GIE and PEIE are all set.

In order to clear TimerX after a time duration of *Period* has elapsed, we must solve for PRx in the following equation:

$$Period = \left(PRx + 1\right) \times 4T_{OSC} \times \left(Timer \times Prescale\,Value\right) \tag{1}$$

This implies that

$$PRx = \frac{Period}{4T_{OSC} \times \left(Timer \times Prescale\,Value\right)} - 1 \tag{2}$$

Table 3 explains the control register TxCON pertaining to TimerX.

Figure 3. Timer2/4/6 block diagram

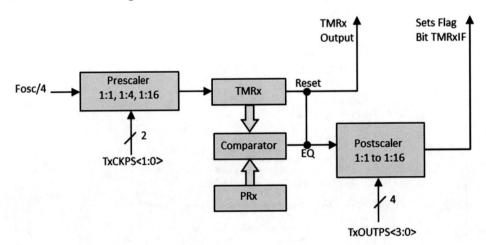

Table 3. TxCON: TimerX control register

TxCON: **TIMER2/4/6 CONTROL REGISTER (x = 2, 4, 6)**

U-0	R/W-0	R/W-0	R/W-0	R/W-0	R/W-0	R/W-0	R/W-0
–	TxOUTPS<3:0>				TMRxON	TxCKPS<1:0>	

bit 7   bit 0

R = Readable bit   W = Writable bit   U = Unimplemented bit, read as '0'

bit 7   **Unimplemented**: Read as '0'

bit 6-3   **TxOUTPS<3:0>**: TimerX Output Postscale Select bits
               0000 = 1:1   Postscale
               0001 = 1:2   Postscale
               ...
               1111 = 1:16 Postscale

bit 2   **TMRxON**: TimerX On bit
               1 = TimerX is on
               0 = TimerX is off

bit 1-   **TxCKPS<1:0>**: TimerX Clock Prescale Select bits
               00 = Prescaler is 1
               01 = Prescaler is 4
               10 = Prescaler is 16

Table 4. Program listing of Example 1

```
Program that generates a 2/10 KHz square wave on RC2 using TMR2
 1  #include      <p18cxxx.h>
 2  #define       Cycles          250-1                 // use (50 - 1) for 10 Khz
 3
 4  void Setup(void);
 5
 6  void main(void) {
 7      Setup();                                        // system initialization
 8      while (1);                                      // wait for interrupt
 9  }
10
11  #pragma code ISR = 0x0008
12  #pragma interrupt ISR
13
14  void ISR(void) {
15      PIR1bits.TMR2IF = 0;                            // acknowledge interrupt
16      PORTCbits.RC2 = !PORTCbits.RC2;                 // TMR2 cleared upon compare
17  }
18
19  void Setup(void) {
20      ANSELCbits.ANSC2 = TRISCbits.TRISC2 = 0;   // RC2: output pin
21      PR2 = Cycles;                              // PR2 = # of cycles
22      T2CONbits.TMR2ON = 1;                      // 1:1 prescaler/postscaler
23      PIE1bits.TMR2IE = 1;                       // enable interrupt
24      INTCONbits.PEIE = 1;
25      INTCONbits.GIE = 1;
26  }
```

Example 1: In reference to Figure 4, write a program to generate a 2 KHz square wave on **RC2** using **Timer2**. What is the new value of **PR2** for a 10 KHz square wave? Display the waveform on an oscilloscope or use a frequency counter to measure the frequency. Assume F_{osc} = 4 MHz.

Solution: T = 1/f = 500 μs. Hence T/2 = 250 μs is the interrupt period used to toggle RB2. Using *Period = 250 μs* and a prescale value of 1:1 in Equation 2, we get PR2 = 249_{10}. The program is listed in Table 4. The oscilloscope of Figure 4 displays the signal. Note that 5 divisions give a period of 500 μs (f = 2 KHz) for a time base of 100 μs/division.

PULSE WIDTH MODULATION (PWM)

The PWM hardware, shown in Figure 5, uses TimerX[3] to generate a TTL signal having a specified frequency and duty cycle. The generated signal is output on one of the CCPy[4] pins. Therefore the relevant TRIS bit must be cleared to make CCPy an output pin. In order to use CCPy in PWM mode, control bits CCPyM<3:0> in CCPyCON must be 11xx. Note that clearing CCPyCON register will force the CCPy output to the default low level.

Figure 4. Hardware setup used to display a signal's frequency and shape

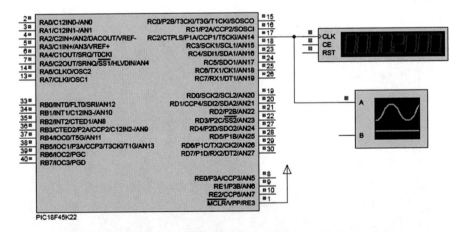

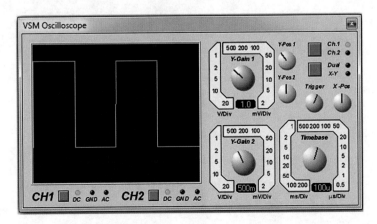

Figure 5. PWM block diagram. 'X' or 'x' = 2, 4, 6. 'y' = 1, 2, 3, 4, 5, 6

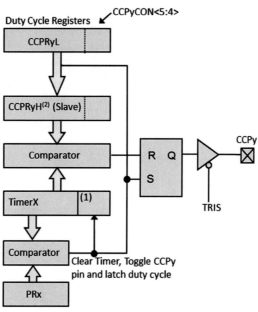

Note 1: The 8-bit timer TimerX register is concatenated with the 2-bit internal system clock (F_{OSC}), or 2 bits of the prescaler, to create the 10-bit time base.

2: In PWM mode, CCPRyH is a read-only register.

The 8-bit timer is concatenated with 2 bits of the prescaler to create a 10-bit time-base. Assuming a prescale value of 1:1, the resulting 10-bit counter runs at a rate of F_{osc} whereas the 8-bit counter TimerX runs at a rate of $F_{osc}/4$. The hardware works as follows:

- When TimerX reaches the value in PRx, the bottom comparator fires a pulse that sets the S-R latch (exception: if PWM duty cycle = 0%, CCPy will not be set) and clears TimerX. This indicates the start of a period (TimerX = PRx in Figure 6). Simultaneously, the 10-bit duty cycle in CCPRyL:CCPyCON<5:4> is loaded into the 10-bit slave register.
- When the upper comparator detects a match between the timer and the slave register, the S-R latch is reset and the pulse is ended. If the PWM duty cycle is longer than the PWM period, CCPy will not be cleared (100% duty cycle).

Noting that the frequency of the PWM signal is the inverse of the period and the pulse width PW is the time the output stays high, the values to be stored in PRx and CCPRyL:CCPyCON<5:4> are obtained through the following equations:

$$Period = \left(PRx + 1\right) \times 4T_{OSC} \times \left(Timer \times Prescale\,Value\right) \qquad (3)$$

$$PW = \left(CCPRyL : CCPyCON\left\langle 5:4\right\rangle\right) \times T_{OSC} \times \left(Timer \times Prescale\,Value\right) \qquad (4)$$

Figure 6. PWM output

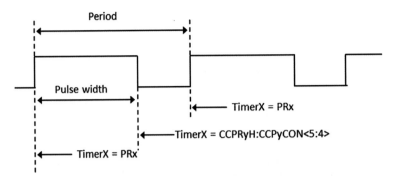

Solving for PRx and [CCPRyL:CCPyCON<5:4>], we get the following expressions:

$$PRx = \frac{Period}{4T_{osc} \times \left(Timer \times Prescale\,Value\right)} - 1 \tag{5}$$

$$CCPRyL : CCPyCON\left\langle 5:4\right\rangle = \frac{PW}{T_{osc} \times \left(Timer \times Prescale\,Value\right)} = \beta \tag{6}$$

β is the numerical result obtained via Equation 6. CCPRyL and CCPyCON<5:4> are the quotient and remainder of the integer division of β by 4. In other words,

$$CCPRyL = \beta\,\text{div}\,4\;\text{and}\;CCPyCON\left\langle 5:4\right\rangle = \beta\,\text{mod}\,4 \tag{7}$$

where *div* and *mod* provide the quotient and remainder of the integer division of β by 4.

Here are the steps needed to configure the CCPy module for PWM operation:

1. Set the PWM period by writing the appropriate value to the PRx register.
2. Set the PWM pulse width by writing to CCPRyL register and CCPyCON<5:4> (or DCyB<1:0>) bits (Table 5).
3. Make the CCPy pin an output by clearing the relevant TRIS pin.
4. Select the timer to use (2, 4, or 6) by configuring registers CCPTMRS0/1 (*PWM Timer Selection Control Register 0/1*). Refer to Tables 6 and 7.
5. Enable TimerX and set its prescale value in TxCON.
6. Configure CCPy module for PWM operation (CCPyCON<3:0> = 11xx).

For instance, if CCP1/RC2 (y = 1) is to be the PWM output employing Timer2 (x = 2), then

●   The PWM period is specified in PR2 in accordance with Equation 5.

Table 5. Capture/Compare/PWM control register

CCPyCON: STANDARD CCPy CONTROL REGISTER (y = 1, 2, 3, 4, 5)

U-0	U-0	R/W-0	R/W-0	R/W-0	R/W-0	R/W-0	R/W-0
-	-	DCyB<1:0>		CCPyM<3:0>			

bit 7   bit 0

bit 7-6	**Unused in standard mode**
bit 5-4	**DCyB<1:0>:** PWM Duty Cycle Least Significant bits
	<u>Capture mode:</u> Unused
	<u>Compare mode:</u> Unused
	<u>PWM mode:</u> These bits are the two LSBs of the PWM duty cycle. The eight MSBs are found in CCPRyL.
bit 3-0	**CCPyM<3:0>:** CCPy Mode Select bits
	0000 = Capture/Compare/PWM off (resets the module)
	0001 = Reserved
	0010 = Compare mode: toggle output on match
	0011 = Reserved
	0100 = Capture mode: every falling edge
	0101 = Capture mode: every rising edge
	0110 = Capture mode: every 4th rising edge
	0111 = Capture mode: every 16th rising edge
	1000 = Compare mode: set output on compare match (CCPy pin is set, CCPyIF is set)
	1001 = Compare mode: clear output on compare match (CCPy pin is cleared, CCPyIF is set)
	1010 = Compare mode: generate software interrupt on compare match (CCPy pin is unaffected, CCPyIF is set)
	1011 = Compare mode: Special Event Trigger (CCPy pin is unaffected, CCPyIF is set) TimerX (selected by CyTSEL bits) is reset, ADON is set, starting A/D conversion if A/D module is enabled[1]
	11xx = PWM mode
Note 1:	This feature is available on CCP5 only.

Table 6. PWM timer selection control register 0

CCPTMRS0:   PWM TIMER SELECTION CONTROL REGISTER 0

R/W-0	R/W-0	U-0	R/W-0	R/W-0	U-0	R/W-0	R/W-0
C3TSEL<1:0>		–	C2TSEL<1:0>		–	C1TSEL<1:0>	

bit 7   bit 0

R = Readable bit	W = Writable bit	U = Unimplemented bit, read as '0'
-n = Value at POR	'1' = Bit is set	'0' = Bit is cleared x = Bit is unknown

bit 7-6	**C3TSEL<1:0>:** CCP3 Timer Selection bits
	00 = CCP3 – Capture/Compare modes use Timer1, PWM modes use Timer2
	01 = CCP3 – Capture/Compare modes use Timer3, PWM modes use Timer4
	10 = CCP3 – Capture/Compare modes use Timer5, PWM modes use Timer6
	11 = Reserved
bit 5	**Unused**
bit 4-3	**C2TSEL<1:0>:** CCP2 Timer Selection bits
	00 = CCP2 – Capture/Compare modes use Timer1, PWM modes use Timer2
	01 = CCP2 – Capture/Compare modes use Timer3, PWM modes use Timer4
	10 = CCP2 – Capture/Compare modes use Timer5, PWM modes use Timer6
	11 = Reserved
bit 2	**Unused**
bit 1-0	**C1TSEL<1:0>:** CCP1 Timer Selection bits
	00 = CCP1 – Capture/Compare modes use Timer1, PWM modes use Timer2
	01 = CCP1 – Capture/Compare modes use Timer3, PWM modes use Timer4
	10 = CCP1 – Capture/Compare modes use Timer5, PWM modes use Timer6
	11 = Reserved

Table 7. PWM timer selection control register 1

CCPTMRS1:   PWM TIMER SELECTION CONTROL REGISTER 1

U-0	U-0	U-0	U-0	R/W-0	R/W-0	R/W-0	R/W-0
–	–	–	–	C5TSEL<1:0>		C4TSEL<1:0>	

bit 7   bit 0

R = Readable bit	W = Writable bit	U = Unimplemented bit, read as '0'	
-n = Value at POR	'1' = Bit is set	'0' = Bit is cleared	x = Bit is unknown

bit 7-4   **Unimplemented:** Read as '0'

bit 3-2   **C5TSEL<1:0>:** CCP5 Timer Selection bits
          00 = CCP5 – Capture/Compare modes use Timer1, PWM modes use Timer2
          01 = CCP5 – Capture/Compare modes use Timer3, PWM modes use Timer4
          10 = CCP5 – Capture/Compare modes use Timer5, PWM modes use Timer6
          11 = Reserved

bit 1-0   **C4TSEL<1:0>:** CCP4 Timer Selection bits
          00 = CCP4 – Capture/Compare modes use Timer1, PWM modes use Timer2
          01 = CCP4 – Capture/Compare modes use Timer3, PWM modes use Timer4
          10 = CCP4 – Capture/Compare modes use Timer5, PWM modes use Timer6
          11 = Reserved

- The pulse width is specified in CCPR1L:CCP1CON<5:4> based upon Equation 6.
- TRISC<2> must be cleared.
- C1TSEL<1:0> in register CCPTMRS0 must be cleared (default value) to select Timer2 for CCP1.
- The suitable prescale value for Timer2 is selected in T2CON. This register also allows Timer2 to be turned on (TMR2ON = 1).
- CCP1CON<3:0> should be loaded with 11xx.

All the registers involved in programming the PWM outputs CCPy are listed in Table 8.

Last but not least, we define the *maximum PWM resolution* (in bits) for a given PWM frequency as:

$$PWM\ Resolution = \frac{\log_{10}\left(F_{OSC}\ /\ F_{PWM}\right)}{\log_{10}\left(2\right)}\,bits \qquad (8)$$

In order to interpret the significance of Equation 8, one can observe that $F_{OSC}\ /\ F_{PWM} = T_{PWM}\ /\ T_{OSC} = n$ where n is the number of cycles of T_{OSC} required to elapse a period of T_{PWM}. Hence, the number of bits required to count n cycles at a rate of F_{OSC} is

$$\log_2\left(n\right) = \log_{10}\left(n\right)/\log_{10}\left(2\right) = \log_{10}\left(F_{OSC}\ /\ F_{PWM}\right)/\log_{10}\left(2\right)\,bits$$

This implies that the resolution determines the number of available duty cycles for a given period. For example, a 10-bit resolution will result in 1024 discrete duty cycles, whereas an 8-bit resolution will result in 256 duty cycles. As a result, the larger the value of $\log_2\left(n\right)$ the higher the PWM resolution. High resolution PWM means that if the duty cycle register is incremented by a count of 1, the duty

Table 8. Registers needed to program the PWM outputs CCPy; TRIS bits are excluded.

SUMMARY OF REGISTERS ASSOCIATED WITH CCPy (y = 1, 2, ..., 5) and TimerX (X = 2, 4, 6)

Name	Bit 7	Bit 6	Bit 6	Bit 4	Bit 3	Bit 2	Bit 1	Bit 0
CCP1CON	P1M<1:0>		DC1B<1:0>		CCP1M<3:0>			
CCP2CON	P2M<1:0>		DC2B<1:0>		CCP2M<3:0>			
CCP3CON	P3M<1:0>		DC3B<1:0>		CCP3M<3:0>			
CCP4CON	-	-	DC4B<1:0>		CCP4M<3:0>			
CCP5CON	-	-	DC5B<1:0>		CCP5M<3:0>			
CCPTMRS0	C3TSEL<1:0>		-	C2TSEL<1:0>		-	C1TSEL<1:0>	
CCPTMRS1	-	-	-	-	C5TSEL<1:0>		C4TSEL<1:0>	
INTCON	GIE	PEIE	TMR0IE	INT0IE	RBIE	TMR0IF	INT0IF	RBIF
PIR1	-	ADIF	RCIF	TXIF	SSPIF	CCP1IF	TMR2IF	TMR1IF
PIR2	OSCFIF	C1IF	C2IF	EEIF	BCL1IF	HLVDIF	TMR3IF	CCP2IF
PIR4	-	-	-	-	-	CCP5IF	CCP4IF	CCP3IF
PIE1	-	ADIE	RCIE	TXIE	SSP1IE	CCP1IE	TMR2IE	TMR1IE
PIE2	OSCFIE	C1IE	C2IE	EEIE	BCL1IE	HLVDIE	TMR3IE	CCP2IE
PIE4	-	-	-	-	-	CCP5IE	CCP4IE	CCP3IE
TMRx	TimerX Register (X or x = 2, 4, 6)							
PRx	TimerX Period Register (X or x = 2, 4, 6)							
TxCON	-	TxOUTPS<3:0>				TMRxON	TxCKPS<1:0>	
CCPRyL	CCPy Register Low Byte (y = 1, 2, ..., 5)							
CCPRyH	CCPy Register High Byte (y = 1, 2, ..., 5)							

Legend: − = unimplemented, read as '0'. Yellow shaded cells are not used by the PWM modules.

cycle time is incremented by a very small amount. When controlling the speed of a DC motor via a PWM signal, the tiny incremental duty cycle will lead to a slight increase in the motor's speed. This is important in control systems requiring precision in the desired motor speed.

> **Example 2:** Write a program to generate a 1 KHz square wave on **CCP2/RC1** (50 % duty cycle). Use a prescale value of 4. Would a prescale value of 1:1 work? Explain.

Solution: Substituting *Period = 1/f = 1000 µs* and *PW = 0.5 * (1000 µs) = 500 µs* in Equations 5 and 6, we get:

$$PR2 = 249_{10} \text{ and } CCPR2L:CCP2CON<5:4> = 500_{10},$$

which implies CCPR2L = (500 div 4) = 125_{10} and CCP2CON<5:4> = (500 mod 4) = 00_2. The program is listed in Table 9. A 1:1 prescale value will not work simply because the values obtained for PR2 and CCPR2L would not fit into 8-bit registers.

> **Example 3:** Write a program to generate a 250 Hz PWM signal with a duty cycle of 80%, 60% and 20% on **CCP1/RC2**. The prescale value used is 16.

Solution: Table 10 lists the complete program with the required modifications for different duty cycles. Figures 7 and 8 display the PWM signal on the simulated oscilloscope. A meticulous look at the division show that the required duty cycles are met indeed.

Table 9. Program to generate a 1 KHz PWM signal with 50% duty cycle

```
Program that uses CCP2 to generate a 1 KHz square wave with 50 % duty cycle
1    #include     <p18cxxx.h>        // CCP2: f = 1 KHz, DC = 50%, Fcy = 1 MHz
2
3    #define      Period      250-1  // T = (PR2+1).4.Tosc.4
4    #define      DC_high     125    // DC = CCPR2L:CCP2CON<5:4>.Tosc.4
5
6    void main(void)
7    {
8        TRISCbits.TRISC1 = 0;       // RC1: output pin
9        PR2 = Period;               // load period
10       CCPR2L = DC_high;           // load duty cycle
11       T2CONbits.TMR2ON = 1;       // enable Timer2
12       T2CONbits.T2CKPS0 = 1;      // clock it with (Fosc/4) / 4
13       CCP2CON = 0x0C;             // PWM mode
14       while (1);                  // PWM signal will run forever
15   }
```

OUTPUT COMPARE

Figure 9 illustrates the compare mode configuration of CCPy (y = 1, 2, …, 5). The 16-bit register CCPRyH:CCPRyL is constantly compared against TimerX (X = 1, 3, 5) (as specified by CyTSEL<1:0> in CCPTMRS0/1). When a match occurs, the compare pin CCPy is affected in accordance with the options of Table 11. The action on pin CCPy is programmed via control bits CCPyM<3:0> in CCPyCON. Upon a true compare, the interrupt flag bit CCPyIF is set and an interrupt occurs if CCPyIE, GIE and PEIE are asserted.

The user must configure the CCPy pin as an output by clearing the appropriate TRIS bit. Note that clearing the CCPyCON register will force the CCPy pin to start with a low level. CCPyCON is cleared upon reset.

In order to use the compare feature, TimerX (X = 1, 3, 5) must be running in synchronous mode when an external clock is used. In the *special event trigger* mode, an internal hardware trigger is generated. This may be used to create an action. The special trigger output of CCPy resets TimerX. Additionally, the CCPy special event trigger will start an A/D conversion if the A/D module is turned on.

Table 10. Code to generate a 250 Hz PWM signal with 80%, 60% and 20% duty cycle

```
Program to generate a 250 Hz PWM signal with 80%, 60% and 20% duty cycle on CCP1/RC2
1    #include     <p18cxxx.h>           // CCP1: f = 250 Hz, DC = 80%
2
3    #define      Period     250-1     // T = (PR2+1).4.Tosc.16
4    #define      DC_high    200       // DC = CCPR1L:CCP1CON<5:4>.Tosc.16
5                                       // DC = 200/125/50 for 80%/50%/20% DC
6    void main(void) {
7        ANSELCbits.ANSC2 = TRISCbits.TRISC2 = 0;  // RC2: output pin
8        PR2 = Period;                             // load period
9        CCPR1L = DC_high;                         // load duty cycle
10       T2CONbits.TMR2ON = 1;                     // enable Timer2
11       T2CONbits.T2CKPS1 = 1;                    // clock it with (Fosc/4) / 16
12       CCP1CON = 0x0C;                           // PWM mode
13       while (1);                                // PWM signal will run forever
14   }
```

Figure 7. f = 250 Hz, duty cycle = 80%

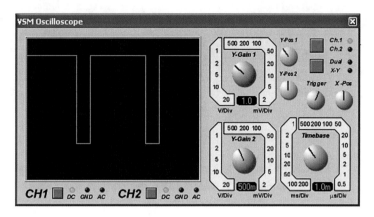

Figure 8. f = 250 Hz, duty cycle = 20%

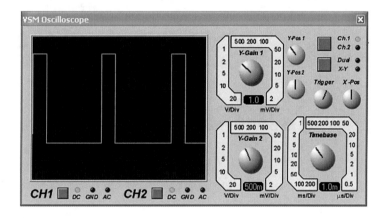

Figure 9. Compare mode block diagram

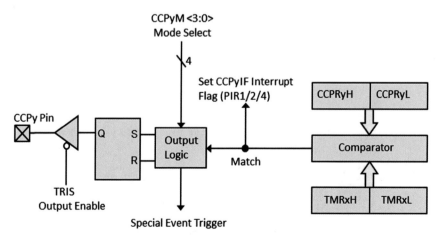

Note 1: Special Event Trigger function on CCPy resets TimerX
(TMRxL:TMRxH = 0x0000). TMRxIF is not set.

2: CCP5 has an additional function. It will set $GO/\overline{DONE}$
bit to start an ADC conversion if ADON = 1.

Table 11. Options of pin CCPy upon true compare. CCPyIF is set for all these options

CCPyM<3:0>	CCPy (x = 1, 2, ..., 5) Pin Status
0010	Toggle output on match
1000	Initialize CCP pin Low. On compare match, force **CCPy** pin High
1001	Initialize CCP pin High. On compare match, force **CCPy** pin Low
1010	Generate software interrupt on compare match. **CCPy** pin is unaffected
1011	On compare match, trigger special event without affecting **CCPy** pin

CyTSEL<1:0> in CCPTMRS0/1 are used to select which timer is associated with which compare unit. These flags are reproduced in Table 12. The control registers pertaining to the CCPy modules are listed in Table 13.

> **Example 4:** The program listed in Table 14 uses the output compare feature (special event) to generate a 50 Hz square wave on **RC2/CCP1**. **Timer1** is used to trigger the compare feature.

> **Example 5:** The program listed in Table 15 uses the output compare (toggle output on match) to generate a 50 Hz square wave on **RC2/CCP1**. **Timer1** is used to trigger the compare feature.

> **Example 6:** *CCP1, Compare mode – Pulse generation:* The program of Table 16 generates a 500 μs pulse on **RC2/CCP1**. The pulse starts 50 μs after **Timer1** is enabled.

INPUT CAPTURE

Figure 10 shows the capture mode block diagram. In this mode, CCPRy (y = 1, 2, ..., 5) captures the 16-bit value of TimerX (X = 1, 3, 5) when an event occurs on CCPy pin. The event is selected by control bits CCPyM<3:0> as listed in Table 17. When a capture is made, the interrupt flag CCPyIF is set. If another capture occurs before the value in CCPRy is read, the old captured value is overwritten by the newly captured value.

Table 12. CyTSEL<1:0> in CCPTMRS0/1 that associate timers with CCP modules

CyTSEL<1:0>	CCPy (y = 1, 2, ..., 5) Pin Status
00	Capture/Compare modes use Timer1
01	Capture/Compare modes use Timer3
10	Capture/Compare modes use Timer5
11	Reserved

Table 13. Registers associated with CCPy: Capture/Compare modes

SUMMARY OF REGISTERS ASSOCIATED WITH CCPy (y = 1, 2, ..., 5) and TimerX (X = 1, 3, 5)

Name	Bit 7	Bit 6	Bit 6	Bit 4	Bit 3	Bit 2	Bit 1	Bit 0
CCP1CON	P1M<1:0>		DC1B<1:0>		CCP1M<3:0>			
CCP2CON	P2M<1:0>		DC2B<1:0>		CCP2M<3:0>			
CCP3CON	P3M<1:0>		DC3B<1:0>		CCP3M<3:0>			
CCP4CON	-	-	DC4B<1:0>		CCP4M<3:0>			
CCP5CON	-	-	DC5B<1:0>		CCP5M<3:0>			
CCPTMRS0	C3TSEL<1:0>		-	C2TSEL<1:0>		-	C1TSEL<1:0>	
CCPTMRS1	-	-	-	-	C5TSEL<1:0>		C4TSEL<1:0>	
INTCON	GIE	PEIE	TMR0IE	INT0IE	RBIE	TMR0IF	INT0IF	RBIF
PIR1	-	ADIF	RCIF	TXIF	SSPIF	CCP1IF	TMR2IF	TMR1IF
PIR2	OSCFIF	C1IF	C2IF	EEIF	BCL1IF	HLVDIF	TMR3IF	CCP2IF
PIR4	-	-	-	-	-	CCP5IF	CCP4IF	CCP3IF
PIE1	-	ADIE	RCIE	TXIE	SSP1IE	CCP1IE	TMR2IE	TMR1IE
PIE2	OSCFIE	C1IE	C2IE	EEIE	BCL1IE	HLVDIE	TMR3IE	CCP2IE
PIE4	-	-	-	-	-	CCP5IE	CCP4IE	CCP3IE
TMRx	TimerX Register (X or x = 1, 3, 5)							
TxCON	TMRxCS<1:0>		TxCKPS<1:0>		TxSOSCEN	T̄x̄S̄ȲN̄C̄	TxRD16	TMRxON
CCPRyL	CCPy Register Low Byte (y = 1, 2, …, 5)							
CCPRyH	CCPy Register High Byte (y = 1, 2, …, 5)							

Legend: – = unimplemented, read as '0'. Yellow shaded cells are not used by the Capture/Compare modules.

Table 14. 50 Hz waveform on RC2 using Timer1 with the output compare feature

```
Code that generates a 50 Hz square wave on CCP1, CCP1 resets TMR1 upon compare
1   #include    <p18cxxx.h>
2   #define     Cycles  10000                   // T/2 = 10 ms (asynch reset)
3                                               // 1000 for 500 Hz, 100 for 5 KHz
4   void Setup(void);
5
6   void main(void) {
7       Setup();                                // system initialization
8       while (1);                              // wait for interrupt
9   }
10
11  #pragma code ISR = 0x0008
12  #pragma interrupt ISR
13
14  void ISR(void) {
15      PIR1bits.CCP1IF = 0;                    // acknowledge interrupt
16      PORTCbits.RC2 = !PORTCbits.RC2;         // timer1 cleared upon compare
17  }
18
19  void Setup(void) {
20      ANSELCbits.ANSC2 = TRISCbits.TRISC2 = 0;  // RC2: digital output pin
21      CCPR1 = Cycles;                         // CCPR1 = number of cycles
22      CCP1CON = 0x0B;                         // CCP1 resets TMR1
23      T1CONbits.TMR1ON = 1;                   // enable TMR1, CLK = Fosc/4
24      PIE1bits.CCP1IE = 1;                    // enable interrupt
25      INTCONbits.PEIE = INTCONbits.GIE = 1;
26  }
```

Table 15. 50 Hz square wave using the toggle output on match feature

```
Code that generates a 50 Hz square wave on CCP1, toggle output on match
1    #include      <p18cxxx.h>
2    #define    Cycles  10000        // T/2 = 10 ms
3                                    // 1000/100 for 500Hz/5KHz
4    void Setup(void);
5
6    void main(void)
7    {
8        Setup();                    // system initialization
9        while (1);                  // wait for interrupt
10   }
11
12   #pragma code ISR = 0x0008
13   #pragma interrupt ISR
14
15   void ISR(void)
16   {
17       CCPR1 = CCPR1 + Cycles;     // anticipate new compare
18       PIR1bits.CCP1IF = 0;        // acknowledge interrupt
19   }
20
21   void Setup(void)
22   {
23       ANSELCbits.ANSC2 = 0;       // RC2: digital pin
24       TRISCbits.TRISC2 = 0;       // RC2: output pin
25       TMR1H = 0x00; TMR1L = 0x00; // start Timer1 at 0x0000
26       CCPR1 = Cycles;             // CCPR1 = number of cycles
27       CCP1CON = 0x02;             // toggle output on match
28       T1CONbits.TMR1ON = 1;       // enable TMR1, CLK = Fosc/4
29       PIE1bits.CCP1IE = 1;        // enable interrupt
30       INTCONbits.PEIE = 1;
31       INTCONbits.GIE = 1;
32   }
```

Table 16. Program to generate a 500 μs pulse on RC2/CCP1

```
Program to generate a 500 us pulse on CCP1 (hardware set/clear)
1    #include      <p18cxxx.h>
2
3    #define    Wait4Match()  {PIR1bits.CCP1IF = 0; while (!PIR1bits.CCP1IF);}
4
5    #define    Ncycles    50        // 50 cycles after TMR0 is reset
6    #define    PW         500       // pulse width of 500 microsecs
7
8    void main(void) {
9        ANSELCbits.ANSC2 = 0;       // RC2: digital pin
10       TRISCbits.TRISC2 = 0;       // RC2: output pin
11       // while (1)                // uncomment to see pulse on scope
12       {
13           TMR1H = 0x00; TMR1L = 0x00; // clear 16-bit TMR1 register
14           CCPR1 = Ncycles;        // 1st compare occurs at Ncycles
15           CCP1CON = 0x08;         // force CCP1 high on match
16           T1CONbits.TMR1ON = 1;   // enable TMR1, Fck = Fosc/4
17           Wait4Match();           // wait for 1st match to occur
18           CCP1CON = 0x09;         // clear output on 2nd match
19           CCPR1 = CCPR1 + PW;     // 2nd compare at PW + Ncycles
20           Wait4Match();           // wait for 2nd match to occur
21       }
22       Sleep();                    // halt clock to save power
23   }
```

Figure 10. Capture mode block diagram

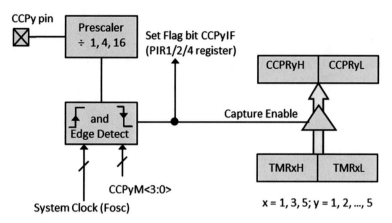

In Capture mode, the CCPy pin should be configured as an input by setting the corresponding TRIS pin. If the CCPy pin is configured as an output, a write to the port can cause a capture condition. In order to use the capture feature, TimerX must be running in synchronous mode when an external clock is used.

CyTSEL<1:0> in CCPTMRS0/1 are used to select which timer is associated with which capture unit (see Table 12). Table 13 lists the registers by the CCP modules in capture mode.

When the Capture mode is changed, a false capture interrupt may be generated. The user should keep the relevant bit CCPyIE clear to avoid false interrupts and should clear the flag bit CCPyIF, following any such change in operating mode.

> **Example 7:** *CCP1, Capture mode:* The program listed in Table 18 measures the period of a waveform in µs and displays it on the LCD. PROTEUS is used to generate a 5 KHz square wave (Figure 11). In order to measure T, the counts of **Timer1** on the first edge (edge1) and the second edge (edge2) are captured. The period is (edge2 − edge1).

CONCLUSION

There are numerous applications involving the CCP units. The PWM feature is used to specify the frequency and duty cycle of a signal. Varying the duty cycle of a PWM signal is of fundamental importance in speed control of DC motors. Varying the frequency of the PWM signal is used in speed control of AC

Table 17. Options of the capture mode; CCPyM<3:0> belong to CCPyCON.

CCPyM3:CCPyM0	Capture mode options
0100	Capture mode, every falling edge
0101	Capture mode, every rising edge
0110	Capture mode, every 4th rising edge
0111	Capture mode, every 16th rising edge

Figure 11. Hardware setup used to measure the period of a waveform

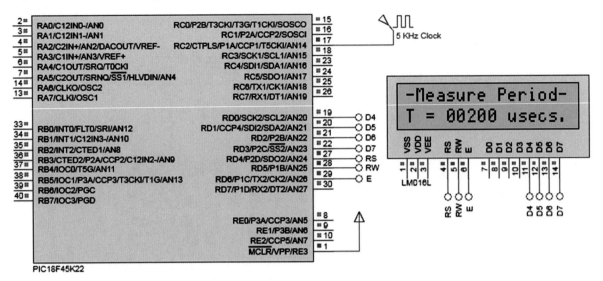

PIC18F45K22

Table 18. Program to measure the period of a waveform in μs

```
Program to measure the period of a waveform in μs via CCP1. The period is displayed on a LCD.
1   #include    <p18cxxx.h>
2   #include    <LCD4lib.h>
3
4   unsigned char Period;
5   char Digits[5];
6
7   #define     Wait4Edge()     {PIR1bits.CCP1IF = 0; while (!PIR1bits.CCP1IF);}
8
9   void Setup(void);
10  void Measure(void);
11
12  void main(void) {
13      Setup();
14      while (1)
15          Measure();
16  }
17
18  void Setup(void) {
19      InitLCD();                      // init LCD display
20      DispRomStr(Ln1Ch0, (ROM *) "-Measure Period-");
21      DispRomStr(Ln2Ch0, (ROM *) "T =        usecs.");
22      CCP1CON = 0x05;                 // capture every +ve edge
23      T1CONbits.TMR1ON = 1;           // enable TMR1, CK = Fosc/4
24  }
25
26  void Measure(void) {
27      TMR1H = 0x00;
28      TMR1L = 0x00;                   // start with timer1 = 0
29      Wait4Edge()                     // wait for edge
30      Period = CCPR1;                 // Period holds 1st edge
31      Wait4Edge()                     // wait for edge
32      Period = CCPR1L - Period;       // Period = edge2 - edge1
33      Bin2AscE(Period, Digits);       // convert to 5 ASCII digits
34      DispVarStr(Digits, Ln2Ch4, 5);  // display period
35  }
```

motors. Another typical application of variable duty cycle PWM signals is in dimmers or heaters. This allows the control of either the intensity of light or the amount of generated heat.

One may also use PWM in infrared communication systems. For instance, a PWM signal representing a sampled signal may be easily fed through an infrared LED and transmitted wirelessly. At the receiver end, the signal may be demodulated via the capture feature. In other words, the pulse width is used to drive a D/A converter thereby reconstructing the original signal. Such schemes have been used in remote controls, wireless speakers, etc.

ENDNOTES

[1]   The 'x' or 'X' variable used in this section is intended to designate Timer1, Timer3 or Timer5. For example TxCON references T1CON, T3CON, or T5CON. TMRxIF references TMR1IF, TMR3IF, or TMR5IF.

[2]   The 'x' or 'X' variable used in this section is intended to designate Timer2, Timer4 or Timer6. For example TxCON references T2CON, T4CON, or T6CON. PRx references PR2, PR4, or PR6.

[3]   The 'x' or 'X' variable used in this section is intended to designate Timer2, Timer4 or Timer6. For example TxCON references T2CON, T4CON, or T6CON. PRx references PR2, PR4, or PR6.

[4]   The 'y' variable used in this section is intended to designate CCP1, CCP2, CCP3, CCP4, or CCP5. For example CCPyCON references CCP1CON, CCP2CON, CCP3CON, CCP4CON, or CCP5CON. CyTSEL<1:0> references C1TSEL<1:0>, C2TSEL<1:0>, C3TSEL<1:0> in CCPTMRS0 or C4TSEL<1:0>, C5TSEL<1:0> in CCPTMRS1.

Chapter 11
State Machines

INTRODUCTION

State diagrams are used to implement Moore or Mealy machines having a number of inputs, outputs and states. These diagrams pictorially describe the algorithms to be realized in hardware. A state diagram consists of the following:

- The states of the machine.
- The inputs which take the machine from one state to another.
- Moore and/or Mealy outputs. Moore outputs change at the clock transition whereas Mealy outputs change immediately as a function of the inputs applied and the current state of the machine.

In brief, state diagrams summarize the behavior of a state machine with all pertaining details. Commonly, they are used to implement sequential circuits via MSI/LSI components or programmable chips such as PALs, GALs or FPGAs. This chapter emphasizes the software realization of state machines through a number of microcontroller applications.

GARAGE DOOR OPENER

A garage door opener is a motorized device that opens and closes garage doors. Most are controlled by switches on the garage wall, as well as by remote controls carried by the owner. A simple model of the whole system, illustrated in Figure 1, consists of:

1. A rolling door controlled by a DC motor. The motor is driven by an H-bridge with two control signals MotorUp and MotorDn that specify the direction: MotorUp = 1 rolls the door up and MotorDn = 1 rolls it down. If none of these signals is asserted then the motor stands still.

DOI: 10.4018/978-1-68318-000-5.ch011

2. A push-button B (Button) which serves to either start the motor when it is stopped or simply to reverse the door's motion direction when the motor is running.

3. Two limit switches that can detect whether the door is in the rolled-up position or in the rolled down position. These sensors are "ORed" together to provide one input signal C (Complete) to the controller; cause in both cases the motor must be stopped.

4. An infrared sensor whose role is to detect any obstruction (car, human, animal, etc.) in the door path. This consists of an IR transmitter which emits a beam of invisible light between the door's rails. If this beam is obstructed, a signal S (Stalled) applied to the controller is asserted. This reverses the door's direction in case it is going down.

5. Last but not least is the microcontroller that implements the state machine of the garage door opener.

The three switches emulating the actual sensors use internal pull-up resistors. Obviously, these switches provide active-low logic levels when pressed. However, since they are tied to the INTx (x = 0, 1, 2) pins, the associated flags INTxIF (x = 0, 1, 2) not only offer active-high logic levels but also they memorize the button pressing event.

The H-bridge is used to reverse the motor's direction. For instance, if MotorDn is driven high, the MOSFETs P2G and N1G conduct and hence they provide a current path to the motor via terminals 2 and 1. As a result, the door rolls down.

The state diagram of the garage door opener is shown in Figure 2. Again, the machine has three inputs: Button (B), Complete (C) and Stalled (S) along with four states:

- **State0 – Up:** The garage door is rolled all the way up. When Button is pressed, the machine goes to state "GoingDn" (or State1) at the clock transition.
- **State1 – GoingDn:** The motor is commanded to roll down the door (MotorUp = 0, MotorDn = 1). If Button is pressed again, the motor changes direction at the clock transition. This condition also occurs when the door encounters an obstacle as it rolls down (Stalled = 1). The door continues to roll down until it triggers the level switch at the bottom (Complete = 1). In this case, the machine goes to state "Down" at the clock transition. In this state, the motor is obviously stopped.

Figure 1. Hardware for the garage door opener

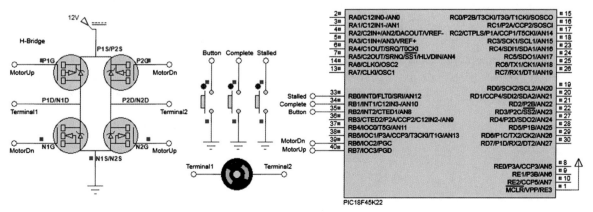

Figure 2. State diagram of garage door opener (Moore machine)

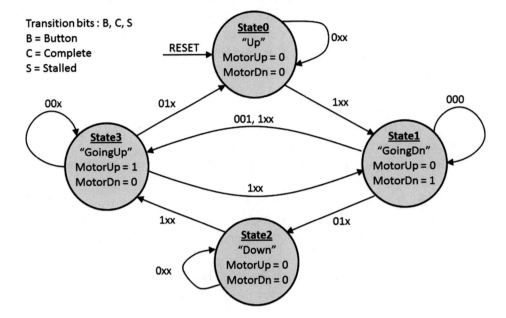

- **State2 – Dn:** The garage door is closed all the way. When Button is pressed, the machine goes to state "GoingUp" (or State3) at the clock transition.
- **State3 – GoingUp:** The motor rolls the door up (MotorUp = 1, MotorDn = 0). If Button is pressed, it changes direction at the clock transition ("GoingDn"). The door continues to go up until it triggers a level switch at the top position (Complete = 1). In this case, the machine goes to state "Up" and the motor is stopped.

Clock transitions are implemented via periodic interrupts. When the machine is in state x, the inputs are tested and the state is updated accordingly. The next state is involved at the next interrupt by analogy with the next clock transition in hardware. The software structure of a state machine is shown in Table 1.

The periodic interrupt provides the looping part or sequencing whereas the switch statement takes care of the decision-making part of the state machine.

For the garage door opener, the clock ticks are implemented via periodic interrupts of Timer0 every 250 ms. The three buttons implementing the sensors (Button, Complete and Stalled) are detected via INT2IF, INT1IF and INT0IF respectively. This means that any of these events will be latched and hence their corresponding flags must be cleared. The macro ClearFlags() clears these flags all together.

Table 2 lists the complete program. The processor cannot be operated in sleep mode since Timer0 is running. However, the idle mode may be employed for that purpose or simply the watchdog timer to provide periodic interrupts while the processor sleeps.

Table 1. State machine program skeleton

```
enum {S0, S1, S2, ...} State = S0;   // initial state = S0

// variables, definitions, etc.

void main(void)
{
    Setup();                         // system initialization
    while (1);                       // wait for interrupt
}

void Setup(void)
{
    ...                              // configure input/output ports
    ...                              // initialize system variables
    ...                              // enable timer interrupt
}

#pragma code ISR = 0x0008
#pragma interrupt ISR

void ISR(void)
{
    ...                              // acknowledge timer interrupt
    ...                              // reload timer

    switch (State) {
        case S0:    ...              // next state logic, Moore/Mealy outputs
                    break;

        case S1:    ...              // next state logic, Moore/Mealy outputs
                    break;

        case S2:    ...              // next state logic, Moore/Mealy outputs
                    break;

        ...                          // more states (if any)
    }
}
```

Table 2a. Software for garage door opener: Moore state machine

```
Software implementation of garage door opener: Moore state machine
1   #include      <p18cxxx.h>    // Moore State Machine: garage door opener
2
3   #define    Stalled      INTCONbits.INT0IF    // stalled indicator
4   #define    Complete     INTCON3bits.INT1IF   // Complete indicator
5   #define    Button       INTCON3bits.INT2IF   // push button (up/down)
6   #define    MotorUp      LATBbits.LATB7       // motor up control signal
7   #define    MotorDn      LATBbits.LATB6       // motor down control signal
8   #define    ClearFlags()  {Button = 0; Complete = 0; Stalled = 0;}
9
10  enum {Up, GoingDn, Down, GoingUp} State = Up;    // initial state = Up
11
12  void Setup(void);
13
14  void main(void) {
15      Setup();                              // system initialization
16      while (1);                            // wait for interrupt
17  }
18
19  void Setup(void) {
20      ANSELB = 0x00;                        // PORTB: digital port
21      INTCON2bits.INTEDG0 = 0;              // INT0 react to -ve edge
22      INTCON2bits.INTEDG1 = 0;              // INT1 react to –ve edge
23      INTCON2bits.INTEDG2 = 0;              // INT2 react to –ve edge
24      TRISBbits.TRISB7 = 0;                 // MotorUp: output
25      TRISBbits.TRISB6 = 0;                 // MotorDn: output
26      INTCON2bits.RBPU = 0;                 // enable internal pull-ups
27
28      TMR0H = 0xFF; TMR0L = 0xFF;           // speed up first interrupt
29      T0CON = 0b10010011;                   // 1/16, 16-bit mode
30      INTCONbits.TMR0IE = 1;                // enable TMR0 interrupt
31      INTCONbits.GIE = 1;                   // global interrupt enable
32  }
33
34  #pragma code ISR = 0x0008
35  #pragma interrupt ISR
36
37  void ISR(void) {
38      INTCONbits.TMR0IF = 0;                // clear interrupt flag
39      TMR0H = (65536 - 15625) / 256;        // 16 us * 15,625 = 0.25 sec
40      TMR0L = (65536 - 15625) % 256;
41
42      switch (State) {
43          case Up:
44              MotorUp = 0; MotorDn = 0;     // motor off
45              if (Button) {                 // 0xx: stay in state
46                  ClearFlags();             // acknowledge "Button"
47                  State = GoingDn;          // 1xx: next state = GoingDn
48              }
49              break;
50
```

continued on following page

Table 2b. Software for garage door opener: Moore state machine continued

```
51          case GoingDn:
52              MotorUp = 0; MotorDn = 1;              // going down
53              if (Button) {
54                  ClearFlags();                      // acknowledge "Button"
55                  State = GoingUp;                   // 1xx: next state = GoingUp
56              }
57              else if (Complete) {
58                  ClearFlags();                      // acknowledge "Complete"
59                  State = Down;                      // 01x: next state = Down
60              }
61              else if (Stalled) {
62                  ClearFlags();                      // acknowledge "Stalled"
63                  State = GoingUp;                   // 001: next state = GoingUp
64              }
65              break;                                 // 000: stay in state
66
67          case Down:
68              MotorUp = 0; MotorDn = 0;              // motor off
69              if (Button) {                          // 0xx: stay in state
70                  ClearFlags();                      // acknowledge "Button"
71                  State = GoingUp;                   // 1xx: next state = GoingUp
72              }
73              break;
74
75          case GoingUp:
76              MotorUp = 1; MotorDn = 0;              // going up
77              if (Button) {
78                  ClearFlags();                      // acknowledge "Button"
79                  State = GoingDn;                   // 1xx: next state = GoingDn
80              }
81              else if (Complete) {
82                  ClearFlags();                      // acknowledge "Complete"
83                  State = Up;                        // 01x: next state = Up
84              }
85              break;                                 // 00x: stay in state
86      }
87 }
```

THUNDERBIRD TAILLIGHTS

Our second example is a state machine that controls the tail lights of a 1972 Ford Thunderbird sketched in Figure 3.

There are three lights on each side, and for turns they operate in sequence to show the turning direction (refer to Figure 4). The microcontroller-based state machine is illustrated in Figure 5. It has two input signals LEFT and RIGHT that indicate the driver's request for a left turn or a right turn. It also has an emergency-flasher input HAZ, that requests the tail lights to be operated in hazard mode – all six lights flashing on and off. It is assumed that the clock triggering the state machine equals the desired flashing rate for the lights.

Figure 3. T-bird tail lights

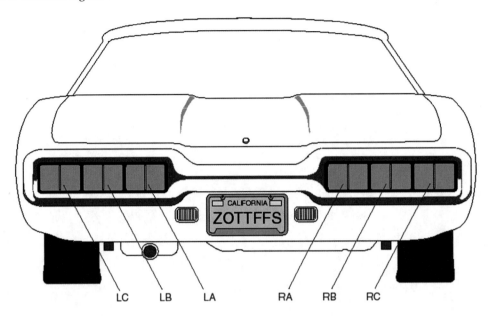

Figure 4. Flashing sequence for T-bird tail lights: (a) left turn; (b) right turn

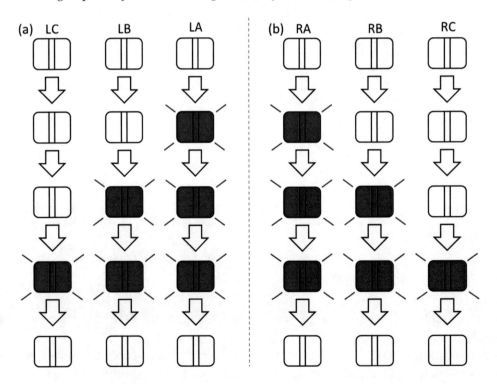

Figure 5. Hardware used to test the T-bird tail lights on PROTEUS

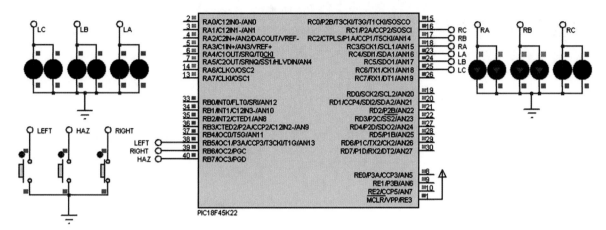

Figure 6 shows the state diagram of the T-bird tail lights. It is also explained thoroughly in the textbook "Digital Design Principles and Practices" by John F. Wakerly (Prentice Hall). The complete program is listed in Table 3.

Figure 6. State diagram for T-bird tail lights

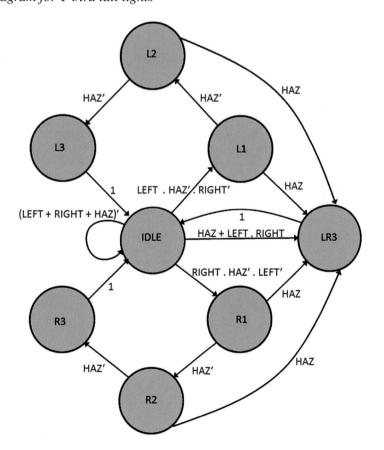

Table 3a. Software implementation of the T-bird tail lights

```
Software implementation of Thunderbird taillights: Moore state machine.
1   #include        <p18cxxx.h>
2
3   #define         HAZ         !PORTBbits.RB7
4   #define         RIGHT       !PORTBbits.RB6
5   #define         LEFT        !PORTBbits.RB5
6
7   enum {IDLE, L1, L2, L3, R1, R2, R3, LR3} State = IDLE; // Initial state IDLE
8
9   void Setup(void);
10
11  void main(void) {
12      Setup();                            // system initialization
13      while (1);                          // wait for interrupt
14  }
15
16  void Setup(void) {
17      INTCON2bits.RBPU = 0;               // internal PUs
18      ANSELB = 0x00                       // PORTB: digital port
19      ANSELC = 0x00; TRISC = 0x00;        // PORTC: digital output port
20      T0CON = 0b10010100;                 // 1/32, 16-bit mode
21      INTCONbits.TMR0IE = 1;              // enable TMR0 interrupt
22      INTCONbits.GIE = 1;                 // global interrupt enable bit
23      TMR0H = 0xFF; TMR0L = 0xFF;         // goto initial state ASAP
24  }
25
26  #pragma code InterruptVector = 0x0008
27  #pragma interrupt ISR
28
29  void ISR(void) {
30      TMR0H = (65536 - 15625) / 256;      // high part of Timer0
31      TMR0L = (65536 - 15625) % 256;      // low part of Timer0
32      INTCONbits.TMR0IF = 0;              // clear interrupt flag
33
34      switch (State) {
35      case IDLE:
36          PORTC = 0b00000000;                     // IDLE State
37          if (LEFT && !HAZ && !RIGHT)
38              State = L1;                          // goto State L1
39          else if (RIGHT && !HAZ && !LEFT)
40              State = R1;                          // goto State R1
41          else if (HAZ || LEFT && RIGHT)
42              State = LR3;                         // goto State LR3
43          else if (!(LEFT || RIGHT || HAZ))        // default state
44              State = IDLE;                        // stay in IDLE state
45          break;
46      case L1:
47          PORTC = 0b00010000;                     // State L1
48          State = (HAZ ? LR3 : L2);               // HAZ = 1, goto LR3,
49          break;                                  // else goto State
50      case L2:
```

continued on following page

Table 3b. Software implementation of the T-bird tail lights continued

```
51          PORTC = 0b00110000;              // State L2
52          State = (HAZ ? LR3 : L3);        // HAZ = 1, goto LR3,
53          break;                           // else goto State L3
54      case L3:
55          PORTC = 0b01110000;              // State L3
56          State = IDLE;                    // goto IDLE state
57          break;
58      case R1:
59          PORTC = 0b00001000;              // State R1
60          State = (HAZ ? LR3 : R2);        // HAZ = 1, goto LR3
61          break;                           // else goto State R2
62      case R2:
63          PORTC = 0b00001100;              // State R2
64          State = (HAZ ? LR3 : R3);        // HAZ = 1, goto LR3
65          break;                           // else goto State R3
66      case R3:
67          PORTC = 0b00001110;              // State R3
68          State = IDLE;                    // goto IDLE state
69          break;
70      case LR3:
71          PORTC = 0b01111110;              // State LR3
72          State = IDLE;                    // goto IDLE State
73          break;
74      }
75  }
```

TRAFFIC-LIGHT CONTROLLER

This controller has been adopted from the textbook "Fundamentals of Logic Design" by Charles. Roth. A traffic-light controller represents a rather complex control function: A busy highway is intersected by a little-used farm road (or side road), as illustrated in Figure 7. Detectors placed along the side road raise a signal C (CAR) as long as a vehicle is waiting to cross the highway. The controller operates as

Figure 7. Highway and a side road (or farm road) intersection

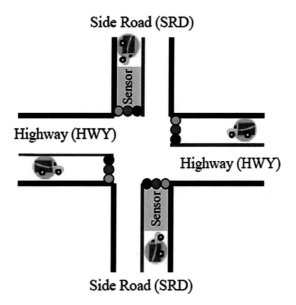

Table 4. Table describing inputs, outputs and states of the traffic-light controller

Input Signal	Description
RESET	Place controller in initial state
C	Car: Detects vehicle on farm road in either direction
TS	Time Short: Short timer interval has expired
TL	Time Long: Long timer interval has expired
Output Signal	**Description**
HG, HY, HR	Highway green, highway yellow and highway red lights
FG, FY, FR	Farm road green, farm road yellow and farm road red lights
ST	Reset timer and start timing long and short intervals.
State	**Description**
HGstate	Highway green state (farm road red)
HYstate	Highway yellow state (farm road red)
FGstate	Farm road green state (highway red)
FYstate	Farm road yellow state (highway red)

follows: as long as no vehicle is detected on the farm road, the lights should remain green in the highway direction. If a vehicle is detected on the farm road, the highway lights should change from green to yellow to red, allowing the farm road lights to become green. The farm road lights stay green as long as a vehicle is detected on the farm road and never longer than a set interval so as not to block traffic along the highway for too long. If these conditions are met, the farm road lights change from green to yellow to red, allowing the highway lights to return to green. Even if vehicles are waiting to cross the highway, the highway should remain green for a minimum time interval.

It is important to ensure that the lights stay yellow for a predetermined amount of time. Thus, we will need to measure a few intervals: one for the amount of time the highway light is yellow, one for the minimum time the highway light is green, and one for the longest amount of time the farm road light can stay green. We will set the two yellow light durations to be the same and also make the two longer time intervals for minimum highway green and maximum farm road green be the same. Therefore, we will need a timer with the ability to signal two time intervals: time short TS (3 to 6 seconds) and time long TL (20 to 255 seconds).

Figure 8. Complete hybrid Moore/Mealy state diagram for the traffic-light controller

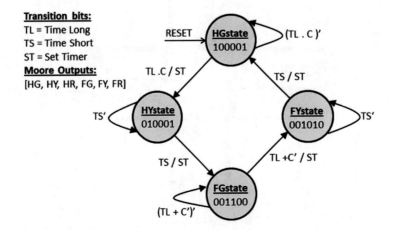

Figure 9. Hardware setup of the traffic light controller

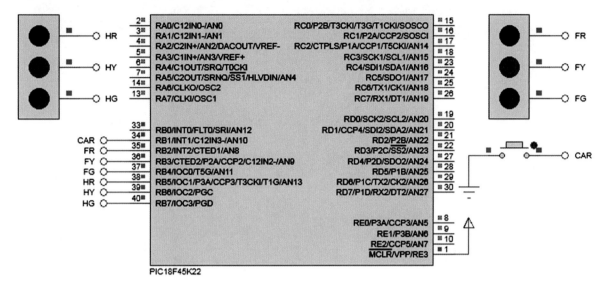

PIC18F45K22

To understand the problem statement, a good starting point is to identify the inputs and outputs as well as the different states of the controller. In terms of the unique output combinations, there are only four. When the highway light is green or yellow, the farm road light must be red, and similarly, when the farm road light is green or yellow, the highway light must be red. Table 4 lists the inputs, the outputs and the states of the traffic-light controller. The relevant state diagram is shown in Figure 8. The hardware setup is depicted in Figure 9. The program is listed in Table 5. The interrupt period is 1 second (1 Hz clock). TS and TL are implemented by counting interrupts.

ELECTRONIC PING-PONG GAME

Our fourth example covers an electronic Ping-Pong game using eight lamps and two push buttons. The lamps emulate the bouncing ball and the push buttons emulate the left and right paddles (LPB and RPB). Figure 10 shows the hardware configuration of the Ping-Pong game. Here is how it works:

1. Upon reset, the BCD displays start with a count of zero on both sides to indicate that the score is zero for both players (left and right). Besides this, all the lamps are initially turned off waiting for the "coin to be tossed".
2. When one of the players presses the TOSS push button, the MCU randomly decides which player must start first. It uses the random value read from Timer0 when TOSS is pressed: if the value read is odd, the left player starts (the leftmost lamp is turned on and the remaining lamps are turned off). By the same token, if the read value is even, it is the right player's turn to start.
3. Under the assumption that it is the left player's turn to start, the MCU waits for the left push button *LPB* to be pressed by the left player. When this occurs, the ball will bounce from left to right. The interrupt period equals the bouncing rate.

Table 5a. Traffic-lights program using a state machine approach

Software implementation of the electronic Ping-Pong game (Mealy machine).

```
1    #include      <p18cxxx.h>
2
3    void Setup(void);
4
5    #define    TL          FLAGS.B0            // time long
6    #define    TS          FLAGS.B1            // time short
7    #define    TimeLong     20                 // 20 seconds for green
8    #define    TimeShort    03                 // 03 seconds for yellow
9    #define    CAR          !PORTBbits.RB1     // car sensor (active low)
10
11   unsigned char TLcount, TScount;
12
13   enum { HG, HY, FG, FY} State = HG;          // initial state = HG
14
15   void main(void) {
16       Setup();                                // system initialization
17       while (1);                              // wait for interrupt
18   }
19
20   void Setup(void) {
21       TL = TS = 0;
22       PORTB = 0x00;                           // all lights initially off
23       ANSELB = 0x00; TRISB = 0b00000011;      // all but RB0/RB1 are outs
24       INTCON2bits.RBPU = 0;                   // enable pullup
25       T0CON = 0b10010011;                     // 1/16, 16-bit mode
26       TLcount = TimeLong;                     // elapse TimeLong
27       INTCONbits.TMR0IE = 1;                  // enable TMR0 interrupt
28       INTCONbits.GIE = 1;                     // global interrupt enable
29   }
30
31   #pragma code ISR = 0x0008
32   #pragma interrupt ISR
33
34   void ISR(void) {
35       INTCONbits.TMR0IF = 0;                  // clear interrupt flag
36       TMR0H = (65536 - 62500) / 256;          // 16 us * 62,500 = 1 sec
37       TMR0L = (65536 - 62500) % 256;
38
39       switch (State) {
40           case HG: PORTB = 0b10000100;        // HG = 1, FR = 1
41               if (--TLcount == 0)
42                   TL = 1;                     // time long has elapsed
43               if (TL && CAR) {
44                   State = HY;                 // TL = CAR = 1, goto HY
45                   TScount = TimeShort;        // elapse TS
46                   TS = 0;
47               } else if (!(TL && CAR))        // check redundancy
48                   State = HG;
49               break;
50           case HY: PORTB = 001000100;         // HY = 1, FR = 1
```

continued on following page

Table 5b. Traffic-lights program using a state machine approach continued

```
51       if (--TScount == 0)
52           TS = 1;                          // time short has elapsed
53       if (TS) {
54           State = FG;                       // TS = 1, next state = FG
55           TLcount = TimeLong;               // elapse TL
56           TL = 0;
57       }
58       break;
59   case FG: PORTB = 0b00110000;              // HR = 1, FG = 1
60       if (--TLcount == 0)
61           TL = 1;                           // time long has elapsed
62       if (TL || !(CAR)) {
63           State = FY;                       // TL = 1 or CAR = 0 goto FY
64           TScount = TimeShort;              // elapse TS
65           TS = 0;
66       }
67       break;
68   case FY: PORTB = 0b00101000;              // HR = 1, FY = 1
69       if (--TScount == 0)
70           TS = 1;                           // time short has elapsed
71       if (TS) {
72           State = HG;                       // TS = 1, next state = HG
73           TLcount = TimeLong;               // elapse TL
74           TL = 0;
75       }
76       break;
77   }
78 }
```

4. 4. As the ball (or lamp) bounces from left to right, the right player is expected to return the ball only when the rightmost lamp is on. If he/she presses the paddle *RPB* during this time slot (*RLAMP.RPB* = 1), the ball bounces back in the opposite direction (right to left in this case). If the right player presses *RPB* before the rightmost lamp *RLAMP* is on, or if *RLAMP* is on and the player ignores it, he/she loses. In this case, the left player's score is incremented by 1 and the left lamp *LLAMP* is turned on waiting for the left player to hit the ball. The condition for which the right player loses is:

$$RLAMP \, . \, \overline{RPB} + \overline{RLAMP} \, . \, RPB = 1$$

Similarly, the condition for which the left player loses is:

$$LLAMP \, . \, \overline{LPB} + \overline{LLAMP} \, . \, LPB = 1$$

5. The players continue to play until one of them reaches the maximum score (15 or so). When the game is over the display is flashed for a few seconds. Afterwards, the machine prompts the user to toss the coin in order to start a new game.

Figure 10. Hardware setup of the electronic Ping-Pong game

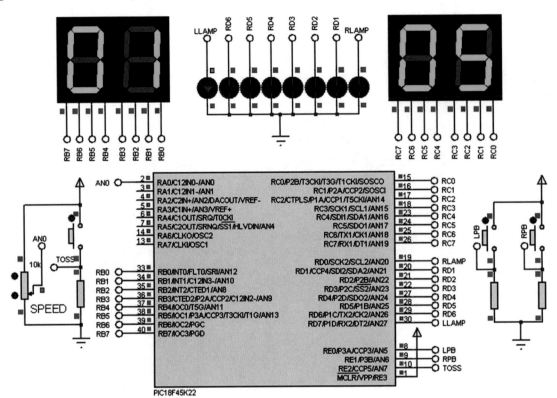

The Ping-Pong state machine has four states, four inputs and two outputs. Table 6 summarizes the states as well as the inputs/outputs of the machine. Figure 11 lays out the basic state diagram of the machine. An extra state used to flash the display upon game over condition will be added in software.

Table 6. States, inputs and outputs of the electronic Ping-Pong game

States	Description
State0 (STOPL)	Left lamp is on. Awaits left push button to be pressed to go to state RUNR.
State1 (RUNR)	Ball bounces from left to right. If (RPB.RLAMP = 1) next state = RUNL.
State2 (RUNL)	Ball bounces from right to left. If (LPB.LLAMP = 1) next state = RUNR.
State3 (STOPR)	Right lamp is on. Awaits right push button to be pressed to go to state RUNL.
Inputs	**Description**
LPB	Left push button. LBP = 1 when the left push button is pressed.
RPB	Right push button. RBP = 1 when the right push button is pressed.
LLAMP	Left lamp. LLAMP = 1 when the leftmost lamp is turned on.
RLAMP	Right lamp. RLAMP = 1 when the rightmost lamp is turned on.
Outputs	**Description**
IncLeft	Increments left 2-digit counter if $RLAMP . \overline{RPB} + \overline{RLAMP} . RPB = 1$.
IncRight	Increments right 2-digit counter if $LLAMP . \overline{LPB} + \overline{LLAMP} . LPB = 1$.

Figure 11. State diagram of the electronic Ping-Pong game

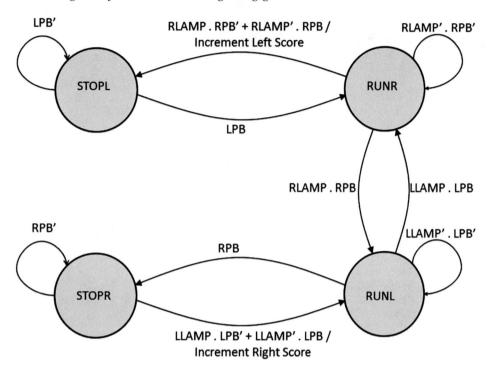

The program is listed in Table 7. An extra state (FLASH) to flash the display has been added. This state is reached if the score has reached the maximum score (15 in the program). The flashing rate of 2 Hz is used when the GameOver indicator is asserted. Flashing is performed by toggling the configuration of PORTB and PORTC from output to input and vice versa for a few seconds. The game speed is specified via analog channel AN0: the potentiometer is tied to a voltage divider between 0 and 5 Volts. In order to provide variable speed to the game through periodic interrupts, the number of cycles to be counted by Timer0 at a rate of 16 μs/cycle has been designed to be:

$$Cycles = 31250 - 110 \times ADRESH$$

where ADRESH is the A/D result in 8-bit mode. The interrupt period (or clock rate of the state machine) in milliseconds is given by the expression:

$$Interrupt\ Period = \left(31250 - 110 \times ADRESH\right) cycles \times \frac{16 \mu s}{cycle} \times \frac{10^{-3} ms}{\mu s}$$

This gives the minimum and maximum interrupt periods of 51.2 ms (ADRESH = 0xFF) and 500 ms (ADRESH = 0x00) respectively. The speed of the game will increase as the wiper of the analog pot is moved from 0V to 5V. The GetSpeed() function computes the 2's complement of $31250 - 110 \times ADRESH$ given by the expression:

Table 7a. Program listing of the electronic Ping-Pong game (Mealy machine)

```
     Software implementation of the electronic Ping-Pong game (Mealy machine).
1    #include      <p18cxxx.h>
2    #include      <BCDlib.h>
3
4    #define       GameOver        FLAGS.B0
5    #define       MaxScore        0x15
6    #define       LPB             PORTEbits.RE0
7    #define       RPB             PORTEbits.RE1
8    #define       TOSS            PORTEbits.RE2
9    #define       LLAMP           LATDbits.LATD7
10   #define       RLAMP           LATDbits.LATD0
11
12   unsigned char LoopCount = 8;
13   enum {STOPL, RUNR, RUNL, STOPR, FLASH} State;      // random initial state
14
15   void Setup(void);
16   void TossCoin(void);
17   void GetSpeed(void);
18   void LeftScore(void);
19   void RightScore(void);
20
21   void main(void) {
22       Setup();                                       // system initialization
23       while (1);                                     // wait for interrupt
24   }
25
26   void Setup(void) {
27       ANSELB = ANSELC = ANSELD = ANSELE = 0x00;      // all but PORTA are digital
28       LATB = LATC = 0x00;                            // left & right scores are 0
29       TRISB = TRISC = 0x00;                          // PORTB/PORTC: output ports
30       LATD = 0x00; TRISD = 0x00;                     // all LEDs are off
31
32       ADCON0bits.ADON = 1;                           // A/D on, channel AN0
33       ADCON2 = 0b00001001;                           // left justify, Tad = 2 us
34
35       T0CON = 0b10010011;                            // 1/16, 16-bit mode
36       TossCoin();                                    // decide initial state
37       GameOver = 0;                                  // initial status is false
38       INTCONbits.TMR0IE = 1;                         // enable TMR0 interrupt
39       INTCONbits.GIE = 1;                            // global interrupt enable
40       TMR0H = 0xFF; TMR0L = 0xFF;                    // goto initial state ASAP
41   }
42
43   void TossCoin(void) {
44       while (!TOSS);                                 // wait for TOSS push button
45       State = (TMR0L & 0x01)? STOPL: STOPR;          // random initial state
46   }
47
48   #pragma code ISR = 0x0008
49   #pragma interrupt ISR
50
```

continued on following page

Table 7b. Program listing of the electronic Ping-Pong game (Mealy machine) continued

```
51   void ISR(void) {
52       INTCONbits.TMR0IF = 0;
53       GetSpeed();
54       switch (State) {
55           case STOPL: LATD = 0b10000000;
56               if (LPB) State = RUNR;
57               break;
58           case RUNR: if (RLAMP && RPB)
59                   State = RUNL;
60               else if ((RLAMP && !RPB) || (!RLAMP && RPB))
61                   LeftScore();
62               else if (!RLAMP && !RPB)
63                   LATD >>= 1;
64               break;
65           case RUNL: if (LLAMP && LPB)
66                   State = RUNR;
67               else if ((LLAMP && !LPB) || (!LLAMP && LPB))
68                   RightScore();
69               else if (!LLAMP && !LPB)
70                   LATD <<= 1;
71               break;
72           case STOPR: LATD = 0b00000001;
73               if (RPB) State = RUNL;
74               break;
75           case FLASH: TRISB = ~TRISB;
76               TRISC = ~TRISC;
77               LATD = ~LATD;
78               if (--LoopCount == 0) Reset();
79               break;
80       }
81   }
82
83   void LeftScore(void) {
84       IncBcd(LATB);
85       if (LATB == MaxScore) {
86           LATD = 0xFF;                        // turn all LEDs on
87           GameOver = 1;
88           State = FLASH;                      // flash score
89       } else
90           State = STOPL;                      // back to STOPL
91   }
92
93   void RightScore(void) {
94       IncBcd(LATC);
95       if (LATC == MaxScore) {
96           LATD = 0xFF;                        // turn all LEDs on
97           GameOver = 1;
98           State = FLASH;                      // flash score
99       } else
100          State = STOPR;                      // back to STOPR
101  }
102
103  void GetSpeed(void) {
104      unsigned int Cycles;
105
```

continued on following page

Table 7c. Program listing of the electronic Ping-Pong game (Mealy machine) continued

```
106    if (!GameOver) {                              // compute speed
107        Cycles = (unsigned) 110*ADRESH - 31250;  // 31250 - 110.ADRESH cycles
108        TMR0H = Cycles / 256;                     // min: 51.2 ms, max: 0.5 s
109        TMR0L = Cycles % 256;                     // dt = 1.76 ms
110        ADCON0bits.GO = 1;                        // convert new sample
111    } else {                                      // 16 us * 31,250 = 0.5 sec
112        TMR0H = (65536 - 31250) / 256;            // high part of Timer0
113        TMR0L = (65536 - 31250) % 256;            // low part of Timer0
114    }
115 }
```

$$110 \times ADRESH - 31250$$

This 16-bit result is stored in Timer0. Hence, the state machine has an adjustable speed controlled by the potentiometer.

PROGRAMMABLE TIMER

This section reproduces Example 5 from Chapter 8 which consists of a programmable timer whose period is determined by the A/D converter as illustrated in Figure 12. The period is between 0 and 255_{10} seconds. The output interface uses a 2x16 LCD.

Figure 12. Programmable timer's hardware; sounder is used to signal time-out.

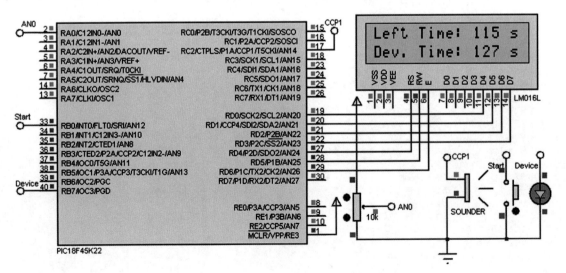

Table 8a. Programmable timer using state machine approach

```
Software implementation of 3-digit programmable timer via a state machine
1    #include      <p18cxxx.h>
2    #include      <LCD4lib.h>
3
4    #define       Device        PORTBbits.RB7
5    #define       Period        250 - 1        // T = (PR2+1).4.Tosc.16, 250Hz
6    #define       DutyCycle     125            // CCPR1L:CCP1CON<5:4>.Tosc.16
7    #define       NSECS         3              // # of seconds sounder is ON
8
9    char Seconds, Digits[3];                   // seconds in binary and ASCII
10
11   enum {SetTime, DeviceON, SounderON} State = SetTime;
12
13   void Setup(void);
14
15   void main(void) {
16       Setup();                               // system initialization
17       while (1);                             // wait for interrupt
18   }
19
20   void Setup(void) {
21       ANSELBbits.ANSB0 = ANSELCbits.ANSC3 = 0;// RB0 and RC3 are digital
22       Device = 0;                            // turn device off initially
23       TRISBbits.TRISB7 = 0;                  // RB7 output pin
24       INTCON2bits.RBPU = 0;                  // enable pull-ups
25       INTCON2bits.INTEDG0 = 0;               // negative edge of INT0
26       InitLCD();                             // initialize LCD in 4-bit mode
27       DispRomStr(Ln1Ch0, (ROM *) "Set T then START");
28       DispRomStr(Ln2Ch0, (ROM *) "Dev. Time:    s");
29       ADCON0bits.ADON = 1;                   // turn on A/D, channel AN0
30       ADCON2 = 0b00001001;                   // left justify, Tad = 2 us
31       T0CON = 0b10010100;                    // divide by 32, 16-bit mode
32       TMR0H = 0xFF; TMR0L = 0xFF;            // goto initial state ASAP
33       INTCONbits.TMR0IE = 1;                 // enable TMR0 interrupt
34       INTCONbits.GIE = 1;                    // global interrupt enable
35   }
36
37   #pragma code ISR = 0x0008
38   #pragma interrupt ISR
39
40   void ISR(void) {
41       INTCONbits.TMR0IF = 0;
42       switch (State) {
43           case SetTime:
44               TMR0H = (65536 - 3125) / 256;  // 32 us * 3,125 = 100 ms
45               TMR0L = (65536 - 3125) % 256;
46               Seconds = ADRESH;              // read Seconds from ADC
47               ADCON0bits.GO = 1;             // start ADC for next ISR
48               Bin2Asc(Seconds, Digits);      // convert to 3 ASCII chars
49               DispVarStr(Digits, Ln2Ch11, 3);// send Digits[] to LCD
50               if (INTCONbits.INT0IF) {       // start PB not pressed, exit
```

continued on following page

Table 8b. Programmable timer using state machine approach continued

```
51              INTCONbits.INT0IF = 0;      // acknowledge START PB
52              if (Seconds != 0) {
53                  Device = 1;                 // turn on device
54                  TMR0H = (65536 - 31250) / 256; // 32 us * 31,250 = 1 sec
55                  TMR0L = (65536 - 31250) % 256;
56                  DispRomStr(Ln1Ch0, (ROM *) "Left Time:      s");
57                  DispVarStr(Digits, Ln1Ch11, 3);
58                  State = DeviceON;           // invokes "run" mode
59              }
60          }
61          break;
62
63      case DeviceON:
64          TMR0H = (65536 - 31250) / 256;      // 32 us * 31,250 = 1 sec
65          TMR0L = (65536 - 31250) % 256;
66          Bin2Asc(--Seconds, Digits);         // convert to ASCII
67          DispVarStr(Digits, Ln1Ch11, 3);     // send Digits[] to LCD
68          if (Seconds == 0) {                 // seconds = 0? turn off dev.
69              Device = 0;
70              Seconds = NSECS;                // # of secs sounder is ON
71              State = SounderON;              // goto SounderON state
72              TRISCbits.TRISC2 = 0;           // set RC2/CCP1 as output
73              PR2 = Period;                   // load period
74              CCPR1L = DutyCycle;             // load duty cycle
75              T2CONbits.T2CKPS1 = 1;          // clock T2 with (Fosc/4)/16
76              CCP1CON = 0b00001100;           // use CCP1 in PWM mode
77              T2CONbits.TMR2ON = 1;           // enable Timer2 for sounder
78          }
79          break;
80
81      case SounderON:
82          TMR0H = (65536 - 31250) / 256;      // 32 us * 31,250 = 1 sec
83          TMR0L = (65536 - 31250) % 256;
84          if (--Seconds == 0)
85              Reset();                        // if Secs = 0 reset CPU
86          break;
87      }
88  }
```

The program is re-written using a state machine implementation. Here is a description of the three states of the machine:

- **SetTime:** Sets the time specified by the wiper of the analog pot. This state waits for the Start push button to be pressed to go to state DeviceON.
- **DeviceON:** Turns on the device and displays a down counter until the set time elapses. Upon termination, the device is turned off and the system goes to state SounderON.
- **SounderON:** Applies a 250 Hz square wave with 50% duty cycle to the sounder for NSECS seconds (3 secs in the program). The square wave is generated via the PWM output of CCP1.

The complete program is listed in Table 8. The sounder is driven by CCP1. The period and duty cycle of the square wave (250 Hz, 50% DC) that drives it are T = 4000 μs and DC = 2000 μs. Using a divide by 16 prescaler for solving the PWM expressions:

$$T = \left(PR2 + 1\right) \times 4T_{osc} \times 16\left(\mu s\right)$$

$$DC = \left[CCPR1L : CCP1CON \left\langle 5 : 4\right\rangle\right] \times T_{osc} \times 16\left(\mu s\right)$$

gives $PR2 = 249_{10}$ and $\left[CCPR1L : CCP1CON \left\langle 5 : 4\right\rangle\right] = 500_{10}$. Therefore,

$$PR2 = 249_{10}$$
$$CCPR1L = 125_{10}$$
$$CCP1CON \left\langle 5 : 4\right\rangle = 00_{2}$$

CONCLUSION

This chapter covered a number of important and practical state machines. When a problem becomes too complicated to describe with words, we tend to resort to state diagrams. These pictorially summarize the algorithm to be implemented in hardware. As it turns out, the software implementation of a state machine is straight forward and systematic. State machines are employed in control systems, digital communications, instrumentation, industrial applications, video games, etc. The following is a list of some applications that can be described with state diagrams:

- Elevator controller.
- Vending machine.
- Washing machine.
- Electronic games.
- Magnetic card reader.
- Error correction in digital receivers.
- Process control.
- Security alarms.
- Home automation.

The list can go on. It is important to note that software implementation of state machines provides a flexible way to change system parameters which is usually a harder task when the machine is implemented with MSI/LSI components or programmable chips like PALs, GALs, or FPGAs.

Chapter 12
Asynchronous Serial Communications

INTRODUCTION

The PIC18F45K22 MCU integrates two EUSART (Enhanced Universal Synchronous Asynchronous Receiver Transmitter) modules which can run concurrently. This chapter restricts the EUSART discussion to asynchronous mode. Communication between a PC and a microcontroller as well as communication among MCUs will be covered thoroughly.

In asynchronous mode, data is transmitted without a synchronizing clock between both ends of the communication channel. This requires only two data lines: TX (Transmit) and RX (Receive). Since there is no synchronizing clock, the transmitter and receiver must be configured to have the same baud rate before they start to communicate. The absence of the clock promotes wireless communications between devices.

DATA PACKET

Since data is transmitted asynchronously, it is framed between the so-called START and STOP bits as illustrated in Figure 1. Initially, the transmission line is idle high, that is to say, when no data is being transmitted the line's logic level is high. To initiate transmission, the data must be written to a transmit register (TXREGx). The EUSART drops the line (logic low) for one bit duration known as the *start bit*. This indicates to the receiver that a byte of data is being transmitted and hence it starts to sample the upcoming data bits. The transmitted information may be a byte or a 9-bit word. The 9th bit, called P in the figure, may be part of the data or it may simply be the *parity bit* used for error detection. The frame is terminated with the *stop bit* which is a logic high level for one time slot. The stop bit followed by the start bit creates a falling edge to indicate to the receiver that new data will be transmitted.

DOI: 10.4018/978-1-68318-000-5.ch012

Figure 1. One EUSART data packet, asynchronous mode

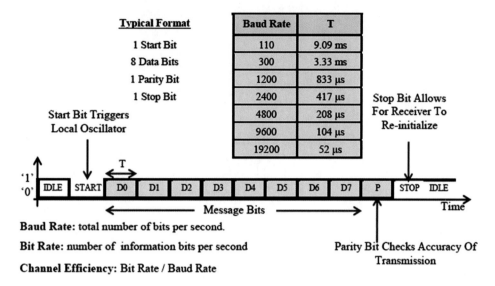

Baud Rate	T
110	9.09 ms
300	3.33 ms
1200	833 μs
2400	417 μs
4800	208 μs
9600	104 μs
19200	52 μs

The baud rate is 1/T where T is the bit duration. The bit rate is the actual transmission rate excluding the START, STOP and Parity bits. Figure 1 shows that if data is transmitted continuously or "back-to-back", the bit rate would be eight eleventh of the baud rate and hence the channel efficiency (Bit Rate / Baud Rate) is about 73%. Note that the parity bit is optional and is usually excluded. In this case, the channel efficiency is 80% at its best.

EUSART TRANSMIT BLOCK

The transmit block diagram of Figure 2 shows that TXEN must be set to enable the clock of the Transmit Shift Register TSR. In order to configure TXx as a serial port pin, SPEN must be set. The baud rate is specified by writing to SPBRGx in the Baud Rate Generator (BRG) block in accordance with the formulas listed in Table 1.

Control bit BRGH (*High Baud Rate Select*), in the Transmit Status and Control register (TXSTAx), selects between low baud rates (BRGH = 0) and high ones (BRGH = 1). Note that the numerical values obtained by any of the formulas of Table 1 must be rounded.

The user has the option of transmitting either a byte or a 9-bit word. This extra bit, which might be a data bit or a parity bit, must be stored in TX9D. The 9-bit mode is enabled by setting TX9. The byte to be transmitted must be loaded in TXREGx. Consequently, this byte is transferred to the Transmit Shift Register TSR provided it is empty (TRMT = 1). At this point, the whole bit packet (START, Data and STOP) will be serialized at the specified baud rate as illustrated in Figure 3. At the beginning of transmission, TRMT is cleared to denote that TSR is busy kicking bits out. The Transmit Buffer Register Empty flag TXIF is set to indicate that a new byte may be written to TXREGx even before TSR pops out all its bits. When the STOP bit is shifted out, the TRMT bit is set to denote that TSR is empty. In order not to wait for the TSR to flush out its data bits, the user may test TXIF. If it is set, a new byte may be written to TXREGx. This allows back-to-back transmission.

Figure 2. EUSART transmit block diagram; TX1/2 is pin RC6/RD6 (EUSART1/2).

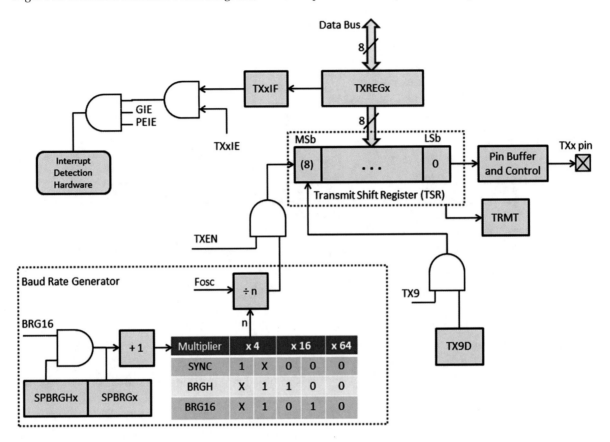

Table 1. Baud rate formulas, 8-bit uses SPBRGx only, 16-bit uses SPBRGHx:SPBRGx

Configuration Bits			BRG/EUSART Mode	SPBRGx Formula (x = 1, 2)
SYNC	BRG16	BRGH		
0	0	0	8-bit / Asynchronous	$\dfrac{F_{osc}}{64 \times Baud\ Rate} - 1$
0	0	1	8-bit / Asynchronous	$\dfrac{F_{osc}}{16 \times Baud\ Rate} - 1$
0	1	0	16-bit / Asynchronous	
0	1	1	16-bit / Asynchronous	$\dfrac{F_{osc}}{4 \times Baud\ Rate} - 1$

Note: 16-bit mode (**BRG16** = 1) uses **SPBRGHx:SPBRGx** to specify baud rate.

Figure 4 illustrates back to back transmission. If TXIF is set (TXREG is empty), a write of word 1 to this buffer transfers the data to TSR and initiates the transmission process. The small pulse in the timing diagram of TXIF signals this transfer. Since TXREG is now "empty", TXIF will be set again to notify the user that a new word can be written to TXREG. If the user decides to write word 2 before word 1 is shifted out, word 2 will be held in TXREG until word 1 is transmitted. In this case, TXIF will remain clear until word 1 is transmitted. At that particular instance of time, word 2 is transferred to TSR and

Figure 3. Asynchronous transmission

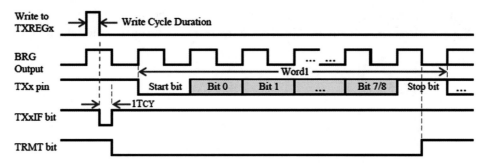

Figure 4. Timing diagram showing two consecutive transmissions

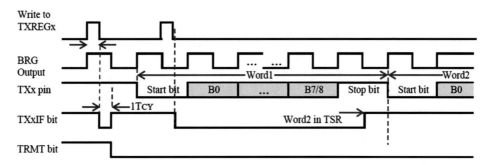

the new word is sent out without any delay. The timing diagram shows that the TRMT flag will remain cleared until both words are sent out.

It is important to note that TXIF is set or cleared by the hardware and hence the user may only poll it to find out the EUSART status. For data transmission on an interrupt basis, the user would have to set GIE and PEIE in INTCON and TXIE in PIE1 (EUSART1) or TXIE in PIE3 (EUSART2).

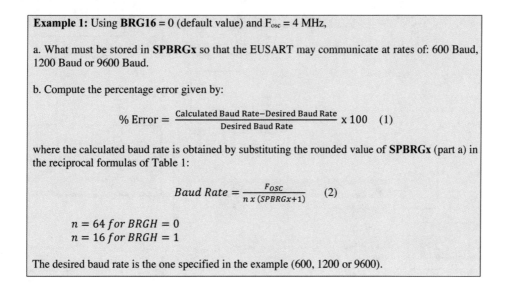

Example 1: Using **BRG16** = 0 (default value) and F_{osc} = 4 MHz,

a. What must be stored in **SPBRGx** so that the EUSART may communicate at rates of: 600 Baud, 1200 Baud or 9600 Baud.

b. Compute the percentage error given by:

$$\% \text{ Error} = \frac{\text{Calculated Baud Rate} - \text{Desired Baud Rate}}{\text{Desired Baud Rate}} \times 100 \quad (1)$$

where the calculated baud rate is obtained by substituting the rounded value of **SPBRGx** (part a) in the reciprocal formulas of Table 1:

$$Baud\ Rate = \frac{F_{osc}}{n \times (SPBRGx+1)} \quad (2)$$

$$n = 64\ for\ BRGH = 0$$
$$n = 16\ for\ BRGH = 1$$

The desired baud rate is the one specified in the example (600, 1200 or 9600).

Solution: Table 2 has been filled up using Equations 1 and 2. Notice that for BRGH = 0 (low speed), the 7% error becomes unacceptable for a baud rate of 9600. This error is reduced to 0.16% for BRGH = 1 (high speed). It can be shown[1] that the maximum error that can be tolerated should not exceed 4%.

EUSART RECEIVE BLOCK

The EUSART receiver is enabled by setting the continuous receive enable bit CREN shown in Figure 5. The receiver is synchronized on the high-to-low transition of the RX line. The incoming data bits are sampled using a high speed clock. This way the hardware gathers three samples of each bit and feeds

Table 2. SPBRG contents plus error as a function of baud rate

Desired BR	BRGH	SPBRG	Actual BR	error	BRGH	SPBRG	Actual BR	error
600	0	103	600.96	+0.16%	1	NA	NA	-
1,200	0	51	1201.92	+0.16%	1	207	1201.92	+0.16%
9,600	0	06	8928.57	-7%	1	25	9615.38	+0.16%

BR = Baud Rate.

Figure 5. EUSART receive block diagram; RX1/2 is pin RC7/RD7 (EUSART1/2).

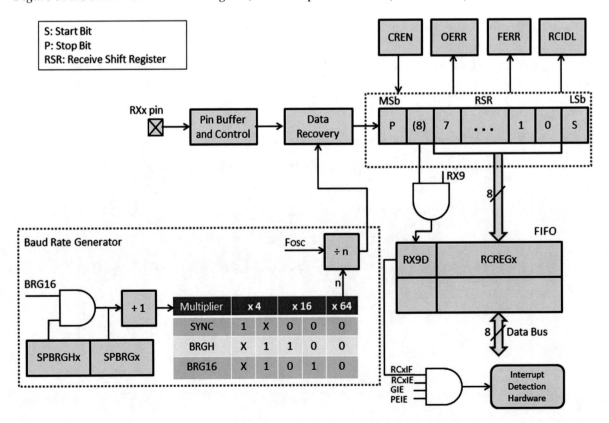

them to a majority circuit to decide upon the bit's logic level. This approach has the advantage of reducing bit error rate in a noisy environment. The bits coming out of the data recovery block are clocked into the receive shift register at the pre-programmed baud rate. Once the Receive Shift Register RSR is filled with bits, the received byte is transferred to the receive register RCREGx implemented as a 2-level deep FIFO (first-in, first-out). The buffer allows the user to hold 2 bytes in the FIFO during the time a byte is being shifted in. If the user reads at least one byte from the filled-up FIFO before it is time to store a new byte, no data will be lost. Otherwise, the new byte will be lost and the overrun error flag OERR is set. The framing error flag FERR is set when the received byte is not followed by the STOP bit.

The receive flag RCIF is set upon reception of a new word and is cleared by reading RCREGx. When two consecutive words are received, the user must read RCREGx twice to clear RCIF. An interrupt will take place if RCIE, GIE and PEIE are set upon occurrence of a reception event (RCIF = 1).

For 9-bit reception (RX9 = 1), the 9th bit received is stored in RX9D. Note that the 9th bit is not only used for parity but also as part of a 9-bit address when the ADDEN bit in RCSTA is set. This is used in applications requiring one master and a number of slaves. In this case, the receive buffer is loaded with new data only when RSR<8> is set. All the slaves tied to the bus will check the received address. Only the addressed slave will put itself in data mode by clearing ADDEN. The subsequent data transfer between the master and the selected slave will not interfere with other slaves since these will continue to operate in Address mode.

Figure 6 describes a situation in which three words are received in sequence. The figure shows that RCIF is set as soon as the first received word is stored in RCREGx. If the program ignores this event and waits until the third word is received, OERR is set and the received word is lost. OERR is cleared by clearing CREN. As to RCIF, it will not be cleared until RCREGx is read twice.

CONTROL REGISTERS

For all modes of EUSART operation, the TRIS control bits corresponding to the RXx and TXx pins should be set to '1'. The EUSART control will automatically reconfigure the pin from input to output

Figure 6. Reception of three consecutive bytes causes OERR bit to be set

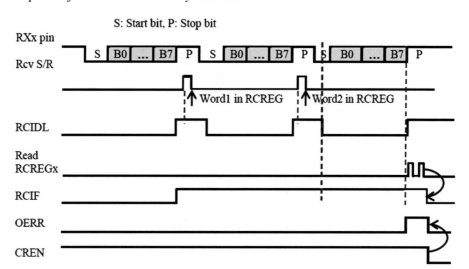

as needed. If the TXx and RXx pins are shared with an analog peripheral, the analog I/O function must be disabled by clearing the corresponding ANSEL bit. When the receiver or transmitter is disabled, the corresponding RXx or TXx may be used as a general purpose I/O pin. Table 3 enumerates all the registers associated with the EUSARTs.

The essential control registers TXSTAx, RCSTAx and BAUDCONx are explained in details in Tables 4, 5 and 6. The remaining ones listed in Table 3 are described bit-by-bit in Appendix 2.

EUSART INTERFACE TO A PERSONAL COMPUTER

The serial port on a personal computer consists of a EUSART plus a level shifter to convert the TTL levels to RS232 levels and vice versa. That is to say that logic high (5V) and logic low (0V) of TX are converted to -12V (or lower) and +12V (or higher) respectively. This way voltage drop becomes less pronounced when using long transmission lines. On the receive side, a shifted voltage level is converted back to TTL level. There are many components available on the market for this purpose. The DS275 level shifter, manufactured by MAXIM Dallas Semiconductor, is a popular level shifter that requires no external components. A microcontroller wanting to communicate with a PC through its serial port requires a level shifter interface as illustrated in Figure 7. The power and ground (pins 8 and 4) of the level shifter as well as the ground pin of the DB-9 connector (pin 5) are not shown in the figure for the sake of simplicity.

Microsoft HyperTerminal is a program that runs under Windows and is used by the PC to communicate serially with other computers or microcontrollers. One can easily setup a session and specify the baud rate and the serial port in use (i.e. com1, com2, etc.). Nowadays since most computers have only USB ports, an inexpensive USB to RS232 converter may be installed as a substitute the missing serial

Table 3. Control registers needed to configure EUSARTx (x = 1, 2)

SUMMARY OF REGISTERS ASSOCIATED WITH EUSARTx (x = 1, 2)

Name	Bit 7	Bit 6	Bit 5	Bit 4	Bit 3	Bit 2	Bit 1	Bit 0
BAUDCONx	ABDOVF	RCIDL	DTRXP	CKTXP	BRG16	–	WUE	ABDEN
INTCON	GIE	PEIE	TMR0IE	INT0IE	RBIE	TMR0IF	INT0IF	RBIF
PIE1	–	ADIE	RC1IE	TX1IE	SSP1IE	CCP1IE	TMR2IE	TMR1IE
PIE3	SSP2IE	BCL2IE	RC2IE	TX2IE	CTMUIE	TMR5GIE	TMR3GIE	TMR1GIE
PIR1	–	ADIF	RC1IF	TX1IF	SSP1IF	CCP1IF	TMR2IF	TMR1IF
PIR3	SSP2IF	BCL2IF	RC2IF	TX2IF	CTMUIF	TMR5GIF	TMR3GIF	TMR1GIF
PMD0	UART2MD	UART1MD	TMR6MD	TMR5MD	TMR4MD	TMR3MD	TMR2MD	TMR1MD
RCSTAx	SPEN	RX9	SREN	CREN	ADDEN	FERR	OERR	RX9D
SPBRGx	EUSARTx Baud Rate Generator Register Low Byte							
SPBRGHx	EUSARTx Baud Rate Generator Register High Byte							
TRISB(2)	TRISB7	TRISB6	TRISB5	TRISB4	TRISB3	TRISB2	TRISB1	TRISB0
TRISC	TRISC7	TRISC6	TRISC5	TRISC4	TRISC3	TRISC2	TRISC1	TRISC0
TRISD(1)	TRISD7	TRISD6	TRISD5	TRISD4	TRISD3	TRISD2	TRISD1	TRISD0
TXREGx	EUSARTx Transmit Register							
TXSTAx	CSRC	TX9	TXEN	SYNC	SENDB	BRGH	TRMT	TX9D

Legend: – = unimplemented cells, read as '0'. Yellow cells are not used by EUSART.

Notes: (1) PIC18(L)F4XK22 devices. (2) PIC18(L)F4XK22 devices have EUSART2 implemented on PORTB (TX2/RB7 and RX2/RB6).

Table 4. Register used to configure the EUSART as a transmitter

TXSTAx: **TRANSMIT STATUS AND CONTROL REGISTER (x = 1, 2)**

R/W-0	R/W-0	R/W-0	R/W-0	R/W-0	R/W-0	R-1	R/W-0
CSRC	TX9	TXEN	SYNC	SENDB	BRGH	TRMT	TX9D
bit 7							**bit 0**

bit 7   **CSRC:** Clock Source Select bit
          <u>Asynchronous mode:</u>
          Don't care
          <u>Synchronous mode:</u>
          1 = Master mode (clock generated internally from BRG)
          0 = Slave mode (clock from external source)

bit 6   **TX9:** 9-bit Transmit Enable bit
          1 = Selects 9-bit transmission
          0 = Selects 8-bit transmission

bit 5   **TXEN:** Transmit Enable bit
          1 = Transmit enabled
          0 = Transmit disabled

bit 4   **SYNC:** EUSART Mode Select bit
          1 = Synchronous mode
          0 = Asynchronous mode

bit 3   **SENDB:** Send Break Character bit
          <u>Asynchronous mode:</u>
          1 = Send Sync Break on next transmission (cleared by hardware upon completion)
          0 = Sync Break transmission completed
          <u>Synchronous mode:</u>
          Don't care

bit 2   **BRGH:** High Baud Rate Select bit
          <u>Asynchronous mode:</u>
          1 = High speed
          0 = Low speed
          <u>Synchronous mode:</u>
          Unused in this mode

bit 1   **TRMT:** Transmit Shift Register Status bit
          1 = TSR empty
          0 = TSR full

bit 0   **TX9D:** Ninth bit of Transmit Data
          Can be address/data bit or a parity bit.

Table 5. Register used to configure the EUSART as a receiver

RCSTAx: **RECEIVE STATUS AND CONTROL REGISTER (x = 1, 2)**

R/W-0	R/W-0	R/W-0	R/W-0	R/W-0	R-0	R-0	R-0
SPEN	RX9	SREN	CREN	ADDEN	FERR	OERR	RX9D
bit 7							**bit 0**

bit 7   **SPEN:** Serial Port Enable bit
1 = Serial port enabled (configures RXx/DTx and TXx/CKx pins as serial port pins)
0 = Serial port disabled (held in Reset)

bit 6   **RX9:** 9-bit Receive Enable bit
1 = Selects 9-bit reception
0 = Selects 8-bit reception

bit 5   **SREN:** Single Receive Enable bit
<u>Asynchronous mode:</u>
Don't care
<u>Synchronous mode – Master:</u>
1 = Enables single receive
0 = Disables single receive
This bit is cleared after reception is complete.
<u>Synchronous mode – Slave</u>
Don't care

bit 4   **CREN:** Continuous Receive Enable bit
<u>Asynchronous mode:</u>
1 = Enables receiver
0 = Disables receiver
<u>Synchronous mode:</u>
1 = Enables continuous receive until enable bit CREN is cleared (CREN overrides SREN)
0 = Disables continuous receive

bit 3   **ADDEN:** Address Detect Enable bit
<u>Asynchronous mode 9-bit (RX9 = 1):</u>
1 = Enables address detection, enable interrupt and load the receive buffer when RSR<8> is
     set
0 = Disables address detection, all bytes are received and ninth bit can be used as parity bit
<u>Asynchronous mode 8-bit (RX9 = 0):</u>
Don't care

bit 2   **FERR:** Framing Error bit
1 = Framing error (can be updated by reading RCREGx register and receive next valid byte)
0 = No framing error

bit 1   **OERR:** Overrun Error bit
1 = Overrun error (can be cleared by clearing bit CREN)
0 = No overrun error

bit 0   **RX9D:** Ninth bit of Received Data
This can be address/data bit or a parity bit and must be calculated by user firmware.

Table 6. Register used to configure the EUSART's polarity, auto-baud detection, etc.

BAUDCONx:　　　　　　　　**BAUD RATE CONTROL REGISTER (x = 1, 2)**

R/W-0	R-1	R/W-0	R/W-0	R/W-0	U-0	R/W-0	R/W-0
ABDOVF	RCIDL	DTRXP	CKTXP	BRG16	–	WUE	ABDEN
bit 7							**bit 0**

bit 7　　**ABDOVF:** Auto-Baud Detect Overflow bit
　　　　<u>Asynchronous mode:</u>
　　　　1 = Auto-baud timer overflowed
　　　　0 = Auto-baud timer did not overflow
　　　　<u>Synchronous mode:</u> Don't care

bit 6　　**RCIDL:** Receive Idle Flag bit
　　　　<u>Asynchronous mode:</u>
　　　　1 = Receiver is Idle
　　　　0 = Start bit has been detected and the receiver is active
　　　　<u>Synchronous mode:</u> Don't care

bit 5　　**DTRXP:** Data/Receive Polarity Select bit
　　　　<u>Asynchronous mode:</u>
　　　　1 = Receive data (RXx) is inverted (active-low)
　　　　0 = Receive data (RXx) is not inverted (active-high)
　　　　<u>Synchronous mode:</u>
　　　　1 = Data (DTx) is inverted (active-low)
　　　　0 = Data (DTx) is not inverted (active-high)

bit 4　　**CKTXP:** Clock/Transmit Polarity Select bit
　　　　<u>Asynchronous mode:</u>
　　　　1 = Idle state for transmit (TXx) is low
　　　　0 = Idle state for transmit (TXx) is high
　　　　<u>Synchronous mode:</u>
　　　　1 = Data changes on the falling edge of the clock and is sampled on its rising edge
　　　　0 = Data changes on the rising edge of the clock and is sampled on its falling edge

bit 3　　**BRG16:** 16-bit Baud Rate Generator bit
　　　　1 = 16-bit Baud Rate Generator is used (SPBRGHx:SPBRGx)
　　　　0 = 8-bit Baud Rate Generator is used (SPBRGx)

bit 2　　**Unimplemented:** Read as '0'

bit 1　　**WUE:** Wake-up Enable bit
　　　　<u>Asynchronous mode:</u>
　　　　1 = Receiver is waiting for a falling edge. No character will be received but RCxIF will be set
　　　　　　on the falling edge. WUE will automatically clear on the rising edge.
　　　　0 = Receiver is operating normally
　　　　<u>Synchronous mode:</u> Don't care

bit 0　　**ABDEN:** Auto-Baud Detect Enable bit
　　　　<u>Asynchronous mode:</u>
　　　　1 = Auto-Baud Detect mode is enabled (clears when auto-baud is complete)
　　　　0 = Auto-Baud Detect mode is disabled
　　　　<u>Synchronous mode:</u> Don't care

Figure 7. Microcontroller's interface to PC via the DS275; V_{cc} and GND are not shown.

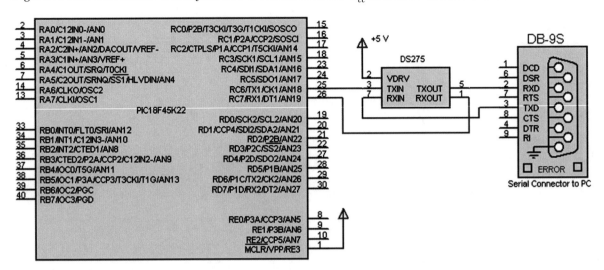

port. Figure 8 shows a typical HyperTerminal session displaying the famous "Hello World!" message on the PC.

Example 2: Using the hardware setup of Figure 9, design a library <Hyperterm.h> to transmit strings from the microcontroller via EUSART1 (pin **RC6/TX1**). The received data is collected and displayed using the PROTEUS virtual terminal which emulates HyperTerminal:

a. Design the function

```
void InitUART(void)
```

to configure EUSART1 to run at a rate of 19,200 Baud for Fcy = 1 MHz.

b. Design the function

```
void TxRamStr(char *Str)
```

to transmit a null-terminated string stored in RAM to the PC.

c. Code the function

```
void TxRomStr(ROM *Str)
```

to transmit a null-terminated string stored in program space to the PC. Recall that ROM has been added to the library <p18cxxx.h> via the statement:

```
typedef  const far rom char      ROM;
```

d. Test the designed functions by displaying a 3-digit up counter on the virtual terminal. You will need to add the function Bin2Asc() designed in chapter 8 (LCD display) to the newly designed library <Hyperterm.h>.

Solution: The fundamental functions of <Hyperterm.h> are listed in Table 7 and reproduced in Appendix 9. Table 8 lists the program of part (d).

Figure 8. HyperTerminal session showing received message

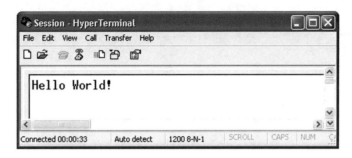

Figure 9. Hardware to emulate serial communications between the MCU and the PC

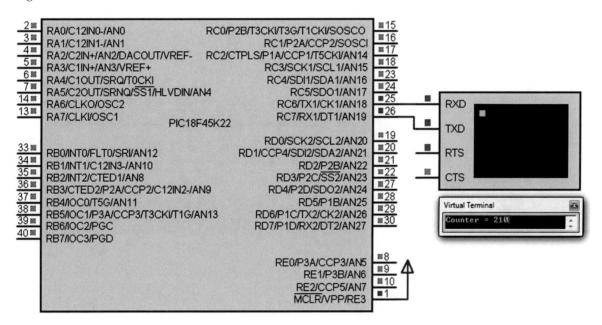

Note also that the designed functions do not explicitly make any reference to EUSART1. In fact, the index '1' has been dropped in registers like TXREG1, RCREG1, etc. The include library <P18F45K22. h> has taken care of this issue. However, if EUSART2 were selected instead, the index '2' would have to be explicitly specified (TXREG2, RCREG2, etc.).

REMOTE CONTROL APPLICATION

Figure 10 illustrates a remote control application. The handheld remote control with hex keypad waits for a key to be pressed. When this occurs, the keyboard encoder chip 74C922 provides the *master* MCU with the hex code. This, in turn, transmits it serially via the serial port (TX line). Upon data reception, the *slave* MCU sets RCIF and stores the new byte (or command) in RCREG. The receiver then displays the pressed key on its BCD display. The transmitter/receiver programs are listed in Tables 9 and 10. Two versions are shown: one using the polling concept and the other using interrupts.

Table 7. Basic EUSART functions in <Hyperterm.h>

```
Initialize the EUSART to run at 19,200 baud.
void InitUART(void)                    // UART (TX/RX) runs at 19,200 baud
{
    ANSELCbits.ANSC6 = 0;              // TX digital pin
    ANSELCbits.ANSC7 = 0;              // RX digital pin
    TXSTAbits.TXEN = 1;                // transmit enable
    RCSTAbits.CREN = 1;                // receive enable
    TXSTAbits.BRGH = 1;                // high speed mode
    SPBRG = 12;                        // 19,200 baud @ 4MHz
    RCSTAbits.SPEN = 1;                // enable UART
}
```

```
Transmit null-terminated string in RAM (data space) via the EUSART
void TxRamStr(char *Str)
{
    while (*Str != '\0')               // if '\0' is encountered exit loop
    {
        while (!PIR1bits.TXIF);
        TXREG = *Str++;                // serialize byte to be sent
    }
}
```

```
Transmit null-terminated string in ROM (program space) via the EUSART
void TxRomStr(ROM *Str)
{
    while (*Str != '\0')               // if "\0" is encountered exit loop
    {
        while (!PIR1bits.TXIF);
        TXREG = *Str++;                // serialize byte to be sent
    }
}
```

Table 8. Solution of Example 2 part (4)

```
Simple example to test serial communication of the EUSART's transmitter
1   #include      <p18cxxx.h>                    // Testing Hyperterminal
2   #include      <delays.h>
3   #include      <Hyperterm.h>
4
5   void main(void)
6   {
7       unsigned char count = 0;
8       char Message[] = "\fCounter =     ";
9
10      InitUART();                               // at 19,200 Baud
11      while (1)                                 // infinite loop
12      {
13          Bin2Asc(count++, &Message[11]);       // binary to ASCII
14          TxRamStr(Message);                    // transmit to terminal
15          Delay10KTCYx(25);                     // 250 ms delay
16      }
17  }
```

Figure 10. Implementation of a remote control

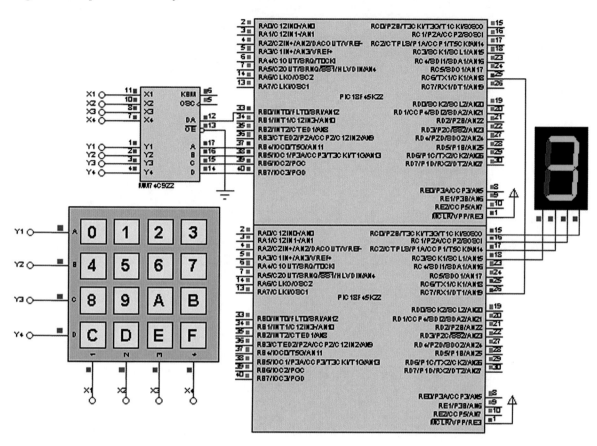

In wireless communications, the transmission line is substituted by an infrared LED at the transmitter side and an infrared detector at the receiver side (Figure 11). If the receiver is matched to a frequency of 38 KHz (TSOP1838), the LED should be driven by a 38 KHz square wave for logic '1' and should be turned off for logic '0'. The received optical signal is demodulated and fed to the RX input of the MCU via the TSOP1838 IC. This chip is designed in a way so as unexpected output pulses due to noise are avoided.

Figure 11. Infrared transmitter (TSAL6200 series) and detector (TSOP1838)

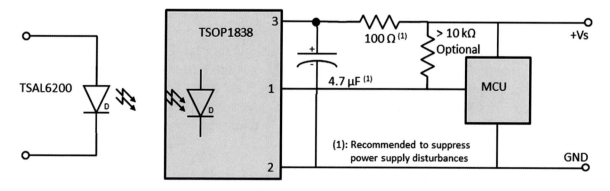

Table 9. Remote control transmitter/receiver programs (polling mode)

Transmitter program for remote control (polling mode)

```
1   #include      <p18cxxx.h>
2   #include      <Hyperterm.h>
3
4   void main(void)
5   {
6       ANSELB = 0x00;                  // PORTB: digital input
7       InitUART();                     // at 19,200 Baud
8       while (1) {
9           while (!INTCONbits.INT0IF); // wait for data available
10          INTCONbits.INT0IF = 0;      // acknowledge pressed key
11          while (!PIR1bits.TXIF);     // wait until transmission is allowed
12          TXREG = PORTB >> 4;         // read keypad, align bits then transmit
13      }
14  }
```

Receiver program for remote control (polling mode)

```
1   #include      <p18cxxx.h>
2   #include      <Hyperterm.h>
3
4   void main(void)
5   {
6       InitUART();                     // at 19,200 Baud
7       PORTC &= 0xF0;                  // start with 0 on display
8       ANSELC &= 0xF0; TRISC &= 0xF0;  // RC<3:0>: digital outputs
9       while (1)                       // infinite loop
10      {
11          while (!PIR1bits.RCIF);     // wait until data is received
12          PORTC = RCREG;              // received key on PORTC
13      }
14  }
```

SHORT MESSAGE SERVICE

Figure 12 shows the hardware required to send short messages from a personal computer to a handheld device. Before cellular phones became popular, doctors, businessmen and VIPs employed pagers to be alerted of any urgent event. In order to send a short message to someone, one had to call a central office and convey the message to the destination's pager via an operator. Although this system has become obsolete, it can be employed to send short messages to end users in a smaller environment: hospital, university, factory, etc.

A quick and dirty way to implement such a system is straight forward. The transmitter is a personal computer with an RS-232 serial port (com1 or com2). The user interface can be as rudimentary as HyperTerminal or as sophisticated as a C Sharp graphical user interface.

In the hardware setup of Figure 12, the user writes the message on HyperTerminal presuming both ends of the communication line run at the same speed. The characters being typed are sent one-by-one via the serial port. Once received, these characters are displayed right away on the LCD. The wireless

Table 10. Remote control transmitter/receiver programs (interrupt mode)

Transmitter program for remote control (interrupt-driven)	
1	`#include        <p18cxxx.h>`
2	`#include        <Hyperterm.h>`
3	
4	`void Setup(void);`
5	
6	`void main(void) {`
7	`    Setup();`
8	`    while (1) Sleep();`
9	`}`
10	
11	`void Setup(void) {`
12	`    ANSELB = 0x00;              // PORTB: digital input`
13	`    InitUART();                 // at 19,200 Baud`
14	`    INTCONbits.INT0IE = 1;      // local mask`
15	`    INTCONbits.GIE = 1;         // global mask`
16	`}`
17	
18	`#pragma code ISR = 0x0008`
19	`#pragma interrupt ISR`
20	
21	`void ISR(void) {`
22	`    INTCONbits.INT0IF = 0;      // acknowledge pressed key`
23	`    while (!PIR1bits.TXIF);     // wait until key has been transmitted`
24	`    TXREG = PORTB >> 4;         // read keypad, align bits then transmit`
25	`}`

Receiver program for remote control (interrupt-driven)	
1	`#include        <p18cxxx.h>`
2	`#include        <Hyperterm.h>`
3	
4	`void Setup(void);`
5	
6	`void main(void) {`
7	`    Setup();`
8	`    while (1);`
9	`}`
10	
11	`void Setup(void) {`
12	`    InitUART();                 // at 19,200 Baud`
13	`    PORTC &= 0xF0;              // start with 0 on display`
14	`    ANSELC &= 0xF0;`
15	`    TRISC &= 0xF0;              // RC<3:0>: digital output`
16	`    PIE1bits.RCIE = 1;          // local mask`
17	`    INTCONbits.PEIE = 1;        // global mask`
18	`    INTCONbits.GIE = 1;         // global mask`
19	`}`
20	
21	`#pragma code ISR = 0x0008`
22	`#pragma interrupt ISR`
23	
24	`void ISR(void) {`
25	`    PORTC = RCREG;              // received key on PORTC`
26	`}`

Figure 12. Transmitter/receiver for short message service

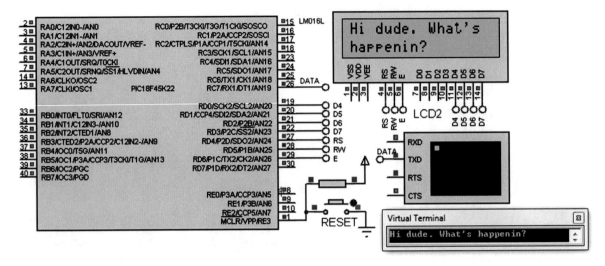

Table 11. Receiver program for short message service

```
Transmitter program for remote control (interrupt-driven)
1    #include      <p18cxxx.h>
2    #include      <string.h>
3    #include      <LCD4lib.h>
4    #include      <Hyperterm.h>
5
6    void main(void)
7    {
8        unsigned char i;
9        char Message[32];
10
11       InitUART();                                  // at 19,200 Baud
12       InitLCD();
13       memset(Message, ' ', 32);                    // fill blanks
14       for (i = 0; i < 32; i++)
15       {
16           while (!PIR1bits.RCIF);                  // wait for data reception
17           Message[i] = RCREG;                      // received key in array
18           DispVarStr(&Message[00], Ln1Ch0, 16);    // display first line
19           DispVarStr(&Message[16], Ln2Ch0, 16);    // display second line
20       }
21       Sleep();
22   }
```

link between the transmitter and the receiver consists of a couple of RF transceivers designed to interface with the serial port. Such transceivers are available on the market at affordable prices.

The receiver's program is listed in Table 11. The message in this case is restricted to 32 characters (for the 16 x 2 LCD). The program is designed to display characters on the LCD as they are being typed in the Virtual Terminal window. Note that characters will not be echoed on this window unless you use the "Echo Typed Characters" option on the virtual terminal.

For a full-blown pager system consisting of one transmitter and a number of receivers, one may resort to the 9-bit mode (RX9 = 1) with address detect (ADDEN = 1). The transmitter sends the pager's address in TXREG along with TX9D = 1. Since address detect is enabled for all receivers, they will all detect the received word. The received byte in RCREG is compared against the device's address determined by the user. The receiver that finds a match is obviously the one being addressed. Consequently, it clears the ADDEN bit to allow all received characters to interrupt the addressed pager. When the transmitter sends data to the addressed receiver, the 9th bit must be set to 0 so that all other receivers will no longer be involved.

CONCLUSION

As a conclusion, the EUSART provides a "quick-and-clean" way of troubleshooting a system's behavior. It is a quick substitute for LCD displays. As to communication between microcontrollers, this can be done via two lines only. In the case of a network of MCUs, this can easily be setup using the 9-bit mode with address detect as explained briefly in section 12.8.

Besides this, the EUSART is well suited for wireless communications. This is true for both infrared transmission as well as radio frequency modulation. There are plenty of EUSART-based transceivers in the market for such a purpose. As to infrared communication, a simple infrared light emitting diode on one end of the communication channel coupled with a photo detector on the other end is capable of transmitting data wirelessly as is the case in TV remote controls.

Finally, the EUSART provides a simple means for a microcontroller to communicate with a PC. Therefore, before USB hubs were adopted as a standard for serial communication between a personal computer and peripheral devices, almost most electronic gadgets (PBX, electronic scales, data acquisition equipment, etc.) had a serial port connector.

ENDNOTE

[1]   A thorough analysis of the maximum tolerated error is covered in the textbook: Embedded design with PIC18F452 microcontroller (chapter 18) by John B. Peatman.

Chapter 13
The Serial Peripheral Interface

INTRODUCTION

The Serial Peripheral Interface (SPI) is an embedded hardware unit in charge of communicating with external peripheral devices and microcontrollers serially. The SPI standard bus was established by Motorola and is supported by various integrated circuit manufacturers. It is based upon a shift register that the user can access in order to send or receive data bytes at a high bit rate. SPI communication is synchronous in the sense that data bits are transmitted and received along with a synchronizing clock. Hence, the receiver does not need to know the bit rate a priori as is the case with the EUSART. The SPI is part of the Master Synchronous Serial Port (MSSP) module on PIC18 microcontrollers. This module may also be used in I²C mode covered in Chapter 14. The SPI is rather simple to work with and is very convenient for low-pin count microcontrollers. For instance, a serial 16-bit A/D converter usurps only 2 microcontroller pins: the data line and the clock line. This is a great advantage in comparison with a parallel 16-bit A/D converter that would appropriate 16 I/O pins.

THE BASIC PRINCIPLE

SPI communication consists of a so-called master and one or more slaves. The master is the communication end that drives the clock line in order to exchange data with the slave. Figure 1 shows a simple configuration depicting only one slave. When the master decides to communicate with the slave, it asserts the Slave Select $\overline{SS}$ pin. Consequently, the slave leaves the high-impedance state and becomes electrically connected to the serial bus. Upon writing a byte to the master's transmit register, an internal shift register pops out these bits one at a time starting with the MSB. The bits transferred from the master on SDO (Serial Data Out) or MOSI (Master Output Slave Input) will in turn "kick-out" the bits residing in the slave's shift register (see Figure 2). The bits out of the slave appear on the master's SDI (Serial Data In) or MISO (Master Input Slave Output). In brief, the shift registers of both the master and the slave act like one circular shift register.

DOI: 10.4018/978-1-68318-000-5.ch013

Figure 1. Master/slave connection between 2 PIC18F25K22 processors

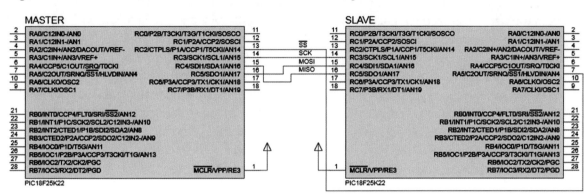

Although the master always initiates data transfer, communication between the master and the slave may take one of the following forms:

- The master sends a dummy byte to the slave. In return, the slave pops out data residing in its shift register. This data is received by the master. The slave may be an analog-to-digital converter (or any other input device) with serial interface. Such a configuration requires the SCK line between master and slave to be connected. The MOSI line becomes redundant and may be disconnected.
- The master sends useful data to the slave which in turn ejects a dummy byte from its shift register. This configuration is applicable whenever the slave is an output device such as a digital-to-analog converter. No physical connection of the MISO line between master and slave is required in this case.

Figure 2. Internal hardware (simplified) of the master and the slave

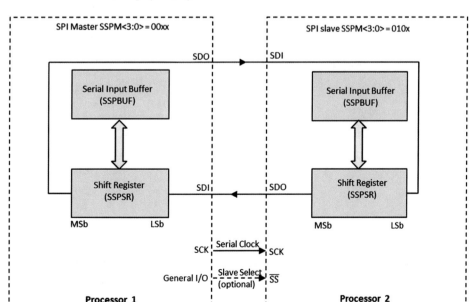

- The master and slave exchange data between each other. A typical example consists of two MCUs, a master and a slave, communicating in full-duplex mode. Obviously, this requires both SDO and SDI to be connected between the master and the slave.

As to the data format or position of the data bits with respect to the clock edge, it is the master's responsibility to setup the appropriate configuration in accordance with the peripheral device connected to the bus. The rule of thumb is simple: if the slave latches the data at the rising edge of the clock, the master must output the data bits at the falling edge and vice versa. One may also need to control the clock rate to match the rate of the slave device. The control registers in charge of setting up the clock polarity/phase and the bit rate are covered in the section 'Control Registers'.

THE MULTI-SLAVE CONFIGURATION

Figure 3 shows a master connected to multiple slaves. It is the duty of the master to insure that no bus contention occurs. The master asserts one of the $\overline{SS}$ lines to select one slave at a time. The SPI devices not selected will have their data lines in a high-impedance state and hence no bus contention results. Besides this, the clock line connected to the non-selected slaves will be inhibited. As a result, the byte transmitted by the master will be transferred to the selected slave only. When the slaves (peripheral devices) have different data formats, the master will have to reconfigure itself each time it needs to communicate with a different slave. This reconfiguration is also required when slave devices communicate at different bit rates. Note that the slave select $\overline{SS}$ pins on the master's side may be any output pin. On the contrary, the $\overline{SS}$ pin on the slave's end is a dedicated pin on the chip.

Figure 3. Single master, multiple slave SPI implementation

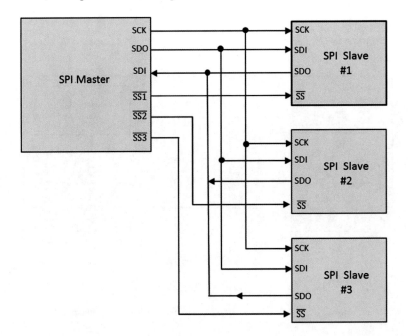

HARDWARE CONFIGURATION/FUNCTIONALITY

The 18F family fully supports SPI as part of its MSSP module. A simplified block diagram of the SPI is shown in Figure 4. The tri-state buffer in the bottom of the figure implies that SCK must be configured as an output pin in order for the SPI to work as a master.

The clock rate options are: $F_{osc}/4$, $F_{osc}/16$ and $F_{osc}/64$. If these rates are inconvenient for a certain application, the hardware provides a more versatile option in which the bit rate may be specified by the Timer2 hardware. Since the master and the slave are driven by the same clock, the shift registers at both ends of the communication channel act like one 16-bit circular shift register. The multiplexer in the middle of the figure selects between the external clock (slave mode) and the internal one (master mode). An elaboration on the data format as specified by SMP, CKE, CKP is covered in the section titled 'SPI Timing Diagram'.

When one slave only is tied to the bus, the slave select pin $RA5 / \overline{SS} / AN4$ is not needed and hence it may be utilized as a general purpose I/O pin. In the multi-slave configuration, $\overline{SS}$ is used to select one slave at a time. When $\overline{SS}$ is not asserted, the data lines at the slave's end are put in a high impedance state and the clock is inhibited.

The SPI is rather simple to use. A byte written by the master to SSPBUF is transferred immediately to the shift register SSPSR. This initiates the serialization of bits out of the data line SDO. Upon the exchange of bytes between master and slave, the received data on both ends is latched into SSPBUF and the processor signals this by setting SSPIF (*Synchronous Serial Port Interrupt Flag*) in register PIR1 (*Peripheral Interrupt Request Register 1*). The application software must read the received byte before it is overwritten by a new one. Besides SSPIF, a flag named *Buffer Full* BF (SSPSTAT<0>) is set whenever a new byte has been transferred to SSPBUF. This flag is automatically cleared when SSPBUF is read.

When using the SPI, the associated pins must be configured as input or output in accordance with their functionality. They must also be set as digital pins as listed in Table 1.

A serial port pin that is not used may be overridden by setting/clearing the appropriate data direction bit. For instance, if the SPI is used as a transmitter only, its SDI pin may be used as a general purpose I/O pin and is configured accordingly. Also in the case where the system has one slave MCU only, the slave's $\overline{SS}$ pin can be spared for use as a general purpose I/O pin.

It is also useful to note that the SPI may be operated in the SLEEP mode when configured as a slave device. Obviously, this is because SCK is driven by the master. When a slave MCU in the SLEEP mode receives a byte, it is awakened and an interrupt may be generated.

SPI TIMING DIAGRAM

In order to use the SPI appropriately, it is essential to understand the data format as illustrated by the timing diagrams of Figure 5. The 3 control bits in charge of this task are:

- **CKP (Clock Polarity):** Specifies the status of the clock line when idle.
- **CKE (Clock Edge Control Bit):** Selects the clock edge that triggers the shift register.
- **SMP (Sample bit):** Indicates the sampling time of the SDI line.

Figure 4. MSSP block diagram in SPI mode

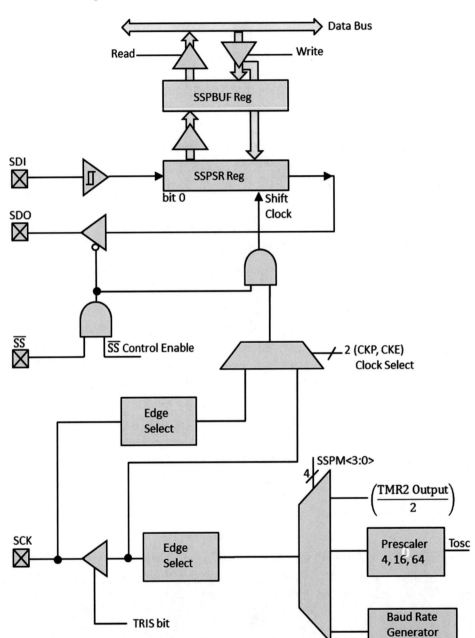

Table 1. Summary of the TRIS and ANSEL bits required to configure the SPI

Pin	Master Mode	Slave Mode	Digital Functionality
SDI	TRISC<4> = 1	TRISC<4> = 1	ANSELC<4> = 0
SDO	TRISC<6> = 0	TRISC<6> = 0	ANSELC<6> = 0
SCK	TRISC<3> = 0	TRISC<3> = 1	ANSELC<3> = 0
$\overline{SS}$	TRISA<5> = 0	TRISA<5> = 1	ANSELA<5> = 0

Figure 5. Timing diagram relating the clock position to the data bits

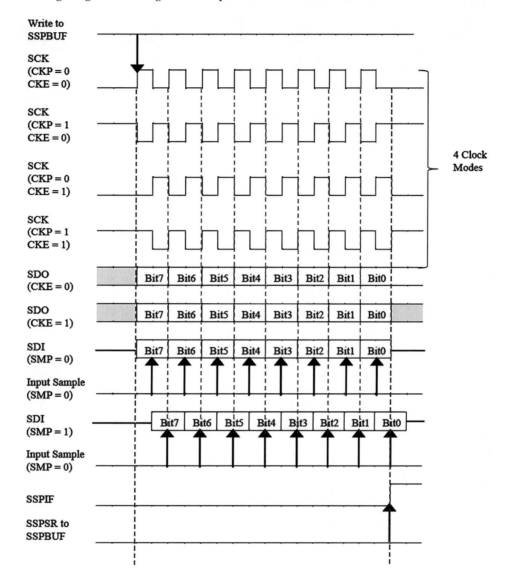

CONTROL REGISTERS

In addition to the data direction bits of Table 1, control registers SSPCON1 and SSPSTAT (Tables 2 and 3) are essential in configuring the MSSP in SPI mode.

It is important to note that WCOL and SSPOV are irrelevant if the user is careful not to allow the conditions that set these flags to occur. Hence these are normally ignored in programming.

Besides this, an important flag (SSPIF in PIR1) is employed extensively to check for termination of an SPI data transfer. The subsequent macro Wait4Flag() waits until SSPIF is set to detect an operation completion:

```
#define  Wait4Flag() {while (!PIR1bits.SSPIF); PIR1bits.SSPIF = 0;}
```

Table 2. Control register SSPCON1

SSPCON1: **SSP CONTROL REGISTER 1**

R/C/HS-0	R/C/HS-0	R/W-0	R/W-0	R/W-0	R/W-0	R/W-0	R/W-0
WCOL	SSPOV	SSPEN	CKP	SSPM<3:0>			
bit 7							bit 0

R = Readable bit	W = Writable bit	U = Unimplemented bit, read as '0'
u = Bit is unchanged	x = Bit is unknown	-n/n = Value at POR and BOR/Value at all other Resets
'1' = Bit is set	'0' = Bit is cleared	HS = Bit set by hardware C = User cleared

bit 7   **WCOL:** Write Collision Detect bit
             Master mode:
             1 = A write to the SSPBUF register was attempted while the I²C conditions were not valid for a
                 transmission to be started
             0 = No collision
             Slave mode:
             1 = The SSPBUF register is written while it is still transmitting the previous word (must be
                 cleared in software)
             0 = No collision

bit 6   **SSPOV:** Receive Overflow Indicator bit[1]
             1 = A new byte is received while the SSPBUF register is still holding the previous data. In case
                 of overflow, the data in SSPSR is lost. Overflow can only occur in Slave mode. In Slave
                 mode, the user must read the SSPBUF, even if only transmitting data, to avoid setting
                 overflow. In Master mode, the overflow bit is not set since each new reception (and
                 transmission) is initiated by writing to the SSPBUF register (must be cleared in software).
             0 = No overflow

bit 5   **SSPEN:** Synchronous Serial Port Enable bit
             1 = Enables serial port and configures SCK, SDO, SDI and $\overline{SS}$ as the source of the serial port
                 pins[2]
             0 = Disables serial port and configures these pins as I/O port pins

bit 4   **CKP:** Clock Polarity Select bit
             1 = Idle state for clock is a high level
             0 = Idle state for clock is a low level

bit 3-0   **SSPM<3:0>:** Synchronous Serial Port Mode Select bits
             0000 = SPI Master mode, clock = Fosc/4
             0001 = SPI Master mode, clock = Fosc/16
             0010 = SPI Master mode, clock = Fosc/64
             0011 = SPI Master mode, clock = TMR2 output/2
             0100 = SPI Slave mode, clock = SCK pin, $\overline{SS}$ pin control enabled
             0101 = SPI Slave mode, clock = SCK pin, $\overline{SS}$ pin control disabled, $\overline{SS}$ can be used as I/O pin
             1010 = SPI Master mode, clock = FOSC/(4 * (SSPADD+1))

Note 1:   In Master mode, the overflow bit is not set since each new reception (and transmission) is
              initiated by writing to the SSPBUF register.
Note 2:   When enabled, these pins must be properly configured as input or output.

Example 1: It is desired to test the master-slave configuration between two microcontrollers as
illustrated in Figure 6. The master is connected to a hex keypad. The slave displays the key pressed
(master's end) on the BCD display (slave's side). When a key is pressed, an interrupt is generated on
the master's side via **INT0**. The master wakes up and transmits the key at a rate of $F_{osc}/16$. Upon data
reception, the slave in interrupted and the received data byte is displayed.

Solution: The transmitter and receiver programs are listed in Table 4.

Table 3. Control register SSPSTAT

SSPSTAT: **SSP STATUS REGISTER**

R/W-0	R/W-0	R-0	R-0	R-0	R-0	R-0	R-0
SMP	CKE	D/$\overline{\text{A}}$	P	S	R/$\overline{\text{W}}$	UA	BF

bit 7   bit 0

R = Readable bit   W = Writable bit   U = Unimplemented bit, read as '0'
-n = Value at POR   '1' = Bit is set   '0' = Bit is cleared   x = Bit is unknown

bit 7   **SMP:** SPI Data Input Sample bit
SPI Master mode:
1 = Input data sampled at end of data output time
0 = Input data sampled at middle of data output time
SPI Slave mode:
SMP must be cleared when SPI is used in Slave mode

bit 6   **CKE:** SPI Clock Edge Select bit (SPI mode only)
In SPI Master or Slave mode:
1 = Transmit occurs on transition from active to idle clock state
0 = Transmit occurs on transition from Idle to active clock state

bit 5   **D/$\overline{\text{A}}$:** Data/$\overline{\text{Address}}$ bit (I²C mode only)

bit 4   **P:** Stop bit (I²C mode only)

bit 3   **S:** Start bit (I²C mode only)

bit 2   **R/$\overline{\text{W}}$:** Read/$\overline{\text{Write}}$ bit information (I²C mode only)

bit 1   **UA:** Update Address bit (I²C mode only)

bit 0   **BF:** Buffer Full Status bit
1 = Receive complete, SSPBUF is full
0 = Receive not complete, SSPBUF is empty

Example 2: It is desired to write a program to have the master read the slave's data (see Figure 7). The slave is interfaced to 8 toggle switches via **PORTB**. The master displays the number of closed toggle switches (logic low) on its BCD display. This is done when the push button on the master's side is pressed. The programs are to be written on an interrupt basis.

Solution: The transmitter and receiver programs are listed in Table 5. The master starts by sending a dummy byte to the slave. In turn, the slave counts the number of closed switches. The master gives the slave 10 ms to count the switches and put the count in SSPBUF. When the master sends the second dummy byte to the slave, it receives the count in SSPBUF.

Example 3: Test the multi-slave setup of Figure 8. The PBs connected to **INT1** and **INT2** are used to transmit the 4-bit binary code (**PORTB<7:4>**) to slave1 and slave2 respectively. For instance, if **PORTB<7:4>** = 1110_2 and **SLAVE2** PB is pressed, the 4-bit code 1110_2 (**E**) is displayed on **SLAVE2**. To do this, the master asserts $\overline{\text{SS2}}$ and transmits the code serially. This awakens **SLAVE2** in order to display the code on the BCD display.

Solution: The master and slave programs are listed in Table 6.

Figure 6. Hardware setup of Example 1

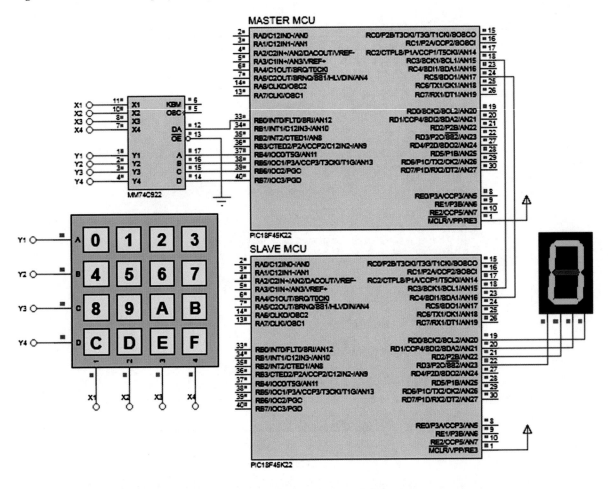

SPI INTERFACE TO THE MAX7219/MAX7221 DISPLAY DRIVERS

The MAX7219/MAX7221 are serial 7-segment display drivers manufactured by MAXIM/DALLAS. They can be interfaced to up to eight common-cathode digits with decimal points as shown in Figure 9. The upcoming chip description comes straight from the manufacturer's datasheet.

The chip requires no current limiting resistors for the segments. Only one external resistor is required to set the segment current for all LEDs. No external transistors are needed to drive the cathodes. The oscillator that drives the multiplexed display is internal and hence no external RC circuit is required. The 8-digit multiplexed display has the following advantages:

1. It usurps only three MCU pins in order to drive up to eight digits. Normally this would require 8 data pins plus 8 cathode drivers, a total of 16 pins.
2. A multiplexed display not only saves pin-count but also power consumption.
3. The serial display relieves the MCU from having to be refreshed periodically. The SPI transmits data serially to the driver at high speed and the driver takes care of the rest: multiplexing, 7-segment decoding, current limiting, etc.

Table 4. Solution of Example 1: master/slave programs

	Transmitter: reads key from keypad on an interrupt basis and transmits to the slave via the SPI
1	`#include        <p18cxxx.h>`
2	`#define        Wait4Flag()     {while (!PIR1bits.SSPIF); PIR1bits.SSPIF = 0;}`
3	
4	`void main(void) {`
5	`    ANSELCbits.ANSC5 = 0; TRISCbits.TRISC5 = 0; // RC5/SDO1 as output`
6	`    ANSELCbits.ANSC3 = 0; TRISCbits.TRISC3 = 0; // RC3/SCK1 as output`
7	
8	`    SSPCON1 = 0b00100001;                       // master, Fosc/16, CKP = 0`
9	`    INTCONbits.INT0IE = 1;                      // local mask`
10	`    INTCONbits.GIE = 1;                         // global mask`
11	
12	`    while (1) Sleep();`
13	`}`
14	
15	`#pragma code ISR = 0x0008`
16	`#pragma interrupt ISR`
17	
18	`void ISR(void) {`
19	`    INTCONbits.INT0IF = 0;              // acknowledge pressed key`
20	`    SSPBUF = PORTB >> 4;`
21	`    Wait4Flag();`
22	`}`

	Receiver: reads key from the master via the SPI and displays it on the BCD display (slave's side)
1	`#include        <p18cxxx.h>            // Receiver program to test SPI`
2	
3	`void main(void)`
4	`{`
5	`    SSPCON1 = 0b00100101;              // SPI as slave, SS: I/O, CKP = 0`
6	`    PORTD &= 0xF0;                     // start with 0 on display`
7	`    ANSELD &= 0xF0; TRISD &= 0xF0;     // RD3:RD0 are outputs`
8	`    ANSELCbits.ANSC3 = 0;              // SCK1: digital input`
9	`    ANSELCbits.ANSC4 = 0;              // SDI1: digital input`
10	`    PIE1bits.SSPIE = 1;                // local mask`
11	`    INTCONbits.PEIE = 1;               // global mask`
12	`    INTCONbits.GIE = 1;                // global mask`
13	
14	`    while (1) Sleep();`
15	`}`
16	
17	`#pragma code ISR = 0x0008`
18	`#pragma interrupt ISR`
19	
20	`void ISR(void)`
21	`{`
22	`    PORTD = SSPBUF;                    // received key on PORTD`
23	`    PIR1bits.SSPIF = 0;                // clear interrupt flag`
24	`}`

Table 5. Solution of Example 2: master/slave programs

Master program: receives number of closed SWs by interrogating the slave via the SPI.

```
1   #include      <p18cxxx.h>
2   #include      <delays.h>
3   #define       Wait4Flag()    {while (!PIR1bits.SSPIF); PIR1bits.SSPIF = 0;}
4
5   void main(void) {
6       ANSELCbits.ANSC3 = 0;
7       TRISCbits.TRISC3 = 0;              // configure RC3/SCK as output
8       SSPCON1 = 0b00110000;             // enable SPI master, Fosc/4, CKP = 1
9       PORTD &= 0xF0;                    // start with 0.
10      ANSELD &= 0xF0; TRISD &= 0xF0;    // Display tied to RD<3:0>
11      INTCON2bits.RBPU = 0;             // enable internal pull-up
12      INTCON2bits.INTEDG0 = 0;          // INT0 reacts to -ve edge
13      INTCONbits.INT0IE = 1;            // local mask
14      INTCONbits.GIE = 1;               // global mask
15      while (1) Sleep();
16  }
17
18  #pragma code ISR = 0x0008
19  #pragma interrupt ISR
20
21  void ISR(void) {
22      INTCONbits.INT0IF = 0;            // acknowledge pressed key
23      SSPBUF = 0x00;                    // send dummy byte
24      Wait4Flag();                      // wait for EOT
25      Delay10KTCYx(1);                  // give slave time to prepare data
26      SSPBUF = 0x00;                    // send dummy byte
27      Wait4Flag();                      // wait for EOT
28      PORTD = SSPBUF;                   // display read data
29  }
```

Slave program: responds to master's request & transmits number of closed SWs via SPI.

```
1   #include      <p18cxxx.h>
2
3   unsigned char i, count, PORTBcopy;
4
5   void main(void) {
6       ANSELCbits.ANSC5 = 0;
7       TRISCbits.TRISC5 = 0;             // configure RC5/SDO as output
8       INTCON2bits.RBPU = 0;             // enable pull-ups.
9       SSPCON1 = 0b00110101;             // enable SPI slave, SS: I/O, CKP = 1
10      PIE1bits.SSPIE = 1;               // local mask
11      INTCONbits.PEIE = 1;              // global mask
12      INTCONbits.GIE = 1;               // global mask
13
14      while (1) Sleep();
15  }
16
17  #pragma code ISR = 0x0008
18  #pragma interrupt ISR
19
20  void ISR(void) {
21      PIR1bits.SSPIF = 0;               // clear interrupt flag
22      for (i = 0,  count = 0, PORTBcopy = PORTB; i < 8; i++, PORTBcopy >>= 1)
23          if ((PORTBcopy & 0x01) == 0) count++;
24      SSPBUF = count;                   // wait master to read SSPBUF
25  }
```

Figure 7. Hardware setup of Example 2

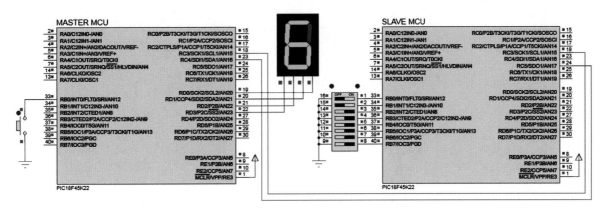

Figure 8. Hardware setup of Example 3 (multi-slave configuration)

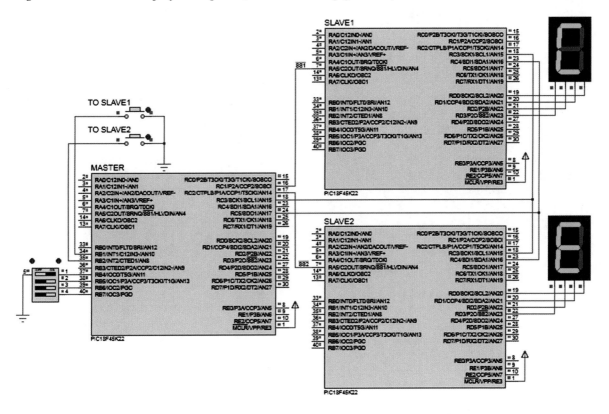

Figure 10 shows the functional diagram of the driver. The DIN and CLK lines are driven by the master (i.e. the PIC18 MCU) to transmit 16 bits (register address plus register data) to the chip. These bits are stored in the 16-bit shift register shown in the bottom of the figure. During transmission, $\overline{CS}$ is driven low. This disables the address register decoder from passing data to the output. When transmission is over, $\overline{CS}$ is negated ($\overline{CS} = 1$). This enables the data stored in the shift register to flow to the

Table 6. Solution of Example 3: programs for the master and the slave

Master program: sends status of toggle switches to a network of slaves

```
1   #include      <p18cxxx.h>
2
3   #define      Wait4Flag()   {while (!PIR1bits.SSPIF); PIR1bits.SSPIF = 0;}
4   #define      SS1    PORTCbits.RC1          // SS (slave select 1)
5   #define      SS2    PORTCbits.RC2          // SS (slave select 2)
6
7   void main(void) {
8       SS1 = 1; SS2 = 1;                      // disable slaves 1 & 2
9       ANSELC = TRISC = 0b11010001;           // SS1, SS2, SDO & SCK: outputs
10      SSPCON1 = 0b00100001;                  // SPI master, Fosc/16, CKP = 0
11      INTCON2bits.RBPU = 0;                  // enable internal pull-up
12      INTCON2bits.INTEDG1 = INTCON2bits.INTEDG2 = 0; // react to -ve edge
13      INTCON3bits.INT1IE = INTCON3bits.INT2IE = 1;    // enable INTx interrupts
14      INTCONbits.GIE = 1;
15      while (1) Sleep();
16  }
17
18  #pragma code ISR = 0x0008
19  #pragma interrupt ISR
20
21  void ISR(void) {
22      if (INTCON3bits.INT1IF)
23         {INTCON3bits.INT1IF = 0; SS1 = 0;}   // enable slave 1
24      else
25         {INTCON3bits.INT2IF = 0; SS2 = 0;}   // enable slave 2
26      SSPBUF = PORTB >> 4;                     // SSPBUF = code
27      Wait4Flag();                             // wait for EOT
28      SS1 = 1; SS2 = 1;                        // disable slaves 1 & 2
29  }
```

Slave program: selected slave receives data from master and outputs it on BCD display

```
1   #include      <p18cxxx.h>
2
3   void main(void) {
4       SSPCON1 = 0b00110100;                  // slave, SS control, CKP = 1
5       PORTD &= 0xF0;                         // start with 0 on display
6       ANSELD &= 0xF0; TRISD &= 0xF0;         // RD3:RD0 are outputs
7       PIE1bits.SSPIE = 1;                    // local mask
8       INTCONbits.PEIE = 1;                   // global mask
9       INTCONbits.GIE = 1;
10      while (1) Sleep();
11  }
12
13  #pragma code ISR = 0x0008
14  #pragma interrupt ISR
15
16  void ISR(void) {
17      PORTD = SSPBUF;
18      PIR1bits.SSPIF = 0;                    // clear interrupt flag
19  }
```

Figure 9. 8-digit multiplexed display driven by the MAX7219/MAX7221 via the SPI

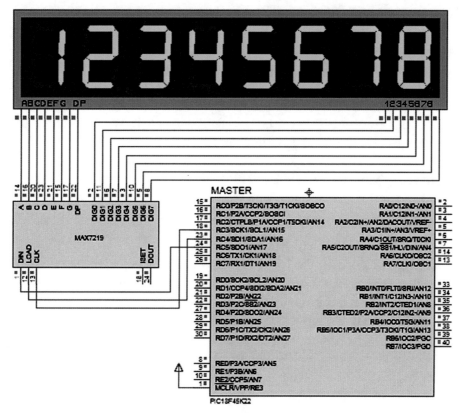

Figure 10. MAX7219/MAX7221 block diagram

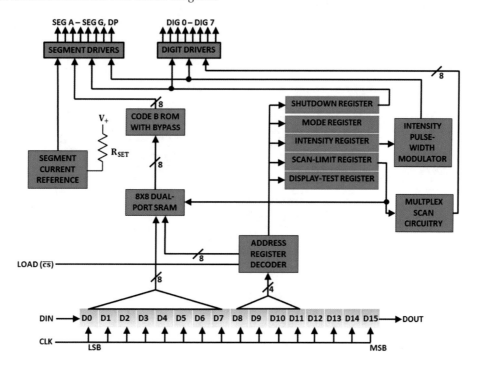

selected register: SHUTDOWN, MODE, INTENSITY, SCAN-LIMIT, DISPLAY-TEST or the digits RAM (8x8 dual-port SRAM).

The multiplex scan circuitry passes one 7-segment code at a time to the segment driver. Simultaneously, it asserts one of the digit drivers. This is a synchronized operation in the sense that when a digit is selected, the 7-segment code pertaining to that digit appears on the segment outputs. The code B ROM with bypass is controlled by the mode register. The 4-bit code may be decoded (7-segment decoder logic) or simply passed as an 8-bit code.

Figure 11 shows how two MAX7219 can be cascaded in order to drive 16 7-segment displays. In this case, **DOUT** of the first chip is used to drive **DIN** of the second.

- **Serial Addressing Mode:** For the MAX7219, serial data at DIN, sent in 16-bit packets, is shifted into the internal 16-bit shift register with each rising edge of CLK regardless of the state of $\overline{LOAD} / \overline{CS}$. For the MAX7221, $\overline{CS}$ must be low to clock data in or out. The data is then latched into either the digit or control registers on the rising edge of $\overline{LOAD} / \overline{CS}$. This signal must go high concurrently with or after the 16th rising clock edge, but before the next rising clock edge or data will be lost. Data at DIN is propagated through the shift register and appears at DOUT 16.5 clock cycle later. Data is clocked out on the falling edge of CLK. Data bits are labeled D0-D15 (Table 7). D8-D11 hold the register address. D0-D7 contain the data, and D12-D15 are "don't care" bits. The most significant bit D15 is the first one received.

- **Digit and Control Registers:** Table 8 lists the 14 addressable digit and control registers. The digit registers are realized with an on-chip, 8x8 dual port SRAM. They are addressed directly so that individual digits can be updated and retain data as long as V+ typically exceeds 2V. The control registers consist of decode mode, display intensity, scan limit (number of scan digits), shutdown, and display test (all LEDs on).

- **Shutdown Mode:** When the MAX7219 is in shutdown mode, the scan oscillator is halted, all segment current sources are pulled to ground, and all digit drivers are pulled to V+, thereby blanking the display. The MAX7221 is identical, except the drivers are high impedance. Data in the digit

Figure 11. Cascading MAX7219 to drive 16 7-segment displays

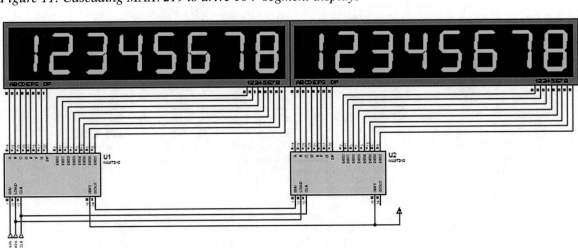

Table 7. Serial data format of the MAX7219/MAX7221 (16-bit)

D15	D14	D13	D12	D11	D10	D9	D8	D7	D6	D5	D4	D3	D2	D1	D0
X	X	X	X	ADDRESS				MSB		DATA				LSB	

Table 8. Register address map of MAX7219/MAX7221 (X: don't care)

REGISTER	ADDRESS					HEX CODE
	D15 - D12	D11	D10	D9	D8	
No-Op	X	0	0	0	0	0xX0
Digit 0	X	0	0	0	1	0xX1
Digit 1	X	0	0	1	0	0xX2
Digit 2	X	0	0	1	1	0xX3
Digit 3	X	0	1	0	0	0xX4
Digit 4	X	0	1	0	1	0xX5
Digit 5	X	0	1	1	0	0xX6
Digit 6	X	0	1	1	1	0xX7
Digit 7	X	1	0	0	0	0xX8
Decode Mode	X	1	0	0	1	0xX9
Intensity	X	1	0	1	0	0xXA
Scan Limit	X	1	0	1	1	0xXB
Shutdown	X	1	1	0	0	0xXC
Display Test	X	1	1	1	1	0xXF

and control registers remain unaltered. Shutdown can be used to save power or as an alarm to flash the display by successively entering and leaving shutdown mode. The shutdown register format is described in Table 9.

- **Decode-Mode Register:** The decode-mode register sets BCD code B (0-9, E, H, L, P, and -) or no-decode operation for each digit. Each bit in the register corresponds to one digit. A logic high selects code B decoding while logic low bypasses the decoder. Examples of decode mode control-register format are listed in Table 10.

When the code B decode mode is used, the decoder looks only at the lower nibble of the data in the digit registers (D3-D0), disregarding bits D4-D6. D7, which sets the decimal point (SEG DP), is independent of the decoder and is positive logic (D7 = 1 turns the decimal point on). Table 11 list the code B font.

Table 9. Shutdown register (X: don't care)

MODE	ADDRESS CODE (HEX)	REGISTER DATA							
		D7	D6	D5	D4	D3	D2	D1	D0
Shutdown	0xXC	X	X	X	X	X	X	X	0
Normal Operation	0xXC	X	X	X	X	X	X	X	1

Table 10. Decode-mode register examples

DECODE MODE	REGISTER DATA								HEX CODE
	D7	D6	D5	D4	D3	D2	D1	D0	
No decode for digits 7-0	0	0	0	0	0	0	0	0	0x00
Code B decode for digit 0 No decode for digits 7-1	0	0	0	0	0	0	0	1	0x01
Code B decode for digit 3-0 No decode for digits 7-4	0	0	0	0	1	1	1	1	0x0F
Code B decode for digits 7-0	1	1	1	1	1	1	1	1	0xFF

Table 11. Code B font

7-SEGMENT CHARACTER	REGISTER DATA						ON SEGMENTS = 1						
	D7*	D6-D4	D3	D2	D1	D0	DP*	A	B	C	D	E	F	G
0		X	0	0	0	0		1	1	1	1	1	1	0
1		X	0	0	0	1		0	1	1	0	0	0	0
2		X	0	0	1	0		1	1	0	1	1	0	1
3		X	0	0	1	1		1	1	1	1	0	0	1
4		X	0	1	0	0		0	1	1	0	0	1	1
5		X	0	1	0	1		1	0	1	1	0	1	1
6		X	0	1	1	0		1	0	1	1	1	1	1
7		X	0	1	1	1		1	1	1	0	0	0	0
8		X	1	0	0	0		1	1	1	1	1	1	1
9		X	1	0	0	1		1	1	1	1	0	1	1
-		X	1	0	1	0		0	0	0	0	0	0	1
E		X	1	0	1	1		1	0	0	1	1	1	1
H		X	1	1	0	0		0	1	1	0	1	1	1
L		X	1	1	0	1		0	0	0	1	1	1	0
P		X	1	1	1	0		1	1	0	0	1	1	1
blank		X	1	1	1	1		0	0	0	0	0	0	0

*The decimal point is set by bit D7 = 1

Figure 12. No-decode mode data bits and corresponding segment lines

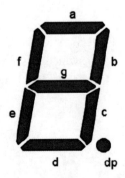

	REGISTER DATA							
	D7	D6	D5	D4	D3	D2	D1	D0
Corresponding Segment Line	dp	a	b	c	d	e	f	g

When no-decode is selected, data bits D7-D0 correspond to the segment lines of the MAX7219/MAX7221. Figure 12 shows the one-to-one pairing of each data bit of the appropriate segment line.

- **Intensity Control and Interdigit Blanking:** The MAX7219/MAX7221 allow display brightness to be controlled with an external resistor (R_{SET}) connected between V+ and ISET. The peak current sourced from the segment drivers is nominally 100 times the current entering ISET. The resistor can either be fixed or variable to allow brightness adjustment. Its minimum value should be 9.63 kΩ, which typically sets the segment current to 40 mA. Display brightness can also be controlled digitally by using the intensity register.

Digital control of display brightness is provided by an internal pulse-width modulator, which is controlled by the lower nibble of the intensity register. The modulator scales the average segment current in 16 steps from a maximum of 31/32 down to 1/32 of the peak current set by R_{SET} (15/16 to 1/16 on MAX7221). Table 12 lists the intensity register format. The maximum interdigit blanking time is set to 1/32 of a cycle.

- **Scan-Limit Register:** The scan-limit register sets how many digits are displayed, from 1 to 8. They are displayed in a multiplexed manner with a typical display scan rate of 800 Hz with 8 digits displayed. If fewer digits are displayed, the scan rate is 8 f_{OSC}/N, where N is the number of digits scanned. Since the number of scanned digits affects the display brightness, the scan limit register should not be used to blank portions of the display (such as leading zero suppression). Table 13 lists the scan-limit register format.

Table 12. Intensity register format

DUTY CYCLE		D7	D6	D5	D4	D3	D2	D1	D0	HEX
MAX7219	MAX7221									CODE
1/32 (min on)	1/16 (min on)	X	X	X	X	0	0	0	0	0xX0
3/32	2/16	X	X	X	X	0	0	0	1	0xX1
5/32	3/16	X	X	X	X	0	0	1	0	0xX2
7/32	4/16	X	X	X	X	0	0	1	1	0xX3
9/32	5/16	X	X	X	X	0	1	0	0	0xX4
11/32	6/16	X	X	X	X	0	1	0	1	0xX5
13/32	7/16	X	X	X	X	0	1	1	0	0xX6
15/32	8/16	X	X	X	X	0	1	1	1	0xX7
17/32	9/16	X	X	X	X	1	0	0	0	0xX8
19/32	10/16	X	X	X	X	1	0	0	1	0xX9
21/32	11/16	X	X	X	X	1	0	1	0	0xXA
23/32	12/16	X	X	X	X	1	0	1	1	0xXB
25/32	13/16	X	X	X	X	1	1	0	0	0xXC
27/32	14/16	X	X	X	X	1	1	0	1	0xXD
29/32	15/16	X	X	X	X	1	1	1	0	0xXE
31/32	15/16 (max on)	X	X	X	X	1	1	1	1	0xXF

Table 13. Scan-limit register format

SCAN LIMIT	REGISTER DATA								HEX CODE
	D7	D6	D5	D4	D3	D2	D1	D0	
Display digit 0 only	X	X	X	X	X	0	0	0	0xX0
Display digits 0 and 1	X	X	X	X	X	0	0	1	0xX1
Display digits 0 1 2	X	X	X	X	X	0	1	0	0xX2
Display digits 0 1 2 3	X	X	X	X	X	0	1	1	0xX3
Display digits 0 1 2 3 4	X	X	X	X	X	1	0	0	0xX4
Display digits 0 1 2 3 4 5	X	X	X	X	X	1	0	1	0xX5
Display digits 0 1 2 3 4 5 6	X	X	X	X	X	1	1	0	0xX6
Display digits 0 1 2 3 4 5 6 7	X	X	X	X	X	1	1	1	0xX7

If the scan-limit register is set for three digits or less, individual digit drivers will dissipate excessive amounts of power. Consequently, the value of RSET resistor must be adjusted according to the number of digits displayed, to limit individual digit driver power dissipation. Table 14 lists the number of digits displayed and the corresponding maximum recommended segment current when the digit drivers are used.

- **Display-Test Register:** The display-test register operates in two modes: normal and display test. Display-test mode turns all LEDs on by overriding, but not altering, all control registers (including the shutdown register). In display-test mode, 8 digits are scanned and the duty cycle is 31/32 (15/16 for MAX7221). Table 15 lists the display-test register format.
- **No-Op Register:** The no-op register is used when cascading MAX7219s or MAX7221s. Connect all devices' $LOAD / \overline{CS}$ inputs together and connect DOUT to DIN on adjacent devices. DOUT is a CMOS logic-level output that easily drives DIN of successively cascaded parts. For example, if four MAX7219s are cascaded, then to write to the fourth chip, send the desired 16-bit word, followed by three no-op codes (hex 0xXX0X, see Table 8). When $LOAD / \overline{CS}$ goes high, data is latched in all devices. The first three chips receive no-op commands, and the fourth receives the intended data.

Table 14. Maximum segment current for 1-, 2-, or 3-digit displays

NUMBER OF DIGITS DISPLAYED	MAXIMUM SEGMENT CURRENT (mA)
1	10
2	20
3	30

Table 15. Display-test register format

MODE	REGISTER DATA							
	D7	D6	D5	D4	D3	D2	D1	D0
Normal Operation	X	X	X	X	X	X	X	0
Display Test Mode	X	X	X	X	X	X	X	1

Figure 13. Multiplexed display interface to the PIC18F45K22

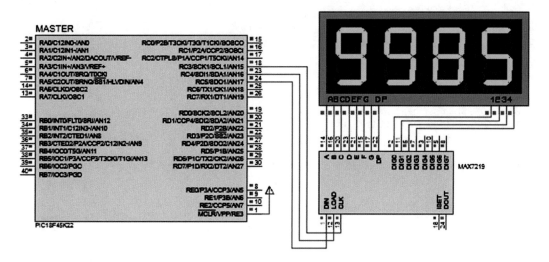

Finally, the MAX7219/MAX7221 is a positive edge-triggered device and hence the SPI must output the data bits on the falling edge of the clock when communicating with the driver. The data set-up time and hold time must be at least 25 ns and 0 ns respectively. The maximum clock rate that can trigger the driver is 10 MHz.

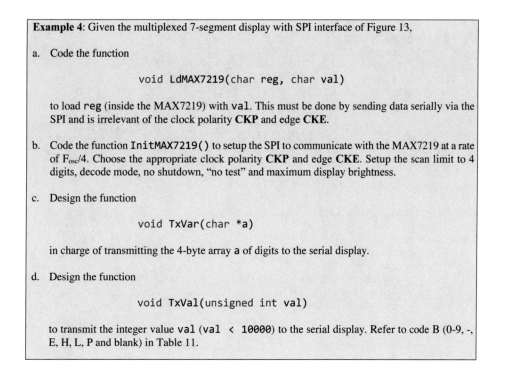

Example 4: Given the multiplexed 7-segment display with SPI interface of Figure 13,

a. Code the function

```
void LdMAX7219(char reg, char val)
```

to load `reg` (inside the MAX7219) with `val`. This must be done by sending data serially via the SPI and is irrelevant of the clock polarity **CKP** and edge **CKE**.

b. Code the function `InitMAX7219()` to setup the SPI to communicate with the MAX7219 at a rate of $F_{osc}/4$. Choose the appropriate clock polarity **CKP** and edge **CKE**. Setup the scan limit to 4 digits, decode mode, no shutdown, "no test" and maximum display brightness.

c. Design the function

```
void TxVar(char *a)
```

in charge of transmitting the 4-byte array `a` of digits to the serial display.

d. Design the function

```
void TxVal(unsigned int val)
```

to transmit the integer value `val` (`val < 10000`) to the serial display. Refer to code B (0-9, -, E, H, L, P and blank) in Table 11.

Solution: InitMAX7219() uses CKE = 0 and CKP = 1 consistent with the timing requirement. The bit rate is $F_{osc}/4 = 1$ MHz (< 10 MHz maximum limit). The required functions are listed in the library <MAX7219.h> of Table 16. An application example that tests these functions is listed in the bottom of the table.

Table 16. Example that uses <MAX7219.h> software library

```
<MAX7219.h>: Display driver software library for the MAX7219 IC
1   #define     Wait4Flag()    {while (!PIR1bits.SSPIF); PIR1bits.SSPIF = 0;}
2   #define     Ld         PORTCbits.RC4      // "Load/CS" signal
3
4   void LdMAX7219(char reg, char val) {   // Load MAX7219 reg with val.
5       Ld = 0;                            // transmit data
6       SSPBUF = reg; Wait4Flag();         // xmit register address
7       SSPBUF = val; Wait4Flag();         // xmit register content
8       Ld = 1;                            // latch data
9   }
10  enum {Decode = 0x09, Intensity = 0x0A, ScanLimit = 0x0B,
11       Shutdown = 0x0C, DisplayTest = 0x0F};
12
13  void InitMAX7219(void) {               // initialize MAX7219
14      TRISC &= 0b11000111;               // RC5/SDO, RC4/ENB, RC3/SCK: outputs
15      SSPCON1 = 0b00110000;              // Fosc/4, CKP = 1, CKE = 0 (default)
16      LdMAX7219(ScanLimit, 3);           // set up to scan 4 digits
17      LdMAX7219(Decode, 0x0F);           // decode for digits 3-0
18      LdMAX7219(Shutdown, 1);            // put MAX7219 in "normal" mode
19      LdMAX7219(DisplayTest, 0);         // put MAX7219 in "no test" mode
20      LdMAX7219(Intensity, 0x0F);        // maximum display brightness
21  }
22
23  void TxVar(char *a) {                  // TX array of 4 digits to MAX7219
24      unsigned char i;
25      for (i = 0x01; i <= 0x04; i++) LdMAX7219(i, a[i-1]);
26  }
27
28  // TX 0xXYZW to MAX7219. A = '-', B = 'E', C = 'H', D = 'L', E = 'P', F = ' '
29  void TxVal(unsigned int val) {
30      LdMAX7219(0x01, (val / 256) / 16); // X = Digit 0 (MSB)
31      LdMAX7219(0x02, (val / 256) % 16); // Y = Digit 1
32      LdMAX7219(0x03, (val % 256) / 16); // Z = Digit 2
33      LdMAX7219(0x04, (val % 256) % 16); // W = Digit 3 (LSB)
34  }
```

```
Counter program to test the MAX7219. The display flashes 9999 whenever this count is reached.
1   #include    <p18cxxx.h>
2   #include    <delays.h>
3   #include    <BCDlib.h>
4   #include    <MAX7219.h>
5
6   char digits[5]; unsigned int counter = 9985;
7
8   void main(void) {
9       InitMAX7219();
10      while (counter < 10000) {
11          Bin2BcdE(counter++, digits);   // convert to BCD
12          TxVar(digits + 1);             // ignore MSD
13          Delay10KTCYx(50);              // 500 ms delay
14      }
15      while (1) {
16          TxVal(0xFFFF);                 // display blanks
17          Delay10KTCYx(50);
18          TxVal(0x9999);                 // display 9999
19          Delay10KTCYx(50);
20      }
21  }
```

Table 17. Major manufacturers of SPI peripherals

Manufacturer	Device Type
Dallas	Real-time clock
Linear Technology	ADC, DAC, temperature sensors
Maxim	ADC, DAC, analog switches
Microchip	MCU, SEEPROM, ADC, CAN controller
Motorola	MCU, DSP
National Semiconductor	LCD controller, temperature sensor, USB controller
Texas Instruments	ADC, DAC, DSP

Table 18. SPI peripheral devices

Device	Type	Features
DS1722	Digital thermometer	-55˚C to 120˚C accuracy ± 2˚C
LM74	Temperature sensor	-55˚C to 150˚C. Max resolution: 1.25˚C
USBN9602	USB controller	DMA-support, several FIFOs
LTC2408	ADC	24-bit sigma/delta, no latency
MAX522	DAC	8-bit, 5 MHz
MAX525	DAC	12-bit, quad DAC
MCP2510	CAN controller	Programmable bit rate up to 1 MHz
MCP3001	ADC	10-bit, 200 ksps, low power, 2.7V to 5V
MCP3002	ADC	10-bit, 200 ksps, 2-channel, 2.7V to 5V

SPI PERIPHERAL DEVICES

There is a wide variety of SPI peripheral devices categorized as follows:

- **Data Converters:** ADC, DAC, Codec, etc.
- Serial EEPROMs.
- **Sensors:** temperature, humidity, pressure, etc.
- Real-Time Clocks (RTC).
- **Others:** CAN controller, USB controller, I/O expansion, digital potentiometer, LCD controller, 7-segment display driver, etc.

Table 17 lists some major manufacturers of SPI peripheral devices whereas Table 18 enumerates some popular SPI integrated circuits.

CONCLUSION

SPI's full duplex communication ability and high bit rate, ranging to several MHz, makes it attractive, simple to use and highly efficient for single slave configurations. For multi-slave configurations, it can be bothersome due to the lack of built-in addressing. Nevertheless, it offers a reliable hardware platform on top of which software protocols can be built. Chapter 14 discusses the I^2C protocol which tends to solve the drawbacks of SPI communications.

Chapter 14
I²C Interface

INTRODUCTION

The utilization of several peripheral devices in microcontroller-based systems has made it almost impossible to connect a reasonable number of these devices to a low pin-count controller. For example, if we were to connect the following I/O devices to a microcontroller:

- Parallel 8-bit A/D converter.
- Parallel 8-bit D/A converter.
- 4x4 hex keypad.
- Alphanumeric LCD in 8-bit mode.

We would usurp at least 36 I/O pins, which is too large for a low pin-count microcontroller. The question that arises here is how can a small MCU accommodate many peripherals without having to add additional hardware. An answer to this question was formerly attempted by introducing the serial peripheral interface (SPI) covered in Chapter 13. Many SPI-type peripheral devices surfaced on the market as a result. Although SPI interfacing offers high speed data transfer between an MCU and a peripheral, it has the following drawbacks:

- Each peripheral component requires a so-called Slave-Select $\overline{SS}$ pin which has to be asserted by the master in order to initiate communication between both ends of the communication link. For instance, if 10 SPI-type peripheral devices were tied to the serial bus, the MCU would have to spare 10 control signals to select amongst them. This is definitely the antithesis of a serial bus.
- SPI interface puts forth some constraints such as clock polarity and clock phase between communicating devices. This is contradictory to the *plug-and-play* philosophy adopted nowadays when adding new hardware to a system.
- The SPI was not originally designed to configure internal registers in a peripheral device and hence it cannot distinguish between data and commands. It was mainly envisioned to transfer high

DOI: 10.4018/978-1-68318-000-5.ch014

speed data between a microcontroller and data acquisition devices. This was the driving force behind seeking a different communication approach between a microcontroller and peripheral devices.

The I²C bus (Inter-Integrated Circuit), which is 2-wire serial bus, was conceived to provide full-blown network capability between a microcontroller and the peripheral devices clustered around it. This bus was developed by Philips Semiconductors in the mid-1980s and has been updated ever since. This chapter lays out the fundamental underpinnings of the I²C bus and emphasizes several applications pertaining to it.

THE I²C DATA FORMAT

As in the case of SPI interfacing, I²C communication is synchronous and is initiated by the master as well. However, there is no such thing as clock polarity and clock phase nor is there a slave select pin. There is one timing requirement relating the clock position to the data and is adopted as a standard by all I²C chip manufacturers. On top of that, data is transferred in both directions between the master and the slave using only one transmission line. Figure 1, shows a system consisting of a network of I²C devices. SDA and SCL are the *open-drain* data and clock lines respectively and hence they require pull-up resistors. The *open-drain* scheme is responsible for ridding the transmission lines SDA and SCL from any bus contention. As a matter of fact, a device not using the bus, electrically disconnects itself from it (high impedance) thereby allowing another one to pull it low (logic '0') or release it (logic '1'). A device that is not "talking" on the bus is in a listening mode waiting to be addressed by the master. Each peripheral device tied to the serial bus is associated with a unique device address provided by the manufacturer. The master communicates with one *slave* at a time by transmitting the *device address* on the bus. The interrogated device acknowledges the master's request by pulling the line low. This is how communication is started between the master and one of the slaves. The subsequent sections elaborate further on the I²C protocol, designed to organize bus communication.

The I²C data format prohibits a level change of a data bit while the clock is high, unless signaling is implied. The high or low levels of the of the data line SDA can only change when the clock signal SCL is low as shown in Figure 2 (top). A setup time and hold time must be satisfied according to the specifications provided in the data sheet of the I²C peripheral device. When the data bit changes while the clock line is high (see Figure 2 (bottom)), one of the following signaling conditions takes place:

- **START Condition:** It initiates data transfer between the master and the slave. Starting with a released bus (SDA = SCL = logic high), the master pulls SDA to ground via an internal transistor. This so-called START condition produces a falling edge of SDA while SCL is high.
- **STOP Condition:** It is used to terminate a transaction between the master and the slave. Starting with a pulled-down bus (SDA = SCL = 0), the master releases SCL first then SDA. This generates a rising edge of SDA while SCL is high.
- **RESTART Condition:** In essence, it is a STOP condition followed by a START condition. It is used to terminate a transaction and restart a new one. This signaling scheme is generally used to change the direction of data flow between the master and the slave.

Figure 1. I²C network showing one master MCU and three slaves

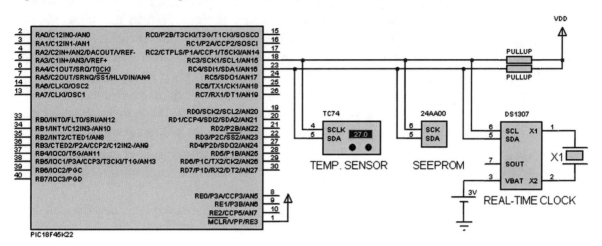

Figure 2. Timing diagrams of data transmission and signaling in I²C communication: (top) timing of the clock SCL versus the data line SDA in I²C communication; (bottom) timing diagram of the START and STOP conditions in I²C communication

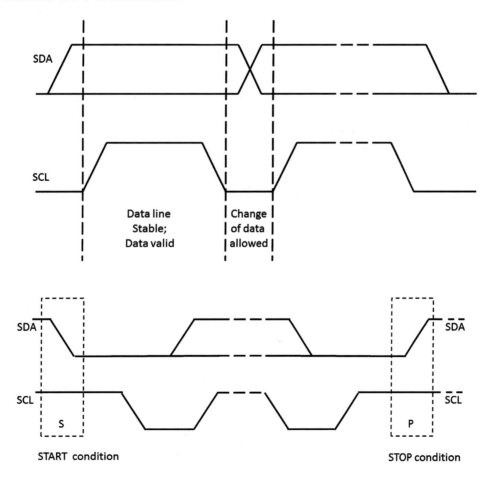

It is worthwhile noting that a *transaction* between the master and the slave is always framed between the START and the STOP conditions. The word master does not necessarily imply transmitter nor does slave imply receiver. The device which can start a *transaction* or information exchange on the I²C bus is the master. The slave can transmit data only upon the master's request. Consequently, both the master and the slave may transmit or receive data under the exclusive control of the master.

As to the information exchange or *transaction* between the master and the slave, it is composed of 8-bit data chunks plus the so-called acknowledge bit (bit 9) generated by the receiver. When a device transmits a byte, the intended receiver acknowledges data reception by pulling down the data line for one clock cycle. This active low $\overline{ACK}$ (Acknowledge) bit informs the transmitter that it is ready for a new byte. If the receiver does not pull down the line, it is due to one of the following reasons:

- The device address has been sent by the master but the destination device is not physically connected to the bus.
- The device address has been sent by the master but the addressed device is malfunctioning despite the fact that it is tied to the serial bus.
- In the case where the master is collecting data from the slave, it may decide it has received enough bytes by releasing the line during the time slot allotted for the acknowledge bit. This "No ACKnowledge" (*NACK*) condition tells the transmitter (the slave in this case) to stop sending data. Upon sending a *NACK* condition to the slave, the master is supposed to initiate a STOP condition to terminate the transaction.

Figure 3 illustrates the position and logic level of the acknowledge bit with respect to the previously transmitted 8-bit *entity*. The word *entity* rather than data has been used deliberately to indicate that different forms of information may flow between the master and the slave. These are summarized in Table 1.

The first entry in the table is the first step to be performed by the master right after the START condition. The 7-bit address of the peripheral chip is trailed by the $R / \overline{W}$ bit. If the master intends to write data to the slave it grounds the data line for one cycle during the 8th bit time slot. Otherwise, if the purpose of the transaction is to read data from the slave, the data line is released (logic high) during the 8th bit time slot. Note that the I²C bus protocol also supports 10-bit device addresses. Since the vast major-

Figure 3. Acknowledge bit on the I²C bus

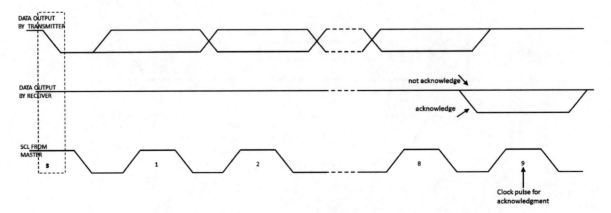

Table 1. Table illustrating all types of data transfer between master and slave

8-bit information transfer between master and slave	Direction flow
7-bit peripheral address + $R/\overline{W}$ bit	Master → Slave
8-bit internal address in peripheral	Master → Slave
8-bit data written to or read from an internal address of peripheral chip	Master ↔ Slave

ity of I²C components utilize 7-bit addresses, we shall restrict our discussion in this chapter to short device addresses.

The second entry in the table is the *internal address* in a peripheral device. Inside an I²C peripheral device, there are configuration and data registers. There registers have internal addresses and hold data. For instance, a real-time clock has to be initialized with the current time and date. If the *seconds* register were to be initialized with data, the master would have to send the address of the *seconds* register followed by the initial data to be stored in it.

The third entry in the table is the byte that has to be written to (or read from) an internal address. It may originate from either end of the communication link. It is the $R/\overline{W}$ bit sent by the master to the slave at an earlier stage that specifies the data direction. The orderly sequence of the *entities* described in Figure 4 along with the $ACK/\overline{NACK}$ signal and the control conditions (START, STOP, RESTART) forms what we have been intuitively calling an I²C *transaction*.

THE I²C TRANSACTIONS

In I²C networks, the master communicates with peripheral devices according to a well-defined protocol. The information exchange between the master and the slave can be called a transaction. In this section several types of transactions will be explained. Evidently, chip designers adhere to these transaction formats when designing I²C peripheral devices.

Figure 4 illustrates the transaction format needed to write to several consecutive registers. The transaction commences with the START condition. The first item transmitted by the master is the 7-bit address of the peripheral chip followed by a logic low $R/\overline{W}$ bit. The addressed device responds with an acknowledgement. Next, the master sends the internal address n inside the peripheral device. This one in

Figure 4. Transaction used to write to several internal registers inside a slave device

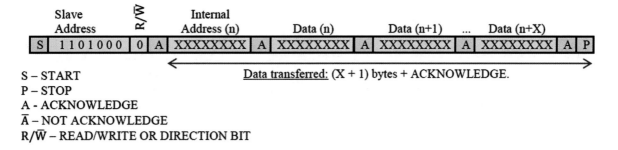

S – START
P – STOP
A - ACKNOWLEDGE
$\overline{A}$ – NOT ACKNOWLEDGE
$R/\overline{W}$ – READ/WRITE OR DIRECTION BIT

turn replies with an acknowledge. The master proceeds by transmitting the data to be written to address n, followed by the data to be written to address n+1, address n+2, ..., address n+X. The slave responds with an acknowledge upon reception of each byte. When it is time to stop dispatching additional data bytes, the master terminates this "bilateral conversation" with a STOP condition.

The transaction of Figure 5 is used by the master to specify the address of an internal register with the intention of reading its contents in a forthcoming transaction. The frame consists of the device address with $R / \overline{W} = 0$ followed by a specific internal address.

Figure 6, on the other hand, illustrates how the master can read the contents of one or more consecutive registers inside a slave device without having to specify the address of each internal register. Here it is assumed that the starting internal address n has been sent to the slave in a previous transaction as in Figure 5. The master broadcasts the device address with $R / \overline{W} = 1$ on the serial bus. Then it puts itself in receive mode in which it may collect data from the addressed slave. The slave acknowledges the read request and consequently transmits the contents of register n. At this point, the master may send an acknowledgement signal in order to receive data from the next consecutive register or simply it may decide that it has received enough data. In the latter case, it will not send an acknowledgement to the slave and in so doing it tells the slave to abort transmission. As usual, the frame ends with the STOP condition.

Figure 7 combines the transactions of Figures 5 and 6 into one. The master specifies the internal address while in the write mode then it puts itself in the read mode by re-transmitting the device address with $R / \overline{W} = 1$. The slave responds to the read command by putting the contents of the specified address on the bus. As long as the master acknowledges byte reception the slave resumes data transmission from the next consecutive internal register. The figure shows only the case of two consecutive registers

Figure 5. Transaction that specifies the internal address of a peripheral device

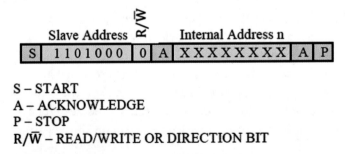

Slave Address $R/\overline{W}$ Internal Address n

| S | 1 1 0 1 0 0 0 | 0 | A | X X X X X X X X | A | P |

S – START
A – ACKNOWLEDGE
P – STOP
R/$\overline{W}$ – READ/WRITE OR DIRECTION BIT

Figure 6. Transaction employed to read consecutive registers inside a slave

Slave Address $R/\overline{W}$ Data (n)   Data (n+1)   Data (n+2)   ...   Data (n+X)

| S | 1 1 0 1 0 0 0 | 1 | A | XXXXXXXX | A | XXXXXXXX | A | XXXXXXXX | A | XXXXXXXX | $\overline{A}$ | P |

S – START
P – STOP
A - ACKNOWLEDGE
$\overline{A}$ – NOT ACKNOWLEDGE
R/$\overline{W}$ – READ/WRITE OR DIRECTION BIT

Data transferred: (X + 1) bytes + ACKNOWLEDGE.
Note: Last data byte is followed by a Not ACKNOWLEDGE $\overline{A}$ signal.

Figure 7. Transaction used to read from consecutive internal registers; R ≡ RESTART

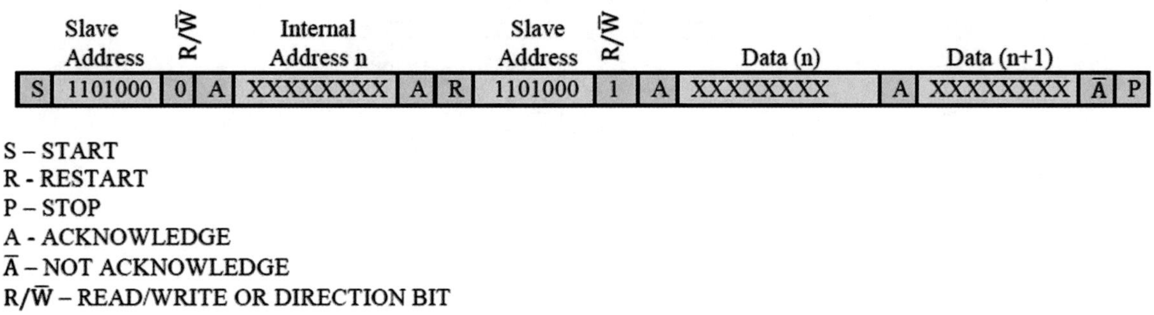

| S | 1101000 | 0 | A | XXXXXXXX | A | R | 1101000 | 1 | A | XXXXXXXX | A | XXXXXXXX | Ā | P |

Slave Address | R/W̄ | Internal Address n | Slave Address | R/W̄ | Data (n) | Data (n+1)

S – START
R - RESTART
P – STOP
A - ACKNOWLEDGE
Ā – NOT ACKNOWLEDGE
R/W̄ – READ/WRITE OR DIRECTION BIT

that are read. The master sends a *NACK* signal to inform the slave it has received enough data. The STOP condition emanating from the master obviously terminates the transaction.

For further transactions, the reader is suggested to learn more about the latest version of the I²C bus on the Internet from www.semiconductors.philips.com/i2c/support.

I²C DATA RATE

The I²C bus may be operated in the "standard mode" at bit rates between 0 Hz and 100 KHz or in the "high-speed" mode at bit rates between 0 Hz and 400 KHz. SMBus is more restrictive when it comes to data rate. It allows operating frequencies between 10 KHz and 100 KHz.

A bus running at 100 KHz, transmits a bit in 10 μs or a 9-bit word (data/address + acknowledge cycle) in 90 μs. The transaction of Figure 7 which consists of 5 of these data chunks plus 3 control conditions (START, RESTART and STOP) would require

$$5 \text{ words x } 90 \text{ μs/ word} + 3 \text{ bits x } 10 \text{ μs/bit} = 480 \text{ μs} \approx 0.5 \text{ ms}$$

If the MCU is interrupted periodically at a rate of 20 Hz in order to carry out the 0.5 msec transaction, then only 1% of the sampling time is elapsed for that matter.

PIC18F45K22 HARDWARE SUPPORT

The PIC18 family fully supports I²C as part of its MSSP module. A simplified block diagram of the relevant hardware is shown in Figure 8.

In master mode, SSPADD is used to specify the I²C clock rate. In this case, the MCU is in charge of generating the START and STOP conditions and of shifting out the data bits. The double buffering scheme of SSPSR and SSPBUF allows the MCU to send data back to back when operating as a master. In the slave mode, this scheme allows the MCU to receive new data in SSPSR while the slave is reading the present byte in SSPBUF. The Schmidt triggers shown in the figure sharpen the rising and falling edges of both the data and the clock in order to satisfy timing constraints. It is worthwhile noting that

Figure 8. MSSP block diagram in I²C Mode: x refers to two I²C blocks on the chip.

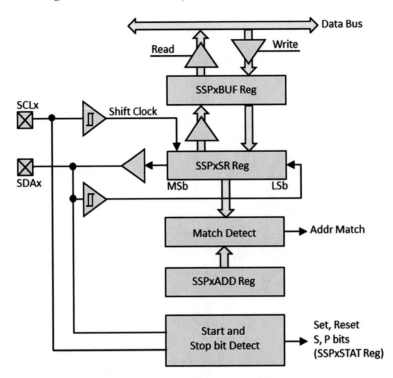

data is sent out most significant bit first. This piece of information is helpful whenever the I²C hardware is non-existent on the chip and the programmer attempts to implement the 2-wire bus in software.

REGISTERS INVOLVED

Since the MCU is generally configured as a master and controls data transfer to or from the slave devices clustered around it, we shall restrict our discussion of the relevant registers to the master mode. In this mode, SSPADD is used to configure the clock rate F_{I2C} as follows:

$$SSPADD = \frac{F_{CY}}{F_{I2C}} - 1$$

where $F_{CY} = F_{OSC} / 4$ is the instruction frequency. For instance, If F_{CY} is 1 MHz and the required clock rate F_{I2C} of the I²C bus is 100 KHz, the value to be stored in SSPADD is 9.

RC4/SDA and RC3/SCL must be configured as inputs (TRISC<4:3> = 11) to allow the I²C hardware (module 1) to change their direction as needed. As a result, SDA drives the data line when the master talks to the slave and switches to input mode to receive data from the slave.

The control registers SSPxCON1 and SSPxCON2 shown in Tables 2 and 3 are indispensable in configuring the I²C bus (master/slave) and in initiating a transaction between the master and the slave.

Table 2. SSPxCON1 used to configure the I²C module. 'x' is dropped for module 1

SSPxCON1:   SSPx CONTROL REGISTER 1 (x = 1, 2)

R/C/HS-0	R/C/HS-0	R/W-0	R/W-0	R/W-0	R/W-0	R/W-0	R/W-0
WCOL	SSPxOV	SSPxEN	CKP	SSPxM<3:0>			
bit 7							**bit 0**

R = Readable bit   W = Writable bit   U = Unimplemented bit, read as '0'
'1' = Bit is set   '0' = Bit is cleared   HS = Bit set by hardware   C = User cleared

bit 7   **WCOL:** Write Collision Detect bit
<u>Master mode:</u>
1 = A write to the SSPxBUF register was attempted while the I²C conditions were not valid for a transmission to be started
0 = No collision
<u>Slave mode:</u>
1 = The SSPxBUF register is written while it is still transmitting the previous word (must be cleared in software)
0 = No collision

bit 6   **SSPxOV:** Receive Overflow Indicator bit[1]
1 = A byte is received while the SSPxBUF register is still holding the previous byte. SSPxOV is a "don't care" in mode (must be cleared in software).
0 = No overflow

bit 5   **SSPxEN:** Synchronous Serial Port Enable bit
1 = Enables the serial port and configures the SDAx and SCLx pins as the source of the serial port pins[2]
0 = Disables serial port and configures these pins as I/O port pins

bit 4   **CKP:** Clock Polarity Select bit
SCLx release control (used only in I²C slave mode)
1 = Enable clock
0 = Holds clock low (clock stretch). (Used to ensure data setup time.)

bit 3-0   **SSPxM<3:0>:** Synchronous Serial Port Mode Select bits
0110 = I²C Slave mode, 7-bit address
0111 = I²C Slave mode, 10-bit address
1000 = I²C Master mode, clock = FOSC / (4 * (SSPxADD+1))[3]
1011 = I²C firmware controlled Master mode (slave idle)
1110 = I²C Slave mode, 7-bit address with Start and Stop bit interrupts enabled
1111 = I²C Slave mode, 10-bit address with Start and Stop bit interrupts enabled

Note 1:   In Master mode, the overflow bit is not set since each new reception (and transmission) is initiated by writing to the **SSPxBUF** register.
Note 2:   When enabled, the **SDAx** and **SCLx** pins must be configured as inputs
Note 3:   **SSPxADD** values of 0, 1 or 2 are not supported for I²C Mode.

The remaining control register SSPSTAT indicates the status of the serial line when the MCU is used as a slave. It has flags that indicate whether a START condition or a STOP condition, among others, has been detected. You may refer to this register in Appendix 2.

Table 3. SSPxCON2 used to implement I²C transactions. 'x' is dropped for module 1

SSPxCON2:   **SSPx CONTROL REGISTER 2 (x = 1, 2)**

R/W-0	R-0	R/W-0	R/S/HC-0	R/S/HC-0	R/S/HC-0	R/S/HC-0	R/S/HC-0
GCEN	ACKSTAT	ACKDT	ACKEN[(1)]	RCEN[(1)]	PEN[(1)]	RSEN[(1)]	SEN[(1)]
bit 7							**bit 0**

R = Readable bit	W = Writable bit	U = Unimplemented bit, read as '0'
u = Bit is unchanged	x = Bit is unknown	-n/n = Value at POR and BOR/Value at all other Resets
'1' = Bit is set	'0' = Bit is cleared	HC = Cleared by hardware S = User set

bit 7   **GCEN:** General Call Enable bit (in I²C Slave mode only)
          1 = Enable interrupt when a general call address (0x00) is received in the SSPxSR
          0 = General call address disabled

bit 6   **ACKSTAT:** Acknowledge Status bit (in I²C mode only)
          1 = Acknowledge was not received
          0 = Acknowledge was received

Bit 5   **ACKDT:** Acknowledge Data bit (in I²C mode only)
          <u>In Receive mode:</u>
          Value transmitted when the user initiates an Acknowledge sequence at the end of a receive
          1 = Not Acknowledge
          0 = Acknowledge

bit 4   **ACKEN**[(1)]**:** Acknowledge Sequence Enable bit (in I²C Master mode only)
          <u>In Master Receive mode:</u>
          1 = Initiate Acknowledge sequence on SDAx and SCLx pins, and transmit ACKDT data bit.
              Automatically cleared by hardware.
          0 = Acknowledge sequence idle

bit 3   **RCEN**[(1)]**:** Receive Enable bit (in I²C Master mode only)
          1 = Enables Receive mode for I²C
          0 = Receive idle

bit 2   **PEN**[(1)]**:** Stop Condition Enable bit (in I²C Master mode only)
          <u>SCKx Release Control:</u>
          1 = Initiate Stop condition on SDAx and SCLx pins. Automatically cleared by hardware.
          0 = Stop condition Idle

bit 1   **RSEN**[(1)]**:** Repeated Start Condition Enabled bit (in I²C Master mode only)
          1 = Initiate Repeated Start condition on SDAx and SCLx pins. Automatically cleared by
              hardware.
          0 = Repeated Start condition Idle

bit 0   **SEN**[(1)]**:** Start Condition Enabled bit (in I²C Master mode only)
          <u>In Master mode:</u>
          1 = Initiate Start condition on SDAx and SCLx pins. Automatically cleared by hardware.
          0 = Start condition Idle
          <u>In Slave mode:</u>
          1 = Clock stretching is enabled for both slave transmit and slave receive (stretch enabled)
          0 = Clock stretching is disabled

Note 1:   **SEN, RSEN, PEN, RCEN** and **ACKEN** are control bits and indicators (flags) as well. These bits
          are cleared by the hardware to indicate that the command, i.e. **START, RESTART, STOP,**
          receive, etc., has been performed. In order to relieve the user from having to poll all these flags,
          the **SSPIF** flag in **PIR1** is set upon termination of any of these I²C commands and hence it may be
          polled as well. **SSPIF** is also set upon termination of a write or read operation.

Figure 9. Block diagram and pin configuration of the TC74 temperature sensor

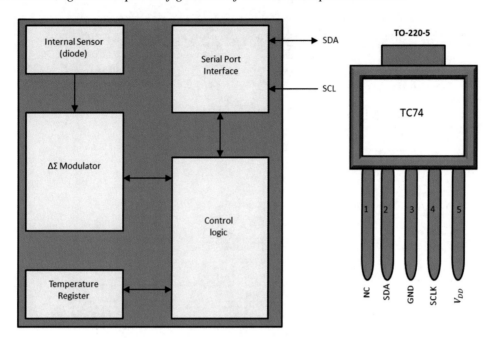

THE TC74 DIGITAL THERMAL SENSOR

The TC74 is a low cost digital thermal sensor with I²C interface particularly suited for temperature measurement between -40 °C and 125 °C. Figure 9 shows the functional block diagram and pin configuration of the sensor.

The TC74A5-5.0VCT comes in a TO-220 package and may be mounted on an enclosure or a heat sink for convenience. Here is a run-down of its essential characteristics:

- **Operating Voltage:** 5.0 V.
- **Accuracy:** $\pm$ 2°C from +25°C to +85°C, $\pm$ 3°C from 0°C to +125°C.
- **Operating Current:** 200 µA in normal mode, 5 µA in standby mode .
- **Temperature Resolution:** 1°C.
- **Conversion Rate:** 8 samples / second.
- **Output Temperature:** 8-bit digital word.
- **Device Address:** 1001101.
- **Internal Registers:** The read only temperature register TEMP at address 0x00 and the Read/Write configuration register CONFIG (Table 4) at address 0x01.

In most applications, the CONFIG register is not tampered with since the TC74 is operated in normal mode upon reset. The need to wait for a ready flag is also irrelevant if an application does not require more than one sample per second. Table 5 illustrates the relationship between the actual temperature and the digital code read from the TC74. For instance, a temperature of 25 °C will give a binary reading of

Table 4. Description of the configuration register

BIT	POR	FUNCTION	TYPE	OPERATION
D[7]	0	STANDBY switch	Read / Write	1 = standby, 0 = normal
D[6]	0	Data Ready	Read only	1 = ready, 0 = not ready
D[5] - D[0]	0	Reserved – Always returns zero when read.	N/A	N/A

Table 5. Table showing the temperature to binary value relationships

Temperature to Digital Value Conversion (TEMP)		
ACTUAL TEMPERATURE	REGISTERED TEMPERATURE	BINARY HEX
+130.00 °C	+127 °C	0111 1111
+127.00 °C	+127 °C	0111 1111
+126.50 °C	+127 °C	0111 1111
+25.25 °C	+25 °C	0001 1001
+0.50 °C	+1 °C	0000 0001
+0.25 °C	0 °C	0000 0000
0.00 °C	0 °C	0000 0000
-0.25 °C	0 °C	0000 0000
-0.50 °C	0 °C	0000 0000
-0.75 °C	-1 °C	1111 1111
-1.00 °C	-1 °C	1111 1111
-25.00 °C	-25 °C	1110 0111
-25.25 °C	-25 °C	1110 0110
-54.75 °C	-55 °C	1100 1001
-55.00 °C	-55 °C	1100 1001
-65.00 °C	-65 °C	1011 1111

$00011001_2 = 0x19 = 25_{10}$. Negative temperatures are represented in 2's complement format. For T = -25 °C, the binary reading is $11100111_2 = 0xE7$. The 2's complement of 0xE7 (231_{10}) is $256_{10} - 231_{10} = 25_{10}$.

Example 1: In accordance with Figure 10, write a program to display the temperature measured by the TC74 temperature sensor. The transaction to be followed is similar to the one of Figure 7 with the exception that the *NACK* occurs right after the first received byte. For low current consumption, use the processor in the *sleep* mode. For that purpose, you need to awaken it periodically via the WDT in order to read the temperature and display it.

Solution: The complete program is listed in Table 6.

Figure 10. Hardware setup to test the I²C temperature sensor TC74

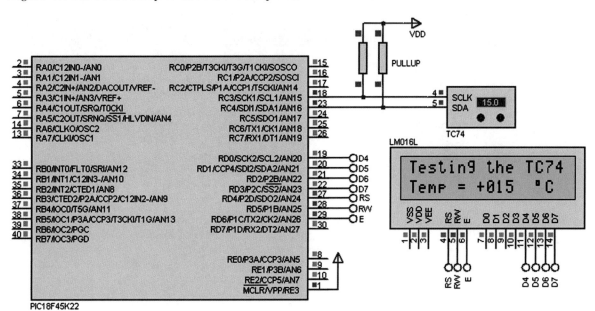

THE DS1307 I²C REAL-TIME CLOCK

The DS1307 serial real-time clock of Figure 11 is a low-power, BCD clock/calendar with 56 bytes of nonvolatile static RAM. The chip's 7-bit address is 1101000. It is manufactured by DALLAS SEMI-CONDUCTOR and requires a 32.768 KHz external crystal. It may be supplied by either the 5V supply or a 3V rechargeable battery for continuous operation. The chip has an SQW/OUT pin whose output frequency can be programmed to have 4 different values. Data is transferred serially to the internal registers listed in Figure 14a via the SDA and SCK lines.

The Control register (address 0x07) is used to program the *open drain* OUT/SQW pin in accordance to the status of SQWE (square wave enable):

Figure 11. Pin configuration of the DS1307 Real-Time Clock

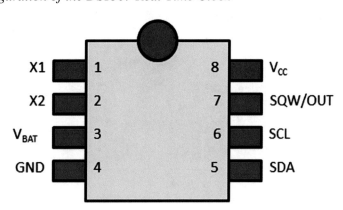

Table 6. Program listing of digital thermometer using the TC74 I²C temperature sensor

Program to test the TC74 temperature sensor. Looping is done via periodic interrupts of the watchdog timer.

```
1    #include    <p18cxxx.h>
2    #include    <i2c.h>
3    #include    <LCD4lib.h>
4
5    #pragma config WDTEN = ON        // watchdog timer Enabled
6    #pragma config WDTPS = 8         // WDT postscale select bits (1:8)
7
8    char Temperature;                // read temperature
9    char Line2[] = "Temp =        C ";
10
11   void Setup(void);
12   void ReadTC74(void);
13   void DispTemp(void);
14
15   void main(void) {
16       Setup();
17       ReadTC74();
18       DispTemp();
19       Sleep();
20   }
21
22   void Setup(void) {
23       InitLCD();                              // init LCD display
24       DispRomStr(Ln1Ch0, (ROM *) "Testing the TC74"); // display line 1
25       Line2[13] = 0xDF;                       // 0xDF: degree symbol
26       SSPADD = 9;                             // 100 Khz I2C frequency
27       SSPCON1 = 0b00111000;                   // MCU in master mode
28       ANSELCbits.ANSC3 = 0; ANSELCbits.ANSC4 = 0;
29   }
30
31   void ReadTC74(void) {
32       StartI2C();                             // start condition
33       putcI2C(0b10011010);                    // send device address with R/W = 0
34       putcI2C(0x00);                          // send internal address
35       RestartI2C();                           // restart condition
36       putcI2C(0b10011011);                    // send device address with R/W = 1
37       Temperature = getcI2C();                // read temperature data
38       NotAckI2C();                            // send a NACK
39       while (SSPCON2bits.ACKEN);              // wait until NACK sequence is over
40       StopI2C();                              // stop condition
41   }
42
43   void DispTemp(void) {
44       Line2[7] = (Temperature < 0? '-': '+'); // store + or - sign
45       if (Temperature < 0)
46           Temperature = -Temperature;         // abs. value of temperature
47       Bin2Asc(Temperature, &Line2[8]);        // convert to 3 ASCII digits
48       DispRamStr(Ln2Ch0, Line2);              // display temperature
49   }
```

- If SQWE = 0, the OUT/SQW pin follows the status of the OUT bit in register Control.
- If SQWE = 1, the OUT/SQW outputs a square wave whose frequency is selected according to RS1:RS0 as depicted in Table 7b.

As to the remaining registers, they hold time and calendar information in packed BCD format. The only irregularity is in register 0x02 which may hold the hour in either the 12-hour mode or 24-hour mode. In the 12-hour mode, bit 5 of the register stores the PM/AM status where logic low and high imply AM and PM respectively. Bit 6 of the hours register must be set to select the 12-hour mode. In the 24-hour mode, bit 6 must be cleared and bit 5 is part of the BCD digit indicating the 10's of hours.

The CLOCK HALT bit CH or bit 7 of the seconds register must be cleared to enable the real-time clock to be triggered by the clock signal. Otherwise, the clock is halted.

In configuring the RTC, one would normally have to load the eight internal registers with the appropriate time and date information. Once this is done, these registers should be read periodically every second. A good idea would be to place the MCU in sleep mode and have the SQW output of the RTC interrupt the CPU at a rate of 1 Hz. This can be accomplished by clearing both RS1 and RS0 and connecting SQW to one of the edge-triggered interrupt pins on the MCU. Care must be taken to pull-up the open-drain SQW pin. If a backup battery is not used, V_{BAT} may be tied to ground.

Table 7a. Timekeeper registers

ADDRESS	Bit7	Bit6	Bit5	Bit4	Bit3	Bit2	Bit1	Bit0	FUNCTION	RANGE
0x00	CH		10 Seconds			Seconds			Seconds	00 - 59
0x01	0		10 Minutes			Minutes			Minutes	00 - 59
0x02	0	12	10 Hour	10 Hour		Hours			Hours	1 - 12 +AM/PM 00 - 23
		24	PM / AM							
0x03	0	0	0	0	0		DAY		DAY	01 - 07
0x04	0	0	10 Date			Date			Date	01 - 31
0x05	0	0	0	10 Month		Month			Month	01 - 12
0x06		10 Year				Year			Year	00 - 99
0x07	OUT	0	0	SQWE	0	0	RS1	RS0	Control	-
0x08 - 0x3F									RAM 56 x 8	0 - 255

Table 7b. Square-wave output frequency selection

RS1	RS0	SQUARE WAVE OUTPUT FREQUENCY
0	0	1Hz
0	1	4.096kHz
1	0	8.192kHz
1	1	32.768kHz

Figure 12. Hardware setup to test the real-time clock

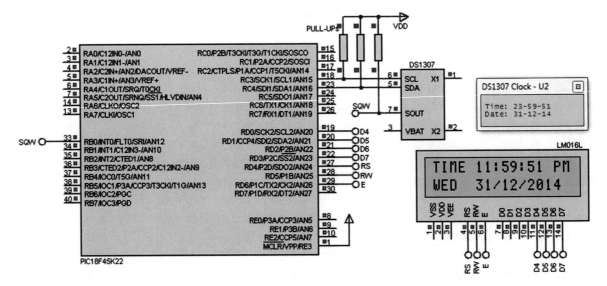

Example 2: Given the hardware setup of Figure 12, write a program to test the DS1307 real-time clock. The program should display the time `HH:MM:SS` on the LCD using the 12-hour mode. It is suggested to tackle it as follows:

a. Assuming the `TimeDate[]` declaration below (Time: Wed 11:59:50 PM, Date: 31/12/2014):

```
unsigned char TimeDate[] = {0x50,0x59,0x23,0x04,0x31,0x12,0x14};
```

Write the function `SetTime()` to transfer this data to the DS1307. This function also configures `SQW` to generate a 1 Hz square wave. Use a transaction like the one in Figure 4.

b. Code the function `ReadTime()` to transfer the contents of the RTC's internal registers to the time/date array `TimeDate[]`. *Hint*: use a transaction similar to the one in Figure 7.

c. Using parts (a) and (b) as well as the LCD library, write the complete program to update the time and date every second. Configure the MCU as a master device running at a clock rate of 100 KHz with F_{CY} = 1 MHz.

Solution: The complete program is listed in Table 8.

MODULAR HARDWARE

One of the hassles that might be encountered by a system designer is the fact that new hardware additions to the system require new microcontroller I/O pins. This would be a problem if the utilized MCU has a low pin-count, set aside the inconvenience of having to redraw the printed circuit board to accommodate the new addition. With the I²C bus, one may design a simple and small-size CPU board populated only by the microcontroller, the crystal oscillator, the reset circuitry and the power supply circuit. On the CPU board, the designer may mount several USB-like connectors dedicated to I/O additions. The connector would supply V_{cc} and ground to the peripheral device as well as SDA and SCL. This way a hardware

Table 8a. Program listing of digital clock using the DS1307 real-time clock

```
Program to test the DS1307 real-time clock. Looping is done via periodic interrupts of SQW on INT0.
1    #include     <p18cxxx.h>
2    #include     <string.h>
3    #include     <i2c.h>
4    #include     <LCD4lib.h>
5    #include     <BCDlib.h>
6
7    void Setup(void);                          // initialize system
8    void SetTime(void);                        // set initial time interactively
9    void ReadTime(void);                       // read time from RTC
10
11   char Line1[] = "TIME Hr:Mn:Sc  M";         // line 1
12   char Line2[] = "DoW  Dy/Mo/20Yr ";         // line 2
13   char DoW[][4] = {"SUN","MON","TUE","WED","THU","FRI","SAT"};    // DOW in ASCII
14   unsigned char TimeDate[] = {0x50,0x59,0x23,0x04,0x31,0x12,0x14}; // 2014-2015
15
16   void main(void)
17   {
18       Setup();
19       while (1)
20           Sleep();
21   }
22
23   void Setup(void)
24   {
25       InitLCD();                             // init LCD display
26       SSPADD = 9;                            // 100 KHz I2C frequency
27       SSPCON1 = 0b00111000;                  // MCU in master mode
28       ANSELCbits.ANSC3 = 0;
29       ANSELCbits.ANSC4 = 0;
30
31       SetTime();                             // turn on the 1 Hz frequency
32
33       ANSELBbits.ANSB0 = 0;                  // RB0: digital input
34       INTCONbits.INT0IE = 1;                 // enable INT0 interrupt
35       INTCONbits.GIE = 1;                    // global mask
36   }
37
38   #pragma code ISR = 0x0008
39   #pragma interrupt ISR
40
41   void ISR(void)
42   {                                          // interrupt every second
43       INTCONbits.INT0IF = 0;
44
45       ReadTime();                            // read time/date information
46       Line1[14] = (TimeDate[2] >= 0x12) ? 'P': 'A'; // decide PM/AM
47       PBCD2Asc(TimeDate[0], &Line1[11]);     // seconds data
48       PBCD2Asc(TimeDate[1], &Line1[8]);      // minutes data
49
50       if (TimeDate[2] >= 0x13)
51           BcdAdd(&TimeDate[2], -12);         // convert to 12-hour mode
52       else if (TimeDate[2] == 0)
53           TimeDate[2] = 0x12;                // Hr = 00 becomes 12 AM
54       PBCD2Asc(TimeDate[2], &Line1[5]);      // hours data
55
56       memcpy(&Line2[0], (void *) DoW[TimeDate[3]-1], 3);  // weekday data
57
58       PBCD2Asc(TimeDate[4], &Line2[5]);      // date data
59       PBCD2Asc(TimeDate[5], &Line2[8]);      // month data
60       PBCD2Asc(TimeDate[6], &Line2[13]);     // year data
61       DispRamStr(Ln1Ch0, Line1);             // display Line1
62       DispRamStr(Ln2Ch0, Line2);             // display Line2
```

Table 8b. Program listing of digital clock using the DS1307 real-time clock continued

```
63    }
64
65    void SetTime(void)
66    {
67        unsigned char i;
68
69        StartI2C();                           // start condition
70        putcI2C(0b11010000);                  // send device address with R/W = 0
71        putcI2C(0x00);                        // send seconds address
72
73        for (i = 0; i < 7; i++)
74                putcI2C(TimeDate[i]);         // init Time[3], Date[4]
75        putcI2C(0x10);                        // control byte: 1 Hz data
76        StopI2C();                            // stop condition
77    }
78
79    void ReadTime(void)
80    {
81        unsigned char i;
82
83        StartI2C();                           // start condition
84        putcI2C(0b11010000);                  // send device address with R/W = 0
85        putcI2C(0x00);                        // send internal address
86        RestartI2C();                         // restart condition
87        putcI2C(0b11010001);                  // send device address with R/W = 1
88
89        for (i = 0; i < 6; i++)               // read Time/Date information
90        {
91            TimeDate[i] = getcI2C();
92            AckI2C();                         // acknowledge to receive more data
93            while (SSPCON2bits.ACKEN);        // wait until ACK sequence is over
94        }
95
96        TimeDate[6] = getcI2C();              // read last byte in Time/Date array
97        NotAckI2C();
98        while (SSPCON2bits.ACKEN);            // wait until NACK sequence is over
99        StopI2C();                            // stop condition
100   }
```

addendum does not require modification of the CPU board and is powered-up from the connector. The I/O units may be innate I²C components such as the TC74 sensor or the DS1307 RTC described earlier in the chapter.

On the other hand, some non-I²C devices may be transformed to receive I²C commands. For instance, a multiplexed 4-digit display may be interfaced to a low-cost MCU with 2-wire interface. When the display module is physically connected on the bus, it can communicate with the CPU board using the serial protocol. In a way, this works like the plug-and-play philosophy of the Windows operating system. To avoid bus contention, each I/O device on the bus has a unique address. In parallel with the added hardware, one needs to design the pertinent software driver. The advantages of adopting this approach are:

• The concept of modularity is extended to the hardware as well. The master delegates responsibilities to the dedicated slaves like a good manager would do. This simplifies and speeds up system development tremendously.

- With the addition of a low-cost microcontroller on the I/O board, the program running on the CPU board becomes smaller. It is now the role of the I/O board to be in charge of all the intricacies required by a specific hardware configuration, i.e. multiplexed display, LCD, etc. The CPU board would only send "high-level" commands to the I/O card. Subsequently, the system designer concentrates his/her efforts on the particular software algorithm being implemented rather than the tedious I/O peculiarities.
- The system designer is freed from having to purchase a costly high pin-count MCU to accommodate a large number of peripherals. As a result, the CPU board may use a low cost MCU as well. The program memory requirements are also less stringent since the bulk of the I/O tasks is handled by the specific I/O board.

Here is a list of some typical I/O cards that can be designed for a variety of applications using an on-board low-cost MCU with I²C capabilities:

1. LCD display module.
2. 4-digit (or more) multiplexed 7-segment display.
3. Keypad module.
4. Dot matrix display.
5. High voltage interface card (with relays, triacs or SCRs).
6. General purpose I/O card.

I²C SUPPORT CHIPS AND MANUFACTURERS

In addition to the custom-made hardware modules listed above, one may use a wide variety of dedicated I²C support chips available on the market. Table 9 lists some of these components along with a brief description of each. Here is a list of some companies that manufacture I²C components:

- Microchip.
- Phillips.
- MAXIM/DALLAS.
- Cadex Electronics.
- Texas Instruments.
- Xicor.

CONCLUSION

The I²C bus standard has led to the surfacing of numerous components on the market due to its reliability, convenience and simplicity. An I²C network is reliable because of its master-slave functionality which guarantees that no bus contention will ever occur unless two devices with the same physical address are part of the network. The reliability also stems from the fact that data is sent to the master in digital format. This is particularly important in applications requiring the use of sensors. Suppose that a temperature sensor with an analog output is connected to the A/D input of an MCU via a long set of

Table 9. Table listing popular I²C components and their functionality

I2C device	Description
PCA9554 I/O expander	Used to add 8 parallel I/O pins to a low-pin count MCU. 8 such devices may be connected on the same serial bus.
MAX 518 Dual 8-bit DAC	2-channel digital-to-analog converter. 4 such devices may be connected on the same serial bus.
DS1621 Thermometer	Digital thermometer that can measure temperatures from -55°C to 125°C in 0.5°C increments. 8 such devices may be tied to the same bus.
AT24C18 Serial EEPROM	128 bytes serial EEPROM optimized for automotive applications where low power and low voltage operation are essential.
MAX6958 Display Driver	Drives a 4-digit multiplexed common-cathode 7-segment displays. It can also scan and debounce a matrix of up to 8 switches.
MAX6955 Display Driver	Drives up to 16 digits 7-segment, 8 digits 14-segment, or 128 discrete LEDs. It can also scan and debounce a matrix of up to 32 switches.
MAX6953 Display Driver	Cathode-row display driver that interfaces MCUs to four 5x7 dot-matrix LED displays through a 2-wire interface.
DS1855 Digital Pot	Dual non-volatile digital potentiometer and secure memory with 256 bytes of EEPROM cells.

wires (say 6 meters or more). The voltage drop incurred by the transmission line is normally remedied by software or hardware calibration. This is definitely a hassle especially when one has to interface the MCU to a large number of such sensors each having a different wire length.

The I²C bus is convenient because of its expandability. One can place many sensors on the bus without having to upgrade the processor. All this is achieved via 2 wires only. The designer would no longer have to conceive sophisticated I/O interfaces but rather he/she can use what is already available in the form of a 2-wire interface. If a processor does not have enough I/O pins, the designer may use an I/O expander chip. In a way, the MCU passes the buck to specialized peripheral devices thereby liberating itself from putting on a one-man show.

Last but not least is the issue of simplicity. As you may have observed, the I²C bus is relatively simple to work with. Once the underlying routines are developed, using them to communicate with peripheral devices turns out to be a trivial task. After being exposed to two or three such peripheral devices, you will find a great ease in learning about and utilizing new components. System designers went a long way from having to decode an added external device (allocate to it one or more logical addresses) to simply plugging the new device onto the serial bus and establishing instant communication.

Appendix 1

GLOSSARY

Absolute Address: A number that specifies the address of an instruction in memory, as opposed to a relative address, which specifies a displacement with respect to the program counter.

Active Low: A designation meaning that the function is performed when the appropriate line or signal is at a low voltage and not when the line is at a high voltage.

Address: A number that identifies a single location in program or data memory.

Address Bus: A bus (set of wires used to transmit information among 2 or more devices) that transmits an address and lets the MCU select an individual location in program or data memory.

Addressing Mode: Method of specifying exactly how the operand of an instruction identifies the data.

Address Word: A set of bits used to determine an address.

Algorithm: A series of logical steps to be followed sequentially in order to solve a problem or perform a task.

American Standard Code for Information Interchange (ASCII): A 7-bit binary code that identifies characters and digits. ASCII codes are used as a standard for the transmission of characters.

Architecture: A description of a microprocessor system's hardware parts, how they are connected, and how they communicate with each other.

Arithmetic Logic Unit (ALU): That part of a CPU that performs arithmetic and logical operations.

Assembler: A program that translates an assembly language program into a machine language program.

Assembler Directive: An instruction to the assembler, not translated into machine code.

Assembling: Translating an assembly language program into a machine language program.

Assembly (Symbolic) Language: A language in which symbols are used instead of numbers to represent operation codes (opcodes) and operands.

Base: A number used as a reference for constructing a number system.

Base Sixteen: Number system having sixteen digits, 0-9 and A-F.

Base Ten: Number system having ten digits, 0-9.

Base Two: Number system having two digits, 0-1.

Binary: Having two states.

Binary-Coded-Decimal (BCD): A number system in which a set of 4 bits represent 1 decimal digit.

Binary Logic: A system of data manipulation using a set of variables (1 and 0) and a series of logical operations.

Binary Representation: Base 2 number system.

Bit: A binary digit.

Bit Time: The amount of time to transmit a single digit.

Block Diagram: A graphic description of individual parts of a system and how they interact.

Breakpoint: A point in a program where the MPU stops executing.

Bus: A set of wires used to transmit information among two or more devices.

Byte: A set of 8 bits.

Call: To transfer control from a main program to a subroutine.

Carry Bit: A flag in the STATUS register that is set if the result of an ALU operation is a number too large to be contained in an 8-bit register.

Cascade: To connect the output of one device to the input of the next.

Central Processor Unit (CPU): That part of a computer that fetches, decodes, and executes instructions; it contains the control, calculating, and decision making sections of a computer.

Clock: A device, typically a crystal oscillator, which produces a series of regular pulses that synchronize the operations within a microcomputer.

Clock Cycle: The interval between successive positive or negative transitions in a clock pulse.

Clock Frequency: The reciprocal of cycle time; or, the number of clock cycles per second.

Comment Field: Field in an assembly language program that contains a comment.

Computer Program: A series of instructions that direct a computer to perform a specific task.

Conditional Branch: An instruction that loads the PC with an address (usually out-of-sequence) based upon a condition.

Control Bus: A bus that transmits control signals.

Control Unit: That part of the CPU that directs the fetching and execution of instructions, by providing timing and control signals.

Cross Assembler: An assembler that assembles a program to be run on another computer.

Data Bus: A bus that transmits data into and out of memory.

Delay Routine: A routine used in any program where a specific time delay is desired.

Destination: In a data transfer, the final location of the data.

Digit Carry: A flag in the STATUS register that is set if there is a carry from the least significant nibble during an addition.

Direct Addressing Mode: An addressing mode in which the data to be processed is specified by an address within the instruction.

Double-Precision Arithmetic: Arithmetic using two computer words (2 bytes for PIC18 devices) to represent one number.

Dual In-Line Package (DIP): A type of IC packaging having two parallel rows of pins.

Edge-Triggered: A response triggered by either the rising or falling edge of a signal and not the level.

Erasable Programmable Read-Only Memory (EPROM): A type of Read-Only Memory that can be erased by applying ultraviolet light and then reprogrammed.

Execute: To carry out instructions in a computer program.

Extended Addressing Mode: An addressing mode in which the data to be processed is in a memory location identified by a 2-byte address.

Fetch: The reading of an instruction by a computer.

Glitch (Noise Spike): Extraneous noise picked up on a wire.

Hand-Assembling: The process of translating an assembly language program into a machine language program by hand rather than by an assembler.

Hardware: The physical parts of a computer.

Hardware Interrupt: An interrupt caused by an external device connected to one of the MCU's interrupt pins.

High Impedance State: A state in which a device is disabled or electrically disconnected from the circuit.

High-Order Byte: The leftmost byte, or leftmost 2 hexadecimal digits.

Immediate Addressing Mode: An addressing mode in which the data to be processed is the operand that is stored within the instruction next to the OP code. On the PIC18, these instructions are the ones referring to a literal (movlw, addlw, etc.) among others.

Indexed Addressing Mode: An addressing mode where the address of the operand is computed by adding an offset to the index register contents (i.e. movf PLUSW0, W).

Index Register: A register whose contents are used in computing an indexed address (i.e. **FSR0**, **FSR1** and **FSR2**).

Inherent (or Implicit) Addressing Mode: An addressing mode in which either the data to be processed is found in an internal register or there is no data (i.e. daw, nop, clrwdt, sleep).

Input/Output Port: The place where data comes into and goes out of a device.

Instruction: A statement that tells the microprocessor what to do. It consists of an opcode plus one or more operands.

Instruction Set: A set of operations and opcodes characteristic of a specific microprocessor.

Interface Circuitry: An assembly of electrical circuit element that provides the necessary connection between a microcomputer and an external device (i.e. relay, transistor, optocoupler, etc.).

Integrated Circuit (IC): A piece of silicon that has several electronic parts on it (a complete circuit).

Internal Bus: A set of conductors within the MCU over which signals are exchanged among its components.

Interrupt: A temporary suspension of a computer's executing program so that it can deal with a higher priority task.

Interrupt Flag: A flip-flop that is set to indicate that an external device is requesting immediate service.

Interrupt Pin: A microprocessor pin that provokes an interrupt when triggered by an edge or a logic level.

Interrupt Mask: A bit that is used to either enable an interrupt to occur or disable it from (mask it out) disrupting the CPU.

Interrupt Service Routine: A routine to be executed in the event of an interrupt.

Interrupt Vectors: Locations assigned to interrupts, containing the starting address of their service routines.

Kilobyte (Kbyte): 1,024 bytes.

Label: A group of characters, of which the first must be alphabetic, used to identify a program name, statement, or memory location.

Level-Sensitive: A response triggered by the level (high or low voltage) of a line, and not by the edge.

LIFO: Last-In-First-Out.

Listing: A document that shows a side-by-side comparison of the assembly language program and the machine language resulting from it.

Load: To copy a number from a memory location into a register.

Look-Up Table: A table that contains two equivalent sets of values stored side by side so that any one of them can be retrieved at will.

Low-Order Byte: The rightmost byte, or 2 hexadecimal digits.

Machine Code: Binary or hexadecimal numbers used to convey instructions to a microprocessor (a "machine").

Machine Language: Same as machine code.

Megabyte (Mbyte): 1,048,676 bytes.

Memory: A set of physical locations that can contain numbers.

Microcontroller (MCU): A microprocessor plus memory and I/O. It is also called single chip micro-computer.

Microprocessor (MPU): A single small device that performs the functions of a CPU.

Microprocessor System: A microprocessor plus other devices needed to perform a specific task.

Mnemonic: A group of letters that symbolize an instruction.

Negative Status Bit (N): It is a flag in the STATUS register that is set if the result of an operation is negative.

Nested Loops: Loops within loops.

Nested Subroutines: Subroutines within subroutines.

Nibble: Half a byte (4 bits).

Nonvolatile Memory: A type of memory where data is retained even when the power is shut off.

Object Code: The hexadecimal or binary numbers contained in an object program.

Object Program: The machine language program resulting from assembling a source program.

Offset: An 8-bit number (signed or unsigned) that, when added to the index register contents, gives an indexed address (i.e. **WREG** is an offset to **FSR0** when using **PLUSW0** addressing mode).

Operand: The quantity that is operated on or the object of the instruction.

Operation Code (OP Code): A binary number recognized by the control unit to identify the type of instruction to be executed.

Overflow Status Bit (V): It is a flag in the **STATUS** register that is set if the result of an operation generates an overflow condition. This can happen when 2 signed numbers of the same polarity are added and the result is of the opposite sign.

Passing Parameters: Giving data and getting data from subroutines.

Peripheral: A unit of processing equipment external to the CPU, such as a keypad, display or printer.

Pin-Out: A diagram showing the pins of an IC and what they represent.

Polling: To interrogate each I/O device to determine whether or not it needs service.

Prioritize: To assign priorities to interrupt devices.

Program Counter (PC): A 21-bit register that holds the address of the next instruction to be executed.

Pulling from the Stack: Copying the top value from a microprocessor's stack into a specific register.

Pushing onto the Stack: Storing a value in the top memory location of a microprocessor's stack.

Random Access Memory (RAM): A type of memory in which any individual location may be accessed directly. Usually Read/Write Memory.

Read-Only Memory (ROM): A type of memory having only read capabilities.

Read/Write memory: A type of memory that has both read and write capabilities.

Register: A physical location implemented with storage cells (usually flip-flops) that can contain a binary value.

Relative Address: A signed displacement (or offset) that is added to the current program counter contents. The result of the addition is placed back in the program counter to affect a transfer of control.

Relative Addressing Mode: An addressing mode where the address of the next instruction to be executed is computed at run time based upon the current PC and a signed offset stored within the instruction.

Return Instruction: An instruction that causes a return to the calling routine. This is done by pulling the return address from the hardware stack.

Retlw Instruction: It is similar to the return instruction with the addition that the immediate value (literal) specified within the instruction is returned as an output parameter in **WREG**.

Routine: A program segment that performs a specialized task and can be part of a larger program.

Serial I/O: The transmission of a group of bits one bit at a time.

Sign Bit: The most significant bit in a signed binary number.

Signed Binary Number: A binary number that can be interpreted as either positive or negative.

Sign Extension: Filling out the most significant bits with all 0s if the number is positive and with all ones if the number is negative.

Software: Computer programs.

Source Code: A program written in assembly language or any high level language (versus machine code).

Stack: A set of contiguous memory locations used in Last-In-First-Out (LIFO) fashion. It is used to save variables or registers for later retrieval.

Stack Pointer: A register whose contents determine the location where data is to be pushed on the stack.

Subroutine: A set of instructions assigned to perform a certain task and is invoked with the call or rcall instruction. Subroutines are essential in providing modularity to computer programs.

Three-State Buffer: A buffer that has three possible states: 1, 0, and disabled (high impedance).

Toggle: To reverse the state of a bit or switch.

Two's Complement: A binary notation that represents signed numbers.

Unidirectional: Data may flow in one direction only.

Unsigned Binary Number: A binary number interpreted as a positive number. Its most significant bit is not treated as a sign bit but rather as part of the number.

Volatile Memory: A type of memory where stored data is retained as long as power is supplied.

Word: A set of bits of varying length, usually a multiple of 4 or 8.

Working Register: A register closely associated with the ALU. In most instructions, it is one of the operands the ALU uses for arithmetic and logic operations. It can be the source and the destination register of an instruction.

Zero Status Bit: It is a flag in the **STATUS** register that is set if the result of an ALU operation is 0 and cleared otherwise.

288

Appendix 2

SPECIAL FUNCTION REGISTERS

B.1: SFRs OF PIC18(L)F2X/4XK22 DEVICES. GREEN BLOCK USES BANKED MODE

Name	Bit 7	Bit 6	Bit 5	Bit 4	Bit 3	Bit 2	Bit 1	Bit 0	Value on POR, BOR
ANSELA	–	–	ANSA5	–	ANSA3	ANSA2	ANSA1	ANSA0	--1- 1111
ANSELB	–	–	ANSB5	ANSB4	ANSB3	ANSB2	ANSB1	ANSB0	--11 1111
ANSELC	ANSC7	ANSC6	ANSC5	ANSC4	ANSC3	ANSC2	–	–	1111 11--
ANSELD[1]	ANSD7	ANSD6	ANSD5	ANSD4	ANSD3	ANSD2	ANSD1	ANSD0	1111 1111
ANSELE[1]	–	–	–	–	–	ANSE2	ANSE1	ANSE0	---- -111
PMD2	–	–	–	–	CTMUMD	CMP2MD	CMP1MD	ADCMD	---- 0000
PMD1	MSSP2MD	MSSP1MD	–	CCP5MD	CCP4MD	CCP3MD	CCP2MD	CCP1MD	00-0 0000
PMD0	UART2MD	UART1MD	TMR6MD	TMR5MD	TMR4MD	TMR3MD	TMR2MD	TMR1MD	0000 0000
VREFCON2	–	–	–	DACR4	DACR3	DACR2	DACR1	DACR0	---0 0000
VREFCON1	DACEN	DACLPS	DACOE	–	DACPSS1	DACPSS0	–	DACNSS	000-00-0
VREFCON0	FVREN	FVRST	FVRS1	FVRS0	–	–	–	–	0001 ----
CTMUICON	ITRIM5	ITRIM4	ITRIM3	ITRIM2	ITRIM1	ITRIM0	IRNG1	IRNG0	0000 0000
CTMUCONL	EDG2POL	EDG2SEL1	EDG2SEL0	EDG1POL	EDG1SEL1	EDG1SEL0	EDG2STAT	EDG1STAT	0000 0000
CTMUCONH	CTMUEN	–	CTMUSIDL	TGEN	EDGEN	EDGSEQEN	IDISSEN	CTTRIG	0000 0000
SRCON1	SRSPE	SRSCKE	SRSC2E	SRSC1E	SRRPE	SRRCKE	SRRC2E	SRRC1E	0000 0000
SRCON0	SRLEN	SRCLK2	SRCLK1	SRCLK0	SRQEN	SRNQEN	SRPS	SRPR	0000 0000
CCPTMRS1	–	–	–	–	C5TSEL1	C5TSEL0	C4TSEL1	C4TSEL0	---- 0000
CCPTMRS0	C3TSEL1	C3TSEL0	–	C2TSEL1	C2TSEL0	–	C1TSEL1	C1TSEL0	00-0 0-00
T6CON	–	T6OUTPS3	T6OUTPS2	T6OUTPS1	T6OUTPS0	TMR6ON	T6CKPS1	T6CKPS0	-000 0000
PR6	Timer6 Period Register								1111 1111
TMR6	Timer6 Register								0000 0000
T5GCON	TMR5GE	T5GPOL	T5GTM	T5GSPM	T5GGO/DONE	T5GVAL	T5GSS1	T5GSS0	0000 0x00
T5CON	TMR5CS1	TMR5CS0	T5CKPS1	T5CKPS0	T5SOSCEN	T5SYNC	T5RD16	TMR5ON	0000 0000
TMR5L	Timer5 Register Low Byte								0000 0000
TMR5H	Timer5 Register High Byte								0000 0000
T4CON	–	T4OUTPS3	T4OUTPS2	T4OUTPS1	T4OUTPS0	TMR4ON	T4CKPS1	T4CKPS0	-000 0000
PR4	Timer4 Period Register								1111 1111
TMR4	Timer4 Register								0000 0000
CCP5CON	–	–	DC5B1	DC5B0	CCP5M3	CCP5M2	CCP5M1	CCP5M0	--00 0000
CCPR5L	Capture/Compare/PWM Register 5, Low Byte								xxxx xxxx
CCPR5H	Capture/Compare/PWM Register 5, High Byte								xxxx xxxx
CCP4CON	–	–	DC4B1	DC4B0	CCP4M3	CCP4M2	CCP4M1	CCP4M0	--00 0000
CCPR4L	Capture/Compare/PWM Register 4, Low Byte								xxxx xxxx
CCPR4H	Capture/Compare/PWM Register 4, High Byte								xxxx xxxx
PSTR3CON	–	–	–	STR3SYNC	STR3D	STR3C	STR3B	STR3A	---0 0001
ECCP3AS	CCP3ASE	CCP3AS2	CCP3AS1	CCP3AS0	PSS3AC1	PSS3AC0	PSS3BD1	PSS3BD0	0000 0000
PWM3CON	P3RSEN	P3DC6	P3DC5	P3DC4	P3DC3	P3DC2	P3DC1	P3DC0	0000 0000
CCP3CON	P3M1	P3M0	DC3B1	DC3B0	CCP3M3	CCP3M2	CCP3M1	CCP3M0	0000 0000
CCPR3L	Capture/Compare/PWM Register 3, Low Byte								xxxx xxxx
CCPR3H	Capture/Compare/PWM Register 3, High Byte								xxxx xxxx
SLRCON[1]	–	–	–	SLRE	SLRD	SLRC	SLRB	SLRA	---1 1111
SLRCON[2]	–	–	–	–	–	SLRC	SLRB	SLRA	---- -111
WPUB	WPUB7	WPUB6	WPUB5	WPUB4	WPUB3	WPUB2	WPUB1	WPUB0	1111 1111
IOCB	IOCB7	IOCB6	IOCB5	IOCB4	–	–	–	–	1111 ----
PSTR2CON	–	–	–	STR2SYNC	STR2D	STR2C	STR2B	STR2A	---0 0001
ECCP2AS	CCP2ASE	CCP2AS2	CCP2AS1	CCP2AS0	PSS2AC1	PSS2AC0	PSS2BD1	PSS2BD0	0000 0000

Legend: x = unknown, u = unchanged, –= unimplemented, q = value depends on condition.
Note 1: PIC18(L)F4XK22 devices only.
Note 2: PIC18(L)F2XK22 devices only.
Note 3: PIC18(L)F23/24K22 and PIC18(L)F43/44K22 devices only.
Note 4: PIC18(L)F26K22 and PIC18(L)F46K22 devices only.

	Bit 7	Bit 6	Bit 5	Bit 4	Bit 3	Bit 2	Bit 1	Bit 0	
PWM2CON	P2RSEN	P2DC6	P2DC5	P2DC4	P2DC3	P2DC2	P2DC1	P2DC0	0000 0000
CCP2CON	P2M1	P2M0	DC2B1	DC2B0	CCP2M3	CCP2M2	CCP2M1	CCP2M0	0000 0000
CCPR2L	Capture/Compare/PWM Register 2, Low Byte								xxxx xxxx
CCPR2H	Capture/Compare/PWM Register 2, High Byte								xxxx xxxx
SSP2CON3	ACKTIM	PCIE	SCIE	BOEN	SDAHT	SBCDE	AHEN	DHEN	0000 0000
SSP2MSK	SSP2 MASK Register bits								1111 1111
SSP2CON2	GCEN	ACKSTAT	ACKDT	ACKEN	RCEN	PEN	RSEN	SEN	0000 0000
SSP2CON1	WCOL	SSPOV	SSPEN	CKP	SSPM3	SSPM2	SSPM1	SSPM0	0000 0000
SSP2STAT	SMP	CKE	D/$\overline{\text{A}}$	P	S	R/$\overline{\text{W}}$	UA	BF	0000 0000
SSP2ADD	SSP2 Address Register in I²C Slave Mode. SSP2 Baud Rate Reload Register in I²C Master Mode								0000 0000
SSP2BUF	SSP2 Receive Buffer/Transmit Register								xxxx xxxx
BAUDCON2	ABDOVF	RCIDL	DTRXP	CKTXP	BRG16	–	WUE	ABDEN	01x0 0-00
RCSTA2	SPEN	RX9	SREN	CREN	ADDEN	FERR	OERR	RX9D	0000 000x
TXSTA2	CSRC	TX9	TXEN	SYNC	SENDB	BRGH	TRMT	TX9D	0000 0010
TXREG2	EUSART2 Transmit Register								0000 0000
RCREG2	EUSART2 Receive Register								0000 0000
SPBRG2	EUSART2 Baud Rate Generator Register Low Byte								0000 0000
SPBRGH2	EUSART2 Baud Rate Generator Register High Byte								0000 0000
CM2CON1	MC1OUT	MC2OUT	C1RSEL	C2RSEL	C1HYS	C2HYS	C1SYNC	C2SYNC	0000 0000
CM2CON0	C2ON	C2OUT	C2OE	C2POL	C2SP	C2R	C2CH1	C2CH0	0000 1000
CM1CON0	C1ON	C1OUT	C1OE	C1POL	C1SP	C1R	C1CH1	C1CH0	0000 1000
PIE4	–	–	–	–	–	CCP5IE	CCP4IE	CCP3IE	---- -000
PIR4	–	–	–	–	–	CCP5IF	CCP4IF	CCP3IF	---- -000
IPR4	–	–	–	–	–	CCP5IP	CCP4IP	CCP3IP	---- -000
PIE5	–	–	–	–	–	TMR6IE	TMR5IE	TMR4IE	---- -000
PIR5	–	–	–	–	–	TMR6IF	TMR5IF	TMR4IF	---- -111
IPR5	–	–	–	–	–	TMR6IP	TMR5IP	TMR4IP	---- -111
PORTA	RA7	RA6	RA5	RA4	RA3	RA2	RA1	RA0	xx0x 0000
PORTB	RB7	RB6	RB5	RB4	RB3	RB2	RB1	RB0	xxx0 0000
PORTC	RC7	RC6	RC5	RC4	RC3	RC2	RC1	RC0	0000 00xx
PORTD[1]	RD7	RD6	RD5	RD4	RD3	RD2	RD1	RD0	0000 0000
PORTE[1]	–	–	–	–	RE3	RE2	RE1	RE0	---- x000
PORTE[2]	–	–	–	–	RE3	–	–	–	---- x---
LATA	PORTA Data Latch Register (Read and Write to Data Latch)								xxxx xxxx
LATB	PORTB Data Latch Register (Read and Write to Data Latch)								xxxx xxxx
LATC	PORTC Data Latch Register (Read and Write to Data Latch)								xxxx xxxx
LATD[1]	PORTD Data Latch Register (Read and Write to Data Latch)								xxxx xxxx
LATE[1]	–	–	–	–	–	LATE2	LATE1	LATE0	---- -xxx
TRISA	PORTA Data Direction Register								1111 1111
TRISB	PORTB Data Direction Register								1111 1111
TRISC	PORTC Data Direction Register								1111 1111
TRISD[1]	PORTD Data Direction Register								1111 1111
TRISE	WPUE3	–	–	–	–	TRISE2[1]	TRISE1[1]	TRISE0[1]	1--- -111
OSCTUNE	INTSRC	PLLEN	TUN5	TUN4	TUN3	TUN2	TUN1	TUN0	00xx xxxx
HLVDCON	VDIRMAG	BGVST	IRVST	HLVDEN	HLVDL3	HLVDL2	HLVDL1	HLVDL0	0000 0000
PIE1	–	ADIE	RC1IE	TX1IE	SSP1IE	CCP1IE	TMR2IE	TMR1IE	-000 0000
PIR1	–	ADIF	RC1IF	TX1IF	SSP1IF	CCP1IF	TMR2IF	TMR1IF	-000 0000
IPR1	–	ADIP	RC1IP	TX1IP	SSP1IP	CCP1IP	TMR2IP	TMR1IP	-111 1111
PIE2	OSCFIE	C1IE	C2IE	EEIE	BCL1IE	HLVDIE	TMR3IE	CCP2IE	0000 0000
PIR2	OSCFIF	C1IF	C2IF	EEIF	BCL1IF	HLVDIF	TMR3IF	CCP2IF	0000 0000
IPR2	OSCFIP	C1IP	C2IP	EEIP	BCL1IP	HLVDIP	TMR3IP	CCP2IP	1111 1111
PIE3	SSP2IE	BCL2IE	RC2IE	TX2IE	CTMUIE	TMR5GIE	TMR3GIE	TMR1GIE	0000 0000
PIR3	SSP2IF	BCL2IF	RC2IF	TX2IF	CTMUIF	TMR5GIF	TMR3GIF	TMR1GIF	0000 0000
IPR3	SSP2IP	BCL2IP	RC2IP	TX2IP	CTMUIP	TMR5GIP	TMR3GIP	TMR1GIP	0000 0000

Legend: x = unknown, u = unchanged, — = unimplemented, q = value depends on condition.

Note 1:   PIC18(L)F4XK22 devices only.
Note 2:   PIC18(L)F2XK22 devices only.
Note 3:   PIC18(L)F23/24K22 and PIC18(L)F43/44K22 devices only.
Note 4:   PIC18(L)F26K22 and PIC18(L)F46K22 devices only.

EECON1	EEPGD	CFGS	–	FREE	WRERR	WREN	WR	RD	xx-0 x000
EECON2	EEPROM Control Register 2 (not a physical register)								---- --00
EEDATA	EEPROM Data Register								0000 0000
EEADR	EEADR<7:0>								0000 0000
EEADRH[4]	–	–	–	–	–	–	EEADR9	EEADR8	---- --00
RCSTA1	SPEN	RX9	SREN	CREN	ADDEN	FERR	OERR	RX9D	0000 000x
TXSTA1	CSRC	TX9	TXEN	SYNC	SENDB	BRGH	TRMT	TX9D	0000 0010
TXREG1	EUSART1 Transmit Register								0000 0000
RCREG1	EUSART1 Receive Register								0000 0000
SPBRG1	EUSART1 Baud Rate Generator Register Low Byte								0000 0000
SPBRGH1	EUSART1 Baud Rate Generator Register High Byte								0000 0000
T3CON	TMR3CS1	TMR3CS0	T3CKPS1	T3CKPS0	T3SOSCEN	$\overline{\text{T3SYNC}}$	T3RD16	TMR3ON	0000 0000
TMR3L	Timer3 Register Low Byte								xxxx xxxx
TMR3H	Timer3 Register High Byte								xxxx xxxx
T3GCON	TMR3GE	T3GPOL	T3GTM	T3GSPM	T3GGO/$\overline{\text{DONE}}$	T3GVAL	T3GSS1	T3GSS0	0000 0x00
ECCP1AS	CCP1ASE	CCP1AS2	CCP1AS1	CCP1AS0	PSS1AC1	PSS1AC0	PSS1BD1	PSS1BD0	0000 0000
PWM1CON	P1RSEN	P1DC6	P1DC5	P1DC4	P1DC3	P1DC2	P1DC1	P1DC0	0000 0000
BAUDCON1	ABDOVF	RCIDL	DTRXP	CKTXP	BRG16	–	WUE	ABDEN	0100 0-00
PSTR1CON	–	–	–	STR1SYNC	STR1D	STR1C	STR1B	STR1A	---0 0001
T2CON	–	T2OUTPS3	T2OUTPS2	T2OUTPS1	T2OUTPS0	TMR2ON	T2CKPS1	T2CKPS0	-000 0000
PR2	Timer2 Period Register								1111 1111
TMR2	Timer2 Register								0000 0000
CCP1CON	P1M1	P1M0	DC1B1	DC1B0	CCP1M3	CCP1M2	CCP1M1	CCP1M0	0000 0000
CCPR1L	Capture/Compare/PWM Register 1, Low Byte								xxxx xxxx
CCPR1H	Capture/Compare/PWM Register 1, High Byte								xxxx xxxx
ADCON2	ADFM	–	ACQT2	ACQT1	ACQT0	ADCS2	ADCS1	ADCS0	0-00 0000
ADCON1	TRIGSEL	–	–	–	PVCFG1	PVCFG0	NVCFG1	NVCFG0	0--- 0000
ADCON0	–	CHS4	CHS3	CHS2	CHS1	CHS0	GO/$\overline{\text{DONE}}$	ADON	--00 0000
ADRESL	A/D Result Register Low Byte								xxxx xxxx
ADRESH	A/D Result Register High Byte								xxxx xxxx
SSP1CON2	GCEN	ACKSTAT	ACKDT	ACKEN	RCEN	PEN	RSEN	SEN	0000 0000
SSP1CON1	WCOL	SSPOV	SSPEN	CKP	SSPM3	SSPM2	SSPM1	SSPM0	0000 0000
SSP1STAT	SMP	CKE	D/$\overline{\text{A}}$	P	S	R/$\overline{\text{W}}$	UA	BF	0000 0000
SSP1ADD	SSP1 Address Register in I²C Slave Mode. SSP1 Baud Rate Register in I²C Master Mode								0000 0000
SSP1BUF	SSP1 Receive Buffer/Transmit Register								xxxx xxxx
SSP1MSK	SSP1 MASK Register bits								1111 1111
SSP1CON3	ACKTIM	PCIE	SCIE	BOEN	SDAHT	SBCDE	AHEN	DHEN	0000 0000
T1GCON	TMR1GE	T1GPOL	T1GTM	T1GSPM	T1GGO/$\overline{\text{DONE}}$	T1GVAL	T1GSS1	T1GSS0	0000 xx00
T1CON	TMR1CS1	TMR1CS0	T1CKPS1	T1CKPS0	T1SOSCEN	$\overline{\text{T1SYNC}}$	T1RD16	TMR1ON	0000 0000
TMR1L	Timer1 Register Low Byte								xxxx xxxx
TMR1H	Timer1 Register High Byte								xxxx xxxx
RCON	IPEN	SBOREN	–	$\overline{\text{RI}}$	$\overline{\text{TO}}$	$\overline{\text{PD}}$	$\overline{\text{POR}}$	$\overline{\text{BOR}}$	01-1 1100
WDTCON	–	–	–	–	–	–	–	SWDTEN	---- ---0
OSCCON2	PLLRDY	SOSCRUN	–	MFIOSEL	SOSCGO	PRISD	MFIOFS	LFIOFS	00-0 01x0
OSCCON	IDLEN	IRCF2	IRCF1	IRCF0	OSTS	HFIOFS	SCS1	SCS0	0011 q000
T0CON	TMR0ON	T08BIT	T0CS	T0SE	PSA	T0PS2	T0PS1	T0PS0	1111 1111
TMR0L	Timer0 Register Low Byte								xxxx xxxx
TMR0H	Timer0 Register High Byte								0000 0000
STATUS	–	–	–	N	OV	Z	DC	C	---x xxxx
FSR2L	Indirect Data Memory Address Pointer 2 Low Byte								xxxx xxxx
FSR2H	–	–	–	–	Indirect Data Memory Address Pointer 2 High Byte				---- 0000

Legend: x = unknown, u = unchanged, – = unimplemented, q = value depends on condition.
Note 1: PIC18(L)F4XK22 devices only.
Note 2: PIC18(L)F2XK22 devices only.
Note 3: PIC18(L)F23/24K22 and PIC18(L)F43/44K22 devices only.
Note 4: PIC18(L)F26K22 and PIC18(L)F46K22 devices only.

Register									Reset Value
PLUSW2	Use contents of FSR2 to address data memory – value of FSR2 is offset by W (not a physical register)								---- ----
PREINC2	Use contents of FSR2 to address data memory – value of FSR2 pre-incremented (not a physical register)								---- ----
POSTDEC2	Use contents of FSR2 to address data memory – value of FSR2 post-decremented (not a physical register)								---- ----
POSTINC2	Use contents of FSR2 to address data memory – value of FSR2 pre-incremented (not a physical register)								---- ----
INDF2	Use contents of FSR2 to address data memory – value of FSR2 not changed (not a physical register)								---- ----
BSR	–	–	–	–	Bank Select Register				---- 0000
FSR1L	Indirect Data Memory Address Pointer 1 Low Byte								xxxx xxxx
FSR1H	–	–	–	–	Indirect Data Memory Address Pointer 1 High Byte				---- 0000
PLUSW1	Use contents of FSR1 to address data memory – value of FSR1 is offset by W (not a physical register)								---- ----
PREINC1	Use contents of FSR1 to address data memory – value of FSR1 pre-incremented (not a physical register)								---- ----
POSTDEC1	Use contents of FSR1 to address data memory – value of FSR1 post-decremented (not a physical register)								---- ----
POSTINC1	Use contents of FSR1 to address data memory – value of FSR1 pre-incremented (not a physical register)								---- ----
INDF1	Use contents of FSR1 to address data memory – value of FSR1 not changed (not a physical register)								---- ----
WREG	Working Register								xxxx xxxx
FSR0L	Indirect Data Memory Address Pointer 0, Low Byte								xxxx xxxx
FSR0H	–	–	–	–	Indirect Data Memory Address Pointer 0, High Byte				---- 0000
PLUSW0	Use contents of FSR0 to address data memory – value of FSR0 is offset by W (not a physical register)								---- ----
PREINC0	Uses contents of FSR0 to address data memory – value of FSR0 pre-incremented (not a physical register)								---- ----
POSTDEC0	Uses contents of FSR0 to address data memory – value of FSR0 post-decremented (not a physical register)								---- ----
POSTINC0	Uses contents of FSR0 to address data memory – value of FSR0 pre-incremented (not a physical register)								---- ----
INDF0	Uses contents of FSR0 to address data memory – value of FSR0 not changed (not a physical register)								---- ----
INTCON3	INT2IP	INT1IP	–	INT2IE	INT1IE	–	INT2IF	INT1IF	11-0 0-00
INTCON2	RBPU	INTEDG0	INTEDG1	INTEDG2	–	TMR0IP	–	RBIP	1111 -1-1
INTCON	GIE/GIEH	PEIE/GIEL	TMR0IE	INT0IE	RBIE	TMR0IF	INT0IF	RBIF	0000 000x
PRODL	Product Register Low Byte								xxxx xxxx
PRODH	Product Register High Byte								xxxx xxxx
TABLAT	Program Memory Table Latch								0000 0000
TBLPTRL	Program Memory Table Pointer Low Byte (TBLPTR<7:0>)								0000 0000
TBLPTRH	Program Memory Table Pointer High Byte (TBLPTR<15:8>)								0000 0000
TBLPTRU	–	–	Program Memory Table Pointer Upper Byte (TBLPTR<21:16>)						--00 0000
PCL	PC Low Byte (PC<7:0>)								0000 0000
PCLATH	Holding Register for PC<15:8>								0000 0000
PCLATU	–	–	–	Holding Register for PC<20:16>					---0 0000
STKPTR	STKFUL	STKUNF	–	STKPTR<4:0>					00-0 0000
TOSL	Top-of-Stack Low Byte (TOS<7:0>)								0000 0000
TOSH	Top-of-Stack High Byte (TOS<15:8>)								0000 0000
TOSU	–	–	–	Top-of-Stack Upper Byte (TOS<20:16>)					---0 0000

Legend: x = unknown, u = unchanged, — = unimplemented, q = value depends on condition.

Note 1: PIC18(L)F4XK22 devices only.

Note 2: PIC18(L)F2XK22 devices only.

Note 3: PIC18(L)F23/24K22 and PIC18(L)F43/44K22 devices only.

Note 4: PIC18(L)F26K22 and PIC18(L)F46K22 devices only.

B.2 SFR MAP OF PIC18(L)F2X/4XK22 DEVICES. GREEN BLOCK USES BANKED MODE

Address	Name	Address	Name	Address	Name	Address	Name
0xF38	ANSELA	0xF6A	SSP2MSK	0xF9C	HLVDCON	0xFCE	TMR1L
0xF39	ANSELB	0xF6B	SSP2CON2	0xF9D	PIE1	0xFCF	TMR1H
0xF3A	ANSELC	0xF6C	SSP2CON1	0xF9E	PIR1	0xFD0	RCON
0xF3B	ANSELD	0xF6D	SSP2STAT	0xF9F	IPR1	0xFD1	WDTCON
0xF3C	ANSELE	0xF6E	SSP2ADD	0xFA0	PIE2	0xFD2	OSCCON2
0xF3D	PMD2	0xF6F	SSP2BUF	0xFA1	PIR2	0xFD3	OSCCON
0xF3E	PMD1	0xF70	BAUDCON2	0xFA2	IPR2	0xFD4	_(2)
0xF3F	PMD0	0xF71	RCSTA2	0xFA3	PIE3	0xFD5	T0CON
0xF40	VREFCON2	0xF72	TXSTA2	0xFA4	PIR3	0xFD6	TMR0L
0xF41	VREFCON1	0xF73	TXREG2	0xFA5	IPR3	0xFD7	TMR0H
0xF42	VREFCON0	0xF74	RCREG2	0xFA6	EECON1	0xFD8	STATUS
0xF43	CTMUICON	0xF75	SPBRG2	0xFA7	EECON2(3)	0xFD9	FSR2L
0xF44	CTMUCONL	0xF76	SPBRGH2	0xFA8	EEDATA	0xFDA	FSR2H
0xF45	CTMUCONH	0xF77	CM2CON1	0xFA9	EEADR	0xFDB	PLUSW2(3)
0xF46	SRCON1	0xF78	CM2CON0	0xFAA	EEADRH(4)	0xFDC	PREINC2(3)
0xF47	SRCON0	0xF79	CM1CON0	0xFAB	RCSTA1	0xFDD	POSTDEC2(3)
0xF48	CCPTMRS1	0xF7A	PIE4	0xFAC	TXSTA1	0xFDE	POSTINC2(3)
0xF49	CCPTMRS0	0xF7B	PIR4	0xFAD	TXREG1	0xFDF	INDF2(3)
0xF4A	T6CON	0xF7C	IPR4	0xFAE	RCREG1	0xFE0	BSR
0xF4B	PR6	0xF7D	PIE5	0xFAF	SPBRG1	0xFE1	FSR1L
0xF4C	TMR6	0xF7E	PIR5	0xFB0	SPBRGH1	0xFE2	FSR1H
0xF4D	T5GCON	0xF7F	IPR5	0xFB1	T3CON	0xFE3	PLUSW1(3)
0xF4E	T5CON	0xF80	PORTA	0xFB2	TMR3L	0xFE4	PREINC1(3)
0xF4F	TMR5L	0xF81	PORTB	0xFB3	TMR3H	0xFE5	POSTDEC1(3)
0xF50	TMR5H	0xF82	PORTC	0xFB4	T3GCON	0xFE6	POSTINC1(3)
0xF51	T4CON	0xF83	PORTD(1)	0xFB5	_(2)	0xFE7	INDF1(3)
0xF52	PR4	0xF84	PORTE	0xFB6	ECCP1AS	0xFE8	WREG
0xF53	TMR4	0xF85	_(2)	0xFB7	PWM1CON	0xFE9	FSR0L
0xF54	CCP5CON	0xF86	_(2)	0xFB8	BAUDCON1	0xFEA	FSR0H
0xF55	CCPR5L	0xF87	_(2)	0xFB9	PSTR1CON	0xFEB	PLUSW0(3)
0xF56	CCPR5H	0xF88	_(2)	0xFBA	T2CON	0xFEC	PREINC0(3)
0xF57	CCP4CON	0xF89	LATA	0xFBB	PR2	0xFED	POSTDEC0(3)
0xF58	CCPR4L	0xF8A	LATB	0xFBC	TMR2	0xFEE	POSTINC0(3)
0xF59	CCPR4H	0xF8B	LATC	0xFBD	CCP1CON	0xFEF	INDF0(3)
0xF5A	PSTR3CON	0xF8C	LATD(1)	0xFBE	CCPR1L	0xFF0	INTCON3
0xF5B	ECCP3AS	0xF8D	LATE(1)	0xFBF	CCPR1H	0xFF1	INTCON2
0xF5C	PWM3CON	0xF8E	_(2)	0xFC0	ADCON2	0xFF2	INTCON
0xF5D	CCP3CON	0xF8F	_(2)	0xFC1	ADCON1	0xFF3	PRODL
0xF5E	CCPR3L	0xF90	_(2)	0xFC2	ADCON0	0xFF4	PRODH
0xF5F	CCPR3H	0xF91	_(2)	0xFC3	ADRESL	0xFF5	TABLAT
0xF60	SLRCON	0xF92	TRISA	0xFC4	ADRESH	0xFF6	TBLPTRL
0xF61	WPUB	0xF93	TRISB	0xFC5	SSP1CON2	0xFF7	TBLPTRH
0xF62	IOCB	0xF94	TRISC	0xFC6	SSP1CON1	0xFF8	TBLPTRU
0xF63	PSTR2CON	0xF95	TRISD	0xFC7	SSP1STAT	0xFF9	PCL
0xF64	ECCP2AS	0xF96	TRISE	0xFC8	SSP1ADD	0xFFA	PCLATH
0xF65	PWM2CON	0xF97	_(2)	0xFC9	SSP1BUF	0xFFB	PCLATU
0xF66	CCP2CON	0xF98	_(2)	0xFCA	SSP1MSK	0xFFC	STKPTR
0xF67	CCPR2L	0xF99	_(2)	0xFCB	SSP1CON3	0xFFD	TOSL
0xF68	CCPR2H	0xF9A	_(2)	0xFCC	T1GCON	0xFFE	TOSH
0xF69	SSP2CON3	0xF9B	OSCTUNE	0xFCD	T1CON	0xFFF	TOSU

Note 1: PIC18(L)F4XK22 devices only.
Note 2: Unimplemented registers are read as '0'.
Note 3: This is not a physical register.
Note 4: PIC18(L)F26K22 and PIC18(L)F46K22 devices only.

B.3 SPECIAL FUNCTION REGISTERS IN ALPHABETIC ORDER (BIT-BY-BIT DISCUSSION)

ADCON0:   A/D CONTROL REGISTER 0

U-0	R/W-0	R/W-0	R/W-0	R/W-0	R/W-0	R/W-0	R/W-0
-			CHS<4:0>			GO/$\overline{\text{DONE}}$	ADON
bit 7							**bit 0**

R = Readable bit	W = Writable bit	U = Unimplemented bit, read as '0'
-n = Value at POR	'1' = Bit is set	'0' = Bit is cleared x = Bit is unknown

bit 7   **Unimplemented**: Read as '0'

Bit 6-2   **CHS<4:0>: Analog Channel Select bits**
00000 = AN0
00001 = AN1GO/$\overline{\text{DONE}}$
00010 = AN2
00011 = AN3
00100 = AN4
00101 = AN5[1]
00110 = AN6[1]
00111 = AN7[1]
01000 = AN8
01001 = AN9
01010 = AN10
01011 = AN11
01100 = AN12
01101 = AN13
01110 = AN14
01111 = AN15
10000 = AN16
10001 = AN17
10010 = AN18
10011 = AN19
10100 = AN20[1]
10101 = AN21[1]
10110 = AN22[1]
10111 = AN23[1]
11000 = AN24[1]
11001 = AN25[1]
11010 = AN26[1]
11011 = AN27[1]
11100 = Reserved
11101 = CTMU
11110 = DAC
11111 = FVR BUF2 (1.024V/2.048V/2.096V Volt Fixed Voltage Reference)[2]

bit 1   **GO/$\overline{\text{DONE}}$:** A/D Conversion Status bit
1 = A/D conversion cycle in progress. Setting this bit starts an A/D conversion cycle.
    This bit is automatically cleared by hardware when the A/D conversion has completed.
0 = A/D conversion completed / not in progress)

bit 0   **ADON:** ADC Enable bit
1 = ADC is enabled
0 = ADC is disabled and consumes no operating current

Note 1:   Available on PIC18(L)F4XK22 devices only.
Note 2:   Allow greater than 15 μs acquisition time when measuring the Fixed Voltage Reference.

ADCON1: **A/D CONTROL REGISTER 1**

R/W-0	U-0	U-0	U-0	R/W-0	R/W-0	R/W-0	R/W-0
TRIGSEL	–	–	–	PVCFG<1:0>		NVCFG<1:0>	

bit 7   bit 0

R = Readable bit	W = Writable bit	U = Unimplemented bit, read as '0'	
-n = Value at POR	'1' = Bit is set	'0' = Bit is cleared	x = Bit is unknown

bit 7   **TRIGSEL**: Special Trigger Select bit
                1 = Selects the special trigger from CTMU
                0 = Selects the special trigger from CCP5

bit 6-4   **Unimplemented:** Read as '0'

bit 3-2   **PVCFG<1:0>:** Positive Voltage Reference Configuration bits
                00 = A/D V$_{REF+}$ connected to internal signal, AV$_{DD}$
                01 = A/D V$_{REF+}$ connected to external pin, V$_{REF+}$
                10 = A/D V$_{REF+}$ connected to internal signal, FVR BUF2
                11 = Reserved (by default, A/D V$_{REF+}$ connected to internal signal, AV$_{DD}$)

bit 1-0   **NVCFG<1:0>:** Negative Voltage Reference Configuration bits
                00 = A/D V$_{REF-}$ connected to internal signal, AV$_{SS}$
                01 = A/D V$_{REF-}$ connected to external pin, V$_{REF-}$
                10 = Reserved (by default, A/D V$_{REF-}$ connected to internal signal, AV$_{SS}$)
                11 = Reserved (by default, A/D V$_{REF-}$ connected to internal signal, AV$_{SS}$)

ADCON2: **A/D CONTROL REGISTER 2**

R/W-0	U-0	R/W-0	R/W-0	R/W-0	R/W-0	R/W-0	R/W-0
ADFM	–	ACQT<2:0>			ADCS<2:0>		

bit 7   bit 0

R = Readable bit	W = Writable bit	U = Unimplemented bit, read as '0'	
-n = Value at POR	'1' = Bit is set	'0' = Bit is cleared	x = Bit is unknown

bit 7   **ADFM**: A/D Result Format Select bit
                1 = Right justified
                0 = Left justified

bit 6   Unimplemented: Read as '0'

bit 5-3   **ACQT<2:0>:** A/D Acquisition time select bits. Acquisition time is the duration that the A/D charge holding capacitor remains connected to A/D channel from the instant the GO/$\overline{DONE}$ bit is set until conversions begins.
                000 = 0[1]
                001 = 2 TAD
                010 = 4 TAD
                011 = 6 TAD
                100 = 8 TAD
                101 = 12 TAD
                110 = 16 TAD
                111 = 20 TAD

bit 2-0   **ADCS<2:0>:** A/D Conversion Clock Select bits
                000 = F$_{OSC}$/2
                001 = F$_{OSC}$ /8
                010 = F$_{OSC}$ /32
                011 = F$_{RC}$[1] (clock derived from a dedicated internal oscillator = 600 kHz nominal)
                100 = F$_{OSC}$ /4
                101 = F$_{OSC}$ /16
                110 = F$_{OSC}$ /64
                111 = F$_{RC}$[1] (clock derived from a dedicated internal oscillator = 600 kHz nominal)

Note 1:   When the A/D clock source is selected as F$_{RC}$ then the start of conversion is delayed by one instruction cycle after the GO/$\overline{DONE}$ bit is set to allow the SLEEP instruction to be executed.

ADRESH: ADC RESULT REGISTER HIGH (ADRESH) ADFM = 0

R/W-x	R/W-x	R/W-x	R/W-x	R/W-x	R/W-x	R/W-x	R/W-x
ADRES<9:2>							

bit 7   bit 0

R = Readable bit   W = Writable bit   U = Unimplemented bit, read as '0'
-n = Value at POR   '1' = Bit is set   '0' = Bit is cleared   x = Bit is unknown

bit 7-0   **ADRES<9:2>**: ADC Result Register bits
                Upper 8 bits of 10-bit conversion result

ADRESL: ADC RESULT REGISTER LOW (ADRESL) ADFM = 0

R/W-x	R/W-x	R/W-x	R/W-x	R/W-x	R/W-x	R/W-x	R/W-x
ADRES<1:0>		-	-	-	-	-	-

bit 7   bit 0

R = Readable bit   W = Writable bit   U = Unimplemented bit, read as '0'
-n = Value at POR   '1' = Bit is set   '0' = Bit is cleared   x = Bit is unknown

bit 7-6   **ADRES<1:0>**: ADC Result Register bits
                Lower 2 bits of 10-bit conversion result

bit 5-0   **Reserved**: Do not use.

ADRESH: ADC RESULT REGISTER HIGH (ADRESH) ADFM = 1

R/W-x	R/W-x	R/W-x	R/W-x	R/W-x	R/W-x	R/W-x	R/W-x
-	-	-	-	-	-	ADRES<9:8>	

bit 7   bit 0

R = Readable bit   W = Writable bit   U = Unimplemented bit, read as '0'
-n = Value at POR   '1' = Bit is set   '0' = Bit is cleared   x = Bit is unknown

bit 7-2   **Reserved**: Do not use.

bit 1-0   **ADRES<9:8>**: ADC Result Register bits
                Upper 2 bits of 10-bit conversion result

ADRESL: ADC RESULT REGISTER LOW (ADRESL) ADFM = 1

R/W-x	R/W-x	R/W-x	R/W-x	R/W-x	R/W-x	R/W-x	R/W-x
ADRES<7:0>							

bit 7   bit 0

R = Readable bit   W = Writable bit   U = Unimplemented bit, read as '0'
-n = Value at POR   '1' = Bit is set   '0' = Bit is cleared   x = Bit is unknown

bit 7-6   **ADRES<7:0>**: ADC Result Register bits
                Lower 8 bits of 10-bit conversion result

ANSELA: PORTA ANALOG SELECT REGISTER

U-0	U-0	R/W-1	U-0	R/W-1	R/W-1	R/W-1	R/W-1
-	-	ANSA5	-	ANSA3	ANSA2	ANSA1	ANSA0

bit 7   bit 0

R = Readable bit   W = Writable bit   U = Unimplemented bit, read as '0'
-n = Value at POR   '1' = Bit is set   '0' = Bit is cleared   x = Bit is unknown

bits 7, 6, 4   **Unimplemented**: Read as '0'

bits 5, 3-0   **ANSAx**: RAx Analog Select bit (x = 5, 3, 2, 1, 0)
                   1 = Digital input buffer disabled (analog pin)
                   0 = Digital input buffer enabled (digital pin)

ANSELB: PORTB ANALOG SELECT REGISTER

U-0	U-0	R/W-1	R/W-1	R/W-1	R/W-1	R/W-1	R/W-1
–	–	ANSB<5:0>					

bit 7   bit 0

R = Readable bit	W = Writable bit	U = Unimplemented bit, read as '0'
-n = Value at POR	'1' = Bit is set	'0' = Bit is cleared x = Bit is unknown

bit 7-6   **Unimplemented**: Read as '0'

bit 5-0   **ANSB<5:0>**: RB<5:0> Analog Select bit
            1 = Digital input buffer disabled (analog pin)
            0 = Digital input buffer enabled (digital pin)

ANSELC: PORTC ANALOG SELECT REGISTER

R/W-1	R/W-1	R/W-1	R/W-1	R/W-1	R/W-1	U-0	U-0
ANSC<7:2>						–	–

bit 7   bit 0

R = Readable bit	W = Writable bit	U = Unimplemented bit, read as '0'
-n = Value at POR	'1' = Bit is set	'0' = Bit is cleared x = Bit is unknown

bit 7-2   **ANSC<7:2>**: RC<7:2> Analog Select bit
            1 = Digital input buffer disabled (analog pin)
            0 = Digital input buffer enabled (digital pin)

bit 1-0   **Unimplemented**: Read as '0'

ANSELD: PORTD ANALOG SELECT REGISTER

R/W-1	R/W-1	R/W-1	R/W-1	R/W-1	R/W-1	R/W-1	R/W-1
ANSD<7:0>							

bit 7   bit 0

R = Readable bit	W = Writable bit	U = Unimplemented bit, read as '0'
-n = Value at POR	'1' = Bit is set	'0' = Bit is cleared x = Bit is unknown

bit 7-0   **ANSD<7:0>**: RD<7:0> Analog Select bit
            1 = Digital input buffer disabled (analog pin)
            0 = Digital input buffer enabled (digital pin)

ANSELE: PORTE ANALOG SELECT REGISTER

U-0	U-0	U-0	U-0	U-0	R/W-1	R/W-1	R/W-1
–	–	–	–	–	ANSE2 [1]	ANSE1[1]	ANSE0[1]

bit 7   bit 0

R = Readable bit	W = Writable bit	U = Unimplemented bit, read as '0'
-n = Value at POR	'1' = Bit is set	'0' = Bit is cleared x = Bit is unknown

bit 7-3   **Unimplemented**: Read as '0'

bit 2-0   **ANSE<2:0>**: RE<2:0> Analog Select bit[1]
            1 = Digital input buffer disabled (analog pin)
            0 = Digital input buffer enabled (digital pin)

Note 1:   Available on PIC18(L)F4XK22 devices only.

BAUDCONx: **BAUD RATE CONTROL REGISTER** (x = 1, 2)

R/W-0	R-1	R/W-0	R/W-0	R/W-0	U-0	R/W-0	R/W-0
ABDOVF	RCIDL	DTRXP	CKTXP	BRG16	–	WUE	ABDEN

bit 7   bit 0

R = Readable bit	W = Writable bit	U = Unimplemented bit, read as '0'	
-n = Value at POR	'1' = Bit is set	'0' = Bit is cleared	x = Bit is unknown

bit 7   **ABDOVF:** Auto-Baud Detect Overflow bit
<u>Asynchronous mode:</u>
1 = Auto-baud timer overflowed
0 = Auto-baud timer did not overflow
<u>Synchronous mode:</u> Don't care

bit 6   **RCIDL**: Receive Idle Flag bit
<u>Asynchronous mode:</u>
1 = Receiver is Idle
0 = Start bit has been detected and the receiver is active
<u>Synchronous mode:</u> Don't care

bit 5   **DTRXP**: Data/Receive Polarity Select bit
<u>Asynchronous mode:</u>
1 = Receive data (RXx) is inverted (active-low)
0 = Receive data (RXx) is not inverted (active-high)
<u>Synchronous mode:</u>
1 = Data (DTx) is inverted (active-low)
0 = Data (DTx) is not inverted (active-high)

bit 4   **CKTXP**: Clock/Transmit Polarity Select bit
<u>Asynchronous mode:</u>
1 = Idle state for transmit (TXx) is low
0 = Idle state for transmit (TXx) is high
<u>Synchronous mode:</u>
1 = Data changes on the falling edge of the clock and is sampled on its rising edge
0 = Data changes on the rising edge of the clock and is sampled on its falling edge

bit 3   **BRG16**: 16-bit Baud Rate Generator bit
1 = 16-bit Baud Rate Generator is used (SPBRGHx:SPBRGx)
0 = 8-bit Baud Rate Generator is used (SPBRGx)

bit 2   **Unimplemented:** Read as '0'

bit 1   **WUE:** Wake-up Enable bit
<u>Asynchronous mode:</u>
1 = Receiver is waiting for a falling edge. No character will be received but RCxIF will be set
on the falling edge. WUE will automatically clear on the rising edge.
0 = Receiver is operating normally
<u>Synchronous mode:</u> Don't care

bit 0   **ABDEN:** Auto-Baud Detect Enable bit
<u>Asynchronous mode:</u>
1 = Auto-Baud Detect mode is enabled (clears when auto-baud is complete)
0 = Auto-Baud Detect mode is disabled
<u>Synchronous mode:</u> Don't care

BSR   **BANK SELECT REGISTER**

–	–	–	–	BSR<3:0>			
bit 7							**bit 0**

R = Readable bit	W = Writable bit	U = Unimplemented bit, read as '0'
-n = Value at POR	'1' = Bit is set	'0' = Bit is cleared x = Bit is unknown

bit 7-4   **Unimplemented:** Read as '0'

bit 3-0   **BSR<3:0>:** Bank number 0, 1, 2, …, 15

CCPxCON: **STANDARD CCPx CONTROL REGISTER (x = 1, 2, 3, 4, 5)**

U-0	U-0	R/W-0	R/W-0	R/W-0	R/W-0	R/W-0	R/W-0
-	-	DCxB<1:0>		CCPxM<3:0>			
bit 7							**bit 0**

R = Readable bit	W = Writable bit	U = Unimplemented bit, read as '0'
-n = Value at POR	'1' = Bit is set	'0' = Bit is cleared x = Bit is unknown

bit 7-6   **Unused**

bit 5-4   **DCxB<1:0>:** PWM Duty Cycle Least Significant bits

Capture mode: Unused

Compare mode: Unused

PWM mode: These bits are the two LSBs of the PWM duty cycle. The eight MSBs are found in CCPRxL.

bit 3-0   **CCPxM<3:0>:** ECCPx Mode Select bits

0000 = Capture/Compare/PWM off (resets the module)
0001 = Reserved
0010 = Compare mode: toggle output on match
0011 = Reserved

0100 = Capture mode: every falling edge
0101 = Capture mode: every rising edge
0110 = Capture mode: every 4th rising edge
0111 = Capture mode: every 16th rising edge

1000 = Compare mode: set output on compare match (CCPx pin is set, CCPxIF is set)
1001 = Compare mode: clear output on compare match (CCPx pin is cleared, CCPxIF is set)
1010 = Compare mode: generate software interrupt on compare match (CCPx pin is unaffected, CCPxIF is set)
1011 = Compare mode: Special Event Trigger (CCPx pin is unaffected, CCPxIF is set) TimerX (selected by CxTSEL bits) is reset, ADON is set, starting A/D conversion if A/D module is enabled[1]

11xx = PWM mode

Note 1:   This feature is available on CCP5 only.

CCPxCON: ENHANCED CCPx CONTROL REGISTER (x = 1, 2, 3, 4, 5)

R/W-0	R/W-0	R/W-0	R/W-0	R/W-0	R/W-0	R/W-0	R/W-0
PxM<1:0>		DCxB<1:0>		CCPxM<3:0>			

bit 7							bit 0

R = Readable bit	W = Writable bit	'0' = Bit is cleared	'1' = Bit is cleared

bit 7-6   **PxM<1:0>:** Enhanced PWM Output Configuration bits
   If CCPxM<3:2> = 00, 01, 10: (Capture/Compare modes)
xx = PxA assigned as Capture/Compare input; PxB, PxC, PxD assigned as port pins

Half-Bridge ECCP Modules[1]:
   If CCPxM<3:2> = 11: (PWM modes)
0x = Single output; PxA modulated; PxB assigned as port pin
1x = Half-Bridge output; PxA, PxB modulated with dead-band control

Full-Bridge ECCP Modules[1]:
   If CCPxM<3:2> = 11: (PWM modes)
00 = Single output; PxA modulated; PxB, PxC, PxD assigned as port pins
01 = Full-Bridge output forward; PxD modulated; PxA active; PxB, PxC inactive
10 = Half-Bridge output; PxA, PxB modulated with dead-band control; PxC, PxD assigned as
   port pins
11 = Full-Bridge output reverse; PxB modulated; PxC active; PxA, PxD inactive

bit 5-4   **DCxB<1:0>:** PWM Duty Cycle Least Significant bits

<u>Capture mode:</u> Unused

<u>Compare mode:</u> Unused

<u>PWM mode:</u> These bits are the two LSBs of the PWM duty cycle. The eight MSBs are found in CCPRxL.

bit 3-0   **CCPxM<3:0>:** ECCPx Mode Select bits

0000 = Capture/Compare/PWM off (resets the module)
0001 = Reserved
0010 = Compare mode: toggle output on match
0011 = Reserved

0100 = Capture mode: every falling edge
0101 = Capture mode: every rising edge
0110 = Capture mode: every 4th rising edge
0111 = Capture mode: every 16th rising edge

1000 = Compare mode: set output on compare match (CCPx pin is set, CCPxIF is set)
1001 = Compare mode: clear output on compare match (CCPx pin is cleared, CCPxIF is set)
1010 = Compare mode: generate software interrupt on compare match (CCPx pin is
   unaffected, CCPxIF is set)
1011 = Compare mode: Special Event Trigger (CCPx pin is unaffected, CCPxIF is set)
   TimerX is reset

Half-Bridge ECCP Modules[1]:
1100 = PWM mode: PxA active-high; PxB active-high
1101 = PWM mode: PxA active-high; PxB active-low
1110 = PWM mode: PxA active-low; PxB active-high
1111 = PWM mode: PxA active-low; PxB active-low

Full-Bridge ECCP Modules[1]:
1100 = PWM mode: PxA, PxC active-high; PxB, PxD active-high
1101 = PWM mode: PxA, PxC active-high; PxB, PxD active-low
1110 = PWM mode: PxA, PxC active-low; PxB, PxD active-high
1111 = PWM mode: PxA, PxC active-low; PxB, PxD active-low

Note 1:   See subsequent table to determine Full-Bridge and Half-Bridge ECCPs for device being used.

PWM RESOURCES

Device Name	ECCP1	ECCP2	ECCP3	CCP4	CCP5
PIC18(L)F23K22	Enhanced PWM Full-Bridge	Enhanced PWM Half-Bridge	Enhanced PWM Half-Bridge	Standard PWM	Standard PWM (Special Event Trigger)
PIC18(L)F24K22					
PIC18(L)F25K22					
PIC18(L)F26K22					
PIC18(L)F43K22	Enhanced PWM Full-Bridge	Enhanced PWM Full-Bridge	Enhanced PWM Half-Bridge	Standard PWM	Standard PWM (Special Event Trigger)
PIC18(L)F44K22					
PIC18(L)F45K22					
PIC18(L)F46K22					

CCPRxH: CAPTURE/COMPARE/PWM REGISTER x, HIGH BYTE (x = 1, 2, 3, 4, 5)

R/W-x	R/W-x	R/W-x	R/W-x	R/W-x	R/W-x	R/W-x	R/W-x

bit 7   bit 0

R = Readable bit   W = Writable bit   x = Bit is unknown

bit 7-0   **CCPRxH<7:0>:** High order byte of CCPx (x = 1, 2, 3, 4, 5)

CCPRxL: CAPTURE/COMPARE/PWM REGISTER x, LOW BYTE (x = 1, 2, 3, 4, 5)

R/W-x	R/W-x	R/W-x	R/W-x	R/W-x	R/W-x	R/W-x	R/W-x

bit 7   bit 0

R = Readable bit   W = Writable bit   x = Bit is unknown

bit 7-0   **CCPRxL<7:0>:** Low order byte of CCPx (x = 1, 2, 3, 4, 5)

CCPTMRS0:   PWM TIMER SELECTION CONTROL REGISTER 0

R/W-0	R/W-0	U-0	R/W-0	R/W-0	U-0	R/W-0	R/W-0
C3TSEL<1:0>		–	C2TSEL<1:0>		–	C1TSEL<1:0>	

bit 7   bit 0

R = Readable bit   W = Writable bit   U = Unimplemented bit, read as '0'
-n = Value at POR   '1' = Bit is set   '0' = Bit is cleared   x = Bit is unknown

bit 7-6   **C3TSEL<1:0>:** CCP3 Timer Selection bits
00 = CCP3 – Capture/Compare modes use Timer1, PWM modes use Timer2
01 = CCP3 – Capture/Compare modes use Timer3, PWM modes use Timer4
10 = CCP3 – Capture/Compare modes use Timer5, PWM modes use Timer6
11 = Reserved

bit 5   **Unused**

bit 4-3   **C2TSEL<1:0>:** CCP2 Timer Selection bits
00 = CCP2 – Capture/Compare modes use Timer1, PWM modes use Timer2
01 = CCP2 – Capture/Compare modes use Timer3, PWM modes use Timer4
10 = CCP2 – Capture/Compare modes use Timer5, PWM modes use Timer6
11 = Reserved

bit 2   **Unused**

bit 1-0   **C1TSEL<1:0>:** CCP1 Timer Selection bits
00 = CCP1 – Capture/Compare modes use Timer1, PWM modes use Timer2
01 = CCP1 – Capture/Compare modes use Timer3, PWM modes use Timer4
10 = CCP1 – Capture/Compare modes use Timer5, PWM modes use Timer6
11 = Reserved

CCPTMRS1:   PWM TIMER SELECTION CONTROL REGISTER 1

U-0	U-0	U-0	U-0	R/W-0	R/W-0	R/W-0	R/W-0
–	–	–	–	C5TSEL<1:0>		C4TSEL<1:0>	
bit 7							**bit 0**

R = Readable bit	W = Writable bit	U = Unimplemented bit, read as '0'	
-n = Value at POR	'1' = Bit is set	'0' = Bit is cleared	x = Bit is unknown

bit 7-4   **Unimplemented:** Read as '0'

bit 3-2   **C5TSEL<1:0>:** CCP5 Timer Selection bits
00 = CCP5 – Capture/Compare modes use Timer1, PWM modes use Timer2
01 = CCP5 – Capture/Compare modes use Timer3, PWM modes use Timer4
10 = CCP5 – Capture/Compare modes use Timer5, PWM modes use Timer6
11 = Reserved

bit 1-0   **C4TSEL<1:0>:** CCP4 Timer Selection bits
00 = CCP4 – Capture/Compare modes use Timer1, PWM modes use Timer2
01 = CCP4 – Capture/Compare modes use Timer3, PWM modes use Timer4
10 = CCP4 – Capture/Compare modes use Timer5, PWM modes use Timer6
11 = Reserved

CMxCON0:   COMPARATOR x CONTROL REGISTER (x = 1, 2)

R/W-0	R-0	R/W-0	R/W-0	R/W-1	R/W-0	R/W-0	R/W-0
CxON	CxOUT	CxOE	CxPOL	CxSP	CxR	CxCH<1:0>	
bit 7							**bit 0**

R = Readable bit	W = Writable bit	U = Unimplemented bit, read as '0'	
-n = Value at POR	'1' = Bit is set	'0' = Bit is cleared	x = Bit is unknown

bit 7   **CxON:** Comparator Cx Enable bit
1 = Comparator Cx is enabled
0 = Comparator Cx is disabled

bit 6   **CxOUT:** Comparator Cx Output bit

If CxPOL = 1 (inverted polarity):
CxOUT = 0 when $CxV_{IN+} > CxV_{IN-}$
CxOUT = 1 when $CxV_{IN+} < CxV_{IN-}$

If CxPOL = 0 (non-inverted polarity):
CxOUT = 1 when $CxV_{IN+} > CxV_{IN-}$
CxOUT = 0 when $CxV_{IN+} < CxV_{IN-}$

bit 5   **CxOE:** Comparator Cx Output Enable bit
1 = CxOUT is present on the CxOUT pin[1]
0 = CxOUT is internal only

bit 4   **CxPOL:** Comparator Cx Output Polarity Select bit
1 = CxOUT logic is inverted
0 = CxOUT logic is not inverted

bit 3   **CxSP:** Comparator Cx Speed/Power Select bit
1 = Cx operates in normal power, higher speed mode
0 = Cx operates in low-power, low-speed mode

bit 2   **CxR:** Comparator Cx Reference Select bit (non-inverting input)
1 = CxV_{IN+} connects to CxV_{REF} output
0 = CxV_{IN} + connects to C12IN+ pin

bit 1-0   **CxCH<1:0>:** Comparator Cx Channel Select bit
00 = C12IN0- pin of Cx connects to CxV_{IN} -
01 = C12IN1- pin of Cx connects to CxV_{IN} -
10 = C12IN2- pin of Cx connects to CxV_{IN} -
11 = C12IN3- pin of Cx connects to CxV_{IN-}

Note 1:   Comparator output requires the following three conditions: CxOE = 1, CxON = 1 and corresponding port TRIS bit = 0.

CM2CON1:   **COMPARATOR 1 AND 2 CONTROL REGISTER**

R-0	R-0	R/W-0	R/W-0	R/W-0	R/W-0	R/W-0	R/W-0
MC1OUT	MC2OUT	C1RSEL	C2RSEL	C1HYS	C2HYS	C1SYNC	C2SYNC

bit 7   **bit 0**

R = Readable bit   W = Writable bit   U = Unimplemented bit, read as '0'
-n = Value at POR   '1' = Bit is set   '0' = Bit is cleared   x = Bit is unknown

bit 7   **MC1OUT:** Mirror Copy of C1OUT bit

bit 6   **MC2OUT:** Mirror Copy of C2OUT bit

bit 5   **C1RSEL:** Comparator C1 Reference Select bit
                1 = FVR BUF1 routed to C1VREF input
                0 = DAC routed to C1VREF input

bit 4   **C2RSEL:** Comparator C2 Reference Select bit
                1 = FVR BUF1 routed to C2VREF input
                0 = DAC routed to C2VREF input

bit 3   **C1HYS:** Comparator C1 Hysteresis Enable bit
                1 = Comparator C1 hysteresis enabled
                0 = Comparator C1 hysteresis disabled

bit 2   **C2HYS:** Comparator C2 Hysteresis Enable bit
                1 = Comparator C2 hysteresis enabled
                0 = Comparator C2 hysteresis disabled

bit 1   **C1SYNC:** C1 Output Synchronous Mode bit
                1 = C1 output is synchronized to rising edge of TMR1 clock (T1CLK)
                0 = C1 output is asynchronous

bit 0   **C2SYNC:** C2 Output Synchronous Mode bit
                1 = C2 output is synchronized to rising edge of TMR1 clock (T1CLK)
                0 = C2 output is asynchronous

CTMUCONH: CTMU CONTROL REGISTER 0

R/W-0	U-0	R/W-0	R/W-0	R/W-0	R/W-0	R/W-0	U-0
CTMUEN	–	CTMUSIDL	TGEN	EDGEN	EDGSEQEN	IDISSEN	CTTRIG
bit 7							bit 0

R = Readable bit   W = Writable bit   U = Unimplemented bit, read as '0'
-n = Value at POR   '1' = Bit is set   '0' = Bit is cleared   x = Bit is unknown

bit 7   **CTMUEN:** CTMU Enable bit
               1 = Module is enabled
               0 = Module is disabled

bit 6   **Unimplemented:** Read as '0'

bit 5   **CTMUSIDL:** Stop in Idle Mode bit
               1 = Discontinue module operation when device enters Idle mode
               0 = Continue module operation in Idle mode

bit 4   **TGEN:** Time Generation Enable bit
               1 = Enables edge delay generation
               0 = Disables edge delay generation

bit 3   **EDGEN:** Edge Enable bit
               1 = Edges are not blocked
               0 = Edges are blocked

bit 2   **EDGSEQEN:** Edge Sequence Enable bit
               1 = Edge 1 event must occur before Edge 2 event can occur
               0 = No edge sequence is needed

bit 1   **IDISSEN:** Analog Current Source Control bit
               1 = Analog current source output is grounded
               0 = Analog current source output is not grounded

bit 0   **CTTRIG:** CTMU Special Event Trigger Control Bit
               1 = CTMU Special Event Trigger is enabled
               0 = CTMU Special Event Trigger is disabled

CTMUCONL: CTMU CONTROL REGISTER 1

R/W-0	R/W-0	R/W-0	R/W-0	R/W-0	R/W-0	R/W-0	R/W-0
EDG2POL	EDG2SEL<1:0>		EDG1POL	EDG1SEL<1:0>		EDG2STAT	EDG1STAT
bit 7							**bit 0**

R = Readable bit   W = Writable bit   U = Unimplemented bit, read as '0'
-n = Value at POR   '1' = Bit is set   '0' = Bit is cleared   x = Bit is unknown

bit 7   **EDG2POL:** Edge 2 Polarity Select bit
               1 = Edge 2 programmed for a positive edge response
               0 = Edge 2 programmed for a negative edge response

bit 6-5   **EDG2SEL<1:0>:** Edge 2 Source Select bits
               11 = CTED1 pin
               10 = CTED2 pin
               01 = ECCP1 Special Event Trigger
               00 = ECCP2 Special Event Trigger

bit 4   **EDG1POL:** Edge 1 Polarity Select bit
               1 = Edge 1 programmed for a positive edge response
               0 = Edge 1 programmed for a negative edge response

bit 3-2   **EDG1SEL<1:0>:** Edge 1 Source Select bits
               11 = CTED1 pin
               10 = CTED2 pin
               01 = ECCP1 Special Event Trigger
               00 = ECCP2 Special Event Trigger

bit 1   **EDG2STAT:** Edge 2 Status bit
               1 = Edge 2 event has occurred
               0 = Edge 2 event has not occurred

bit 0   **EDG1STAT:** Edge 1 Status bit
               1 = Edge 1 event has occurred
               0 = Edge 1 event has not occurred

ECCPxAS: CCPx AUTO-SHUTDOWN CONTROL REGISTER (x = 1, 2, 3)

R/W-0	R/W-0	R/W-0	R/W-0	R/W-0	R/W-0	R/W-0	R/W-0
CCPxASE	CCPxAS<2:0>			PSSxAC<1:0>		PSSxBD<1:0>	
bit 7							**bit 0**

R = Readable bit	W = Writable bit	U = Unimplemented bit, read as '0'	
-n = Value at POR	'1' = Bit is set	'0' = Bit is cleared	x = Bit is unknown

bit 7   **CCPxASE:** CCPx Auto-shutdown Event Status bit
               if PxRSEN = 1;
               1 = An Auto-shutdown event occurred; CCPxASE bit will automatically clear when event
               goes away;
               CCPx outputs in shutdown state
               0 = CCPx outputs are operating
               if PxRSEN = 0;
               1 = An Auto-shutdown event occurred; bit must be cleared in software to restart PWM;
               CCPx outputs in shutdown state
               0 = CCPx outputs are operating

bit 6-4   **CCPxAS<2:0>:** CCPx Auto-Shutdown Source Select bits [1]
               000 = Auto-shutdown is disabled
               001 = Comparator C1 (async_C1OUT) – output high will cause shutdown event
               010 = Comparator C2 (async_C2OUT) – output high will cause shutdown event
               011 = Either Comparator C1 or C2 – output high will cause shutdown event
               100 = FLT0 pin - low level will cause shutdown event
               101 = FLT0 pin or Comparator C1 (async_C1OUT) – low level will cause shutdown event
               110 = FLT0 pin or Comparator C2 (async_C2OUT) – low level will cause shutdown event
               111 = FLT0 pin or Comparators C1 or C2 – low level will cause shutdown event

bit 3-2   **PSSxAC<1:0>:** Pins PxA and PxC Shutdown State Control bits
               00 = Drive pins PxA and PxC to '0'
               01 = Drive pins PxA and PxC to '1'
               1x = Pins PxA and PxC tri-state

bit 1-0   **PSSxBD<1:0>:** Pins PxB and PxD Shutdown State Control bits
               00 = Drive pins PxB and PxD to '0'
               01 = Drive pins PxB and PxD to '1'
               1x = Pins PxB and PxD tri-state

Note 1:   If C1SYNC or C2SYNC bits in the CM2CON1 register are enabled, the shutdown will be
               delayed by Timer1.

EEADR: EEPROM ADDRESS REGISTER

R/W-0	R/W-0	R/W-0	R/W-0	R/W-0	R/W-0	R/W-0	R/W-0
EEADR <7:0>							
bit 7							**bit 0**

R = Readable bit	W = Writable bit	U = Unimplemented bit, read as '0'	
-n = Value at POR	'1' = Bit is set	'0' = Bit is cleared	x = Bit is unknown

bit 7-0   **EEADR <7:0>:**

EEADRH: EEPROM ADDRESS HIGH REGISTER

U-0	U-0	U-0	U-0	U-0	U-0	R/W-0	R/W-0
–	–	–	–	–	–	EEADR9	EEADR8
bit 7							**bit 0**

R = Readable bit	W = Writable bit	U = Unimplemented bit, read as '0'	
-n = Value at POR	'1' = Bit is set	'0' = Bit is cleared	x = Bit is unknown

bit 7-2   **Unimplemented:** Read as '0'

bit 1-0   **EEADR<9:8>:** Most significant bits of EEPROM address. Available only PIC18(L)F26K22
               and PIC18(L)F46K22.

EECON1:   DATA EEPROM CONTROL 1 REGISTER

R/W-x	R/W-x	U-0	R/W-0	R/W-x	R/W-0	R/S-0	R/S-0
EEPGD	CFGS	–	FREE	WRERR	WREN	WR	RD

bit 7   **bit 0**

R = Readable bit   W = Writable bit
S = Bit can be set by software, but not cleared   U = Unimplemented bit, read as '0'
-n = Value at POR   '1' = Bit is set   '0' = Bit is cleared   x = Bit is unknown

bit 7   **EEPGD:** Flash Program or Data EEPROM Memory Select bit
1 = Access Flash program memory
0 = Access data EEPROM memory

bit 6   **CFGS:** Flash Program/Data EEPROM or Configuration Select bit
1 = Access Configuration registers
0 = Access Flash program or data EEPROM memory

bit 5   **Unimplemented:** Read as '0'

bit 4   **FREE:** Flash Row (Block) Erase Enable bit
1 = Erase the program memory block addressed by TBLPTR on the next WR command
(cleared by completion of erase operation)
0 = Perform write-only

bit 3   **WRERR:** Flash Program/Data EEPROM Error Flag bit[1]
1 = A write operation is prematurely terminated (any Reset during self-timed programming in
normal operation, or an improper write attempt)
0 = The write operation completed

bit 2   **WREN:** Flash Program/Data EEPROM Write Enable bit
1 = Allows write cycles to Flash program/data EEPROM
0 = Inhibits write cycles to Flash program/data EEPROM

bit 1   **WR:** Write Control bit
1 = Initiates a data EEPROM erase/write cycle or a program memory erase cycle or write
cycle. (The operation is self-timed and the bit is cleared by hardware once write is
complete. The WR bit can only be set (not cleared) by software.)
0 = Write cycle to the EEPROM is complete

bit 0   **RD:** Read Control bit
1 = Initiates an EEPROM read (Read takes one cycle. RD is cleared by hardware. The RD bit
can only be set (not cleared) by software. RD bit cannot be set when EEPGD = 1 or CFGS
= 1.)
0 = Does not initiate an EEPROM read

Note 1:   When a WRERR occurs, the EEPGD and CFGS bits are not cleared. This allows tracing of the
error condition.

EECON2:   EEPROM CONTROL REGISTER 2 (NOT A PHYSICAL REGISTER)

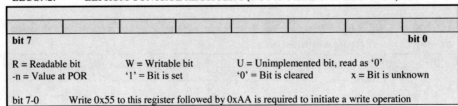

bit 7   **bit 0**

R = Readable bit   W = Writable bit   U = Unimplemented bit, read as '0'
-n = Value at POR   '1' = Bit is set   '0' = Bit is cleared   x = Bit is unknown

bit 7-0   Write 0x55 to this register followed by 0xAA is required to initiate a write operation

EEDATA: **EEPROM DATA REGISTER**

R/W-0	R/W-0	R/W-0	R/W-0	R/W-0	R/W-0	R/W-0	R/W-0

bit 7   bit 0

R = Readable bit	W = Writable bit U = Unimplemented bit, read as '0'
-n = Value at POR	'1' = Bit is set '0' = Bit is cleared x = Bit is unknown

bit 7-0   Hold data to be written to EEPROM or data read from EEPROM

FSRxH: **INDIRECT DATA MEMORY ADDRESS POINTER x, HIGH BYTE (x = 0, 1, 2)**

U-0	U-0	U-0	U-0	R/W-0	R/W-0	R/W-0	R/W-0
-	-	-	-	Indirect Data Memory Address Pointer 0, High Byte			

bit 7   bit 0

R = Readable bit	W = Writable bit U = Unimplemented bit, read as '0'
-n = Value at POR	'1' = Bit is set '0' = Bit is cleared x = Bit is unknown

bit 7-4   **Unimplemented**: Read as '0'

bit 3-0   **FSRxH<3:0>**: High Byte

FSRxL: **INDIRECT DATA MEMORY ADDRESS POINTER x, LOW BYTE (x = 0, 1, 2)**

R/W-x	R/W-x	R/W-x	R/W-x	R/W-x	R/W-x	R/W-x	R/W-x

bit 7   bit 0

R = Readable bit	W = Writable bit x = Bit is unknown

bit 7-0   **FSRxL<7:0>**: Low Byte

HLVDCON: **HIGH/LOW-VOLTAGE DETECT CONTROL REGISTER**

R/W-0	R-0	R-0	R/W-0	R/W-0	R/W-1	R/W-0	R/W-1
VDIRMAG	BGVST	IRVST	HLVDEN	HLVDL<3:0>			

bit 7   bit 0

R = Readable bit   W = Writable bit   '0' = Bit is cleared   '1' = Bit is set

bit 7   **VDIRMAG:** Voltage Direction Magnitude Select bit
                1 = Event occurs when voltage equals or exceeds trip point (HLVDL<3:0>)
                0 = Event occurs when voltage equals or falls below trip point (HLVDL<3:0>)

bit 6   **BGVST:** Band Gap Reference Voltages Stable Status Flag bit
                1 = Internal band gap voltage references are stable
                0 = Internal band gap voltage reference is not stable

bit 5   **IRVST:** Internal Reference Voltage Stable Flag bit
                1 = Indicates that the voltage detect logic will generate the interrupt flag at the specified
                     voltage range
                0 = Indicates that the voltage detect logic will not generate the interrupt flag at the specified
                     voltage range and the HLVD interrupt should not be enabled

bit 4   **HLVDEN:** High/Low-Voltage Detect Power Enable bit
                1 = HLVD enabled
                0 = HLVD disabled

bit 3-0   **HLVDL<3:0>:** Voltage Detection Level bits[1]
                1111 = External analog input is used (input comes from the HLVDIN pin)
                1110 = Maximum setting
                .
                .
                .
                0000 = Minimum setting

Note 1:   See datasheet for specifications.

INDFx: **INDIRECT VIA FSRx REGISTER (x = 0, 1, 2)**

U-0	U-0	U-0	U-0	U-0	U-0	U-0	U-0

bit 7   bit 0

R = Readable bit	W = Writable bit	U = Unimplemented bit, read as '0'	
-n = Value at POR	'1' = Bit is set	'0' = Bit is cleared	x = Bit is unknown

bit 7-0   **Not a physical register**: used for indirect addressing via FSRx (x = 0, 1, 2)

INTCON: **INTERRUPT CONTROL REGISTER**

R/W-0	R/W-0	R/W-0	R/W-0	R/W-0	R/W-0	R/W-0	R/W-x
GIE	PEIE	TMR0IE	INT0IE	RBIE	TMR0IF	INT0IF	RBIF

bit 7   bit 0

R = Readable bit	W = Writable bit	U = Unimplemented bit, read as '0'	
-n = Value at POR	'1' = Bit is set	'0' = Bit is cleared	x = Bit is unknown

bit 7   **GIE:** Global Interrupt Enable bit
                 1 = Enables all unmasked interrupts
                 0 = Disables all interrupts including peripherals

bit 6   **PEIE:** Peripheral Interrupt Enable bit
                 1 = Enables all unmasked peripheral interrupts
                 0 = Disables all peripheral interrupts

bit 6   **TMR0IE:** Timer0 Overflow Interrupt Enable bit
                 1 = Enables the TMR0 overflow interrupt
                 0 = Disables the TMR0 overflow interrupt

bit 4   **INT0IE:** INT0 External Interrupt Enable bit
                 1 = Enables the INT0 external interrupt
                 0 = Disables the INT0 external interrupt

bit 3   **RBIE:** Port B Interrupt-On-Change (IOCx) Interrupt Enable bit[2]
                 1 = Enables the IOCx port change interrupt
                 0 = Disables the IOCx port change interrupt

bit 2   **TMR0IF:** Timer0 Overflow Interrupt Flag bit
                 1 = TMR0 has overflowed (must be cleared in software)
                 0 = TMR0 register did not overflow

bit 1   **INT0IF:** INT0 External Interrupt Flag bit
                 1 = The INT0 external interrupt occurred (must be cleared in software)
                 0 = The INT0 external interrupt did not occur

bit 0   **RBIF:** RB Port Change Interrupt Flag bit[1]
                 1 = At least one of the IOC<3:0> (RB<7:4>) pins changed state (must be cleared in software)
                 0 = None of the IOC<3:0> (RB<7:4>) pins have changed state

Note 1:   A mismatch condition will continue to set the RBIF bit. Reading PORTB will end the mismatch condition and allow the bit to be cleared.

Note 2:   RB port change interrupts also require the individual pin IOCB enables.

INTCON2:   INTERRUPT CONTROL REGISTER 2

R/W-1	R/W-1	R/W-1	R/W-1	U-0	R/W-1	U-0	R/W-1
$\overline{\text{RBPU}}$	INTEDG0	INTEDG1	INTEDG2	–	TMR0IP	–	RBIP
bit 7							bit 0

R = Readable bit   W = Writable bit   U = Unimplemented bit, read as '0'
-n = Value at POR   '1' = Bit is set   '0' = Bit is cleared   x = Bit is unknown

bit 7   **$\overline{\text{RBPU}}$**: PORTB Pull-up Enable bit
                    1 = All PORTB pull-ups are disabled

bit 6   **INTEDG0**: External Interrupt 0 Edge Select bit
                    1 = Interrupt on rising edge
                    0 = Interrupt on falling edge

bit 5   **INTEDG1**: External Interrupt 1 Edge Select bit
                    1 = Interrupt on rising edge
                    0 = Interrupt on falling edge

bit 4   **INTEDG2**: External Interrupt 2 Edge Select bit
                    1 = Interrupt on rising edge
                    0 = Interrupt on falling edge

bit 3   **Unimplemented**: Read as '0'

bit 2   **TMR0IP**: Timer0 Overflow Interrupt Priority bit
                    1 = High priority
                    0 = Low priority

bit 1   **Unimplemented**: Read as '0'

bit 0   **RBIP**: RB Port Change Interrupt Priority bit
                    1 = High priority
                    0 = Low priority

Note: Interrupt flag bits are set when an interrupt condition occurs, regardless of the state of its
                    corresponding enable bit or the global enable bit. User software should insure the appropriate
                    interrupt flag bits are clear prior to enabling an interrupt. This feature allows for software
                    polling.

INTCON3:   INTERRUPT CONTROL REGISTER 3

R/W-1	R/W-1	U-0	R/W-0	R/W-0	U-0	R/W-0	R/W-0
INT2IP	INT1IP	–	INT2IE	INT1IE	–	INT2IF	INT1IF
bit 7							bit 0

R = Readable bit   W = Writable bit   U = Unimplemented bit, read as '0'
-n = Value at POR   '1' = Bit is set   '0' = Bit is cleared   x = Bit is unknown

bit 7   **INT2IP**: INT2 External Interrupt Priority bit
               1 = High priority
               0 = Low priority

bit 6   **INT1IP**: INT1 External Interrupt Priority bit
               1 = High priority
               0 = Low priority

bit 5   **Unimplemented**: Read as '0'

bit 4   **INT2IE**: INT2 External Interrupt Enable bit
               1 = Enables the INT2 external interrupt
               0 = Disables the INT2 external interrupt

bit 3   **INT1IE**: INT1 External Interrupt Enable bit
               1 = Enables the INT1 external interrupt
               0 = Disables the INT1 external interrupt

bit 2   **Unimplemented**: Read as '0'

bit 1   **INT2IF**: INT2 External Interrupt Flag bit
               1 = The INT2 external interrupt occurred (must be cleared in software)
               0 = The INT2 external interrupt did not occur

bit 0   **INT1IF**: INT1 External Interrupt Flag bit
               1 = The INT1 external interrupt occurred (must be cleared in software)
               0 = The INT1 external interrupt did not occur

Note: Interrupt flag bits are set when an interrupt condition occurs, regardless of the state of its corresponding enable bit or the global enable bit. User software should insure the appropriate interrupt flag bits are clear prior to enabling an interrupt. This feature allows for software polling.

IOCB: INTERRUPT-ON-CHANGE PORTB CONTROL REGISTER

R/W-1	R/W-1	R/W-1	R/W-1	U-0	U-0	U-0	U-0
IOCB7	IOCB6	IOCB5	IOCB4	–	–	–	–
bit 7							bit 0

R = Readable bit   W = Writable bit   U = Unimplemented bit, read as '0'
-n = Value at POR   '1' = Bit is set   '0' = Bit is cleared   x = Bit is unknown

bit 7-4   **IOCB<7:4>:** Interrupt-on-Change PORTB control bits
               1 = Interrupt-on-change enabled[1]
               0 = Interrupt-on-change disabled

Bit 3-0   **Unimplemented**: Read as '0'

Note 1:   Interrupt-on-change requires that the RBIE bit (INTCON<3>) is set.

IPR1:   **PERIPHERAL INTERRUPT PRIORITY REGISTER 1**

U-0	R/W-1	R/W-1	R/W-1	R/W-1	R/W-1	R/W-1	R/W-1
–	ADIP	RC1IP	TX1IP	SSP1IP	CCP1IP	TMR2IP	TMR1IP

bit 7   **bit 0**

R = Readable bit	W = Writable bit	U = Unimplemented bit, read as '0'
-n = Value at POR	'1' = Bit is set	'0' = Bit is cleared x = Bit is unknown

bit 7   **Unimplemented:** Read as '0'

bit 6   **ADIP:** A/D Converter Interrupt Priority bit
                      1 = High priority
                      0 = Low priority

bit 5   **RC1IP:** EUSART1 Receive Interrupt Priority bit
                      1 = High priority
                      0 = Low priority

bit 4   **TX1IP:** EUSART1 Transmit Interrupt Priority bit
                      1 = High priority
                      0 = Low priority

bit 3   **SSP1IP:** Master Synchronous Serial Port 1 Interrupt Priority bit
                      1 = High priority
                      0 = Low priority

bit 2   **CCP1IP:** CCP1 Interrupt Priority bit
                      1 = High priority
                      0 = Low priority

bit 1   **TMR2IP:** TMR2 to PR2 Match Interrupt Priority bit
                      1 = High priority
                      0 = Low priority

bit 0   **TMR1IP:** TMR1 Overflow Interrupt Priority bit
                      1 = High priority
                      0 = Low priority

IPR2:   **IPR2: PERIPHERAL INTERRUPT PRIORITY REGISTER 2**

R/W-1	R/W-1	R/W-1	R/W-1	R/W-1	R/W-1	R/W-1	R/W-1
OSCFIP	C1IP	C2IP	EEIP	BCL1IP	HLVDIP	TMR3IP	CCP2IP

bit 7   bit 0

R = Readable bit   W = Writable bit   U = Unimplemented bit, read as '0'
-n = Value at POR   '1' = Bit is set   '0' = Bit is cleared   x = Bit is unknown

bit 7   **OSCFIP:** Oscillator Fail Interrupt Priority bit
                  1 = High priority
                  0 = Low priority

bit 6   **C1IP:** Comparator C1 Interrupt Priority bit
                  1 = High priority
                  0 = Low priority

bit 5   **C2IP:** Comparator C2 Interrupt Priority bit
                  1 = High priority
                  0 = Low priority

bit 4   **EEIP:** Data EEPROM/Flash Write Operation Interrupt Priority bit
                  1 = High priority
                  0 = Low priority

bit 3   **BCL1IP:** MSSP1 Bus Collision Interrupt Priority bit
                  1 = High priority
                  0 = Low priority

bit 2   **HLVDIP:** Low-Voltage Detect Interrupt Priority bit
                  1 = High priority
                  0 = Low priority

bit 1   **TMR3IP:** TMR3 Overflow Interrupt Priority bit
                  1 = High priority
                  0 = Low priority

bit 0   **CCP2IP:** CCP2 Interrupt Priority bit
                  1 = High priority
                  0 = Low priority

IPR3:   **PERIPHERAL INTERRUPT PRIORITY REGISTER 3**

R/W-0	R/W-0	R/W-0	R/W-0	R/W-0	R/W-0	R/W-0	R/W-0
SSP2IP	BCL2IP	RC2IP	TX2IP	CTMUIP	TMR5GIP	TMR3GIP	TMR1GIP

bit 7   **bit 0**

R = Readable bit   W = Writable bit   U = Unimplemented bit, read as '0'
-n = Value at POR   '1' = Bit is set   '0' = Bit is cleared   x = Bit is unknown

bit 7   **SSP2IP:** Synchronous Serial Port 2 Interrupt Priority bit
                       1 = High priority
                       0 = Low priority

bit 6   **BCL2IP:** Bus Collision 2 Interrupt Priority bit
                       1 = High priority
                       0 = Low priority

bit 5   **RC2IP:** EUSART2 Receive Interrupt Priority bit
                       1 = High priority
                       0 = Low priority

bit 4   **TX2IP:** EUSART2 Transmit Interrupt Priority bit
                       1 = High priority
                       0 = Low priority

bit 3   **CTMUIP:** CTMU Interrupt Priority bit
                       1 = High priority
                       0 = Low priority

bit 2   **TMR5GIP:** TMR5 Gate Interrupt Priority bit
                       1 = High priority
                       0 = Low priority

bit 1   **TMR3GIP:** TMR3 Gate Interrupt Priority bit
                       1 = High priority
                       0 = Low priority

bit 0   **TMR1GIP:** TMR1 Gate Interrupt Priority bit
                       1 = High priority
                       0 = Low priority

IPR4:   **PERIPHERAL INTERRUPT PRIORITY REGISTER 4**

U-0	U-0	U-0	U-0	U-0	R/W-0	R/W-0	R/W-0
–	–	–	–	–	CCP5IP	CCP4IP	CCP3IP

bit 7   **bit 0**

R = Readable bit   W = Writable bit   U = Unimplemented bit, read as '0'
-n = Value at POR   '1' = Bit is set   '0' = Bit is cleared   x = Bit is unknown

bit 7-3   **Unimplemented:** Read as '0'

bit 2   **CCP5IP:** CCP5 Interrupt Priority bit
                       1 = High priority
                       0 = Low priority

bit 1   **CCP4IP:** CCP4 Interrupt Priority bit
                       1 = High priority
                       0 = Low priority

bit 0   **CCP3IP:** CCP3 Interrupt Priority bit
                       1 = High priority
                       0 = Low priority

IPR5:   **PERIPHERAL INTERRUPT PRIORITY REGISTER 5**

U-0	U-0	U-0	U-0	U-0	R/W-0	R/W-0	R/W-0
–	–	–	–	–	TMR6IP	TMR5IP	TMR4IP
bit 7							bit 0

R = Readable bit   W = Writable bit   U = Unimplemented bit, read as '0'
-n = Value at POR   '1' = Bit is set   '0' = Bit is cleared   x = Bit is unknown

bit 7-3   **Unimplemented:** Read as '0'

bit 2   **TMR6IP:** TMR6 to PR6 Match Interrupt Priority bit
                  1 = High priority
                  0 = Low priority

bit 1   **TMR5IP:** TMR5 Overflow Interrupt Priority bit
                  1 = High priority
                  0 = Low priority

bit 0   **TMR4IP:** TMR4 to PR4 Match Interrupt Priority bit
                  1 = High priority
                  0 = Low priority

LATx: **LATx: PORTx OUTPUT LATCH REGISTER**[1]

R/W-x	R/W-x	R/W-x	R/W-x	R/W-x	R/W-x	R/W-x	R/W-x
LATx7	LATx6	LATx5	LATx4	LATx3	LATx2	LATx1	LATx0
bit 7							bit 0

R = Readable bit   W = Writable bit   U = Unimplemented bit, read as '0'
-n = Value at POR   '1' = Bit is set   '0' = Bit is cleared   x = Bit is unknown

bit 7-0   **LATx<7:0>:** PORTx Output Latch bit value[2]

Note 1:   Register Description for LATA, LATB, LATC and LATD.
Note 2:   Writes to PORTA are written to corresponding LATA register. Reads from PORTA register is
                  return of I/O pin values.

LATE: **PORTE OUTPUT LATCH REGISTER**[1]

U-0	U-0	U-0	U-0	U-0	R/W-x	R/W-x	R/W-x
–	–	–	–	–	LATE2	LATE1	LATE0
bit 7							bit 0

R = Readable bit   W = Writable bit   U = Unimplemented bit, read as '0'
-n = Value at POR   '1' = Bit is set   '0' = Bit is cleared   x = Bit is unknown

bit 7-3   **Unimplemented:** Read as '0'

bit 2-0   **LATE<2:0>:** PORTE Output Latch bit value[2]

Note 1:   Available on PIC18(L)F4XK22 devices only.
Note 2:   Writes to PORTA are written to corresponding LATA register. Reads from PORTA register is
                  return of I/O pin values.

OSCCON: **OSCILLATOR CONTROL REGISTER**

R/W-0	R/W-0	R/W-1	R/W-1	R-q	R-0	R/W-0	R/W-0
IDLEN		IRCF<2:0>		OSTS [1]	HFIOFS		SCS<1:0>

bit 7   bit 0

R = Readable bit	W = Writable bit	U = Unimplemented bit, read as '0'
-n = Value at POR	'1' = Bit is set	'0' = Bit is cleared x = Bit is unknown

bit 7   **IDLEN:** Idle Enable bit
                       1 = Device enters Idle mode on SLEEP instruction
                       0 = Device enters Sleep mode on SLEEP instruction

bit 6-4   **IRCF<2:0>:** Internal RC Oscillator Frequency Select bits[2]
                       111 = HFINTOSC – (16 MHz)
                       110 = HFINTOSC/2 – (8 MHz)
                       101 = HFINTOSC/4 – (4 MHz)
                       100 = HFINTOSC/8 – (2 MHz)
                       011 = HFINTOSC/16 – (1 MHz)[3]

                       If INTSRC = 0 and MFIOSEL = 0:
                       010 = HFINTOSC/32 – (500 kHz)
                       001 = HFINTOSC/64 – (250 kHz)
                       000 = LFINTOSC – (31.25 kHz)

                       If INTSRC = 1 and MFIOSEL = 0:
                       010 = HFINTOSC/32 – (500 kHz)
                       001 = HFINTOSC/64 – (250 kHz)
                       000 = HFINTOSC/512 – (31.25 kHz)

                       If INTSRC = 0 and MFIOSEL = 1:
                       010 = MFINTOSC – (500 kHz)
                       001 = MFINTOSC/2 – (250 kHz)
                       000 = LFINTOSC – (31.25 kHz)

                       If INTSRC = 1 and MFIOSEL = 1:
                       010 = MFINTOSC – (500 kHz)
                       001 = MFINTOSC/2 – (250 kHz)
                       000 = MFINTOSC/16 – (31.25 kHz)

bit 3   **OSTS:** Oscillator Start-up Time-out Status bit
                       1 = Device is running from the clock defined by FOSC<3:0> of the CONFIG1H register
                       0 = Device is running from the internal oscillator (HFINTOSC, MFINTOSC or LFINTOSC)

bit 2   **HFIOFS:** HFINTOSC Frequency Stable bit
                       1 = HFINTOSC frequency is stable
                       0 = HFINTOSC frequency is not stable

bit 1-0   **SCS<1:0>:** System Clock Select bit
                       1x = Internal oscillator block
                       01 = Secondary (SOSC) oscillator
                       00 = Primary clock (determined by FOSC<3:0> in CONFIG1H).

Note 1:   Reset state depends on state of the IESO Configuration bit.
Note 2:   INTOSC source may be determined by the INTSRC bit in OSCTUNE and the MFIOSEL bit in OSCCON2.
Note 3:   Default output frequency of HFINTOSC on Reset.

OSCCON2:   OSCILLATOR CONTROL REGISTER 2

R-0/0	R-0/q	U-0	R/W-0/0	R/W-0/u	R/W-1/1	R-x/u	R-0/0
PLLRDY	SOSCRUN	–	MFIOSEL	SOSCGO[1]	PRISD	MFIOFS	LFIOFS
bit 7							**bit 0**

R = Readable bit	W = Writable bit	U = Unimplemented bit, read as '0'
q = Depends on condition	'1' = Bit is set	'0' = Bit is cleared x = Bit is unknown

bit 7   **PLLRDY:** PLL Run Status bit
1 = System clock comes from 4xPLL
0 = System clock comes from an oscillator, other than 4xPLL

bit 6   **SOSCRUN:** SOSC Run Status bit
1 = System clock comes from secondary SOSC
0 = System clock comes from an oscillator, other than SOSC

bit 5   **Unimplemented:** Read as '0'.

bit 4   **MFIOSEL:** MFINTOSC Select bit
1 = MFINTOSC is used in place of HFINTOSC frequencies of 500 kHz, 250 kHz and 31.25 kHz
0 = MFINTOSC is not used

bit 3   **SOSCGO**[1] **:** Secondary Oscillator Start Control bit
1 = Secondary oscillator is enabled.
0 = Secondary oscillator is shut off if no other sources are requesting it.

bit 2   **PRISD:** Primary Oscillator Drive Circuit Shutdown bit
1 = Oscillator drive circuit on
0 = Oscillator drive circuit off (zero power)

bit 1   **MFIOFS:** MFINTOSC Frequency Stable bit
1 = MFINTOSC is stable
0 = MFINTOSC is not stable

bit 0   **LFIOFS:** LFINTOSC Frequency Stable bit
1 = LFINTOSC is stable
0 = LFINTOSC is not stable

Note 1:   The SOSCGO bit is only reset on a POR Reset.

OSCTUNE: OSCILLATOR TUNING REGISTER

R/W-0	R/W-0	R/W-0	R/W-0	R/W-0	R/W-0	R/W-0	R/W-0
INTSRC	PLLEN[1]	TUN<5:0>					
bit 7							bit 0

R = Readable bit   W = Writable bit   U = Unimplemented bit, read as '0'
-n = Value at POR   '1' = Bit is set   '0' = Bit is cleared   x = Bit is unknown

bit 7   **INTSRC:** Internal Oscillator Low-Frequency Source Select bit
       1 = 31.25 kHz device clock derived from the MFINTOSC or HFINTOSC source
       0 = 31.25 kHz device clock derived directly from LFINTOSC internal oscillator

bit 6   **PLLEN:** Frequency Multiplier 4xPLL for HFINTOSC Enable bit[1]
       1 = PLL enabled
       0 = PLL disabled

bit 5-0   **TUN<5:0>:** Frequency Tuning bits – use to adjust MFINTOSC and HFINTOSC frequencies
       011111 = Maximum frequency
       011110 =
       • • •
       000001 =
       000000 = Oscillator module (HFINTOSC and MFINTOSC) are running at the factory
               calibrated frequency.
       111111 =
       • • •
       100000 = Minimum frequency

Note 1:   The PLLEN bit is active for all the primary clock sources (internal or external) and is designed
         to operate with clock frequencies between 4 MHz and 16 MHz.

PCL   PC LOW BYTE (PC<7:0>)

R/W-0	R/W-0	R/W-0	R/W-0	R/W-0	R/W-0	R/W-0	R/W-0
bit 7							bit 0

R = Readable bit   W = Writable bit   U = Unimplemented bit, read as '0'
-n = Value at POR   '1' = Bit is set   '0' = Bit is cleared   x = Bit is unknown

bit 7-0   **PC<7:0>):** least significant bits of program counter

PCLATH: HOLDING REGISTER FOR PC<15:8>

R/W-0	R/W-0	R/W-0	R/W-0	R/W-0	R/W-0	R/W-0	R/W-0
bit 7							bit 0

R = Readable bit   W = Writable bit   '1' = Bit is set   '0' = Bit is cleared

bit 7-0   **Holding Register for PC<15:8>**

PCLATU: HOLDING REGISTER FOR PC<20:16>

U-0	U-0	U-0	R/W-0	R/W-0	R/W-0	R/W-0	R/W-0
-	-	-	Holding Register for PC<20:16>				
bit 7							bit 0

R = Readable bit   W = Writable bit   U = Unimplemented bit, read as '0'
-n = Value at POR   '1' = Bit is set   '0' = Bit is cleared   x = Bit is unknown

bit 7-5   **Unimplemented:** Read as '0'.

bit4-0   **Holding Register for PC<20:16>**

PIE1:   **PERIPHERAL INTERRUPT ENABLE (FLAG) REGISTER 1**

U-0	R/W-0	R/W-0	R/W-0	R/W-0	R/W-0	R/W-0	R/W-0
–	ADIE	RC1IE	TX1IE	SSP1IE	CCP1IE	TMR2IE	TMR1IE

bit 7   bit 0

R = Readable bit   W = Writable bit   U = Unimplemented bit, read as '0'
-n = Value at POR   '1' = Bit is set   '0' = Bit is cleared   x = Bit is unknown

bit 7   **Unimplemented:** Read as '0'.

bit 6   **ADIE:** A/D Converter Interrupt Enable bit
1 = Enables the A/D interrupt
0 = Disables the A/D interrupt

bit 5   **RC1IE:** EUSART1 Receive Interrupt Enable bit
1 = Enables the EUSART1 receive interrupt
0 = Disables the EUSART1 receive interrupt

bit 4   **TX1IE:** EUSART1 Transmit Interrupt Enable bit
1 = Enables the EUSART1 transmit interrupt
0 = Disables the EUSART1 transmit interrupt

bit 3   **SSP1IE:** Master Synchronous Serial Port 1 Interrupt Enable bit
1 = Enables the MSSP1 interrupt
0 = Disables the MSSP1 interrupt

bit 2   **CCP1IE:** CCP1 Interrupt Enable bit
1 = Enables the CCP1 interrupt
0 = Disables the CCP1 interrupt

bit 1   **TMR2IE:** TMR2 to PR2 Match Interrupt Enable bit
1 = Enables the TMR2 to PR2 match interrupt
0 = Disables the TMR2 to PR2 match interrupt

bit 0   **TMR1IE:** TMR1 Overflow Interrupt Enable bit
1 = Enables the TMR1 overflow interrupt
0 = Disables the TMR1 overflow interrupt

PIE2: PERIPHERAL INTERRUPT ENABLE (FLAG) REGISTER 2

R/W-0	R/W-0	R/W-0	R/W-0	R/W-0	R/W-0	R/W-0	R/W-0
OSCFIE	C1IE	C2IE	EEIE	BCL1IE	HLVDIE	TMR3IE	CCP2IE

bit 7   **bit 0**

R = Readable bit   W = Writable bit   '1' = Bit is set   '0' = Bit is cleared

bit 7   **OSCFIE:** Oscillator Fail Interrupt Enable bit
                    1 = Enabled
                    0 = Disabled

bit 6   **C1IE:** Comparator C1 Interrupt Enable bit
                    1 = Enabled
                    0 = Disabled

bit 5   **C2IE:** Comparator C2 Interrupt Enable bit
                    1 = Enabled
                    0 = Disabled

bit 4   **EEIE:** Data EEPROM/Flash Write Operation Interrupt Enable bit
                    1 = Enabled
                    0 = Disabled

bit 3   **BCL1IE:** MSSP1 Bus Collision Interrupt Enable bit
                    1 = Enabled
                    0 = Disabled

bit 2   **HLVDIE:** Low-Voltage Detect Interrupt Enable bit
                    1 = Enabled
                    0 = Disabled

bit 1   **TMR3IE:** TMR3 Overflow Interrupt Enable bit
                    1 = Enabled
                    0 = Disabled

bit 0   **CCP2IE:** CCP2 Interrupt Enable bit
                    1 = Enabled
                    0 = Disabled

PIE3: **PERIPHERAL INTERRUPT ENABLE (FLAG) REGISTER 3**

R/W-0	R/W-0	R/W-0	R/W-0	R/W-0	R/W-0	R/W-0	R/W-0
SSP2IE	BCL2IE	RC2IE	TX2IE	CTMUIE	TMR5GIE	TMR3GIE	TMR1GIE
bit 7							bit 0

R = Readable bit   W = Writable bit   U = Unimplemented bit, read as '0'
-n = Value at POR   '1' = Bit is set   '0' = Bit is cleared   x = Bit is unknown

bit 7   **SSP2IE:** TMR5 Gate Interrupt Enable bit
                1 = Enabled
                0 = Disabled

bit 6   **BCL2IE:** Bus Collision Interrupt Enable bit
                1 = Enabled
                0 = Disabled

bit 5   **RC2IE:** EUSART2 Receive Interrupt Enable bit
                1 = Enabled
                0 = Disabled

bit 4   **TX2IE:** EUSART2 Transmit Interrupt Enable bit
                1 = Enabled
                0 = Disabled

bit 3   **CTMUIE:** CTMU Interrupt Enable bit
                1 = Enabled
                0 = Disabled

bit 2   **TMR5GIE:** TMR5 Gate Interrupt Enable bit
                1 = Enabled
                0 = Disabled

bit 1   **TMR3GIE:** TMR3 Gate Interrupt Enable bit
                1 = Enabled
                0 = Disabled

bit 0   **TMR1GIE:** TMR1 Gate Interrupt Enable bit
                1 = Enabled
                0 = Disabled

PIE4: **PERIPHERAL INTERRUPT ENABLE (FLAG) REGISTER 4**

U-0	U-0	U-0	U-0	U-0	R/W-0	R/W-0	R/W-0
–	–	–	–	–	CCP5IE	CCP4IE	CCP3IE
bit 7							bit 0

R = Readable bit   W = Writable bit   U = Unimplemented bit, read as '0'
-n = Value at POR   '1' = Bit is set   '0' = Bit is cleared   x = Bit is unknown

bit 7-3   **Unimplemented:** Read as '0'

bit 2   **CCP5IE:** CCP5 Interrupt Enable bit
                1 = Enabled
                0 = Disabled

bit 1   **CCP4IE:** CCP4 Interrupt Enable bit
                1 = Enabled
                0 = Disabled

bit 0   **CCP3IE:** CCP3 Interrupt Enable bit
                1 = Enabled
                0 = Disabled

PIE5:   **PERIPHERAL INTERRUPT ENABLE (FLAG) REGISTER 5**

U-0	U-0	U-0	U-0	U-0	R/W-0	R/W-0	R/W-0
–	–	–	–	–	TMR6IE	TMR5IE	TMR4IE

bit 7   **bit 0**

R = Readable bit	W = Writable bit	U = Unimplemented bit, read as '0'
-n = Value at POR	'1' = Bit is set	'0' = Bit is cleared x = Bit is unknown

bit 7-3   **Unimplemented:** Read as '0'

bit 2   **TMR6IE:** TMR6 to PR6 Match Interrupt Enable bit
                   1 = Enables the TMR6 to PR6 match interrupt
                   0 = Disables the TMR6 to PR6 match interrupt

bit 1   **TMR5IE:** TMR5 Overflow Interrupt Enable bit
                   1 = Enables the TMR5 overflow interrupt
                   0 = Disables the TMR5 overflow interrupt

bit 0   **TMR4IE:** TMR4 to PR4 Match Interrupt Enable bit
                   1 = Enables the TMR4 to PR4 match interrupt
                   0 = Disables the TMR4 to PR4 match interrupt

PIR1: **PERIPHERAL INTERRUPT REQUEST (FLAG) REGISTER 1**

U-0	R/W-0	R-0	R-0	R/W-0	R/W-0	R/W-0	R/W-0
–	ADIF	RC1IF	TX1IF	SSP1IF	CCP1IF	TMR2IF	TMR1IF

bit 7 **bit 0**

R = Readable bit   W = Writable bit   U = Unimplemented bit, read as '0'
-n = Value at POR   '1' = Bit is set   '0' = Bit is cleared   x = Bit is unknown

bit 7   **Unimplemented:** Read as '0'.

bit 6   **ADIF:** A/D Converter Interrupt Flag bit
    1 = An A/D conversion completed (must be cleared by software)
    0 = The A/D conversion is not complete or has not been started

bit 5   **RC1IF:** EUSART1 Receive Interrupt Flag bit
    1 = The EUSART1 receive buffer, RCREG1, is full (cleared when RCREG1 is read)
    0 = The EUSART1 receive buffer is empty

bit 4   **TX1IF:** EUSART1 Transmit Interrupt Flag bit
    1 = The EUSART1 transmit buffer, TXREG1, is empty (cleared when TXREG1 is written)
    0 = The EUSART1 transmit buffer is full

bit 3   **SSP1IF:** Master Synchronous Serial Port 1 Interrupt Flag bit
    1 = The transmission/reception is complete (must be cleared by software)
    0 = Waiting to transmit/receive

bit 2   **CCP1IF:** CCP1 Interrupt Flag bit
    Capture mode:
    1 = A TMR1 register capture occurred (must be cleared by software)
    0 = No TMR1 register capture occurred
    Compare mode:
    1 = A TMR1 register compare match occurred (must be cleared by software)
    0 = No TMR1 register compare match occurred
    PWM mode:
    Unused in this mode

bit 1   **TMR2IF:** TMR2 to PR2 Match Interrupt Flag bit
    1 = TMR2 to PR2 match occurred (must be cleared by software)
    0 = No TMR2 to PR2 match occurred

bit 0   **TMR1IF:** TMR1 Overflow Interrupt Flag bit
    1 = TMR1 register overflowed (must be cleared by software)
    0 = TMR1 register did not overflow

Note: Interrupt flag bits are set when an interrupt condition occurs, regardless of the state of its corresponding enable bit or the global enable bit. User software should insure the appropriate interrupt flag bits are clear prior to enabling an interrupt. This feature allows for software polling.

PIR2:   PERIPHERAL INTERRUPT REQUEST (FLAG) REGISTER 2

R/W-0	R/W-0	R/W-0	R/W-0	R/W-0	R/W-0	R/W-0	R/W-0
OSCFIF	C1IF	C2IF	EEIF	BCL1IF	HLVDIF	TMR3IF	CCP2IF
bit 7							bit 0

R = Readable bit   W = Writable bit   U = Unimplemented bit, read as '0'
-n = Value at POR   '1' = Bit is set   '0' = Bit is cleared   x = Bit is unknown

bit 7   **OSCFIF:** Oscillator Fail Interrupt Flag bit
         1 = Device oscillator failed, clock input has changed to HFINTOSC (must be cleared by
            software)
         0 = Device clock operating

bit 6   **C1IF:** Comparator C1 Interrupt Flag bit
         1 = Comparator C1 output has changed (must be cleared by software)
         0 = Comparator C1 output has not changed

bit 5   **C2IF:** Comparator C2 Interrupt Flag bit
         1 = Comparator C2 output has changed (must be cleared by software)
         0 = Comparator C2 output has not changed

bit 4   **EEIF:** Data EEPROM/Flash Write Operation Interrupt Flag bit
         1 = The write operation is complete (must be cleared by software)
         0 = The write operation is not complete or has not been started

bit 3   **BCL1IF:** MSSP1 Bus Collision Interrupt Flag bit
         1 = A bus collision occurred (must be cleared by software)
         0 = No bus collision occurred

bit 2   **HLVDIF:** Low-Voltage Detect Interrupt Flag bit
         1 = A low-voltage condition occurred (direction determined by the VDIRMAG bit of the
            HLVDCON register)
         0 = A low-voltage condition has not occurred

bit 1   **TMR3IF:** TMR3 Overflow Interrupt Flag bit
         1 = TMR3 register overflowed (must be cleared by software)
         0 = TMR3 register did not overflow

bit 0   **CCP2IF:** CCP2 Interrupt Flag bit
         <u>Capture mode:</u>
         1 = A TMR1 register capture occurred (must be cleared by software)
         0 = No TMR1 register capture occurred
         <u>Compare mode:</u>
         1 = A TMR1 register compare match occurred (must be cleared by software)
         0 = No TMR1 register compare match occurred
         <u>PWM mode:</u>
         Unused in this mode.

PIR3:   **PERIPHERAL INTERRUPT (FLAG) REGISTER 3**

R/W-0	R/W-0	R/W-0	R/W-0	R/W-0	R/W-0	R/W-0	R/W-0
SSP2IF	BCL2IF	RC2IF	TX2IF	CTMUIF	TMR5GIF	TMR3GIF	TMR1GIF

bit 7   **bit 0**

R = Readable bit	W = Writable bit	U = Unimplemented bit, read as '0'
-n = Value at POR	'1' = Bit is set	'0' = Bit is cleared x = Bit is unknown

bit 7   **SSP2IF:** Synchronous Serial Port Interrupt Flag bit
                 1 = The transmission/reception is complete (must be cleared in software)
                 0 = Waiting to transmit/receive

bit 6   **BCL2IF:** MSSP2 Bus Collision Interrupt Flag bit
                 1 = A bus collision has occurred while the SSP2 module configured in I^2C master was
                    transmitting (must be cleared in software)
                 0 = No bus collision occurred

bit 5   **RC2IF:** EUSART2 Receive Interrupt Flag bit
                 1 = The EUSART2 receive buffer, RCREG2, is full (cleared by reading RCREG2)
                 0 = The EUSART2 receive buffer is empty

bit 4   **TX2IF:** EUSART2 Transmit Interrupt Flag bit
                 1 = The EUSART2 transmit buffer, TXREG2, is empty (cleared by writing TXREG2)
                 0 = The EUSART2 transmit buffer is full

bit 3   **CTMUIF:** CTMU Interrupt Flag bit
                 1 = CTMU interrupt occurred (must be cleared in software)
                 0 = No CTMU interrupt occurred

bit 2   **TMR5GIF:** TMR5 Gate Interrupt Flag bits
                 1 = TMR gate interrupt occurred (must be cleared in software)
                 0 = No TMR gate occurred

bit 1   **TMR3GIF:** TMR3 Gate Interrupt Flag bits
                 1 = TMR gate interrupt occurred (must be cleared in software)
                 0 = No TMR gate occurred

bit 0   **TMR1GIF:** TMR1 Gate Interrupt Flag bits
                 1 = TMR gate interrupt occurred (must be cleared in software)
                 0 = No TMR gate occurred

PIR4:   **PERIPHERAL INTERRUPT (FLAG) REGISTER 4**

U-0	U-0	U-0	U-0	U-0	R/W-0	R/W-0	R/W-0
–	–	–	–	–	CCP5IF	CCP4IF	CCP3IF

bit 7   **bit 0**

R = Readable bit	W = Writable bit	U = Unimplemented bit, read as '0'
-n = Value at POR	'1' = Bit is set	'0' = Bit is cleared x = Bit is unknown

bit 7-3   **Unimplemented:** Read as '0'

bit 2   **CCP5IF:** CCP5 Interrupt Flag bits
<u>Capture mode:</u>
1 = A TMR register capture occurred (must be cleared in software)
0 = No TMR register capture occurred
<u>Compare mode:</u>
1 = A TMR register compare match occurred (must be cleared in software)
0 = No TMR register compare match occurred
<u>PWM mode:</u>
Unused in PWM mode.

bit 1   **CCP4IF:** CCP4 Interrupt Flag bits
<u>Capture mode:</u>
1 = A TMR register capture occurred (must be cleared in software)
0 = No TMR register capture occurred
<u>Compare mode:</u>
1 = A TMR register compare match occurred (must be cleared in software)
0 = No TMR register compare match occurred
<u>PWM mode:</u>
Unused in PWM mode.

bit 0   **CP3IF:** ECCP3 Interrupt Flag bits
<u>Capture mode:</u>
1 = A TMR register capture occurred (must be cleared in software)
0 = No TMR register capture occurred
<u>Compare mode:</u>
1 = A TMR register compare match occurred (must be cleared in software)
0 = No TMR register compare match occurred
<u>PWM mode:</u>
Unused in PWM mode.

PIR5:   **PERIPHERAL INTERRUPT (FLAG) REGISTER 5**

U-0	U-0	U-0	U-0	U-0	R/W-0	R/W-0	R/W-0
–	–	–	–	–	TMR6IF	TMR5IF	TMR4IF

bit 7   **bit 0**

R = Readable bit	W = Writable bit	U = Unimplemented bit, read as '0'
-n = Value at POR	'1' = Bit is set	'0' = Bit is cleared x = Bit is unknown

bit 7-3   **Unimplemented:** Read as '0'

bit 2   **TMR6IF:** TMR6 to PR6 Match Interrupt Flag bit
1 = TMR6 to PR6 match occurred (must be cleared in software)
0 = No TMR6 to PR6 match occurred

bit 1   **TMR5IF:** TMR5 Overflow Interrupt Flag bit
1 = TMR5 register overflowed (must be cleared in software)
0 = TMR5 register did not overflow

bit 0   **TMR4IF:** TMR4 to PR4 Match Interrupt Flag bit
1 = TMR4 to PR4 match occurred (must be cleared in software)
0 = No TMR4 to PR4 match occurred

PLUSWx: OFFSET FSRx BY WREG (EFFECTIVE ADDRESS) (x = 0, 1, 2)

U-0	U-0	U-0	U-0	U-0	U-0	U-0	U-0
bit 7							**bit 0**

R = Readable bit   W = Writable bit   U = Unimplemented bit, read as '0'

bit 7-0   **Not physically implemented**: This register is used to specify offset addressing mode.

PMD0:   PERIPHERAL MODULE DISABLE REGISTER 0

R/W-0	R/W-0	R/W-0	R/W-0	R/W-0	R/W-0	R/W-0	R/W-0
UART2MD	UART1MD	TMR6MD	TMR5MD	TMR4MD	TMR3MD	TMR2MD	TMR1MD
bit 7							**bit 0**

R = Readable bit   W = Writable bit   U = Unimplemented bit, read as '0'
-n = Value at POR   '1' = Bit is set   '0' = Bit is cleared   x = Bit is unknown

bit 7   **UART2MD:** UART2 Peripheral Module Disable Control bit
                 1 = Module is disabled, Clock Source is disconnected, module does not draw digital power
                 0 = Module is enabled, Clock Source is connected, module draws digital power

bit 6   **UART1MD:** UART1 Peripheral Module Disable Control bit
                 1 = Module is disabled, Clock Source is disconnected, module does not draw digital power
                 0 = Module is enabled, Clock Source is connected, module draws digital power

bit 5   **TMR6MD:** Timer6 Peripheral Module Disable Control bit
                 1 = Module is disabled, Clock Source is disconnected, module does not draw digital power
                 0 = Module is enabled, Clock Source is connected, module draws digital power

bit 4   **TMR5MD:** Timer5 Peripheral Module Disable Control bit
                 1 = Module is disabled, Clock Source is disconnected, module does not draw digital power
                 0 = Module is enabled, Clock Source is connected, module draws digital power

bit 3   **TMR4MD:** Timer4 Peripheral Module Disable Control bit
                 1 = Module is disabled, Clock Source is disconnected, module does not draw digital power
                 0 = Module is enabled, Clock Source is connected, module draws digital power

bit 2   **TMR3MD:** Timer3 Peripheral Module Disable Control bit
                 1 = Module is disabled, Clock Source is disconnected, module does not draw digital power
                 0 = Module is enabled, Clock Source is connected, module draws digital power

bit 1   **TMR2MD:** Timer2 Peripheral Module Disable Control bit
                 1 = Module is disabled, Clock Source is disconnected, module does not draw digital power
                 0 = Module is enabled, Clock Source is connected, module draws digital power

bit 0   **TMR1MD:** Timer1 Peripheral Module Disable Control bit
                 1 = Module is disabled, Clock Source is disconnected, module does not draw digital power
                 0 = Module is enabled, Clock Source is connected, module draws digital power

PMD1:   **PERIPHERAL MODULE DISABLE REGISTER 1**

R/W-0	R/W-0	U-0	R/W-0	R/W-0	R/W-0	R/W-0	R/W-0
MSSP2MD	MSSP1MD	–	CCP5MD	CCP4MD	CCP3MD	CCP2MD	CCP1MD
bit 7							**bit 0**

R = Readable bit   W = Writable bit   U = Unimplemented bit, read as '0'
-n = Value at POR   '1' = Bit is set   '0' = Bit is cleared   x = Bit is unknown

bit 7   **MSSP2MD:** MSSP2 Peripheral Module Disable Control bit
               1 = Module is disabled, Clock Source is disconnected, module does not draw digital power
               0 = Module is enabled, Clock Source is connected, module draws digital power

bit 6   **MSSP1MD:** MSSP1 Peripheral Module Disable Control bit
               1 = Module is disabled, Clock Source is disconnected, module does not draw digital power
               0 = Module is enabled, Clock Source is connected, module draws digital power

bit 5   **Unimplemented:** Read as '0'

bit 4   **CCP5MD:** CCP5 Peripheral Module Disable Control bit
               1 = Module is disabled, Clock Source is disconnected, module does not draw digital power
               0 = Module is enabled, Clock Source is connected, module draws digital power

bit 3   **CCP4MD:** CCP4 Peripheral Module Disable Control bit
               1 = Module is disabled, Clock Source is disconnected, module does not draw digital power
               0 = Module is enabled, Clock Source is connected, module draws digital power

bit 2   **CCP3MD:** CCP3 Peripheral Module Disable Control bit
               1 = Module is disabled, Clock Source is disconnected, module does not draw digital power
               0 = Module is enabled, Clock Source is connected, module draws digital power

bit 1   **CCP2MD:** CCP2 Peripheral Module Disable Control bit
               1 = Module is disabled, Clock Source is disconnected, module does not draw digital power
               0 = Module is enabled, Clock Source is connected, module draws digital power

bit 0   **CCP1MD:** CCP1 Peripheral Module Disable Control bit
               1 = Module is disabled, Clock Source is disconnected, module does not draw digital power
               0 = Module is enabled, Clock Source is connected, module draws digital power

PMD2:   **PERIPHERAL MODULE DISABLE REGISTER 2**

U-0	U-0	U-0	U-0	R/W-0	R/W-0	R/W-0	R/W-0
–	–	–	–	CTMUMD	CMP2MD	CMP1MD	ADCMD
bit 7							**bit 0**

R = Readable bit   W = Writable bit   U = Unimplemented bit, read as '0'
-n = Value at POR   '1' = Bit is set   '0' = Bit is cleared   x = Bit is unknown

bit 7-3   **Unimplemented:** Read as '0'

bit 3   **CTMUMD:** CTMU Peripheral Module Disable Control bit
               1 = Module is disabled, Clock Source is disconnected, module does not draw digital power
               0 = Module is enabled, Clock Source is connected, module draws digital power

bit 2   **CMP2MD:** Comparator C2 Peripheral Module Disable Control bit
               1 = Module is disabled, Clock Source is disconnected, module does not draw digital power
               0 = Module is enabled, Clock Source is connected, module draws digital power

bit 1   **CMP1MD:** Comparator C1 Peripheral Module Disable Control bit
               1 = Module is disabled, Clock Source is disconnected, module does not draw digital power
               0 = Module is enabled, Clock Source is connected, module draws digital power

bit 0   **ADCMD:** ADC Peripheral Module Disable Control bit
               1 = Module is disabled, Clock Source is disconnected, module does not draw digital power
               0 = Module is enabled, Clock Source is connected, module draws digital power

PORTx[(1)] :   **PORTx REGISTER (x = A, B, C, D)**

R/W-u	R/W-u	R/W-u	R/W-u	R/W-u	R/W-u	R/W-u	R/W-u
RA7	RA6	RA5	RA4	RA3	RA2	RA1	RA0

bit 7   bit 0

R = Readable bit	W = Writable bit	u = Unknown	
-n = Value at POR	'1' = Bit is set	'0' = Bit is cleared	x = Bit is unknown

bit 7-0   **Rx<7:0>:** PORTx I/O bit values[(2)]

Note 1:   Register Description for PORTA, PORTB, PORTC and PORTD.
Note 2:   Writes to PORTx are written to corresponding LATx register. Reads from PORTx register is return of I/O pin values.

PORTE: **PORTE REGISTER**

U-0	U-0	U-0	U-0	R/W-u	R/W-u	R/W-u	R/W-u
–	–	–	–	RE3[(1)]	RE2[(2), (3)]	RE1[(2), (3)]	RE0[(2), (3)]

bit 7   bit 0

R = Readable bit	W = Writable bit	u = Unknown	
-n = Value at POR	'1' = Bit is set	'0' = Bit is cleared	x = Bit is unknown

bit 7-4   **Unimplemented:** Read as '0'

bit 3   **RE3:** PORTE Input bit value[(1)]

bit 2-0   **RE<2:0>:** PORTE I/O bit values[(2), (3)]

Note 1:   Port is available as input only when MCLRE = 0.
Note 2:   Writes to PORTx are written to corresponding LATx register. Reads from PORTx register is return of I/O pin values.
Note 3:   Available on PIC18(L)F4XK22 devices.

POSTDECx: **INDEXED ADDRESSING WITH POST-DECREMENTATION (x = 0, 1, 2)**

U-0	U-0	U-0	U-0	U-0	U-0	U-0	U-0

bit 7   bit 0

U = Unimplemented bit, read as '0'

bit 7-0   **Unimplemented**: This register is simply used to specify an addressing mode

POSTINCx: **INDEXED ADDRESSING WITH POST-INCREMENTATION (x = 0, 1, 2)**

U-0	U-0	U-0	U-0	U-0	U-0	U-0	U-0

bit 7   bit 0

U = Unimplemented bit, read as '0'

bit 7-0   **Unimplemented**: This register is simply used to specify an addressing mode

PRx: **TIMERx PERIOD REGISTER (x = 2, 4, 6)**

R/W-1	R/W-1	R/W-1	R/W-1	R/W-1	R/W-1	R/W-1	R/W-1

bit 7   bit 0

R = Readable bit	W = Writable bit	'1' = Bit is set	'0' = Bit is cleared

bit 7-0   **PRx<7:0>:** Period register for TMRx (x = 2, 4, 6)

PREINCx: **INDEXED ADDRESSING WITH PRE-INCREMENTATION (x = 0, 1, 2)**

U-0	U-0	U-0	U-0	U-0	U-0	U-0	U-0

bit 7   bit 0

U = Unimplemented bit, read as '0'

bit 7-0   **Unimplemented**: This register is simply used to specify an addressing mode

PRODH: **PRODUCT REGISTER HIGH BYTE**

R/W-x	R/W-x	R/W-x	R/W-x	R/W-x	R/W-x	R/W-x	R/W-x

bit 7   bit 0

R = Readable bit   W = Writable bit   x = Bit is unknown

bit 7-0   **High order bits of product (following a multiply instruction)**

PRODL: **PRODUCT REGISTER LOW BYTE**

R/W-x	R/W-x	R/W-x	R/W-x	R/W-x	R/W-x	R/W-x	R/W-x

bit 7   bit 0

R = Readable bit   W = Writable bit   U = Unimplemented bit, read as '0'
-n = Value at POR   '1' = Bit is set   '0' = Bit is cleared   x = Bit is unknown

bit 7-0   **Low order bits of product (following a multiply instruction)**

PSTRxCON: **PWM STEERING CONTROL REGISTER[1] (x = 1, 2, 3)**

U-0	U-0	U-0	R/W-0	R/W-0	R/W-0	R/W-0	R/W-0
–	–	–	STRxSYNC	STRxD	STRxC	STRxB	STRxA

bit 7   bit 0

R = Readable bit   W = Writable bit   U = Unimplemented bit, read as '0'
-n = Value at POR   '1' = Bit is set   '0' = Bit is cleared   x = Bit is unknown

bit 7-5   **Unimplemented:** Read as '0'

bit 4   **STRxSYNC:** Steering Sync bit
1 = Output steering update occurs on next PWM period
0 = Output steering update occurs at the beginning of the instruction cycle boundary

bit 3   **STRxD:** Steering Enable bit D
1 = PxD pin has the PWM waveform with polarity control from CCPxM<1:0>
0 = PxD pin is assigned to port pin

bit 2   **STRxC:** Steering Enable bit C
1 = PxC pin has the PWM waveform with polarity control from CCPxM<1:0>
0 = PxC pin is assigned to port pin

bit 1   **STRxB:** Steering Enable bit B
1 = PxB pin has the PWM waveform with polarity control from CCPxM<1:0>
0 = PxB pin is assigned to port pin

bit 0   **STRxA:** Steering Enable bit A
1 = PxA pin has the PWM waveform with polarity control from CCPxM<1:0>
0 = PxA pin is assigned to port pin

Note 1:   The PWM Steering mode is available only when the CCPxCON register bits CCPxM<3:2> = 11 and PxM<1:0> = 00.

PWMxCON: **ENHANCED PWM CONTROL REGISTER (x = 1, 2, 3)**

R/W-0	R/W-0	R/W-0	R/W-0	R/W-0	R/W-0	R/W-0	R/W-0
PxRSEN	PxDC<6:0>						
bit 7							bit 0

R = Readable bit	W = Writable bit	U = Unimplemented bit, read as '0'
-n = Value at POR	'1' = Bit is set	'0' = Bit is cleared x = Bit is unknown

bit 7   **PxRSEN:** PWM Restart Enable bit
                   1 = Upon auto-shutdown, the CCPxASE bit clears automatically once the shutdown event
                       goes away; the PWM restarts automatically
                   0 = Upon auto-shutdown, CCPxASE must be cleared in software to restart the PWM

bit 6-0   **PxDC<6:0>:** PWM Delay Count bits
                   PxDCx = Number of FOSC/4 (4 * TOSC) cycles between the scheduled time when a PWM
                   signal should transition active and the actual time it transitions active

RCON: **RESET CONTROL REGISTER**

R/W-0/0	R/W-q/u	U-0	R/W-1/q	R-1/q	R-1/q	R/W-q/u	R/W-0/q
IPEN	SBOREN[1]	–	$\overline{\text{RI}}$	$\overline{\text{TO}}$	$\overline{\text{PD}}$	POR [2]	$\overline{\text{BOR}}$
bit 7							bit 0

R = Readable bit	W = Writable bit	U = Unimplemented bit, read as '0'
'1' = Bit is set	'0' = Bit is cleared	-n/n = Value at POR and BOR/Value at all other Resets
x = Bit is unknown	u = unchanged	q = depends on condition

bit 7   **IPEN:** Interrupt Priority Enable bit
                   1 = Enable priority levels on interrupts
                   0 = Disable priority levels on interrupts (PIC16CXXX Compatibility mode)

bit 6   **SBOREN:** BOR Software Enable bit[1]
                   If BOREN<1:0> = 01:
                   1 = BOR is enabled
                   0 = BOR is disabled
                   If BOREN<1:0> = 00, 10 or 11:
                   Bit is disabled and read as '0'.

bit 5   **Unimplemented:** Read as '0'

bit 4 $\overline{\text{RI}}$: RESET Instruction Flag bit
                   1 = The RESET instruction was not executed (set by firmware or Power-on Reset)
                   0 = The RESET instruction was executed causing a device Reset (must be set in firmware after a
                   code-executed Reset occurs)

bit 3 $\overline{\text{TO}}$: Watchdog Time-out Flag bit
                   1 = Set by power-up, CLRWDT instruction or SLEEP instruction
                   0 = A WDT time-out occurred

bit 2 $\overline{\text{PD}}$: Power-down Detection Flag bit
                   1 = Set by power-up or by the CLRWDT instruction
                   0 = Set by execution of the SLEEP instruction

bit 1 $\overline{\text{POR}}$: Power-on Reset Status bit[2]
                   1 = No Power-on Reset occurred
                   0 = A Power-on Reset occurred (must be set in software after a Power-on Reset occurs)

bit 0 $\overline{\text{BOR}}$: Brown-out Reset Status bit[3]
                   1 = A Brown-out Reset has not occurred (set by firmware only)
                   0 = A Brown-out Reset occurred (must be set by firmware after a POR or Brown-out Reset occurs)

Note 1:   When CONFIG2L[2:1] = 01, then the SBOREN Reset state is '1'; otherwise, it is '0'.
Note 2:   The actual Reset value of POR is determined by the type of device Reset.
Note 3:   See subsequent table.

BOR Configuration		Status of SBOREN (RCON<6>)	BOR Operation
BOREN1	**BOREN0**		
0	0	Unavailable	BOR disabled; must be enabled by reprogramming the Configuration bits.
0	1	Available	BOR enabled by software; operation controlled by SBOREN
1	0	Unavailable	BOR enabled by hardware in Run and Idle modes; disabled during Sleep mode.
1	1	Unavailable	BOR enabled by hardware; must be disabled by reprogramming the Configuration bits.

RCREGx: **EUSARTX RECEIVE REGISTER (x = 1, 2)**

R/W-0	R/W-0	R/W-0	R/W-0	R/W-0	R/W-0	R/W-0	R/W-0

bit 7   **bit 0**

R = Readable bit	W = Writable bit	U = Unimplemented bit, read as '0'
-n = Value at POR	'1' = Bit is set	'0' = Bit is cleared x = Bit is unknown

bit 7-0   **Received data bits**

RCSTAx: **RECEIVE STATUS AND CONTROL REGISTER (x = 1, 2)**

R/W-0	R/W-0	R/W-0	R/W-0	R/W-0	R-0	R-0	R-0
SPEN	RX9	SREN	CREN	ADDEN	FERR	OERR	RX9D

bit 7   bit 0

R = Readable bit	W = Writable bit	U = Unimplemented bit, read as '0'
-n = Value at POR	'1' = Bit is set	'0' = Bit is cleared x = Bit is unknown

bit 7   **SPEN:** Serial Port Enable bit
                      1 = Serial port enabled (configures RXx/DTx and TXx/CKx pins as serial port pins)
                      0 = Serial port disabled (held in Reset)

bit 6   **RX9:** 9-bit Receive Enable bit
                      1 = Selects 9-bit reception
                      0 = Selects 8-bit reception

bit 5   **SREN:** Single Receive Enable bit
                      <u>Asynchronous mode:</u>
                      Don't care
                      <u>Synchronous mode – Master:</u>
                      1 = Enables single receive
                      0 = Disables single receive
                      This bit is cleared after reception is complete.
                      <u>Synchronous mode – Slave</u>
                      Don't care

bit 4   **CREN:** Continuous Receive Enable bit
                      <u>Asynchronous mode:</u>
                      1 = Enables receiver
                      0 = Disables receiver
                      <u>Synchronous mode:</u>
                      1 = Enables continuous receive until enable bit CREN is cleared (CREN overrides SREN)
                      0 = Disables continuous receive

bit 3   **ADDEN:** Address Detect Enable bit
                      <u>Asynchronous mode 9-bit (RX9 = 1):</u>
                      1 = Enables address detection, enable interrupt and load the receive buffer when RSR<8> is
                           set
                      0 = Disables address detection, all bytes are received and ninth bit can be used as parity bit
                      <u>Asynchronous mode 8-bit (RX9 = 0):</u>
                      Don't care

bit 2   **FERR:** Framing Error bit
                      1 = Framing error (can be updated by reading RCREGx register and receive next valid byte)
                      0 = No framing error

bit 1   **OERR:** Overrun Error bit
                      1 = Overrun error (can be cleared by clearing bit CREN)
                      0 = No overrun error

bit 0   **RX9D:** Ninth bit of Received Data
                      This can be address/data bit or a parity bit and must be calculated by user firmware.

SLRCON: **SLEW RATE CONTROL REGISTER**

U-0	U-0	U-0	R/W-1	R/W-1	R/W-1	R/W-1	R/W-1
–	–	–	SLRE [(1)]	SLRD [(1)]	SLRC	SLRB	SLRA

bit 7   bit 0

R = Readable bit	W = Writable bit	U = Unimplemented bit, read as '0'
-n = Value at POR	'1' = Bit is set	'0' = Bit is cleared x = Bit is unknown

bit 7-5   **Unimplemented:** Read as '0'

bit 4   **SLRE:** PORTE Slew Rate Control bit[(1)]
            1 = All outputs on PORTE slew at a limited rate
            0 = All outputs on PORTE slew at the standard rate

bit 3   **SLRD:** PORTD Slew Rate Control bit[(1)]
            1 = All outputs on PORTD slew at a limited rate
            0 = All outputs on PORTD slew at the standard rate

bit 2   **SLRC:** PORTC Slew Rate Control bit
            1 = All outputs on PORTC slew at a limited rate
            0 = All outputs on PORTC slew at the standard rate

bit 1   **SLRB:** PORTB Slew Rate Control bit
            1 = All outputs on PORTB slew at a limited rate
            0 = All outputs on PORTB slew at the standard rate

bit 0   **SLRA:** PORTA Slew Rate Control bit
            1 = All outputs on PORTA slew at a limited rate[(2)]
            0 = All outputs on PORTA slew at the standard rate

Note 1:   These bits are available on PIC18(L)F4XK22 devices.
Note 2:   The slew rate of RA6 defaults to standard rate when the pin is used as CLKOUT

SPBRGx: **EUSARTx BAUD RATE GENERATOR REGISTER LOW BYTE (x = 1, 2)**

R/W-0	R/W-0	R/W-0	R/W-0	R/W-0	R/W-0	R/W-0	R/W-0

bit 7   bit 0

R = Readable bit	W = Writable bit	U = Unimplemented bit, read as '0'
-n = Value at POR	'1' = Bit is set	'0' = Bit is cleared x = Bit is unknown

bit 7-0   **Serial Port Baud Rate generator least significant bits**

SPBRGHx: **EUSARTx BAUD RATE GENERATOR REGISTER HIGH BYTE (x = 1, 2)**

R/W-0	R/W-0	R/W-0	R/W-0	R/W-0	R/W-0	R/W-0	R/W-0

bit 7   bit 0

R = Readable bit	W = Writable bit	U = Unimplemented bit, read as '0'
-n = Value at POR	'1' = Bit is set	'0' = Bit is cleared x = Bit is unknown

bit 7-0   **Serial Port Baud Rate generator most significant bits**

SRCON0:   **SR LATCH CONTROL REGISTER**

R/W-0	R/W-0	R/W-0	R/W-0	R/W-0	R/W-0	R/W-0	R/W-0
SRLEN	\multicolumn{3}{c}{SRCLK<2:0>}			SRQEN	SRNQEN	SRPS	SRPR
bit 7							bit 0

R = Readable bit	W = Writable bit	U = Unimplemented bit, read as '0'
-n = Value at POR	'1' = Bit is set	'0' = Bit is cleared x = Bit is unknown

bit 7   **SRLEN:** SR Latch Enable bit[1]
               1 = SR latch is enabled
               0 = SR latch is disabled

bit 6   **SRCLK<2:0>:** SR Latch Clock Divider Bits
               000 = Generates a 2 TOSC wide pulse on DIVSRCLK every 4 peripheral clock cycles
               001 = Generates a 2 TOSC wide pulse on DIVSRCLK every 8 peripheral clock cycles
               010 = Generates a 2 TOSC wide pulse on DIVSRCLK every 16 peripheral clock cycles
               011 = Generates a 2 TOSC wide pulse on DIVSRCLK every 32 peripheral clock cycles
               100 = Generates a 2 TOSC wide pulse on DIVSRCLK every 64 peripheral clock cycles
               101 = Generates a 2 TOSC wide pulse on DIVSRCLK every 128 peripheral clock cycles
               110 = Generates a 2 TOSC wide pulse on DIVSRCLK every 256 peripheral clock cycles
               111 = Generates a 2 TOSC wide pulse on DIVSRCLK every 512 peripheral clock cycles

bit 3   **SRQEN:** SR Latch Q Output Enable bit
               1 = Q is present on the SRQ pin
               0 = Q is internal only

bit 2   **SRNQEN:** SR Latch $\overline{Q}$ Output Enable bit
               1 = $\overline{Q}$ is present on the SRNQ pin
               0 = $\overline{Q}$ is internal only

bit 1   **SRPS:** Pulse Set Input of the SR Latch bit[2]
               1 = Pulse set input for 2 TOSC clock cycles
               0 = No effect on set input

bit 0   **SRPR:** Pulse Reset Input of the SR Latch bit[2]
               1 = Pulse reset input for 2 TOSC clock cycles
               0 = No effect on Reset input

Note 1:   Changing the SRCLK bits while the SR latch is enabled may cause false triggers to the set and Reset inputs of the latch.

Note 2:   Set only, always reads back '0'.

SRCON1:   **SR LATCH CONTROL REGISTER 1**

R/W-0	R/W-0	R/W-0	R/W-0	R/W-0	R/W-0	R/W-0	R/W-0
SRSPE	SRSCKE	SRSC2E	SRSC1E	SRRPE	SRRCKE	SRRC2E	SRRC1E

bit 7   bit 0

R = Readable bit   W = Writable bit   U = Unimplemented bit, read as '0'
-n = Value at POR   '1' = Bit is set   '0' = Bit is cleared   x = Bit is unknown

bit 7   **SRSPE:** SR Latch Peripheral Set Enable bit
             1 = SRI pin status sets SR Latch
             0 = SRI pin status has no effect on SR Latch

bit 6   **SRSCKE:** SR Latch Set Clock Enable bit
             1 = Set input of SR latch is pulsed with DIVSRCLK
             0 = Set input of SR latch is not pulsed with DIVSRCLK

bit 5   **SRSC2E:** SR Latch C2 Set Enable bit
             1 = C2 Comparator output sets SR Latch
             0 = C2 Comparator output has no effect on SR Latch

bit 4   **SRSC1E:** SR Latch C1 Set Enable bit
             1 = C1 Comparator output sets SR Latch
             0 = C1 Comparator output has no effect on SR Latch

bit 3   **SRRPE:** SR Latch Peripheral Reset Enable bit
             1 = SRI pin resets SR Latch
             0 = SRI pin has no effect on SR Latch

bit 2   **SRRCKE:** SR Latch Reset Clock Enable bit
             1 = Reset input of SR latch is pulsed with DIVSRCLK
             0 = Reset input of SR latch is not pulsed with DIVSRCLK

bit 1   **SRRC2E:** SR Latch C2 Reset Enable bit
             1 = C2 Comparator output resets SR Latch
             0 = C2 Comparator output has no effect on SR Latch

bit 0   **SRRC1E:** SR Latch C1 Reset Enable bit
             1 = C1 Comparator output resets SR Latch
             0 = C1 Comparator output has no effect on SR Latch

SSP1ADD: **SSP1 ADDRESS IN I²C SLAVE MODE**
                 SSP1 BAUD RATE REGISTER IN I²C MASTER MODE

R/W-0	R/W-0	R/W-0	R/W-0	R/W-0	R/W-0	R/W-0	R/W-0

bit 7   bit 0

R = Readable bit   W = Writable bit   U = Unimplemented bit, read as '0'
-n = Value at POR   '1' = Bit is set   '0' = Bit is cleared   x = Bit is unknown

SSP1BUF: **SSP1 RECEIVE BUFFER/TRANSMIT REGISTER**

R/W-x	R/W-x	R/W-x	R/W-x	R/W-x	R/W-x	R/W-x	R/W-x

bit 7   bit 0

R = Readable bit   W = Writable bit   U = Unimplemented bit, read as '0'
-n = Value at POR   '1' = Bit is set   '0' = Bit is cleared   x = Bit is unknown

SSPxCON1:   SSPx CONTROL REGISTER 1 (x = 1, 2)

R/C/HS-0	R/C/HS-0	R/W-0	R/W-0	R/W-0	R/W-0	R/W-0	R/W-0
WCOL	SSPxOV	SSPxEN	CKP	SSPxM<3:0>			
bit 7							**bit 0**

R = Readable bit	W = Writable bit	U = Unimplemented bit, read as '0'
u = Bit is unchanged	x = Bit is unknown	-n/n = Value at POR and BOR/Value at all other Resets
'1' = Bit is set	'0' = Bit is cleared	HS = Bit set by hardware C = User cleared

bit 7 **WCOL:** Write Collision Detect bit
<u>Master mode:</u>
1 = A write to the SSPxBUF register was attempted while the I^{2}C conditions were not valid for a transmission to be started
0 = No collision
<u>Slave mode:</u>
1 = The SSPxBUF register is written while it is still transmitting the previous word (must be cleared in software)
0 = No collision

bit 6 **SSPxOV:** Receive Overflow Indicator bit[1]
<u>In SPI mode:</u>
1 = A new byte is received while the SSPxBUF register is still holding the previous data. In case of overflow, the data in SSPxSR is lost. Overflow can only occur in Slave mode. In Slave mode, the user must read the SSPxBUF, even if only transmitting data, to avoid setting overflow. In Master mode, the overflow bit is not set since each new reception (and transmission) is initiated by writing to the SSPxBUF register (must be cleared in software).
0 = No overflow
<u>In I^{2}C mode:</u>
1 = A byte is received while the SSPxBUF register is still holding the previous byte. SSPxOV is a "don't care" in mode (must be cleared in software).
0 = No overflow

bit 5 **SSPxEN:** Synchronous Serial Port Enable bit
In both modes, when enabled, these pins must be properly configured as input or output
<u>In SPI mode:</u>
1 = Enables serial port and configures SCKx, SDOx, SDIx and $\overline{SSx}$ as the source of the serial port pins[2]
0 = Disables serial port and configures these pins as I/O port pins
<u>In I^{2}C mode:</u>
1 = Enables the serial port and configures the SDAx and SCLx pins as the source of the serial port pins[3]
0 = Disables serial port and configures these pins as I/O port pins

bit 4	**CKP:** Clock Polarity Select bit
	<u>In SPI mode:</u>
	1 = Idle state for clock is a high level
	0 = Idle state for clock is a low level
	<u>In I²C Slave mode:</u>
	SCLx release control
	1 = Enable clock
	0 = Holds clock low (clock stretch). (Used to ensure data setup time.)
	<u>In I²C Master mode:</u>
	Unused in this mode
bit 3-0	**SSPxM<3:0>:** Synchronous Serial Port Mode Select bits
	0000 = SPI Master mode, clock = FOSC/4
	0001 = SPI Master mode, clock = FOSC/16
	0010 = SPI Master mode, clock = FOSC/64
	0011 = SPI Master mode, clock = TMR2 output/2
	0100 = SPI Slave mode, clock = SCKx pin, $\overline{SSx}$ pin control enabled
	0101 = SPI Slave mode, clock = SCKx pin, $\overline{SSx}$ pin control disabled, $\overline{SSx}$ can be used as I/O pin
	0110 = I²C Slave mode, 7-bit address
	0111 = I²C Slave mode, 10-bit address
	1000 = I²C Master mode, clock = FOSC / (4 * (SSPxADD+1))[4]
	1001 = Reserved
	1010 = SPI Master mode, clock = FOSC/(4 * (SSPxADD+1))
	1011 = I²C firmware controlled Master mode (slave idle)
	1100 = Reserved
	1101 = Reserved
	1110 = I²C Slave mode, 7-bit address with Start and Stop bit interrupts enabled
	1111 = I²C Slave mode, 10-bit address with Start and Stop bit interrupts enabled
Note 1:	In Master mode, the overflow bit is not set since each new reception (and transmission) is initiated by writing to the SSPxBUF register.
Note 2:	When enabled, these pins must be properly configured as input or output.
Note 3:	When enabled, the SDAx and SCLx pins must be configured as inputs
Note 4:	SSPxADD values of 0, 1 or 2 are not supported for I²C Mode.

SSPxCON2:   **SSPx CONTROL REGISTER 2 (x = 1, 2)**

R/W-0	R-0	R/W-0	R/S/HC-0	R/S/HC-0	R/S/HC-0	R/S/HC-0	R/S/HC-0
GCEN	ACKSTAT	ACKDT	ACKEN[1]	RCEN[1]	PEN[1]	RSEN[1]	SEN[1]
bit 7							bit 0

R = Readable bit	W = Writable bit	U = Unimplemented bit, read as '0'
u = Bit is unchanged	x = Bit is unknown	-n/n = Value at POR and BOR/Value at all other Resets
'1' = Bit is set	'0' = Bit is cleared	HC = Cleared by hardware S = User set

bit 7   **GCEN:** General Call Enable bit (in I²C Slave mode only)
1 = Enable interrupt when a general call address (0x00) is received in the SSPxSR
0 = General call address disabled

bit 6   **ACKSTAT:** Acknowledge Status bit (in I²C mode only)
1 = Acknowledge was not received
0 = Acknowledge was received

Bit 5   **ACKDT:** Acknowledge Data bit (in I²C mode only)
<u>In Receive mode:</u>
Value transmitted when the user initiates an Acknowledge sequence at the end of a receive
1 = Not Acknowledge
0 = Acknowledge

bit 4   **ACKEN[1]:** Acknowledge Sequence Enable bit (in I²C Master mode only)
<u>In Master Receive mode:</u>
1 = Initiate Acknowledge sequence on SDAx and SCLx pins, and transmit ACKDT data bit.
    Automatically cleared by hardware.
0 = Acknowledge sequence idle

bit 3   **RCEN[1]:** Receive Enable bit (in I²C Master mode only)
1 = Enables Receive mode for I²C
0 = Receive idle

bit 2   **PEN[1]:** Stop Condition Enable bit (in I²C Master mode only)
<u>SCKx Release Control:</u>
1 = Initiate Stop condition on SDAx and SCLx pins. Automatically cleared by hardware.
0 = Stop condition Idle

bit 1   **RSEN[1]:** Repeated Start Condition Enabled bit (in I²C Master mode only)
1 = Initiate Repeated Start condition on SDAx and SCLx pins. Automatically cleared by
    hardware.
0 = Repeated Start condition Idle

bit 0   **SEN[1]:** Start Condition Enabled bit (in I²C Master mode only)
<u>In Master mode:</u>
1 = Initiate Start condition on SDAx and SCLx pins. Automatically cleared by hardware.
0 = Start condition Idle
<u>In Slave mode:</u>
1 = Clock stretching is enabled for both slave transmit and slave receive (stretch enabled)
0 = Clock stretching is disabled

Note 1:   For bits ACKEN, RCEN, PEN, RSEN, SEN: If the I²C module is not in the Idle mode, this bit
may not be set (no spooling) and the SSPxBUF may not be written (or writes to the SSPxBUF are
disabled).

SSPxCON3:   **SSPx CONTROL REGISTER 3 (x = 1, 2)**

R-0	R/W-0	R/W-0	R/W-0	R/W-0	R/W-0	R/W-0	R/W-0
ACKTIM	PCIE	SCIE	BOEN	SDAHT	SBCDE	AHEN	DHEN
bit 7							**bit 0**

R = Readable bit	W = Writable bit	U = Unimplemented bit, read as '0'	
-n = Value at POR	'1' = Bit is set	'0' = Bit is cleared	x = Bit is unknown

bit 7   **ACKTIM:** Acknowledge Time Status bit (I^2C mode only)[3]
                  1 = Indicates the I^2C bus is in an Acknowledge sequence, set on 8th falling edge of SCLx clock
                  0 = Not an Acknowledge sequence, cleared on 9th rising edge of SCLx clock

bit 6   **PCIE:** Stop Condition Interrupt Enable bit (I^2C mode only)
                  1 = Enable interrupt on detection of Stop condition
                  0 = Stop detection interrupts are disabled[2]

bit 5   **SCIE:** Start Condition Interrupt Enable bit (I^2C mode only)
                  1 = Enable interrupt on detection of Start or Restart conditions
                  0 = Start detection interrupts are disabled[2]

bit 4   **BOEN:** Buffer Overwrite Enable bit
                  <u>In SPI Slave mode:</u>[1]
                  1 = SSPxBUF updates every time that a new data byte is shifted in ignoring the BF bit
                  0 = If new byte is received with BF bit of the SSPxSTAT register already set, SSPxOV bit of the SSPxCON1 register is set, and the buffer is not updated
                  <u>In I^2C Master mode:</u>
                  This bit is ignored.
                  <u>In I^2C Slave mode:</u>
                  1 = SSPxBUF is updated and $\overline{ACK}$ is generated for a received address/data byte, ignoring the state of the SSPxOV bit only if the BF bit = 0.
                  0 = SSPxBUF is only updated when SSPxOV is clear

bit 3   **SDAHT:** SDAx Hold Time Selection bit (I^2C mode only)
                  1 = Minimum of 300 ns hold time on SDAx after the falling edge of SCLx
                  0 = Minimum of 100 ns hold time on SDAx after the falling edge of SCLx

bit 2   **SBCDE:** Slave Mode Bus Collision Detect Enable bit (I^2C Slave mode only)
                  If on the rising edge of SCLx, SDAx is sampled low when the module is outputting a high state, the BCLxIF bit of the PIR2 register is set, and bus goes idle
                  1 = Enable slave bus collision interrupts
                  0 = Slave bus collision interrupts are disabled

bit 1	**AHEN:** Address Hold Enable bit (I^2C Slave mode only)
	1 = Following the 8th falling edge of SCLx for a matching received address byte; CKP bit of the SSPxCON1 register will be cleared and the SCLx will be held low.
	0 = Address holding is disabled
Note 1:	For daisy-chained SPI operation; allows the user to ignore all but the last received byte. SSPxOV is still set when a new byte is received and BF = 1, but hardware continues to write the most recent byte to SSPxBUF.
Note 2:	This bit has no effect in Slave modes for which Start and Stop condition detection is explicitly listed as enabled.
Note 3:	The ACKTIM Status bit is active only when the AHEN bit or DHEN bit is set.
bit 0	**DHEN:** Data Hold Enable bit (I^2C Slave mode only)
	1 = Following the 8th falling edge of SCLx for a received data byte; slave hardware clears the CKP bit of the SSPxCON1 register and SCLx is held low.
	0 = Data holding is disabled
Note 1:	For daisy-chained SPI operation; allows the user to ignore all but the last received byte. SSPxOV is still set when a new byte is received and BF = 1, but hardware continues to write the most recent byte to SSPxBUF.
Note 2:	This bit has no effect in Slave modes for which Start and Stop condition detection is explicitly listed as enabled.
Note 3:	The ACKTIM Status bit is active only when the AHEN bit or DHEN bit is set.

SSPxMSK: **SSPx MASK REGISTER (x = 1, 2)**

R/W-1	R/W-1	R/W-1	R/W-1	R/W-1	R/W-1	R/W-1	R/W-1
MSK7	MSK6	MSK5	MSK4	MSK3	MSK2	MSK1	MSK0
bit 7							**bit 0**

R = Readable bit	W = Writable bit	U = Unimplemented bit, read as '0'
-n = Value at POR	'1' = Bit is set	'0' = Bit is cleared x = Bit is unknown

bit 7-1	**MSK<7:1>:** Mask bits
	1 = The received address bit n is compared to SSPxADD<n> to detect I^2C address match
	0 = The received address bit n is not used to detect I^2C address match
bit 0	**MSK<0>:** Mask bit for I^2C Slave mode, 10-bit Address
	I^2C Slave mode, 10-bit address (SSPxM<3:0> = 0111 or 1111):
	1 = The received address bit 0 is compared to SSPxADD<0> to detect I^2C address match
	0 = The received address bit 0 is not used to detect I^2C address match
	I^2C Slave mode, 7-bit address, the bit is ignored

SSPxSTAT: **SSPx STATUS REGISTER (x = 1, 2)**

R/W-0	R/W-0	R-0	R-0	R-0	R-0	R-0	R-0
SMP	CKE	D/$\overline{\text{A}}$	P	S	R/$\overline{\text{W}}$	UA	BF

bit 7   bit 0

R = Readable bit   W = Writable bit   U = Unimplemented bit, read as '0'
-n = Value at POR   '1' = Bit is set   '0' = Bit is cleared   x = Bit is unknown

bit 7   **SMP:** SPI Data Input Sample bit
            <u>SPI Master mode:</u>
            1 = Input data sampled at end of data output time
            0 = Input data sampled at middle of data output time
            <u>SPI Slave mode:</u>
            SMP must be cleared when SPI is used in Slave mode
            <u>In I^{2}C Master or Slave mode:</u>
            1 = Slew rate control disabled for standard speed mode (100 kHz and 1 MHz)
            0 = Slew rate control enabled for high speed mode (400 kHz)

bit 6   **CKE:** SPI Clock Edge Select bit (SPI mode only)
            <u>In SPI Master or Slave mode:</u>
            1 = Transmit occurs on transition from active to Idle clock state
            0 = Transmit occurs on transition from Idle to active clock state
            <u>In I^{2}C mode only:</u>
            1 = Enable input logic so that thresholds are compliant with SMbus specification
            0 = Disable SMbus specific inputs

bit 5   **D/$\overline{\text{A}}$:** Data/$\overline{\text{Address}}$ bit (I^{2}C mode only)
            1 = Indicates that the last byte received or transmitted was data
            0 = Indicates that the last byte received or transmitted was address

bit 4   **P:** Stop bit
            (I^{2}C mode only. This bit is cleared when the MSSPx module is disabled, SSPxEN is cleared.)
            1 = Indicates that a Stop bit has been detected last (this bit is '0' on Reset)
            0 = Stop bit was not detected last

bit 3   **S:** Start bit
            (I^{2}C mode only. This bit is cleared when the MSSPx module is disabled, SSPxEN is cleared.)
            1 = Indicates that a Start bit has been detected last (this bit is '0' on Reset)
            0 = Start bit was not detected last

bit 2	**R/W̄:** Read/Write bit information (I²C mode only) This bit holds the R/W̄ bit information following the last address match. This bit is only valid from the address match to the next Start bit, Stop bit, or not A̅C̅K̅ bit. In I²C Slave mode: 1 = Read 0 = Write In I²C Master mode: 1 = Transmit is in progress 0 = Transmit is not in progress OR-ing this bit with SEN, RSEN, PEN, RCEN or ACKEN will indicate if the MSSPx is in Idle mode.
bit 1	**UA:** Update Address bit (10-bit I²C mode only) 1 = Indicates that the user needs to update the address in the SSPxADD register 0 = Address does not need to be updated
bit 0	**BF:** Buffer Full Status bit Receive (SPI and I²C modes): 1 = Receive complete, SSPxBUF is full 0 = Receive not complete, SSPxBUF is empty Transmit (I²C mode only): 1 = Data transmit in progress (does not include the A̅C̅K̅ and Stop bits), SSPxBUF is full 0 = Data transmit complete (does not include the A̅C̅K̅ and Stop bits), SSPxBUF is empty

SSPxADD: MSSPx ADDRESS AND BAUD RATE REGISTER (I²C MODE) (x = 1, 2)

R/W-0	R/W-0	R/W-0	R/W-0	R/W-0	R/W-0	R/W-0	R/W-0
			ADD<7:0>				
bit 7							**bit 0**

R = Readable bit	W = Writable bit	'1' = Bit is set	'0' = Bit is cleared

SSPxBUF: SSPx RECEIVE BUFFER/TRANSMIT REGISTER (x = 1, 2)

R/W-x	R/W-x	R/W-x	R/W-x	R/W-x	R/W-x	R/W-x	R/W-x
bit 7							**bit 0**

R = Readable bit	W = Writable bit	x = Bit is unknown

STATUS: **STATUS REGISTER**

U-0	U-0	U-0	R/W-x	R/W-x	R/W-x	R/W-x	R/W-x
–	–	–	N	OV	Z	DC [1]	C [1]

bit 7   **bit 0**

R = Readable bit	W = Writable bit	U = Unimplemented bit, read as '0'
-n = Value at POR	'1' = Bit is set	'0' = Bit is cleared x = Bit is unknown

bit 7-5   **Unimplemented:** Read as '0'

bit 4   **N:** Negative bit
This bit is used for signed arithmetic (two's complement). It indicates whether the result was negative (ALU MSB = 1).
1 = Result was negative
0 = Result was positive

bit 3   **OV:** Overflow bit
This bit is used for signed arithmetic (two's complement). It indicates an overflow of the 7-bit magnitude which causes the sign bit (bit 7 of the result) to change state.
1 = Overflow occurred for signed arithmetic (in this arithmetic operation)
0 = No overflow occurred

bit 2   **Z:** Zero bit
1 = The result of an arithmetic or logic operation is zero
0 = The result of an arithmetic or logic operation is not zero

bit 1   **DC:** Digit Carry/$\overline{\text{Borrow}}$ bit (ADDWF, ADDLW,SUBLW,SUBWF instructions)[1]
1 = A carry-out from the 4th low-order bit of the result occurred
0 = No carry-out from the 4th low-order bit of the result

bit 0   **C:** Carry/$\overline{\text{Borrow}}$ (ADDWF, ADDLW, SUBLW, SUBWF instructions) [1]
1 = A carry-out from the Most Significant bit of the result occurred
0 = No carry-out from the Most Significant bit of the result occurred

Note 1:   For $\overline{\text{Borrow}}$, the polarity is reversed. A subtraction is executed by adding the two's complement of the second operand. For rotate (RRF, RLF) instructions, this bit is loaded with either the high-order or low-order bit of the source register.

T0CON: **TIMER0 CONTROL REGISTER**

R/W-1	R/W-1	R/W-1	R/W-1	R/W-1	R/W-1	R/W-1	R/W-1
TMR0ON	T08BIT	T0CS	T0SE	PSA	TOPS<2:0>		

bit 7   bit 0

R = Readable bit	W = Writable bit	U = Unimplemented bit, read as '0'
-n = Value at POR	'1' = Bit is set	'0' = Bit is cleared x = Bit is unknown

bit 7   **TMR0ON**: Timer0 On/Off Control bit
                         1 = Enables Timer0
                         0 = Stops Timer0

bit 6   **T08BIT**: Timer0 8-Bit/16-Bit Control bit
                         1 = Timer0 is configured as an 8-bit timer/counter
                         0 = Timer0 is configured as a 16-bit timer/counter

bit 5   **T0CS**: Timer0 Clock Source Select bit
                         1 = Transition on T0CKI pin
                         0 = Internal instruction cycle clock (CLKOUT)

bit 4   **T0SE**: Timer0 Source Edge Select bit
                         1 = Increment on high-to-low transition on T0CKI pin
                         0 = Increment on low-to-high transition on T0CKI pin

bit 3   **PSA**: Timer0 Prescaler Assignment bit
                         1 = Timer0 prescaler is not assigned. Timer0 clock input bypasses prescaler.
                         0 = Timer0 prescaler is assigned. Timer0 clock input comes from prescaler output.

bit 2-0   **T0PS<2:0>**: Timer0 Prescaler Select bits
                         111 = 1:256   Prescale value
                         110 = 1:128   Prescale value
                         101 = 1:64   Prescale value
                         100 = 1:32   Prescale value
                         011 = 1:16   Prescale value
                         010 = 1:8   Prescale value
                         001 = 1:4   Prescale value
                         000 = 1:2   Prescale value

TxCON: **TIMER1/3/5 CONTROL REGISTER (x = 1, 3, 5)**

R/W-0/u	R/W-0/u	R/W-0/u	R/W-0/u	R/W-0/u	R/W-0/u	R/W-0/0	R/W-0/u
TMRxCS<1:0>		TxCKPS<1:0>		TxSOSCEN	$\overline{\text{TxSYNC}}$	TxRD16	TMRxON

bit 7   bit 0

R = Readable bit   W = Writable bit   U = Unimplemented bit, read as '0'
u = Bit is unchanged   x = Bit is unknown
'1' = Bit is set   '0' = Bit is cleared   -n/n = Value at POR and BOR/Value at all other Resets

bit 7-6   **TMRxCS<1:0>:** Timer1/3/5 Clock Source Select bits
                   11 = Reserved. Do not use.
                   10 = Timer1/3/5 clock source is pin or oscillator:
                   <u>If TxSOSCEN = 0:</u>
                   External clock from TxCKI pin (on the rising edge)
                   <u>If TxSOSCEN = 1:</u>
                   Crystal oscillator on SOSCI/SOSCO pins
                   01 = Timer1/3/5 clock source is system clock (FOSC)
                   00 = Timer1/3/5 clock source is instruction clock (FOSC/4)

bit 5-4   **TxCKPS<1:0>:** Timer1/3/5 Input Clock Prescale Select bits
                   11 = 1:8 Prescale value
                   10 = 1:4 Prescale value
                   01 = 1:2 Prescale value
                   00 = 1:1 Prescale value

bit 3   **TxSOSCEN:** Secondary Oscillator Enable Control bit
                   1 = Dedicated Secondary oscillator circuit enabled
                   0 = Dedicated Secondary oscillator circuit disabled

bit 2   **$\overline{\text{TxSYNC}}$:** Timer1/3/5 External Clock Input Synchronization Control bit
                   <u>TMRxCS<1:0> = 1X</u>
                   1 = Do not synchronize external clock input
                   0 = Synchronize external clock input with system clock (FOSC)
                   <u>TMRxCS<1:0> = 0X</u>
                   This bit is ignored. Timer1/3/5 uses the internal clock when TMRxCS<1:0> = 1X.

bit 1   **TxRD16:** 16-Bit Read/Write Mode Enable bit
                   1 = Enables register read/write of Timer1/3/5 in one 16-bit operation
                   0 = Enables register read/write of Timer1/3/5 in two 8-bit operation

bit 0   **TMRxON:** Timer1/3/5 On bit
                   1 = Enables Timer1/3/5
                   0 = Stops Timer1/3/5
                   Clears Timer1/3/5 Gate flip-flop

TxGCON: **TIMER1/3/5 GATE CONTROL REGISTER (x = 1, 3, 5)**

R/W-0/u	R/W-0/u	R/W-0/u	R/W-0/u	R/W/HC-0/u	R-x/x	R/W-0/u	R/W-0/u
TMRxGE	TxGPOL	TxGTM	TxGSPM	TxGGO/$\overline{\text{DONE}}$	TxGVAL	TxGSS<1:0>	
bit 7							bit 0

R = Readable bit	W = Writable bit	U = Unimplemented bit, read as '0'
u = Bit is unchanged	x = Bit is unknown	-n/n = Value at POR and BOR/Value at all other Resets
'1' = Bit is set	'0' = Bit is cleared	HC = Bit is cleared by hardware

bit 7   **TMRxGE:** Timer1/3/5 Gate Enable bit
                 <u>If TMRxON = 0:</u>
                 This bit is ignored
                 <u>If TMRxON = 1:</u>
                 1 = Timer1/3/5 counting is controlled by the Timer1/3/5 gate function
                 0 = Timer1/3/5 counts regardless of Timer1/3/5 gate function

bit 6   **TxGPOL:** Timer1/3/5 Gate Polarity bit
                 1 = Timer1/3/5 gate is active-high (Timer1/3/5 counts when gate is high)
                 0 = Timer1/3/5 gate is active-low (Timer1/3/5 counts when gate is low)

bit 5   **TxGTM:** Timer1/3/5 Gate Toggle Mode bit
                 1 = Timer1/3/5 Gate Toggle mode is enabled
                 0 = Timer1/3/5 Gate Toggle mode is disabled and toggle flip-flop is cleared
                 Timer1/3/5 gate flip-flop toggles on every rising edge.

bit 4   **TxGSPM:** Timer1/3/5 Gate Single-Pulse Mode bit
                 1 = Timer1/3/5 gate Single-Pulse mode is enabled and is controlling Timer1/3/5 gate
                 0 = Timer1/3/5 gate Single-Pulse mode is disabled

bit 3   **TxGGO/$\overline{\text{DONE}}$:** Timer1/3/5 Gate Single-Pulse Acquisition Status bit
                 1 = Timer1/3/5 gate single-pulse acquisition is ready, waiting for an edge
                 0 = Timer1/3/5 gate single-pulse acquisition has completed or has not been started
                 This bit is automatically cleared when TxGSPM is cleared.

bit 2   **TxGVAL:** Timer1/3/5 Gate Current State bit
                 Indicates the current state of the Timer1/3/5 gate that could be provided to TMRxH:TMRxL.
                 Unaffected by Timer1/3/5 Gate Enable (TMRxGE).

bit 1-0   **TxGSS<1:0>:** Timer1/3/5 Gate Source Select bits
                 00 = Timer1/3/5 Gate pin
                 01 = Timer2/4/6 Match PR2/4/6 output
                 10 = Comparator 1 optionally synchronized output (sync_C1OUT)
                 11 = Comparator 2 optionally synchronized output (sync_C2OUT)

TxCON: **TIMER2/4/6 CONTROL REGISTER (x = 2, 4, 6)**

U-0	R/W-0	R/W-0	R/W-0	R/W-0	R/W-0	R/W-0	R/W-0
–		T2OUTPS	S<3:0>		TMR2ON	T2CKPS	S<1:0>

bit 7   bit 0

R = Readable bit	W = Writable bit	U = Unimplemented bit, read as '0'
-n = Value at POR	'1' = Bit is set	'0' = Bit is cleared x = Bit is unknown

bit 7   **Unimplemented**: Read as '0'

bit 6-3   **TxOUTPS<3:0>**: TimerX Output Postscale Select bits
                      0000 = 1:1   Postscale
                      0001 = 1:2   Postscale
                      .
                      .
                      .
                      1111 = 1:16   Postscale

bit 2   **TMR2ON**: TimerX On bit
                      1 = TimerX is on
                      0 = TimerX is off

bit 1-   **T2CKPS<1:0>**: Timer2 Clock Prescale Select bits
                      00 = Prescaler is 1
                      01 = Prescaler is 4
                      00 = Prescaler is 16

TABLAT: **PROGRAM MEMORY TABLE LATCH**

R/W-0	R/W-0	R/W-0	R/W-0	R/W-0	R/W-0	R/W-0	R/W-0

bit 7   bit 0

R = Readable bit	W = Writable bit	U = Unimplemented bit, read as '0'
-n = Value at POR	'1' = Bit is set	'0' = Bit is cleared x = Bit is unknown

bit 7-0   **Holds result of a TBLRD instruction**

TBLPTRH: **PROGRAM MEMORY TABLE POINTER HIGH BYTE (TBLPTR<15:8>)**

R/W-0	R/W-0	R/W-0	R/W-0	R/W-0	R/W-0	R/W-0	R/W-0

bit 7   bit 0

R = Readable bit	W = Writable bit	'1' = Bit is set '0' = Bit is cleared

bit 7-0   **8 high significant bits of TBLPTR**

TBLPTRL: **PROGRAM MEMORY TABLE POINTER LOW BYTE (TBLPTR<7:0>)**

R/W-0	R/W-0	R/W-0	R/W-0	R/W-0	R/W-0	R/W-0	R/W-0

bit 7   bit 0

R = Readable bit	W = Writable bit	'1' = Bit is set '0' = Bit is cleared

bit 7-0   **8 low significant bits of TBLPTR**

TBLPTRU: **PROGRAM MEMORY TABLE POINTER UPPER BYTE (TBLPTR<21:16>)**

U-0	U-0	R/W-0	R/W-0	R/W-0	R/W-0	R/W-0	R/W-0
–	–	Program Memory Table Pointer Upper Byte (TBLPTR<21:16>)					
bit 7							bit 0

R = Readable bit   W = Writable bit   U = Unimplemented bit, read as '0'
-n = Value at POR   '1' = Bit is set   '0' = Bit is cleared   x = Bit is unknown

bit 7-6   **Unimplemented**: Read as '0'

bit 5-0   **8 upper significant bits of TBLPTR**

TMR0H: **TIMER0 REGISTER HIGH BYTE**

R/W-0	R/W-0	R/W-0	R/W-0	R/W-0	R/W-0	R/W-0	R/W-0
bit 7							bit 0

R = Readable bit   W = Writable bit   '1' = Bit is set   '0' = Bit is cleared

bit 7-0   **8 most significant bits of Timer0 (temporary latch used in read and write operations)**

TMR0L: **TIMER0 REGISTER LOW BYTE**

R/W-x	R/W-x	R/W-x	R/W-x	R/W-x	R/W-x	R/W-x	R/W-x
bit 7							bit 0

R = Readable bit   W = Writable bit   x = Bit is unknown

bit 7-0   **8 least significant bits of Timer0**

TMRxH: **TIMER1/3/5 REGISTER HIGH BYTE (x = 1, 3, 5)**

R/W-x	R/W-x	R/W-x	R/W-x	R/W-x	R/W-x	R/W-x	R/W-x
bit 7							bit 0

R = Readable bit   W = Writable bit   x = Bit is unknown

bit 7-0   **8 most significant bits of TimerX**

TMRxL: **TIMER1/3/5 REGISTER LOW BYTE (x = 1, 3, 5)**

R/W-x	R/W-x	R/W-x	R/W-x	R/W-x	R/W-x	R/W-x	R/W-x
bit 7							bit 0

R = Readable bit   W = Writable bit   x = Bit is unknown

bit 7-0   **8 least significant bits of TimerX**

TMRx: **TIMERx REGISTER (x = 2, 4, 6)**

R/W-0	R/W-0	R/W-0	R/W-0	R/W-0	R/W-0	R/W-0	R/W-0
bit 7							bit 0

R = Readable bit   W = Writable bit   '1' = Bit is set   '0' = Bit is cleared

bit 7-0   **8 bits of TIMERx (x = 2, 4, 6)**

TOSH: **TOP-OF-STACK HIGH BYTE (TOS<15:8>)**

R/W-0	R/W-0	R/W-0	R/W-0	R/W-0	R/W-0	R/W-0	R/W-0
bit 7							bit 0

R = Readable bit	W = Writable bit	'1' = Bit is set	'0' = Bit is cleared

bit 7-0   **High significant bits of stack**

TOSL: **TOP-OF-STACK LOW BYTE (TOS<7:0>)**

R/W-0	R/W-0	R/W-0	R/W-0	R/W-0	R/W-0	R/W-0	R/W-0
bit 7							bit 0

R = Readable bit	W = Writable bit	'1' = Bit is set	'0' = Bit is cleared

bit 7-0   **Low significant bits of stack**

TOSU: **TOP-OF-STACK UPPER BYTE (TOS<20:16>)**

U-0	U-0	U-0	R/W-0	R/W-0	R/W-0	R/W-0	R/W-0
–	–	–	Top-of-Stack Upper Byte (TOS<20:16>)				
bit 7							bit 0

R = Readable bit	W = Writable bit	U = Unimplemented bit, read as '0'	
-n = Value at POR	'1' = Bit is set	'0' = Bit is cleared	x = Bit is unknown

bit 7-5   **Unimplemented:** Read as '0'.
bit 4-0   **Upper significant bits of stack**

TRISx: **PORTx TRI-STATE REGISTER**[1]

R/W-1	R/W-1	R/W-1	R/W-1	R/W-1	R/W-1	R/W-1	R/W-1
TRISx7	TRISx6	TRISx5	TRISx4	TRISx3	TRISx2	TRISx1	TRISx0
bit 7							bit 0

R = Readable bit	W = Writable bit	'1' = Bit is set	'0' = Bit is cleared

bit 7-0   **TRISx<7:0>:** PORTx Tri-State Control bit
            1 = PORTx pin configured as an input (tri-stated)
            0 = PORTx pin configured as an output
Note 1:   Register description for TRISA, TRISB, TRISC and TRISD.

TRISE: **PORTE TRI-STATE REGISTER**

R/W-1	U-0	U-0	U-0	U-0	R/W-1	R/W-1	R/W-1
WPUE3	–	–	–	–	TRISE2[1]	TRISE1[1]	TRISE0[1]
bit 7							bit 0

R = Readable bit	W = Writable bit	U = Unimplemented bit, read as '0'	
-n = Value at POR	'1' = Bit is set	'0' = Bit is cleared	x = Bit is unknown

bit 7   **WPUE3:** Weak Pull-up Register bits
            1 = Pull-up enabled on PORT pin
            0 = Pull-up disabled on PORT pin
bit 6-3   **Unimplemented:** Read as '0'

bit 2-0   **TRISE<7:0>:** PORTE Tri-State Control bit[1]
            1 = PORTE pin configured as an input (tri-stated)
            0 = PORTE pin configured as an output

Note 1:   Available on PIC18(L)F4XK22 devices only.

TXREGx: **EUSARTx TRANSMIT REGISTER (x = 1, 2)**

R/W-0	R/W-0	R/W-0	R/W-0	R/W-0	R/W-0	R/W-0	R/W-0

bit 7   bit 0

R = Readable bit   W = Writable bit   '1' = Bit is set   '0' = Bit is cleared

bit 7-0   **Transmit registers bits**

TXSTAx: **TRANSMIT STATUS AND CONTROL REGISTER (x = 1, 2)**

R/W-0	R/W-0	R/W-0	R/W-0	R/W-0	R/W-0	R-1	R/W-0
CSRC	TX9	TXEN	SYNC	SENDB	BRGH	TRMT	TX9D

bit 7   bit 0

R = Readable bit   W = Writable bit   U = Unimplemented bit, read as '0'
-n = Value at POR   '1' = Bit is set   '0' = Bit is cleared   x = Bit is unknown

bit 7   **CSRC:** Clock Source Select bit
Asynchronous mode:
Don't care
Synchronous mode:
1 = Master mode (clock generated internally from BRG)
0 = Slave mode (clock from external source)

bit 6   **TX9:** 9-bit Transmit Enable bit
1 = Selects 9-bit transmission
0 = Selects 8-bit transmission

bit 5   **TXEN:** Transmit Enable bit[1]
1 = Transmit enabled
0 = Transmit disabled

bit 4   **SYNC:** EUSART Mode Select bit
1 = Synchronous mode
0 = Asynchronous mode

bit 3   **SENDB:** Send Break Character bit
Asynchronous mode:
1 = Send Sync Break on next transmission (cleared by hardware upon completion)
0 = Sync Break transmission completed
Synchronous mode:
Don't care

bit 2   **BRGH:** High Baud Rate Select bit
Asynchronous mode:
1 = High speed
0 = Low speed
Synchronous mode:
Unused in this mode

bit 1   **TRMT:** Transmit Shift Register Status bit
1 = TSR empty
0 = TSR full

bit 0   **TX9D:** Ninth bit of Transmit Data
Can be address/data bit or a parity bit.

Note 1:   SREN/CREN overrides TXEN in Sync mode.

VREFCON0:   FIXED VOLTAGE REFERENCE CONTROL REGISTER

R/W-0	R/W-0	R/W-0	R/W-1	U-0	U-0	U-0	U-0
FVREN	FVRST	FVRS<1:0>		–	–	–	–
bit 7							bit 0

R = Readable bit   W = Writable bit   U = Unimplemented bit, read as '0'
-n = Value at POR   '1' = Bit is set   '0' = Bit is cleared   x = Bit is unknown

bit 7	**FVREN:** Fixed Voltage Reference Enable bit 0 = Fixed Voltage Reference is disabled 1 = Fixed Voltage Reference is enabled
bit 6	**FVRST:** Fixed Voltage Reference Ready Flag bit 0 = Fixed Voltage Reference output is not ready or not enabled 1 = Fixed Voltage Reference output is ready for use
bit 5-4	**FVRS<1:0>:** Fixed Voltage Reference Selection bits 00 = Fixed Voltage Reference Peripheral output is off 01 = Fixed Voltage Reference Peripheral output is 1x (1.024V) 10 = Fixed Voltage Reference Peripheral output is 2x (2.048V)[1] 11 = Fixed Voltage Reference Peripheral output is 4x (4.096V)[1]
bit 3-2	**Reserved:** Read as '0'. Maintain these bits clear.
bit 1-0	**Unimplemented:** Read as '0'.
Note 1:	Fixed Voltage Reference output cannot exceed VDD.

VREFCON1:   VOLTAGE REFERENCE CONTROL REGISTER 1

R/W-0	R/W-0	R/W-0	U-0	R/W-0	R/W-0	U-0	R/W-0
DACEN	DACLPS	DACOE	–	DACPSS<1:0>		–	DACNSS
bit 7							bit 0

R = Readable bit   W = Writable bit   U = Unimplemented bit, read as '0'
-n = Value at POR   '1' = Bit is set   '0' = Bit is cleared   x = Bit is unknown

bit 7	**DACEN:** DAC Enable bit 1 = DAC is enabled 0 = DAC is disabled
bit 6	**DACLPS:** DAC Low-Power Voltage Source Select bit 1 = DAC Positive reference source selected 0 = DAC Negative reference source selected
bit 5	**DACOE:** DAC Voltage Output Enable bit 1 = DAC voltage level is also an output on the DACOUT pin 0 = DAC voltage level is disconnected from the DACOUT pin
bit 4	**Unimplemented:** Read as '0'
bit 3-2	**DACPSS<1:0>:** DAC Positive Source Select bits 00 = VDD 01 = VREF+ 10 = FVR BUF1 output 11 = Reserved, do not use
bit 1	**Unimplemented:** Read as '0'
bit 0	**DACNSS:** DAC Negative Source Select bits 1 = VREF- 0 = VSS

VREFCON2:   VOLTAGE REFERENCE CONTROL REGISTER 2

U-0	U-0	U-0	R/W-0	R/W-0	R/W-0	R/W-0	R/W-0
–	–	–	DACR<4:0>				

bit 7   bit 0

R = Readable bit	W = Writable bit	U = Unimplemented bit, read as '0'
-n = Value at POR	'1' = Bit is set	'0' = Bit is cleared x = Bit is unknown

bit 7-5   **Unimplemented:** Read as '0'

bit 4-0   **DACR<4:0>:** DAC Voltage Output Select bits
               $VOUT = ((VSRC+) - (VSRC-)) * (DACR<4:0> / (2^5)) + VSRC-$

WDTCON: WATCHDOG TIMER CONTROL REGISTER

U-0	U-0	U-0	U-0	U-0	U-0	U-0	R/W-0
–	–	–	–	–	–	–	SWDTEN[1]

bit 7   bit 0

R = Readable bit	W = Writable bit	U = Unimplemented bit, read as '0'
-n = Value at POR	'1' = Bit is set	'0' = Bit is cleared x = Bit is unknown

bit 7-1   **Unimplemented:** Read as '0'

bit 0   **SWDTEN:** Software Enable or Disable the Watchdog Timer bit[1]
               1 = WDT is turned on
               0 = WDT is turned off (Reset value)

Note 1:   This bit has no effect if the Configuration bit, WDTEN, is enabled.

WPUB: WEAK PULL-UP PORTB REGISTER

R/W-1	R/W-1	R/W-1	R/W-1	R/W-1	R/W-1	R/W-1	R/W-1
WPUB7	WPUB6	WPUB5	WPUB4	WPUB3	WPUB2	WPUB1	WPUB0

bit 7   bit 0

R = Readable bit	W = Writable bit	U = Unimplemented bit, read as '0'
-n = Value at POR	'1' = Bit is set	'0' = Bit is cleared x = Bit is unknown

bit 7-0   **WPUB<7:0>:** Weak Pull-up Register bits
               1 = Pull-up enabled on PORTB pin
               0 = Pull-up disabled on PORTB pin

WREG: WORKING REGISTER

R/W-x	R/W-x	R/W-x	R/W-x	R/W-x	R/W-x	R/W-x	R/W-x

bit 7   bit 0

R = Readable bit	W = Writable bit	U = Unimplemented bit, read as '0'
-n = Value at POR	'1' = Bit is set	'0' = Bit is cleared x = Bit is unknown

bit 7-0   **Working register bits**

Appendix 3

INSTRUCTION SET SUMMARY

PIC18(L)F2X/4XK22 devices incorporate the standard set of 75 PIC18 core instructions, as well as an extended set of 8 new instructions, for the optimization of code that is recursive or that utilizes a software stack. The extended set is not discussed in this textbook.

Standard Instruction Set

The standard PIC18 instruction set adds many enhancements to the previous PIC® MCU instruction sets, while maintaining an easy migration from these PIC MCU Instruction sets. Most Instructions are a single program memory word (16 bits), but there are four instructions that require two program memory locations.

Each single-word instruction is a 16-bit word divided into an opcode, which specifies the instruction type and one or more operands, which further specify the operation of the instruction.

The instruction set is highly orthogonal and is grouped into four basic categories:

- Byte-oriented operations.
- Bit-oriented operations.
- Literal operations.
- Control operations.

The PIC18 instruction set summary in Table 3 lists byte-oriented, bit-oriented, literal and control operations. Table 2 shows the opcode field descriptions.

Most byte-oriented instructions have three operands:

1. The file register (specified by 'f').
2. The destination of the result (specified by 'd').
3. The accessed memory (specified by 'a').

The file register designator 'f' specifies which file register is to be used by the instruction. The destination designator 'd' specifies where the result of the operation is to be placed. If 'd' is zero, the result is placed in the WREG register. If 'd' is one, the result is placed in the file register specified in the instruction.

All bit-oriented instructions have three operands:

1.   The file register (specified by 'f').
2.   The bit in the file register (specified by 'b').
3.   The accessed memory (specified by 'a').

The bit field designator 'b' selects the number of the bit affected by the operation, while the file register designator 'f' represents the number of the file in which the bit is located.

The literal instructions may use some of the following operands:

- A literal value to be loaded into a file register (specified by 'k').
- The desired FSR register to load the literal value into (specified by 'f').
- No operand required (specified by '–').

The control instructions may use some of the following operands:

- A program memory address (specified by 'n').
- The mode of the call or return instructions (specified by 's').
- The mode of the table read and table write instructions (specified by 'm').
- No operand required (specified by '–').

All instructions are a single word, except for four double-word instructions. These instructions were made double-word to contain the required information in 32 bits. In the second word, the 4 MSBs are '1's. If this second word is executed as an instruction (by itself), it will execute as a nop.

All single-word instructions are executed in a single instruction cycle, unless a conditional test is true or the program counter is changed as a result of the instruction. In these cases, the execution takes two instruction cycles, with the additional instruction cycle(s) executed as a nop.

The double-word instructions execute in two instruction cycles.

One instruction cycle consists of four oscillator periods. Thus, for an oscillator frequency of 4 MHz, the normal instruction execution time is 1 µs. If a conditional test is true, or the program counter is changed as a result of an instruction, the instruction execution time is 2 µs. Two-word branch instructions (if true) would take 3 µs.

Table 2 shows the general formats that the instructions can have. All examples use the convention '0xnn' to represent a hexadecimal number.

The Instruction Set Summary, shown in Table 3, lists the standard instructions recognized by the Microchip Assembler (MPASM ™).

The datasheet provides a full description of each instruction in the section entitled "Standard Instruction Set".

Table 1. Opcode field descriptions

Field	Description
a	RAM access bit a = 0: RAM location in Access RAM (BSR register is ignored) a = 1: RAM bank is specified by BSR register.
Bbb	Bit address within an 8-bit file register (0 to 7).
BSR	Bank Select Register. Used to select the current RAM bank.
C, DC, Z, OV, N	ALU Status bits: **C**arry, **D**igit Carry, **Z**ero, **O**verflow, **N**egative.
D	Destination select bit d = 0: store result in WREG; d = 1: store result in file register f
Dest	Destination: either the WREG register or the specified register file location.
F	8-bit Register file address (0x00 to 0xFF) or 2-bit FSR designator (00_2 to 11_2).
f_s	12-bit Register file address (0x000 to 0xFFF). This is the source address.
f_d	12-bit Register file address (0x000 to 0xFFF). This is the destination address.
GIE	Global Interrupt Enable bit.
K	Literal field, constant data or label (may be either an 8-bit, 12-bit or a 20-bit value).
Label	Label name.
mm * *+ *_ +*	The mode of the TBLPTR register for the table read and table write instructions. Only used with table read and table write instructions. No change to register (such as TBLPTR with table reads and writes) Post-Increment register (such as TBLPTR with table reads and writes) Post-Decrement register (such as TBLPTR with table reads and writes) Pre-Increment register (such as TBLPTR with table reads and writes)
N	The relative address (2's complement number) for relative branch instructions or the direct address for Call/Branch and Return instructions.
PC	Program Counter
PCL	Program Counter Low Byte
PCH	Program Counter High Byte.
PCLATH	Program Counter High Byte Latch
PCLATU	Program Counter Upper Byte Latch.
$\overline{PD}$	Power-down bit.
PRODH	Product of Multiply High Byte.
PRODL	Product of Multiply Low Byte.
S	Fast Call/Return mode select bit s = 0: do not update into/from shadow registers s = 1: certain registers loaded into/from shadow registers (Fast mode)
TBLPTR	21-bit Table Pointer (points to a Program Memory location).
TABLAT	8-bit Table Latch.
$\overline{TO}$	Time-out bit.
TOS	Top-of-Stack.
U	Unused or unchanged.
WDT	Watchdog Timer.
WREG	Working register (accumulator).
X	Don't care ('0' or '1'). The assembler will generate code with x = 0. It is the recommended form of use for compatibility with all Microchip software tools.
Z_s	7-bit offset value for indirect addressing of register files (source).
Z_d	7-bit offset value for indirect addressing of register files (destination).
{ }	Optional argument.
[text]	Indicates an indexed address.
(text)	The contents of text.
(expr) <n>	Specifies bit n of the register indicated by the pointer expr.
→	Assigned to.
< >	Register bit field.
∈	In the set of.
Italics	User-defined term (font is Courier New).

Table 2. General format for instructions

Byte-oriented file register operations	Example Instruction

Byte-oriented file register operations

```
16          10  9  8  7              0
|  OPCODE       | d | a | f(FILE #)    |
```

d = 0 for result destination to be WREG register
d = 1 for result destination to be file register (f)
a = 0 for force Access Bank
a = 1 for BSR to select bank
f = 8-bit file register address

addwf RegA, W

Byte to Byte move operations (2-word)

```
16       12  11                   0
| OPCODE    | f (Source FILE #)      |
```

```
16       12  11                   0
| 1111      | f (Destination FILE #) |
```

f = 12-bit file register address

movff RegA, RegB

Bit-oriented file register operations

```
16       12  11   9  8  7           0
| OPCODE    | b (BIT #) | a | f (file #) |
```

b = 3 bit position of bit in file register (f)
a = 0 to force Access Bank
a = 1 for BSR to select bank
f = 8-bit file register address

bsf   RegA, 7

Literal operations

```
16              8  7              0
| OPCODE          | k (literal )     |
```

k = 8-bit immediate value

movlw 0x7F

Control operations (`call`, `goto` and Branch operations)

```
16              8  7              0
| OPCODE          | n <7:0> (literal) |
```

```
16       12  11                   0
| 1111      | n<19:8> (literal)      |
```

n = 20-bit immediate value

goto   Label

```
16           9  8  7              0
| OPCODE       | S | n<7:0> (literal) |
```
S =
Fast bit

```
16       12  11                   0
| 1111      | n<19:8> (literal)      |
```

call   MyFunc

```
16       11  10                   0
| OPCODE    | n<10:0> (literal)      |
```

bra   MyFunc

```
16              8  7              0
| OPCODE          | n <7:0> (literal) |
```

bc   MyFunc

Table 3a. PIC18FXXXX instruction set

Mnemonic, Operands		Description	Cycles	16-Bit Instruction Word				Status Affected	Notes
				MSB			LSB		
BYTE-ORIENTED OPERATIONS									
addwf	f, d, a	Add WREG and f	1	0010	01da	ffff	ffff	C, DC, Z, OV, N	1, 2
addwfc	f, d, a	Add WREG and Carry bit to f	1	0010	00da	ffff	ffff	C, DC, Z, OV, N	1, 2
andwf	f, d, a	AND WREG and f	1	0001	01da	ffff	ffff	Z, N	1, 2
clrf	f, a	Clear f	1	0110	101a	ffff	ffff	Z	2
comf	f, d, a	Complement f	1	0001	11da	ffff	ffff	Z, N	1, 2
cpfseq	f, a	Compare f with WREG, Skip =	1 (2 or 3)	0110	001a	ffff	ffff	None	4
cpfsgt	f, a	Compare f with WREG, Skip >	1 (2 or 3)	0110	010a	ffff	ffff	None	4
cpfslt	f, a	Compare f with WREG, Skip <	1 (2 or 3)	0110	000a	ffff	ffff	None	1, 2
decf	f, d, a	Decrement f	1	0000	01da	ffff	ffff	C, DC, Z, OV, N	1, 2, 3, 4
decfsz	f, d, a	Decrement f, Skip if 0	1 (2 or 3)	0010	11da	ffff	ffff	None	1, 2, 3, 4
dcfsnz	f, d, a	Decrement f, Skip if Not 0	1 (2 or 3)	0100	11da	ffff	ffff	None	1, 2
incf	f, d, a	Increment f	1	0010	10da	ffff	ffff	C, DC, Z, OV, N	1, 2, 3, 4
incfsz	f, d, a	Increment f, Skip if 0	1 (2 or 3)	0011	11da	ffff	ffff	None	4
infsnz	f, d, a	Increment f, Skip if Not 0	1 (2 or 3)	0100	10da	ffff	ffff	None	1, 2
iorwf	f, d, a	Inclusive OR WREG with f	1	0001	00da	ffff	ffff	Z, N	1, 2
movf	f, d, a	Move f	1	0101	00da	ffff	ffff	Z, N	1
movff	fs, fd	Move fs (source) to 1st word	2	1100	ffff	ffff	ffff₅	None	
		fd (destination) 2nd word		1111	ffff	ffff	ffff_d		
movwf	f, a	Move WREG to f	1	0110	111a	ffff	ffff	None	
mulwf	f, a	Multiply WREG with f	1	0000	001a	ffff	ffff	None	1, 2
negf	f, a	Negate f	1	0110	110a	ffff	ffff	C, DC, Z, OV, N	
rlcf	f, d, a	Rotate left f through Carry	1	0011	01da	ffff	ffff	C, Z, N	1, 2
rlncf	f, d, a	Rotate left f (No Carry)	1	0100	01da	ffff	ffff	Z, N	
rrcf	f, d, a	Rotate right f through Carry	1	0011	00da	ffff	ffff	C, Z, N	
rrncf	f, d, a	Rotate right f (No Carry)	1	0100	00da	ffff	ffff	Z, N	
setf	f, a	Set f	1	0110	100a	ffff	ffff	None	1, 2
subfwb	f, d, a	Subtract f from WREG with borrow	1	0101	01da	ffff	ffff	C, DC, Z, OV, N	
subwf	f, d, a	Subtract WREG from f	1	0101	11da	ffff	ffff	C, DC, Z, OV, N	1, 2
subwfb	f, d, a	Subtract WREG from f with borrow	1	0101	10da	ffff	ffff	C, DC, Z, OV, N	
swapf	f, d, a	Swap Nibbles in f	1	0011	10da	ffff	ffff	None	4
tstfsz	f, a	Test f, Skip if 0	1 (2 or 3)	0110	011a	ffff	ffff	None	1, 2
xorwf	f, d, a	Exclusive OR WREG with f	1	0001	10da	ffff	ffff	Z, N	

Note 1: When a PORT register is modified as a function of itself (e.g., movf PORTB, F), the value used will be that value present on the pins themselves. For example, if the data latch is '1' for a pin configured as input and is driven low by an external device, the data will be written back with a '0'.

Note 2: If this instruction is executed on the TMR0 register (and where applicable, 'd' = 1), the prescaler will be cleared if assigned.

Note 3: If the program Counter (PC) is modified or a conditional test is true, the instruction requires two cycles. The second instruction is executed as a nop.

Note 4: Some instructions are two-word instructions. The second word of these instructions will be executed as a nop unless the first word of the instruction retrieves the information embedded in these 16 bits. This ensures that all program memory locations have a valid instruction.

Table 3b. PIC18FXXXX instruction set continued

Mnemonic, Operands	Description	Cycles	16-Bit Instruction Word MSB		LSB		Status Affected	Notes
BIT-ORIENTED OPERATIONS								
bcf f, b, a	Bit Clear f	1	1001	bbba	ffff	ffff	None	1, 2
bsf f, b, a	Bit Set f	1	1000	bbba	ffff	ffff	None	1, 2
btfsc f, b, a	Bit Test f, Skip if Clear	1 (2 or 3)	1011	bbba	ffff	ffff	None	3, 4
btfss f, b, a	Bit Test f, Skip if Set	1 (2 or 3)	1010	bbba	ffff	ffff	None	3, 4
btg f, b, a	Bit Toggle f	1	0111	bbba	ffff	ffff	None	1, 2
CONTROL OPERATIONS								
bc n	Branch if Carry	1 (2)	1110	0010	nnnn	nnnn	None	
bn n	Branch if Negative	1 (2)	1110	0110	nnnn	nnnn	None	
bnc n	Branch if Not Carry	1 (2)	1110	0011	nnnn	nnnn	None	
bnn n	Branch if Not Negative	1 (2)	1110	0111	nnnn	nnnn	None	
bnov n	Branch if Not Overflow	1 (2)	1110	0101	nnnn	nnnn	None	
bnz n	Branch if Not Zero	1 (2)	1110	0001	nnnn	nnnn	None	
bov n	Branch if Overflow	1 (2)	1110	0100	nnnn	nnnn	None	
bra n	Branch Unconditionally	2	1101	0nnn	nnnn	nnnn	None	
bz n	Branch if Zero	1 (2)	1110	0000	nnnn	nnnn	None	
call n, s	Call Subroutine 1st word	2	1110	110s	k_7kkk	$kkkk_0$	None	
	2nd word		1111	$k_{19}kkk$	kkkk	$kkkk_7$		
clrwdt	Clear Watchdog Timer	1	0000	0000	0000	0100	$\overline{TO}, \overline{PD}$	
daw	Decimal Adjust WREG	1	0000	0000	0000	0111	C	
goto n	Go to Address 1st word	2	1110	1111	k_7kkk	$kkkk_0$	None	
	2nd word		1111	$k_{19}kkk$	kkkk	$Kkkk_8$		
nop	No Operation	1	0000	0000	0000	0000	None	
nop	No Operation	1	1111	xxxx	xxxx	xxxx	None	4
pop	Pop Top of Return Stack (TOS)	1	0000	0000	0000	0110	None	
push	Push Top of Return Stack (TOS)	1	0000	0000	0000	0101	None	
rcall n	Relative Call	2	1101	1nnn	nnnn	nnnn	None	
reset	Software Device Reset	1	0000	0000	1111	1111	All	
retfie s	Return from Interrupt Enable	2	0000	0000	0001	000s	GIE, PEIE	
retlw k	Return with Literal in WREG	2	0000	1100	kkkk	kkkk	None	
return s	Return from Subroutine	2	0000	0000	0001	001s	None	
sleep	Go into Standby mode	1	0000	0000	0000	0011	$\overline{TO}, \overline{PD}$	

Note 1: When a PORT register is modified as a function of itself (e.g., movf PORTB, F), the value used will be that value present on the pins themselves. For example, if the data latch is '1' for a pin configured as input and is driven low by an external device, the data will be written back with a '0'.

Note 2: If this instruction is executed on the TMR0 register (and where applicable, 'd' = 1), the prescaler will be cleared if assigned.

Note 3: If the program Counter (PC) is modified or a conditional test is true, the instruction requires two cycles. The second instruction is executed as a nop.

Note 4: Some instructions are two-word instructions. The second word of these instructions will be executed as a nop unless the first word of the instruction retrieves the information embedded in these 16 bits. This ensures that all program memory locations have a valid instruction.

Table 3c. PIC18FXXXX instruction set continued

Mnemonic, Operands	Description	Cycles	16-Bit Instruction Word MSB		LSB		Status Affected	Notes
LITERAL OPERATIONS								
addlw k	Add Literal and WREG	1	0000	1111	kkkk	kkkk	C, DC, Z, OV, N	
andlw k	AND Literal with WREG	1	0000	1011	kkkk	kkkk	Z, N	
iorlw k	Inclusive OR Literal with WREG	1	0000	1001	kkkk	kkkk	Z, N	
lfsr f, k	Move 12-bit literal to FSRf	1	1110	1110	00ff	$k_{11}kkk$	None	
			1111	0000	k_7kkk	$kkkk_0$		
movlb k	Move Literal to BSR<3:0>	1	0000	0001	kkkk	kkkk	None	
movlw k	Move Literal to WREG	1	0000	1110	kkkk	kkkk	None	
mullw k	Multiply Literal with WREG	1	0000	1101	kkkk	kkkk	None	
retlw k	Return with Literal in WREG	1	0000	1100	kkkk	kkkk	None	
sublw k	Subtract WREG from Literal	1	0000	1000	kkkk	kkkk	C, DC, Z, OV, N	
xorlw k	Exclusive OR Literal with WREG	1	0000	1010	kkkk	kkkk	Z, N	
DATA MEMORY ↔ PROGRAM MEMORY OPERATIONS								
tblrd*	Table Read	2	0000	0000	00000	1000	None	
tblrd*+	Table Read with Post-Increment	2	0000	0000	00000	1001	None	
tblrd*-	Table Read with Post-Decrement	2	0000	0000	00000	1010	None	
tblrd+*	Table Read with Pre-Increment	2	0000	0000	00000	1011	None	
tblwt*	Table Write	2	0000	0000	00000	1100	None	
tblwt*+	Table Write with Post-Increment	2	0000	0000	00000	1101	None	
tblwt*-	Table Write with Post-Decrement	2	0000	0000	00000	1110	None	
tblwt+*	Table Write with Pre-Increment	2	0000	0000	00000	1111	None	

Appendix 4

<MyMacros.asm>

Preamble

This appendix puts together all the macros and subroutines developed in chapter 4. These are categorized as follows:

- Basic.
- Extended or 16-bit type.
- Stack related.
- Binary-to-BCD and BCD-to-Binary conversion.
- Delay routines.
- Swap type.
- 8/16-bit logical shift.
- Pointing to program space.

These macros are packaged in the file <MyMacros.asm> to be included at the beginning of assembly language programs. The subroutines invoked by the macros are also placed together in a library. For instance, subroutines pertaining to conversion from binary to BCD and vice versa, are bundled together in the *include file* <BCDlib.asm>. The ones relevant to the EEPROM are put together in the file <EE-PROM.asm>, etc. These libraries must be included, as needed, at the end of a program before the end directive (see Figure 1).

Figure 2 shows a skeleton of <MyMacros.asm>. Note the directive (radix dec) appearing on top of the file. It simply tells the assembler to interpret constants as decimal. For example, in the instruction:

```
movlw        64
```

the constant 64 will be interpreted as $(01000000_2 = 0x40)$. If the intention is to use 64 in base 16, then one of the following instructions will do:

```
movlw        0x64              ; constant in hexadecimal

movlw        B'01100100'       ; constant in binary
```

Figure 1. Assembly language program structure depicting include files

```
Structure of an assembly language program using <MyMacros.asm> and<BCDlib.asm>
#include    <P18F45K22.inc>     ; P18F45K22 SFRs & accessories
#include    <MyMacros.asm>      ; macros/predeclared variables

            cblock      0x000
                . . .                  ; user-defined variables
            endc

            org         0x0000
            InitSP                     ; initialize stack pointer
            . . .
            bra         $

#include    <BCDlib.asm>         ; library of subroutines
            end
```

Figure 2. Structure of <MyMacros.asm>

```
<MyMacros.asm> with indispensable directives, pre-declared variables and macros
        radix       dec             ; choose base 10
        config      PBADEN = OFF    ; <RB5:RB0> digital at POR

        cblock      0x040
            RegA, RegB, RegC, RegD   ; 8-bit GP registers
            RegE:2, RegF:2           ; 16-bit GP registers
            RegG:2, RegH:2           ; 16-bit GP registers
            wE:2                     ; 16-bit working register
        endc

Load    macro       reg, val        ; load reg with val
        movlw       val             ; move val to WREG
        movwf       reg             ; move WREG to reg
        endm

IncBcd  macro       f
        incf        f, W            ; store incremented f in W
        daw                         ; decimal adjust W
        movwf       f               ; store adjusted value in f
        endm

            . . .                    ; more macros, some are
                                     ; self-contained, others
                                     ; call subroutines
```

The second directive, you ought to use in <MyMacros.asm> is:

```
config      PBADEN = OFF
```

Its purpose is to configure the dual purpose pins (analog/digital) of PORTB as digital at power up reset (POR). These pins are <RB5:RB0>. PBADEN stands for PORTB A-to-D Enable.

Basic Macros

This section lists the basic macros discussed in Chapter 4 along with their codes. Table 1 groups these macros into four categories: register load, 8-bit BCD increment/decrement, compare and branch type, and bit-test and branch instructions. Table 2 lists the implementation of these macroinstructions.

Extended Macros

Since 16-bit macros are numerous, they are subdivided into two categories: (1) Data move and arithmetic type, and (2) conditional branch macroinstructions.

Tables 3 and 4 list the data move and arithmetic operations (prototypes and implementation respectively) while Tables 5 and 6 list the second category which is essentially a set of macroinstructions used to compare a register against another or against a constant. As a result of the comparison, the CPU branches to an address or executes the next instruction in sequence.

Software Stack Macros

Table 7 lists the stack related macros. These macroinstructions allow protection of variables against side effects as explained in Chapter 4. Here is a basic description of these macroinstructions.

- **InitSP:** Initialize SP to point to address 0x0FF.
- **PushB reg:** Push 8-bit register on the stack, then decrement SP.
- **PullB reg:** Increment SP then retrieve 8-bit value pointed to by SP into 8-bit reg.
- **PushD reg:** Push 16-bit register on the stack, then decrement SP by 2.
- **PullD reg:** Increment SP then retrieve 16-bit value pointed to by SP into 16-bit reg. Since the stack is pulled twice, the SP is incremented twice upon completion.

Binary-to-BCD and BCD-to-Binary

Table 8 lists the macros and subroutines that convert 8-bit and 16-bit binary numbers to Binary-Coded-Decimal (BCD) and vice versa. The subroutines belong to the library <BCDlib.asm> whereas the macros are part of <MyMacros.asm>.

Delay Routines

Table 9 tabulates the delay macros developed in Chapter 4 and more: DelayS, DelayL and DelayUS (microseconds delay).

Swap, Logical Shift (8/16-Bit) and Point to PS

Tables 10, 11 and 12 implement swap macros, 8/16-bit logical shift macros and the Point macroinstruction. Since Lslf and Lsrf specify a destination (F or W), F <u>must</u> be equated to 1 in file <P18F45K22.inc>.

Table 1. Prototypes of basic macros

Macro Prototype	Performed Task	Cycles
Load reg, val	Load an 8-bit register with a constant value	2
IncBcd reg	Increment packed BCD register, destination: F or W	2/3
DecBcd reg	Decrement packed BCD register, destination: F or W	3/4
Cpfblt reg, label	PC ← label if reg < WREG, else execute next instruction	3/4
Cpfbeq reg, label	PC ← label if reg = WREG, else execute next instruction	3/4
Cpfbneq reg, label	PC ← label if reg != WREG, else execute next instruction	2/3
Cpfbgt reg, label	PC ← label if reg > WREG, else execute next instruction	3/4
Brclr reg, flag, label	PC ← label if flag = 0, else execute next instruction	2/3
Brset reg, flag, label	PC ← label if flag = 1, else execute next instruction	2/3

Table 2. Implementation of basic macros

Load an 8-bit register reg in data space with an 8-bit constant val			
Load	macro	reg, val	; load reg with val
	movlw	val	; move val to WREG
	movwf	reg	; move WREG to reg
	endm		
Increment packed BCD register by 1. Uses the daw instruction to adjust the result.			
IncBcd	macro	f	
	incf	f, W	; store incremented f in W
	daw		; decimal adjust W
	movwf	f	; store adjusted value in f
	endm		
Decrement packed BCD register by 1. Uses the daw instruction to adjust the result.			
DecBcd	macro	f	
	movlw	0x99	; 10s complement of -1: 0x99
	addwf	f, W	; store decremented f in W
	daw		; decimal adjust W
	movwf	f	; store adjusted value in f
	endm		
Compare reg against WREG, branch to label if reg < WREG (unsigned comparison)			
Cpfblt	macro	reg, label	
	cpfslt	reg	
	bra	$+4	; skip next instruction
	bra	label	
	endm		
Compare reg against WREG, branch to label if reg = WREG			
Cpfbeq	macro	reg, label	
	cpfseq	reg	
	bra	$+4	; skip next instruction
	bra	label	
	endm		
Compare reg against WREG, branch to label if reg != WREG			
Cpfbneq	macro	reg, label	
	cpfseq	reg	; skip next instruction if equal
	bra	label	; else branch
	endm		
Compare reg against WREG, branch to label if reg > WREG (unsigned comparison)			
Cpfbgt	macro	reg, label	
	cpfsgt	reg	
	bra	$+4	; skip next instruction
	bra	label	
	endm		
Branch to label if flag (or bit number) in reg is clear			
Brclr	macro	reg, flag, label	
	btfss	reg, flag	
	bra	label	
	endm		
Branch to label if flag (or bit number) in reg is set			
Brset	macro	reg, flag, label	
	btfsc	reg, flag	
	bra	label	
	endm		

Table 3. Prototypes of 16-bit data move and arithmetic operations

Macro Prototype		Performed Task	Cycles
LoadE	reg, val	Load extended register with 16-bit literal	4
MovffE	Src, Dst	Extended move of Src to Dst	4
ClrE	reg	Clear 16-bit register	2
ComE	reg	1's complement 16-bit register	2
IncE	reg	Increment 16-bit register by 1	2
NegE	reg	Negate 16-bit register (2's complement)	4
AddE	reg, val	Add 16-bit value to 16-bit register	4
AddwfE	reg	Add WREG to 16-bit variable register	3
AddwEf	reg	Add 16-bit wE to 16-bit variable register	4
DecE	reg	Decrement 16-bit register by 1	3
SubE	reg, val	Subtract 16-bit literal from 16-bit register	4
SubwfE	reg	Subtract WREG from 16-bit register	3
SubwEf	reg	Subtract 16-bit wE from 16-bit register	4
IncBcdE	reg	Increment 4-digit packed BCD register by 1	6/8
DecBcdE	reg	Decrement 4-digit packed BCD register by 1	8/11

Table 4a. Implementation of 16-bit data move and arithmetic operations

Load 16-bit register `reg` in data space with 16-bit constant `val` in little-endian format			
LoadE	macro	reg, val	
	Load	reg+1, high(val)	; high(val) = MS byte
	Load	reg+0, low(val)	; low(val) = LS byte
	endm		

Transfer 16-bit register `SrcReg` to 16-bit register `DstReg` (byte order is preserved)		
MovffE	macro	SrcReg, DstReg
	movff	SrcReg+0, DstReg+0
	movff	SrcReg+1, DstReg+1
	endm	

Clear 16-bit register `reg`		
ClrE	macro	reg
	clrf	reg+1
	clrf	reg+0
	endm	

1's complement 16-bit register `reg`		
ComE	macro	reg
	comf	reg+0, F
	comf	reg+1, F
	endm	

Increment 16-bit register `reg` by 1			
IncE	macro	reg	
	infsnz	reg+0, F	; increment LS byte by 1
	incf	reg+1, F	; increment MS byte if needed
	endm		

Negate 16-bit register `reg` (2's complement)		
NegE	macro	reg
	ComE	reg
	IncE	reg
	endm	

Add 16-bit value `val` to 16-bit register `reg`			
AddE	macro	reg, val	
	movlw	low(val)	; get LS value
	addwf	reg+0, F	; add it to LS register
	movlw	high(val)	; get MS value
	addwfc	reg+1, F	; add it to MS register
	endm		

Add 8-bit value in **WREG** to 16-bit register `reg`			
AddwfE	macro	reg	
	addwf	reg+0, F	; add W to LS register
	btfsc	STATUS C	; if a carry is generated,
	incf	reg+1, F	; increment MS register
	endm		

Add `wE` to 16-bit register `reg`		
AddwEf	macro	reg
	movf	wE+0, W
	addwf	reg+0, F
	movf	wE+1, W
	addwfc	reg+1, F
	endm	

Table 4b. Implementation of 16-bit data move and arithmetic operations continued

Decrement 16-bit register reg by 1			
DecE	macro	reg	
	decf	reg+0, F	; decrement LS byte by 1
	btfss	STATUS C	
	decf	reg+1, F	; dec. MS byte if needed
	endm		

Subtract 16-bit value val from 16-bit register reg			
SubE	macro	reg, val	
	movlw	low(val)	; get LS value
	subwf	reg+0, F	; subtract it from LS reg.
	movlw	high(val)	; get MS value
	subwfb	reg+1, F	; subtract it from MS reg.
	endm		

Subtract 8-bit unsigned value in **WREG** from 16-bit register reg			
SubwfE	macro	reg	
	subwf	reg+0, F	; subtract W from LS byte
	btfss	STATUS, C	; if a borrow is generated,
	decf	reg+1, F	; decrement MS byte
	endm		

Subtract wE from 16-bit register (little-endian format)			
SubwEf	macro	reg	
	movf	wE+0, W	
	subwf	reg+0, F	
	movf	wE+1, W	
	subwfb	reg+1, F	
	endm		

Increment 16-bit packed BCD register reg			
IncBcdE	macro	reg	
	local	ExitAddr	
	IncBcd	reg	
	bnc	ExitAddr	
	IncBcd	reg+1	
ExitAddr			
	Endm		

Decrement 16-bit packed BCD register reg			
DecBcdE	macro	reg	
	local	ExitAddr	
	DecBcd	reg	
	movlw	0x99	
	subwf	reg, W	
	bnz	ExitAddr	
	DecBcd	reg+1	
ExitAddr			
	endm		

Table 5. Prototypes of 16-bit conditional branch macroinstructions

Macro Prototype	Performed Task	Cycles
`BnzE    reg, label`	PC ← label if **reg** ≠ 0, else execute next instruction	3/4/5
`BzE     reg, label`	PC ← label if **reg** = 0, else execute next instruction	3/4/5
`BltE    reg, val, label`	PC ← label if **reg** < value, else execute next instruction	4/5/7/8
`BgeE    reg, val, label`	PC ← label if **reg** ≥ value, else execute next instruction	4/5/7/8
`BeqE    reg, val, label`	PC ← label if **reg** = value, else execute next instruction	4/6/7
`CpEblt  reg, label`	PC ← label if **reg** < wE, else execute next instruction	4/5/7/8
`CpEbeq  reg, label`	PC ← label if **reg** = wE, else execute next instruction	4/6/7
`CpEbgt  reg, label`	PC ← label if **reg** > wE, else execute next instruction	4/5/8/9
`TstEsz  reg`	Skip next instruction if **reg** = 0, else execute it	3/4
`TstEsnz reg`	Skip next instruction if **reg** ≠ 0, else execute it	4/5

Table 6a. Implementation of 16-bit conditional branch macroinstructions

```
Branch to label if 16-bit register reg is different than zero
BnzE        macro       reg, label
            movf        reg+0, F     ; Set Z if lower byte = 0
            bnz         label        ; if LS byte != 0, bra to label
            movf        reg+1, F     ; Set Z if upper byte = 0
            bnz         label        ; if MS byte is != 0, bra to label
            endm                     ; else next

Branch to label if 16-bit register reg is equal to zero
BzE         macro       reg, label
            local       ExitAddr
            movf        reg+0, F     ; Set Z if LS reg. = 0
            bnz         ExitAddr     ; LS register != 0,continue
            movf        reg+1, F     ; Set Z if MS register = 0
            bz          label        ; MS register = 0, bra to label
ExitAddr                             ; else continue
            endm

Compare 16-bit register against 16-bit value, branch if reg < val (unsigned comparison)
BltE        macro       reg, val, label
            local       ExitAddr
            movlw       high(val)    ; put high order data in W
            subwf       reg+1, W     ; compare (reg)hi with (val)hi
            bnc         label        ; reg < val, goto label
            bnz         ExitAddr     ; result != 0, bra to ExitAddr
            movlw       low(val)     ; compare (reg)lo with (val)lo
            subwf       reg+0, W     ; if reg >= val, bra to ExitAddr
            bnc         label        ; else branch to label
ExitAddr
            endm

Unsigned compare 16-bit register reg against a 16-bit constant val, skip if reg ≥ val
BgeE        macro       reg, val, label
            local       ExitAddr
            movlw       high(val)    ; put high order data in W
            subwf       reg+1, W     ; (REG)hi - (Value)hi
            bnc         ExitAddr     ; Reg < Value, resume
            bnz         label        ; Reg > Value, branch
            movlw       low(val)     ; (REG)lo - (Value)lo
            subwf       reg+0, W     ; if C = 0, REG < Value
            bc          label
ExitAddr
            endm
```

Table 6b. Implementation of 16-bit conditional branch macroinstructions

Compare 16-bit register reg against 16-bit value val, branch if reg < val			
BeqE	macro	reg, val, label	
	local	ExitAddr	
	movlw	high(val)	; put high order data in W
	subwf	reg+1, W	; compare (REG)hi with (Value)hi
	bnz	ExitAddr	; (REG)hi != (Value)hi, to ExitAddr
	movlw	low(val)	; is (REG)lo = (Val)lo?
	subwf	reg+0, W	; REG != Value, branch to ExitAddr
	bz	label	; else branch to label
ExitAddr			
	endm		

Unsigned compare 16-bit reg against wE, branch to label if reg < wE. Does not modify wE.			
CpEblt	macro	reg, label	
	local	ExitAddr	
	movf	wE+1, W	; (Reg)hi - (wE)hi
	subwf	reg+1, W	
	bnc	label	; (Reg)hi < (wE)hi
	bnz	ExitAddr	; (Reg)hi > (wE)hi, continue
	movf	wE+0, W	; (Reg)hi = (wE)hi
	subwf	reg+0, W	; (Reg)lo - (wE)lo
	bnc	label	; (Reg)lo < (wE)lo
ExitAddr			; continue
	endm		

Unsigned compare 16-bit reg against wE, branch to label if reg = wE. Does not modify wE.			
CpEbeq	macro	reg, label	
	local	ExitAddr	
	movf	wE+1, W	; (Reg)hi - (wE)hi
	subwf	reg+1, W	
	bnz	ExitAddr	; (Reg)hi != (wE)hi, resume
	movf	wE+0, W	; (Reg)hi = (wE)hi
	subwf	reg+0, W	; (Reg)lo - (wE)lo
	bz	label	; (Reg)lo = (wE)lo
ExitAddr			; continue
	endm		

Unsigned compare 16-bit reg against wE, branch to label if reg > wE. Does not modify wE.			
CpEbgt	macro	reg, label	
	local	ExitAddr	
	movf	wE+1, W	; (Reg)hi - (wE)hi
	subwf	reg+1, W	
	bnc	ExitAddr	; (Reg)hi < (wE)hi, resume
	bnz	label	; (Reg)hi > (wE)hi
	movf	wE+0, W	; (Reg)hi = (wE)hi
	subwf	reg+0, W	; (Reg)lo - (wE)lo
	bz	ExitAddr	; (Reg)lo = (wE)lo, resume
	bc	label	; (Reg)lo > (wE)lo
ExitAddr			; continue
	endm		

Test 16-bit register, skip next instruction if reg is zero			
TstEsz	macro	reg	
	movf	reg+0, F	; Set Z if lower byte = 0
	bnz	$+4	; if LS byte is != 0, don't skip
	tstfsz	reg+1	; if MS byte is != 0, don't skip
	endm		

Test 16-bit register, skip next instruction if reg is non-zero			
TstEsnz	macro	reg	
	movf	reg+0, F	; Set Z if LS reg. = 0
	btfsc	STATUS, Z	; Z bit = 0, skip
	movf	reg+1, F	; Z = 1 test MS register
	btfsc	STATUS, Z	; Z bit = 0, skip
	endm		

Table 7. Implementation of stack related macros

Macro Implementation			Performed Task	Cycles
InitSP	macro lfsr endm	 2, 0x0FF 	SP ← 0x0FF, initialize SP to 0x0FF	2
PushB	macro movff endm	reg reg, POSTDEC2 	*SP ← reg, SP--	2
PullB	macro movff endm	reg PREINC2, reg 	SP++, reg ← *SP	2
PushD	macro movff movff endm	reg reg+1, POSTDEC2 reg+0, POSTDEC2 	*SP ← reg+1, SP--, *SP ← reg, SP--	4
PullD	macro movff movff endm	reg PREINC2, reg+0 PREINC2, reg+1 	SP++, reg ← *SP, SP++, reg+1 ← *SP	4

Table 8b. Conversion macros and subroutines

Convert `SrcReg` to BCD digits `DstAddr`, `DstAddr+1` and `DstAddr+2` - 115 cycles max			
Bin2Bcd	macro	SrcReg, DstAddr	
	PushB	RegA	
	PushD	FSR0L	
	movff	SrcReg, RegA	; RegA = binary value
	lfsr	0, DstAddr	; FSR0 = destination address
	call	_Bin2Bcd	; subroutine in "BCDlib.asm"
	PullD	FSR0L	
	PullB	RegA	
	endm		
Convert RegA to BCD digits at address pointed to by FSR0. Library: `<BCDlib.asm>`			
_Bin2Bcd	clrf	POSTINC0	
	clrf	POSTDEC0	
	movlw	100	; compute 100s
	rcall	CmpDig	
	movlw	10	
	rcall	CmpDig	; compute 10s
	movff	RegA, POSTDEC0	; get single digit
	movf	POSTDEC0, F	; adjust pointer
	return		
CmpDig	Cpfblt	RegA, ExitCmp	
	incf	INDF0, F	
	subwf	RegA, F	; subtract 100 or 10
	bra	CmpDig	
ExitCmp	movf	POSTINC0, F	; increment pointer
	return		
Convert `SrcReg` to BCD digits `DstAddr`, `DstAddr+1` ... `DstAddr+4` - 460 cycles max			
Bin2BcdE	macro	SrcReg, DstAddr	
	PushD	RegE	
	PushD	FSR0L	
	MovffE	SrcReg, RegE	; RegE = binary value
	lfsr	0, DstAddr	; FSR0 = destination address
	call	_Bin2BcdE	; subroutine in "BCDlib.asm"
	PullD	FSR0L	
	PullD	RegE	
	endm		
Convert RegE to 5 BCD digits stored at the address pointed to by FSR0.			
_Bin2BcdE	PushD	FSR0L	
	fill	(clrf POSTINC0), 4*2	; 4 instructions
	PullD	FSR0L	; recover initial ptr value
	LoadE	wE, 10000	; compute 10 Ks
	rcall	CmpDigE	
	LoadE	wE, 1000	
	rcall	CmpDigE	; compute Ks
	LoadE	wE, 100	
	rcall	CmpDigE	;compute 100s
	LoadE	wE, 10	
	rcall	CmpDigE	; compute 10s
	movff	RegE, INDF0	; get single digit
	return		
CmpDigE	CpEblt	RegE, ExitCmpE	
	incf	INDF0, F	
	SubwEf	RegE	; subtract 10K, 1K, 100, 10
	bra	CmpDigE	
ExitCmpE	movf	POSTINC0, F	; increment pointer
	return		

Table 8b. Conversion macros and subroutines

Convert the 3-byte BCD array at SrcAddr to binary. Result is in DstReg:2 (13 cycles)			
Bcd2Bin	macro	SrcAddr, DstReg	
	movf	SrcAddr+0, W	; W = D2
	mullw	10	; PRODL = 10*D2
	movf	SrcAddr+1, W	; W = D1
	addwf	PRODL, W	; W = 10*D2 + D1
	mullw	10	; PROD = 100*D2 + 10*D1
	movf	SrcAddr+2, W	; W = D0
	AddwfE	PRODL	; PROD = 100*D2+10*D1+D0
	MovffE	PRODL, DstReg	; result to DstReg
	endm		
Convert the 4-byte BCD array at SrcAddr to binary. Result is in DstReg:2 (16 cycles)			
Bcd2BinE	macro	SrcAddr, DstReg	
	movf	SrcAddr+0, W	; W = D3
	mullw	10	; PRODL = 10*D3
	movf	SrcAddr+1, W	; W = D2
	addwf	PRODL, W	; W = 10*D3 + D2
	mullw	100	; PROD = 1000*D3 + 100*D2
	MovffE	PRODL, DstReg	; save result
	movf	SrcAddr+2, W	; W = D1
	mullw	10	; PRODL = 10*D1
	movf	SrcAddr+3, W	; W = D0
	addwf	PRODL, W	; W = 10*D1 + D0
	AddwfE	DstReg	; 1000D3 + 100D2 + 10D1 + D0
	endm		

Table 9. Implementation of delay macros

Macro DelayS: provides short delays (1ms to 255 ms). Max error = 0.3 %			
DelayS	macro	msecs	
	local	InnerLoop, OuterLoop	
	PushB	RegA	
	Load	RegA, msecs	; RegA = msecs
OuterLoop	movlw	250	; to elapse 1 ms
InnerLoop	nop		
	addlw	-1	
	bnz	InnerLoop	
	decf	RegA, F	; msecs down counter
	bnz	OuterLoop	
	PullB	RegA	
	endm		
Macro DelayL: provides long delays (1 ms to 65.535 sec). Max error = 0.8 %			
DelayL	macro	msecs	
	local	InnerLoop, OuterLoop	
	PushD	RegE	
	LoadE	RegE, msecs	; RegE = msecs
OuterLoop	movlw	250	; to elapse 1 ms
InnerLoop	nop		
	addlw	-1	
	bnz	InnerLoop	
	DecE	RegE	; msecs down counter
	BnzE	RegE, OuterLoop	
	PullD	RegE	
	endm		
Macro that provides microseconds delays in multiples of 5us: 5us to 1275 us (100% accurate)			
DelayUS	macro	usecs	; specifies # of usecs
	local	Loop	
	movlw	usecs / 5	; W used as down counter
Loop	nop		
	nop		
	addlw	-1	
	bnz	Loop	
	endm		

Table 10. Implementation of Swap and SwapE macros

Swap the two 8-bit registers arg1 and arg1 passed as arguments - 4 cycles			
Swap	macro	arg1, arg2	; swap arg1 & arg2
	movf	arg1, W	
	movff	arg2, arg1	
	movwf	arg2	
	endm		
Swap the two 16-bit registers pointed to by FSR0 and FSR1 – 12 cycles			
SwapE	macro		
	movff	POSTINC0, wE+0	; wE = a[i]
	movff	POSTDEC0, wE+1	
	movff	POSTINC1, POSTINC0	; a[i] = a[j]
	movff	POSTDEC1, POSTDEC0	
	movff	wE+0, POSTINC1	; a[j] = wE
	movff	wE+1, POSTDEC1	
	endm		

Table 11. Logical shift macros Lslf, Lsrf, LslE, and LsrE

Logical shift left 8-bit register reg and specify destination (W or F) – 2 cycles		
Lslf	macro	reg, dest
	bcf	STATUS, C
	rlcf	reg, dest
	endm	
Logical shift right 8-bit register reg and specify destination (W or F) – 2 cycles		
Lsrf	macro	reg, dest
	bcf	STATUS, C
	rrcf	reg, dest
	endm	
Logical shift left 16-bit register reg – 3 cycles		
LslE	macro	reg
	bcf	STATUS, C
	rlcf	reg+0, F
	rlcf	reg+1, F
	endm	
Logical shift right 16-bit register reg – 3 cycles		
LsrE	macro	reg
	bcf	STATUS, C
	rrcf	reg+1, F
	rrcf	reg+0, F
	endm	

Table 12. Implementation of the Point macro

Load TBLPTR with AddrPS (Address in program space) – 6 cycles
Point   macro   AddrPS
Load   TBLPTRU, upper(AddrPS)
Load   TBLPTRH, high(AddrPS)
Load   TBLPTRL, low(AddrPS)
endm

Appendix 5

C18 REFERENCE SHEET

Basic Data Types

Table 1. C18 basic data types

Type	Size	Minimum	Maximum
char[1]	8 bits	-128	127
unsigned char	8 bits	0	255
int	16 bits	-32,768	32,767
unsigned int	16 bits	0	65,535
short	16 bits	-32,768	32,767
unsigned short	16 bits	0	65,535
short long	24 bits	-8,388,608	8,388,607
unsigned short long	24 bits	0	16,777,215
long	32 bits	-2,147,483,648	2,147,483,647
unsigned long	32 bits	0	4,294,967,295
float	32 bits	$\pm2^{-126} \approx \pm1.17549435e\text{-}38$	$\pm2^{128}*(2\text{-}2^{-15}) \approx \pm6.80554349e\text{+}38$
Double	32 bits	$\pm2^{-126} \approx \pm1.17549435e\text{-}38$	$\pm2^{128}*(2\text{-}2^{-15}) \approx \pm6.80554349e\text{+}38$

Conversion Characters

Table 2. Standard C conversion characters

Conversion Character	Meaning
%c	Single character
%s	String (all characters until '\0')
%d	Signed decimal integer
%i	Signed decimal integer
%o	Unsigned octal integer
%u	Unsigned decimal integer
%x	Unsigned hexadecimal integer with lower case digits (1a5e)
%X	As **x**, but with upper case digits (e.g. 1A5E)
%f	Floating point value
%e	Floating point value with exponent (e.g. **1.26e-5**)
%E	As **e**, but uses **E** for exponent
%g	As **e** or **f**, but depends on size and precision of value
%G	As **g**, but uses **E** for exponent

Table 3. Formatted print in standard C

Example	Output
printf("%d 0x%02x", 0xFF, 12);	255 0x0C
printf("%c 0x%02x", 'A', 'B');	A 0x42
printf("%d %d", '0', '2');	48 50
printf("%d %d", (unsigned char) -1, -2);	255 -2
printf("%s", "Hello World");	Hello World
printf("%.5s", "Hello World");	Hello
printf("0x%X 0x%x", 250, 254);	0xFA 0xfe
printf("%f %1.2f", 1.0/3, 2.0/3);	0.333333 0.67
printf("%1.4f %1.3e", 1.0/3, 1.0/3);	0.3333 3.333e-001
printf("%f %1.3E", 1.26e-3, 1.26e-3);	0.001260 1.260E-003

C Operators

If two operators of the same precedence are in the same expression, the computer will evaluate the expression from left to right. Example: d = a * b % c is equivalent to d = (a * b) % c.

Table 4. Listing of C operators

Operator	Operator Meaning
+	Addition operator
+=	Addition assignment operator, **x += y**, is the same as **x = x + y**
&=	Bitwise AND assignment operator, **x &= y**, is the same as **x = x & y**
&	Bitwise AND operator
^=	Bitwise XOR assignment operator, **x ^= y**, is the same as **x = x ^ y**
^	Bitwise XOR operator
|=	Bitwise inclusive OR assignment operator, **x |= y**, is the same as **x = x | y**
|	Bitwise inclusive OR operator
?:	Conditional expression operator
--	Decrement
/=	Division assignment operator, **x /= y**, is the same as **x = x / y**
/	Division operator
==	Equality
>	Greater than operator
>=	Greater than or equal to operator
++	Increment
*	Indirection operator
!=	Inequality
<<=	Left shift assignment operator, **x <<= y**, is the same as **x = x << y**
<	Less than operator
<<	Left shift operator
<=	Less than or equal to operator
&&	Logical AND operator
!	Logical negation operator
||	Logical OR operator
%=	Modulus assignment operator, **x %= y**, is the same as **x = x % y**
%	Modulus operator
*=	Multiplication assignment operator, **x *= y**, is the same as **x = x * y**
*	Multiplication operator
~	One's complement operator
>>=	Right shift assignment operator, **x >>= y**, is the same as **x = x >> y**
>>	Right shift operator
->	Structure pointer operation
-=	Subtraction assignment operator, **x -= y**, is the same as **x = x - y**
-	Subtraction operator, **x = x - y** (binary operation)
-	2's complement operator or negation, **-x** (unary operation)
sizeof	Determines size in bytes of operand

Table 5. Major operators (grouped by precedence)

Category	Symbol
increment/decrement	++, --
multiply/divide/modulus	*, /, %
add/subtract	+, -
relational comparisons	>, >=, <, <=
equality comparisons	==, !=
And	&&
Or	||
Assignment	=, +=, -=, *=, /=, %=

Decision Statements

Table 6. Decision statements (if and switch/case)

Statement	Syntax	Example

if	```if (expression)```
	``` statement²;```
	```// endif```
		```if (x < y)```
		``` printf("x < y");```
		```// endif```

if / else	```if (expression)```
	``` statement;```
	```else```
	``` statement;```
	```// endif```
		```if (x < y)```
		``` printf("x < y");```
		```else```
		``` printf("x >= y");```
		```// endif```

if / else if	```if (expression)```
	``` statement;```
	```else if³ (expression)```
	``` statement;```
	```else⁴```
	``` statement;```
	```// endif```
		```if (x < y)```
		``` printf("x < y");```
		```else if (x > y)```
		``` printf("x > y");```
		```else```
		``` printf("x = y");```
		```// endif```

Nested if	```if (expression)```
	```{```
	``` statement;```
	``` if (expression)```
	``` statement;```
	```}```
	```else if```
	``` …```
		```if (abs(a*a + b*b - c*c) < eps)```
		```{```
		``` printf("ABC is right-angled");```
		``` if (a == b)```
		``` printf(" and isosceles");```
		```}```
		```else if ((a == b) && (b == c))```
		``` printf("ABC is equilateral");```
		```else if ((a == b) || (b == c))```
		``` printf("ABC is isosceles");```
		```else```
		``` printf("ABC is scalene");```
		```// endif```

Conditional expression	```expr? statement1: statement2```
	
	```// is equivalent to```
	
	```if (expr)```
	``` statement1;```
	```else```
	``` statement2;```
	```// endif```
		```a > 5? c += 2: c -= 3;```
		
		```// is equivalent to```
		
		```c += a > 5? 2: -3;```
		
		```// or```
		
		```if (a > 5)```
		``` c = c + 2;```
		```else```
		``` c = c - 3;```
		```// endif```

switch / case	```switch (constant-expression)⁵```
	```{```
	``` case const1: statement(s);```
	``` break;```
	``` case const2: statement(s);```
	``` break;```
	``` ...```
	``` default: statement(s);```
	```}```
		```switch (choice) {```
		``` case 0: printf("Zero");```
		``` break;```
		``` case 1: printf("One");```
		``` break;```
		``` case 2: printf("Two");```
		``` break;```
		``` default: printf("What?");```
		```}```

Loops

Table 7. Conditional loops and auto indexed loops

Statement	Syntax	Example

`while loop`	```while (expression)```
	``` statement⁶;```
		```i = 0;```
		```sum = 0;```
		```while (i < 10)```
		```{```
		``` sum = sum + 2*i + 1;```
		``` i++;```
		```}```

`do-while loop`	```do {```
	``` statement;```
	``` statement;```
	```} while (expression);⁷```
		```i = 0;```
		```sum = 0;```
		```do {```
		``` sum = sum + 2*i + 1;```
		``` i++;```
		```} while (i < 10);```

`for loop`	```for (initialize; test; update)```
	``` statement;⁸```
		```sum = 0;```
		```for (i = 0; i < 10; i++)```
		``` sum = sum + 2*i + 1;```
		```// or```
		```for (i = 0, sum = 0; i < 10; i++)```
		``` sum = sum + 2*i + 1;```

`Loop with break`	```while (expression)```
	```{```
	``` statement;```
	``` if (condition) break;```
	``` statement;```
	```}```
		```i = 0;```
		```while (++i < 10)```
		```{```
		``` printf("%d ", i);```
		``` if (i == 5) break;```
		```} // prints: 1 2 3 4 5```

`Loop with continue`	```while (expression)```
	```{```
	``` statement;```
	``` if (condition) continue;```
	``` statement;```
	```}```
		```i = 0;```
		```while (++i < 10)```
		```{```
		``` if (i < 5) continue;```
		``` printf("%d ", i);```
		```} // prints: 5 6 7 8 9```

`Nested loops⁹`	```for (init; test; update) {```
	```statement(s);```
	``` for (init; test; update)```
	``` { statement(s);}```
	```statement(s);```
	```}```
		```for (i = 1; i <= 9; i++) {```
		``` printf("%d| ", i);```
		``` for (j = 1; j <= 9; j++)```
		``` printf("%3d ", i*j);```
		``` if (i != 9) printf("\n");```
		```} // prints multiplication table```

`Infinite loop`	```while (1)```
	```{```
	``` statement(s);```
	```}```
	``` // or```
	```for (;;)```
	```{```
	``` statement(s);```
	```}```
	``` // or```
	```do {```
	``` statement(s);```
	```} while (1)```
		```i = 0;```
		```while (1)```
		```{```
		``` printf("i = 0x%02x\n", i++);```
		``` Sleep(250);```
		```}```
		``` // or```
		```i = 0;```
		```for (;;)```
		```{```
		``` printf("i = 0x%02x\n", i++);```
		``` Sleep(250);```
		```}```

Functions

Functions return at most one value. A function that does not return a value has a return type of void. Values needed by a function are called parameters or arguments. Passing parameters by value (*in only*) - Variable is passed to the function but changes to p1 are not passed back:

```
return_type function(type p1)      // p1: in only parameter
```

Passing parameters by reference (*in out*) - Variable is passed to the function and changes to p1 are passed back:

```
return_type function(type *p1)      // p1: in out parameter
```

Table 8. Functions with a variety of argument types as well as return types

1. Non-void function with *in-only* parameter	`a = xCube(5);` // function call

<pre>return_type function(type p1, type p2, ...)
{
    statement;
    statement;
    ...
}</pre>
	<pre>int xCube(int x)
	{
	    int y;
	    y = x * x * x;
	    return y;
	}</pre>

2. void function with *in-only* parameters	`printAverage(20, 40);` // function call

<pre>void function(type p1, type p2, ...)
{
    statement;
    statement;
    ...
}</pre>
	<pre>void printAverage(int x, int y)
	{
	    int z;
	    z = (x + y) / 2.0 + 0.5;
	    printf("Average = %d", z);
	}</pre>

3. void function with *in-out* parameters	`swap(&a, &b);` // function call

<pre>void function(type *p1, type *p2, ...)
{
    statement;
    statement;
    statement;
    ...
}</pre>
	<pre>void swap(int *x, int *y)
	{
	    int temp;
	    temp = *x;
	    *x = *y;
	    *y = temp;
	}</pre>

4. Function with *in-only* & *in-out* parameters	`Unpack(0x98, &D1, &D2);` // function call

<pre>void function(type p1, type *p2, type *p3)
{
    statement;
    ...
}</pre>
	<pre>void Unpack(char N, char *D1, char *D0)
	{
	    *D1 = (unsigned char) N >> 4;
	    *D0 = N & 0x0F;
	}</pre>

4. Nested functions	`Sort3(&x, &y, &z);` // function call

<pre>void function1(type p1, type p2)
{
    statement(s);
    function2(p1, p2);
    statement(s);
}
 	
void function2(type x, type y)
{
    statement(s);
    function3(&x, &y);
}
 	
void function3(type *x, type *y)
{
    statement(s);
}</pre>
	<pre>void Sort3(int *a, int *b, int *c)
	{
	    Sort2(a, b);
	    Sort2(a, c);
	    Sort2(b, c);
	}
	
	void Sort2(int *arg1, int *arg2)
	{
	    int temp;
	    if (*arg1 > *arg2)
	    {
	        temp = *arg1;
	        *arg1 = *arg2;
	        *arg2 = temp;
	    }
	}</pre>

One-Dimensional Arrays

Arrays are variables that can store many items of the same type. The individual items known as *elements* are stored sequentially and are uniquely identified by the array *index* (or *subscript*). Arrays:

- May contain any number of elements.
- Elements must be of the same type.
- The index is zero based.
- Array size (number of elements) must be specified at declaration.

Arrays are declared much like ordinary variables. The general syntax is:

```
type arrayName[size];
```

where size refers to the number of elements and must be a constant integer (Example 1 in Table 9). Arrays may be initialized with a list when declared:

```
type arrayName[size] = {item_1, item_2, … , item_n};
```

where item_1, item_2, … must match the type of the array (Examples 2 and 4 in Table 9).

Arrays are accessed like variables, but with an index as in arrayName[index], where index may be a variable or a constant (Example 3 in Table 9). Note that the first element in the array has an index of 0. Beware that C does not provide any bounds checking.

Arrays are passed by reference rather than by value for greater efficiency. A pointer to the array, rather than the array itself is passed to the function (Examples 5 and 6 in Table 9).

Table 9. Examples of one-dimensional arrays

1. Array declaration	`int a[10];    // an array that can hold 10 integers`
	`char a[25];   // an array that can hold 25 characters`

2. Initialization at compilation time	`char a[5] = {'a', 'b', 'c', 'd', 'e'};` `int  b[5] = {10, 20, 30, 40, 50};`

3. Initialization at run-time	`for (i = 0; i < 5; i++)    // i is of type char`
	`    a[i] = 'a' + i;        // a[0] = 'a', a[1] = 'b', …`
	`for (i = 0; i < 5; i++)    // i is of type int`
	`    b[i] = 10 * (i + 1);   // b[0] = 10, b[1] = 20, …`

4. Declaration of strings	`char Message[6] = "Hello"; // extra byte for '\0'`
	`char Str[] = "Hello world";// allocates bytes as needed`

5. Function to find the maximum value of an array	`int maximum(int a[], int N)`
	`{`
	`    int max, i;`
	``
	`    max = a[0];                  // assumed maximum`
	`    for (i = 1; i < N; i++)`
	`        if (a[i] > max)`
	`            max = a[i];          // assumed maximum`
	`    return max;                  // return max value`
	`}`

6. Function to find the average value of an array (using a pointer parameter)	`int average(int *a, int N) {`
	`    int i, sum = 0;              // accumulated sum = 0`
	``
	`    for (i = 0; i < N; i++)`
	`        sum = sum + *a++;        // sum = sum + a[i]`
	`    return (float) sum / N + 0.5; // rounded average value`
	`}`

Character Arrays and Strings

Strings are arrays of char whose last element is a null character '\0' with an ASCII value of 0. C has no native string data type, so strings must always be treated as character arrays. Strings:

- Are enclosed in double quotes "string".
- Are terminated by a null character '\0'.
- Must be manipulated as arrays of characters (treated element by element).
- May be initialized with a string literal.

Strings are created like any other array of type char (char arrayName[length]). length must be one larger than the length of the string to accommodate the terminating null character '\0'. A char array with n elements holds strings with n-1 char (example 1 in Table 10).

Character arrays may be initialized with string literals. In this case, the array size is not required for it is automatically determined by the length of the string (example 2 in Table 10). The NULL character '\0' is automatically appended to a string.

At run-time, strings must be initialized element by element. The NULL character '\0' must be appended manually.

Strings cannot be compared using relational operators (==, !=, etc.). One must use standard C library string manipulation functions. strcmp() returns 0 if strings equal.

Table 10. String declaration and pertaining functions

1. String declaration	`char str1[10];      // holds 9 characters plus '\0'`
	`char str2[6];       // holds 9 characters plus '\0'`

2. Initialization at compilation time	`char str1[] = "Balamand";   // 9 chars "Balamand\0"`
	`char str2[6] = "Hello";     // 6 chars "Hello\0"`
	`char str3[4] = {'P', 'I', 'C', '\0'}; // size required`

3. Initialization at run-time	`Str[0] = 'H'; Str[1] = 'e'; Str[2] = 'l';` `Str[3] = 'l'; Str[4] = 'o'; Str[5] = '\0';`

4. String functions (in string.h). s and s1 are C strings, c is a char.	`strlen(s): length of s.`
	`strcpy(s, s1): copy s1 to s.`
	`strncpy(s, s1, n): copy s1 to s up to n characters.`
	`strcat(s, s1): concatenate s1 after s.`
	`strncat(s, s1): concatenate s1 after s up to n characters.`
	`strcmp(s, s1): compare s to s1.`
	`strncmp(s, s1): compare s to s1, only first n characters.`
	`strchr(s, c): pointer to first c in s.`
	`strrchr(s, c): pointer to last c in s.`
	`strstr(s, s1): pointer to first s1 in s.`
	`memcpy(s, s1, n): copy n chars from s1 to s.`
	`memmove(s, s1, n): copy n chars from s1 to s (may overlap).`
	`memcmp(s, s1, n): compare n chars of s with s1.`
	`memchr(s, c, n): pointer to first c in first n chars of s.`
	`memset(s, c, n): put c into first n chars of s.`

5. String comparison	`char str[] = "Bye";`
	
	`if (!strcmp(str, "Bye"))          // returns 0 if str = "Bye"`
	`    printf("The string is %s", str);`

6. Character count	`int CountCh(char *str, char ch) { // counts # of ch in str`
	`    int i, count = 0;`
	
	`    for (i = 0; i < strlen(str); i++)`
	`        if (str[i] == ch) count++;`
	`    return count;`
	`}`

Character Classification and Conversion Functions (ctype.h)

Table 11. Built-in character functions

1. unsigned char isalnum(unsigned char ch);		8. unsigned char isgraph(unsigned char ch);	
Function:	Determine if character ch is alphanumeric.	**Function:**	Determine if ch is a graphical character.
Remarks:	A character is considered to be alphanumeric if it is in the range of 'A' to 'Z', 'a' to 'z' or '0' to '9'.	**Remarks:**	A character is a graphical case alphabetic if it is any printable character except space.
Returns:	Non-zero if the character is alphanumeric, zero otherwise.	**Returns:**	Non-zero if the character is graphical, zero otherwise.
2. unsigned char isalpha(unsigned char ch);		**9. unsigned char isspace(unsigned char ch);**	
Function:	Determine if ch is alphabetic.	**Function:**	Determine if ch is a white space character.
Remarks:	A character is considered to be alphabetic if it is in the range 'A' to 'Z' or 'a' to 'z'.	**Remarks:**	White spaces: space, '\t', '\r', '\n', '\f' and '\v'.
Returns:	Non-zero if the character is alphabetic, zero otherwise.	**Returns:**	Non-zero if character is white space, zero otherwise.
3. unsigned char islower(unsigned char ch);		**10. unsigned char isblank(unsigned char ch);**	
Function:	Determine if character ch is a lower alphabetic character.	**Function:**	Determine if ch is a blank (space) character (typed with the space bar).
Remarks:	A character is considered to be lowercase alphabetic if it is in the range of 'a' to 'z'.	**Returns:**	Non-zero if character is blank, zero otherwise.
Returns:	Non-zero if the character is a lower alphabetic character, zero otherwise.	**Remarks:**	Not a standard C18 function and hence it must be coded as: {return ch == ' '? 1: 0}
4. unsigned char isupper(unsigned char ch);		**11. unsigned char isprint(unsigned char ch);**	
Function:	Determine if a character is an uppercase alphabetic character.	**Function:**	Determine if character ch is a printable character.
Remarks:	A character is considered to be uppercase alphabetic if it is in the range of 'A' to 'Z'.	**Remarks:**	A character is considered to be printable if it is in the range of 0x20 to 0x7E, inclusive.
Returns:	Non-zero if the character is an uppercase alphabetic character, zero otherwise.	**Returns:**	Non-zero if the character is a printable character, zero otherwise.
5. unsigned char isdigit(unsigned char ch);		**12. unsigned char ispunct(unsigned char ch);**	
Function:	Determine if ch is a decimal character.	**Function:**	Determine if character ch is a punctuation character.
Remarks:	A character is considered to be a digit character if it is in the range of '0' to '9'.	**Remarks:**	Punctuation character is printable & is neither a space nor alphanumeric.
Returns:	Non-zero if the character is a digit character, 0 otherwise.	**Returns:**	Non-zero if ch is punctuation character, zero otherwise.
6. unsigned char isxdigit(unsigned char ch);		**13. char tolower(char ch);**	
Function:	Determine if a character ch is a hexadecimal digit.	**Function:**	Convert ch to a lowercase alphabetical ASCII character.
Remarks:	A character is considered to be a hexadecimal digit if it is in the range '0' to '9', 'a' to 'f' or 'A' to 'F'.	**Remarks:**	Function converts ch to lowercase if the argument is a valid uppercase character.
Returns:	Non-zero if ch is hexadecimal, zero otherwise.	**Returns:**	Lower case character if ch is a valid uppercase character, otherwise it returns same ch.
7. unsigned char iscntrl(unsigned char ch);		**14. char toupper(char ch);**	
Function:	Determine if ch is a control character.	**Function:**	Convert ch to uppercase.
Remarks:	A character is considered to be a control character if it is not a printable character.	**Remarks:**	Function converts ch to uppercase if the argument is a valid lowercase character.
Returns:	Non-zero if the character is a control character, 0 otherwise.	**Returns:**	Upper case character if ch is a valid lowercase character, otherwise it returns same ch.

Two-Dimensional Arrays

Syntax: `type arrayName[size1][size2];`   `// see first 2 entries in table E.12`

size1 and size2 are the y and x dimensions respectively. A 3x3 array is visualized in Figure 1.

Figure 1. Visualization of a 3 x 3 two-dimensional array

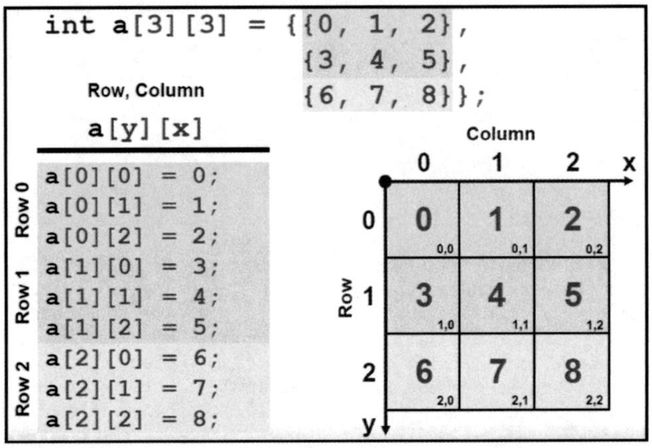

Table 12. Examples of two-dimensional arrays

Array declaration	`int a[10][10];` `// 10x10 array of 100 integers`

Initialization at compilation time	`int a[3][3] = {{0, 1, 2},`
	`              {3, 4, 5},`
	`              {6, 7, 8}};`

Initialization at run-time	`for (i = 0; i < 3; i++)     // i & j: integer type`
	`    for (j = 0; j < 3; j++)`
	`        a[i][j] = 3*i + j;`

Declaration of array of strings	`char DoW[][4] = {"SUN","MON","TUE","WED","THU","FRI","SAT"};` `// DoW[0] refers to "SUN", DoW[1] refers to "MON", etc.`

Filling a square matrix with random data at run-time	`void FillMatrix(int a[][10], int N)`
	`{`
	`    int i, j;`
	`    for (i = 0; i < N; i++)`
	`        for (j = 0; j < N; j++)`
	`            a[i][j] = rand();`
	`}`

Adding two square matrices together	`void Add(int a[][10], int b[][10], int c[][10], int N) {`
	`    int i, j;`
	
	`    for (i = 0; i < N; i++)`
	`        for (j = 0; j < N; j++)`
	`            c[i][j] = a[i][j] + b[i][j];`
	`}`

Transposing a square matrix	`void TransposeMatrix(int a[][10], int N) {`
	`    int i, j, temp;`
	`    for (i = 0; i < N; i++)   // swap a(i,j) with a(j,i)`
	`        for (j = i+1; j < N; j++) {`
	`            temp = a[i][j];`
	`            a[i][j] = a[j][i];`
	`            a[j][i] = temp;`
	`        }`
	`}`

Pointers

A pointer variable (or just pointer) is a variable that stores a memory address. Pointers allow the indirect manipulation of data stored in memory. Pointers are declared using *. To set a pointer's value to the address of another variable, use the & operator. Pointers can point to functions as well.

Table 13. Examples of data access via pointers

1. Pointer declaration	12. Array of pointers

`int *iPtr;    // pointer to int`
`float *fPtr;  // pointer to float`
	`char *p[4];   // creates an array of`
	`              // 4 pointers to char`

2. Example 1 – &x refers to address of x	13. Initialization of pointer array. x, y, *p[4]: char type

`int x, *p;    // int & pointer to int`
`p = &x;       // p = address of x`
`*p = 5;       // same as x = 5;`
	`p[0] = &x;    // p[0] points to x`
	`p[1] = "My string"; // p[1] = string address`
	`y = *p[0];    // dereferencing pointer y = x`

3. Post-increment pointer	14. Initializing an array of pointers to point to strings

`z = *(p++);   // z = *p, p = p+1`
`z = *p++;     // z = *p, p = p+1`
	`char *str[] = {"Zero", "One", "Two",`
	`               "Three", "Four", "\0"};`

4. Post-increment data pointed to by pointer	15. Printing element of an array of strings as declared in 14.
`z = (*p)++;   // z = *p, *p = *p+1`	`printf("%s", str[2]); // prints Two`
5. Example 2 – Recall that *(p++) ↔ *p++	16. Example 4 - Printing strings until '0' is encountered

`int x[3] = {1,2,3};`
`int y, z;`
`int *p = &x[0];`
`y = 5 + *(p++);   // y = 6, p = p + 1`
`z = 5 + (*p)++;   // z = 7, x[1] = 3`
	`char *str[] = {"Zero", "One", "Two",`
	`               "Three", "Four", "\0"};`
	`int i = 0;`
	`while (*str[i] != '\0')`
	`    printf("%s\n", str[i++]);`

6. Pre-increment pointer	17. Function pointers

`z = *(++p);   // p = p+1, z = *p`
`z = *++p;     // p = p+1, z = *p`
	`int (*fp) (int); // fp points to a function`
	`having 1 int argument and an int return value`

7. Pre-increment data pointed to by pointer	18. Function pointer assignment
`z = ++(*p);   // *p = *p+1, z = *p`	`fp = square;    // int square(int);`
8. Example 3 – Recall that *(++p) ↔ *++p	19. Passing a function pointer

`int x[3] = {1,2,3};`
`int y, z;`
`int *p = &x[0];`
 	
`y = 5 + *(++p);   // p = p + 1, y = 7`
`z = 5 + ++(*p);   // z = 8, x[1] = 3`
	`int square(int n) {return n*n;}`
	`int cube(int n) {return n*n*n;}`
	`int (*fp) (int); // pointer to function with`
	`…               // 1 argument`
	`fp = cube;       // point to function cube`
	`printf("%d", fp(2)); // prints 8`

9. Pointers and functions (in out parameters)	20. Example 5 – Using a fp to select among 4 functions

`void square (int *n)  // address of n is`
`{                     // passed to function`
`   *n *= *n;          // square n`
`}`
 	
`void main(void) {`
`   int x = 2;`
 	
`   square(&x);        // pass x by reference`
`   printf("%d\n", x); // will print 4`
`}`
	`int sum(int a, int b) {return a + b;}`
	`int product(int a, int b) {return a * b;}`
	`int quotient(int a, int b) {return a / b;}`
	`int remainder(int a, int b) {return a % b;}`
	
	`int op(int a, int b, int (*fp)(int, int))`
	`{return fp(a, b);}  // call function via fp`
	
	`void main(void) {`
	`    printf("%d", op(5, 6, &sum));`
	`}`

10. Pointers and strings (adding an offset)	21. Example 6 – Evaluating a definite integral

`char *Str = "Microsoft"; // Str points to`
`                          // first char`
Str
↓
| M | i | c | r | o | s | o | f | T | \0 |
↑
Str +4
	`float xSquared(float x) {return x * x;}`
	`float I(float a, float b, float (*f) (float))`
	`{`
	`    float x, sum = 0.0; int i, Npts = 10000;`
	`    for (i = 0; i <= Npts; i++) {`
	`        x = (float) i / Npts * (b - a) + a;`
	`        sum += f(x) * (b - a) / (Npts + 1);`
	`    }`
	`    return sum;`
	`}`

11. Pointers and strings (offset addressing)	`// Compute integral of x²dx for |x| ≤ 1`

`char *Str = "Microsoft"; // Str points to`
`                          // first char`
*Str == 'M'
↓
| M | i | c | r | o | s | o | f | T | \0 |
↑
*(Str +4) == 'o'
	`void main(void)`
	`{`
	`    printf("%f", I(-1, 1, xSquared));`
	`}`

Structures

Structures are collections of variables grouped together under a common name. The variables within a structure are referred to as the structure's members, and may be accessed individually as needed. Structures:

- May contain any number of members. These members may be of any data type.
- Allow related variables to be treated as a single unit, even if they have different types.
- Ease the organization of complicated data.

Table 14. Structures declarations and examples

1. Structure declaration	10. Nesting structures
| ```
struct structName
{
    type₁ memberName₁;  // members are declared
    ...                 // like normal variables
    typeₙ memberNameₙ;
}
``` | ```
typedef struct {float x; float y;} point;

typedef struct {point a; point b;} line;
...
line m;
m.a.x = 1; m.a.y = 7; m.b.x = 40; m.b.y = 18;
``` |
| **2. Structure to handle complex numbers** | **11. Structure of strings, assignments are shown to the right** |
| ```
struct complex
{
    float re;       // real part
    float im;       // imaginary part
}
``` | ```
struct strings          str.a[0] = 'B';
{                       str.a[1] = 'a';
    char a[4];          str.a[2] = 'B';
    char *b;            str.a[3] = '\0';
} str;                  str.b = "Good";
``` |
| **3. Declaring a structure variable** | **12. Pointer to structure (2 alternatives)** |
| ```
struct structName
{
    type₁ memberName₁;
    ...
    typeₙ memberNameₙ;
} varName₁, ..., varNameₙ;
``` | ```
typedef struct          struct complex
{                       {
    float re;               float re;
    float im;               float im;
} complex;              }
complex *p;             struct complex *p;
``` |
| **4. Declaring 2 variables x and y of type complex (method 1)** | **13. Using pointer to access structure members (refer to 12)** |
| ```
struct complex
{
    float re;       // real part
    float im;       // imaginary part
} x, y;
``` | ```
complex x;      // complex variable
complex *p;     // pointer to complex
p = &x;
p->re = 1.25; // set x.re = 1.25 via p
p->im = 2.50; // set x.im = 2.50 via p
``` |
| **5. Declaring 2 variables x and y of type complex (method 2)** | **14. Array of structures** |
| ```
struct complex
{
    float re;       // real part
    float im;       // imaginary part
}
struct complex x, y;  // x & y of type complex
``` | ```
typedef struct
{
    float re;
    float im;
} complex;
complex a[3];   // array of 3 complex types
``` |
| **6. Assigning a structure variable** | **15. Initialize array of structures (compilation C & run-time R)** |
| ```
x.re = 1.25;   // initialize real part of x
x.im = 2.50;   // initialize imaginary part of x
y = x;         // set struct y equal to struct x
``` | ```
complex a[3] = {{1, 2}, {3, 6}, {7, 8}}; // C
a[0].re = 6.75; a[0].im = 3.42;      // R
a[1].re = 75.6; a[1].im = 42.3;      // R
``` |
| **7. Creating a structure type using typedef** | **16. Adding 2 complex numbers, z = sum(x, y);** |
| ```
typedef struct structTagₒₚₜᵢₒₙₐₗ
{
    type₁ memberName₁;
    ...
    typeₙ memberNameₙ;
} typeName;
``` | ```
complex sum(complex x, complex y)
{
    complex z;
    z.re = x.re + y.re; z.im = x.im + y.im;
    return z;
}
``` |
| **8. Structure type to handle complex numbers** | **17. Adding 2 complex numbers, sum(a, b, &c);** |
| ```
typedef struct
{
    float re;
    float im;
} complex;
...
complex x, y; // declare x & y of type complex
``` | ```
void sum(complex x, complex y, complex *z)
{
    z->re = x.re + y.re; z->im = x.im + y.im;
}
...
complex c, a = {1.2, 2.6}, b = {2.8, 1.4};
sum(a, b, &c);
``` |
| **9. Initializing a structure variable at declaration** | **18. Printing a complex number x** |
| ```
complex x = {1, 2}; // x.re = 1, x.im = 2
``` | ```
printf("(%f + j%f)\n", x.re, x.im);
``` |

Unions and Bit Fields

Unions are similar to structures but a union's members all share the same memory location. In essence a union is a variable that is capable of holding different types of data at different times. Unions:

- May contain any number of members.
- Members may be of any data type.
- Are as large as their largest member.
- Use exactly the same syntax as structures except struct is replaced with union.

Bit Fields are unsigned int members of structures that occupy a specified number of adjacent bits from one to sizeof(int). They may be used as an ordinary int variable in arithmetic and logical operations. Bit Fields:

- Are ordinary members of a structure.
- Have a specified bit width.
- Are often used in conjunction with unions to provide bit access to a variable without masking operations.

Table 15. Summary of unions and bit fields

1. Union declaration

```
union unionName
{
   type1 memberName1;  // members are declared
   ...                 // like normal variables
   typen memberNamen;
}
```

1. Creating a bit field

```
struct structName
{
   unsigned int memberName1: bitWidth;
   ...
   unsigned int memberNamen: bitWidth;
}
```

2. Union of `char`, `short` and `int` plus variable declaration

```
union mixedBag
{
   char a;  // x.a: lowest byte of union
   short b; // x.b: lowest 2 bytes of union
   int c;   // x.c: all 4 bytes of union
} x;        // x is of type mixedBag
```

2. Bit field may be declared normally or as a `typedef`

```
typedef struct
{
   unsigned int bit0: 1;
   unsigned int bit1to6: 6;
   unsigned int bit7: 1;
} byteBits;
```

3. Creating a structure type using `typedef`

```
typedef union unionTag_optional
{
   type1 memberName1;
   type1 memberName2;
   ...
   typen memberNamen;
} typeName;
```

3. Assigning bits to a bit field

```
struct byteBits
{
   unsigned a: 1;
   unsigned b: 2;
   unsigned c: 3;
   unsigned d: 2;
} x;
```

Bit field x

7	6	5	4	3	2	1	0
1	1	1	0	1	1	0	1
d		c			b		a

```
x.a = 1; x.b = 2;
x.c = 5; x.d = 3;
```

4. Union type to handle `mixedBag`

```
typedef union
{
   char a;  // occupies lowest byte of union
   short b; // occupies lowest 2 bytes of union
   int c;   // occupies all 4 bytes of union
} mixedBag;
...
mixedBag x;     // x is allotted 4 memory bytes
mixedBag y[5];  // array of mixedBag unions
```

4. Union allowing bit field or full byte access plus example

```
union {
   char fullByte;
   struct
   {
      int a: 1;
      int b: 2;
      int c: 3;
      int d: 2;
   } bitField;
} bitByte;
```

```
bitByte.bitField.a = 1;
bitByte.bitField.b = 2;
bitByte.bitField.c = 5;
bitByte.bitField.d = 3;
printf("%X\n", bitByte);
// prints ED

bitByte.fullByte = 170;
printf("%X\n", bitByte);
// prints AA
```

5. Using `mixedBag` data type of part 4

```
x.c = 0x12345678; y[0].c = 0x89ABCDEF;
x.b = 0xABEF;     y[0].b = 0x1256;
x.a = 0xCD;       y[0].a = 0x34;

printf("x = 0x%X and y[0] = 0x%X", x, y[0]);

// prints: x = 0x1234ABCD and 0x89AB1234
```

5. Bit field allowing bitwise or full byte access of PORTB

```
union byteBits {  // union of Bitfield & char
  struct          // structure of bits
  {
    int b0:1; int b1:1; int b2:1; int b3:1;
    int b4:1; int b5:1; int b6:1; int b7:1;
  } bit;
  char val;       // b7, b5, … b0 in one shot
} PORTB;          // variable of type union
```

6. Function to initialize a union type. Use `initX(&x)` to invoke it

```
void initX(mixedBag *x)
{
   x->c = 0x12345678;
   x->b = 0xABEF;
   x->a = 0xCD;
} // x (type mixedBag) is loaded with
0x1234ABCD
```

6. Accessing PORTB (part 11) bit-by-bit or in one shot

```
PORTB.val = 0xFF;
PORTB.bit.b7 = 1;
PORTB.bit.b6 = !PORTB.bit.b6;
PORTB.bit.b4 = 0;
PORTB.val &= 0xF0;
// snippet stores A0 in PORTB
```

Enumerations, Macros

Enumerations are integer data types that you can create with a limited range of values. Each value is represented by a symbolic constant that may be used in conjunction with variables of the same enumerated type. Enumerations:

- Are unique integer data types.
- May only contain a specified list of values.
- Values are specified as symbolic constants .

Macros are text replacements, created with #define, that insert code into your program. Macros may take parameters like a function, but the macro code and parameters are always inserted into code by text substitution. Macros:

- Are evaluated by the pre-processor.
- Are not executable code themselves.
- Provide shortcuts.

Appendix 5

Table 16. Table listing examples on enumerations and macros

1. Enumeration syntax	1. Macros with `#define`
`enum typeName {label`$_0$`, label`$_1$`, …, label`$_n$`};` The compiler sets label$_0$ = 0, label$_1$ = 1, …, label$_n$ = n. Each label value is one greater than the previous value.	`#define label text` Every instance of *label* in the current file will be replaced by *text* which can be any arithmetic or logic expression.
2. Enumeration example	2. Macros examples

`enum weekday {SUN, MON, TUE, …, FRI, SAT};`
 	
Label values:
SUN = 0, MON = 1, TUE = 2, …, FRI = 5, SAT = 6
	`#define Fosc 4000000`
	`#define Tcy (0.25 * (1/Fosc))`
	`#define Setup InitSystem(Fosc, 250, 0x5A)`
	`#define Mask 0xFC`

3. Assigning a label a specific value	3. Syntax of function-like macro with arguments
`enum typeName {label`$_0$` = const`$_0$`, …, label`$_n$`};` The compiler sets label$_0$ = const$_0$, label$_1$ = (const$_0$ + 1), … . Each label value is one greater than the previous value.	`#define label(arg`$_1$`, …, arg`$_n$`) code` The *code* must fit on a single line or use '\' to split lines. Each instance of *label*() is expanded into *code*. This is not a C function.
4. Out-of-sequence assignment of labels	4. Examples of function-like macros

`enum people {Joe, Roy, Paul = 7, Sam, Mike};`
 	
Label values:
Joe = 0, Roy = 1, Paul = 7, Sam = 8, Mike = 9
	`#define min(x, y) (x < y? x: y)`
	`#define square(x) (x)*(x)`
	`#define swap(x, y) {x ^= y; y ^= x; x ^= y;}`
	`#define comp(x) (~x)`

5. Declaring enumeration type variable	5. Argument macros side-effects will give wrong results

Declared along with type:
`    enum typeName {const-list} varName`$_1$`, …;`
 	
Declared independently:
`    enum typeName varName`$_1$`, …, varName`$_n$`;`
	`i = 5;`
	`x = square(i++); // results: x = 25, i = 7`
	
	`// expression expands into x = (i++)*(i++);`
	`// so i is incremented twice instead of once`

6. Example of enumeration type variable	6. Avoid semicolons at the end of a macro definition

`enum weekday {SUN, MON, …, FRI, SAT} today;`
`enum weekday day;    // day is a variable of`
`                     // type weekday`
	`#define a 4;`
	`c = a + b;    // translates into c = 4; + b`
	`&`
	`              // hence a compiler error`

7. Declaring a "tag less" enumeration variable	7. Bit set, bit clear and bit toggle. Operates on bit b in reg. R

`enum {const-list} varName`$_1$`, …, varName`$_n$`;`
 	
No type name is available to declare more `enum` type variables later in code. Example:
 	
`enum {SUN, MON, TUE, WED, THU, FRI, SAT} today;`
	`#define bset(r, b) r = r | (0x01 << b)`
	`#define bclr(r, b) r = r & ~(0x01 << b)`
	`#define btg(r, b) r = r ^ (0x01 << b)`
	`// r: unsigned char, b: bit number (7 … 0)`
	`Example: bset(x, 0); bclr(x, 7); btg(x, 4);`
	`// x = 0xF0 gives x = 0x61 upon execution of:`

8. Declaring enumeration type with `typedef`	8. Swapping nibbles of a register of type `unsigned char`

`typedef enum {const-list} typeName;`
 	
The enumeration may now be used as an ordinary data type (compatible with int). Example:
 	
`typedef enum {SUN, MON, …, FRI, SAT} weekday;`
`weekday day;  // variable of type weekday`
	`#define swapN(r) r = (r << 4) | (r >> 4)`
	`…`
	`unsigned char x = 0xAB, y = 0x34;`
	`…`
	`swapN(x); swapN(y);`
	`printf("x = 0x%02X", x);  // prints x = 0xBA`
	`printf("x = 0x%02X", y);  // prints x = 0x43`

9. Conclusions on enumeration data type	9. Conclusions on macros
Enumerations provide a means of associating a list of constants with one or more variables. They make code easier to read. Variables declared as enum are essentially int types.	#define macros simplify your code and make it easier to maintain. Extreme care must be taken when crafting a macro due to the way they are substituted within your code.

393

ENDNOTES

1   A plain char is signed by default. It could be substituted by signed char.

2   If more than one statement are to be executed when expression is true, then the statements must be preceded by the left curly bracket { and terminated by the right curly bracket }.

3   As many else if may be added as needed by the logic to be implemented.

4   The else clause is optional and may be omitted if not required by the logic.

5   The constant-expression must always be an integer data type (int, char, etc.).

6   If more than one statement are to be executed within the body of the loop, then the statements must be preceded by the left curly bracket { and terminated by the right curly bracket }.

7   The curly brackets { } may be removed if only one statement is in the body of the loop.

8   Same as endnote 6.

9   Nested loops could be nested while, do/while, for or a mixture of these constructs. Table shows nested for.

Appendix 6

CONVERSION, DELAY, AND EEPROM LIBRARIES

Conversion Library

Table 1 lists 8/16-bit BCD increment/decrement C macros using inline Assembly language. Table 2 lists conversion functions. These macros and functions are part of the C library <BCDlib.h>.

Built-in Delay Library

The delay functions execute code for a specific number of processor instruction cycles. For time based delays, the processor operating frequency must be taken into account. The routines are part of the library <delays.h> and are described in Table 3.

EEPROM Library

Table 4 lists the functions of the homemade <eeprom.h> library designed in Chapter 5. The table illustrates 8/16-bit EEPROM read and write routines.

Table 1. 8-bit/16-bit BCD increment/decrement C macros

Inline assembly to increment an 8-bit packed BCD variable using the daw instruction (4 cycles)

```
#define   IncBcd(f)      {_asm                          \
                            movlb      f                \
                            incf       f, 0, 1          \
                            daw                         \
                            movwf      f, 1             \
                         _endasm}
```

Inline assembly to decrement an 8-bit packed BCD variable using the daw instruction (5 cycles)

```
#define   DecBcd(f)      {_asm                          \
                            movlb      f                \
                            movlw      0x99             \
                            addwf      f, 0, 1          \
                            daw                         \
                            movwf      f, 1             \
                         _endasm}
```

Inline assembly to increment a 16-bit packed BCD variable (10 cycles maximum)

```
#define   IncBcdE(f)     {IncBcd(f)                     \
                          _asm                          \
                            tstfsz     f, 1             \
                            bra        4                \
                          _endasm                       \
                          IncBcd(f+1)}
```

Inline assembly to decrement a 16-bit packed BCD variable (13 cycles maximum)

```
#define   DecBcdE(f)     {DecBcd(f)                     \
                          _asm                          \
                            movlw      0x99             \
                            subwf      f, 0, 1          \
                            bnz        5                \
                          _endasm                       \
                          DecBcd(f+1)}
```

Table 2. Conversion functions

Convert 8-bit N to 3 BCD digits. Result at `a[0]` (MSB), `a[1]` & `a[2]` (423 cycles maximum)

```c
void Bin2Bcd(unsigned char N, char *a)
{
    a[2] = N % 10;                      // least significant digit
    N = N / 10;
    a[1] = N % 10;                      // middle significant digit
    a[0] = N / 10;                      // most significant digit
}
```

Convert 16-bit N to 5 BCD digits. Result at `a[0]` (MSB), `a[1]`, …, `a[4]` (2160 cycles)

```c
void Bin2BcdE(unsigned int N, char *a)
{
    unsigned char i;

    for (i = 0; i < 4; i++)
    {
        a[4-i] = N % 10;               // rem of division by 10
        N = N / 10;
    }
    a[0] = N;
}
```

Convert a 3-byte unpacked BCD array to binary. Maximum value returned is 999.

```c
unsigned int Bcd2Bin(char *a)
{
    return (int) a[0] * 100 + a[1] * 10 + a[2];
}
```

Convert a 4-byte unpacked BCD array to binary. Maximum value returned is 9999.

```c
unsigned int Bcd2BinE(unsigned char *a)
{
    return (int) a[0] * 1000 + (int) a[1] * 100 + a[2] * 10 + a[3];
}
```

Increment packed BCD register. Convert to binary, increment, then back to BCD

```c
void BcdInc(unsigned char *reg)
{
    *reg = (*reg / 16) * 10 + (*reg % 16);    // packed BCD to binary
    *reg = *reg != 99? *reg + 1: 0;           // add 1 to reg
    *reg = (*reg / 10) * 16 + (*reg % 10);    // binary to packed BCD
}
```

Decrement packed BCD register. Convert to binary, decrement, then back to BCD

```c
void BcdDec(unsigned char *reg)
{
    *reg = (*reg / 16) * 10 + (*reg % 16);    // packed BCD to binary
    *reg = *reg != 0? *reg - 1: 99;           // sub 1 from reg
    *reg = (*reg / 10) * 16 + (*reg % 10);    // binary to packed BCD
}
```

Add `val` to packed BCD register. Convert to binary, add, then back to BCD

```c
void BcdAdd(unsigned char *reg, unsigned char val)
{
    *reg = (*reg / 16) * 10 + (*reg % 16);   // BCD to binary
    *reg += val;                             // add val to reg
    *reg = (*reg / 10) * 16 + (*reg % 10);// binary to BCD
}
```

Table 3. Delay functions in <delays.h>

Delay1TCY(): Delay 1 instruction cycle (T_{CY})	
Include:	`delays.h`
Prototype:	`void Delay1TCY(void);`
Remarks:	This function is actually a `#define` for the `nop` instruction. When encountered in the source code, the compiler simply inserts a nop.
File Name:	`#define` in `<delays.h>`
Delay10TCYx(): Delay in multiples of 10 instruction cycles (T_{CY})	
Include:	`delays.h`
Prototype:	`void Delay10TCYx(unsigned char unit);`
Arguments:	The value of `unit` can be any 8-bit value. A value in the range [1, 255] will delay (`unit*10`) cycles. A value of 0 causes a delay of 2,560 cycles.
Remarks:	This function creates a delay in multiples of 10 instruction cycles.
File Name:	`d10tcyx.asm`
Delay100TCYx(): Delay in multiples of 100 instruction cycles (T_{CY}).	
Include:	`delays.h`
Prototype:	`void Delay100TCYx(unsigned char unit);`
Arguments:	The value of `unit` can be any 8-bit value. A value in the range [1, 255] will delay (`unit*100`) cycles. A value of 0 causes a delay of 25,600 cycles.
Remarks:	This function creates a delay in multiples of 100 instruction cycles.
File Name:	`d100tcyx.asm`
Delay1KTCYx(): Delay in multiples of 1,000 instruction cycles (T_{CY}).	
Include:	`delays.h`
Prototype:	`void Delay1KTCYx(unsigned char unit);`
Arguments:	The value of `unit` can be any 8-bit value. A value in the range [1, 255] will delay (`unit*1000`) cycles. A value of 0 causes a delay of 256,000 cycles.
Remarks:	This function creates a delay in multiples of 1000 instruction cycles.
File Name:	`d1ktcyx.asm`
Delay10KTCYx(): Delay in multiples of 10,000 instruction cycles (T_{CY}).	
Include:	`delays.h`
Prototype:	`void Delay10KTCYx(unsigned char unit);`
Arguments:	The value of `unit` can be any 8-bit value. A value in the range [1, 255] will delay (`unit*10000`) cycles. A value of 0 causes a delay of 2,560 Kcycles.
Remarks:	This function creates a delay in multiples of 10,000 instruction cycles.
File Name:	`d10ktcyx.asm`

Table 4. EEPROM 8/16-bit read/write functions

ReadEE(): Returns value from EEPROM address SrcReg to a register in data space

```
unsigned char ReadEE(unsigned char SrcReg) {
    EEADR = SrcReg;              // select EE address to read from
    EECON1bits.EEPGD = 0;        // access Data EEPROM memory
    EECON1bits.CFGS = 0;         // don't access config registers
    EECON1bits.RD = 1;           // initiate EEPROM read
    return EEDATA;               // return read value
}
```

Wrt2EE(): Write data from SrcReg in data space to EEPROM address DstReg

```
void Wrt2EE(unsigned char SrcReg, unsigned char DstReg) {
    char interruptSet = 0;       // indicates GIE state

    EEADR = DstReg;              // specify destination register
    EEDATA = SrcReg;             // contents of SrcReg in EEDATA
    EECON1bits.EEPGD = 0;        // access Data EEPROM memory
    EECON1bits.CFGS = 0;
    EECON1bits.WREN = 1;         // enable EEPROM write
    if (INTCONbits.GIE)          // used to recover GIE state
        interruptSet = 1;
    INTCONbits.GIE = 0;          // disable interrupts
    EECON2 = 0x55;               // required sequence
    EECON2 = 0xAA;               // required sequence
    EECON1bits.WR = 1;           // initiates a write cycle
    while (EECON1bits.WR);       // wait for write to terminate
    if (interruptSet)            // recover GIE state
        INTCONbits.GIE = 1;
    EECON1bits.WREN = 0;         // disable EEPROM write
}
```

eReadEE: Returns 16-bit value from EE address SrcReg (extended: 16-bit)

```
unsigned int eReadEE(unsigned int SrcReg)
{
    unsigned char LsByte, MsByte;   // least & most significant bytes

    LsByte = ReadEE(SrcReg + 0);
    MsByte = ReadEE(SrcReg + 1);
    return (unsigned int) MsByte * 256 + LsByte;
}
```

eWrt2EE: Write 16-bit data from SrcReg to EE address DstReg (extended: 16-bit)

```
void eWrt2EE(unsigned int SrcReg, unsigned char DstReg)
{
    Wrt2EE(SrcReg % 256, DstReg + 0);
    Wrt2EE(SrcReg / 256, DstReg + 1);
}
```

Appendix 7

CONFIGURATION REGISTERS

Table 1. Listing of configuration registers along with values on POR and BOR

Name	Bit 7	Bit 6	Bit 5	Bit 4	Bit 3	Bit 2	Bit 1	Bit 0	Value on POR, BOR
CONFIG1L	-	-	-	-	-	-	-	-	0000 0000
CONFIG1H	IESO	FCMEN	PRICLKEN	PLLCFG	FOSC<3:0>				0010 0101
CONFIG2L	-	-	-	BORV<1:0>		BOREN<1:0>		$\overline{\text{PWRTEN}}$	0001 1111
CONFIG2H	-	-	WDPS<3:0>				WDTEN<1:0>		0011 1111
CONFIG3L	-	-	-	-	-	-	-	-	0000 0000
CONFIG3H	MCLRE	-	P2BMX	T3CMX	HFOFST	CCP3MX	PBADEN	CCP2MX	1011 1111
CONFIG4L	$\overline{\text{DEBUG}}$	XINST	-	-	-	LVP[1]	-	STRVEN	1000 0101
CONFIG4H	-	-	-	-	-	-	-	-	1111 1111
CONFIG5L	-	-	-	-	CP3[2]	CP2[2]	CP1	CP0	0000 1111
CONFIG5H	CPD	CPB	-	-	-	-	-	-	1100 0000
CONFIG6L	-	-	-	-	WRT3[2]	WRT2[2]	WRT1	WRT0	0000 1111
CONFIG6H	WRTD	WRTB	WRTC[3]	-	-	-	-	-	1110 0000
CONFIG7L	-	-	-	-	EBTRB3[2]	EBTRB2[2]	EBTRB1	EBTRB0	0000 1111
CONFIG7H	-	EBTRB	-	-	-	-	-	-	0100 0000
DEVID1[4]	DEV<2:0>			REV<4:0>					qqqq qqqq
DEVID2[4]	DEV<10:3>								0101 qqqq

Legend: — = unimplemented, q = value depends on condition. Yellow shaded bits are unimplemented, read as '0'.
Note 1: Can only be changed when in high voltage programming mode.
Note 2: Available on PIC18(L)FX5K22 and PIC18(L)FX6K22 devices only.
Note 3: In user mode, this bit is read-only and cannot be self-programmed.
Note 4: See Register 24-12 and Register 24-23 for DEVID values. DEVID registers are read-only and cannot be programmed by the user.

Table 2. Config registers addresses

Address	Name
0x300000	CONFIG1L
0x300001	CONFIG1H
0x300002	CONFIG2L
0x300003	CONFIG2H
0x300004	CONFIG3L
0x300005	CONFIG3H
0x300006	CONFIG4L
0x300007	CONFIG4H
0x300008	CONFIG5L
0x300009	CONFIG5H
0x30000A	CONFIG6L
0x30000B	CONFIG6H
0x30000C	CONFIG7L
0x30000D	CONFIG7H
0x3FFFFE	DEVID1[4]
0x3FFFFF	DEVID2[4]

Table 3. Config registers bit-by-bit description

CONFIG1H: CONFIGURATION REGISTER 1 HIGH

R/P-0	R/P-0	R/P-1	R/P-0	R/P-0	R/P-1	R/P-0	R/P-1
IESO	FCMEN	PRICLKEN	PLLCFG	FOSC<3:0>			
bit 7							bit 0

R = Readable bit   P = Programmable bit   U = Unimplemented bit, read as '0'
-n = Value when device is not programmed   x = Bit is unknown

bit 7   **IESO** [1]**:** Internal/External Oscillator Switchover bit
               1 = Oscillator Switchover mode enabled
               0 = Oscillator Switchover mode disabled

bit 6   **FCMEN**[1]**:** Fail-Safe Clock Monitor Enable bit
               1 = Fail-Safe Clock Monitor enabled
               0 = Fail-Safe Clock Monitor disabled

bit 5   **PRICLKEN:** Primary Clock Enable bit
               1 = Primary Clock is always enabled
               0 = Primary Clock can be disabled by software

bit 4   **PLLCFG:** 4 x PLL Enable bit
               1 = 4 x PLL always enabled, Oscillator multiplied by 4
               0 = 4 x PLL is under software control, PLLEN (OSCTUNE<6>)

bit 3-0   **FOSC<3:0> :** Oscillator Selection bits
               1111 = External RC oscillator, CLKOUT function on RA6
               1110 = External RC oscillator, CLKOUT function on RA6
               1101 = EC oscillator **(low power, ≤ 500 kHz)**
               1100 = EC oscillator, CLKOUT function on OSC2 **(low power, ≤ 500 kHz)**
               1011 = EC oscillator **(medium power, 500 kHz-16 MHz)**
               1010 = EC oscillator, CLKOUT function on OSC2 **(medium power, 500 kHz - 16 MHz)**
               1001 = Internal oscillator block, CLKOUT function on OSC2
               1000 = Internal oscillator block
               0111 = External RC oscillator
               0110 = External RC oscillator, CLKOUT function on OSC2
               0101 = EC oscillator **(high power, > 16 MHz)**
               0100 = EC oscillator, CLKOUT function on OSC2 **(high power, > 16 MHz)**
               0011= HS oscillator **(medium power, 4 MHz - 16 MHz)**
               0010= HS oscillator **(high power, >16 MHz)**
               0001= XT oscillator
               0000= LP oscillator

Note 1:   When FOSC<3:0> is configured for HS, XT, or LP oscillator and FCMEN bit is set, then the
               IESO bit should also be set to prevent a false failed clock indication and to enable automatic
               clock switch over from the internal oscillator block to the external oscillator when the OST
               times out.

Appendix 7

Table 4.

CONFIG2L: CONFIGURATION REGISTER 2 LOW

U-0	U-0	U-0	R/P-1	R/P-1	R/P-1	R/P-1	R/P-1
-	-	-	BORV<1:0>[1]		BOREN<1:0>[2]		$\overline{\text{PWRTEN}}$ [2]

bit 7   bit 0

R = Readable bit   P = Programmable bit   U = Unimplemented bit, read as '0'
-n = Value when device is not programmed   x = Bit is unknown

bit 7-5   **Unimplemented**: Read as '0'

bit 4-3   **BORV<1:0>:** Brown-out Reset Voltage bits[1]
11 = V_{BOR} set to 1.90 V nominal
10 = V_{BOR} set to 2.20 V nominal
01 = V_{BOR} set to 2.50 V nominal
00 = V_{BOR} set to 2.85 V nominal

bit 2-1   **BOREN<1:0>:** Brown-out Reset Enable bits[2]
11 = Brown-out Reset enabled in hardware only (SBOREN is disabled)
10 = Brown-out Reset enabled in hardware only and disabled in Sleep mode
      (SBOREN is disabled)
01 = Brown-out Reset enabled and controlled by software (SBOREN is enabled)
00 = Brown-out Reset disabled in hardware and software

bit 0   **$\overline{\text{PWRTEN}}$:** Power-up Timer Enable bit[2]
1 = PWRT disabled
0 = PWRT enabled

Note 1:   See datasheet's section 27.1 "DC Characteristics: Supply Voltage, PIC18(L)F2X/4XK22" for specifications.
Note 2:   The Power-up Timer is decoupled from Brown-out Reset, allowing these features to be independently controlled.

403

Table 5.

CONFIG2H: CONFIGURATION REGISTER 2 HIGH

U-0	U-0	R/P-1	R/P-1	R/P-1	R/P-1	R/P-1	R/P-1
-	-	WDTPS<3:0>				WDTEN<1:0>	
bit 7							**bit 0**

R = Readable bit   P = Programmable bit   U = Unimplemented bit, read as '0'
-n = Value when device is not programmed   x = Bit is unknown

bit 7-6   **Unimplemented**: Read as '0'

bit 5-2   **WDTPS<3:0>:** Watchdog Timer Postscale Select bits
                 1111 = 1:32,768
                 1110 = 1:16,384
                 1101 = 1:8,192
                 1100 = 1:4,096
                 1011 = 1:2,048
                 1010 = 1:1,024
                 1001 = 1:512
                 1000 = 1:256
                 0111 = 1:128
                 0110 = 1:64
                 0101 = 1:32
                 0100 = 1:16
                 0011 = 1:8
                 0010 = 1:4
                 0001 = 1:2
                 0000 = 1:1

bit 1-0   **WDTEN<1:0>:** Watchdog Timer Enable bits
                 11 = WDT enabled in hardware; SWDTEN bit disabled
                 10 = WDT controlled by the SWDTEN bit
                 01 = WDT enabled when device is active, disabled when device is in Sleep; SWDTEN bit
                 disabled
                 00 = WDT disabled in hardware; SWDTEN bit disabled

Table 6. CONFIG3H: configuration register 3 high

CONFIG3H: CONFIGURATION REGISTER 3 HIGH

R/P-1	U-0	R/P-1	R/P-1	R/P-1	R/P-1	R/P-1	R/P-1
MCLRE	-	P2BMX	T3CMX	HFOFST	CCP3MX	PBADEN	CCP2MX
bit 7							**bit 0**

R = Readable bit   P = Programmable bit   U = Unimplemented bit, read as '0'
-n = Value when device is not programmed   x = Bit is unknown

bit 7   **MCLRE:** $\overline{\text{MCLR}}$ Pin Enable bit
               1 = MCLR pin enabled; RE3 input pin disabled
               0 = RE3 input pin enabled; MCLR disabled

bit 6   **Unimplemented**: Read as '0'

bit 5   **P2BMX:** P2B Input MUX bit
               1 = P2B is on RB5[1]
                   P2B is on RD2[2]
               0 = P2B is on RC0

bit 4   **T3CMX:** Timer3 Clock Input MUX bit
               1 = T3CKI is on RC0
               0 = T3CKI is on RB5

bit 3   **HFOFST:** HFINTOSC Fast Start-up bit
               1 = HFINTOSC starts clocking the CPU without waiting for the oscillator to stabilize
               0 = The system clock is held off until the HFINTOSC is stable

bit 2   **CCP3MX:** CCP3 MUX bit
               1 = CCP3 input/output is multiplexed with RB5
               0 = CCP3 input/output is multiplexed with RC6[1]
               CCP3 input/output is multiplexed with RE0[2]

bit 1   **PBADEN:** PORTB A/D Enable bit
               1 = ANSELB<5:0> resets to 1, PORTB<5:0> pins are configured as analog inputs on Reset
               0 = ANSELB<5:0> resets to 0, PORTB<4:0> pins are configured as digital I/O on Reset

bit 0   **CCP2MX:** CCP2 MUX bit
               1 = CCP2 input/output is multiplexed with RC1
               0 = CCP2 input/output is multiplexed with RB3

Note 1:   PIC18(L)F2XK22 devices only.
Note 2:   PIC18(L)F4XK22 devices only.

Table 7. CONFIG4L: configuration register 4 low

CONFIG4L: CONFIGURATION REGISTER 4 LOW

R/P-1	R/P-0	U-0	U-0	U-0	R/P-1	U-0	R/P-1
$\overline{\text{DEBUG}}$ (2)	XINST	-	-	-	LVP[1]	-	STRVEN
bit 7							bit 0

R = Readable bit   P = Programmable bit   U = Unimplemented bit, read as '0'
-n = Value when device is not programmed   x = Bit is unknown

bit 7 $\overline{\text{DEBUG}}$: Background Debugger Enable bit[2]
                  1 = Background debugger disabled, RB6 and RB7 configured as general purpose I/O pins
                  0 = Background debugger enabled, RB6 and RB7 are dedicated to In-Circuit Debug

bit 6   **XINST:** Extended Instruction Set Enable bit
                  1 = Instruction set extension and Indexed Addressing mode enabled
                  0 = Instruction set extension and Indexed Addressing mode disabled (Legacy mode)

bit 5-3   **Unimplemented:** Read as '0'

bit 2   **LVP:** Single-Supply ICSP Enable bit
                  1 = Single-Supply ICSP enabled
                  0 = Single-Supply ICSP disabled

bit 1   **Unimplemented:** Read as '0'

bit 0   **STVREN:** Stack Full/Underflow Reset Enable bit
                  1 = Stack full/underflow will cause Reset
                  0 = Stack full/underflow will not cause Reset

Note 1:   Can only be changed by a programmer in high-voltage programming mode.
Note 2:   The $\overline{\text{DEBUG}}$ bit is managed automatically by device development tools including
                  debuggers and programmers. For normal device operations, this bit should be maintained as
                  a '1'.

Table 8. CONFIG5L: configuration register 5 low

CONFIG5L: CONFIGURATION REGISTER 5 LOW

U-0	U-0	U-0	U-0	R/C-1	R/C-1	R/C-1	R/C-1
-	-	-	-	CP3[(1)]	CP2[(1)]	CP1	CP0
bit 7							bit 0

R = Readable bit   P = Programmable bit   U = Unimplemented bit, read as '0'
-n = Value when device is not programmed   C = Clearable only bit

bit 7-4   **Unimplemented**: Read as '0'

bit 3   **CP3:** Code Protection bit[(1)]
          1 = Block 3 not code-protected
          0 = Block 3 code-protected

bit 2   **CP2:** Code Protection bit[(1)]
          1 = Block 2 not code-protected
          0 = Block 2 code-protected

bit 1   **CP1:** Code Protection bit
          1 = Block 1 not code-protected
          0 = Block 1 code-protected

bit 0   **CP0:** Code Protection bit
          1 = Block 0 not code-protected
          0 = Block 0 code-protected

Note 1:   Available on PIC18(L)FX5K22 and PIC18(L)FX6K22 devices.

Table 9. CONFIG5H: configuration register 5 high

CONFIG5H: CONFIGURATION REGISTER 5 HIGH

R/C-1	R/C-1	U-0	U-0	U-0	U-0	U-0	U-0
CPD	CPB	-	-	-	-	-	-
bit 7							bit 0

R = Readable bit   P = Programmable bit   U = Unimplemented bit, read as '0'
-n = Value when device is not programmed   C = Clearable only bit

bit 7   **CPD:** Data EEPROM Code Protection bit
          1 = Data EEPROM not code-protected
          0 = Data EEPROM code-protected

bit 6   **CPB:** Boot Block Code Protection bit
          1 = Boot Block not code-protected
          0 = Boot Block code-protected

bit 5-0   **Unimplemented:** Read as '0'

Table 10. CONFIG6L: configuration register 6 low

CONFIG6L: CONFIGURATION REGISTER 6 LOW

U-0	U-0	U-0	U-0	R/C-1	R/C-1	R/C-1	R/C-1
-	-	-	-	WRT3[1]	WRT3[1]	WRT1	WRT0

bit 7   bit 0

R = Readable bit   P = Programmable bit   U = Unimplemented bit, read as '0'
-n = Value when device is not programmed   C = Clearable only bit

bit 7-4   **Unimplemented**: Read as '0'

bit 3   **WRT3:** Write Protection bit[1]
              1 = Block 3 not write-protected
              0 = Block 3 write-protected

bit 2   **WRT2:** Write Protection bit[1]
              1 = Block 2 not write-protected
              0 = Block 2 write-protected

bit 1   **WRT1:** Write Protection bit
              1 = Block 1 not write-protected
              0 = Block 1 write-protected

bit 0   **WRT0:** Write Protection bit
              1 = Block 0 not write-protected
              0 = Block 0 write-protected

Note 1:   Available on PIC18(L)FX5K22 and PIC18(L)FX6K22 devices.

Table 11. CONFIG6H: configuration register 6 high

CONFIG6H: CONFIGURATION REGISTER 6 HIGH

R/C-1	R/C-1	R-1	U-0	U-0	U-0	U-0	U-0
WRTD	WRTB	WRTC[1]	-	-	-	-	-

bit 7   bit 0

R = Readable bit   P = Programmable bit   U = Unimplemented bit, read as '0'
-n = Value when device is not programmed   C = Clearable only bit

bit 7   **WRTD:** Data EEPROM Write Protection bit
              1 = Data EEPROM not write-protected
              0 = Data EEPROM write-protected

bit 6   **WRTB:** Boot Block Write Protection bit
              1 = Boot Block not write-protected
              0 = Boot Block write-protected

bit 5   **WRTC:** Configuration Register Write Protection bit[1]
              1 = Configuration registers not write-protected
              0 = Configuration registers write-protected

bit 4-0   **Unimplemented:** Read as '0'

Note 1:   This bit is read-only in normal execution mode; it can be written only in Program mode.

Table 12. CONFIG7L: configuration register 7 low

CONFIG7L: CONFIGURATION REGISTER 7 LOW

U-0	U-0	U-0	U-0	R/C-1	R/C-1	R/C-1	R/C-1
-	-	-	-	EBTR3[1]	EBTR2[1]	EBTR1	EBTR0
bit 7							bit 0

R = Readable bit   P = Programmable bit   U = Unimplemented bit, read as '0'
-n = Value when device is not programmed   C = Clearable only bit

bit 7-4   **Unimplemented**: Read as '0'

bit 3   **EBTR3**: Table Read Protection bit[1]
1 = Block 3 not protected from table reads executed in other blocks
0 = Block 3 protected from table reads executed in other blocks

bit 2   **EBTR2**: Table Read Protection bit[1]
1 = Block 2 not protected from table reads executed in other blocks
0 = Block 2 protected from table reads executed in other blocks

bit 1   **EBTR1**: Table Read Protection bit
1 = Block 1 not protected from table reads executed in other blocks
0 = Block 1 protected from table reads executed in other blocks

bit 0   **EBTR0**: Table Read Protection bit
1 = Block 0 not protected from table reads executed in other blocks
0 = Block 0 protected from table reads executed in other blocks

Note 1:   Available on PIC18(L)FX5K22 and PIC18(L)FX6K22 devices.

Table 13. CONFIG7H: configuration register 7 high

CONFIG7H: CONFIGURATION REGISTER 7 HIGH

U-0	R/C-1	U-0	U-0	U-0	U-0	U-0	U-0
-	EBTRB	-	-	-	-	-	-
bit 7							bit 0

R = Readable bit   P = Programmable bit   U = Unimplemented bit, read as '0'
-n = Value when device is unprogrammed   C = Clearable only bit

bit 7   **Unimplemented**: Read as '0'

bit 6   **EBTRB**: Boot Block Table Read Protection bit
1 = Boot Block not protected from table reads executed in other blocks
0 = Boot Block protected from table reads executed in other blocks

bit 5-0   **Unimplemented**: Read as '0'

Table 14. DEVID1: device ID register 1

DEVID1:   DEVICE ID REGISTER 1

R	R	R	R	R	R	R	R
DEV2	DEV1	DEV0	REV4	REV3	REV2	REV1	REV0
bit 7							**bit 0**

R = Readable bit   P = Programmable bit   U = Unimplemented bit, read as '0'
-n = Value when device is not programmed   C = Clearable only bit

bit 7-5   **DEV<2:0>:** Device ID bits
         These bits, together with DEV<10:3> in DEVID2, determine the device ID.
         See Table G.4 for complete Device ID list.

bit 4-0   **REV<4:0>:** Revision ID bits
         These bits indicate the device revision.

Table 15. DEVID2: device ID register 2

DEVID2:   DEVICE ID REGISTER 2

R	R	R	R	R	R	R	R
DEV10	DEV9	DEV8	DEV7	DEV6	DEV5	DEV4	DEV3
bit 7							**bit 0**

R = Readable bit   P = Programmable bit   U = Unimplemented bit, read as '0'
-n = Value when device is not programmed   C = Clearable only bit

bit 7-0   **DEV<10:3>:** Device ID bits
         These bits, together with DEV<2:0> in DEVID1, determine the device ID.
         See Table G.4 for complete Device ID list.

Table 16. Device ID table for the PIC18(L)F2X/4XK22 family

DEV<10:0>	DEV<2:0>	Part Number
0101 0100	000	PIC18F46K22
	001	PIC18LF46K22
	010	PIC18F26K22
	011	PIC18LF26K22
0101 0101	000	PIC18F45K22
	001	PIC18LF45K22
	010	PIC18F25K22
	011	PIC18LF25K22
0101 0110	000	PIC18F44K22
	001	PIC18LF44K22
	010	PIC18F24K22
	011	PIC18LF24K22
0101 0111	000	PIC18F43K22
	001	PIC18LF43K22
	010	PIC18F23K22
	011	PIC18LF23K22

Appendix 8

LCD LIBRARIES

Basic LCD Routines in 4-Bit Mode (Hardware/Code)

Figure 1 displays the needed connections between the MCU and the LCD in 4-bit mode. Table 1 lists the basic functions for the LCD in 4-bit mode. These are packaged in the software library <LCD4lib.h>.

LCD Functions for Displaying Strings, Blanks, and Variables

Table 2 lists some utility functions needed to display character strings or blanks on the LCD. These functions are also part of the library <LCDxlib.h> where x = 4 or 8 (4-bit and 8-bit modes). Note that DispRomStr() employs the ROM data type (added to <p18cxxx.h>) defined as:

```
typedef    const far rom char    ROM;    // strings in PS
```

Table 3 lists some conversion routines needed when working with LCDs. These functions have been added to <LCDxlib.h> (x = 4, 8) as well.

Figure 1. PIC18F45K22 connection with LCD in 4-bit mode

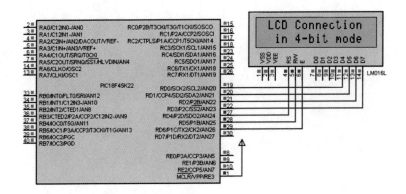

Table 1. Basic functions for the LCD in 4-bit mode <LCD4lib.h>

Include libraries, control signals assignment plus forward declarations.

```
#include        <delays.h>
#include        <LCDdefs.h>

#define      E         PORTDbits.RD6
#define      RW        PORTDbits.RD5
#define      RS        PORTDbits.RD4

void SendCmd(char);
void SendNibble(char);
void Wait4LCD(void);
```

Initialize the LCD in 4-bit mode.

```
void InitLCD(void)
{
    char LCDstr[] = {0x33, 0x32, 0x28, 0x0C, 0x01, 0x06, '\0'};

    ANSELD &= 0x80;                 // RD<6:0> are digital pins
    Delay10KTCYx(10);               // small initial delay
    while (*LCDstr != '\0')
        SendCmd(*LCDstr++);
}
```

Send a command to the LCD display.

```
void SendCmd(char cmd)                 // send a command to the LCD
{
    RS = 0; RW = 0; E = 0;             // set LCD in command mode
    SendNibble((cmd >> 4) & 0x0F);     // send upper nibble of command
    SendNibble(cmd & 0x0F);            // send lower nibble of command
    Wait4LCD();
}
```

Writes a character to the LCD display by sending the upper nibble then the lower nibble.

```
void SendChar(char ch)
{
    RS = 1; RW = 0; E = 0;             // set LCD in data mode
    SendNibble((ch >> 4) & 0x0F);      // send upper nibble of data
    SendNibble(ch & 0x0F);             // send lower nibble of data
    Wait4LCD();
}
```

Send a nibble to the LCD.

```
void SendNibble(char ch)
{
    TRISD &= 0b10000000;               // RD6..RD0 are output pins
    PORTD = (PORTD & 0xF0) | ch;       // upper nibble of not altered
    E = 1;                             // latch control state (RS/R_W)
    Delay10TCYx(2);                    // 20 cycles delay
    E = 0;                             // latch data/command
}
```

Wait for the busy flag (active low) before a new character/command is written to the LCD.

```
void Wait4LCD(void)                    // Wait for busy flag to clear.
{
    unsigned char LoNibble, HiNibble, status;

    TRISD |= 0x0F;                     // switch data port to input
    RW = 1; RS = 0; E = 0;             // read busy flag
    do {
      E = 1;                           // provide logic high on E
      Nop();                           // 1 cycle delay
      HiNibble = PORTD << 4;           // read the high nibble
      E = 0;                           // provide falling edge
      E = 1;                           // provide logic high on E
      Nop();                           // 1 cycle delay
      LoNibble = PORTD & 0x0F;         // read the low nibble
      E = 0;                           // provide falling edge
      status = HiNibble | LoNibble;    // status<7> = busy flag
    } while (status & 0x80);           // test busy flag
}
```

Table 2. Functions to write strings/blanks to LCD; used by <LCDxlib.h> x = 4, 8

Display null-terminated string (in ROM) at StartPos.

```
void DispRomStr(char StartPos, ROM *Str)
{
    SendCmd(StartPos);
    while (*Str != '\0')
        SendChar(*Str++);
}
```

Display null-terminated string (in RAM) at StartPos.

```
void DispRamStr(char StartPos, char *Str)
{
    SendCmd(StartPos);
    while (*Str != '\0')
        SendChar(*Str++);
}
```

Display ASCII variable of specified length at StartPos.

```
void DispVarStr(char *Str, char StartPos, unsigned char NumOfChars)
{
    unsigned char i;

    SendCmd(StartPos);
    for (i = 0; i < NumOfChars; i++)
        SendChar(*Str++);
}
```

Display a number of blank characters at StartPos.

```
void DispBlanks(char StartPos, unsigned char NumOfChars)
{
    unsigned char i;

    SendCmd(StartPos);
    for (i = 0; i < NumOfChars; i++)
        SendChar(' ');                       // send a blank character
}
```

Table 3. Conversion routines added to <LCDxlib.h> x = 4, 8

Convert BCD array of length Len to ASCII.

```
void Bcd2Asc(char *a, unsigned char Len)
{
    unsigned char i;

    for (i = 0; i < Len; i++)
        a[i] += '0';                            // convert to ASCII
}
```

Convert ASCII array of length Len to BCD.

```
void Asc2Bcd(char *a, unsigned char Len)
{
    unsigned char i;

    for (i = 0; i < Len; i++)
        a[i] &= 0x0F;                           // convert to BCD
}
```

Convert from packed BCD to 2 bytes of consecutive ASCII characters. Most significant first.

```
void PBCD2Asc(unsigned char SrcReg, char *DstArr)
{
    *DstArr++ = (SrcReg >> 4) | '0';           // upper nibble to ASCII
    *DstArr-- = (SrcReg & 0x0F) | '0';         // lower nibble to ASCII
}
```

Convert 3-digit ASCII array to binary.

```
unsigned int Asc2Bin(char *a)
{
    return (int) (a[0] & 0x0F) * 100 + (a[1] & 0x0F) * 10 + a[2] & 0x0F;
}
```

Convert 4-digit ASCII array to binary

```
unsigned int Asc2BinE(char *a)
{
    return (int) (a[0] & 0x0F) * 1000 + (a[1] & 0x0F) * 100 +
                 (a[2] & 0x0F) * 10 + (a[3] & 0x0F);
}
```

Convert 8-bit N to ASCII chars and store in array a (MSD first)

```
void Bin2Asc(unsigned char N, char *a)
{
    a[2] = (N % 10) + '0';                  // least significant digit
    N = N / 10;
    a[1] = (N % 10) + '0';                  // middle significant digit
    a[0] = (N / 10) + '0';                  // most significant digit
}
```

Convert 16-bit N to ASCII chars and store in array a (MSD first)

```
void Bin2AscE(unsigned int N, char *a)
{
    unsigned char i;

    for (i = 0; i < 4; i++)
    {
      a[4-i] = (N % 10) + '0';              // rem of N / 10 in ASCII
      N = N / 10;
    }
    a[0] = N + '0';
}
```

Basic LCD Routines in 8-Bit Mode (Hardware/Code)

Figure 2 shows the needed connections between the MCU and the LCD in 8-bit mode. Table 4 lists the basic functions for the LCD in 8-bit mode. These are packaged in the software library <LCD8lib.h>.

LCD Definitions

Table 5 lists all the character positions on the LM016L LCD (16 characters x 2 lines) and the LM044L LCD (20 characters x 4 lines). It allows the use of symbolic addresses to specify characters positions on the LCD. It has been included in <LCD4lib.h> and <LCD8lib.h> to simplify matters. Therefore, there is no need to include <LCDdefs.h> in user programs.

The functions

- `void Bcd2Asc(char *a, unsigned char Len)`
- `void Asc2Bcd(char *a, unsigned char Len)`
- `void PBCD2Asc(unsigned char SrcReg, char *DstArr)`
- `unsigned int Asc2Bin(char *a)`
- `unsigned int Asc2BinE(char *a)`
- `void Bin2Asc(unsigned char N, char *a)`
- `void Bin2AscE(unsigned int N, char *a)`

are common to <LCDxlib.h> (x = 4 or 8) and <Hyperterm.h>. In order to avoid compiler errors when both libraries are used, the file <LCDxlib.h> has the following directive on top:

```
#define     LCD    // to remove conflict with <Hyperterm.h>
```

In addition to this, the library <Hyperterm.h> uses the following directive:

```
#ifndef     LCD
                   // place implementation of above functions in here
#endif
```

This way, if the LCD library is used, the common functions will not be inserted twice in the code. These two libraries have been designed so that duplicate functions appear only once.

Figure 2. PIC18F45K22 connection with LCD in 8-bit mode

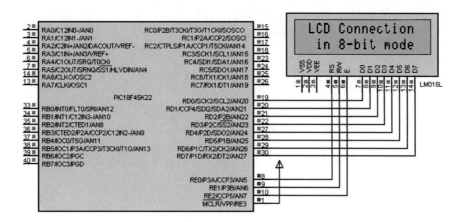

Table 4. Basic functions for the LCD in 8-bit mode <LCD8lib.h>

Include libraries, control signals assignment plus forward declarations.

```
#include     <delays.h>
#include     <LCDdefs.h>

#define       E      PORTEbits.RE2
#define       RW     PORTEbits.RE1
#define       RS     PORTEbits.RE0

void SendCmd(char);
void Wait4LCD(void);
```

Initialize the LCD in 8-bit mode.

```
void InitLCD(void)
{
    char LCDstr[] = {0x38, 0x38, 0x0C, 0x01, 0x06, '\0'};
    unsigned char i = 0;

    ANSELE = 0x00; TRISE = 0x00;    // RE2, RE1, RE0 are output pins
    ANSELD = 0x00;                  // PORTD digital port
    Delay10KTCYx(10);               // small initial delay
    while (LCDstr[i] != '\0')
       SendCmd(LCDstr[i++]);
}
```

Send a command to the LCD display.

```
void SendCmd(char cmd)              // send a command to the LCD
{
    TRISD = 0x00;                   // switch data port to output
    RW = 0; RS = 0; E = 0;          // Command mode, R/W = 0
    PORTD = cmd;                    // write in one shot
    E = 1;                          // +ve edge latches RS & R_W
    Nop();
    E = 0;                          // -ve edge latches data
    Wait4LCD();
}
```

Writes a character to the LCD display.

```
void SendChar(char ch)              // send a character to the LCD
{
    TRISD = 0x00;                   // switch data port to output
    RW = 0; RS = 1; E = 0;          // Data mode, R/W = 0
    PORTD = ch;                     // write in one shot
    E = 1;                          // +ve edge latches RS & R_W
    Nop();
    E = 0;                          // -ve edge latches data
    Wait4LCD();
}
```

Wait for the busy flag (active low) before a new character/command is written to the LCD.

```
void Wait4LCD(void)
{
    unsigned char status;
    TRISD = 0xFF;                   // switch data port to input
    RW = 1; RS = 0; E = 0;          // Command mode with R/W = 1
    do {
        E = 1;                      // provide logic high on E
        Nop();                      // 1 cycle delay
        status = PORTD;             // read status
        E = 0;                      // provide a falling edge
    } while (status & 0x80);        // test busy flag
}
```

Table 5a. <LCDdefs.h> lists all character positions on the LCD; char position ranges from 0 to 19. Valid for LM016L & LM044L.

Char position ranges from 0 to 19. Valid for LM016L & LM044L.				
1	#define	Ln1Ch0	0x80	Line1, character 0
2	#define	Ln1Ch1	0x81	Line1, character 1
3	#define	Ln1Ch2	0x82	Line1, character 2
4	#define	Ln1Ch3	0x83	Line1, character 3
5	#define	Ln1Ch4	0x84	Line1, character 4
6	#define	Ln1Ch5	0x85	Line1, character 5
7	#define	Ln1Ch6	0x86	Line1, character 6
8	#define	Ln1Ch7	0x87	Line1, character 7
9	#define	Ln1Ch8	0x88	Line1, character 8
10	#define	Ln1Ch9	0x89	Line1, character 9
11	#define	Ln1Ch10	0x8A	Line1, character 10
12	#define	Ln1Ch11	0x8B	Line1, character 11
13	#define	Ln1Ch12	0x8C	Line1, character 12
14	#define	Ln1Ch13	0x8D	Line1, character 13
15	#define	Ln1Ch14	0x8E	Line1, character 14
16	#define	Ln1Ch15	0x8F	Line1, character 15
17	#define	Ln1Ch16	0x90	Line1, character 16
18	#define	Ln1Ch17	0x91	Line1, character 17
19	#define	Ln1Ch18	0x92	Line1, character 18
20	#define	Ln1Ch19	0x93	Line1, character 19
21				
22	#define	Ln2Ch0	0xC0	Line2, character 0
23	#define	Ln2Ch1	0xC1	Line2, character 1
24	#define	Ln2Ch2	0xC2	Line2, character 2
25	#define	Ln2Ch3	0xC3	Line2, character 3
26	#define	Ln2Ch4	0xC4	Line2, character 4
27	#define	Ln2Ch5	0xC5	Line2, character 5
28	#define	Ln2Ch6	0xC6	Line2, character 6
29	#define	Ln2Ch7	0xC7	Line2, character 7
30	#define	Ln2Ch8	0xC8	Line2, character 8
31	#define	Ln2Ch9	0xC9	Line2, character 9
32	#define	Ln2Ch10	0xCA	Line2, character 10
33	#define	Ln2Ch11	0xCB	Line2, character 11
34	#define	Ln2Ch12	0xCC	Line2, character 12
35	#define	Ln2Ch13	0xCD	Line2, character 13
36	#define	Ln2Ch14	0xCE	Line2, character 14
37	#define	Ln2Ch15	0xCF	Line2, character 15
38	#define	Ln2Ch16	0xD0	Line2, character 16
39	#define	Ln2Ch17	0xD1	Line2, character 17
40	#define	Ln2Ch18	0xD2	Line2, character 18
41	#define	Ln2Ch19	0xD3	Line2, character 19
42				
43	#define	Ln3Ch0	0x94	Line3, character 0
44	#define	Ln3Ch1	0x95	Line3, character 1
45	#define	Ln3Ch2	0x96	Line3, character 2
46	#define	Ln3Ch3	0x97	Line3, character 3
47	#define	Ln3Ch4	0x98	Line3, character 4
48	#define	Ln3Ch5	0x99	Line3, character 5
49	#define	Ln3Ch6	0x9A	Line3, character 6
50	#define	Ln3Ch7	0x9B	Line3, character 7
51	#define	Ln3Ch8	0x9C	Line3, character 8
52	#define	Ln3Ch9	0x9D	Line3, character 9

Table 5b. <LCDdefs.h> lists all character positions on the LCD; char position ranges from 0 to 19. Valid for LM016L & LM044L continued.

53	#define	Ln3Ch10	0x9E	Line3, character 10
54	#define	Ln3Ch11	0x9F	Line3, character 11
55	#define	Ln3Ch12	0xA0	Line3, character 12
56	#define	Ln3Ch13	0xA1	Line3, character 13
57	#define	Ln3Ch14	0xA2	Line3, character 14
58	#define	Ln3Ch15	0xA3	Line3, character 15
59	#define	Ln3Ch16	0xA4	Line3, character 16
60	#define	Ln3Ch17	0xA5	Line3, character 17
61	#define	Ln3Ch18	0xA6	Line3, character 18
62	#define	Ln3Ch19	0xA7	Line3, character 19
63				
64	#define	Ln4Ch0	0xD4	Line4, character 0
65	#define	Ln4Ch1	0xD5	Line4, character 1
66	#define	Ln4Ch2	0xD6	Line4, character 2
67	#define	Ln4Ch3	0xD7	Line4, character 3
68	#define	Ln4Ch4	0xD8	Line4, character 4
69	#define	Ln4Ch5	0xD9	Line4, character 5
70	#define	Ln4Ch6	0xDA	Line4, character 6
71	#define	Ln4Ch7	0xDB	Line4, character 7
72	#define	Ln4Ch8	0xDC	Line4, character 8
73	#define	Ln4Ch9	0xDD	Line4, character 9
74	#define	Ln4Ch10	0xDE	Line4, character 10
75	#define	Ln4Ch11	0xDF	Line4, character 11
76	#define	Ln4Ch12	0xE0	Line4, character 12
77	#define	Ln4Ch13	0xE1	Line4, character 13
78	#define	Ln4Ch14	0xE2	Line4, character 14
79	#define	Ln4Ch15	0xE3	Line4, character 15
80	#define	Ln4Ch16	0xE4	Line4, character 16
81	#define	Ln4Ch17	0xE5	Line4, character 17
82	#define	Ln4Ch18	0xE6	Line4, character 18
83	#define	Ln4Ch19	0xE7	Line4, character 19

Appendix 9

HYPERTERMINAL FUNCTIONS

This appendix summarizes all the functions developed in Chapter 12 and pertaining to serial communications via the UART. Table 1 lists all these functions which belong to the library <Hyperterm.h>.
The functions

```
void Bcd2Asc(char *a, unsigned char Len)
void Asc2Bcd(char *a, unsigned char Len)
void PBCD2Asc(unsigned char SrcReg, char *DstArr)
unsigned int Asc2Bin(char *a)
unsigned int Asc2BinE(char *a)
void Bin2Asc(unsigned char N, char *a)
void Bin2AscE(unsigned int N, char *a)
```

are common to the libraries <LCDxlib.h> (x = 4 or 8) and <Hyperterm.h>. In order to avoid compiler errors when both libraries are used together, the file <LCDxlib.h> has the following directive on top:

```
#define      LCD          // to remove conflict with <Hyperterm.h>
```

In addition to this, the library <Hyperterm.h> uses the following directive:

```
#ifndef      LCD

                          // place implementation of above functions in here
#endif
```

This way, if the LCD library is used (LCD defined), then the common functions will not be inserted twice in the code. These two libraries have been designed carefully so that conflicting functions appear only once.

Table 1a. Listing of the UART functions belonging to the library <Hyperterm.h>

Initialize the EUSART to run at 19,200 baud.	

```
void InitUART(void)                        // UART (TX/RX) runs at 19,200 baud
{
   ANSELCbits.ANSC6 = 0;                   // TX digital pin
   ANSELCbits.ANSC7 = 0;                   // RX digital pin
   TXSTAbits.TXEN = 1;                     // transmit enable
   RCSTAbits.CREN = 1;                     // receive enable
   TXSTAbits.BRGH = 1;                     // high speed mode
   SPBRG = 12;                             // 19,200 baud @ 4MHz
   RCSTAbits.SPEN = 1;                     // enable UART
}
```

Transmit null-terminated string in RAM (data space) via the EUSART

```
void TxRamStr(char *Str)
{
   while (*Str != '\0')                    // if '\0' is encountered exit loop
   {
      while (!PIR1bits.TXIF);
      TXREG = *Str++;                      // serialize byte to be sent
   }
}
```

Transmit null-terminated string in ROM (program space) via the EUSART

```
void TxRomStr(ROM *Str)
{
   while (*Str != '\0')                    // if "\0" is encountered exit loop
   {
      while (!PIR1bits.TXIF);
      TXREG = *Str++;                      // serialize byte to be sent
   }
}
```

Send data packet serially via the EUSART

```
void TxPacket(char *Packet, unsigned char Len)
{
   unsigned char i;

   for (i = 0; i < Len; i++)
   {
      while (!PIR1bits.TXIF);
      TXREG = *Packet++;                   // serialize byte to be sent
   }
}
```

Table 1b. Listing of the UART functions belonging to the library <Hyperterm.h> continued

Receive data packet serially via the EUSART

```
void RxPacket(char *Packet, unsigned char Len)
{
    unsigned char i;

    for (i = 0; i < Len; i++)
    {
        while (!PIR1bits.RCIF);             // wait until character is received
        *Packet++ = RCREG;                  // store received data in Packet[]
    }
}
```

Convert 8-bit N to ASCII characters (hex digits) and store in array a (starting with MSD).

```
void Byte2Asc(unsigned char N, char *a)
{
    a[0] = N >> 4;                          // most significant digit
    a[1] = N & 0x0F;                        // least significant digit
    a[0] += (a[0] < 10? '0': 'A' - 10);     // convert MSD to ASCII
    a[1] += (a[1] < 10? '0': 'A' - 10);     // convert LSD to ASCII
}
```

Convert 16-bit N to ASCII characters (hex digits) and store in array a (starting with MSD).

```
void Word2Asc(unsigned int N, char *a)
{
    unsigned char i, digit;

    for (i = 0; i < 4; i++)
    {
        digit = N % 16;                     // digit = LCD of N
        N = N / 16;                         // remove LSD of N
        digit += (digit < 10? '0': 'A' - 10); // convert digit to ASCII
        a[3-i] = digit;                     // MSD on top (a[0]), LSD on a[3]
    }
}
```

Convert BCD array of length Len to ASCII.

```
void Bcd2Asc(char *a, unsigned char Len)
{
    unsigned char i;

    for (i = 0; i < Len; i++)
        a[i] += '0';                        // convert to ASCII
}
```

Table 1c. Listing of the UART functions belonging to the library <Hyperterm.h> continued

Convert ASCII array of length Len to BCD.

```
void Asc2Bcd(char *a, unsigned char Len)
{
    unsigned char i;
    for (i = 0; i < Len; i++)
        a[i] &= 0x0F;                        // convert to BCD
}
```

Convert from packed BCD to 2 bytes of consecutive ASCII characters. Most significant first.

```
void PBCD2Asc(unsigned char SrcReg, char *DstArr)
{
    *DstArr++ = (SrcReg >> 4) | '0';          // upper nibble to ASCII
    *DstArr-- = (SrcReg & 0x0F) | '0';        // lower nibble to ASCII
}
```

Convert 3-digit ASCII array to binary.

```
unsigned int Asc2Bin(char *a)
{
    return (int) (a[0] & 0x0F) * 100 + (a[1] & 0x0F) * 10 +
            (a[2] & 0x0F);
}
```

Convert 4-digit ASCII array to binary

```
unsigned int Asc2BinE(char *a)
{
    return (int) (a[0] & 0x0F) * 1000 + (a[1] & 0x0F) * 100 +
            (a[2] & 0x0F) * 10 + (a[3] & 0x0F);
}
```

Convert 8-bit N to ASCII chars and store in array a (MSD first)

```
void Bin2Asc(unsigned char N, char *a)
{
    a[2] = (N % 10) + '0';                    // least significant digit
    N = N / 10;
    a[1] = (N % 10) + '0';                    // middle significant digit
    a[0] = (N / 10) + '0';                    // most significant digit
}
```

Convert 16-bit N to ASCII chars and store in array a (MSD first)

```
void Bin2AscE(unsigned int N, char *a)
{
    unsigned char i;

    for (i = 0; i < 4; i++)
    {
        a[4-i] = (N % 10) + '0';              // rem of N / 10 in ASCII
        N = N / 10;
    }
    a[0] = N + '0';
}
```

Compilation of References

Freescale Semiconductor Inc. (2005). *M68HC11E family data sheet*. Austin, TX: Freescale Semiconductor Inc.

Labcenter Electronics. (2003). *Intelligent schematic input system*. North Yorkshire, UK: Labcenter Electronics.

Microchip. (2005a). *MPLAB C18 C compiler user's guide*. Phoenix, AZ: Microchip Technology Incorporated.

Microchip. (2005b). *MPLAB C18 C compiler getting started*. Phoenix, AZ: Microchip Technology Incorporated.

Microchip. (2005c). *MPLAB C18 C compiler getting libraries*. Phoenix, AZ: Microchip Technology Incorporated.

Microchip. (2010-2012). *PIC18(L)F2X/4XK22 data sheet*. Phoenix, AZ: Microchip Technology Incorporated.

Peatman, J. (2002). *Embedded design with the PIC18F452 microcontroller*. New York, NY: Pearson.

Roth, C. (1995). *Fundamentals of logic design* (4th ed.). Boston, MA: PWS Publishing Company.

Wakerly, J. (1999). *Digital design: Principles and practices* (3rd ed.). Upper Saddle River, NJ: Prentice Hall.

About the Author

Nicolas K. Haddad is a professor of Computer Engineering at the University of Balamand, Lebanon. He received his B.S. from the University of Louisiana at Lafayette and his M.S. and Ph.D. from Ohio University before being appointed as an assistant professor at the New Mexico Institute of Mining and Technology. After his fifteen-year stay in the United States, Dr. Haddad returned to his home land Lebanon, where he taught as a full-timer at two Universities: Université Saint Joseph (past) and University of Balamand (present). In addition to teaching, Dr. Haddad has always worked as an electronics consultant for several local firms. He also established a Microcontroller Training Center for engineers who were not exposed to this area while in college. Dr. Haddad is the recipient of the 1994 distinguished teacher award at the New Mexico Institute of Mining and Technology. He speaks, reads and writes four languages fluently. He currently resides in Beirut, Lebanon with his wife, two daughters, and son.

Index

7-bit address 266-267, 275

A

amplifier 167, 180
architectures 7, 9
arithmetic logic 13, 33
automobiles 1

B

buffers 100, 114, 116
bytes 3, 7-8, 10-11, 13, 26, 28, 46, 48, 66, 72-73, 80, 88, 148, 227, 240, 243, 268, 275

C

C language 25, 32, 71-74, 91, 108
C language programs 72
cell phone 1
circuitry 7, 11, 100, 108, 167, 254, 278
code 7, 9, 11, 36, 38, 40, 47-49, 58, 65, 69, 71-72, 90, 102, 116, 119, 123, 148, 158, 164, 166-168, 171, 175, 177, 233, 254-255, 273
compiler 9, 71-72, 74, 80, 84, 90-91, 116
complete program 119, 158, 202, 207, 221
computer 1-3, 7, 9, 25, 40, 43, 228, 236, 239
configuration 15, 94, 109, 116, 119, 122, 125, 171, 192, 211, 215, 240, 242-243, 251, 267, 273, 275
Controllers 1-2
Conversion 59, 85-86, 158, 166-170, 172, 174, 192

D

data transfer 145, 227, 241, 245, 263, 270
data types 72-73, 108
datasheet 11, 15, 48, 88, 146, 148, 248
digital camera 1
dishwashers 1

E

electronics 1

F

functions 71, 84, 88, 99, 102, 109, 116, 144, 148, 150, 233

H

hardware 5, 9, 11-13, 25, 35-36, 38, 44-46, 58-59, 79, 81, 86, 91, 94, 98, 100, 102-105, 108-109, 116, 120-121, 125, 127, 130, 132-133, 141, 143, 158, 164, 169, 181, 186-187, 192, 198, 200-202, 207, 211, 214, 218, 221, 225-226, 233, 236, 240-241, 243, 248, 251, 262-263, 269-270, 275, 278, 280-282
high level 25, 48, 51, 59, 61, 69, 74, 91, 140, 222
HyperTerminal 228, 232-233, 236

I

initialization 148
Instruction Set 3, 7, 9, 25, 48, 50

L

library 59, 74, 84, 86, 88, 90-91, 233
liquid-crystal displays 144

M

memory 3, 7-13, 19, 25-26, 28, 30, 38, 40, 42, 45-47, 50-51, 58, 66, 68, 72, 83, 90
Microchip 2-3, 10, 180
microcontroller 1-5, 8, 13, 23, 30, 33, 38, 54, 66, 71, 88, 119-120, 122, 140, 145, 166, 180, 200, 222, 228, 232, 239-240, 263-264, 278
microprocessor 2, 8-9

microwave 1, 3
modular blocks 69

O

operations 7, 11, 13, 29-36, 38, 42, 46, 50, 54, 56, 58,
74, 86, 88, 94, 116, 126, 142, 174, 182, 188, 227,
245, 254, 275
operators 73-74
oscillator 7, 11, 14-17, 19, 97, 117, 119, 172, 248, 278

P

plug-and-play philosophy 280
power saving 123, 125, 139, 142
printers 1
processor's throughput 7
processors 3, 9, 13, 24-25, 30, 58, 72, 94, 241
program 2-3, 5, 8-12, 19, 25, 35, 38, 40, 44-46, 48-51,
54, 59, 66, 69, 71, 80, 82-83, 86, 90, 92, 116,
119-120, 123, 130, 155, 158, 176, 180, 182, 191,
202, 207, 211, 215, 220-221, 227-228, 238, 275
programming 3, 43, 48-49, 54, 69, 72, 91-92, 97, 116-
117, 127, 190, 245

R

refrigerators 1
Routine 44, 46, 59, 69, 120-121, 123, 142, 155

S

scanners 1

Serial Peripheral Interface 240, 263
sleep mode 22, 123, 125, 130, 142, 180-182, 202,
243, 277
software 5, 9, 16, 32, 49-50, 58, 65, 68-69, 71, 86,
143, 200, 202, 214, 221, 243, 262, 270, 280, 282
subprograms 49-50, 59, 92, 148
subroutine 11-12, 43-45, 49-50, 58-59, 69
syntax 50, 61, 74, 83, 90

T

technology 2-3, 10, 19
temperature 15, 166-167, 180, 273, 275, 281
trigger 14, 97, 102, 114, 116, 121, 172, 182, 192, 259

U

user 1, 3, 5, 27, 31, 40, 44, 48-49, 51, 58, 72-73, 96,
100, 102, 123, 126, 132, 136, 144, 146, 150,
158, 165, 170, 182, 192, 197, 223-225, 227, 236,
239-240, 245

V

voltage sample 166-167

W

wireless telephone 1
writing 46, 48, 126, 182, 223, 240

Stay Current on the Latest Emerging Research Developments

Become an IGI Global Reviewer for Authored Book Projects

Premier Reference Source

Solutions for High-Touch Communications in a High-Tech World

Premier Reference Source

Advanced Research on Biologically Inspired Cognitive Architectures

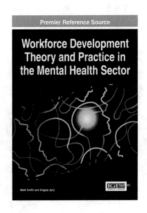
Premier Reference Source

Workforce Development Theory and Practice in the Mental Health Sector

Premier Reference Source

Resource Management and Efficiency in Cloud Computing Environments

The overall success of an authored book project is dependent on quality and timely reviews.

In this competitive age of scholarly publishing, constructive and timely feedback significantly decreases the turnaround time of manuscripts from submission to acceptance, allowing the publication and discovery of progressive research at a much more expeditious rate. Several IGI Global authored book projects are currently seeking highly qualified experts in the field to fill vacancies on their respective editorial review boards:

Applications may be sent to:
development@igi-global.com

Applicants must have a doctorate (or an equivalent degree) as well as publishing and reviewing experience. Reviewers are asked to write reviews in a timely, collegial, and constructive manner. All reviewers will begin their role on an ad-hoc basis for a period of one year, and upon successful completion of this term can be considered for full editorial review board status, with the potential for a subsequent promotion to Associate Editor.

If you have a colleague that may be interested in this opportunity, we encourage you to share this information with them.

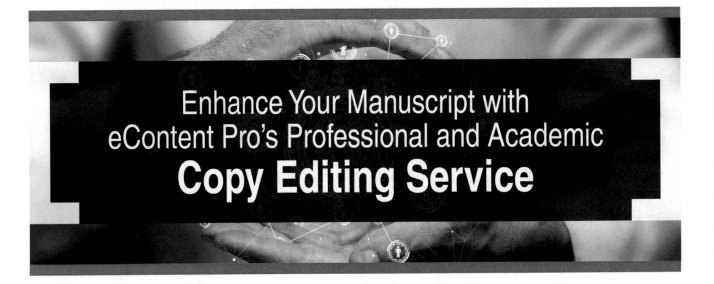

Become an IRMA Member

Members of the **Information Resources Management Association (IRMA)** understand the importance of community within their field of study. The Information Resources Management Association is an ideal venue through which professionals, students, and academicians can convene and share the latest industry innovations and scholarly research that is changing the field of information science and technology. Become a member today and enjoy the benefits of membership as well as the opportunity to collaborate and network with fellow experts in the field.

IRMA Membership Benefits:

- **One FREE Journal Subscription**

- **30% Off Additional Journal Subscriptions**

- **20% Off Book Purchases**

- Updates on the latest events and research on Information Resources Management through the IRMA-L listserv.

- Updates on new open access and downloadable content added to Research IRM.

- A copy of the Information Technology Management Newsletter twice a year.

- A certificate of membership.

IRMA Membership $195

Scan code or visit **irma-international.org** and begin by selecting your free journal subscription.

Membership is good for one full year.